CRITICAL COMPANION TO

Toni Morrison

Toni Morrison

A Literary Reference to Her Life and Work

CARMEN GILLESPIE

Facts On File
An imprint of Infobase Publishing

Critical Companion to Toni Morrison

Facts On File, Inc.
An imprint of Infobase Publishing
132 West 31st Street
New York NY 10001

Library of Congress Cataloging-in-Publication Data

Gillespie, Carmen.
Critical companion to Toni Morrison : a literary reference to her life and work /
Carmen Gillespie.
p. cm.
Includes bibliographical references and index.
ISBN 978-0-8160-6276-8 (hc : acid-free paper) 1. Morrison, Toni. I. Title. II.
Title: Facts On File critical companion to Toni Morrison.
PS3563.O8749Z653 2007
813'.54—dc22   2006038231

Facts On File books are available at special discounts when purchased in bulk
quantities for businesses, associations, institutions, or sales promotions.
Please call our Special Sales Department in New York at (212) 967-8800 or
(800) 322-8755.

You can find Facts On File on the World Wide Web at http://www.factsonfile.com

Text design by Erika K. Arroyo
Cover design by Cathy Rincon/Anastasia Plé

Printed in the United States of America

VB Hermitage 10 9 8 7 6 5 4 3 2 1

This book is printed on acid-free paper.

The mothers soar and the children must know their names.
—To Professor Toni Morrison, with awe and gratitude.

Contents

ACKNOWLEDGMENTS

Special thanks go to all of the many students with whom I have been fortunate to share the experience of exploring Morrison's work. J. Scott, I am grateful for our many conversations about Morrison and her works and for your sending me the announcement about this publication. My appreciation and admiration go to the members of the Toni Morrison Society, the Wintergreen Women, and Cave Canem for their support, encouragement, and example.

I am indebted to the wonderful and accommodating staff at the Lorain Public Library, especially Sandra Ruth and Valerie Smith, who patiently and expertly responded to all of my requests. This book was finished expediently with the expert research and transcription skills of my graduate research assistant, Adam Tavel.

I extend thanks to my friend Vincent Stephens for endless pep talks, insight, and feedback.

Finally, and most importantly, I gratefully acknowledge my family: my husband, Harold Bakst, who always believed that I could rise to this challenge and helped me every step of the way, my daughter, Chelsea, who patiently and cheerfully endured the sight of her mother perpetually glued to the computer, and Delaney, the new addition to our family.

INTRODUCTION

In her novel *Paradise* (1997), Toni Morrison has a character named Patricia Best who becomes consumed with documenting the detailed genealogy of the residents of her town, Ruby, Oklahoma. For the past few years, I have felt a bit like Patricia Best as I have attempted to document the personal, literary, and contextual genealogies of Toni Morrison. Like Patricia Best, I came to a conclusion even before I began: that the details of the life and works of this exceptionally accomplished artist could never add up to the whole. The story of Toni Morrison's life and works can never be inscribed or contained in a single work.

Eventually, Pat Best gives up on her work and, in frustration, burns the documents she has so fastidiously gathered. Although at times the complexity and abundance of Morrison's seemingly inexhaustible abilities made me sympathetic to Patricia Best's feelings of futility, I continued working with the hope that *Critical Companion to Toni Morrison* would be a useful guide for those wishing to explore the multi-faceted creations that emerge from the intense and productive pressure of Morrison's expansive imagination.

Adding to the many acknowledgments her work has received, Morrison has been recognized by the *New York Times Review of Books* as having written the best novel of the last 25 years, *Beloved*. Toni Morrison has also recently decided to retire from her position as the Robert E. Goheen Professor in the Council of Humanities at Princeton University. Undoubtedly, this is the beginning of a new phase of endeavor for Professor Morrison. Her new novel, *Mercy*, is scheduled for publica-

tion in the coming year. Even now, I am certain that she is at work on other projects that will prove, as Patricia Best learned and as Morrison has said, that nothing, certainly no single volume, can pin down the complexities of human experience, particularly of the life and work of an artist with the intellectual vigor and inventive tenacity of Toni Morrison.

It has been a privilege to work on this volume. I hope that it will function as an incentive to encourage exploration of the generative and verdant worlds contained in the many varieties of intellectual production fashioned by Toni Morrison.

About This Book

Part I of this book provides a biography of Toni Morrison. Part II offers detailed entries on Morrison's works, focusing on her novels but also including her short story "Recitaf," children's and non-fiction books, essays and interviews, theatrical adaptations, librettos, lyrics, and more. Entries on the novels and "Recitatif" contain major synopses and critical commentary subsections and subentries on the individual characters in the work. Part III contains entries on people, terms, and topics related to Morrison and her work. Part IV contains the appendices, including a chronology of Morrison's life, chronologies of the events in each of her novels, a bibliography of Morrison's works, and a bibliography of secondary sources.

Any reference to a person, term, or topic that is the subject of its own entry in Part III is given in SMALL CAPITAL LETTERS the first time it appears in another entry.

PART I

Biography

Toni Morrison

(1931–   )

The Nobel Prize–winning author known to the world as Toni Morrison was born with another name. At her birth on February 18, 1931, the name given to the infant who would become Toni Morrison was, according to her birth certificate, Chloe Ardelia Wofford. There is much speculation about the origin of Morrison's name change from Chloe Wofford to Toni Morrison. Morrison herself has said that Toni was a nickname that she acquired as a young adult and that she regrets having used the name when she published her first novel, *The Bluest Eye*, in 1970. To Morrison's friends and family, she is still referred to by the name she was born with, Chloe Wofford. Publicly, she is known as Toni Morrison.

Toni Morrison's family had a profound influence on her development as a writer. Morrison spent a great deal of time with her extended family, particularly with her maternal grandparents. Both sides of Morrison's family had moved north from southern states, as so many African Americans did in the exodus known historically as the Great Migration. All four of her grandparents left the South and headed to Ohio in search of better economic

The Wofford family home in Lorain, Ohio, where Chloe Wofford (Toni Morrison) was born in 1931. *(Photograph by Carmen R. Gillespie)*

opportunities and greater freedom from the often violent manifestations of southern racism.

Morrison's grandparents on her mother's side were Ardelia and John Solomon Willis. The Willises were farmers from Alabama. Early in the century, the Willises abandoned the South when racism and economic realities forced them from their farm in Greenville. John Solomon Willis inherited the land the farm was located on from his grandmother who was Native American in origin.

The family relocated to Kentucky with their children, one of whom was Ella Ramah Willis, Toni Morrison's mother. While in Kentucky, John Willis worked as a coal miner. After facing disillusionment with the racial climate and lack of economic opportunities for African Americans in Kentucky, the family settled in Lorain, Ohio. John Solomon Willis and his wife Ardelia deeply valued education and stressed its importance to their children. John Willis taught himself to read and to play the violin. He was also an avid storyteller. Morrison recalled the stories of her mother's family and used them as a springboard for her novel *Song of Solomon* (1977).

Morrison's paternal grandparents died before she was born, and so she did not have firsthand experience of them. Many years after her father, George Wofford died, Morrison discovered that her grandfather was forced from his position as a train engineer shortly before his family relocated from

Toni Morrison greets an admirer following the performance of the opera *Margaret Garner* in Cincinnati, Ohio, July 2005. *(Photograph by Carmen R. Gillespie)*

Cartersville, Georgia, to Lorain. The family's move may also have been motivated by three lynchings of African-American men that occurred in the town. Witnessing these injustices may have left a lifelong impression on George Wofford. Morrison describes her father as having a deep and unwavering suspicion of white people, feeling that they were inferior and brutal—unworthy of serious consideration. Although a staunch advocate for equality, Morrison's mother, Ramah Willis Wofford, was more willing to evaluate individuals on the basis of their particular behavior.

Ramah Willis Wofford was a gifted singer and was active in the church. Morrison recalls her mother's resistance to the racism of Lorain. She says that her mother refused, for example, to sit in the segregated section of the movie theater. Between her father and mother's response to the world they lived in and her grandparent's stories, Morrison's world was richly imbued with a sense of place, community, purpose, and identity that would, in time, infuse the rich fabric of her imaginative, eventually narrative, universe.

According to Morrison's first teachers, she was an extraordinary and mature student who, as the only African American in her first grade class at Hawthorne Elementary School, was also the only student who came to school already able to read.

Morrison has said that she cannot remember a time when she did not know how to read. Race relationships in Lorain, a small, industrial town of immigrants, were complicated. Morrison went to integrated schools and often was called upon to help other students learn to read. That was particularly true of the new immigrants whose command of English was not particularly strong.

As might be imagined, Morrison excelled in her school work and was well-liked by both her peers and her teachers. While Morrison was growing up in Lorain, she was particularly close to her sister, Lois, who is only a year and a half older than Morrison. The girls also had two younger brothers, George and Raymond. Their parents, George and Ramah, were protective. They encouraged their children to pursue education. George Sr. worked several jobs to ensure the financial security of his family. His primary occupation was as a welder in the local Lorain shipyard. When she was not primarily occupied with raising her four children, Ramah Wofford, like her husband, held a variety of jobs including working at the American Stove Works. Ramah Wofford was also employed for a time as a Lorain Public Schools custodian. Ramah Wofford was also very involved in the family's church, the Greater St. Matthew African Methodist Episcopal Church (A.M.E.). Mrs. Wofford was

The steel plant where George Wofford, Chloe Wofford's (Toni Morrison's) father worked during her childhood
(Photograph by Carmen R. Gillespie)

active in many church groups and was noted in the community for her participation in the choir. Morrison has said that the musical talents of her family made her feel deficient since she did not believe that she possessed an equivalent gift.

Morrison continued to excel throughout her school career. As a teen, she worked as a helper in the Lorain Public Library. She recalls that the library was one of her favorite places. She often spent leisure time there and received advice from helpful librarians who assisted her in molding her developing intellectual life. Morrison read widely in the classics. Some of the writers Morrison admired while in high school were Tolstoy and Dostoevsky. Morrison worked on her high school newspaper and yearbook and was interested in theater. In fact, when Morrison graduated with honors from Lorain High School, she had aspirations to become a dancer.

Morrison credits her mother with inspiring her to attend college. Although Morrison was an excellent student, the decision to attend college was not automatic. Morrison was the first person in her family to graduate from college. In 1949 she left Lorain to pursue an undergraduate education at Howard University in Washington, D.C. Morrison has said that she was genuinely surprised by the color and class consciousness and social (as opposed to intellectual) environment she discovered there. While at Howard, Morrison majored in English and minored in Classics. Morrison studied with author and intellectual Alain Locke and with the poet Sterling Brown. She joined the African-American sorority, Alpha Kappa Alpha, and was a member of the theatrical group, the Howard University Players. At the time Morrison attended Howard, poet Amiri Baraka (LeRoi Jones) was also a student there. Upon graduation, Morrison moved to Ithaca, New York, to earn a master's degree from Cornell University.

While at Cornell, Morrison studied literature and completed her master's degree in 1955. Morrison's master's thesis was written on suicide as a literary construct in the fiction of William Faulkner and Virginia Woolf. Following completion of her master's degree, Morrison began her long career as a university professor with an appointment at Texas Southern University.

Toni Morrison's (Chloe Wofford's) senior year high school yearbook photograph *(Courtesy of the Lorain Public Library, Toni Morrison Collection)*

In Houston, at Texas Southern, Morrison expanded her understanding of the African-American experience in ways that she had not experienced as a student at Howard. Morrison remained at Texas Southern for two years, leaving in 1957 to return to Washington, D.C., and Howard University as an instructor on the faculty. While at Howard, Morrison met the man she would eventually marry, Harold Morrison. Morrison was an architect from Jamaica. Morrison took her husband's name and began to use the first name of Toni, a name she would later

The original Lorain Public Library, dedicated in 1904, where young Chloe Wofford (Toni Morrison) often went to read and study. Morrison credits the thoughtful librarians here with steering her burgeoning intellectual growth. *(Photograph by Carmen R. Gillespie)*

call a nickname. Morrison remained at Howard until 1965. She had several students who would eventually be prominent in their own right, such as Andrew Young, Claude Brown, and Stokely Carmichael. While on faculty at Howard, Morrison became a member of a writer's group, through which she began a draft of what eventually became her first published novel, *The Bluest Eye* (1970).

In 1961, Toni and Harold Morrison welcomed their first child, a son, Harold Ford, into the world. For reasons Morrison has attributed to cultural differences, the Morrison marriage was unhappy. Pregnant, Morrison traveled to Europe in 1964 and lived there briefly before traveling back to the States to divorce her husband and to return tempo-

rarily to her parents' home in Lorain, Ohio. Morrison's second son, Kevin Slade, was born while the family was in Lorain. Eventually, Morrison's ex-husband returned to the Caribbean, and established an architectural firm, and made his residence in Barbados and Jamaica.

Although Morrison's mother expressed concern about her daughter's move to a place where she had no family, Morrison took a job as a textbook editor at Random House in Syracuse, New York, with hopes that, in time, she would be promoted and transferred to the main office of Random House in New York City. In spite of the difficulties involved in raising children as a single mother while working full time, Morrison also managed to continue work on her first novel, *The Bluest Eye* (1970).

In 1967, Morrison's ambitions were realized when her hard work at Random House paid off and she was promoted to senior editor and relocated to New York City. Morrison was the first African-American woman to hold the position of senior editor at Random House. While an editor at Random House, Morrison was responsible for shepherding the writing careers of a generation of young African-American writers, including Toni Cade Bambara, Henry Dumas, Michelle Cliff, and Angela Davis.

In 1970, Toni Morrison published her first novel, *The Bluest Eye*. Although she received critical praise for the book, it was not a commercial success. The novel details the coming of age of a young protagonist, Pecola Breedlove, who is marginalized by her race, gender, and class. Pecola's eventual destruction haunts the narrator, Claudia MacTeer, who feels retrospectively that there was something more she should have done or should have been able to do to prevent Pecola's downfall. Morrison says that she wrote *The Bluest Eye,* in part, because it was a book that she would have wanted to read but that did not exist in another form at the time she was writing. The book is an important contribution to the outpouring of African-American women's writ-

Toni Morrison (Chloe Wofford) high school yearbook photograph. Morrison is pictured working as a member of the newspaper staff. *(Courtesy of the Lorain Public Library, Toni Morrison Collection)*

ings that emerged during the late 1960s and early 1970s and would become what is now known as the Afra American literary renaissance. In addition to Toni Morrison, the AFRA AMERICAN LITERARY RENAISSANCE includes writers such as Alice Walker, Toni Cade Bambara, Gayle Jones, Shirley Ann Williams, Gloria Naylor, Ntozake Shange, and Nikki Giovanni.

While still an editor at Random House and raising two young children on her own, Morrison resumed her teaching career. In 1971, she began teaching literature and creative writing at the State University of New York at Purchase as an associate professor. Morrison continued her successful emergence as a writer with the publication of her second novel, *Sula,* in 1973.

Sula is the story of a friendship between two African-American women that begins in childhood and is damaged by the inability of the surrounding community and of the women themselves to recognize the primary significance of that relationship. *Sula* is an examination of conformity and of tradition. The novel questions the assumptions that limit women's lives and leave them with no sense of themselves outside of their roles as mothers, wives, and daughters.

Like *The Bluest Eye, Sula* was well received critically, but did not find a large audience. The novel was featured in the national women's magazine *Redbook*. Although it did not win, in 1975 the novel was nominated for a National Book Award, one of the most prestigious awards for fiction in the United States. The novel did win the Ohioana Book Award. Although 1975 was a banner year for Toni Morrison in many ways, her joy was overshadowed by the death of her father in Lorain on September 9.

Following in her parent's footsteps, Morrison continued to work at more than one job. Yale University offered Morrison a visiting lectureship in 1976. She accepted, and traveled back and forth from New York to New Haven, Connecticut, in order to fulfill her responsibilities as an editor and as a professor. Morrison published her third novel, *Song of Solomon* (1977), based loosely on the stories Morrison learned from listening to her maternal grandfather, John Solomon Willis. The narrative is the first of Morrison's novels to feature a male persona as the primary protagonist.

The novel tells the tale of the Dead family, who are deeply disconnected as a result of their collective ignorance about their family's narrative and, therefore, themselves. The son of the family, Milkman Dead, undergoes tremendous growth as he uncovers the narrative of the Deads and trades his avariciousness and selfishness for true self-knowledge and wisdom. The novel also confronts one of the central dilemmas of the post–Civil Rights era—the question of whether justice should occur, to quote Malcolm X, "by any means necessary." *Song of Solomon* received the National Book Critics Circle Award. It was also Morrison's first novel to receive commercial as well as critical validation.

Morrison's fame and reputation continued to grow with President Jimmy Carter's appointment of her to the National Council on the Arts in 1980. In 1981, Morrison published her fourth novel, *Tar Baby. Tar Baby* (1981) is a deceptively simple novel that interrogates the complex conflicts inherent in colonialism, neo-colonialism, post-colonialism, nationalism, assimilation, global economics, identity, and essentialism. Taking its foundation from the metaphor of the TAR BABY, the novel asks important question about race, class, relationships, and migration. The interactions of the primary characters, Jadine Childs and Son (William Green), provide the stage for working out these modern conflicts. Jadine represents the colonized person who longs for authenticity and is plagued with insecurity and self-doubt about her character and worth. Son represents another extreme. He is a sort of contemporary Caliban—a natural man who is enmeshed in folk culture and wisdom. The central question the novel ponders is whether these two characters can coexist without destroying each other or impeding each other's growth and progress. Morrison sets most of the action of *Tar Baby* outside of the United States, on a fictional island in the Caribbean.

Following the publication of *Tar Baby,* Morrison's fame reached new levels, including her selection to appear on the cover of *Newsweek* magazine in March 30, 1981. Morrison decided to dedicate her time completely to writing and teaching; to that end, in 1983, she left her position as a senior editor at Random House. She also published her lone short story "Recitatif" (1983).

In 1984, Morrison accepted an endowed chair at the State University of New York at Albany and became the Albert Schweitzer Professor of the Humanities. Morrison's decision to devote more of her time to writing proved fruitful. In 1986, Morrison saw the production of her first play, *Dreaming Emmett,* in Albany. *Dreaming Emmett* concerns the questions surrounding the historical narrative of EMMETT TILL, a young Chicago teen who was murdered in 1955 while visiting family in Money, Mississippi. Till's murderers were acquitted of the crime, but several months after the trial, they confessed to the deed in a story published in *Look* magazine.

During this incredibly productive time in her life, Morrison turned again to history as a source when she chose the story of MARGARET GARNER as a springboard for her fifth novel, *Beloved* (1987). Margaret Garner was a slave in Kentucky in 1851 when she and her husband decided to try to escape with their children to the other side of the Ohio River and freedom. The story of Margaret Garner was an inspiration for Morrison, but the novel that she wrote, *Beloved,* is more than a replication of the Margaret Garner story.

Beloved (1987) is the story of Sethe Garner and Paul D Garner, two former slaves whose traumatic experiences as slaves on a Kentucky farm called Sweet Home cause them to share critical memories. Sweet Home binds them together even after they are no longer enslaved. Paul D's traumas emerge in part from the emasculation inherent in slavery. He is uncertain about what it means to be a man since the autonomy and strength traditionally attributed to that label have been denied to him for most of his life. Sethe tries to live in the wake of her decision to kill her children rather than to have them returned to slavery after her successful escape with them is undone. Sethe tries to manage the consequences of her decision and finds herself isolated and living half a life.

At the novel's beginning, Paul D arrives at 124 Bluestone Road, the home Sethe claims as a free woman. *Beloved* (1987) is the story of the two and of their attempt to find true freedom through the achievement of a kind of equilibrium between the memory of the horrors of the past, the demands

Maplewood Farm on Richwood Road in Boone County, Kentucky, was home to Margaret Garner and provided Toni Morrison with the inspiration for the farm Sweet Home in her novel *Beloved*. *(Photograph by Carmen R. Gillespie)*

of the present, and the fear of the uncertainty of the future. Morrison's artful handling of the difficult issues *Beloved* raises solidified her reputation as a figure of major significance in the pantheon of American letters.

The recognition Morrison received in the wake of the publication of *Beloved* (1987) was not without controversy or without protest. Although Morrison was nominated for the National Book and National Book Critics Circle awards, she did not win the prizes. Morrison's exclusion led June Jordan, Houston Baker, and nearly 50 other prominent African-American writers to write a public letter protesting the lack of acknowledgment of Morrison's writing. The letter solidified Morrison's position as the dean of contemporary African-American literature. In March of 1988, Morrison was selected to receive the Pulitzer Prize for *Beloved*. She was also invited

to become a Tanner lecturer at the University of Michigan.

Toni Morrison continued in her role as a path breaker when she became the first African-American woman to hold an endowed chair at an Ivy League university. In 1989, Morrison became the Robert E. Goheen Professor in the Council of Humanities at Princeton University in Princeton, New Jersey.

Morrison's role as a professor at one of the major universities in the country did not affect her literary output. In 1992 she published her sixth novel, *Jazz*. The novel became a *New York Times* best-selling novel. *Jazz* (1992) is the second of a trilogy of Morrison's novels reflecting on the idea of love and its manifestations. The idea for the novel originated with a James Van Der Zee photograph of a dead, teenaged woman who, knowing she was dying, told her friends that tomorrow she would give them the name of the man who shot her during a rent party with a silenced gun. By the next day, the woman was dead and so did not betray her lover, the man who had murdered her.

The novel tells the story of the New York neighborhood, Harlem, from the perspective of its ordinary inhabitants, namely Joe and Violet Trace. The couple is at the center of the novel's investigation of the complexities faced by the millions of African Americans who moved from the rural South to the North during the Great Migration in search of jobs and a better life in the cities. Joe and Violet have to negotiate the stories from their pasts they bring with them to the city. These foundational tales continue to haunt and to define who they are even as they begin, or try to begin, new lives in the city. The skills, knowledge, and information that they acquire as they mature in the southern countryside both equip and disable them for their lives as urban residents. The novel bridges the post–Civil War era and the post–World War I generation in its portrait of the HARLEM RENAISSANCE and the NEW NEGRO from the inside out. *Jazz* (1992) received largely positive reviews and added to Morrison's literary stature and reputation. Also in 1992, Toni Morrison became a founding member of Elie Wiesel's Académie Universelle des Cultures.

Morrison contributed to the richness of life on the Princeton University campus when she established her Atelier program. Morrison began the Atelier program as an interdisciplinary arts program that brings artists from various disciplines together to work closely with students to produce a work of art or an artistic production. Atelier artists-in-residence since 1993 have included Robert Danielpour, Gabriel García Márquez, Yo Yo Ma, Maria Tucci, Peter Sellars, Lars Jann, and Roger Babb. Also in 1993, Morrison published her critical text, *Playing in the Dark: Whiteness and the Literary Imagination.* The text is now revered as a classic work of American literary criticism.

Continuing 1993's status as a landmark year in Toni Morrison's life, the now world-famous author joined American Nobel Prize laureates in literature Sinclair Lewis, Eugene O'Neill, Pearl S. Buck, William Faulkner, Ernest Hemingway, John Stein-

beck, Saul Bellow, Isaac Bashevis Singer, Czeslaw Milosz, and Joseph Brodskey when she won the award in 1993. She became the first black woman to win the prize.

Also in 1993, literary critic and professor Carolyn Denard initiated the Toni Morrison Society at the annual convention of the American Literature Association in Baltimore, Maryland. The official founding date of the Toni Morrison Society is May 28, 1993. According to its literature, the purpose of the society is "to initiate, sponsor, and encourage critical dialogue, scholarly publications, conferences and projects devoted to the study of the life and works of Toni Morrison." The Toni Morrison Society currently has more than 200 members worldwide. It convenes at biennial meetings devoted to the analysis and exploration of the works of Toni Morrison. Conferences have been held since 1998 in the cities of Atlanta, Georgia; Lorain, Ohio; Washington, D.C.; and Cincinnati, Ohio, each of which has a special relevance to Toni Morrison and/or her work.

The series of fortunate events in Toni Morrison's career was undercut when, on Christmas Day, 1993, her much-loved house on the Hudson River burned. As a result of the fire, the author lost some original manuscripts and irreplaceable family heirlooms and mementos. The author's grief continued when her mother, Ella Ramah Wofford, died on February 17, 1994, the day before Morrison's birthday.

Continuing to develop her interests in theater, dance, and music, in 1995 Morrison created the interdisciplinary work entitled *Degga* with composer Max Roach and dancer/choreographer BILL T. JONES. The work premiered at Lincoln Center. When Toni Morrison's hometown of LORAIN decided to honor her, Morrison suggested that they create a reading room in her name in the Lorain Public Library. The room was dedicated in 1995 in Lorain and Morrison returned to her hometown for the ceremony.

In 1995, Morrison also edited and published an edition of the writings of Huey P. Newton in a volume entitled *To Die for the People: The Writings of Huey P. Newton.* In the same year, the libretto she composed to the song cycle entitled *Honey and Rue*, with composer ANDRE PREVIN, was recorded by African-American opera singer KATHLEEN BATTLE.

When, in 1995, Toni Morrison was awarded the National Book Foundation Medal for Distinguished Contribution to American Letters, she gave one of her most important and well-known speeches, *The Dancing Mind: Speech upon Acceptance of the National Book Foundation Medal for Distinguished Contribution to American Letters on the Sixth of November, Nineteen Hundred and Ninety-Six.* The speech was published in 1996 as a book.

Toni Morrison's fame and popularity, as well as sales of all of her novels, increased when *Song of Solomon* was chosen in 1996 by talk-show personality Oprah Winfrey for her show's book club. In the same year, Morrison edited and published the multi-genre collection of Toni Cade Bambara's

writings *Deep Sightings and Rescue Missions: Fiction, Essays and Conversations* (1996).

In response to the national conversation about the racial issues raised by the O. J. Simpson murder trial, Morrison edited and published *Birth of a Nation'hood: Gaze, Script, and Spectacle in the O. J. Simpson Case* in 1997. She coedited the text with Claudia Brodsky Lacour, a comparative literature professor at Princeton. Toni Morrison also wrote the libretto for *Sweet Talk: Four Songs on Text*, with composer Richard Danielpour.

In 1997, Toni Morrison published her seventh novel, *Paradise*, the final installment of her trilogy on the question of love in its myriad forms. In the novel, Morrison examined the ways in which love

When the Toni Morrison Reading Room of the Lorain Public Library was dedicated on January 22, 1995, Morrison returned to Ohio for the ribbon-cutting ceremony. Pictured left to right in the photo are her nephew Kenneth Brooks, Lorain Library Board president Norman Herschelman, Morrison's son Harold Ford, poet Sonia Sanchez, Ohio member of Congress Sherrod Brown, and Lorain Library director Kenneth Cromer. *(Courtesy of the Lorain Public Library, Toni Morrison Collection)*

is abused and/or fulfilled. The novel demonstrates the way that the manifestations of love determine not only the course of individual and familial interactions, but also can affect the character, direction, and health of whole communities.

Specifically, *Paradise* (1997) tells the story of lost women who find themselves at the edge of an all-black town called Ruby. The members of the town, as descendants of historical outcasts, might find common connections with the women living in the Convent, just beyond Ruby's limits. Instead, the town leaders, enmeshed in fear of change and of the world outside of Ruby, perceive the women as threatening. They are so shaken by the women's presence and potential influence that they attempt to kill them rather than grapple with the realities of inevitable change.

In 1998, Oprah Winfrey produced and starred in a cinematic version of *Beloved.* The movie, directed by Jonathan Demme, and also starring Danny Glover, was a critical and commercial failure. In the same year, Toni Morrison edited and published the collected works of James Baldwin under the title *James Baldwin: Collected Essays: Notes of a Native Son / Nobody Knows My Name / The Fire Next Time / No Name in the Street / The Devil Finds Work / Other Essays* (1998).

Toni Morrison and her youngest son, Slade, began a literary collaboration in 1999 with their joint authorship of *The Big Box,* the first in a series of children's books the mother and son have produced. The book was illustrated by Giselle Potter. In the first year of the new century, Toni Morrison was nominated for and received the National Humanities Medal. She also published the poems "I Am Not Seaworthy," "The Lacemaker," "The Perfect Ease of Grain," and "The Town Is Lit" in the literary magazine *Ploughshares.*

In 2001, Toni Morrison published *The Book of Mean People,* her second collaboration with her son, Slade Morrison. In 2002, she published the poem "black crazies" in *Ms.* magazine.

Toni Morrison published her eighth novel, *Love,* in 2003. *Love* appeared to mixed reviews and to date the novel does not enjoy the same reputation as some of Morrison's earlier novels. *Love* is another chronicle in Morrison's continuing explo-

ration of the lives, communities, and histories of African Americans.

The story specifically questions the meanings of love for post–Civil Rights movement African-American communities. The novel has as its center the pre-integration gathering site of Cosey's Hotel and Resort, a beach escape for middle-class African Americans. This site becomes the locale for both the very particular conflict between the novel's main characters, Heed and Christine Cosey, as well as a stage for the exploration of the larger issues of assim-

In November 2006, Toni Morrison was invited to be a guest curator at the Louvre Museum in Paris, France. The exhibit she conceived was entitled *The Foreigner's Home.* This poster, outside the gates of the Louvre, was one of the advertisements for the event. *(Photograph by Carmen R. Gillespie)*

ilationism vs. nationalism, class conflicts, and sexism as they affect African-American communities.

In 2003, Morrison's third collaboration with son Slade Morrison appeared when the mother/son team wrote and published the children's book, *The Lion or the Mouse? (Who's Got Game?)*. In 2004, the Slade and Toni Morrison collaboration continued with the publication of the children's book, *The Poppy or the Snake? (Who's Got Game?)*. Also in 2004, in commemoration of the 50th anniversary of the *Brown v. Board of Education of Topeka, Kansas* Supreme Court decision that declared unconstitutional the legal practice of "separate but equal" established in the 1896 *Plessy v. Ferguson* Supreme Court decision, Toni Morrison published the book *Remember: The Journey to School Integration* for young readers.

In 2005, Toni Morrison served as a Feature Films Jury Member of the 2005 Cannes Festival. Another major event for 2005 was the public performance of the opera, *Margaret Garner*. Morrison wrote the libretto with composer Richard Danielpour. The opera premiered to rave reviews in Detroit, Michigan; Philadelphia, Pennsylvania; and Cincinnati, Ohio. Toni Morrison received an honorary doctor of letters degree in 2005 from the University of Oxford.

In the spring of 2006, after a 17-year tenure as the Robert E. Goheen Professor in the Council of Humanities in creative writing at Princeton University, Toni Morrison retired. The same year the *New York Times Book Review* named *Beloved* as the best work of American fiction of the past 25 years.

In November 2006, Morrison served as guest curator at the Louvre in Paris at an event entitled *The Foreigner's Home,* cosponsored by the Toni Morrison Society, at which Toni Morrison read from her forthcoming novel, *Mercy.*

BIBLIOGRAPHY

Fultz, Lucy. *Toni Morrison: Playing with Difference.* Urbana and Chicago: University of Illinois Press, 2003.

Jordan, June, and Houston Baker. "Black Writers in Praise of Toni Morrison." *New York Times Book Review,* January 24, 1988, 36.

RM Artists Presents Profile of a Writer: Toni Morrison (1987). Home Vision, DVD/VHS, 1987.

Morrison, Toni, as told to Michelle Lodge. "Pride and Joy." *Time* (March 15, 2004). Available online: URL: http://www.time.com/time/magazine/article /0,9171,993628,00.html. Accessed on September 10, 2006.

PART II

Works A to Z

NOVELS AND SHORT FICTION

Beloved (1987)

Beloved is the story of what happens in the silences of trauma. The novel reveals the lives of its two main characters, Sethe and Paul D. Both are former slaves and both are trying to create lives for themselves in the wake of decimating and pervasive personal histories. Both are forever marked by the legacy of their individual experiences with American slavery.

The portraits of Paul D and Sethe created by Toni Morrison in *Beloved* confront the questions of what it means to be a man and also what it means to be a mother when the basic elements of freedom and humanity are denied. These questions are always difficult but are rendered nearly impossible to answer with the lack of autonomy and choice that defines slavery. Even when the characters are no longer literally enslaved, their thoughts and actions are haunted by their memories of their earliest and formative experiences as someone else's property.

In *Beloved*, there is an attempt to enter the consciousness of individuals who were enslaved and to animate the feelings that must have been associated with so much uncertainty, loss, and violation. In the novel, that personification is made manifest in the character Beloved. Beloved can be seen as a representation, a personification of all the trauma and catastrophic human cost of the Middle Passage and slavery.

According to Morrison, the idea for the novel *Beloved* originated with the historical narrative of MARGARET GARNER, a woman who in 1856 ran away from the farm where she was enslaved in Kentucky. When she and the others she escaped with were followed and discovered by their owner, Garner tried to kill her children rather than have them re-enslaved. She succeeded in killing one of her children, and her subsequent trial became the subject of national controversy particularly as concerned the issue of ABOLITION.

Toni Morrison wrote the libretto for an opera based on the story of Margaret Garner. The opera, *Margaret Garner,* with music by composer RICHARD DANIELPOUR, premiered in Philadelphia, Detroit,

The cabin on Maplewood Farm in Boone, Kentucky, where Margaret Garner, the real-life inspiration for Sethe in Morrison's novel *Beloved,* is thought to have lived. *(Photograph by Carmen R. Gillespie)*

and Cincinnati in 2005. The novel *Beloved* was awarded the Pulitzer Prize in 1988. *Beloved* was also produced as a major Hollywood motion picture in 1998.

SYNOPSIS

Beloved has three main sections, but the novel does not have chapter titles. Breaks are indicated in this synopsis with additional line breaks.

One
Beloved begins with the house that is the centerpoint of the narrative, 124 Bluestone Road. This house outside of CINCINNATI is the home of Sethe Garner and her family. The members of her family—her sons, Howard and Buglar, and her mother-in-law, Baby Suggs—gradually leave the house or die. So by the beginning of the novel, the year

1873, Sethe and her daughter Denver are the sole occupants of the house.

The house is said to be spiteful and is, apparently, haunted. The haunting drives away Sethe's sons, who can no longer bear the fear and uncertainty of their home. Their grandmother on their father's side, Baby Suggs, died not long after the boys left. Baby Suggs, after a lifetime of hardship and agonizing personal traumas, gave up on life.

The current occupants of 124 Bluestone Road—Sethe and her daughter Denver—are convinced that the haunt roaming their home is Sethe's dead daughter, Denver's sister, who is unnamed in the novel except for the word on her tombstone, Beloved. When the infant died, Sethe traded her body in a sexual exchange with the engraver to have the letters etched on her dead daughter's tombstone.

Sethe is a former slave who escaped to 124 Bluestone Road, while pregnant with Denver. Denver was born just as Sethe arrived on the banks of the Ohio River. As previously mentioned, after the departure of Sethe's sons and the death of Baby Suggs, Sethe and Denver are alone at 124, alienated from the community and kept company only by a ghost. The isolation of the two women is disrupted as Sethe returns to her house one afternoon and finds Paul D waiting for her on the porch. Paul D is one of the men enslaved on the same farm with Sethe in Kentucky, called Sweet Home. At the time of the escape, there were six people enslaved at Sweet Home, Sethe, Paul D, Paul A, Paul F, Sixo, and Halle, Sethe's husband.

As Sethe is the only woman on the farm, all of the Sweet Home men dream of partnering with her. The Sweet Home men, as they were called by their owner, Mr. Garner, allowed her to choose which one of them she wanted to have as a partner and she chose Baby Suggs's son, Halle. When Paul D arrives at 124, he and Sethe have not seen each other in 18 years.

Almost from the moment of Paul D's arrival, Denver is threatened by his relationship with her mother and by the memories that they share but she does not. Sethe invites Paul D to stay for dinner and tells him about the scars on her back. Sethe says that the scars trailing her back resemble a chokecherry tree. She also tells him that the young white men on Sweet Home violated her by suckling her breasts and then beating her. In a gesture of consolation and affection, Paul D kisses the scars Sethe has named after a tree and holds her breasts as he does so. Almost immediately, the ghost begins to manifest itself, and Paul D fights it by throwing furniture and yelling. He seems to rid the house of the presence, but the leaving saddens Denver, who sees the ghost as a comrade.

Sethe and Paul D consummate their relationship, and Paul D, after all of his years of imagining the sexual encounter, finds Sethe and the experience disappointing. As he reflects on their love-making, he remembers Sixo, one of the other Sweet Home men, and the lengths to which he would go to meet a woman he loved. Sixo found a hiding place for himself and his love that was one-third of the 34 miles between them and, in spite of some initial confusion, would meet her there for brief rendezvous. As a result, Sixo was the only black man at Sweet Home who was not longing for Sethe.

Denver—Sethe and Halle's daughter—has had her whole life defined by her mother's stories, by the absence of other people, and by the tangible presence of the ghost she believes is her sister. She has been told the story of her own birth so many times that she experiences it as a memory.

Sethe escaped from Sweet Home by herself and walked as long as she could at six-months pregnant and with no shoes. At one point, she falls to the ground and is prepared to lay there until she dies when out of the woods comes a young singing white woman named Amy Denver. Amy Denver tells Sethe stories, particularly about her plans to travel to Boston to get some carmine-colored velvet. By distracting Sethe from her pain with her songs and stories, Amy Denver helps her to get to shelter where the two women spend the night. Amy rubs Sethe's feet until they regain their feeling.

Even though it no longer haunts 124 Bluestone and traumatizes its occupants, Denver is still able to see the ghost and tells Sethe that it looks like a white dress holding onto her mother. Sethe tells her daughter about rememory—the tangible presence of the past in everyday experience. The women both conclude that nothing ever dies, including memory. Because of Paul D's arrival, Denver realizes that she has not heard the whole story of Sethe's escape from Sweet Home.

Sethe tells her daughter about schoolteacher, the overseer at Sweet Home and brother to Garner, who took over the farm after Mr. Garner's death. Schoolteacher arrived at Sweet Home shortly after Mr. Garner's mysterious death, bringing with him two young men, both called nephew. Schoolteacher wrote down all of his observations about the slaves at Sweet Home. At one point, Sethe overhears him discussing the animal and human characteristics of the Sweet Home slaves and she realizes the extent of schoolteacher's inhumanity and the danger that his disregard presents for herself and her family and friends, especially for her children.

After Paul D rids 124 of its ghost, Sethe begins to imagine that she, Paul D, and Denver might make a life with each other, a life safe from the ever-menacing presence of the past. Denver is not at all pleased by the proposition that Paul D might stay with them for an extended amount of time. Paul D says to Sethe that if he is going to stay with them, he has to be able to interact with Denver honestly and to respond if she is rude. He says to Sethe that he believes that the three of them can share a life.

The three go to a local carnival. Paul D serves as connection to a community from which Sethe and Denver have been estranged and alienated. Denver enjoys the carnival and begins to think that having Paul D around may not be so unbearable. As they walk home, the shadows of their hands are connected.

The next chapter begins with the description of a woman walking out of a body of water who, through great effort, finds herself sitting on a tree stump in front of 124 Bluestone Road. Paul D, Sethe, and Denver find the woman there when they return from the carnival. Upon seeing the woman, Sethe runs to go urinate. The woman is insatiably thirsty, well-dressed, and relatively young. Later the woman reveals her age to be 19. She tells the three that her name is Beloved, with no last name.

After arriving, Beloved sleeps for four days, and then she is struck with an insatiable appetite. Paul D is suspicious of Beloved and perplexed by the contradiction between her healthy appearance and infirm behavior. The rift between Paul D and Denver grows larger when Sethe asks Denver about an incident the two witnessed, where Beloved shows she is not really impaired as she picks up a chair with one hand. Denver lies to Sethe and says that she did not see Beloved pick up the chair as Paul D reported, deepening the divide between Denver and Paul D.

Beloved adores Sethe and wants nothing more than to hear the stories Sethe sometimes tells. Sethe tells her about a pair of crystal earrings she once had and the dress she made for her impromptu wedding to Halle. When Mrs. Garner sees her in the dress, she gives Sethe the present of the earrings. Sethe also tells Beloved and Denver about her own mother and one of her very few memories of her. Sethe's mother shows her daughter a brand mark that she has on her ribs in case the child ever needs to be able to identify her. Sethe, not realizing the brand had been burned into her mother by her master, asks her mother for a similar mark. Her mother responds by slapping Sethe. Sethe tells the girls that eventually her mother was hanged. Denver is jealous of the sharing between Beloved and her mother.

In the next chapter, Paul D's suspicions continue and he questions Beloved and her motivations. He is particularly disturbed by the incongruity between the girl's new shoes and the story of her long journey to 124. Paul D confronts Sethe and says to her that he thinks Beloved needs to go. Sethe disagrees. They get into a conversation about the past, and Paul D tells Sethe why Halle did not meet her as was planned when she ran away from Sweet Home: Halle saw the moment when schoolteacher and his nephews tied Sethe down, beat her, and suckled her breast. Witnessing this perverse violence and not being able to act to prevent it or to effectively intervene sent Halle into insanity.

Like Sethe, Paul D has his own painful memories. The last time Sethe saw Paul D before she left Sweet Home, he had a bit in his mouth. Sethe asks him about that experience and Paul D says that the most humiliating element of the episode was seeing Mister, the rooster, who was free while he was constrained like an animal.

Denver and Beloved dance in the attic. Beloved tells Denver that the place that she came from was dark and crowded. Denver makes her promise that she will not leave. Then Beloved asks Denver to tell her the story of her birth. Denver tells the story with the hope of ensuring that Beloved will not leave, a fear that haunts her growing relationship with the girl. Denver hopes that her own stories will be as compelling to Beloved as Sethe's and that the stories will help bind Beloved to her side.

Denver also tells Beloved the story Sethe has told to her about her arrival in the world on the banks of the Ohio. Denver speaks of Amy Denver's hands and their skill at restoring Sethe's feet. She tells Beloved how Sethe trusted Amy Denver and believed that the girl would help and not betray her. After Amy tended to Sethe's feet, she worked on her injured back. It was at this point that Amy told Sethe that she had a tree on her back and described it in great detail, again distracting Sethe from her agony. Amy also sang to Sethe songs her own mother had sung to her.

Sethe slept through the night and in the morning was able to walk a bit. Amy helped her walk most of the day until they got to the river and found there an abandoned boat. As Sethe neared the river, her water broke and she went into labor. The baby, Denver, was born in the boat alongside the Ohio River. Amy asked Sethe to tell the newborn child about her, and Sethe decided as she drifted off to sleep to name her child Denver.

Sethe is still trying to resolve the news Paul D gave her about Halle. She tries to grapple with yet another irreconcilably horrible event. As she struggles with this new and painful knowledge, she reflects back on the years at 124 and in particular, the loss of Baby Suggs, Halle's mother. Baby Suggs gained her freedom and release from Sweet Home because Halle worked off the farm to raise enough money to purchase her freedom. When she arrived to freedom in Ohio, Baby Suggs became a freeform, nondenominational preacher who taught lessons of self-affirmation and compassion. Her church was a clearing in the woods where the people came to dance, laugh, sing, cry, and celebrate themselves and each other.

Sethe misses Baby Suggs and the cathartic healing of the Clearing. So she takes Denver and Beloved to the space in the woods where Baby Suggs once held worship. As Sethe walks to the Clearing, she remembers the details of the time of her first encounter with this community, when she was rescued from the banks of the river by Stamp Paid.

After Amy left, Sethe walked a bit down the river and happened upon some other black people. They offered her food and drink and then took her to a spot on the free side of the Ohio. Another woman, Ella, came to get her from that spot and delivered her to Baby Suggs's house, where Sethe had sent her other children with another group of runaways.

At Baby Suggs's, Sethe was nursed back to health and reunited with her children. She managed to bring the earrings with her that were a wedding present from Mrs. Garner by keeping them knotted in her petticoat. She dangled the earrings for the baby girl who arrived before Sethe with her brothers. Sethe has 28 days of freedom once she arrives at 124. She gets to know people in the community and is able to be a mother to her children for the first time in her life. She also learns what it is like to have choices and not to always be told what to do.

At the Clearing, Sethe tries to accept the final reality that Halle will never arrive at 124. She craves Baby Suggs's touch and feels her gently massaging fingers even in death. Suddenly, the fingers that were once comforting begin to strangle Sethe. The girls come running, and Sethe is able to breathe again. She has bruises on her neck where she was choked. Then Beloved begins to massage and kiss Sethe. Sethe stops her, telling the girl that what she is doing is not appropriate for someone her age. As the three walk back to the house, Sethe begins to feel that the terrible details of her story are not so unbearable with someone to share them with, Paul D.

When she gets back to the house, Paul D kisses Sethe and they begin to make love. Beloved enters the house and is filled with jealousy toward Paul D for the attention he receives from Sethe. Beloved runs back outside and is confronted by Denver who accuses her of trying to kill Sethe. Beloved runs off to the woods alone.

Denver remembers when she was not so lonely—when she went to school and learned how to read and write until a young boy, Nelson Lord, asks her about her mother and Denver stops going to school forever. Following the incident, Denver hears nothing at all for two years until she hears the ghost crawling on the stairs. Denver goes to the woods to find Beloved and discovers her watching two turtles make love.

This chapter begins to tell the story of Paul D's experience after the failed escape from Sweet Home. Paul D is sold to a man named Brandywine. After Paul D tries to kill the man, he is sent to work on a CHAIN GANG in Alfred, Georgia. The men on the gang sleep chained together in separate wooden cages embedded in the earth. While in Alfred, Georgia, Paul D and his fellow slave/prisoners are forced to endure every type of torture and abuse, from starvation to sodomy.

The men's salvation is their communication through the songs they sing as they work. They sing about their lives, their longings, and their loves, and, through this ritual, they preserve their humanity. They experience a seemingly endless rain that threatens to drown the men in their in-ground prisons. One man discovers that the earth underneath the boxes is soft enough to get through, but in order for one to escape, they all must. So the men communicate through the chain and all 46 come up through the mud to safety.

The men get help from a group of infirm Cherokee who feed them and help them to break the chains that so fiercely bind them together. Paul D follows the blooming trees north to freedom. He attempts to lock all of his experiences away in a rusty recess of his heart. He calls his heart a tobacco tin and stores his feelings and memories there in order to avoid encountering the painful past.

Beloved seems to have a kind of control over Paul D. One night, rather than joining Sethe in bed, he sleeps all night in the rocking chair downstairs.

Although he continues having sex with Sethe at other times, he begins to sleep each night in the chair. From the chair, he finds himself sleeping in the storeroom, and then he moves to the cold house to sleep. Paul D's movement is not associated with a change in his feelings toward Sethe. He genuinely loves the woman. Even he finds his behavior inexplicable.

Eventually, Beloved finds her way out to the cold room while Paul D is sleeping there. Despite Paul D's efforts to control himself, Beloved and Paul D have sex. During the act, Beloved asks Paul D to call out her name. Afterward, Paul D's carefully protected past bursts out of containment and begins to affect his every action.

When speculating about where Beloved comes from, Sethe believes that the girl has been kept in confinement by a white man for his perverse gratification. Sethe knows people who have been in similar situations and believes that such an explanation helps to make sense of the incongruities between Beloved's story and the details of her appearance and behavior.

Denver, on the other hand, is certain that Beloved is the ghost of her sister come to life. Denver lives in dread that Beloved will disappear or will go away, leaving her alone again. Beloved does vanish one day while the girls play in the keeping house, only to reappear again.

Paul D tries to understand his behavior with Beloved and his examinations send him reeling into the past he has tried to seal away since he left Sweet Home. In an attempt to regain control, he tries to be a better companion to Sethe. He goes to pick her up after work and walks her home like she is a schoolgirl.

In the alley outside of the restaurant where Sethe works, Paul D asks Sethe if she will have a baby with him. As the two playfully walk home, it begins to snow and they both wonder at the beauty of the moment. As they near home, Beloved is waiting for Sethe not far from the house. She stands out in the snow without a coat or hat.

That evening, Sethe suggests that Paul D come back up to the bedroom to sleep and Paul D feels that the problem has been solved.

After dinner, Denver and Beloved discuss Paul D's presence. Beloved wants him to leave. Almost as she says it, she pulls a tooth out of her mouth. Beloved is afraid that she, literally, will fall into pieces, and Denver shares her fear. She cries about the tooth and about her longing for Sethe and more while the snow continues to fall deep and heavy outside.

This chapter begins with a flashback of Baby Suggs's thoughts. After the unparented arrival of her three grandchildren to 124 Bluestone Road, Baby Suggs is pleased but afraid that their parents might not survive the escape. Sethe's arrival with another granddaughter makes Baby Suggs believe that it might be possible for her family to arrive intact.

Spurred by Stamp Paid's gift of a bucket of blackberries, Baby Suggs decides to have a little celebration with her friends and neighbors to mark the arrival of most of her family. Baby Suggs cooks an enormous feast of pies and turkeys and corn pudding and rabbits and feeds 90 people.

The unintended consequence of the party is jealousy and resentment. Baby Suggs's friends and neighbors begin to wonder why she seems to be so fortunate and are deeply jealous of the generous and big-hearted woman. The next morning, Baby Suggs feels something is amiss, but cannot put her finger on the source of the discontent she senses. Then Baby Suggs has another premonition about something larger and more dangerous approaching.

Baby Suggs is the mother of seven children. Halle is the only one she is allowed to keep for any length of time. When Garner purchases her and Halle, Halle is 10 years old and more expensive than Baby Suggs because she has a bad hip. At the Garners, Baby Suggs receives better treatment than she did at any of the other places she has been enslaved. She works alongside Mrs. Garner and does not receive the physical and verbal abuse she is used to from other places.

Eventually Halle purchases Baby Suggs's freedom from the Garners and Mr. Garner takes her to Cincinnati himself and leaves her in the care of an abolitionist family named the Bodwins. Baby Suggs keeps her name when she gains freedom because

it is the name she has from her husband, and she hopes that he might be able to find her. She also looks for her other children in hopes that she might be able to locate them.

The Bodwins give Baby Suggs a house and set her up as a cobbler and washerwoman and, eventually, as a preacher. Although she never learns any information about her lost children, Baby Suggs has a reasonably good life at 124 until the day after the celebration with the blackberry pies.

What Baby Suggs senses on the morning following her feast is the approach of schoolteacher and three other men to take Sethe and her children back to slavery. When the men arrive at the shed where Sethe has taken her children, they discover that Sethe has tried to kill her children rather than have them returned to slavery. Sethe tries to hit the baby against a wall when Stamp Paid runs in and saves the infant, Denver, from death.

Schoolteacher immediately gives up his claim to Sethe and her children, seeing her as ruined and "untamable." Baby Suggs enters the shed, binds the boys' wounds, and tries to get Sethe to hand her the dead baby girl; eventually, Sethe takes her surviving baby girl, Denver, with her off to jail.

At 124, Paul D does not know about Sethe's attempt to save her children from slavery, so when Stamp Paid shows him the photograph from the newspaper detailing the event, he is in disbelief. Stamp Paid reads the story to Paul D, and Paul D still cannot believe that the words are associated with the Sethe he knows and loves.

Sethe tries to explain herself to Paul D. She circles the room as she tells him about the baby and how, when Sethe arrived at 124, the baby was crawling already. She speaks of trying to raise her children at Sweet Home, of trying to keep them out of harm's way. She tells him what it was like to have gotten all of her children and herself safely out of slavery. She talks of the joy of the freedom to love her children, which was a new experience when she arrived at 124. With all of that, Sethe tells Paul D she could not go back to slavery or let her children go. For her the truth is simple: She would not let her children be slaves, so she put them where she thought they would be safe, on the other side of this life.

Paul D tells Sethe that her love is too much. He tells her that what she did was wrong. Then, as if adding insult, he tells her that she is not an animal but a person. Paul D then leaves Sethe, her story, and her house.

Two

Stamp Paid is regretful about his decision to tell Paul D about Sethe. He wonders at his motivations. He is sorry that he did not consider Sethe's feelings and that he did not think of Denver, the child he saved, and how Paul D's departure might affect her. He also feels that he has betrayed Baby Suggs, the woman he so deeply admires.

As Stamp Paid approaches 124, he hears choruses of loud voices of what he believes are spirits. Stamp never actually visits Sethe because he cannot bring himself to knock on the door. The doors of all of the houses in the community have always been open to him, and he does not know what to do with the silent and shut door of 124 or about his uncertain welcome.

Sethe tries to reconcile herself to Paul D's decision to leave and decides not to dwell on the departure. Sethe, Denver, and Beloved go ice skating on mismatched skates left over from Baby Suggs's cobbling work. When they return from the skating and huddle before the warm fire, Beloved begins to hum a tune that Sethe created as a lullaby for her children. The fact that Beloved knows the song confirms for Sethe her belief that this woman-child is her dead child come back to life.

Stamp Paid tries again to visit Sethe and remembers Baby Suggs's exhaustion and her retreat from the world and from her preaching. Baby Suggs wanted to think about something that would not cause her pain. She goes to bed to think about color. Stamp understands that Baby Suggs gives up on life for two reasons: She thinks her preaching makes no difference in what happened to those that she loves and she also cannot decide whether or what Sethe did was right. Having to think about those two impossible dilemmas, coupled with all of her losses is too much, and Baby Suggs gives up on all of it and takes to bed to study color.

Stamp Paid fails to get into 124. He also is tired. While fishing in the river, he finds a red ribbon still attached to hair and scalp. This discovery exhausts him and makes him empathize with Baby Suggs's despair.

Sethe wakes and begins to prepare breakfast for her daughters. She decides that everything that she needs is within her home and that the outside world holds no interest for her any longer. Believing that her daughter has returned makes Sethe feel redeemed, as if she can be free from the guilt and anguish of her decision. Her perceptions of Beloved's return give her a second chance.

During one of his attempts to visit Sethe, Stamp notices Beloved and wonders who she is and when she came to Sethe's home. He also reflects on his own transitions. Stamp Paid's original name is Joshua. He changed it himself when he lost his wife to the lustful desires of his master's son. The name indicates his feeling that, following that trauma, he has no more obligations. The situation with Sethe and his inability to get into her house make him feel, for the first time since the loss of his wife, that perhaps he is more indebted than he believes. He goes to visit his old friend Ella to ask her who the new woman at 124 is, but Ella does not know. She tells him, to his horror, that Paul D is sleeping in the basement of the church. Stamp Paid goes to see him immediately.

Sethe arrives at work late for the first time since beginning the job. She finds herself at the end of the day without food to take home to the girls, and she contemplates stealing some food. This dilemma reminds her of Sweet Home and Sixo's theft of a young pig. Sixo said that since both he and the pig were property, that he was not stealing the pig but enriching the wealth of the farm. For the first time since her child's death, Sethe is filled with excitement and joy. She cannot wait to get home. She remembers details of Sweet Home that made it clear to her that she could not let her children return there. Sethe once overheard schoolteacher talking to the nephews, instructing them on the difference between the slaves' human and animal characteristics. She remembers that the men of Sweet Home started planning to escape after they learned from Sixo about the UNDERGROUND RAILROAD.

Stamp Paid decides to stop trying to visit Sethe and Denver. He cannot overcome his sorrow at not being able to enter the house without knocking. No one is left to check on or care about the women.

Sethe explains her relationship to the woman she believes is her dead daughter and claims the woman as her lost daughter. She wants to explain to the girl everything that has happened. She reflects on the horrors of her own experience—looking for her mother's brand on hanging bodies. Having back the woman she believes is her dead child, Sethe begins to enjoy and experience the world in ways that she has not allowed herself since the death of her child.

She also remembers the last day on Sweet Home—how she did not want to leave without Halle and how she told Mrs. Garner that school-teacher and the nephews had beaten her and stolen her milk. She speaks about how she sold her body, her sex, for Beloved's headstone and recognizes that she came close to being a prostitute and probably would have had it not been for the Bodwins getting the job for her cooking at Sawyer's restaurant. But for Sethe none of that matters anymore because she believes her daughter has returned to her and she can claim her place as Beloved's mother.

Denver also claims Beloved, as she has since her arrival, as her sister. She reveals her love for her mother but also admits that she fears Sethe because she knows that Sethe killed her sister and tried to kill her brothers. Denver comments on the fact that, except for two times after she stopped attending school, she has never left the house.

She thinks that Beloved came to her—that Beloved belongs to her. Denver thinks that she has to protect Beloved from Sethe. She remembers being in prison with Sethe and knows how tangible bad events can be. Denver imagines that when Sethe combs Denver's hair each night, she cuts her head off.

Denver reveals that she spends a great deal of time imagining that her father is coming back. When Paul D arrives, she thinks that he might be Halle and is disappointed to find out that he is not and that he came looking for Sethe, not Denver.

Baby Suggs told Denver about her father—how much he loved soft fried eggs, what a good man he was, how well he could read and do figures—what kind of man he was. Denver thinks Beloved came to wait with her for Halle's return. She claims Beloved as her own.

The next chapter contains Beloved's internal thoughts and memories. She remembers a woman gathering flowers in a basket, and she longs for a clear view of and connection to the woman's face. She seems to experience time as a perpetual simultaneity, where all things happen at once and forever. She remembers being in a small place where she cannot stand up and where she is crowded in with others and where some of the others are dying. The place she describes resembles accounts of slave ships.

Beloved also remembers a time when they are not crouching. She seems to recount the experiences on the deck of a slave ship with some dead piled up nearby. The woman she longs for earlier is there, and Beloved wants to free her from the chains that are around her neck. The woman is lost to the sea. Then Beloved returns to the crouching space.

The woman Beloved longs for has something shining by her ears. Clouds separate her from the woman. Beloved longs for the woman's face. The men and women are separated until a storm mixes everybody together and Beloved ends up on the back of a man who sings to her. He sings about the place before the clouds where a woman is gathering flowers. The man dies.

The dead man and his song reconnect Beloved to the woman she has lost to the sea. The woman jumps into the sea. She goes into the water of her own accord.

Later, Beloved is standing in the rain and trying not to fall apart while someone or something unnamed is violating her. Then she is alone at a bridge for some time. Everything that she has experienced is in the water, including the face that she craves. She sees the face she loves in the water and wants to join with it. The woman seems to consume her, and they are one and then they are not. The connection is short. Then she is alone.

Beloved comes out of the water. She is not dead. She says that Sethe is the face that she lost. Now

Beloved believes that she can have the face that she lost, that she can join with Sethe.

The next chapter conflates the individual perspectives of each of the women: Sethe, Denver, and Beloved. Beloved explains that Sethe is the woman that she lost three different times in her dream-like memories. She believes she has found her and is determined not to lose Sethe again.

The three enter into a conversation where each woman tries to define herself based on their relationship with the other. Repeatedly, the women locate and relocate each other in their pasts. Their needs, desires, and losses create a circle of connection that is fueled by the interaction of love and possession.

Paul D is staying in the Church of the Holy Redeemer feeling as if everything has fallen apart. His strategy of keeping the past at bay, locked up in his heart, his tobacco tin, failed and now he finds himself haunted by a past that will not be managed. Because of slavery, Paul D has been separated from most of his family all of his life. Sweet Home was a kind of surrogate family where, for 20 years, he lived with his brothers, two friends, and was treated better than most slaves. When Garner died, or was murdered, the vulnerability of their situation became apparent.

When Garner died, the Sweet Home men realized that their fate had been entirely in his hands, their lives lived at his whim. Paul D tries to remember the things that went wrong with their escape plan from Sweet Home. They did not count on Sethe's pregnancy, unexpected visits from neighbors, Sethe having more demands on her time, and Sixo being locked up at night. Each of these complications combined to make the plan, which was doable, fail with terrible consequences.

When they got the signal to meet the other runaways in the cornfield, Halle went to tell Sethe that she needed to bring the children to the corn that night. No one knew what happened to Halle. The next time anyone saw him, he had already lost his mind after seeing Sethe molested by the nephews and beaten by schoolteacher. Paul A never showed up. The Thirty-Mile Woman escaped. Schoolteacher caught Paul D and Sixo. They tried to burn

Sixo alive. As he died, he called out Seven-O in acknowledgment of the pregnancy of the Thirty-Mile Woman. Because the fire was not hot enough, they ended up shooting Sixo to kill him. Paul D was destined for Alfred, Georgia.

Stamp Paid comes to find Paul D to apologize to him for telling him what Sethe did. He says that the people should have offered Paul D some place to stay and that he apologizes on behalf of the community. Paul D tells Stamp that the minister did offer his house to him but that he, Paul D, wanted to stay by himself. Stamp Paid then tells Paul D the story of his wife, Vashti. He tells how he was powerless when the master wanted his way with her. When the master tires of her, Stamp Paid restrains himself from killing her and escapes.

All of this conversation is but an introduction to what Stamp Paid really wants to talk to Paul D about: Sethe and what happened with her when schoolteacher came to recapture her and her children. Stamp tells Paul D that he was there and that what Sethe did, she did out of love. Stamp Paid also asks Paul D about the girl who is staying in Sethe's house, and Paul D tells what he knows about Beloved. Stamp Paid says that around the time of Beloved's arrival, a dead white man was discovered. The man was known to have kept a young black girl locked up in his house against her will. The girl disappeared. Stamp Paid speculates that Beloved might be that girl. Paul D shivers in the recollection of all of that misery and asks Stamp how much a person is supposed to be able to take. Stamp answers that a person has to take all he is capable of managing.

Three

The house on Bluestone Road is quiet at the beginning of *Three*. The circle of passion among the three women has worn them all out. Denver, however, is the only one of the three capable of stepping outside of the circle and into the company of others in order to get the real things that they need to exist—food, clothing, and the like. Sethe and Beloved establish an insatiable rhythm of need that consumes them both. Eventually Sethe's only impulse is to satisfy all of Beloved's needs completely. Beloved becomes utterly consuming of everything Sethe possesses. Denver begins to realize that it is not Beloved who is vulnerable but Sethe. Denver decides that she is going to have to leave the yard of 124.

Denver remembers her grandmother and her comforting words. Baby Suggs acknowledged that the world was not safe, but told her granddaughter that all that she could do was to recognize that truth and, with that knowledge, keep going. Denver seeks out the last adult person she had any contact with, Lady Jones, the schoolteacher. Lady Jones is a mixed race woman who hates her complexion and marries a dark-skinned man. She has always been kind to Denver and helps her out again in this situation.

When they learn of Sethe and Denver's plight, the women of the community rally and begin leaving food for them. Denver takes over the care for her mother and Beloved. Sethe continues to try to persuade Beloved that she did the right and only thing in response to schoolteacher's arrival in the yard. Beloved does not understand or care and continues to demand all of Sethe's attention and resources.

Denver visits the Bodwins and asks them for help securing a job. Their housekeeper, Janey, talks them into letting Denver work there at night. From Janey, the women of the town hear more of the story of Beloved and 124 and are convinced that Beloved is the dead child returned from beyond to plague Sethe. Although they do not like Sethe and what they perceive as her excessive pride, they also have ghosts in their own respective closets and are offended at the thought of the past asserting itself in such a tangible way.

Some of the women of the town gather to go and confront the specter they believe has overtaken Sethe's home and life. Thirty of them gather and walk down Bluestone Road at three in the afternoon. When they arrive at 124, some of the women drop to their knees and start a wordless singing sound. Just then, Edward Bodwin approaches the house to pick up Denver for her new job working for him and his sister. When Beloved and Sethe appear outside, the women see Beloved as a beautiful, pregnant, dark-black, naked woman.

When Sethe sees Edward Bodwin approach, she is immediately taken back psychologically to the day the schoolteacher appeared in her yard and runs toward him wielding the ice pick she is holding. The women stop her before she can hurt Bodwin and he never knows what happened.

Paul D returns to 124 to see if Sethe is all right and to discover if anything can be resurrected from their aborted relationship. Before Paul D returns to the house, he runs into Denver in town. The two converse. Paul D asks Denver who she thinks Beloved was. Denver is uncertain and replies that Beloved may have been her sister but that she also was more. Denver tells Paul D he can visit Sethe, but that he has to be careful what he says to her.

Paul D reenters the house slowly reflecting on his behavior while there and the mistakes he made. He looks for Sethe and finds her in Baby Suggs's old room singing the lullaby she created for her children. Sethe tells him that she is tired. The statement reminds Paul D of what Sethe told him about Baby Suggs's death, how she finally gave up, and he realizes that he has to pull Sethe out of her resignation. Sethe thinks of all of the people she has lost and tells Paul D that Beloved has left her too. She says that her child, the one she killed, is the most valuable thing in her life. Paul D, believing that the two can build a life together, tells her that she is her own most important thing.

The novel ends with a conclusion that is more like a refrain. It describes two kinds of loneliness, loneliness that can be contained and loneliness that drifts and spreads. Then it tells of a lost woman who has no name and, not belonging, breaks into pieces.

Beloved eventually is forgotten. She blurs at the edges of memory until she is indistinct and hazy. Yet she remains at the margin of things that cannot be explained. Her footprints appear and disappear, however, and the human choice for explaining the inexplicable most often is in the shifts and changes of the natural world and elements, not in something as difficult and incomprehensible as the supernatural desire of a lost beloved.

CRITICAL COMMENTARY

One of the keys to understanding *Beloved* is found in the title of the novel. The novel's title can be broken into three parts—the words be and *love* and the letter d.

To Be

The word *be* is critical to understanding the novel in that it highlights one of the central questions of the novel, what does it mean to be a human being and then, particularly, what does it mean to be a human being when one's primary humanity is denied. Each of the primary characters in the novel must confront this question on their own terms and come to their own conclusions regarding the purpose of their own lives as well as the particularities of the specific denials of their humanity. Although it involves all of the characters, the question of what it means *to be* is the particular concern of Sethe and Paul D. Throughout the novel, the primary setting, 124 Bluestone Road, is referred to as a house with two stories. Although the description refers to the physical structure of the house, it is also applicable to the novel itself. Even though *Beloved* contains multiple overlapping and interwoven narratives, arguably the novel primarily explores the stories of Sethe and Paul D.

Sethe is at the center of the novel's questions about what it means to be a human being. These questions for Sethe revolve around how one can be a mother, a wife, a friend, a daughter—a woman—while a slave. After her arrival at Sweet Home, unlike most slaves, Sethe has to make the decision about whom among the Sweet Home men she will love—whom she will choose as her partner. She is able, within the limitations of Sweet Home's confines, to choose Halle as her husband. Lillian Garner's gift to her at the time of her "wedding," the crystal earrings, seems to signify to Sethe Garner's endorsement of the marriage and of Sethe's ability to choose a husband even though enslaved. Although they are not legally wedded, from Sethe's youthful and inexperienced perspective, she has made a choice and she believes that her decision means something permanent and lasting because she believes the mythology that Garner has created about Sweet Home—that she and the men who are enslaved there are allowed to live as humans.

As time progresses and Sethe becomes a mother, she begins to realize that the freedom that she thinks she has at Sweet Home is indeed an illusion. She misses the companionship of other women. With such a limited range of individuals to interact with, Sethe lacks critical sources of knowledge. Without a community of one's own choosing and without the autonomy to make decisions for oneself, it is impossible to know what choices you might have made and therefore impossible to know what kind of person one might become. Sethe does not know if she would be a good wife, mother, friend, or daughter because she is not given the opportunity to explore these options.

Even more specifically, the world Sethe, Halle, Sixo, and the Pauls inhabit is completely dependant upon the wiles of one man, Garner. When Garner dies, so does all of the stability and relative sense of self-possession of the slaves at Sweet Home.

The reality is that Sethe is not allowed to "be" at Sweet Home. The time that she is able to spend with her husband and her children is not her own. She is required to attend to Lillian Garner rather than to watch her own children. During such a time, the young Howard has an incident with the cow, Red Cora, where his thumb is dislocated. Not only is Sethe unable to watch her children adequately to prevent such mishaps from occurring, but also she does not know how to help Howard once he is injured. Sixo is the one who is able to assist Sethe, resetting Howard's thumb and binding it so that it will heal adequately. Significantly, Sixo is the only member of the Sweet Home community who has any experience as a free man. As such, he has an identity that comes from living a life and having experiences that derive from the exercise of free will. Sixo knows himself and has a sense of his identity beyond the confines of Sweet Home and its inhabitants. It is Sixo, for example, who, rather than limiting himself to sexual release with cows, finds a woman other than Sethe, the Thirty-Mile Woman, on another farm with whom to have a relationship.

Sethe does not process the extent of the precariousness of the situation at Sweet Home and the true degree of the inhabitants' enslavement until she overhears schoolteacher instructing the nephews about the animal and human characteristics of each of the blacks on the farm. At that point, she understands that schoolteacher, the man who is ultimately in charge of her fate and that of her children, does not regard her as human. When she makes this realization, she understands that if her existence is controlled by another person, she is not free to be. She determines that she and her children will be free to determine their own identities and lives away from Sweet Home.

After her escape from Sweet Home, Sethe has nearly a month of freedom and self-discovery. The short time between her escape and the arrival of schoolteacher at 124 Bluestone Road is the only period in which Sethe has an opportunity to explore her identity. During this time, she is able to play with her children, to have conversations with other women, to develop friendships and relationships, to explore her understanding of spirituality, to grieve the losses of her life, to reflect upon her future and make plans. Sethe is allowed to be.

Schoolteacher's arrival at 124 Bluestone Road changes everything. Ironically, the arrival of Sethe's former master demonstrates the extent to which Sethe has become a free person. The arrival of the slave master into Baby Suggs's yard sparks Sethe's understanding of herself and her children as autonomous individuals with agency. She refuses to return to slavery, to once again having no control over what happens to her body, her self, and also to having no say over what happens to her children's bodies and selves. Rather than allowing their recapture, Sethe makes the only decision she feels she has at her disposal—her only opportunity to act rather than to react—and she decides to take the lives of her children into her own hands rather than return them to the control of schoolteacher and a life of slavery.

Sethe's choice also may speak to a different sensibility the character possesses regarding the meaning of death. Sethe's decision to end the lives of her children rather than see them recaptured may suggest that her understanding of what it means to be may not be defined by the traditional definitions of boundaries between life and death. Sethe suggests that she is putting her children in a better place, pushing them to safety. Rather than ending their lives, she seems to believe that she is assisting their passage into another state of being. Sethe's discus-sions about her actions imply that she does not see death as an end to life, but as a continuation of existence in another form. Sethe truly believes that her actions toward her children are preferable to their potential fates should they be allowed to be reenslaved.

Unknowingly, however, Sethe's choice enters her into another kind of slavery. The guilt she feels about her decision prohibits her from allowing herself to live. Sethe is enslaved by responsibility for the consequences of her action. After the misery, as Baby Suggs calls it, Sethe refuses to allow herself to be defined in anyway other than as a mother. By limiting her identity to motherhood, she still is not able to fully explore the question of what it means to be Sethe. At the end of the novel, when Paul D suggests to Sethe that she is her own most important priority, the possibility exists that Sethe might develop the other parts of her identity that have been so long neglected.

Paul D also struggles with the question of what it means to be. Like the rest of the Sweet Home men, Paul D is lured into the delusion of independence and security that the farm, under Garner's control, seems to promise. With Garner as master, Paul D is allowed to carry his own gun. Garner gives Halle permission to earn money to buy Baby Suggs's freedom and he does not force the men to mate with Sethe; rather, she is allowed to choose from among the men which one she will have as a husband. Garner brags to his neighbors that the slaves of Sweet Home are "nigger men." All of these factors combine to make Paul D and the others believe that there is something unique about their situation—that they are truly able to be men.

Once Garner dies, everything changes for Paul D and for all of the enslaved residents of Sweet Home. When schoolteacher arrives, he takes away the primary symbol of Paul D's manhood and independence, his gun. He, Sethe, and the rest of the Sweet Home men suffer the disintegration of their ephemeral and transient world. They determine to change their situation by running away from Sweet Home to freedom.

When their plans are foiled, Paul D's sense of himself and of his being in the world further decays. When schoolteacher decides to sell Paul D, Paul D learns his precise quantitative value. Hearing his worth spoken aloud reinforces his feeling of unworthiness and his understanding that, legally and in the eyes of a great number of people, he is no better than an animal. Paul D has that feeling reinforced time and again after he is sold. Almost immediately, Paul D is chained and made to wear a bit. As he sits awaiting his fate, Paul D sees the rooster at Sweet Home, whose name, significantly, is Mister. The freedom and independence of the rooster makes Paul D feel the weight and seeming permanence of his own shackles. Later, when Paul D finds himself in Alfred, Georgia, not only is he chained, but also he is held underground. All of the pain and trauma of his experiences combine so that Paul D believes that he has to contain his memories and keep on the move. He is not able simply to be because his refusal to confront the pain of his past prevents him from living fully.

Both Sethe and Paul D are hampered in the human struggle to be—to find and create a meaningful subjective experience—because of their categorization and experiences as chattel.

Love

A foundational question Morrison engages in *Beloved* is, who is the beloved and what does it mean to be loved? Morrison reflects upon the question of love and its meanings and manifestations through her examination of various types of love. Among the many types of love the novel examines are mother love and the love between adults. Obviously, both types of love are seriously complicated by slavery and its aftermath.

There are many examples of relationships between mothers and children throughout the novel. Each example demonstrates how complicated the relationship always is, but emphasizes the near impossibility of mother love when the mother has no ability to protect either herself or her children from the violating dangers of slavery.

Sethe recounts to Denver and Beloved her fragmented memories of her own mother. Sethe's primary caretaker when she is a small girl is named Nan. Although Nan is a friend of her mother's and is, like her mother, originally from Africa, she is not Sethe's mother. Sethe vaguely remembers encountering her

mother a few times. One time Sethe remembers that her mother shows her a mark that has been branded upon her chest. Sethe's Ma'am shows her the mark so that if something happens to her, Sethe will be able to identify her body. Sethe does not understand, yet the absence of her mother does mark her in profound ways and affects her own ability to mother and her perceptions of motherhood.

As a mother at Sweet Home, Sethe is frustrated by her inability to watch her children. She often has to leave them on their own when she is performing her many responsibilities. Sethe's concern for her children's well-being is her primary motivation for leaving Sweet Home even when the plans that they make go so badly awry. Sethe takes her children to the corn before she returns to find out what happened to Halle. Getting her children to safety is her primary objective. Later, as she collapses while trying to escape at the end of her pregnancy, Sethe sees herself only as a mother and is motivated to survive because she wants to get her milk to her daughter who is still breastfeeding. Significantly, Sethe remembers that her own mother was not able to breastfeed her because she was forced to return to the fields. For Sethe, one of the ultimate expressions of freedom and of mother love is having the ability, the time, and the freedom to provide milk for her children—a basic function often denied to women who were enslaved. Sethe's mother love is not sentimental; it is pragmatic because of the circumstances she finds herself in as property claimed by another. It is this pragmatism that makes Sethe's actions toward her children when schoolteacher arrives at 124 Bluestone Road an extension of her mother love.

Baby Suggs's experiences also provide insight into the complexities of mother love during slavery. Baby Suggs has eight children, all of whom eventually are lost to her. Through Baby Suggs's losses, the cost of slavery and the damage that the institution does to the primary relationships between human beings is made plain. Showing much determination of character and personal strength when she first becomes a free woman, Baby Suggs searches for her lost children, but, when she discovers the task to be impossible, she does not give up on life; rather, she becomes a kind of mother-figure for others, becoming a preacher and healer who exhorts a community that has been damaged by the ravages of slavery to love themselves and each other. Baby Suggs does eventually give up in despair after Sethe's decision to try to kill her children rather than return them to slavery. Baby Suggs cannot decide whether what Sethe did was right or not.

Although certainly not traditional, *Beloved* is a kind of love story. As previously mentioned, the two stories of Paul D and Sethe form the structural foundation for the novel and their narratives ask whether it is possible for two individuals, traumatized and violated by experiences that are beyond their control, to come together and love each other.

Paul D's arrival at 124 is one of the first occurrences in the novel. His arrival changes the dynamic of Sethe and Denver's lives and offers the possibility of partnership and life beyond the shadow of guilt and responsibility within which Sethe lives after she takes the life of her daughter. Paul D's instinctual response upon learning of Sethe's abuse at the hands of schoolteacher and the nephews is to hold her, to lift her breasts, and to caress her scarred back with his mouth. This loving attention signals that Paul D is perhaps the one person who understands enough about Sethe's past and what she has been through for the two of them to be able to love each other.

In order for Paul D to love Sethe and for her to be able to love him the two both have to come to terms with the impact of the past and to integrate that trauma into their sense of self rather than suppressing or denying the reality of the horrific events they have both experienced.

D—The Past
In order to be able to move forward, to be together, and to love each other both Paul D and Sethe must confront the horrors of their individual and collective pasts. The end of the title of the novel *Beloved* is the letter d, which usually functions linguistically in English to signify past tense. It is that past that the character Beloved forces both Paul D and Sethe to address in order to create a future for themselves in which they can begin to be on their own terms and by their own definitions.

When Beloved arrives, Sethe inexplicably has to urinate copiously. This act can be seen as a recre-

ation of the events of labor. When Sethe's "water breaks" when she first sees Beloved, her physical reaction can be seen as her giving birth to the manifestation of her dead child. Whether Beloved is actually Sethe's dead child or not, Sethe's eventual belief that she is allows her to confront all of her feelings about what she did to her child.

Paul D also has his own ghosts to confront. Paul D tries to contain the past—Sweet Home, the loss of his brothers, Alfred, Georgia—in his heart, sealed, he believes, so that it cannot affect him; however, Paul D's sexual encounter with Beloved demonstrates to him that it is not possible to keep everything inside. That encounter destroys his resolve and he is forced to acknowledge that he has no control over his own feelings and responses to what has happened to him. He has to mull over the events, process them, and incorporate them into a self-created honest identity.

When Paul D learns from Stamp Paid what Sethe did to her children, at first he is in denial about the reality of what the man is telling him. When he confronts Sethe with the information, he says to her that her actions are those of an animal. Paul D's statement returns the novel to the fundamental question of being and highlights Paul D's own insecurity about his humanity as well as his guilt about having slept with Beloved. Paul D's lack of compassion toward Sethe and his subsequent departure demonstrate the extent of his own fears and the weight of the past that does not allow him to act lovingly and sympathetically toward Sethe.

After Paul D leaves, Sethe falls into the vortex of the past through her relationship with Beloved. The balance of the promise of a future that Paul D represented is gone. Sethe neglects Denver who represents the present and becomes obsessed with assuaging the needs and desire of the past in the form of Beloved. Sethe becomes consumed, both literally and figuratively, with the need to compensate for the death of her child by indulging her every whim. Such an urgent engagement with the past is self-destructive and never progresses beyond the reality of the act that can never be changed. As such, Sethe and Beloved become trapped in a vicious cycle that threatens to destroy Sethe.

The inadvertent reenactment of schoolteacher's arrival at 124 Bluestone Road by Edward Bodwin, as well as the presence of the 30 community women, catalyze Beloved's departure. The difference in the two events is critical. Sethe does not turn the knife toward her children this time; rather, she attempts to destroy what she perceives as the actual threat, the real enemy—the white man. Although misguided, Sethe's action brings the narrative full circle and establishes Sethe's agency and demonstrates her newfound ability to choose. This act can be seen as the exorcism of Sethe's past—she can move forward and let the specter of what she did remain in the past.

When Paul D returns to 124 Bluestone Road, he comes having acquired new humility. Having wrestled with his demons, Paul D is able to return to Sethe without judgment and with the knowledge and acceptance of the complex and impossible circumstances that lead an individual to the choices that Sethe made that were, in actuality, not choices at all. When Paul D returns, it is with new respect for Sethe's experiences and for the ability of the two to connect and to have a loving life together. Paul D knows that Sethe is capable of helping him to order his past and to move into the future. Through their love for each other, the two can help each other to be—to develop the autonomy and relative freedom from the decimating legacies of the past necessary to create selfhood.

SOME IMPORTANT THEMES AND SYMBOLS IN *BELOVED*

The Cyclical Movement of Human Experience

Throughout *Beloved*, the unfolding narratives of the characters move in intersecting and overlapping circles. Sethe, for example, mistakenly reenacts her defense of her children when Edward Bodwin comes to 124 Bluestone Road, recreating and bringing full circle her response to schoolteacher's attempt to recapture her family. When Paul D returns to 124 Bluestone Road after his departure upon learning of Sethe's attempt to kill her children, his return follows the path of his departure as he comes back to Sethe's side. When Sethe tries to explain to Paul D why she takes the actions she does when

schoolteacher arrives, she circles repeatedly around him as he sits at her kitchen table. In her resignation after Paul D leaves, Sethe takes Denver and Beloved ice skating and the three go around and around the pond representing the vortex of obsession with the past to which Sethe and Beloved ultimately succumb. The novel's circlings reflect the book's often repeated idea that the past, present, and future coexist and that the patterns of human experience move in orbits through these terrains. These rotations are represented symbolically in the novel in many ways, including the cycles of the seasons and of women's bodies.

The Disinterest and Richness of the Natural World

The natural world functions in *Beloved* as both an indifferent backdrop and a well of knowledge and information for the characters. Both Sethe and Paul D remain astonished by the natural beauty of Sweet Home in spite of the terrible loss and devastation that occurred there. Although water is absolutely critical to human survival, water in *Beloved* delivers up the red ribbons of lynched children and seems to be a burial ground for the forgotten and lost of the Middle Passage and the slave trade. Similarly, when schoolteacher arrives at 124 Bluestone Road to recapture Sethe and her children, it is a beautiful, clear day with no warning about what is to come.

On the other hand, Paul D is able to find his way north by following the blooming trees. The trees provide the critical information he needs in order to find his way to sanctuary and safety away from the brutality of Alfred, Georgia. Likewise, Sethe goes to the Clearing, the beautiful chapel of trees where the community used to worship with Baby Suggs, in order to find solace and peace. On one occasion when she goes there, however, she is strangled. This choking may be a warning, or at least a foreshadowing of the dangers of her relationship with Beloved.

Throughout *Beloved*, the natural world is frequently a neutral backdrop to the experiences of the character. On the other hand, the natural world does provide vital information to the characters if they are able to read and understand it. Some of the important symbolic uses of nature in the novel include Amy Denver's renaming of Sethe's scars as a tree, the freedom and seeming independence of Mister, the rooster, as Paul D is sold from Sweet Home, and the mating turtles from whom Beloved learns the secrets of sexual consummation.

The Fragmented Nature of Human Understanding and Perception

One of the critical tasks for the reader of Morrison's fiction, particularly of *Beloved*, is the work of assembling the narrative from the disparate pieces of the story that are dispensed slowly to the reader as the novel unfolds. Using this technique, the responsibility for the coherence and meaning of the novel belongs to the reader. The novel emphasizes the fragmented nature of human experience by telling the story in discrete bits. Denver, for example, learns upon Paul D and Beloved's arrival that the story of her birth that Sethe has told her has other parts, pieces of the narrative that Sethe has never shared with the girl. Although Paul D and Sethe both have parts of the story about what happened on the day of their attempted escape from Sweet Home, neither has the complete story. There are critical details, like what happened to Halle after Paul D last sees him that neither of them ever knows. Similarly, through her memories, Baby Suggs has parts of the experience of being a mother, yet, because of the artificial disconnect brought about by their status as property, Baby Suggs does not have a complete narrative knowledge of any of her offspring.

Through its structural fragmentation, *Beloved* makes the point that all human beings experience existence in starts and fits rather than as a smooth and continuous linear narrative. The expected fragmentation of experience is further complicated and pulverized by the crushing realities of slavery and, for that reason, the characters in the novel struggle continuously to make sense—to make a coherent narrative of their lives. The significant symbolic representations of human fragmentation are Baby Suggs's quilt that she uses to contemplate color at the end of her life, the unintelligible voices that Stamp Paid hears surrounding 124 Bluestone Road, and Paul D's understanding at the novel's end that, like Sixo's discovery about the Thirty-Mile Woman, Sethe is one of the few people in the world who can help him to order and make sense of the violent jumble of his life.

Sexuality, Night, Freedom, and Slavery

In *Beloved*, Morrison links night and sexuality. For many of the characters, because of the restrictions imposed during the day by slavery, the night is the only time for connection and often the only time for reflection. Additionally, *Beloved* often links nighttime sexuality with freedom and daytime sexuality with slavery.

There are many examples of night functioning as a space for intimacy in *Beloved*. The men of Sweet Home dream at night of bedding Sethe while she decides which one of them to love. Sixo visits the Thirty-Mile Woman at night in an empty stone place. Halle and Sethe touch and talk with each other only at night. Sethe and Halle "marry" at night. Paul D and Sethe walk to work together in the dark. Denver is born on the banks of the Ohio River in the evening.

The connection in the novel between night and self-reflection is most apparent with the character Beloved herself. During the night, Beloved repeatedly asks Denver to say her name. Beloved loses form and identity in the dark. At night, Beloved's insatiable hunger for Sethe's company, particularly for Sethe's stories, becomes strongest. The night also transforms Paul D. When Beloved and Paul D have sex, the contents of his tobacco tin—his heart—open.

Enslaved African Americans often used the cover of night to escape. Morrison reflects this historical reality with her use of night as a space where freedom becomes possible. The Sweet Home men and Sethe and her children plan their escape from slavery at night. During Sethe's escape, Amy Denver assures her that if she makes it through the night, she will live to experience freedom. Paul D and the other men on the chain gang escape during a rainy night. At the end of the novel, Paul D urges Sethe to fight to stay alive and promises always to be with her through the night. With this assurance, Sethe has the possibility of living and escaping the fate of Baby Suggs.

Sexuality is also pervasive in the novel as a symbol of the connection and disconnection, often violent disconnection, between human beings. For example Sethe has sex in exchange for having the words engraved on her child's gravestone. In order to signify, in a permanent way, the existence of her child, Sethe feels she has no choice but to engage in a humiliating and exploitative sexual encounter. Significantly, this exploitative sexual experience happens during the day.

Unnaturally separated from potential women partners, the Sweet Home men have sex with cows until Sethe decides whom she wants to "marry." She chooses Halle and the men enviously watch the couple making love in the corn field.

Upon their reunion, Sethe and Paul D have sex upstairs while Denver is left lonely in the kitchen. Sethe reveals that she remembers desire but had forgotten how it worked until having sex with Paul D. Although they have waited years for this encounter, Paul D finds the reality disappointing; however, after their initial sexual encounter, Paul D and Sethe have sex regularly in order to stave off the pain of the circumstances of their lives and to begin to establish a kind of normalcy.

Before escaping from Sweet Home, Sethe is raped during the day by the nephews while her husband watches. She feels that the rape, the nephews' sucking on her breast, is like having her children's milk stolen.

The prison guards in Alfred, Georgia, where Paul D is imprisoned, sodomize the prisoners during the morning line up on a regular basis, leaving open the possibility of Paul D's history as a rape victim. This possibility is connected to Paul D's questions about his status as a man. Complicating his relationship to sexuality is his sexual coupling with Beloved. The mysterious girl may function in the novel as a type of succubus, a demon figure, extracting semen and vitality from Paul D and, ultimately, becoming pregnant with his child.

CHARACTERS

124 Bluestone Road   124 Bluestone Road is the Baldwins' home that they rent to Baby Suggs and then to Sethe. The house used to be a way station for fugitive slaves. The house fills with spite and the red light of the ghost. 124 is at first a waiting place, as it was in the years before Sethe was there. Later

in the novel, the house is said to be, alternately, loud and then quiet.

ailing Cherokee   When Paul D escapes from the prison chain gang in Alfred, Georgia, he and the other men meet up with and are assisted by a group of Cherokee who are themselves ill and destitute. Rather than follow the so-called Trail of Tears westward, this group of Cherokee remain in Georgia as fugitives. Their experience had been marked by a series of betrayals by the government with which they had made many treaties, each one eventually and illegally negated.

The group Paul D and his men take up with no longer have any faith in the government and have decided to go it alone. Although the disease the Cherokee suffer from goes unnamed in the novel, the description of their condition sounds like smallpox. The Cherokee free Paul D and his companions from their chains and offer them food and shelter. Paul D is the last of the Alfred, Georgia, men to leave the Cherokee. Eventually he decides to run to the North, to freedom. They tell him how to get there. As it is spring, they advise him to follow the blossoming trees, which he does, all the way to Delaware.

The alliance between the Cherokee and the escaped slaves echoes the real affiliations between Native American groups and enslaved and free African Americans. There are many historical instances of Native Americans and African Americans joining forces and resources to assist each other.

Amy Denver   Amy Denver is the white girl who helps Sethe deliver Denver. She assists Sethe to a lean-to, props her up on leaves, and rubs her feet. Amy Denver also puts spider webs on Sethe's recently whipped back. She says she has slept with the sun on her face before, and asks Lu (Sethe) if she has done so. She sings the "Lady Button Eyes" song to Sethe. She is a servant girl of a man named Buddy. Like Sethe, she is running away. Amy Denver wants to go to Boston where she has heard that they have the best velvet. She and Sethe also have in common having been beaten. After Sethe gives birth on the banks of the Ohio River with Amy's assistance, Amy continues on her journey. Sethe decides to name her daughter after her.

Ardelia Ardelia is Baby Suggs's lost child who loved the burned bottom of bread. Baby Suggs never discovers what happens to the child although she searches for information about Ardelia and her other lost children after Halle, her sole remaining child, purchases her freedom. The last Baby Suggs hears of the child is that she was purchased by someone named Dunn and taken west.

Aunt Phyllis Aunt Phyllis is one of the people for whom the suffering of slavery results in permanent insanity. Aunt Phyllis is said to sleep with her eyes open. From the examples of people like Jackson Till and Aunt Phyllis, Sethe learns what can happen when a person reaches the breaking point. Sethe does not want to lose touch with reality, although her perpetual struggles with the emotional traumas of her life seem to push her in that direction.

Before Aunt Phyllis loses her faculties, she is the midwife for the African-American women in the community in Kentucky where Sweet Home is located. Aunt Phyllis lives in Minnowville and, in her desire to talk to another woman about mothering, Sethe wants to arrange to have Mrs. Garner drop her off at Aunt Phyllis's when Mrs. Garner goes to church so that she can speak with the woman regarding some questions she has about raising her children.

Baby Suggs (Jenny Whitlow; Baby Suggs, holy)
Baby Suggs has had eight children (Patty, Rosa Lee, Ardelia, Tyree, John, Nancy, Famous, and Halle) by six different fathers, and all of her children are taken away by the vagaries of slavery except her son Halle who eventually buys her freedom. The only things that she can remember of her children are the details, like the fact that her firstborn loved the burnt bottom of bread. After she is free, she unsuccessfully tries to find out what happened to her children.

Before Halle buys her freedom, Baby Suggs is the house slave at the Garner farm, Sweet Home. She was called Jenny Whitlow on her bill of sale to the Garners, and they always called her Jenny.

When she is freed, Mr. Garner drives her to his friends, the Bodwins, in Ohio. The Bodwins help Baby Suggs get her life started by providing her with a house and with work. The house, 124 Bluestone Road, was where Edwin Bodwin spent his first years.

After being freed, Baby Suggs starts preaching in the Clearing, a beautiful outdoor sanctuary. She is an unchurched preacher who speaks and dances in the Clearing. There she cries for the living and the dead and tells the community to do the same. Her house is one of the centers of the community, where people stop by to share news and leave messages. She helps her neighbors in many ways and is referred to often as Baby Suggs, holy.

When Sethe arrives at 124 after running away, Baby Suggs pierces Sethe's ears so she can wear the earrings given her by Mrs. Garner. Baby Suggs provides great joy to her community and is a stabilizing influence in Sethe's life. She mends shoes, items that allow people to escape and take journeys. After she receives her daughter-in-law and the four children, Baby gives a party for all the neighbors where she supplies food in such abundance that it stirs up feelings of resentment in the neighbors, as if she were making herself better than they were—that she could afford to be so generous with her resources. She smells disapproval after she has the blackberry party and people see her as too proud. According to some, Baby Suggs is not a real slave since Halle bought her from the Garners and sent her across the Ohio.

After Sethe's "misery," Baby Suggs withdraws to her deathbed. She comes to believe that she has let herself get too involved in life—that she has begun to feel that things might go well for her; that she has let herself care and somehow has tempted God to smack her down because she has presumed too much. When close to her death after Sethe's difficult act, Baby Suggs focuses her attention on colors. Sethe follows her on this path at the end of the novel, but is presented with another possibility through the love of Denver and Paul D.

Beloved (the Crawling-already? baby) The name Beloved comes from the word that Sethe had engraved on her dead daughter's sparkling pink tombstone and that name comes from the only two words Sethe hears the preacher say when the baby is buried: "Dearly Beloved." Sethe pays for the engraving of the name Beloved on the tombstone by letting the engraver have sex with her for 10 minutes, with his son watching them. It is as if the name is given to the spirit of Sethe's child coincidentally.

Beloved arrives at 124 Bluestone Road after coming out of the water. Sethe and Denver believe that she is the ghost of the daughter Sethe killed. Beloved is ill when she arrives at 124. The whites of her eyes are so white, they appear blue. She wears a white dress and has new, lineless skin like a baby. She has three scratches on her forehead. Beloved has a craving for sugar and loves to ask Sethe questions about the past, like what happened to Sethe's earrings, which she thinks are diamonds. She pulls out her tooth and Denver has to tell her to cry because it should hurt. Beloved knows the song that Sethe made up for her children, and when she sings it, Sethe believes that Beloved is her lost daughter. Beloved seems to become pregnant by Paul D after asking him to touch her on the inside and call her by her name.

While at 124, Beloved both coddles Sethe and attempts to make her suffer. Denver's unfailing loyalty goes unnoticed. Beloved vacillates between behaving like a woman and acting like a child. Her actions are filled with anger and confusion.

Beloved feeds off of Sethe's love, leaving the older woman emaciated and shrunken. Sethe seems to become the child while Beloved becomes the mother. In one of the novel's final scenes, the community women who see her believe that she is pregnant. Beloved is, apparently, finally cast out of Sethe's house by the prayers and cries of 30 black women from the community. She is last seen as a blur, running naked through the forest next to a stream, with fish for hair. Eventually she disappears, leaving the reader and the characters in the novel unclear about her identity and her fate. Some critics have suggested that the character Beloved reappears as the character Wild in the novel *Jazz*.

Billy   Billy is the bull at Sweet Home. When Garner is alive, he lets the bull mate with Red Cora only periodically. On the other hand, schoolteacher

is greedy and allows the cow to become pregnant repeatedly. This lack of consideration for the well-being of the cow demonstrates the lack of compassion inherent in schoolteacher's personality.

Bodwin   See MR. AND MISS BODWIN

Brandywine   Brandywine is the man to whom schoolteacher sells Paul D after Paul D tries to escape from Sweet Home. Brandywine puts a bit in Paul D's mouth. Paul D tries to kill Brandywine and, subsequently, is sold to the chain gang in Alfred, Georgia.

Brother   Brother is the tree Paul D feels a connection to at Sweet Home. The tree is also the gathering place for the Sweet Home men.

Buglar   Buglar is Sethe and Halle's son and Baby Suggs's grandson. When Buglar is 13, he runs away to join the Civil War. He leaves as soon as a mirror shatters at 124 Bluestone, an event he sees as a sign. Sethe tries to kill him when schoolteacher comes to 124 Bluestone to return them to slavery. After his mother kills his sister, he is afraid to touch Sethe or to have her touch him. Both he and his brother Howard try to warn Denver about Sethe so that she does not suffer the same fate as their other sister.

Clearing, the   The Clearing is where Baby Suggs preaches on Saturdays until Sethe kills Beloved. The community gathers there to hear Baby's healing and redemptive words. After Baby Suggs's death and Paul D's arrival, Sethe returns to the Clearing with Beloved and Denver. While they are there, Sethe feels as if she is being choked by invisible hands. Bruises appear on her neck after the incident.

Denver   Denver is Sethe's daughter. Sethe is pregnant with Denver when she escapes Sweet Home. Amy Denver helps Sethe give birth to Denver on a leaky boat on the edge of the Ohio River. Sethe names the child after the woman who helped her escape.

Denver was a tiny baby when Sethe killed her older sister so she never knows what it is like to grow up without that shadow hanging over her family's life. It is also significant that Denver ingests her dead sister's blood as she breastfeeds right after Sethe kills her sister. After Sethe gets out of jail, the neighbors abandon Baby Suggs, Sethe, and Sethe's children. As a result, Denver grows up rarely leaving her own yard and seeing few people outside the family except for Stamp Paid. Since she is so lonely after her grandmother, Baby Suggs, dies and her brothers run away, Denver actually enjoys the company of the ghost who haunts the house. Denver is deaf for two years after Nelson Lord asks her about her mother at Lady Jones's school. She fantasizes that her father, Halle, will eventually come to her rescue.

Toward the end of the novel, Denver breaks free from the trance that Beloved has cast over 124 Bluestone Road. Denver feels displaced by Paul D and then by Beloved in Sethe's affections until she finally leaves 124 Bluestone Road in order to save Sethe's life. She ventures out into the world and learns to get along and communicate with her community. She becomes a more confident and strong woman. Paul D even comments that Denver reminds him of Halle now that she has grown up a little.

Ella   Ella and her husband, John, are waiting on the other side of the Ohio to help Sethe and Denver after they escape from Sweet Home. When Ella was a slave, she was locked up and abused by her master. Out of that abusive situation, Ella gives birth to a child that she allows to die. Spitefully, she wonders if Sethe and the children are really Halle's family or not. Because of her own guilt, Ella is much more judgmental than the other people who help Sethe along the way. She is very opinionated and makes her opinions known. After holding a grudge against Sethe for years, she convinces some of the women of the town that Sethe needs rescuing from Beloved. Because of her own history, she will not tolerate the idea of the dead returning to seek revenge.

Famous   Famous is one of Baby Suggs's lost children. According to Baby Suggs's fragmented memories of her children, his skin color was still in the process of acquiring a permanent hue the last time she saw him. Unlike most of her other children, Baby Suggs knows what happened to Famous. He and one of her other children, Nancy, died in the hold of a slave ship while it was in the harbor waiting to be packed with individuals for sale before sailing from the Virginia coast.

Four Horsemen, the   The Four Horsemen in *Beloved* are schoolteacher, his nephew, the slave catcher, and the sheriff who come for Sethe and the children at 124 Bluestone Road. They come the day after the blackberry party. Following Sethe's attempt to kill her children, the sheriff stays after the rest leave 124. The sheriff takes Sethe to jail.

The phrase the four horsemen calls to mind the four horsemen of the apocalypse mentioned in the book of Revelation in the Bible. The biblical four horsemen are agents of global destruction who ride horses of four different colors, each horse representing a different type of catastrophe.

Halle   Halle is the last of Baby Suggs's children and the only one that she gets to see live to adulthood. Halle and Baby Suggs are purchased by Mr. Garner and are brought to work at Sweet Home when Halle is 10 years old. Halle grows up thinking that he and the other Sweet Home men, Paul A, Paul F, Paul D, and Sixo, are in fact independent and able to live with some degree of freedom unavailable to other slaves.

When Sethe is purchased by Garner to come to work at Sweet Home, eventually she chooses Halle to be her husband. The two have a makeshift wedding and the consummation of their union in the corn field is witnessed by all of the inhabitants of Sweet Home. Although it is not a legal union, Halle is Sethe's husband and the father of her children. Halle Suggs buys his mother out of slavery by working at farms near Sweet Home on Sundays. Baby Suggs resettles in Cincinnati and lives in a house owned by abolitionists at 124 Bluestone Road.

When the Sweet Home slaves decide to run away to Ohio, their plan goes badly awry. Halle, for reasons unknown, is in the barn when the nephews suckle and beat Sethe. He is a witness to the entire event. Apparently, seeing the brutality leveled at his wife combined with his inability to intervene sends Halle past the breaking point and he seems to lose touch with reality. Later, Paul D sees Halle slathering clabber on his face and, after he arrives at 124 years later, he tells Sethe what he saw. Halle was the most respected of the Sweet Home men. Sethe expects that he is dead but never really knows for sure. The novel does not offer any conclusive knowledge of Halle's whereabouts. His daughter, Denver, fantasizes about him and wishes for his return.

Here Boy   Here Boy is the dog at 124 Bluestone Road. The ghost throws him against a wall and hurts him so badly that Sethe has to put his eye back in the socket. The whole time that Beloved is living at 124, Here Boy is gone. The dog returns after she leaves. When Paul D returns and sees Here Boy, he knows Beloved is gone for good.

Hi-Man   Hi-Man announces when work starts for the chain gang in Alfred, Georgia. In the evening, he also lets the men know when work is to end. Hi-Man is the leader of the men and helps them to survive. More than simply functioning as the coordinator of the chain gang, Hi Man is a kind of spiritual guide. He seems to know intuitively when the men need additional support in order to keep going.

When the rain comes and the men escape through the mud of their individual cells, Hi-Man is the signal man who keeps them all together and moving in the right direction. Without Hi Man's guidance and the trust and faith that each of the men place in him, escape would have been impossible.

Hi-Man leads the men safely to an encampment of ailing Cherokee where the men are able to find shelter, food, and to make plans about where they will go. Hi-Man decides to find the remainder of this group of Cherokee who are not ill and to cast his lot with them.

Howard   Howard is the son of Sethe and Halle and the grandson of Baby Suggs. Like his brother, he runs away and joins the Civil War. For Howard, the catalyst for his departure is seeing two

tiny handprints appear in a cake. Sethe tries to kill him when schoolteacher comes to 124 Bluestone Road to return them to slavery. He is afraid of his mother, Sethe, after he witnesses her kill his sister. Both he and his brother Buglar try to teach Denver how to protect herself from Sethe.

Jackson Till   Jackson Till is one of the people to whom the suffering of slavery brings permanent insanity. Jackson Till is said to sleep under his bed as a result of his experiences. Through her experiences with people like Jackson Till and Aunt Phyllis, Sethe learns what can happen when a person reaches the breaking point. Sethe does not want to lose touch with reality, although her perpetual struggle with the emotional traumas of her life seems, at times, to push her in that direction.

Janey Wagon   Janey is the first free black that Baby Suggs encounters when she gets to Ohio. She is a cook for the Bodwins. Toward the end of the novel, remembering Baby Suggs, Janey encourages the sister and brother to give Denver a job after Denver ventures out of 124 Bluestone Road in order to save Sethe.

Jenny Whitlow (see Baby Suggs)   Jenny is the name that Garner gives to Baby Suggs because it is the name provided for her on the sales ticket when he purchases her and Halle. Even after he learns of his mistake as he is driving Baby Suggs to freedom, he does not approve of her name and advises her to keep Jenny. After Mrs. Garner grows ill, she begins to call Sethe Jenny as well.

Joe Nathan   Joe Nathan is a servant for Mr. Buddy along with Amy Denver. Amy Denver tells Sethe that Joe Nathan has been kind to her. Joe Nathan tells Amy that Mr. Buddy is her father, but she does not believe him.

John   John is Ella's husband. The couple helps Sethe and Denver after their escape from Sweet Home.

Johnny   Johnny is Baby Suggs's lost child whose features are so undeveloped when she last sees him that she does not know whether his cleft chin is permanent or a dimple that would have faded with his babyhood. Baby Suggs never discovers what happens to her child. Despite her desire to know what has happened to Johnny, she knows that, since he ran away more than 30 years ago, searching for him might cause him trouble and so she decides not to attempt to discover his whereabouts.

Joshua See STAMP PAID.

Judy (Judith) While drunk, sitting on the church steps, Paul D asks Stamp Paid if Judy, who lives down Plank Road, will take him into her home. Stamp Paid replies with the story of his wife, Vashti.

Lady Jones Lady Jones teaches Denver and many African-American children in the community to read and write. Lady Jones is a very light-skinned African-American woman who hates her skin color. When Denver decides that she needs to help to prevent her mother's deterioration at the hands of Beloved, she goes to Lady Jones for help. Lady Jones helps to get food to Denver and Sethe from the women of the community.

Lu Sethe tells Amy Denver that her name is Lu when Amy happens upon her while she is trying to escape. Lu is the only name Amy ever knows for Sethe.

Ma'am Ma'am is Sethe's little-known mother. Sethe has vague memories of the woman who gave birth to her and she tells Denver and Beloved what she remembers. According to Sethe's memories, her mother worked the indigo fields and was gone early in the morning and away until late into the night. As such, Sethe rarely saw her. Sethe says that her mother was not able to do the things with her that form the traditional foundation of the mother-daughter bond such as fixing her hair, sleeping with her, even nursing her as an infant.

The one major interaction Sethe does remember with her mother is when the woman shows her daughter the brand mark she received. Ma'am shows Sethe the mark in case she is killed and

her child should need to identify her body. As a very young girl, Sethe does not understand her mother's serious message and says that she wants a mark of her own. Her mother slaps Sethe out of frustration.

Eventually, Sethe's mother is hanged. Sethe never learns the reason her mother and many others who died with her were killed. As Sethe recounts the story of her Ma'am to Denver and Beloved, she remembers that her mother and her mother's companions spoke another language. She also remembers her primary caretaker, Nan, telling her about her mother—that Nan and her mother came from across the sea, that they had been raped on the ship, and that Ma'am had many children by the white men who raped her. Nan tells Sethe that of all of these children, Ma'am kept only Sethe, the one child conceived with a man Ma'am loved. Sethe wanted to be Ma'am's daughter, but never had the chance.

Mister Mister, the rooster at Sweet Home, serves as a contrast to Paul D. The sight of the bird, while Paul D wears a bit after being captured during the foiled attempt to run away, humiliates and haunts Paul D.

M. Lucille Williams After Miss Lady Jones alerts the African-American women of Cincinnati to Denver, Sethe, and Beloved's situation, the women begin to contribute food to the household. On one occasion, a basket of eggs is left with a note attached that reads M. Lucille Williams. In that way, Denver knows to return the basket or container to its rightful owner. Denver pays a visit to M. Lucille Williams and returns the basket and thanks the woman.

Mr. Able Woodruff Able Woodruff, along with Janey Wagon, is a black employee of the Bodwins. He does the work outside of the house for the brother and sister, while Janey performs the work indoors. Eventually, Denver comes to work for the Bodwins as well, but Denver has yet to be born when Baby Suggs first meets Janey and Able when Garner brings her to the Bodwins when Halle purchases her freedom.

Woodruff takes Baby Suggs out to 124 Bluestone Road for the first time. During the ride, Baby Suggs notices the scar on the young man's cheek. He tells Baby Suggs that he was born in Virginia.

Mr. Buddy   Mr. Buddy is the man Amy Denver is running away from when she encounters Sethe. She tells Sethe of Mr. Buddy's cruel treatment of her, including beatings and verbal abuse. She says that her beatings from Mr. Buddy were never as severe as the ones that produced the scars on Sethe's back.

Amy has been told but is uncertain whether Mr. Buddy is her father or not. She fervently hopes that he is not. According to Amy, her mother was given to Mr. Buddy and that is how Amy comes to be in his service.

Mr. Garner   Mr. Garner is the master at Sweet Home. Mr. Garner claims to treat his enslaved men like men instead of slaves. He listens to their opinions. Garner does not sell their stud services as others do. He allows Halle to go to other farms to hire out and earn money to buy Baby Suggs's freedom. The man has a cheerful attitude toward life, as if it is something to be enjoyed; one way in which he enjoys it is by baiting his neighbors on the subject of how they handle their slaves.

Garner prides himself on being a kind master and never using a whip. Garner drives Baby Suggs to Ohio after Halle purchases her freedom and, during the ride, tells Baby to keep the name Jenny Whitlow, the name he and his sister call her because Baby Suggs is not a proper name. In spite of Garner's advice, Baby Suggs decides to keep her name so that her husband can find her if he is still alive.

It seems possible that Garner might have died from something other than natural causes. When the Sweet Home men talk about how he died, Sixo thinks he has been shot in the ear, but the others do not think so because there is no blood. The general consensus seems to be that Garner had a stroke and that his brain exploded out of his ear, but it seems quite possible that someone put a small bullet into his ear hole. With Mr. Garner's death, his slaves suffer because it was his personality alone that had created the illusion of bearable life for them.

All-in-all, no matter how humane Mr. Garner tries to be, he still benefits from the labor of his slaves, and he still keeps them as slaves rather than giving them their freedom. When he dies, the lives of his slaves are handed over to the whims of his brother-in-law, schoolteacher.

Mr. and Miss Bodwin   Mr. and Miss Bodwin are brother and sister abolitionists who live together and help fugitive slaves once they get to Ohio. When Baby Suggs arrives newly freed from slavery, Miss Bodwin gives her a wool dress. The Bodwins, supporters of the UNDERGROUND RAILROAD, are still racist and epitomize that double standard by having racist figurines in their home.

Janey is their servant and after Sethe's downfall at the hands of Beloved, Janey convinces the Bodwins to provide Denver with a job taking care of the house at night. The Bodwins hire Denver. As Mr. Bodwin is on his way to pick her up for work, he encounters the group of women standing outside of 124 Bluestone Road exorcising Beloved from the house. Sethe attacks him with an ice pick because she believes he is schoolteacher come back to collect her children. By the end of the novel, Miss Bodwin wants to sell the house.

Mr. Sawyer   See SAWYER

Mr. Scripture Woodruff   Mr. Scripture Woodruff is the black man who escorts Baby to her new home from the Bodwins' house. He tells Baby about Reverend Pike who Baby later asks to write letters for her to help Baby find her lost children. None of the letters result in Baby Suggs reuniting with any of her children.

Mrs. Lillian Garner   Lillian Garner is the wife of Mr. Garner. She has a tumor in her neck, which eventually makes her so ill that she is confined to the bed. Sixo believes that schoolteacher poisons her. Garner gives Sethe a pair of earrings as a wedding present. Lillian Garner sells Paul F to keep Sweet Home going after her husband's death. After she receives pressure from her neighbors about being the only white woman at Sweet Home, she invites schoolteacher, her brother, to run the farm.

Because Mrs. Garner, despite being kind, acquiesces to the status quo and believes that a woman cannot run a farm alone with a group of black people, everyone suffers. She has great sympathy for Sethe when she tells her about the nephew stealing her milk, and tears roll down her face, but she cannot speak out against it—literally because she has some kind of growth in her neck, but also figuratively because she has allowed herself to be defined by societal expectations.

Nan Nan is Sethe's caretaker. Nan nurses various children at the farm where Sethe is born. Although she is missing an arm, Nan is a good caretaker of young children and Sethe has much more of an attachment to Nan than she does to Ma'am. Sethe's mother and Nan know each other from the time of their kidnapping in Africa. Nan speaks a language other than English, probably from her home of origin in Africa.

After Sethe's Ma'am is killed, Nan takes Sethe away before she has time to identify her mother's body, although Sethe knows that her mother has been hanged. Sethe remembers her when Beloved asks her about her mother.

Nancy Nancy is one of Baby Suggs's lost children. Unlike most of her other children, Baby Suggs knows what happened to Nancy. Nancy and one of Baby Suggs's other children, Famous, died in a Virginia harbor, in the hold of a slave ship while it was being packed with individuals to be sold elsewhere.

Nelson Lord Nelson Lord is one of Lady Jones's pupils. He is as smart as Denver and asks her the questions about Sethe that cause Denver to go deaf for two years and stop attending school. He has a birthmark like a nickel on his cheek.

nephews, the Schoolteacher's given name as well as the names of his nephews are never provided. It is possible that their relative anonymity occurs in the novel because they are meant to represent a type of person. The nephews are vicious and vulgar bullies. They are secure in acting out and they remain unaccountable for their actions because they are relatives of white landowners. Schoolteacher is the only person they seem to listen to and they acquire much of their way of being and inhumane behavior from his example and tutelage. The nephews beat Sethe while she is pregnant and suck milk from her breasts.

Schoolteacher blames one nephew for "overbeating" Sethe before she tries to escape. The punishment the nephew receives for that crime is that he must stay at home and tend the ill Mrs. Garner while schoolteacher and the other nephew go out to hunt Sethe down in order to try to bring her back to Sweet Home.

Old Whitlow Old Whitlow is the name of Halle and Baby Suggs's owner before they are purchased by Garner.

Patsy See Thirty-Mile Woman

Patty Patty is one of Baby Suggs's lost children. In Baby Suggs's memory, the one thing she recalls about Patty is her lisp. Baby Suggs wonders if the child ever lost the lisp when she became an adult. Despite her efforts after she becomes free, Baby Suggs does not learn anything about the whereabouts of Patty or about her other lost children, whose fates remain uncertain.

Paul A Garner Paul A is a half brother to Paul D and Paul F. Paul A is captured while trying to escape from Sweet Home and is lynched by schoolteacher.

Paul D Garner Paul D Garner is the last of the Sweet Home men. He is said to listen to women and to be able to make them cry. When he was a slave, he overheard how much he was worth. This knowledge haunts him and makes him insecure about his humanity. Paul D has been silenced by a bit and, therefore, there is a wildness in his eyes. Paul D is captured as he tries to run away from Sweet Home along with the rest of the Sweet Home family. Paul D is captured after he delays leaving because he wants to wait for Paul A. After he is caught, Paul D is sold to a man named Brandywine. After he tries to kill Brandywine, he is sold again to a chain gang in Alfred, Georgia.

During a rainstorm, he and the rest of the chain gang escape. They end up living with sick Cherokee for several months. Paul D then travels like a wanderer around the country. Paul D walks from Georgia to Delaware. His heart has been replaced by what he calls a buried tobacco tin that is rusted shut and he feels nothing for some time.

Eventually, Paul D ends up at 124 Bluestone Road looking for Sethe. He and Sethe become lovers. Paul D begins to open up the lives of the women who live at 124. He takes Sethe and Denver to a carnival. Paul D is there when Beloved first appears on a stump outside the house. Paul D. thinks that Beloved bewitches him and that he cannot go up the steps in the evening to be with Sethe. He begins to stay in the cold house where, eventually, Beloved comes to him. Having sex with Beloved and learning about Sethe's attempt to murder her children opens up his tobacco tin and scares him away from the house and Sethe.

After leaving 124, Paul D begins sleeping in the church. Stamp Paid is upset that no one in the community takes Paul D in, but the truth is that he refuses their offers. After some time, Paul D returns to 124 and reminds Sethe that they can and must go on with their lives and learn to live with the realities of their pasts.

Paul F Garner   Paul F is the half brother of Paul A and Paul D. Paul F is the first Sweet Home slave sold after Mr. Garner's death.

Private Keane   Keane is a private in the Union army who travels with Paul D as Paul D leaves Alabama and heads north at the end of the Civil War. Keane had served earlier in the war in the MASSACHUSETTS 54TH REGIMENT, the first all-black Union regiment. Keane tells Paul D of the soldiers' struggle to acquire equal pay, but Paul D is simply astonished by the idea of a group of black men being paid to fight.

Later, Keane secures a boat for Paul D and another soldier, Sergeant Rossiter, by which the three men board a Union gunboat. The three men part ways in Memphis as the soldiers set off in search of their units. Paul D remains aboard the ship until it docks in Wheeling, West Virginia.

Red Cora   Red Cora is the cow on Sweet Home who is responsible for stepping on Howard's hand

and dislocating his thumb. Sixo resets the child's finger and splints it so it will heal correctly. Sethe tells this story to Paul D to demonstrate to him the extent of what she did not know how to do as a mother as she tries to explain to him why she killed her daughter and tried to kill her other children.

red-headed boy and yellow-hairdo girl, the   Immediately after Sethe and Denver are taken away to jail, two children arrive in a wagon and bring some muddy shoes to Baby Suggs to repair. They are the red-headed boy and the yellow-hairdo girl. The boy orders Baby Suggs around and calls her by her first name—treating her without any respect. Even though Baby Suggs has just tragically lost one grandchild and does not know what will happen to her daughter-in-law and other granddaughter, it is business as usual for the children.

There is no sympathy for her loss and pain as a human being—she is just an object to be ordered around. Baby Suggs feels as if she has brought all this destruction upon herself by lacking humility and inviting her neighbors to a party so lavish it made them jealous.

Reverend Willie Pike   Reverend Willie Pike is a preacher in the black community who can read and write and who Baby Suggs asks to help her locate her lost children. After the townspeople refuse to enter the yard of 124 Bluestone Road, Sethe, from the community's perspective, adds insult to injury by refusing to attend Reverend Pike's services.

Rosa Lee   Rosa Lee is one of Baby Suggs's lost children. Baby Suggs never discovers what happened to the child although she searches for information about and her other lost children after Halle, her sole remaining child, purchases her freedom.

Sawyer   Sawyer is the man who owns the restaurant that Sethe works in as a cook. The Bodwins get Sethe her job working for Sawyer. He is a relatively reasonable man to his employees until after his son is killed in the Civil War; then he becomes unpleasant. As Sethe gets more and more involved in pleasing Beloved, her attendance at work becomes erratic and Mr. Sawyer fires her.

schoolteacher Schoolteacher is a ruthless and vicious man who cares for nothing but money. He is Lillian Garner's brother and comes to Sweet Home after Garner dies and Lillian comes to believe that she cannot be alone with the black slaves of Sweet Home. He sees the slaves of Sweet Home as animals and treats them that way. Sethe overhears him discussing the human and animal characteristics of the slaves at Sweet Home. At this point, Sethe fully understands the extent of schoolteacher's dangerous disregard. After the foiled escape attempt, schoolteacher is responsible for the murders of Sixo and Paul A and verbally and physically abuses the others.

After Sethe's escape from Sweet Home, schoolteacher tries to recapture Sethe and her children in order to reap the full benefits of what he calls her breeding, meaning her ability to reproduce. After Sethe kills her baby, schoolteacher feels that Sethe is ruined and has lost her value and he returns to Kentucky.

Sergeant Rossiter Sergeant Rossiter is a friend of Paul D's companion, Private Keane. The three men meet at the end of the Civil War. Sergeant Rossiter helps Keane to secure a boat in which the men reach a Union gunboat and there gain sanctuary.

Sethe Garner Suggs Sethe is born a slave on a farm where her mother works in the rice fields and cannot even breast-feed her. Another woman, Nan, nurses Sethe. Although Sethe does not know her mother very well, she does remember that her mother, Ma'am, showed her a brand on her side so that Sethe could identify her if she was killed. Naively, Sethe asks for her own mark and her mother slaps her. When her mother is murdered, Sethe cannot find the mark.

When she is 13, Sethe is sold to Sweet Home, a farm in Kentucky owned by Mr. and Mrs. Garner. They purchase Sethe to take the place of the house slave, Baby Suggs, whose freedom has been purchased by Halle, her son. While at Sweet Home, Sethe gives birth to Denver, Howard, Buglar, and the crawling-already? baby. She also becomes the wife of Halle Suggs.

As slaves, Sethe and Halle never have an official wedding ceremony or legal marriage. Sethe makes a dress she calls a bedding dress out of bits and pieces she scrapes together for her first night of married life with Halle. Mrs. Garner, seeing her efforts, gives her a pair of crystal earrings.

While at Sweet Home, the Garners' farm, Sethe overhears schoolteacher instructing the nephews to differentiate between Sethe's animal and human qualities. Sethe was supposed to run away with the men of Sweet Home, but the plans they make are foiled. Sethe cannot find Halle when it is time to leave. After she takes her children to the corn field and to the others who are running away, one of the nephews holds her down and the other takes her milk.

When Sethe makes her escape from Sweet Home, she is pregnant with Denver. During her escape, Sethe has the assistance of a white girl, Amy Denver. Sethe has been beaten so badly by schoolteacher that she has a scar on her back that Amy says resembles a chokecherry tree. With Amy Denver's encouragement, Sethe makes it to the Ohio River, where she goes into labor. She delivers Denver in a leaking boat in the river. Amy leaves, and she and Denver are delivered to the other side, to freedom, by Stamp Paid and Ella.

While Sethe experiences her 28 days of freedom living with Baby Suggs, schoolteacher, a sheriff, and one of the nephews come to get Sethe and her children. Because she cannot let her children live in slavery, she attempts to save them from that possibility by killing them. By the time the posse arrives, Sethe has killed Beloved and has tried to kill her other children. The repercussions of that act and how she and the rest of her family and community deal with them form the story of this novel.

After her actions, schoolteacher thinks her worthless, so he and the nephew leave. The sheriff then arrests Sethe for murder. She holds on tightly to Denver so the baby goes to jail with her. Eventually, the Bodwins help to get her released from jail.

In the wake of her actions, Sethe talks about rememory, disrememory, and memory and tries to forget what happened in the shed. When Paul D arrives at 124, he feels that it might be possible for them to have a life together. Sethe and Paul D become lovers.

When Beloved shows up, Sethe feels compelled to take her in and care for her. When Sethe begins to believe that Beloved is her dead daughter come to life, she spoils her and does everything to make her happy. She becomes so servile to Beloved that her own health becomes endangered. She stops taking care of and paying attention to Denver and eventually loses her job at Sawyer's Restaurant.

When Mr. Bodwin comes to pick Denver up for work, Sethe thinks that he is coming to take her children. Repeating her earlier act and still trying to defend her children, Sethe attempts to attack Bodwin. After Sethe's attack on Bodwin, Beloved disappears, leaving Sethe despondent. With the help of Denver and Paul D, however, Sethe may have a chance to claim and live her own life.

Sixo   Sixo is born in Africa and brings with him the language and customs of his native land. Sixo is considered the wild man of the Sweet Home men. Sixo is the only one other than Halle to be with a woman sexually while they are at Sweet Home. He teaches Sethe a great deal about raising children. He, for example, ties Howard's hand up when he breaks his finger. After he is caught stealing, Sixo tells schoolteacher that he steals food only to improve schoolteacher's property. He has a knowing tale about everything and fights back when schoolteacher's posse tries to capture him when he tries to escape.

At first, schoolteacher wants Sixo alive, but then he decides Sixo is no good. Sixo travels more than 30 miles in a night to be with his woman, called the Thirty-Mile Woman. She is pregnant when schoolteacher tries to burn Sixo to death. As they kill Sixo, he cries "seven-o" in celebration of his unborn child.

Stamp Paid (Joshua)   Stamp Paid is the name that a former slave, Joshua, gives himself because he feels the price has been paid for his freedom. He does not kill his wife, Vashti, after his master's son sleeps with her. His original name was Joshua, but he changes it after the loss of Vashti. He changes his name to hide his shame and disgrace over his

inability to intervene in the situation with his wife. Stamp Paid helps Sethe, all of her children, and hundreds of others cross the Ohio River to freedom.

Stamp Paid brings two pails of blackberries he has picked over to 124 Bluestone Road. The blackberries spawn a feast that causes the rest of the town to be jealous of Baby Suggs's good fortune. Stamp Paid is considered to be a savior and fisherman by his community and is welcome at anyone's home.

Stamp Paid's character is lovingly pitiful. Stamp Paid shows Paul D the newspaper clipping of Sethe after she has killed her daughter. Feeling guilty, afterward he goes to Sethe's house to try to explain his actions but cannot force himself to knock on the door. After Beloved takes over at 124 Bluestone Road, Stamp Paid does not feel welcome at the house anymore. He tries three times to knock on the door, but he is not heard. Stamp Paid eventually redeems himself by helping Paul D.

Thirty-Mile Woman (Patsy)   The Thirty-Mile Woman is the woman Sixo walks 30 miles at night to see. She is described as not unusual looking, but Paul D remembers that she lit up the dark with her love when she saw Sixo. She is 14 years old and already promised to another man.

She finds the wrong location when trying to meet Sixo and weeps because she believes that he decided not to come. Sixo hears her crying and finds and reassures her. In order to provide an excuse for her absence from the field, Sixo pierces her leg to simulate a snakebite.

When Sixo is burned to death during the foiled escape from Sweet Home, he sings out his solace in knowing that Patsy has escaped and is pregnant with his child.

Tyree   Tyree is one of Baby Suggs's lost children. Despite her desire to know what has happened to her child, she knows that, since he ran away more than 30 years ago, searching for him might cause him trouble and so she decides not to attempt to discover his whereabouts.

Vashti   Vashti is Stamp Paid's wife when he was called Joshua. The master's son on the plantation where Stamp Paid and Vashti lived forces Vashti to have sex with him over the course of a year. She will not let Joshua do anything about it because he will be killed and she will have no one to return to after the master's son is done with her. Joshua does not have relations with her for the whole period of time that this forced sex is going on. When Joshua comes to the point that he feels that he would like to snap her thin neck, he changes his name to Stamp Paid instead. His chosen name indicates something about the emotional costs of this incident and of slavery generally.

FURTHER READING

Capuano, Peter J. "Truth in Timbre: Morrison's Extension of Slave Narrative Song in *Beloved*," *African American Review* 37, no. 1 (Spring 2003): 95–104.

Fuston, Jeanna. "From the Seen to the Told: The Construction of Subjectivity in Toni Morrison's *Beloved*," *African American Review* 36, no. 3 (Fall 2002): 461–474.

Mandel, Naomi. "I Made the Ink: Identity, Complicity, 60 Million, and More," *Modern Fiction Studies* 48, no. 3 (Fall 2002): 581–614.

Spargo, R. Clifton. "Trauma and the Specters of Enslavement in Morrison's *Beloved*," *Mosaic: A Journal for the Interdisciplinary Study of Literature* 35, no. 1 (March 2002): 113–132.

Story, Ralph D. "Sacrifice and Surrender: Sethe in Toni Morrison's *Beloved*," *CLA Journal* 46, no. 1 (September 2002): 21–30.

Taylor, Deborah. "Toni Morrison's *Beloved* and the Apotropaic Imagination," *Utopian Studies* 15, no. 2 (2004): 251–254.

Wolfe, Joanna. "Ten Minutes for Seven Letters: Song as Key to Narrative Revision in Toni Morrison's *Beloved*," *Narrative* 12, no. 3 (October 2004): 263–281.

The Bluest Eye (1970)

The Bluest Eye is Toni Morrison's first published novel. The novel takes place in the 1940s in the industrial northeast of LORAIN, OHIO, and tells the story of Pecola Breedlove, a young African-American woman who is marginalized by her community and the larger society. Individually and collectively people mark Pecola and her dysfunctional family as falling outside the boundaries of what is normal and, thus, as undesirable. Pecola's story intersects with and contrasts with that of the novel's primary narrator, Claudia MacTeer, whose coming of age, while challenging, is not the alienating, ultimately impossible situation experienced by Pecola.

The novel addresses the social forces that drive understanding and definition of cultural constructs such as beauty, normalcy, family, and sexuality. These constructs are a particular issue for African-American communities that often are excluded from representation. Through exposure of the embedding of the dangerous hierarchies associated with these concepts into our primary narratives—reading primers, movies, and products—the novel demonstrates the difficulties of growing up and of surviving for African-American young women. Morrison examines the impact of this exclusion on individuals and on the community as a whole. Using Pecola's story as a focal point, *The Bluest Eye* reveals the destructive impact of social hierarchies and of social invisibility.

The Bluest Eye, written during the 1960s, reflects the increasing awareness during that time of the impact of representation on identity formation. Many African Americans during that time rejected cultural stereotypes and worked to create a more accurate and affirmative understanding of African-American life. *The Bluest Eye* also echoes the public expressions of many African-American women in the late 1960s and early 1970s that addressed their particular situation and concerns.

SYNOPSIS

The Bluest Eye is a coming-of-age narrative that tells the parallel, but very different stories, of its protagonists, Pecola Breedlove and Claudia MacTeer, two African-American young girls faced with a world that disregards their existence and undermines their sense of self-worth during the adolescent years that are central to healthy identity formation. Unlike Pecola, Claudia survives the damaging impacts of this invisibility. Claudia has her family, which, while challenged by the post depression realities of African-American life, manages to convey to their daughter the knowledge that her intact survival to adulthood is one of their central concerns. Pecola, having no such reassurance, falls through the cracks created by history, racism, and sexism, and, at the novel's end, is permanently psychologically fractured.

The Bluest Eye begins with a replication of the DICK AND JANE READERS that were one of the primary instruments used to teach generations of American children how to read. By reproducing the primers at the beginning of the novel, *The Bluest Eye* questions the story told in the primers of the lives of the fictional Dick and Jane and their family. This narrative of family life is artificial and flat, yet, in its use as such a central tool in teaching millions of children to read, the narrative became a powerful sign of what is normal and desirable—a story that inevitably impresses itself upon the child who is in the process of acquiring literacy.

In *The Bluest Eye*, the DICK AND JANE narrative represents an accepted, almost invisible controlling narrative, against which each of the primary characters unconsciously evaluates her own existence. The story becomes a litmus test against which the characters measure their self-worth. Both of these primary characters, Claudia MacTeer and Pecola Breedlove, move through the four seasons of the novel, autumn, winter, spring, and summer, in search of validation of their lives.

The plot of the novel begins with an invitational narrative voice that tells the reader the secret of Pecola's rape and impregnation by her father. Presumably, this voice is the adult Claudia looking back on her childhood and trying to reconcile her successful survival of childhood with the tragedy of Pecola's life. The novel, in part, is Claudia's revisiting the details of Pecola's story as well as her own acquisition of adult understandings. Claudia explains to the reader that she and her sister, with childlike belief, feel that they will be able to save Pecola and her unborn child/sister by planting marigold seeds. The seeds they plant, like all of the other marigolds that year, never bloom. Likewise, Pecola and her child/sister are doomed to stillbirth. The novel is, in part, the adult Claudia's desire to come to terms with her helplessness and, perhaps, to do the only thing she possibly can for Pecola: tell her story.

Autumn

The first chapter of the *Autumn* section of the novel presents the details of Claudia MacTeer's life with her family. The chapter begins with the revelation of Claudia and her sister Frieda's envy of their next door neighbor, Rosemary Villanucci. Rosemary flaunts her family's superior economic position by sitting in her family's 1939 Buick. Rosemary taunts Claudia and Frieda by telling them that they cannot come into the Buick. The girls retaliate by beating Rosemary up when she emerges from the car. Rosemary inexplicably responds by offering to pull down her pants. Claudia and Frieda do not allow Rosemary to expose herself, understanding that the act would be demeaning to her, but even more demeaning for them. Rosemary's behavior may be the first introduction to the issue of incest, an issue that pervades *The Bluest Eye*. Rosemary may respond to Claudia and Frieda's violence by offering her sexuality because that is a way in which she has successfully averted physical violence in the past.

Claudia's experience of the world is infused with the presence of her mother, Mrs. MacTeer. Claudia speaks of a childhood illness that she believes is a source of irritation to her mother. In retrospect, she concludes that her mother is simply busy and overwhelmed with the work of keeping her family healthy and intact, and that her impatience is a sign not of indifference but of profound love and concern. Claudia learns from her mother's conversations with other adult women in the town. She and her sister do not always understand the words of the women, but they learn from the sounds, the intonations of their conversations, valuable information about becoming an adult woman.

In order to make ends meet, the MacTeers take a boarder into their home, Mr. Henry. Claudia and Frieda adore Mr. Henry because, unlike the other adults in their lives, he pays attention to them, speaks to them directly, and calls them by the names of famous movie stars. The MacTeers also have another visitor about the same time as the arrival of Mr. Henry. Cholly Breedlove, Pecola's father, burns down the Breedlove home, and so Pecola Breedlove temporarily lives with the MacTeers.

While Pecola is at the MacTeers', Claudia contrasts Pecola and Frieda's adoration of white girlhood—in the form of white baby dolls and the child star, SHIRLEY TEMPLE—with her own disdain for white girls. Claudia does not understand what makes white girls more acceptable, more adored. This adoration comes from all the adults she knows, black and white. When Claudia receives a white doll for Christmas, she destroys it in an attempt to discover what it contains that makes it so desirable. All she discovers is the metal cylinder that makes the doll bleat.

Instead of receiving a white baby doll, Claudia wants a more sensual experience. She wants to eat peaches in her grandmother's kitchen, smelling violets while her grandfather plays the violin just for her. Claudia also rebels against the mandatory cleanliness of her nightly bath. She feels that the bath removes all of her inventiveness and creativity, the essence of herself; however, Claudia discovers that conformity is a necessary element of maturity and, eventually, she learns to love her white dolls and Shirley Temple, and to take baths without complaint.

While at the MacTeers', Pecola marks one of the passages from girlhood to womanhood when she begins her menstrual period. The incident is traumatic for Claudia and Frieda as well. Rosemary Villanucci sees the girls trying to help Pecola and accuses them of playing inappropriately. Mrs. MacTeer, hearing Rosemary's accusation, begins to punish her children by spanking them until she realizes what has occurred. Claudia and Frieda are impressed with Pecola's emerging womanhood. As the girls fall asleep that night, Pecola, after having been informed that she can now have a baby, ponders how that happens. Claudia innocently tells her that she has to be loved. Pecola, who never has been loved, wonders how someone gets another to love them.

*HEREISTHEHOUSEITISGREENANDWH
ITEITHASAREDDOORITISVERYPRETT
YITISVERYPRETTYPRETTYPRETTYP*
The novel shifts focus to the Breedloves and to their house and their lives. The family lives in a storefront that has been converted to a two-room apartment. Even the Breedloves' furniture reflects their status because it is torn and undesirable. The family believes that they themselves are, like the house and the furniture, ugly—the opposite of the fictional Dick and Jane. They are defined as ugly because they do not look like the culture's definition of beautiful. They are black and poor and do not see any affirmation of their reality anywhere.

*HEREISTHEHOUSEITISGREENANDWH
ITEITHASAREDDOORITISVERYPRETT
YITISVERYPRETTYPRETTYPRETTYP*
The Breedloves' self-definition as ugly confirms the messages they receive from both the African-American and white communities. The contempt and exclusion they experience in the world becomes a template for their internal interactions. The family's exchanges consist almost entirely of verbal, physical, and ultimately sexual abuse. Pecola's brother, Sammy Breedlove, copes with the bleak realities of the family's life by regularly escaping, running away. Pecola uses the exact opposite strategy and internalizes her feelings, transforming them into self-hatred and an overwhelming longing to disappear. It is this longing that is the source of Pecola's craving for blue eyes, for the bluest eyes possible. She believes that if she, like SHIRLEY TEMPLE and Jane, has blue eyes, a central marker for beauty in the dominant culture, then she will be loved and her life will be bearable.

*HERE ISTHERFAMILYMOTHERFATHER
DICKANDJANETHEYLIVEINTHEGREE
NANDWHITEHOUSETHEYAREVERYH*
The disregard and abuse Pecola experiences within her home are echoed in her encounters in the world beyond the storefront. When she journeys to the candy store to purchase her favorite candy, MARY JANES, the storekeeper Mr. Yacobowski does not even look at her and tries to avoid touching her when they exchange money. The candy provides Pecola with an artificial respite from her misery. Consuming the Mary Janes becomes for her a fleeting opportunity to imagine herself to be the little girl depicted on the wrapper, a girl who is desirable enough to be consumed.

Like the MacTeers, the prostitutes Marie, China, and Poland, who live in an apartment above the

Breedloves' storefront home, acknowledge Pecola's humanity and treat the child decently. The women tell Pecola stories of their lives and her conversations with them feed her curiosity to discover what love is and how one becomes lovable.

Winter

The section of the novel entitled *Winter* follows the first section entitled, *Autumn*. Like the *Autumn* section, *Winter* begins with Claudia's narration. She describes her father's protective stance toward his family and the elements, including winter weather, that threaten it. One of those external threats presents a danger to Claudia's self-esteem and sense of well-being. A new girl, Maureen Peal, arrives in town from the big city of Toledo, Ohio. The response that Maureen, an upper-middle-class, light-skinned, green-eyed, well-dressed child receives from the adults and the children in the community leads Claudia to question the source of their adoration and to recognize that characteristics as superficial as physical appearance are often determiners of the treatment one receives in the world.

Maureen Peal and Pecola Breedlove present opposing points on the spectrum of acceptability, with Claudia falling somewhere between the extremes of adoration and rejection the other two girls receive. One day, Claudia, Frieda, and Maureen Peal are walking home from school and encounter a bunch of boys taunting Pecola. The boys tease Pecola about her skin color and her poverty. Particularly, the boys repeat over and over that Pecola's daddy sleeps with no clothes on, a jibe that refers both to the family's poverty and suggests some sort of sexual impropriety. In defense of Pecola, Frieda breaks up the circle of boys, and the girls invite Pecola to join them. Maureen Peal offers to buy an ice cream cone for Pecola. Since the MacTeer girls have no money, they do not eat ice cream and are envious of Maureen's seeming wealth.

As the girls continue to walk, their conversation turns to the adolescent topics of menstruation, pregnancy, and male nakedness. Maureen and Pecola begin to quarrel about whether Pecola has ever seen her father naked as the boys earlier accused. This conversation leads to a larger argument that ends with Maureen Peal accusing all of the girls of the same thing the boys had earlier accused Pecola of—being dark-skinned, poor, and, most pointedly, of falling outside normative behavior. Maureen defends herself by distinguishing herself from the girls and asserting that she is cuter than them and, therefore, better than them. After this event, Claudia and Frieda are left to grapple with the question of the role and hierarchies of physical beauty—hierarchies that mark them as less valuable, desirable, and worthy than those who are perceived as more beautiful.

Immediately following the incident with Maureen Peal, Claudia and Frieda have another discovery that impacts their understanding of the world and their corresponding loss of innocence. The girls find Mr. Henry in their house with the prostitutes China and Miss Marie. Mr. Henry encourages the girls to lie to their mother—to not tell her about his transgression. The girls decide not to reveal Mr. Henry's secret.

The last chapter of the *Winter* section again contrasts the coming-of-age experiences of Claudia and Frieda and Pecola. Although Claudia and Frieda have difficult situations to negotiate, none of them are as destructive as the circumstances Pecola faces. This final chapter of *Winter* begins with an account of a type of middle-class African-American woman who traveled north in the GREAT MIGRATION in search of education and better opportunities. Here Morrison critiques the premise of assimilation—the idea that one has to conform completely to the ideal constructions of the dominant culture and, in that process, abandon all of the markers of identity that are associated with the marginalized culture. In order to bolster their own sense of self, the women make clear distinctions between colored people and niggers and firmly disassociate themselves from the latter.

The character, Geraldine, is the representative of this group of women. She is obsessed with appearance—her house, her clothes, her hair—and values the order of her life above relationships with her husband and her child, Junior. Junior is, therefore, malicious and abusive. The family lives next to the playground of the school, and Junior, in his isolation, longs to interact with his peers but is forbidden to do so. His frustration manifests itself in his treatment of those with less power, the cat his mother loves and, during one afternoon, Pecola.

Junior lures Pecola into his house and then throws his mother's cat in her face. The cat scratches Pecola, and she tries to escape the house, but Junior will not let her go. Junior again throws the cat at nearly the same moment his mother arrives. Geraldine blames the entire situation on Pecola and, seeing her as a representative of all that she is trying to escape—poverty, disorder, despair—calls the child a bitch and orders her out of the house.

Spring

The third section of *The Bluest Eye*, *Spring*, contrasts the traditional expectations of the season—hopefulness, regeneration—with the realities of human existence. Mr. Henry molests Frieda by fondling her breasts. The MacTeers once again demonstrate their clear affection for their daughters and investment in their safety by violently throwing Mr. Henry out of the house. Frieda overhears a neighbor, Mrs. Dunion, suggesting that some permanent damage may have occurred to Frieda. The idea of being ruined frightens Frieda, mainly because she does not understand what is meant by the word. The only association the girls have with the words is its use in reference to the prostitutes they have heard described as ruined and so they think that being ruined means being fat. They believe that whiskey will prevent Frieda from becoming fat, so they go on a quest for alcohol.

Claudia and Frieda believe that Pecola will know where they can get alcohol, so they go to her house. She is not there, and Miss Marie tells them that Pecola is with her mother at a house by the lake. Miss Marie offers them a pop and suggests that they wait for Pecola with her on the porch. Frieda tells her that they are not allowed to come into her house, and Miss Marie laughs and throws a glass bottle at them. The girls find Pecola at the lake in front of the house where Pauline works as a maid and they decide to walk home together. While they are waiting, Pecola knocks over a blueberry pie her mother has made and the blueberries stain Pauline's floor and burn Pecola's legs. Rather than showing the girl compassion and concern, Pauline beats and

violently scolds her daughter. Pauline's affection and consideration is reserved for the white daughter of the family for whom she works.

SEEMOTHERMOTHERISVERYNICEMO THERWILLYOUPLAYWITHJANEMOTH ERLAUGHSLAUGHMOTHERLAUGHLA

The next three chapters of *Spring* tell the stories of Pauline, Cholly, and Soaphead Church. Pauline's story traces her origins from rural Alabama where she is born as the ninth of 11 Williams children. She is treated differently from the rest of the children, a difference the narrator speculates might stem from a limp Pauline develops as a child following an accident where she steps on a rusty nail. Pauline receives comfort from ordering and cleaning items in her parents' home. She also loves church music and conflates the images of a savior with her teenage romantic fantasies. This conception of romantic love establishes her expectations for the relationship she eventually develops with Cholly.

Pauline and Cholly's relationship begins with high expectation and a move north to Lorain, Ohio. In Lorain, Pauline feels excluded by women who see her as country and unsophisticated. Pauline begins to purchase clothes and makeup to bolster her self-esteem, while Cholly begins to drink heavily. The two begin to argue and Pauline turns to motion pictures for comfort. She tries to imitate the appearance of the movie stars until she breaks a front tooth eating candy. Pauline then gives up on trying to imitate the beauty ideals of the dominant culture and settles on adopting the role of wronged wife. This role makes her a perpetual victim and gives her a way to justify and organize her emotional and psychological life. Along with giving up on creating her identity, Pauline stops trying to create a home. She prefers the order she can create in the homes of her white employees where she feels in control and valued.

SEEFATHERHEISBIGANDSTRONGFATH ERWILLYOUPLAYWITHJANEFATHER ISSMILINGSMILESMILEFATHERSMILESMILE

Cholly's story is bleaker than Pauline's. Cholly is abandoned at four days old by his mother who has some mental deficiency. Cholly's Aunt Jimmy rescues the baby and raises him until her death, when

Cholly is 13. Following Aunt Jimmy's funeral, Cholly has an encounter that defines the rest of his life. Cholly embarks on his first sexual encounter in the woods with a young woman named Darlene. As the two young people begin to discover how sexuality works, hunters stumble upon them and force the two to copulate under their violating gaze. Cholly, unable to defend himself or Darlene against this attack, turns his anger and impotence toward Darlene. This channeling of frustration to those weaker than him is a pattern he will repeat throughout his life with devastating consequences for those close to him.

Following the funeral and the incident in the woods, Cholly erroneously thinks he has impregnated Darlene and runs off to find a man he believes is his father, Sampson Fuller. Fuller's rejection of Cholly is another definitive moment in his maturation. He is utterly alone and free of obligations to or responsibility for anyone else. In such a state, Cholly is outside of the boundaries of human interaction and, with no moral framework, is inevitably doomed to be a destructive force in the lives of others.

At the end of Cholly's life story, the chapter concludes with Cholly's rape of Pecola. The act is told entirely from Cholly's perspective. He looks at his child as she washes dishes and is disturbed by the defeat written into her posture. He feels it is an indictment of his parenting. Pecola's gesture of scratching the back of her calf with her foot reminds Cholly of Pauline and the vulnerability that attracted him to her. Since Cholly has such a limited range of emotions and of ways to express his feelings, he translates his possible compassion and affection for Pecola into a sexual expression and repeats his seduction of Pauline on his helpless daughter. Pecola is silent throughout the encounter and is left unconscious on the floor of the kitchen.

SEETHEDOGBOWWOWGOESTHEDOG DOYOUWANTTOPLAYDOYOUWANT TOPLAYWITHJANESEETHEDOGRUNR

The final chapter in *Spring* details the life story of the pedophile and self-proclaimed psychic and spiritualist, Soaphead Church, also known by his given name, Elihue Micah Whitcomb. Soaphead disdains human contact except for that of little girls, whom he finds have not yet descended into the dirtiness of humanity. Soaphead's peculiar assessment of the world stems from his childhood and the assumptions he internalizes. Born in the British West Indies, Soaphead adopts the racial hierarchies that place whiteness at the top. As light-skinned black people, Soaphead and his family gain privilege from their relative whiteness, and Soaphead, therefore, feels he is superior.

This sense of superiority is at the core of his failed marriage. Despondent upon having lost the one genuine love of his life, his wife Velma, as well as the support of his relatively wealthy family, Soaphead tries a wide array of occupations, traveling salesman, insurance agent, and desk clerk before he moves to Lorain to become a fortune-teller.

When Pecola seeks his services, Soaphead is genuinely moved by her desire for blue eyes and, for the first time, sincerely wishes for the power to grant her wish. He writes a letter to God asking for the ability to grant her wish. He is not selfless enough, however, to avoid using Pecola to kill Bob, his landlady's dog who so repulses him.

Summer

The final section of *The Bluest Eye* is *Summer*. In the first of the two final chapters, the invitational narrative voice introduced at the beginning of the novel returns as the adult Claudia reflects upon her discovery of the truth of what happened to Pecola. The truth about what happened to Pecola is shocking to Claudia, but what is more disturbing to her is the response of the town. The adults in the community only gossip about the rape of Pecola and do not do anything to intervene on her behalf. Claudia and Frieda invoke the only power they think they have, planting seeds, to try to assist Pecola and her unborn child.

LOOKLOOKHERECOMESAFRIENDTHE FRIENDWILLPLAYWITHJANETHEYWI LLPLAYAGOODGAMEPLAYJANEPLAY

The next chapter consists of the internal dialogue between Pecola and the alter ego that emerges in the wake of her rape and pregnancy by Cholly. The split personality is Pecola's way of coping with the devastating impact of the rape. The dialogue reveals that Cholly rapes Pecola more than once. The chapter also exposes Pecola's persistent insecurity in spite of the fact that she seems to believe that she has at last acquired her much-desired blue eyes. Pecola fears that her eyes are not the bluest and will not achieve the love and acceptance she so desperately craves.

The adult Claudia concludes the novel with her reflections about the situation. Pecola is a casualty of the malignant love of her father, the failures of her mother, the disinterest of her community, and a culture that defines her as disposable, insignificant, and ugly.

CRITICAL COMMENTARY

Morrison's first novel, *The Bluest Eye*, outlines the coming-of-age of an African-American female protagonist, Pecola Breedlove, who originates in circumstances that make her success, her survival even, unlikely. Of great significance in understanding the major themes of the novel is Pecola's struggle to exist within the narrow spaces in which her community places her. Pecola is not accepted by blacks or whites. In this in-between nowhere land, the child is ultimately lost, unable to root herself in the firm ground of love and understanding that is necessary for any successful maturation.

Pecola Breedlove is largely voiceless throughout the novel. There is little access to her first-person internal thoughts until the end of the novel when her psyche has become irreparably fractured. As such, the narrative constructs Pecola's world by exploring the experiences of those around her. The two major deterministic forces in Pecola's young life are her mother and father, Cholly and Pauline Breedlove. Significantly, Pecola never calls either of her parents mom or dad, demonstrating the psychological and emotional distance between the young girl and her parents.

Cholly and Pauline's lives are revealed in the novel through flashback sequences of their lives. In each of the chapters detailing the histories of Pecola's parents, their narratives reveal vastly differing, yet significantly overlapping experiences. Cholly is a throwaway child whose mother abandons him upon his birth. This abandonment colors and determines Cholly's entire future. Raised by his Aunt Jimmy,

Cholly loses her when he is at a critical point in his maturation. Following Aunt Jimmy's funeral, Cholly has his first sexual experience when he and a young girl, Darlene, wander off into the nearby woods and wind up having sex. While in the midst of this encounter, hunters stumble upon the couple and violate them by shining a flashlight upon them and forcing them to continue. This event is a critical turning point in Cholly's life. Rather than turning his rage on the hunters, against whom he is powerless, Cholly turns his ire upon the young girl, Darlene. Throughout his life, Cholly confuses love and affection with violence and will take out his frustrations and bitterness on those who are less powerful than himself—namely his family.

Unlike Cholly, Pauline comes from a large and intact family, but she does not feel a part of the group. Like Cholly, Pauline is an outcast and is not embraced or claimed by her family in the ways that she needs in order to feel valued. Pauline grows up longing for rescue and for love from an unknown and mysterious lover who will rescue her from her disconnection. When Cholly arrives in her life, Pauline is susceptible to believing that he is what she has been longing for and missing. Her marriage to Cholly, migration to the North, and birth of her children leave her disappointed and disillusioned. The argumentative and violent home life of Pauline and Cholly speaks to a clash of different coping mechanisms. When Cholly loses interest in his marriage, his life, and his children, he turns to drink and idleness. Utilizing an opposite approach, Pauline greets her despair by becoming a staunch and devoted church member and a tireless worker for her employers for whom she works as a domestic. In the midst of the collision of these extremes exists the life of their daughter, Pecola Breedlove.

Pecola exists in the narrow spaces between the opposite extremes of her parents and of the various communities she inhabits. Morrison's conjoining of seemingly opposite ideas creates the tension between *The Bluest Eye*'s opening line, "Nuns go by quiet as lust," and the narrator's statement near the end of the text that describes the incestuous rape of Pecola by her father, "he fucked her tenderly" (162–63). By conjoining jarring, polarized, and overtly sexualized language, Morrison embeds in these descriptions a reflection of the violent differences that traditionally characterize human desire, aggression, and submission. Morrison's artful language defies simplistic categorization and compartmentalization. Her phrases expose the complexity and primacy of desire and its inextricable connection to the fundamental problems of oppression—sexism, racism, and classism.

Throughout the novel, Pecola is located in spaces in between two oppositions. Significantly, there is a crack in the sidewalk that repeatedly causes Pecola to trip. The Y-shaped crack seems to belong to her, perhaps the only thing that does. Pecola finds herself in the middle of taunting school boys who surround her and plague her with their mean verbal jabs. Perhaps, most significantly, Pecola is in the space between the black and white communities that surround her, unaccepted by and alienated from both.

At the end of *The Bluest Eye*, Pecola is in that messy, uncomfortable, disordered space Morrison claims as paradise, the only possible honest and lived paradise, a space in which the rubble and collapse of oppressive categories dismantle patriarchal notions of contradiction, of difference—black/white, male/female, good/evil, sexual/pure, rich/poor—the structural pillars and hierarchies of meaning that encourage Pecola's isolation.

Pecola's ultimate psychological break stems from the brutally she has experienced, but, more fundamentally, her psychological fragmentation has roots in the absence of relationships—with self, with family, with community. Pecola lacks the rootedness that, by contrast, allows Claudia to survive the difficulties of growing up as a little black girl. *The Bluest Eye*'s protagonist/narrator Claudia recalls the abrasive quality of her mother's hands as the overworked woman anxiously applies balm to her ailing daughter. ". . . [I]t was a productive and fructifying pain. Love thick and dark as Alaga syrup eased into that cracked window. I could smell it—taste it—sweet, musty, with an edge of WINTERGREEN in its base—everywhere in that house" (12). Although the experience is painful for Claudia, she recognizes that the discomfort her mother's efforts engender is rooted in a sincere urgency and a zealous, if hasty and abrasive, compassion.

Claudia, the adolescent, dreams of simple sensual pleasures; instead she is given things—particularly, white dolls—that are supposed to substitute for connection and affection. The lessons of *The Bluest Eye* reveal the complexities of coming-of-age in a culture that does not value your existence. Such maturation is always difficult, but it is impossible if one does not have the foundational support and love of primary caretakers.

SOME IMPORTANT THEMES AND SYMBOLS IN *THE BLUEST EYE*

House and Home

Throughout *The Bluest Eye*, the question of house and of home is central to the narrative. The DICK AND JANE READER begins with the line, "Here is the house" (1). The simple phrase resonates with questions about the nature of the family: What is a family? What roles do members of the family play? With Dick and Jane those answers are easy, simple, and exclusive. "Normal" houses have families with a mother, father, and children with strictly defined rules and roles. *The Bluest Eye*, through its exploration of other types of houses—homes—reveals that the answers to those questions are not so straightforward and easily apparent.

The novel also demonstrates that the pervasiveness of the ideal of the house/family as depicted in stories, films, and songs can make individuals feel deficient. As the young women characters in *The Bluest Eye* come of age, each of them has to confront these ideals and to explain and justify for themselves the differences between their lived realities and the picture of houses/homes as presented in the dominant culture.

The Failure of Community

The failure of community is directly connected to the demise of childhood innocence in Toni Morrison's *The Bluest Eye*. It is the community's abandonment of the protagonist Pecola Breedlove and her family that ultimately results in her psychological destruction. The Breedloves are disconnected from their communities of origin and fail to connect with their fellow townspeople. These multiple disconnections disable the normal boundaries of behavior and Cholly Breedlove impregnates his daughter Pecola when she is 12. Rather than embrace her after this horrific trauma, the community rejects Pecola and contributes to her downfall.

> They were disgusted, amused, shocked, outraged, or even excited by the story. But we listened for the one who would say, "Poor little girl," or, "poor baby," but there was only head wagging where those words should have been. We looked for eyes creased with concern, but saw only veils. (190)

In the case of the Breedloves, it is the failure of community that enables their loss. Community abandonment is both the catalyst and the final blow to both the family and Pecola's disintegration.

The Role of Environment in Growth and Development

The Bluest Eye explores the question of environment, the atmosphere in which the main characters, Claudia and Pecola, are nurtured. The unyielding nature of the protagonists' environments may refer to their immediate families, their peers, their communities, and their culture. Each of these elements is in some way unyielding and uncompromisingly resistant to the girls' healthy maturation. Both Claudia and Pecola have to battle against racism, sexism, poverty, and cultural mythologies in order to protect their psychological health. Claudia, although struggling with her own issues, has a more supportive environment than Pecola, and thus is able to work her way through the unyielding earth while Pecola, like the marigold seeds, is not.

Acquiring Discernment

Some of the most precarious work of maturation is the task of figuring out what messages to believe and follow. As Claudia, Pecola, and Frieda explore their world, adults often give them advice and tell them about the world. The phrase, "truth in timbre," refers to the ability of the girls to understand the world more honestly and truthfully from adults' sounds, the tones in their voices, rather than from the literal meanings of the words themselves (15). An example of this clarity occurs when Mr. Henry lies to Claudia about the reasons why the prostitutes, Marie and China, are in the MacTeers' house. Although he says that the women are there for Bible study, Claudia and Frieda know, from the sound of his voice, that he is lying to them. Throughout the novel, Morrison questions the frequent differential between what people say and what they actually mean, and she suggests that acquiring this discernment is one of the primary tasks of becoming an adult.

Displacement

The Bluest Eye explores the theme of outdoors as it exposes the vulnerability of the community depicted in the novel. Subjected to the whims of racism and classism, particularly potent in the post-Depression 1930s and early 1940s, the people of Lorain have to work hard to ensure that their existence is secure. Their actions are often controlled by their legitimate fear of being displaced, of losing the central marker of stability and identity, the house.

Learning to Love and Be Loved

Throughout the novel, the characters are able to survive adversity and psychological erosion in direct correlation to the extent that they feel loved. At the end of the novel, the narrator states that "Love is never any better than the lover" (206). Although Pauline and Cholly believe that they love each other, neither is capable of transcending their own immediate needs and insecurities because neither of them has ever been well loved or appreciated.

On the other hand, Claudia knows from her mother's care of her when she is ill that she is loved. As a result, Claudia is able to show affection for and love people in her life, namely Frieda and Pecola. This ability to love transcends her coming of age and explains her sense of responsibility for Pecola even after she is an adult and Pecola is beyond help.

Morrison's references to reproduction in *The Bluest Eye* are sharply divided between positive and negative experiences. When Morrison shifts in her narration to the history of some of her characters, like Pauline and Cholly, the characters often refer to reproduction in terms of their hopes for creating family. Conversely, in the present tense of the novel, adult characters tend to refer to reproduction as something beyond their control and often as undesirable.

The Destructive Impact of the Construct of Physical Beauty

Throughout *The Bluest Eye*, the destructive impact of the construct of physical beauty affects the self-esteem of almost every character. The novel suggests that objective definitions of physical beauty are created by the ideals of the dominant culture in order to reinforce power dynamics. African Americans traditionally have been excluded even from consideration as attractive and, as such, suffer from the resultant lack of affirmation. For example, Pauline does not ever see an image of herself in the films she views. She tries to replicate the notions of beauty she finds on the screen only to find such imitation impossible because she has different hair, skin, and features—a different aesthetic. African-American communities often internalize definitions of beauty from the dominant culture and find beautiful its members that most closely match those ideals, individuals such as Maureen Peal, and exclude and isolate those of its own who least resemble the dominant ideals, marginalized souls like Pecola Breedlove.

Night and Day

In *The Bluest Eye* Morrison distinguishes between night and day, darkness and light, and night becomes a time to be feared.

The first reference to night in *The Bluest Eye* is Claudia's description of her home. She says that most of her house is clouded in darkness during the night, a darkness that invites roaches and mice. For the remainder of the novel, the roaches and mice evolve into images of death and despair. Pauline suffers through Cholly's unloving intercourse in the night. Cholly's Aunt Jimmy dies from eating a peach cobbler she receives at night. White men objectify and sexually abuse Cholly and Darlene during the night and, at the turning point of his life, Cholly lays in his own feces until dark. The devil is compared to night when Cholly refers to Satan as a strong black figure that blots out the sun.

Morrison uses night in compound words as well. Geraldine's nightgown represents her resistance to sex, and Soaphead Church writes his blasphemous letter to God on a night table. Claudia utters the novel's final reference to night, completing the circle she began by saying that the summer of Pecola's

misfortune, the summer of selling seeds that would never grow, was just a series of sticky nights.

Hands

Mrs. MacTeer's hands are ambiguous to her daughter as they cause her pain, yet, under the surface, they convey to Claudia a deep, abiding mother love. Similarly, Claudia and Frieda learn the meaning behind the conversations of their mother and her friends not by listening to the words they say but instead by reading the motion and nuance of their hands. Another instance of hands functioning as a tool for diagnosis occurs in Cholly's youth. When Cholly's Aunt Jimmy becomes ill, the women in the community send for M'Dear, a local conjure/medicine woman. She runs her hands over Jimmy's body to determine the cause of the woman's illness. She also examines Jimmy's hands for further diagnosis.

Although hands convey important information in the cases of Mrs. MacTeer and M'Dear, *The Bluest Eye* also reveals that children are not always attuned to the information they may need in order to read someone's character. For example, when Mr. Henry comes to the MacTeer house to live, the children run their hands over his body looking for a quarter. Their parents look on approvingly, not suspecting Mr. Henry's inclination toward pedophilia and neither Claudia nor Frieda has a negative sense of the man.

Significantly, the hands of Claudia's white baby doll, the hated Christmas present, are rough and scratch her as she sleeps. This may provide information about the nature of the African-American characters' encounters with whiteness in the larger culture. Mr. Yacobowski's red and lumpy hands symbolize his contempt for Pecola. He tries to avoid touching her hand when taking her money. His hand scratches hers when he finally reaches to take the pennies she tries to give him to pay for the Mary Janes.

In *The Bluest Eye*, hands also represent character traits. Maureen Peal, the perfect, light-skinned girl at school, has six fingers on one hand. Claudia and Frieda relish this imperfection and tease her. To stand up to Maureen, Frieda strikes a proud pose with her hand on her hip. The southern black women who fight off the "funkiness" sleep with their hands folded across their stomachs, exemplifying their desire for order and control, and their attempt to bar the sexual advances of their husbands. Junior, the son of one of these "perfect" women, is a product of her lack of emotion and caring. He forces Pecola to stay in the house with his hands. Upset by Junior, Pecola holds her face with her hands as she cries. She touches Geraldine's cat, the cat that Junior detests, with tear soaked hands. When frightened by the prostitute, the MAGINOT LINE, Claudia and Frieda reach for each other's hands. The Maginot Line's hands are dimpled with fat. As a boy, Cholly idolizes a man named Blue. As he watches Blue hold a melon up in the air, Cholly watches Blue's hands and wonders if this is what God looks like, but he decides that Blue better represents the devil.

The Breedloves are said to take their ugliness into their hands like a cape they then don. Before ugliness becomes the family's self-definition, Cholly gets into bed with Pauline and she feels the grooves of his rough callused hands even before he touches her. When he does begin to touch her, she gives all of her strength into his hands. When she is having an orgasm, she places her hands on him. After their marriage begins to fail, and both Pauline and Cholly adopt ugliness as a way of being, Cholly uses his hands to fight Pauline. Like a coward, he hits her with the palm of his hand. When the marriage between Cholly and Pauline begins to fail and Pauline's romantic hopes fade, Pauline cannot seem to keep her hands off Cholly. She uses violence as a vent for her frustrations. Pauline uses her hands to hit Pecola after she knocks over the blueberry cobbler. Pauline then proceeds to use the same hands to comfort the white child of her employers. When Pauline is a young and lonely child, she dreams of a stranger coming simply to hold her hand.

Older Morrisonian African-American women characters are a study in strength and contradiction. The work of their hands consists of felling trees, cutting umbilical cords, killing animals, as well as coaxing flowers to bloom. (138)

Lips and Mouths

In *The Bluest Eye*, the lips of various characters provide important information about the meanings of their words and/or their intentions.

Lips provide a great deal of information and foreshadowing about Mr. Henry and his perversions. Disembodied lips state that Mr. Henry will be a boarder in the MacTeer home. In the next line, Mrs. MacTeer is revealed as the source of this information. The original lack of identification of the speaker may represent Mrs. MacTeer's uncharacteristic inability to discern the true nature and intentions of Mr. Henry. Frieda's instincts about Mr. Henry may be better than her mother's. The girl makes an odd noise with her lips when Claudia suggests that she, Pecola, and Frieda look at Mr. Henry's pornographic magazines or at the Bible. The MacTeer girls return home following Mr. Henry's encounter with China and the Maginot Line. When the girls ask Mr. Henry who the women are, he takes a drink of pop with his lips and this gesture makes the girls intuitively unsettled.

When a situation is imbalanced or precarious in *The Bluest Eye*, there are indicators of this state by portrayals of unusual or contrasting lips. In a description cataloging the ugliness of the Breedloves, the narrator states that the "shapely lips" of Mrs. Breedlove, Sammy, and Pecola only reinforces their unattractiveness (39). China applies a "cupid-bow" mouth and changes her hairstyle repeatedly. Despite her attempts at make-up, the narrator describes the woman's painted face as unflattering. Mr. MacTeer's face reflects the harsh realities faced by the family during winter. As winter begins, Claudia notes that he will not "unrazor" his lips until the seasons change (61). As she tries to defend Pecola against the taunts of Bay Boy and his friends, Bay Boy threatens Claudia with a fat lip (66).

The narrator describes women who have "lost their funkiness," women like Geraldine who put lipstick on in thin lines as only part of their mouths because they do not want their lips to be too big (83). When Cholly and Darlene begin to have sex, Darlene kisses Cholly on the mouth and he finds her "muscadine-lipped" mouth unpleasant.

In *The Bluest Eye*, Morrison also uses lips to indicate a boundary or border. Before throwing her pop bottle at Claudia, Frieda, and Pecola in disgust when she learns that the MacTeer girls are not allowed to enter her apartment, the Maginot Line puts the bottle to her lips for a last sip. According to the narrator, Pauline sees Lorain, Ohio, as "the melting pot on the lip of America" and she is disappointed with the realities of the town and of her life there (117).

Lip references also occur in the novel as an external indication of the internal feelings and responses of characters. For example, early in their relationship, the sound of Cholly's whistle "pulls" Pauline's lips into a smile. During Aunt Jimmy's final illness, Miss Alice visits her. Alice reads First *Corinthians* while amens "drop" from Aunt Jimmy's lips (136). Neighborhood women gather at Aunt Jimmy's house to help take care of her. As they do so they lick their lips and empathize with Jimmy's pains by remembering their own. The women who visit Jimmy remember their young lips, "relaxed and content."

In her final deliberate act, Pecola goes to Soaphead Church to request blue eyes. As he contemplates her request, he purses his lips. For the first time in his life, Church wants to act with sincerity and tries to fulfill his promise. In spite of this temporary lapse in his normal selfishness, Church returns to his typical behavior and uses Pecola self-interestedly to rid himself of the plague of his landlady's dog, Bob. As such, Soaphead moves his lips as he pretends to pray.

Of course, the most significant meaning lips can convey is the affect of a person—the representation of their emotions on the canvas of the face. As such, smiles, genuine or artificial, are crucial to Morrison's character development in *The Bluest Eye*. As he arrives at the MacTeer home, Mr. Henry is described as smiling frequently and with his teeth. Mr. Henry's smile evokes that of the minstrel character, masking his true identity and intent behind a wide deceptive smile. Mrs. MacTeer smiles twice during Mr. Henry's introduction to the family. She is not a woman given to smiling, but is taken in by Mr. Henry's seeming jocularity. The experience of watching their mother respond in this manner is disconcerting for both Claudia and Frieda.

Claudia's interactions with Pecola foreshadow the ill-fated child's eventual psychological dissociation as Claudia is described as entertaining Pecola and the girl's smile as separate entities. Similarly, Claudia is disturbed by the false, almost macabre smiles of her dolls.

Genuine smiles are not always benign, however. The Maginot Line smiles with a "genuine" smile at Claudia, Pecola, and Frieda—a smile that is, ironically, more sincere than that of other adults who interact with the children—but her smile fades when she learns that Claudia and Frieda are not allowed to come into her apartment. In the wake of the Coke bottle the Maginot Line throws at them, Claudia and Frieda meet Pecola at the house on the lake and are surprised to find her smiling.

Interestingly, Morrison differentiates between lips and mouths in her use of the body as a symbol in *The Bluest Eye*. The mouth is capable of language and therefore of major significance in Morrison's depiction of her characters in the novel.

Even as a girl, Claudia MacTeer is aware of the indignities associated with racial discrimination. Her next-door neighbor, Rosemary Villanucci, embodies that discrimination when she informs Claudia and her sister Frieda that they cannot come into her house. As she makes this statement, Rosemary is eating bread and butter. Claudia responds with an unrealized desire to humiliate Rosemary by hitting her in the mouth while she chews. By envisioning hitting Rosemary in the mouth, Claudia imagines a violent response to the hurtful impact of Rosemary's words. Similarly, the physical is used to counter words when Frieda tries to explain to Pecola about her first menstrual period and Pecola responds by placing her fingers on her mouth.

During a childhood illness, Mrs. MacTeer rubs Vick's salve on Claudia's chest and puts some in her mouth, telling her to swallow it. With this instruction, Mrs. MacTeer symbolically encourages Claudia to ingest her healing love. In this instance, the mouth becomes a space for access to the authentic self or soul. The mouth functions as such a space in other instances in the novel as well. Following Mr. Henry's molestation of Frieda, Mr. and Mrs. MacTeer attack him physically. As they pummel him, he begins to sing "Nearer My God to Thee." Mrs. MacTeer tells him to keep God's name out of his mouth. After Pecola feeds Bob the poisoned meat, the dog moves his mouth strangely. Pecola opens her mouth in horror and then covers her mouth to prevent herself from vomiting. While pregnant with Sammy, Pauline loses a tooth as she eats candy during a Gable and HARLOW film. This loss signifies her self-perception as an ugly woman with an imperfect mouth, so unlike those on the screen. This experience of a loss within the mouth totally changes Pauline's self-perception.

Pauline is perhaps most revelatory in a series of flashback memories. In one of them, she tells of a white employer who spoke out of one side of her mouth and casually informs Pauline that she should leave her marriage to Cholly. The woman's husband is said to have a slash instead of a mouth. In another flashback memory, Pauline describes making love with Cholly. She likes the feeling of Cholly's mouth under her chin.

The mouth can also function as a symbol of a character's condition. Earlier in the novel, during Aunt Jimmy's illness, the sick woman briefly begins to feel better. She then eats a piece of peach cobbler that the neighbors believe causes her death. Aunt Jimmy's mouth is in an O shape the next morning when she is found dead. On the day of Aunt Jimmy's funeral, mouths were "set down" (150). A fly settles in the corner of her mouth until Cholly waves it away. After Aunt Jimmy's funeral, Cholly plays with some of his cousins. One of them, Jake, offers him a cigarette. Cholly embarrasses himself by placing the cigarette over the match instead of placing it in his mouth. After an adventure with Darlene, Jake, and Suky in the grape patch, Cholly's mouth tastes of muscadine. This taste mirrors his feeling of belonging and contentment. After he runs away, in search of his father, Cholly is "dry-mouthed" in anticipation of the ill-fated meeting.

When Claudia encounters the Maginot Line, she is unable to speak, finding her mouth immobile. In a moment of sincere self-revelation, Soaphead Church writes a letter to God saying that it is difficult for him to keep his mouth and hands off girl children.

CHARACTERS

Aunt Jimmy Aunt Jimmy is Cholly's aunt, his mother's sister. She rescues Cholly as a baby after his mother abandons him and subsequently raises Cholly on her own. She is the sole source of affec-

tion for Cholly during his childhood. Despite her care, Cholly is often repulsed by Aunt Jimmy's age, appearance, and smell. Cholly does, however, respect Aunt Jimmy and has sincere affection for her. In the spring of Cholly's 13th year, Aunt Jimmy falls ill after sitting on a damp bench at a camp meeting. The women of the community, who are clearly attached to Aunt Jimmy, gather around, sit with her, bring her food, and attempt to nurse her back to health. The women's concern shows Aunt Jimmy's position as a center and a stalwart in her community. Out of concern one of the women, Essie Foster, prepares and brings a peach cobbler to Aunt Jimmy. M'Dear, the town midwife and healer, warns Jimmy not to eat solid food. Aunt Jimmy does not comply, eats a piece of peach pie, and is dead the next morning. The community and members of Jimmy's family gather for her funeral. Aunt Jimmy's death leaves Cholly completely orphaned.

Aunt Julia Aunt Julia is an aunt to Della Jones and is said to aimlessly drift up and down Sixteenth Street in an old bonnet, startling passersby. Mrs. Breedlove and her friends are ambivalent about whether Aunt Julia should be committed to the county mental hospital.

Bay Boy Bay Boy is one of the boys in town who harass and torment Pecola as she walks with Claudia, Frieda, and Maureen Peal. The boys surround Pecola and taunt her with jibes about her family and the darkness of her skin color. The boys' mockery indicates their insecurity and, like their role models in the town, they compensate for their fear by positioning themselves as superior to Pecola and the Breedlove family. When Frieda and Claudia stop the boys' abuse of Pecola, the boys act in typical male macho style by leaving and pretending that standing up to the girls is not worth the trouble. Louis Junior, Geraldine's son, idolizes Bay Boy.

Bertha Reese Bertha Reese is the older and deeply religious woman who owns a candy shop and rents a room to Soaphead Church. Hard of hearing, Bertha Reese leaves her tenant to his own devices. She owns a mangy dog named Bob that Soaphead finds disgusting. Soaphead deceives Pecola into killing the dog when he tells her that feeding Bob a piece of meat will fulfill her request for blue eyes. Bertha is upset when she discovers the dead dog.

Big Mama Big Mama is Mrs. MacTeer's mother and Claudia and Frieda's grandmother. Claudia wishes that, instead of presents for Christmas, she could sit in Big Mama's kitchen, a warm safe space, and eat Big Mama's food.

Big Papa Claudia and Frieda call their grandfather, Mrs. MacTeer's father, Big Papa. Big Papa plays the violin and one of Claudia's fondest wishes is to have him play the violin for her alone.

Blue Jack Described as old and as a ladies' man, Blue Jack is a former slave and one of the few people for whom Cholly expresses affection. In fact, Cholly loves Blue. Blue works as a drayman at Tyson's Feed and Grain store where Cholly also works. Blue pays attention to Cholly and is a storyteller who captivates young Cholly with tales of what it felt like to be emancipated. Blue also tells a peculiar tale about a dead white woman who was beheaded by her husband and who haunted her former home blindly in search of a comb.

The most significant encounter between Blue and Cholly occurs at a Fourth of July church picnic. After the father of a family attending the picnic breaks a watermelon against a rock in order to open it for his children, Blue retrieves the heart, the seedless sweet core of the melon, and gives it to Cholly. Cholly and Blue eat the melon together.

When Aunt Jimmy dies and Cholly, with no information about sex, thinks that his ill-fated sexual encounter with Darlene may have impregnated her, the young man seeks out Blue for advice. Blue, an alcoholic, is incoherent and incapable of responding to or providing guidance to Cholly.

Bob Bertha Reese owns Bob the dog. Bob is so old and ill that he smells and oozes fluid from his various orifices. Soaphead obsesses about what he sees as the disturbing physical infirmities of the mutt and desires nothing more than to bring about the dog's demise. Soaphead, however, finds the prospect of actually killing the dog himself too dis-

tasteful to enact. Soaphead gives Pecola poisoned meat to feed him. Soaphead tells Pecola that feeding the meat to the dog will help her to get the blue eyes she desires. Soaphead tricks Pecola into killing the dog and convinces himself that the act is for the greater good. After Pecola feeds Bob the poisoned meat, the dog moves his mouth strangely. Pecola opens her mouth in horror and then covers her mouth to prevent herself from vomiting.

Buddy Wilson Buddy Wilson is one of the boys in town who harass and torment Pecola as she walks with Claudia, Frieda, and Maureen Peal. The boys surround Pecola and taunt her with jibes about her family and the darkness of her skin color. The boys' mockery indicates their insecurity and, like their role models in the town, they compensate for their fear by positioning themselves as superior to Pecola and the Breedlove family. When Frieda and Claudia stop the boys' abuse of Pecola, the boys enact male machismo by leaving and pretending that standing up to the girls is not worth the trouble.

China China is a prostitute who shares a residence and companionship with two other prostitutes, Miss Marie and Poland. They live in the same building as the Breedloves and share conversations with Pecola. China is very interested in her own appearance and is always transforming her looks by changing her makeup from one style to another. China applies a "cupid-bow" mouth and changes her hairstyle repeatedly. Despite her attempts at make up, the narrator describes her face as unflattering. Aging, China is resistant to being thought of as old. She is thin with brown teeth and bandy legs. Like Miss Marie and Poland, she hates men.

Cholly Breedlove (Mr. Breedlove) Named after his Aunt Jimmy's dead brother, Charles Breedlove, Cholly, begins his life inauspiciously when his mentally impaired mother abandons him at a railroad track when he is four days old. This singular event becomes a defining moment in Cholly's life history as he can aptly be described as alone in every sense of the word. Although Aunt Jimmy rescues him from the tracks, she is able to provide a home for him only until his early adolescence, as a result of her death in Cholly's 13th year. When Aunt Jimmy dies, Cholly is again an orphan and without a home. His father, said by Aunt Jimmy to be Samson Fuller, rejects him cruelly when Cholly seeks him out after Aunt Jimmy's death. After this rejection, Cholly acquires a freedom, a detachment unconstrained by responsibility or conscience and therefore becomes dangerous and destructive.

Perhaps the defining moment in Cholly's life occurs at the funeral banquet following Aunt Jimmy's burial. After Aunt Jimmy's funeral, Cholly plays with some of his cousins. One of them, Jake, offers him a cigarette. Cholly embarrasses himself by placing the cigarette over the match instead of placing it in his mouth. Cholly and newfound cousin, Jake, begin a youthful flirtation with two girls, Darlene and Suky. The foursome go on a walk and discover an unripe muscadine grape grove. In the wake of their feasting on the grapes, renowned for their dark sweetness, Cholly and Darlene kiss and, eventually, begin to have intercourse. When Cholly and Darlene initiate their love making, Darlene kisses Cholly on the mouth and he finds her mouth unpleasant. The subsequent humiliating interruption and exploitation of this first sexual experience by racist and abusive white hunters leaves Cholly powerless to defend himself or to retaliate. As a result, he channels his frustration and anger toward Darlene, establishing a lifelong pattern of venting his rage at the oppression he experiences on those more powerless and impotent than himself.

This habitual redirection of his anger at relatively helpless individuals occurs most frequently with his family. Cholly meets and marries Pauline Williams and, for a brief period, seems to genuinely connect with her as they begin to build a life together. The complicated transition from the rural South to the relatively urban North, coupled with Cholly's complete lack of knowledge of how to be a husband and father, as well as his excessive drinking, snuff out his desire for Pauline and his capacity to bond with or care for his children Sammy and Pecola. The constant in the Breedlove home is the perpetual emotional, verbal, and physical battle between Cholly and Pauline, whom he always refers to as Mrs. Breedlove. Cholly merely responds

to stimuli in his environment and is incapable of functioning as anything other than an abuser.

Cholly's most troubling act is the rape of his daughter Pecola. Ironically, his violation of Pecola is complicated by Cholly's perverse, alcohol-bleary perception that he is somehow demonstrating tenderness toward his daughter. Cholly's rape of Pecola results in her pregnancy and miscarriage and instigates Pecola's mental collapse. Later, Cholly dies in the workhouse.

Claudia MacTeer Claudia MacTeer is the daughter of Mrs. MacTeer (Mama) and Mr. MacTeer (Daddy) and the primary narrator of the novel. Claudia MacTeer is nine years old at the beginning of the novel. Claudia lives in a green house, which connects her to the Dick and Jane story at the beginning of the novel. She shares with the fictional and flat Dick and Jane the same family structure. She is a daughter with a father and a mother and a sister and she, like Jane, plays. But Claudia's world is filled with realities unexpressed in the stereotypical world inhabited by Dick and Jane.

Claudia's house is green, but it is also old and cold. These characteristics reflect the very real difficulties Claudia and her family face. The family, while stable and solid, has to contend with the challenges of life as African Americans in the post-DEPRESSION era. Resources are valued and her parent's anxieties about their ability to sustain their family permeate Claudia's existence. In the tension of her parent's concern lies evidence of their deep and abiding love for both Claudia and her sister Frieda. This love manifests in the things that they do for Claudia rather than in the things that they say to her. Through her experience of their actions, Claudia grows secure in her belief in the relative safety of her immediate world. She is not coddled by her parents, but she is protected and cared for by them. In many ways Claudia functions as a contrast to Pecola who is without parental protection and nurturance.

The Bluest Eye can be characterized as a bildungsroman, or a coming-of-age story, featuring Claudia as the primary character undergoing the transition between childhood and womanhood. The novel traces Claudia's development through a series of problems she encounters. Each incident, while often unresolved, demonstrates to Claudia the norms of her community and the rules that govern the behavior of the adults in that community. Often Claudia, in her innocence, finds conflict between the values articulated by adults and their actions. In her acceptance of or acquiescence to these inconsistencies, Claudia learns how to conform to the expectations of those around her.

The conflicts Claudia navigates teach her primarily about what behaviors are acceptable and which are not, as well as what the consequences are for straying beyond the boundaries of communally defined normalcy. For example, Claudia learns that it is not alright to destroy a gift even if, fundamentally, the gift is distasteful to her. When she is given a white baby doll for Christmas, those around her expect that she, like they, will value it and cherish the gift. Claudia is disturbed by the false, almost macabre smiles of her dolls. Claudia does not understand what the doll represents and why those around her are so enamored of it. As a result, she dismantles the toy in an attempt literally to get at the heart of what is so attractive about the doll.

Claudia also learns how to read her environment, a lesson vital to internalizing behaviors and adapting to adult ways of behaving. She observes her mother's women friends; by hearing the tone of their conversation, she understands not *what* they say, but how they say it. She notices her father's face and the way in which the concern about keeping his family warm and fed in the winter symbolically freezes his expression. Likewise, she receives notification of her mother's state of mind each day by listening to the songs that Mrs. MacTeer sings. The sound of the song signals to Claudia her mother's state of mind. Often, however, there is a decided difference between what Claudia perceives and what she is told.

Claudia's major conflicts often come from the difference between what she has been told is acceptable and the contradictory ways in which she sees those around her behaving. Claudia's final act in the novel demonstrates this ambivalence as well as her attempt to act on what she believes is right— what she has been told to do rather than what she observes adults doing. Following Pecola's rape and

pregnancy, Claudia notices that the adults in the community talk about the violation of the child, but do not express sympathy for Pecola and her unborn child. This lack of compassion prompts Claudia and Frieda to act in the only way they know and that is accessible to them. Relying on what remains of childhood belief and faith, the sisters plant marigold seeds with the hope that this act will somehow ensure Pecola's baby's survival.

Ultimately, the failure of the marigolds to grow may represent the futility of Claudia's attempt to defy the realities of maturity that the adults in her life have already accepted. The marigolds do not grow. She cannot save Pecola or change the environment in which they both exist, a world where the reality is that people are bound by the stories they believe—stories like DICK AND JANE that create hierarchies and, most frequently, place those without blue eyes at the bottom of the heap.

Daddy (Mr. MacTeer) Mr. MacTeer, called Daddy by Claudia, is a man invested in the well-being of his family. Although not such a central character as Mama (Mrs. MacTeer), Mr. MacTeer is a powerful force in his daughters' lives and, in contrast to Cholly and some other fathers in the novel, is responsible for and contributes to his family's well-being. Claudia describes her father's physical features in terms that ground him in the natural world. The most significant act he performs in the novel occurs when Henry Washington molests Frieda. He assaults the man physically and shoots after him in an attempt to defend his daughter.

The MacTeer girls experience some shame about their father as well. Remembering one evening when their father checks on them while he is naked, the girls are embarrassed by Maureen Peal's question asking whether they have seen a man naked.

Darlene Mimicking the behavior of his older cousin, Jake, Cholly shyly approaches Darlene during Aunt Jimmy's funeral banquet. Although Cholly asks Darlene to go on a walk with him, it is Darlene who is the one in control of the situation. While the two share a feast of muscadine grapes,

Darlene stains her dress with the dark juice of the fruit.

Darlene instigates the sexual interaction between the two and the encounter might have proven pleasurable and fulfilling for both of them if hunters had not intruded and turned their intercourse into a degrading spectacle. Darlene is broken by the event and by Cholly's hostile response to her as they walk back to the banquet. During their walk, it begins to rain. This event helps Darlene to explain her stained and dirty dress to her mother, who does not react with excessive anger. Darlene is the first in a long series of women that Cholly will use as the focus of his frustration and anger at the oppression he experiences.

Della Jones   Della Jones is the subject of gossip by Mrs. MacTeer's women friends as they discuss why Henry Washington is coming to board at the MacTeers' home. This conversation reveals that Della Jones is a "good" woman who regularly attends church, keeps a clean home, and perfumes herself with violet water. Despite these qualities, she succumbs to her family's tendency toward mental illness when her husband leaves her for Trifling Peggy from Elyria. In addition to this emotional trauma, Della also suffers a series of strokes that leave her unable to communicate effectively or to recognize those around her. A sister, who is thought to have intentions of claiming Della's house, is said to be coming from North Carolina to care for Della in Henry Washington's absence.

Dewey Prince   Dewey Prince is the great love of Miss Marie (Maginot Line). Marie tells Pecola stories of this man. Marie tells Pecola that she met Dewey when she was 14 and that she ran away from Jackson, Mississippi, to Cincinnati, Ohio, with him and that they lived together like a married couple for three years. The couple has children that Marie refuses to speak about. Marie's stories about Dewey Prince make Pecola curious about love between adults.

Dick   The novel begins with a replication of the DICK AND JANE texts that were widely used by American educators in the 1940s and 1950s to teach primary school students how to read. Dick is a character in the Dick and Jane book series. The series was designed to help children learn how to read. The books are characterized by simple phrases that describe the activities and feelings of the characters in a way that is accessible to pre-readers. These books present a sanitized version of family life and normalcy. Their function as the first books in children's lives and as the books that introduce them to written narrative underscores their cultural significance. Dick's only role in the recreation of the primer at the beginning of *The Bluest Eye* is that he lives in the same green and white house as the rest of the family. The house in the Dick and Jane narrative has a red door.

Essie Foster   Essie Foster is a wonderful cook and well-intentioned woman who brings Aunt Jimmy a peach cobbler when Aunt Jimmy is ill. M'Dear has prescribed a diet solely of POT LIQUOR for Aunt Jimmy. Because Aunt Jimmy eats the pie in defiance of M'Dear's advice, the town attributes her death to the ingestion of the peach cobbler. Although Aunt Jimmy's women friends do not blame her, Essie Foster is said to feel responsible for Aunt Jimmy's death. She even offers to hold the funeral banquet at her house.

Father   Father is a character in the Dick and Jane book series. The series was designed to help children learn how to read. The books are characterized by simple phrases that describe the activities and feelings of the characters in a way that is accessible to pre-readers. These books present a sanitized version of family life and normalcy. Their function as the first books in children's lives and as the books that introduce them to written narrative underscores their cultural significance. Father's only role in the recreation of the primer at the beginning of *The Bluest Eye* is that he lives in the same green and white house as the rest of the family and that, rather than playing with Jane, he smiles. He is described physically as big and strong.

Fisher girl, the   The Fishers' young daughter is a favorite of Pauline as she works as a maid in the Fisher home, a place where she finds order and respite from the dysfunction and chaos of her life with her own family. Pauline showers the little Fisher girl with endearments and affectionate nicknames while she does not provide the same nurturance for her own children, Sammy and Pecola. Pauline's disproportionate adoration of the little Fisher girl in comparison to her harsh and distant demeanor toward Pecola reinforces Pecola's view of herself as unworthy and unloved.

Frieda and Claudia also witness Pauline's favoritism and neglect of Pecola as they are present at the Fisher home when Pecola, out of childish curiosity, accidentally spills a hot blueberry pie her mother has just made. Despite the burns Pecola receives from the hot berries, Pauline hits and violently rebukes her child while consoling and comforting the little Fisher girl who is unsettled but unharmed by the event.

Fishers, the   Pauline's employers, the Fishers, represent an extreme opposite of her life at home with her family. The Fishers' house is neat, well-decorated, and orderly. Pauline finds both a purpose and solace through her work as their maid. In a possible allusion to the film *Imitation of Life,* Mr. Fisher claims that Pauline's blueberry pies would be more lucrative than real estate. In return for the comfort the family represents, Pauline is a loyal, protective, and self-effacing servant. The Fishers give Pauline a nickname, Polly, a gesture she missed and did not receive from her own family.

Frieda MacTeer   Frieda MacTeer is the older daughter of the MacTeers and Claudia's sister. She is 10 years old at the beginning of the novel. Although Frieda is more reserved and shy than Claudia, she is a bit more savvy and informed about the machinations of the adult world than is Claudia. Even though Frieda is more withdrawing than Claudia, she often demonstrates an enormous strength of character. She, for example, defends Pecola when she is pestered by a group of boys and also intervenes when her mother misunderstands what is happening when Pecola begins to menstruate. Frieda consistently defends those who are weaker than she is and who are abused and oppressed. Frieda makes an odd noise with her lips

when Claudia suggests that she, Pecola, and Frieda look at Mr. Henry's pornographic magazines or at the Bible.

Frieda is the victim of sexual abuse at the hands of Mr. Henry Washington, a boarder in her family's home. When Henry Washington inappropriately pinches her breast, characteristically, she protects herself by telling her parents. Frieda's expectation that her parents will defend her and shield her from harm stands in marked contrast to Pecola's rape at the hands of Cholly. After the incident of abuse, Frieda is despondent because she believes she may be ruined. Frieda participates in Claudia's hopeful but futile planting of marigold seeds for Pecola's unborn baby.

Geraldine   Geraldine is a migrant from the South who relocates to Lorain with her husband Louis. Geraldine, socialized to conform unquestioningly to the definitions of normalcy, rigidly adheres to convention. She is deeply invested in appearance and channels all of her feeling and emotion into the work of creating order and fighting against anything—dirt, poverty, free expression—that threatens her efforts. She is one of the southern black women who fight off the "funkiness" and sleep with their hands folded across their stomachs, exemplifying their desire for order and control and their attempt to bar the sexual advances of their husbands.

Geraldine's investment in assimilation leads her to avoid and despise blacks that she deems unacceptable. She passes this way of thinking on to her son, Louis Junior, who is isolated from his peers as a result. Geraldine is an overbearing but disinterested mother who saves her fondest attention and adoration for her cat.

When Geraldine finds Pecola in her home and her cat injured, the woman loses all pretense of graciousness and hurls expletives at the child. Pecola represents a dangerous intrusion into her neatly arranged life. Geraldine has no compassion or sympathy for the child. She only wants Pecola out of her house.

Grinning Hattie   Grinning Hattie is one of Della Jones's sisters who never seems mentally competent.

Henry Washington   See MR. HENRY

hunters   The hunters are the men in the woods who make a spectacle of Darlene and Cholly's sexual encounter. From their actions and their broken and monosyllabic use of English, the men appear to be extremely limited. Their voyeurism and vicarious rape of both Darlene and Cholly is an action meant to affirm their power and serves as a way for the men to assert their assumed superiority. The incident is marked by the disturbing staccato laughter of the men as they sadistically watch the helpless pair obey their commands.

Ivy   Ivy is a member of the choir in Pauline's hometown in Kentucky, Ivy has a voice that seems to resonate with Pauline's imaginative perceptions of the world. Ivy's singing seems to Pauline to give sound to a range of feelings that Pauline associates with romantic love and with her hopes for a prince to come and rescue her from her situation at home.

Jake   Jake, a young man of 15, is O.V.'s son. Cholly meets Jake for the first time at Aunt Jimmy's funeral. After Jake gives Cholly his first cigarette, the two quickly bond and Jake suggests that Cholly should introduce him to some of the local girls who are attending the funeral. Jake, Suky, Cholly, and Darlene then go for a walk to eat muscadine grapes. After eating the grapes, Jake and Suky return to the gathering, leaving Cholly and Darlene alone. This very short interaction with Jake seems to be the only genuine camaraderie Cholly experiences in his life.

Jane   *(Dick and Jane)*   The novel begins with a replication of the Dick and Jane texts that were widely used by American educators into the 1940s and 1950s to teach primary school students how to read. Jane is a character in the Dick and Jane book series. The series was designed to help children learn how to read. The books are characterized by simple phrases that describe the activities and feelings of the characters in a way that is accessible to pre-readers. These books present a sanitized version of family life and normalcy. Their function as

the first books in children's lives and as the books that introduce them to written narrative underscores their cultural significance.

Jane is the central figure in the recreation of Dick and Jane at the beginning of *The Bluest Eye*. In addition to living happily in the green and white house with Father, Mother, and Dick, Jane wants to play. The house in the Dick and Jane narrative has a red door. The plot of the narrative involves Jane's attempt to find a playmate. She asks the cat, Mother, Father, and the dog to play and they are unresponsive. At the end of the story, Jane finds a friend and they play.

Junie Bug   Junie Bug is one of the boys in town who harass and torment Pecola as she walks with Claudia, Frieda, and Maureen Peal. The boys surround Pecola and taunt her with jibes about her family and the darkness of her skin color. The boys' mockery indicates their insecurity and, like their role models in the town, they compensate for their fear by positioning themselves as superior to Pecola and the Breedlove family. When Frieda and Claudia stop the boys' abuse of Pecola, the boys enact male machismo by leaving and pretending that standing up to the girls is not worth the trouble.

Junior   See LOUIS JUNIOR

Listerine and Lucky Strike Breath   Listerine and Lucky Strike Breath is the descriptive name given to the man who sells a sofa to Cholly Breedlove. The sofa, when delivered, is slit in the back. The salesman refuses to replace the damaged goods and therefore the Breedloves receive the defective furniture rather than a new, inviting sofa. The incident illustrates the ways in which disadvantaged African Americans were often cheated and powerless to change their circumstances.

Louis Junior (Junior)   Obsessively cared for by his mother, Geraldine, Louis Junior feels the care is physical only, and he longs for her affection and warmth—attentions his mother seems to be able to express only to the family cat. Living next door to the elementary school gives Louis a false sense of ownership and an arrogance that bolsters his mean behavior. Geraldine's discrimination against poor and/or darker skinned blacks contributes to Junior's frustration and isolation. Junior is a boy who goes to school with Pecola. Junior's major flaw comes from the fact that his mother has taught him to hate and shun other African-American people who do not meet certain "ideal" class and skin color characteristics. Junior uses violence as a means to express his anger and hurt. Like Pecola, Junior is abused, but in a different way. Junior has been given everything he needs to survive. He is not beaten or yelled at, but Junior never receives affection or love from his mother.

One lonely afternoon, Junior lures Pecola into his house, under the guise of wanting to play with her. When he gets her in the house, he throws his mother's cat, whom he jealously hates, in Pecola's face. He is gleeful at her injury and at her panic as he tells her she is locked in the house and is his prisoner. When Geraldine walks in on the scene, Junior blames Pecola for everything that has happened. Geraldine responds by calling Pecola a bitch.

Maginot Line   See MISS MARIE

Mama (Mrs. MacTeer)   Claudia and Frieda's mother, Mama, or Mrs. MacTeer, is a fierce woman who works hard to keep her family fed, clothed, well, and respectable. Claudia misreads her abrupt and straightforward mannerisms for disregard. When Claudia is ill, for example, Mrs. MacTeer fusses at her and does not fit a model or stereotype of motherhood; however, her way of communicating is simply her way of dealing with frustration and anxiety about her daughter's health. Claudia's mother's hands are ambiguous to the little girl as they cause her pain, yet convey to Claudia a deep abiding motherlove.

Both Mr. and Mrs. MacTeer are deeply invested in their family's well-being and love their daughters, but the expression of their affection is plagued by the financial difficulties the family faces. Both Claudia and Frieda know that their parents will protect them as evidenced by Frieda's impulse to tell her parents immediately when Henry Washington molests her. Both parents unhesitatingly defend their daughter.

Mrs. MacTeer is a singer, and her songs convey information to her daughters that is both practical and generative. By listening to her songs, the girls know what her mood is, but they also think about the words, words that serve as a catalyst for the girls' imaginations. Although not traditionally nurturing, Mrs. MacTeer is a strong woman who provides for her children an environment in which they learn to value themselves.

Maureen Peal   Maureen Peal is the new girl in town. She arrives in Lorain in the middle of winter from the comparatively big city of Toledo, Ohio, and is assigned the locker next to Claudia's. Both Frieda and Claudia are perplexed by the adoration Maureen Peal receives. Maureen Peal is light-skinned with long straight hair and green eyes. Her family is economically more comfortable than the MacTeers and most of the town's African-American residents. She wears clothes that the MacTeer girls only dream about owning. The black and white adults and children in LORAIN treat the girl with the deference and adoration associated with whiteness and, by doing so, reveal the skin color and class hierarchies that influence the community.

The MacTeer girls dwell on Maureen's imperfections, namely a dogtooth and evidence of an extra finger on each hand, in order to balance the injury to their self-esteem caused by the disparity in the way people treat Maureen and themselves. Claudia and Frieda relish Maureen's imperfections and tease her about them. Maureen has more information than the girls about some things like menstruation and seems worldlier.

Like the boys who taunt Pecola, Maureen Peal also calls her names and adds Frieda and Claudia to her insults, which all focus on the sisters' darker skin color. Unlike Pecola, though, the MacTeer girls have enough self-esteem to fight back. They call Maureen names as she runs down the street away from them. Maureen's main defense is her cry that she is cute.

M'Dear M'Dear is the midwife and healer in Cholly's hometown. The name M'Dear is an African-American slang term for mother dear. Older than the memory of most of the townspeople, the town depends on M'Dear in cases of illness that are particularly difficult to overcome. M'Dear is also the town midwife. M'Dear resembles other powerful female figures in African-American literature as she possesses knowledge and ability that seem nearly supernatural. Living alone in a decrepit structure on the edge of the woods, she is a mysterious and awesome figure, especially to young Cholly.

When Aunt Jimmy falls ill and the remedies of her friends fail to enact a cure, M'Dear is summoned to render a diagnosis and prescribe a cure. M'Dear, taller than the preacher who accompanies her, arrives holding a hickory stick. She wears her hair in four white knots of gray hair. She runs her hands over Jimmy's body to determine the cause of the woman's illness. She also examines Jimmy's hands for further signs. She diagnoses Aunt Jimmy seemingly intuitively, feeling the sick woman's head, looking at her fingernails and palms, scratching her scalp, listening to her chest and stomach, and looking at her stools.

Following the examination, M'Dear tells Jimmy to drink pot liquor, the fluid that remains in the pot after cooking greens, and nothing else. After M'Dear leaves with the preacher, the women at Aunt Jimmy's house remark about the reliability and consistency of M'Dear's diagnoses and urge Aunt Jimmy to follow the wise woman's advice.

Miss Alice Miss Alice is one of the women friends of Aunt Jimmy's who gather to care for and comfort her when she falls ill. Aunt Jimmy singles out Miss Alice's Bible reading as the one remedy that she will accept. Miss Alice reads to Aunt Jimmy from FIRST CORINTHIANS and, although it does not help Aunt Jimmy's condition, Miss Alice's reading does soothe the sick woman to sleep. Cholly runs first to Miss Alice's house with the news of Aunt Jimmy's death.

Miss Bertha Reese The proprietor of a neighborhood candy and tobacco store, Miss Bertha has a reputation for selling stale candy and for frequently running out of stock. Bertha's store is in a one-room brick building in her yard and it is close to the MacTeer home.

Miss Dunion After Henry Washington molests Frieda, Miss Dunion is present at the MacTeer home. She witnesses Mr. MacTeer's assault of Henry Washington and advises Mrs. MacTeer to take Frieda to the doctor to see if she has lost her virginity. Miss Dunion refers to this possibility as being ruined, a term both Frieda and Claudia misunderstand. They have heard the word "ruined" only used in reference to the prostitutes Miss Marie (Maginot Line) and China, and so think that the term refers to Frieda's pending physical transformation to resemble the women. They think that Frieda will grow fat.

Miss Erkmeister Miss Erkmeister, a woman with bow legs, is Maureen Peal and Pecola's gym teacher. During a conversation with Pecola, Maureen Peal expresses some bitterness that Miss Erkmeister wears shorts instead of bloomers during the girls' gym class.

Miss Marie (Maginot Line) Miss Marie is one of the three prostitutes who live above the Breedloves in the storefront. Pecola enjoys visiting Marie and Marie treats the girl with affection and tells her stories. The Maginot Line's hands are dimpled with fat. As an obese and unapologetic prostitute, Marie garners the censure of the community. Marie is the symbol of a "bad" woman, and Claudia and Frieda are forbidden to speak with her or go into her home. When Miss Marie invites the girls up to her apartment, they tell her so. The Maginot Line smiles authentically at Claudia, Pecola, and Frieda—a smile that is more sincere than that of other adults who interact with the children, but her smile fades when she learns that Claudia and Frieda are not allowed to come into her apartment. She then throws a pop bottle at them and laughs. Before throwing her pop bottle at Claudia, Frieda, and Pecola in disgust when she learns that the MacTeer girls are not allowed to enter her apartment, she puts the bottle to her lips for a last sip. In spite of this, Claudia thinks that Marie has kind eyes that remind the child of water.

Marie peppers her conversations with references to food. She also gives Pecola food nicknames.

Marie is the only person to give Pecola a nickname. One of the stories that Marie tells Pecola is of her lost love, Dewey Prince. This man travels with Marie when she is 14 from Jackson, Mississippi, to Cincinnati, Ohio, and, although unmarried, they live together as a couple. At the time, Marie is so unworldly that she has never owned a pair of underwear. When the woman she works for gives her a pair, she thinks that it is a hat. Dewey Prince is the only man that Miss Marie likes. She tells Pecola that she had children with Dewey Prince, but gives no other information about what happened to them or to her relationship.

Mother   Mother is a character in the DICK AND JANE book series. The series was designed to help children learn how to read. The books are characterized by simple phrases that describe the activities and feelings of the characters in a way that is accessible to pre-readers. These books present a sanitized version of family life and normalcy. Their function as the first books in children's lives and as the books that introduce them to written narrative underscores their cultural significance. Mother's only role in the recreation of Dick and Jane at the beginning of *The Bluest Eye* is that she lives in the same green and white house as the rest of the family and, that, rather than playing with Jane, she laughs. She is described as very nice.

Mr. Breedlove   See CHOLLY BREEDLOVE

Mr. Buford   After the MacTeers discover that Henry Washington has molested Frieda, Mr. Buford gives Mr. MacTeer a gun to shoot Henry Washington.

Mr. Henry (Henry Washington)   Henry Washington is a charming and manipulative child abuser who comes to live in the MacTeer home in the autumn as a result of the parents' attempt to secure more money for the family. Interestingly, he has a stuttering laugh that is similar to the perverse laughter of the hunters who torture Cholly and Darlene. He moves from the Thirteenth Street home of Della Jones, who is reputedly losing touch with reality. At first, Mr. and Mrs. MacTeer think

he is an ideal boarder as he playfully teases Frieda and Claudia, does magic tricks, and calls them by the names of famous white female movie stars like GRETA GARBO and GINGER ROGERS. The MacTeers trust Henry Washington as a boarder in their home because of his reputation as a hard worker and as one who does not live a life outside the strict public rules of the community.

The reality of Henry Washington's character is more evidence that the public face of the town hides a very different reality. Despite the impression the town holds of him, Henry Washington reads pornography, cavorts with prostitutes in the MacTeer house, and, ultimately, molests Frieda by touching her breasts. When he arrives at the MacTeer home, Mr. Henry is described as smiling frequently with his teeth. The MacTeer girls return home following Mr. Henry's encounter in their home with China and the Maginot Line. When they ask him who the women are, he takes a drink of pop with his lips and this gesture makes the girls intuitively unsettled. Henry Washington's calculated abuse of Frieda contrasts with Cholly Breedlove's spontaneous violation of Pecola and helps to extend the reality of child abuse beyond the particular context of poverty and abnormal behavior and to position abuse as a pervasive social problem.

When Mr. MacTeer learns of Henry Washington's abuse of Frieda, he assaults the man and shoots at him. Ironically, Henry Washington reacts by singing the hymn, "Nearer My God to Thee." Mrs. MacTeer tells him to keep God's name out of his mouth. He is last seen running in sock feet down the street in the wake of Mr. MacTeer's gun shot.

Henry Washington is a major catalyst in Frieda and Claudia's loss of innocence. Troubling, however, is Claudia's revelation of the psychological seduction Henry Washington enacts on the girls with his mannerisms. She says that neither she nor Frieda felt anger or bitterness toward Henry Washington when they thought back on the incident.

Mr. MacTeer   See DADDY

Mrs. Breedlove   See PAULINE WILLIAMS BREEDLOVE

Mrs. MacTeer   See MAMA

Mr. Yacobowski   Mr. Yacobowski is the white, 52-year-old immigrant man who owns the Fresh Vegetable, Meat, Sundries store. He is phlegmatic, with blue eyes that gaze blankly at Pecola when she comes to his store to buy the peanut butter–filled caramel candies called MARY JANES. He does not even want to touch her hand as he takes Pecola's money. Mr. Yacobowski's red and lumpy hands symbolize his contempt for Pecola. He tries to avoid touching her hand when taking her money. His hand scratches hers when he finally reaches to take the pennies.

Old Slack Bessie   Old Slack Bessie is a resident of Elyria and the mother of Trifling Peggy.

O.V.   O.V. is Aunt Jimmy's half-brother and is not biologically related to Cholly who is the son of Jimmy's sister, O.V.'s other half-sister. O.V. is reputed to be a Christian who has a house worthy of admiration. When Aunt Jimmy dies, O.V. brings his wife and children to the funeral to pay his respects and to claim Aunt Jimmy's possessions. As the nearest relative to Cholly, he would be the one to assume responsibility for Cholly. Cholly hates him.

Pauline Williams Breedlove   Pauline Williams Breedlove, the mother of Sammy and Pecola and the wife of Cholly Breedlove, is one of the nine children of Ada and Fowler Williams. Born as the ninth child of the Williams family, Pauline begins life in Alabama before her family moves to Kentucky. As with many African-American migrations north, the move improves the Williams' economic situation and they move into a house, a space that Pauline uses as an outlet for her energy and creativity.

Perhaps the defining characteristic of Pauline's childhood is the relative disregard she experiences. Unlike her brothers and sisters, Pauline was not noticed or made to feel special. She attributes this invisibility to a deformed foot that manifests after she steps on a rusty nail at the age of two. Left to her own imagination, Pauline embraces a fantasy about romantic love, particularly with the notion that an ideal man will come and rescue her from her obscurity.

Pauline is perhaps most revelatory in a series of flashback memories. In one of them, she tells of a white employer who spoke out of one side of her mouth and casually informed Pauline that she should leave her marriage to Cholly. The woman's husband is said to have a slash instead of a mouth. While pregnant with her son Sammy, Pauline loses a tooth as she eats candy during a Gable and Harlow film. This loss signifies her self-perception as ugly with an imperfect mouth, so unlike those on the screen. In a flashback memory, Pauline describes making love with Cholly. She likes the feeling of Cholly's mouth under her chin.

When the marriage between Cholly and Pauline begins to fail and Pauline's romantic hopes fade, she cannot seem to keep her hands off Cholly. She uses violence as a vent for her frustrations. In a description cataloging the ugliness of the Breedloves, the narrator states that the "shapely lips" of Mrs. Breedlove, Sammy, and Pecola only reinforce their unattractiveness. Pauline sees Lorain, Ohio, as "the melting pot on the lip of America" and she is disappointed with the realities of the town and of her life there.

Pecola Breedlove   Pecola Breedlove is the second child of Cholly and Pauline Breedlove. Pecola is 11 years old at the beginning of the novel. Pauline is enamored of Hollywood films and may have gotten her daughter's name from the character Peola in the 1934 version of the movie *Imitation of Life*. Pecola may be a misspelling of Peola, the character from the film named Peola, played by actress Freddi Washington. The character from the film has in common with Pecola the desire to be white.

From the beginning of her daughter's life Pauline describes Pecola as eager, but ugly. Neither Pecola nor her brother, Sammy, receive the love, attention, and support they need from their parents, who are preoccupied, abusive, and dysfunctional. Pecola internalizes their neglect and, believing the reason for her suffering to come from some personal deficiency and longs to understand what it is that makes her so unlovable. Observing the culture around her that seems to embrace and adore little girls with blue eyes, Pecola comes to believe that if she had blue eyes, she would have a different experience of the world and would have the love and attention that she needs and desires.

In a drunken, lustful moment, Cholly notices his daughter Pecola and her vulnerability. He is so driven by his own desires and by his complete inability to identify with another and to adhere to moral boundaries that he rapes his daughter in an act that, in his delirium, he believes is tender. Pecola is fractured psychologically by this event. She is also impregnated and even more desperate to acquire her blue eyes.

She journeys to the local spiritualist/psychic Soaphead Church, who is also a pedophile. Although he does not sexually abuse Pecola, he manipulates her into killing his landlady's dog, Bob. He tells Pecola that if she feeds Bob meat, she will receive the blue eyes that she desires. Watching Bob die is yet another trauma Pecola endures.

After her visit to Soaphead, Pecola seems to believe that she has blue eyes; however, her psyche is utterly fragmented and she communicates only with an alter ego, a critical voice in her head. Even the imagined acquisition of her long desired blue eyes does not ease Pecola's pain and anxiety. She continues to wonder if her eyes are the bluest.

P.L.   P.L. is a companion of Bay Boy and is idolized, for a time, by Geraldine's son, Louis Junior.

Poland   Poland is the name of one of the prostitutes that live in the apartment above the Breedloves' storefront. Poland delights Pecola with her singing and gives the little girl food nicknames. Like Mrs. MacTeer, Poland sings all of the time. Despite some of her crudeness, Poland seems to care for Pecola and asks her questions that seem to suggest genuine concern for the girl. Poland seems to be an alcoholic. Poland's songs make Pecola wonder about love and how it comes about.

Ralph Nisensky   Ralph Nisensky is the lone playmate of Louis Junior. Ralph is not a very interesting partner to Louis as Ralph is thoughtful rather than active.

Rosemary Villanucci   Next door to the MacTeers lives Rosemary Villanucci and her family. Although Rosemary is a frequent playmate of the MacTeer girls, they find her irritating and aggravating. The novel begins with a display of hostility from Claudia and Frieda generated as Rosemary taunts the girls while eating bread in her family's 1939 Buick. The child's arrogance irritates the sisters and they promise to hit her out of frustration. The most peculiar aspect of this incident, however, is Rosemary's response. In response to Claudia and Frieda's assault, Rosemary offers to pull down her underwear, an offer that perplexes Frieda and Claudia. The girls sense that Rosemary's sexuality is somehow valuable and that they preserve their own self-esteem by refusing to see her nakedness. Rosemary's first instinct to remove her underwear in response to violence may indicate that there is also some sexual abuse in her history.

Another incident involving Rosemary Villanucci occurs when Pecola has her first menstrual period while she is staying at the Breedloves' house. Rosemary observes Claudia and Frieda trying to help Pecola and shouts out to Mrs. MacTeer that the girls are playing in inappropriate way. Rosemary's screams result in Mrs. MacTeer misunderstanding the situation and punishing her girls until Frieda tells her what is really happening. When Mrs. MacTeer learns of Pecola's situation, she immediately stops scolding the children and goes to help Pecola. She also castigates Rosemary and sends her home.

Sammy Breedlove   Sammy Breedlove is 14 years old. He is the oldest child of Pauline and Cholly Breedlove and the brother of Pecola, with whom he seems to have no relationship. Sammy is born at home and is difficult for Pauline to feed. Pauline does not deliberately become pregnant with Sammy. When he is a boy, Pauline often yells at and physically abuses her son. Like his sister and father, Sammy calls Pauline Mrs. Breedlove.

Like the rest of his family, Sammy is burdened with the label of ugliness. This imposed identity permeates Sammy's sense of self and informs his interactions with others. Sammy acts out because he is perceived as ugly, and his appearance draws his friends to him as they are daunted and awed by the intimidation his looks cause.

During his parents' endless fights, Sammy often pretends to sleep. At other times, he participates in their conflicts in an attempt to defend Pauline. During one violent interaction, he angrily encourages his mother to kill Cholly. Pauline responds by scolding her son. Sammy's response to the violence of his home is to run away more than 27 times. Eventually, he leaves town permanently.

Sampson Fuller   Before Cholly is born, his father, Sampson Fuller, leaves town. Cholly learns about Sampson Fuller from Aunt Jimmy, who only speculates that Sampson Fuller is Cholly's father and barely remembers his name. Later, after Aunt Jimmy's death, when Cholly believes he has impregnated Darlene, he follows in his father's footsteps and also leaves town. He goes in search of his unseen father in Macon, Georgia. When Cholly finds Sampson Fuller, the man humiliates him and, after throwing money at him, abusively tells the boy to leave. This rejection marks an important turning point in Cholly's life. From that point on, he is rootless and without context.

Soaphead Church (Elihue Micah Whitcomb)   Soaphead Church is a self-proclaimed psychic healer who is born into a West Indian family that is deeply invested in the white elements of their racially mixed heritage. Soaphead despises people and physical contact, messiness, and slovenliness. A misanthropic pedophile, he is the product of a misguided and brutal father. Although Soaphead momentarily transcends his emotional inertia while in a relationship with a woman he loves named Velma, he succumbs to even greater isolation and despondency when she leaves him in frustration.

Like Cholly and Henry Washington, Soaphead is also a child molester who convinces himself that his abuse of young girls is beautiful, even noble. Claudia and Frieda think that he is scary and crazy. When people come to see Soaphead for healing, they seem to acquire peace of mind and he enjoys a regular clientele. Soaphead has a profound distaste for human excretion of all kinds, a distaste that comes from his fear of his own inevitable demise. In spite of his general loathing of people, Soaphead Church collects their personal effects. He is an array of opposites, but always is able to assure himself that he is in the right. Particularly problematic to Soaphead is the dog, Bob, owned by his landlord, Bertha Reese, also known as Miss Bertha. The dog is old and physically repulsive to Soaphead and seems to represent all that he despises about existence.

Pecola comes to see Soaphead after her rape by Cholly. She comes to ask him for blue eyes, a gift she believes will change her life and make her adored. Soaphead sees Pecola's request as an opportunity for him to rid himself of the presence of Bob, the dog. Soaphead tells Pecola that she will acquire her blue eyes if she feeds Bob a piece of meat, which she does not know is poisoned, bringing about the dog's death. While Pecola watches, Soaphead moves his lips as he pretends to pray. Soaphead maintains that this is a charitable act that will grant Pecola's wish, at least within the confines of her own perceptions.

Suky   Suky is a girl from Cholly's hometown who is known for her sharp tongue. She is attracted to Jake and ventures into the woods with him and Cholly and Darlene during the repast following Aunt Jimmy's funeral.

Trifling Peggy   The daughter of Old Slack Bessie, Trifling Peggy is the allegedly promiscuous woman from Elyria who leaves town with Della Jones's husband. Della Jones's husband says that Trifling Peggy's smell is the one a real woman should have.

Velma   Velma is Soaphead Church's former wife. She is affectionate, strong, and full of life. When she discovers that her husband is trying to convert her to his gloomy outlook and lifestyle, she abandons him. The marriage between Velma and Soaphead Church is a union of opposites and her positive energy stands in opposition to his pessimism, despair, and enervation.

Williams family, the (Ada, Foster, Pauline, Chicken, and Pie and nine other children)   The Williamses are Pauline's family of origin. Originally the family lives in Alabama. They then move to

Kentucky around the beginning of World War I. The move improves the family's situation. They are able to own a house that does not suffer from the limitations of the economicaly deprived environment they had before.

Woodrow Cain Woodrow Cain is one of the boys in town who harass and torment Pecola as she walks with Claudia, Frieda, and Maureen Peal. The boys surround Pecola and taunt her with jibes about her family and the darkness of her skin color. The boys' mockery indicates their insecurity; like their role models in the town, they compensate for their fear by positioning themselves as superior to Pecola and the Breedlove family. When Frieda and Claudia stop the boys' abuse of Pecola, the boys enact male machismo by leaving and pretending that standing up to the girls is not worth their trouble.

Claudia learns, from overhearing a conversation between Mrs. MacTeer and Woodrow's mother, that he still wets the bed.

FURTHER READING

Cormier-Hamilton, Patrice. "Black Naturalism and Toni Morrison: The Journey Away from Self-Love in *The Bluest Eye*," *MELUS* 19, no. 4 (Winter 1994): 109–128.

Douglas, Christopher. "What the Bluest Eye Knows about Them: Culture, Race, Identity," *American Literature: A Journal of Literary History, Criticism, and Bibliography* 78 (March 2006): 141–168.

Kuenz, Jane. "*The Bluest Eye*: Notes on History, Community, and Black Female Subjectivity," *African American Review* 27, no. 3 (1993): 421.

Malmgren, Carl D. "Texts, Primers, and Voices in Toni Morrison's *The Bluest Eye*," *Critique* 41, no. 3 (Spring 2000): 251–273.

Mayo, James "Morrison's *The Bluest Eye*," *Explicator* 60, no. 4 (Summer 2002): 231–234.

McKittrick, Katherine. "Black and 'Cause I'm Black I'm Blue: Transverse Racial Geographies in Toni Morrison's *The Bluest Eye*," *Gender Place and Culture: A Journal of Feminist Geography* 7, no. 2 (June 2000): 125–143.

Mermann-Jozwiak, Elisabeth. "Re-membering the Body: Body Politics in Toni Morrison's *The Blu-est Eye*," *Literature Interpretation Theory* 12, no. 2 (2001): 189–194.

Moses, Cat. "The Blues Aesthetic in Toni Morrison's *The Bluest Eye*," *African American Review* 33, no. 4 (Winter 1999): 623–638.

Jazz (1992)

Jazz is the second of a trilogy of Morrison's novels reflecting on the idea of love and its manifestations. The idea for the novel originated with a JAMES VAN DER ZEE photograph of a dead teenaged woman who, knowing she was dying, told her friends that tomorrow she would give them the name of the man who had shot her with a silenced gun at a rent party. The woman was dead the next day and so intentionally did not betray her lover, the man who had murdered her.

The novel tells the story of the New York neighborhood HARLEM from the perspective of its ordinary inhabitants, namely Joe and Violet Trace. The couple is at the center of the novel's investigation of the complexities faced by those millions of African Americans who moved from the rural South to the North during the GREAT MIGRATION in search of jobs and a better life in the cities.

Joe and Violet have to negotiate the stories from their pasts that continue to haunt them and to define who they are even as they begin, or try to begin, new lives in the city. The skills, knowledge, and information that they acquire as they mature in the southern countryside both equip and disable them for their lives as urban residents. The novel bridges the post–Civil War era and the post–World War I generation in its portrait of the HARLEM RENAISSANCE and the NEW NEGRO from the inside out.

SYNOPSIS

Jazz does not have chapter titles. Breaks are indicated in this synopsis with additional line breaks.

The unnamed narrator is a central, if mysterious, character in *Jazz*. Throughout the novel, she provides the vantage point and perspective for the reader's experience of the characters and their lives. Whether her perspectives and analyses are accurate is a matter of decision for the reader who becomes an active participant in the unfolding and meaning of the story.

The narrator introduces the novel's primary protagonists, Violet and Joe Trace, with a conversational first line. She tells of Violet's birds and of her behavior at the funeral of Joe's girlfriend. Joe murdered his girlfriend Dorcas because she did not love him any more. Furious but unable to be angry at Joe, Violet turns her anger and pain on the dead girl and goes to her funeral, illogically, to cut and hurt her. Unsuccessful at this, she releases her pet tropical birds to the winter cold.

Violet is 50 at the beginning of the novel and very thin. She is determined to get revenge for the affair between Joe and Dorcas and she has an affair that lasts only a few weeks and does not achieve her aim. Failing to either anger or reconnect with Joe, Violet decides to focus her attention on the dead girl, and she and Joe begin to share an obsession with his murdered mistress.

Violet tries to learn everything she can about the girl—what she wore, how she danced, who her friends were—and uses that information to begin to imitate her. She is so persistent that, eventually, she befriends the dead girl's aunt, Alice Manfred. Alice gives Violet a picture of Dorcas. Violet places it on her mantel where she and Joe spend hours looking at it and crying.

The narrator waxes on about the city, the way the light hits it at angles, and the actions and energies of its inhabitants. Clearly, she controls the narrative and directs the reader's attention to the particular hopefulness of blacks in 1926, when racial opportunities seemed more abundant than ever and the world had declared an end to all wars.

Violet and Joe spend their nights taking turns looking at the picture of Dorcas. Each sees something different in the face of the dead girl. Joe sees his lover, forgiving and kind, even in death. Violet imagines a selfish, greedy, sneaky overindulged child.

During the day, Violet works as a hairdresser and Joe is a traveling cosmetics salesman. Violet becomes so obsessed with Dorcas that she even imagines how she would cut her hair. Violet may have become a hairdresser because of her grandmother, Vera Louise, who told stories about the blonde hair of a boy she took care of named Golden Gray.

Violet has had a series of slips that make people around her doubt her sanity. Even before Joe's affair with Dorcas, Violet, one day, simply and inexplicably sits down in the street. She does not accept help from anyone and rolls over on her side. People carry her to some nearby steps until she gets up of her own accord and goes to an appointment to do hair.

Another time Violet is waiting for two women who are late for an appointment when she picks up a baby she is supposed to be watching from its carriage and begins to walk away with it. She thinks that Joe will love the baby. As she walks away, the baby's sister, who is supposed to be watching the child, begins to scream. Violet says that she was not taking, but walking the baby. Some people in the crowd believe her. Others feel that Violet actually meant to take the child. Her husband never knows about these strange events and the impression that Violet makes on those who hear about them.

The narrator explains that sometimes Violet falls into the spaces where the light of her reality is not smooth. When there is a break, Violet reacts. This behavior is not typical of Violet who once was a self-possessed, self-assured woman who was active in the world, but her world grows increasingly still and silent.

After she tries to injure Dorcas's corpse during the girl's funeral, Violet forces her pet birds out of the window. The act robs her of the important ritual of caring for something living. All that she thinks she now possesses is the flat photograph of the dead girl to obsess over. For Joe the photograph is different. It is a representation of a live person that was dynamic and real for him. The photograph sends him into a reverie of details about Dorcas— how her eyelids looked when they made love, her dreams and aspirations, the particular pitch of her voice.

Joe tries so hard to remember the details about Dorcas because he cannot remember the details of his early love and passion for Violet and the loss of those memories disturbs him greatly. Violet and Joe first encountered each other as they worked as migrant laborers in Vesper County, Virginia. The couple boarded a train for New York in 1906 and, like so many others, rode into the city on a wave of eager anticipation. By 1926, the passion and excitement that had drawn them together and fueled their exodus from Virginia to New York was not even a memory. Joe, looking to recapture that feeling of joy and excitement, found a woman who he thought would provide that spark.

Dorcas was not just a fling for Joe, though. Something about the girl made him want to share the deepest parts of himself and his story. He wanted to tell her about his hunts for the mother he never knew, how he thought he saw his mother in a cave, and how desperately he wanted for this imagined meeting to affirm some affection this unknown woman might have had for her son.

The couple has motherlessness in common because Dorcas, too, is an orphan. Dorcas's mother died in a fire. She told Joe about that loss and she cried with him before they made love.

Their love making was passionate and enflamed by the shared deep ache of loss. Their meetings took place in an apartment Joe rented from a woman named Malvonne. The affair with Dorcas provided what Joe needed: companionship, excitement, and connection.

Malvonne, the woman Joe rents the apartment from where he and Dorcas meet, lives her life through her intrusion in the doings of others in a way that is possible only in a city where people live in close proximity to each other. When her nephew, Sweetness, leaves for another city, she learns that he is a thief. One of the things that he stole was mail and, after he leaves, Malvonne finds a bag of letters he had taken. At first inclined to mail them, Malvonne opens them instead. She tries to make amends where possible for the theft and the time delay.

When Joe tries to convince Malvonne to rent the room to him, he justifies his decision by saying that Violet does not take care of him anymore and that he deserves some pleasure in life. Malvonne agrees largely because she wants the money and

because she dislikes Violet. So Joe and Dorcas meet in Malvonne's apartment on Thursdays, and Joe becomes a Thursday man.

The next chapter recalls the silent march that tens of thousands of blacks made down Fifth Avenue in July of 1917 in protest of racial discrimination and violence. The march was a response to the riots that had just happened in East St Louis, Illinois. Alice Manfred, Dorcas's aunt, recalls the march and standing with Dorcas, whose parents had just been killed in the rioting. Alice Manfred's response to this tragedy is to try to protect Dorcas (and herself) from what she calls Imminent Demise.

For Alice, the signs of the coming apocalypse are everywhere. In the new way that women dressed and danced, there is ample proof that all is not well. The music—JAZZ and the BLUES—particularly disturbs Alice and seems to justify her sense that everything is falling apart. In fact, she blames the music for the riots that killed her sister and brother-in-law. Alice cannot, however, reconcile the dignity and power she feels when she hears the drums at the march with their inevitable connection to the lowdown music she so despises.

Dorcas has a different experience of the march. She hears the beat as a signal of the promise of her life to come after she escapes from the over-ardent gaze of her fearful aunt. When Dorcas thinks of the riots, she remembers her house burning and, from a child's perspective, thinks of her paper dolls and imagines how quickly they must have burned. Like the dolls, Dorcas is vulnerable to ignition by any one of the many sparks of the city.

Dorcas and her best friend, Felice, attend a party while Alice is out of town. While there, Dorcas is rejected by two popular brothers. This rejection sends her into an adolescent tailspin of insecurity. Joe Trace, an older man, with more money than her peers, seems the perfect antidote to her bruised ego.

Joe and Dorcas meet at Alice Manfred's house. He boldly whispers something in Dorcas's ear as he leaves after collecting some money owed to him. After Dorcas's death this fact drives Alice to distraction as she had been so focused on keeping Dorcas in the house and under her watchful eye that it never occurred to her that someone or something dangerous could have met her there.

Mourning and genuinely fearful of the turn of events that has resulted in the death of her niece, Alice is astonished to find Violet, the wife of the man who killed her niece, knocking at her front door. Violet and Alice gradually begin to get to know each other out of a shared interest in Dorcas, and, particularly, in Dorcas and Joe. During one conversation, while trying to explain her behavior to Alice, Violet asks her if she would fight another woman for her man. This question gives Alice pause and makes her consider that she may in fact have more in common with Violet than she thinks. Alice had a husband who left her for another woman and, although she does not commit physical violence against this woman, she dreams of killing her over and over again.

Violet is like a person split in two. She does not recognize the woman who goes to Dorcas's funeral to stab the dead girl in the face. That other woman earns the name Violent from the community. She remembers that her parrot did not fly away immediately after she puts it out in the cold. It lingers outside saying to Violet the only words it knows, "love you." After two days, the parrot is gone and she does not know what happened to it.

Violet spends considerable energy consuming calories in order to regain the hips that she has lost as she ages. She imagines what Dorcas and Joe did together. Violet knows another Joe, the Virginia Joe, and feels that Dorcas could not possibly have understood Joe the way that she does. As she thinks about the past, though, she realizes that her ideas of love were tainted and tailored by her grandmother, True Belle, who told stories about Golden Gray, the object of Violet's adoration. With those expectations and unrealistic ideals, Joe could only disappoint.

Violet also remembers her mother, Rose Dear, who when faced with disaster, killed herself. Violet does not judge her mother, but she does not want to be like her, broken by circumstances and by the absence of a man. Before Rose Dear killed herself, she, along with Violet and her siblings, were put out of their home. Rose Dear's mother, True Belle,

comes to take care of the family. Violet wonders what was the final indignity or horror that sent Rose Dear to the well forever. Her mother's situation discourages Violet from having children.

During her reflections, Violet also muses on her first meeting with Joe who fell out of a tree she was sleeping beneath. From that moment, the two were inseparable. After they arrived in the city, they were both happy to be childless as it allowed them to feel free with their time and energy. As Violet grows older and more distant from Joe, she begins to crave children and to regret not having any. Her desire becomes so strong that she buys a doll as a surrogate. After Joe's murder of Dorcas, she occasionally thinks of the doll as the daughter she never had.

During her visit, Violet asks Alice Manfred what she should do. Both women turn toward imagined and dead mothers for the answer and are surprised, embarrassed, and amused by their own responses. Then Alice tells Violet to love what she has instead of wishing to change reality. While Alice gives Violet this advice, she inadvertently burns the shirt she is ironing. This uncharacteristic carelessness surprises and then, somehow, delights the women, who break into uncontrolled laughter. As a result Violet remembers the power and value of laughter.

As she leaves the drugstore where she has had all of these liberating thoughts, Violet notices that it is spring.

Spring brings change to the city. The narrator reflects on Joe's affair. She contends that, having been faithful all of his married life, Joe is cocky and self-righteous enough to feel justified in having had an affair.

Joe gives his account of the affair and begins by talking about how he cannot speak to anyone about it. He approaches that whole situation like the salesman that he is. Dorcas excited him, but he did not know what it was that made him speak with her that day at her aunt's house.

Joe speaks of his origins, of his birth in Vesper County, Virginia, in 1873. The Williams family adopts him when he was three months old, but they do not give him their last name. He eventually names himself Trace, after what his parents left without. Joe grows up with the Williams' son,

Victory, who was almost the same age (15). Joe counts this self-naming as his first change. He says that the second came when the best hunter in the county chose him as an apprentice. A fire in Joe's home town accounts for another major transformation. The fire gets him to travel to the nearby town of Palestine where he meets Violet. He and Violet decide to move from the South to New York and this relocation changes Joe once again. When the couple move uptown, Joe has his fifth, and, he believes at the time, final transformation. When he is attacked and beaten by whites in 1917, however, he changes again. The year 1925 brings the last change when Joe, disturbed by his wife's sleeping with a doll, turns to an 18-year-old for comfort.

Joe enjoys everything about Dorcas, including her acne-scarred skin. He sees her marks as a path for him to track. Ultimately, that trail leads Joe to the party where he shoots Dorcas in the heart. Joe recounts the details of Dorcas's breakup with him and of his attempt to recapture all that they shared as it falls apart. Joe embraced the relationship he had with Dorcas because, for the first time in his life, he exercises choice: With Dorcas, life did not happen to him. He made it happen. Joe changes seven times to become his own NEW NEGRO.

The novel shifts to True Belle, Violet's grandmother, and to the story of her departure from and return to Rome, Virginia. True Belle leaves Virginia for Baltimore, Maryland, as the slave of Vera Louise when Vera Louise becomes pregnant with a black man's child.

True Belle lives 11 years with Violet and her siblings before she dies. For Violet, those 11 years are filled with stories of Golden Gray.

Although Vera Louise tells her neighbors in Baltimore that Golden Gray is an orphan she adopted, the boy in fact is her child. Vera Louise denies her son because his father is a black man. When Vera Louise's parents discover her pregnancy and its source, they give her a large sum of money, the slave True Belle, and tell her never to return.

True Belle does not return home or to the children she is forced to leave for more than two decades. She goes back to Rome when her daughter, Rose Dear, needs her help. She fills her grandchil-

dren's minds with stories of Golden Gray, Vera Louise's child, who she helps to raise. The stories detail how the child was treated like a prince, bathed in scented water, and was a perfect gentleman.

Golden Gray receives his name from his prodigious blonde curls that his mother tells him to always wear long. When he is 18, she finally tells him that his father is a black man. Upon learning the truth, Golden Gray leaves Baltimore to find his father and, presumably, to kill him.

The narrator tells the story of Golden Gray's journey to meet his father, starting off for Virginia in a two-seated carriage. At some point in the journey, he believes his trunk has come loose and stops the carriage to fix it. As he gets back into the carriage, he sees, coming out of the woods, a naked, pregnant, and very black woman. As the woman runs away from him, she hits her head on a tree. The self-absorbed and fastidious Golden Gray is at a loss as to what to do. He has more compassion for his horse than he does for the injured woman. Needing to believe in himself as chivalrous, however, he cannot leave the woman as he would like to do.

Covering the woman with his coat, he places her in the carriage. When he arrives at his destination, he first removes his trunk and takes it into the house that, he discovers, is empty. He then returns to the carriage and to the woman to bring her into the house. He worries about his coat and if it will be wearable.

Golden Gray believes that his father's name is Henry LesTroy and that he has arrived at his father's cabin. Golden Gray still grapples with the new knowledge that he is not only white but also black.

The narrator intervenes in her own storytelling and begins to question Golden Gray's actions and motivations. She notes that he behaves as if someone is watching him, as if he is crafting the story for the father he awaits. Golden Gray hears the approach of mule hooves and discovers a young black boy, Honor, who thinks that Golden Gray is white. The boy looks after LesTroy's animals when he is gone.

Golden Gray goes to change his clothes before the boy returns from his work of feeding the animals. As he lays out his clothes, he reflects that not until he knew he had a father did he miss him. When he learns of his parentage, Golden Gray is unhinged. Only True Belle's suggestion that he travel to find his father helps to give his confusion, anger, and crisis a focal point and a purpose.

The interventions by the narrator force the reader to consider all aspects of the story rather than simply dismissing Golden Gray as a self-centered cad. She notes his hurt and perplexity and asks, indirectly, that the reader factor those realities into the evaluation and judgment of this character.

Golden Gray brings Honor to the woman he found in the woods. The child determines from the woman's temperature that she needs water. The boy tries to give her some water. He also washes the blood off of her face.

The woman Golden Gray finds in the woods and Golden himself become a local legend and everything that happens in the community that is negative gets construed as something the woman has done or brought about. The community comes to call the woman Wild. But Henry LesTroy experiences the woman and Golden Gray as real people.

When LesTroy, also known as Hunter's Hunter, returns to his cabin, he finds Golden Gray, Wild, and the boy—Honor—in his cabin. Golden Gray confronts the man immediately, accusing him of being his father. Taken aback, LesTroy tells Golden that he did not know about him. Almost immediately, Wild goes into labor and delivers a newborn that she will not touch.

Finally, the father and son have an opportunity to speak with one another. LesTroy asks who told him that he was his father. LesTroy smiles fondly when he hears True Belle's name. The whole story makes sense to him when he hears that True Belle left with Vera Louise. Golden Gray is mocking and sarcastic. LesTroy does not tolerate the boy's tone and tells him to behave or leave his house. Golden Gray still wants to kill him.

As a young adult, Joe, the baby Wild gave birth to, tries to find her with no success. Once, he hears human singing from a cave. When he calls out to the singer, she disappears. All of his efforts to locate his mother are in vain and, despairing, he gives up searching for her. In his despondency, he decides to marry Violet.

It is the hunting impulse that sends Joe after Dorcas with a gun. Clearly, his love for Dorcas and his inability to let her go is also connected to the loss and absence of his mother. Just as Joe does not understand how a mother can abandon her child and have no love for it, Joe cannot understand why Dorcas would leave him for one of the young men he sees as incapable of treating her the way she deserves. He imagines that when he finds Dorcas, she will be repentant and will want to come back to him.

The chapter ends with Joe's memory of finding the spot where he believes his mother, Wild, lives. The stone crevasse opens to a smooth walled space that is colored by the changing sky. Her things are there, tools for cooking, a green dress, earrings, but the person he seeks is nowhere to be found.

Joe walks into the party where he finds Dorcas. She is happy because she has overcome the initial social rejection that attracted her to Joe. Now Dorcas is with a popular boy her own age, Acton, who is desired by the other girls she knows. Dorcas's contentment also comes from knowing that Joe still wants her, that she is the object of desire and drama.

Dorcas recalls their last conversation and her cruel, complete rejection of Joe. He offers to leave Violet, and Dorcas repeats that she does not want Joe anymore. Dorcas tires of Joe because he does nothing for her social status. Her relationship with him was not only secret but also she believes that, if made public, the romance would be a joke among her peers. For Dorcas, Joe is too easy to please. He presents no challenge. What she now likes about Acton is his investment in how she looks and in her ability to conform to what he wants. Dorcas is too superficial to appreciate Joe's adoration. After their conversation, Dorcas is sure that Joe will come for her. She believes that if he sees her with Acton, he will understand that their relationship is over.

Dorcas sees Joe, who proceeds to shoot her. She loses consciousness. When she awakens in a bedroom, she sees Acton, unconcerned with her status, anxiously trying to get her blood off of his jacket. People ask her who shot her. She will not tell.

On a beautiful day in the city, Violet is so moved by the weather that she does not care about her slight body and her belief that it is her lack of a behind that causes Joe to lose interest. She has taken the photograph of Dorcas back to Alice Manfred. As she stands outside on her porch, a girl, carrying a record, walks up to her looking very much like Dorcas.

The girl is Dorcas's friend Felice. Like Joe, Violet, and Dorcas, Felice is raised without her parents as primary caretakers. The girl's parents work away from home, and she sees them only occasionally. They are too tired and preoccupied to parent her when they are with her.

Felice fills in some of the information about Dorcas, how superficial the girl was, how concerned she was about what people wore and how they smelled. Felice knows that the kids at school would tease her because of the difference in skin color between her and Dorcas. Felice thinks that Dorcas was interested in Joe because of the secrecy of the relationship.

Felice goes to see Violet because she is looking for a ring her mother gave her. Felice thinks that her mother stole the ring from Tiffany's for her daughter. Felice loaned the ring to Dorcas, who had wanted to wear it to impress Acton.

Felice is different from Dorcas. She is not looking for a good time and has concern and respect for other people. It is also more important to her to have a job and a way to support herself than to have a boyfriend or husband.

Felice finds Violet pretty and, after she meets Joe, she understands what Dorcas may have seen in him. Felice begins to spend time with the couple and they all seem to learn and grow from each other. Felice learns from Violet that the countryside might also be a valuable place to be. Violet asks the girl to try to figure out the gender of the trees around her. The point Violet is making is that the perception of reality can be a creative process that can improve and nurture the experience of the world. Violet tells Felice that she wasted a lot of time wanting to be something other than whom and what she was. She says that she had to rid herself of the picture of Golden Gray in her mind in order to own her own life.

Felice tells Violet and Joe that Dorcas would not accept any help because she wanted to die.

Joe talks to Felice about Dorcas and tells the girl that Dorcas had a vulnerable and caring side that no one saw but him because no one else had tried to love her. Joe tells Felice that he shot Dorcas because he was afraid she would leave him and that he did not know how to keep her or truly love her. He says that he still does not know how to love truly, but that he is trying to learn. Felice also tells Joe that Dorcas's last words were about him. Felice learns from Violet that the ring she was looking for, that her mother had given to her, was buried with Dorcas.

The novel ends with the same narrative voice that begins the book. In addition to the usual revelations, the narrator notes that Alice Manfred moves back to Springfield. Felice continues to grow in her own self-determined way. Joe gets a new job, and he and Violet renew their companionship. The couple also acquires a new bird. The bird loves music, so they take it to the roof at night in its cage so it can hear the music coming from the streets. The couple finds a quiet contentment in each other. The narrator then reveals herself to be the book, the narrative itself.

CRITICAL COMMENTARY

Toni Morrison's sixth novel, *Jazz,* is like the music it is named after, a study of the complex blending and melding that becomes the United States. The United States is many things, but is often conceptualized as a coming together of opposites, of the synthesis of urban and rural, black and white, rich and poor, male and female, and young and old. All of these polarities combine in a unique formulation that creates the sound, the look, and the character of the country known as the United States—in other words, JAZZ. In *Jazz,* Toni Morrison examines this definition of America by creating characters that can provide access to the experience of what it means to live in a space that is defined by the idea of opposition.

Morrison describes these particularly American coming together in her novel *Jazz* as an attempted union that is primarily characterized by cycles of yearning, movement, desire, and loss that affect the entire country as well as the individuals who call it home. The novel moves in its journey through the small orbits of the individual characters, to ever larger circles of concern. This movement metaphorically replicates the inscription of music on a record—the text upon which all music but especially jazz would have been imprinted in years past. The reader of the novel *Jazz* becomes, then, like the needle on a record player, gently caressing the surface of the words in order to discern the meaning of the text as it moves slowly toward the center—all the while revealing more and more, pieces, notes of the entire score of the novel.

The novel begins with a sound whose meaning may become more transparent when the record analogy is applied. This beginning sound may be the scratching hiss of a record needle making contact with the surface of the record. With this introduction, the reader begins the interactive process of reading the novel. The word "Sth" that begins the novel requires the reader to pause to consider the meaning of this ambiguous introduction. With this introduction, Morrison requires readers' active participation in the novel. Although the sound that she writes suggests the inception of the record player's interaction with the record, variously it could also stand for the sucking of the teeth that people make when disgusted at an event they experience. The word could also be Morrison's way of bridging, creating a segue, between *Jazz* and her previous novel, *Beloved.* The central character in *Beloved* is Sethe. *Jazz*'s first word, Sth, therefore, may call the reader's attention to the connections between *Beloved* and *Jazz. Jazz* engages some of the central questions raised in *Beloved*—the meaning and relevance of love and freedom, the centrality of memory in the formation of identity, and the circular nature of experience. The word could even be Morrison's wry way of referring to *Jazz* as the sixth contribution to her literary canon.

The record Morrison creates with the novel *Jazz* begins with the musical line of a single character, Violet Trace. Morrison has said that she got the idea for *Jazz* from a story of a photograph taken by Harlem photographer James Van Der Zee. Van Der Zee was a popular and inspired photographer who is credited with creating some of the most important visual documentation of the period in African-American history known as the HARLEM RENAISSANCE. In the early years of photography, taking pictures of the dead was a fairly common occurrence. Families would hold on to the photos as a way of commemorating the loved one. It was just such a photograph and the story behind it that Morrison claims as the inspiration for the novel *Jazz.* According to Morrison, James Van Der Zee's photo from his book, *The Harlem Book of the Dead* (1978), was of a young girl who died after being shot by her boyfriend. According to legend, the girl, knowing she was dying, was asked to reveal the identity of the man who shot her. Although she knew that death was imminent, the girl reportedly replied, "I'll tell you tomorrow." This statement is loaded with the complex contradictions that inform *Jazz.*

As previously mentioned, Violet is the central character of the novel and she is a woman who embodies the difficult objectives of the novel—the quest to inhabit the space in between. Violet is middle-aged, a position that is sometimes difficult for women who have often been defined as useless and unappealing once they have passed their childbearing years. Violet is haunted by the girl that she once was and uncertain of the woman she wants to become.

As a young woman, Violet chose not to have children as a direct result of her observation of her mother's, Rose Dear, experience of motherhood as unrelenting burden. Violet's conflict between her past and her future is compounded by her relocation in her 30s from South to North. Violet perceives herself as fundamentally different in the country than she is in the city. Violet perceives herself when she lived in the country as someone strong and capable. During the last years of life in her new home in the city, Violet seems to undergo a kind of breakdown—the fracture of self that seems to correlate in part with her move north begins to manifest in her actions. The community notes her peculiar behavior—she is said to have attempted to steal a baby and to have sat down randomly in the middle of the street—both inexplicable and ambiguous actions that match Violet's state of mind as well as her inability to fix on a self. The source of Violet's rootless self can be found in the abandonment she experiences as a child as the result of her father's involuntary, life-preserving absence and her mother's suicide. As a woman, these losses manifest in Violet as a fissure or crack. Violet is between the spaces, like the dark, ever-moving lanes or spaces between the lines of a record.

Like the needle on a record, the reader goes in and out of lines of sound—the characters' songs—while reading the novel. This experience may help to illuminate some of the meaning of the novel's epigraph, "I am the name of the sound/ and the sound of the name. / I am the sign of the letter/ and the designation of the division." The enigmatic quotation comes from the GNOSTIC GOSPELS and, like the rest of the novel, forces the reader to contemplate contradiction. In this instance, the sound of the name may refer to JAZZ, which both names a kind of music and onomatopoetically replicates the sound of that music. The sign of the letter may refer to the distinction between what things and people seem to be and what they actually are, the connection between identity and self that plagues each of these characters as they try to move through their lives. At mid-life, Violet tries to understand who she is and, like a scratched record, gets stuck. The designation of the division referred to in the epigraph may be the artificial barriers of identity placed between groups of people in order to create the sign—name, race, religion, gender, sexuality—that defines an individual. These artificial barriers are constructed, yet are powerful determiners of experience, just as the silences between the notes of a song and between the songs on a record become an indistinguishable element of the music.

The central male character in the novel, Joe, has a song/story that is interwoven with Violet's and yet is distinguishable from it. The characters' narratives combine to create a complete work yet function like the improvisational solos common to JAZZ music. Joe's story is more like a BLUES. His problems, like a blues riff, can be stated in three parts, his wife will not talk to him, which makes him deeply lonely, and motivates him to seek out love somewhere else. Like Violet, Joe is in emotional crisis and is torn between his younger, southern, country self and the older, northern, urban man he has become. Both Violet and Joe are yearning for

something that they cannot identify. Violet thinks that it is a baby that she desires and Joe thinks that it is a lover. Interestingly, for a while, they both come to believe that Dorcas is the answer for what they seek, but their longing is of a deeper and less specific nature.

Returning to the record analogy, *Jazz*, circles through the improvisations of its various characters, each contributing to create the sound of the city, of Harlem. In part, the sound of the city is a cry of loss. Like Joe and Violet, almost all of the residents of Harlem have come from somewhere else, and so the sound of the city, jazz, becomes a way to express the loss of and longing for home, as well as a celebration of the new home the North has become. As the novel moves ever-closer to the center of the story, it must make the journey back to the South, back home, in order to understand the pieces of the whole. At the narrative heart of the novel is the story of the interaction of Golden Gray and Wild. This interaction is not only the source of Joe and Violet's crises, but also is the fundamental contradiction and conflict the novel slowly brings the reader to consider—the coming together of blacks and whites in the formation of the United States.

Jazz music is often spoken of as quintessentially American since it is an art form that seems to have originated on this continent. Jazz also is the fusion or mixing of different musical traditions—particularly European and African. Morrison's novel, *Jazz*, takes on the questions and problems raised by that fusion and represents them with the characters Golden Gray and Wild. Although Golden Gray appears white, he is of mixed racial heritage. When he discovers this reality, it sends him into a crisis, and he angrily seeks revenge on his black father. Golden Gray, particularly in light of the way he dresses and acts, can be seen as a representation of America's founding fathers, men like Jefferson and Washington, who, although believing themselves to be white, in fact were descended from the same African ancestor as the rest of humanity. Wild, is the personification of a composite of beliefs about Africans and African Americans. She is unkempt. She is fertile. She is preverbal and illiterate. She is dangerous. She is motherless. She is wild. All of these ideas have, at one time or another, been held as common currency about black people. Significantly, Wild's description bears a striking resemblance to the character Beloved in her novel of the same name. Since *Jazz* is the second in the series of three novels Morrison has called a trilogy, it follows that the character might exist in both books. In *Beloved,* the titular character comes to represent all of the souls lost during slavery. So in *Jazz,* that character becomes reproductive and gives birth. As the cumulative spirit of loss, Beloved/Wild embodies the impact of slavery and the omnipresence of that loss. Wild echoes and replicates for others her own experiences. She abandons, yet haunts.

The encounter between Golden Gray and Wild becomes the clash between narratives and between representations of the other. Although the two characters are representations of seeming oppositions, they are strangely drawn to each other. Like the violent coming together of blacks and whites in the United States throughout the brutal enterprise of slavery, Wild and Golden Gray's encounter creates a hierarchy in which Golden Gray feels superior, even though what is most noticeable in his behavior toward Wild is his inhumanity. Golden Gray values honor over humanity. He demonstrates this preference by the revulsion he shows toward Wild as well as the attention and care he lavishes on his horse rather than the laboring woman. This intriguing narrative comes and goes in riffs. The reader discovers that the baby Wild gives birth to, yet will not nurse, is Joe. Through information revealed in this section of the novel, the reader learns that Golden Gray's father, Hunter's Hunter, becomes Joe's surrogate father. The information from True Belle that sends Golden Gray on his journey to find his father connects the narrative to Violet. As there is no resolution to the conflict between the races in the United States, however, there is no conclusion to the story of the encounter between Golden Gray and Wild. The two figures enter into memory and mythology and haunt both Joe and Violet as the couple move from the South to the city. The unresolved story of Wild and Golden Gray is the deeply rooted and buried tale of the country—a story whose ambigu-

ity and uncertainty continues to affect and haunt all Americans.

In order to resolve the crises that threaten their existence, both Joe and Violet have to confront this primary narrative and to begin to understand its impact on their self-construction. For Violet, True Belle's stories of Golden Gray make her feel insignificant and unattractive. True Belle's adoration of Golden Gray, particularly of his golden locks, echoes the privileging of whiteness in the larger culture. Violet's fundamental insecurity comes from abandonment and a devaluing of self that catches up with her as she enters middle age and begins to reassess her life and its meaning. Mistakenly, Violet diagnoses her sense of insecurity, loss, and worthlessness as grief over not having had a child. She begins withdrawing, acting strangely, and sleeping with dolls. After she learns of Joe's affair with and murder of Dorcas, she channels all of her energy into that loss. Dorcas becomes the child she never had.

For Joe, his relationship with Dorcas provides access to the lost mother, Wild, that he mourns. Joe tells Dorcas the tale of his loss—how he hunted for the woman that he believes is his mother in the backwoods. Like Wild, and unlike Violet, Dorcas is a mystery to Joe. The illusive and fleeting nature of Dorcas's interactions with Joe is familiar and attractive to him as they mirror the unresolved feelings that he has about his unknown mother. The crisis happens for Joe when Dorcas decides to end their relationship.

When Dorcas abandons Joe, he experiences the breakup as a resurrection of all of the feelings of loss he has had all of his life as an orphaned child. As soon as the relationship is over, Joe reverts to the ways that were most familiar to him as a young man and decides to hunt and track Dorcas the way that he hunted his mother through the woods. This hunting behavior leads him to the rent party where Dorcas is with Acton. Since he can no longer have her, he does what any hunter would do when discovering the tracked prey—he shoots and kills the girl.

Joe's actions coupled with Violet's crises bring the couple to a point where they can begin to write their own song rather than to continue their dancing to music written for them by others. Dorcas's friend Felice is instrumental in the couple's recovery and in the composition of their original melody. Felice means happy in Spanish. Like acquiring a foreign language, Joe and Violet have to learn a new way of attaining and understanding happiness. When the two abandon their distinct but mutual longings for imposed impossibilities, the couple, with Felice's assistance, comes to create their own quiet contentment.

With the resolution of Violet and Joe's longings—the feelings that come from their shared history as orphans—the album that is *Jazz* gently drifts to its final note. The final passages of the novel, reveal the deeply interactive structure of the story when the narrator reveals herself as the book itself and professes that, like a record, there is no life without the active and compassionate participation of the listening reader.

SOME IMPORTANT THEMES AND SYMBOLS IN *JAZZ*

Nighttime and the Hunt

Morrison uses night in *Jazz* as a marker of routine and ritual, as a time for passion and love, and as a space for questing to fulfill deeply held needs and desires. The music, JAZZ, has always had an association with night as an illicit and sensual time, and thus, nighttime figures prominently throughout the narrative.

Sleeplessness marks the lives of Violet and Joe at the beginning of the novel. The specter of Dorcas haunts the couple. Her picture is the focus of their nighttime prowling. By the end of the novel, as Violet and Joe gradually resolve the troubles of their marriage, the two become more routine in their actions and, as a result, begin to treat the night as a time of companionship. Joe takes a job that starts at midnight and so he and Violet spend the evenings comfortably in each other's company. The two overcome the restlessness and disorder that the night originally represents for them.

The night is also a site for love and passion. This is particularly true during the early period of Joe and Violet's relationship, which begins in the South. Violet and Joe meet one night when he falls out of a tree in front of her. Their love develops during night meetings, and nighttime becomes a

special time for them. Later, because Joe also has his affair with Dorcas at night, Violet feels that the love she and Joe shared during long ago nights is tainted. While he is having the affair with Dorcas, Joe begins to live for their nightly encounters.

Unfulfilled desire motivates each of the characters in *Jazz*. Often the quest for fulfillment of these needs occurs at night. These nocturnal quests often result in unpredicted outcomes. Golden Gray sets out on a journey to find his black father and, as the sun begins to set, he crosses paths with the naked woman, Wild, who is pregnant with Joe. Golden Gray cares for Wild at night in his father's cabin. As a hunter, Joe habitually spends much of his nighttime stalking prey. This activity is appropriate for the country hunter but becomes a problem when, as a city-dweller, he reclaims his identity and authority as a hunter and shoots Dorcas at an after-hours rent party after she tells him that she no longer wants to be in their relationship.

Birds and Flight

Violet and Joe own several birds. The birds serve as a symbolic connection between the couple's rural past and urban present. Although the couple find in HARLEM the economic security and relative safety they lacked in the South, they are both haunted by loss and yearning—loss of home and longing for their absent mothers. The birds seem to function temporarily as a substitute for the couples' losses. Violet talks to her birds more than to anyone else. Violet's parrot even tells her that he loves her and, as such, may temporarily replace the love she does not receive from Joe. Joe continues to take care of the birds, even when he is with Dorcas, so as not to disturb the routine of his stale marriage to Violet. The birds seem to represent a solid ritual that replaces the hunting to which he is accustomed.

Joe also believes that Violet cares more about her birds than her own husband. Joe feels threatened by Violet's relationship with her parrot because she gives more love to the bird than to him. This realization partially motivates Joe's search for love and affection elsewhere.

When Violet discovers that Joe has killed Dorcas, she runs back to the apartment and lets the birds fly out into the cold. This action may be symbolic of throwing love out of the window, letting go of and not appreciating the love she has. After Violet releases the birds, she and Joe are left alone in the silent apartment. The couple is lonely without the birds.

Love, Lust, and Longing

In *Jazz*, the apple becomes the symbol of unrequited desire. When Joe and Dorcas make love, the two cast Dorcas as the apple, the forbidden fruit. Joe is attracted to the girl, and yet, even when their relationship is thriving, Dorcas and the feelings she evokes make Joe wish that he was never born. Dorcas dangles just out of Joe's reach. Although the two have a fully sexual relationship, Dorcas never completely is satisfied with it. Even when they make love, Dorcas wants Joe to take her out places and to do things with her, while Joe is entirely satisfied just being in her presence. All Joe desires is Dorcas's company, while Dorcas longs for affirmation that she is an adult, something her relationship with Joe cannot provide.

Despite her desire for something and some place else, Dorcas's relationship with Joe does provide her with one aspect of what she longs for, an adult drama. At the rent party before she is shot, Dorcas is aware of Joe's intentions to come and do her harm, yet she does nothing about it. She also does not reveal Joe's identity after he shoots her at the party. Before she dies, Dorcas whispers to Felice to tell Joe that there is only one apple. This cryptic remark may refer to Dorcas's acknowledgment that the longing that she had for adult experiences and for public recognition were in fact fulfilled by the relationship she had with Joe. When Dorcas dies, ironically, she receives the attention and celebrity she longs for in life.

When Joe learns from Felice of Dorcas's last words, he smiles sadly. But the next words that Joe utters, after learning of Dorcas's pronouncement, are the repetitions of Felice's name, possibly indicating that he will have some happiness and satisfaction knowing that the relationship with Dorcas meant something to his former lover in spite of all of the destructiveness that resulted from it.

Sexuality

The word "jazz" has, since its origins, been associated with sexuality, temptation, and taboo. As

such, it follows that Morrison's novel should be rooted in passion. Sexuality is at the center of the novel as are other forms of desire and longing.

Sexuality manifests itself as a central current throughout the narrative. Joe Trace is moved, literally and metaphorically, by what he imagines is Dorcas's innocence, freedom, youth, and sweetness. This attraction culminates in a sexual union that has its roots in both characters' motherlessness. As a refrain or echo to the activities of Joe and Dorcas, the city sky reminds the novel's narrator of the illegal love of sweethearts before they are caught. Tantalizingly, while Dorcas paints Joe's fingernails, the two experience a metaphoric orgasm.

Malvonne reads from love letters she has never sent—letters that have been stolen and have not reached their intended destinations. Malvonne's voracious consumption of the letters may represent an unrequited love and/or her unfulfilled desires. Contradictorily, she thinks of sex as "a low down sticky thing" (44).

Forbidden or taboo love manifests in the text in the sexual relationship that reaches fruition in the birth of the mythical Golden Gray. Vera Louise Gray, the white plantation mistress, seduces a black man, Henry LesTroy, and becomes pregnant. As a result of her pregnancy, she is disowned by her family and relocates to Baltimore with the family slave, True Belle.

The end of the text suggests the possibility of a quieter and more sober sexuality with the reconciliation of Joe and Violet and the quiet simmer of their twilight passion. The intimacy of their sexuality at the end of the novel is notable and contrasts sharply with the spectacle of Joe and Dorcas's affair. Joe and Violet's undercover whispers and public love are mysterious to the narrator.

CHARACTERS

Acton   Acton is the boy Dorcas dates after she breaks up with Joe. Dorcas tries so hard to win Acton's affection, but nothing she does pleases him. The boy is superficial and does not really care about Dorcas. His relative disinterest excites Dorcas who is looking for someone whose interest in her more closely matches her own relatively low self-esteem. Dorcas also is deeply invested in the approval of her peers. Although Joe treats her with adulation and respect, Dorcas prefers Acton who is not solicitous of her needs.

Dorcas is with Acton at the party where Joe hunts her in order to commit murder. Acton and Dorcas are dancing when Joe appears and shoots her with a silencer. After discovering Dorcas's injuries, Acton remains self-absorbed. He seems much more upset with the fact that Dorcas's blood stains his clothing than he is with the girl's injuries. He disappears from the narrative after the night of the party during which Joe shoots Dorcas.

Alice Manfred Alice Manfred is the aunt who raises Dorcas after the girl's parents are killed in a race riot. Alice Manfred emphasizes modesty and decorum in her home. Her housekeeping represents her take on life. She seems to want, more than anything, to have some control over what happens and so maintains rigid control over her home and tries to extend that control to her niece.

Alice Manfred was left by her husband and never fully recovers from his abandonment. After he leaves, she dreams of revenge and fantasizes about killing her husband's mistress. Alice's inability to forgive either her husband or the woman paralyzes her and prevents her from progressing or making changes in her life. After Violet tries to attack dead Dorcas at the girl's funeral for having an affair with Joe, Alice Manfred calls Violet Violent.

On the other hand, Alice eventually seems to forgive Violet after the women bond. Ultimately, Alice sees that both she and Violet are wounded by life in very similar ways and that they both suffer from terrible losses that have warped their characters. There is some evidence that the relationship with Violet may even help Alice to recover from her past.

Alice's apprehensions are not only personal. She sees evil doing and danger in the world, and the music, jazz and the BLUES, comes to represent all that is wrong. Alice keeps newspapers as a kind of proof of what she calls Imminent Demise. After Dorcas's death, Alice begins to obsess about defenseless women. She is a perfectionist. She sews to make money. Eventually, Alice leaves Harlem and returns to her home in Springfield.

Bud Bud and C.T. are acquaintances of Joe's. The two play checkers and exchange friendly insults with each other. Joe enjoys their company. The day that Joe meets Dorcas for the first time, he is delayed in the delivery he is making to her aunt's house because the conversation between Bud and C.T. is so compelling. On that day, the two argue over the S.S. *Ethiopia*, MARCUS GARVEY's ship, a discussion from which Joe has a hard time tearing himself away.

Clayton Bede Clayton Bede is a landowner in Virginia who takes over Harlon Rick's place. He exploits Joe and Violet to the point that they decide to move to Harlem.

Colonel Wordsworth Gray Colonel Wordsworth Gray is the novel's representative of the southern master class. Colonel Wordsworth Gray is Vera Louise Gray's father. The man disowns his daughter after he learns that she is pregnant by an African-American man. Even though Colonel Wordsworth Gray has children himself with some of the slave women on his plantation, he is unforgiving in his treatment of his daughter after the discovery of her pregnancy. Both he and his wife send Vera Louise away. They provide her with money and tell her never to return to her home.

C.T. C.T. and Bud are acquaintances of Joe's. The two play checkers and exchange friendly insults with each other. Joe enjoys their company. The day that Joe meets Dorcas for the first time, he is delayed in the delivery he is making to her aunt's house because the conversation between C.T. and Bud is so compelling. On that day, the two argue over the S.S. *Ethiopia*, Marcus Garvey's ship, a discussion from which Joe has a hard time tearing himself away.

Dorcas Manfred Dorcas Manfred is 18 years old at the beginning of *Jazz*. Dorcas is the other woman in the novel's central love triangle. The three members of the triangle are Dorcas Manfred and Joe and Violet Trace. Although the triangle forms the center of the novel, Dorcas is dead at the novel's inception. Dorcas dies when Joe shoots her with a silencer at a rent party.

Dorcas has simple and superficial interests and tastes. Her favorite band is Slim Bates' Ebony Keys. She goes frequently to have her hair done by legally licensed beauticians. Dorcas is, in part, interested in Joe because he sells cosmetics. During the course of their brief relationship, Dorcas enjoys giving Joe manicures. Dorcas asks Joe to take her to Mexico, a night club, but he does not want to be seen in public with her and have Violet learn of their tryst.

Dorcas's father is killed in riots in East St. Louis, Illinois. Her mother is killed later that day when the family's house burns down while the woman is inside. During the riot, Dorcas stays across the street at a friend's house when her house incinerates. While the house is burning down, Dorcas wants to go back to her room to get her paper dolls. After the fire, she is sent to New York City, to Harlem, to live with Alice Manfred, her aunt.

Partially because of the experiences of Alice's parents and also because of her own negative life experiences, Alice Manfred fears the world and all that might happen. As a result the woman tries to control everything that she can, including her environment and her niece. Dorcas does not understand her aunt's fears and rebels against the woman's misguided attempts at protection. One evening when Dorcas is 16 and her aunt is out of town, she sneaks out to go to a party for the first time. She has a difficult time finding something to wear since her aunt forces her to wear very modest clothes. When Dorcas is out of her aunt's sight, she frequently makes a habit of dressing in ways that her aunt would find inappropriate.

At the party, Dorcas dances with a boy named Martin. She discovers that she is a good dancer. Sometime later, Dorcas meets Joe at her aunt's house while Alice hosts a Civic Daughters meeting. Joe comes to Alice's in his capacity as a door to door cosmetics salesman. Dorcas answers the door when Joe arrives. This meeting signals the beginning of the courtship between Dorcas and Joe.

There is no particular or obvious reason for Joe to be attracted to Dorcas. She has long hair and bad skin. The girl wears glasses, but not around Joe. She also changes her voice when she is around

Joe. Dorcas is young enough to be one of Joe and Violet's miscarried children. She feels that the body she inhabits is unworthy of the love and attention Joe lavishes.

Joe makes her feel valuable because of his immense hunger for her. His hunger stems from the absences and hollows that formed in him as the result of his status as an orphan like Dorcas. After Dorcas grows tired of Joe and of his unfailing adulation, she chooses a second lover who is closer to her age named Acton.

Acton does not treat Dorcas well or genuinely care for the girl, but she still likes Acton better than she does Joe because he is in demand. Dorcas is immature and asks the boys she dates to do foolhardy things to impress her, like slapping white sales ladies. Frequently, she gives Acton presents and acts toward him with the deference and care she learned from Joe's treatment.

Dorcas is with Acton at a party the night that she is killed. Joe comes to the party and shoots the girl with a silencer. Joe does not shoot Dorcas out of anger, but because he cannot stand the idea of her living without him and no longer returning his love and affection. When Dorcas's friend, Felice, asks her who shot her, she refuses to tell her or anyone else of Joe's guilt. Dorcas's refusal suggests that her feelings for Joe may have been more profound than was apparent in her breakup with and subsequent cruelty to the man.

Dorcas dies as a result of the injuries she receives at Joe's hands. Alice Manfred is beside herself at the news of the death of her niece. Alice Manfred cannot forgive herself when she learns that Dorcas met Joe at her house. Violet is so angry when she learns of Joe's affair with Dorcas that she goes to Dorcas's funeral and impotently attempts to stab the girl while she lies in her coffin.

Violet becomes obsessed with Dorcas and borrows a photograph of her from Alice Manfred, who loans Violet the photograph to get Violet to leave her apartment. Joe and Violet take turns looking at the girl's photograph and projecting on to her their imaginings and desires. Eventually, Dorcas's friend Felice helps to free Joe and Violet from the spell of Dorcas when she gives them more information about what the girl was really like in life.

Duggie Duggie is the owner of the malt shop that Violet frequents. Violet goes there to drink the malts she thinks will help her to have hips. She believes that having hips like she used to have when she first met Joe will help save her marriage and will affirm her womanhood. Before the couple actually meet at Alice Manfred's, Joe first sees Dorcas in Duggie's where she goes to buy the peppermint candy that she loves and that makes her skin break out.

Dumfrey women, the The Dumfrey women are Harlem residents. The women are a mother and daughter who imagine themselves to be the epitome of what it means to be urbane. The two women are Violet's customers and have relocated to Harlem from Cottown, which is near Memphis. Their origins in the country may help to explain the airs that the women adopt when they arrive in the city. They appear to be what Harlem residents refer to as citified.

Their father and husband owns a store on 136th Street and the money that he brings in contributes to the sense of status the women feel. Both women have the good fortune of having desk jobs, jobs that also confer a type of status. Violet comes to their home every other Tuesday to do their hair. They are the customers Violet is waiting for when she is accused of stealing the baby, Phil, from the girl with the records.

Faye Faye is Stuck's new wife. Stuck is Joe's best friend.

Felice Felice is Dorcas's best friend and goes with Dorcas to the rent party where Joe kills her. Trying to save her friend, Felice calls the ambulance twice. She does not go to Dorcas's funeral because she is mad at Dorcas. She believes that Dorcas wanted to die. Before the party, Felice loans Dorcas a ring Felice's mother stole for her daughter from Tiffany's. Felice's mother steals the ring for her daughter as the result of a racial slur that she experiences while in the store. Much to Felice's chagrin and distress, Dorcas wears the ring to her grave. Felice lives with her grandmother, although her parents come home when they can from their employment in a town called Tuxedo Junction.

Before she learns that the ring her mother gave her has been buried with Dorcas, Felice visits Violet and Joe to inquire about the ring. Felice thinks that they might have some information about where Dorcas might have left it. After her first visit to Violet and Joe, Felice feels that the experience with the elderly couple helps her to understand Dorcas better. She even almost understands why Dorcas had a relationship with Joe. Felice and the couple become friends and, unintentionally, Felice helps them to recover their marriage and get over what happed between Joe and Dorcas. After Felice's embrace of them, the couple no longer haunt Dorcas's picture at night looking for answers. They find comfort in each other's arms and in a newfound appreciation of their long-term love.

Felice's mother Felice's mother is away from Felice working most of the time when Felice is young. She, along with Felice's father, Walter, works in a town called Tuxedo Junction. Felice's mother, who remains unnamed in the novel, misses going to church when she and Walter are working in Tuxedo Junction. As a result the woman is filled with regrets whenever Felice sees her mother. The woman loves to dance.

Apparently, Felice's mother is bitter about the racism she experiences as a part of her work and is sensitive to racially based insults and slights. When injured by a racial slur, she steals a ring from Tiffany's and gives it to Felice. This is the ring that Felice loans to Dorcas and it is, inadvertently, buried with the girl.

Felice's mother grows too ill to work in Tuxedo. Felice empathizes and helps both her mother and grandmother with the things they need that require her assistance.

Frances Miller Frances Miller and her sister tend small children during the day. They belong to a group called the Doomsdayers. The women keep a list of nightclubs that sell liquor. Even though the nightclubs often are owned and/or frequented by other African Americans, the women are willing to report the lawbreakers to the authorities. When Dorcas is young and has moved to New York to live with Alice after the death of her parents, the sisters watch the child while Alice works. Frances Miller gives the kids in her care, including Dorcas, apple butter sandwiches and tells them stories about love. Dorcas's romantic notions about love that she acts out later may have roots in the stories that she hears from the Miller sisters while she is a young, impressionable girl.

Frank Williams Frank Williams is the father of Victory Williams and the husband of Rhoda Williams. He and his wife adopt Joe after the child is abandoned as a baby by his mother, Wild. Frank Williams is good to Joe and treats him like one of his own children.

Gistan Gistan is a friend of Joe. When Joe has problems with Violet, and later with Dorcas, he cannot talk with his friend about it. When Joe kills Dorcas at the rent party, Gistan comes by Joe and Violet's house with Stuck, Joe's other friend, to tell Joe that they cannot play cards with him anymore. The two friends shun him because of his murder of Dorcas. The girl's death, however, does not end the men's relationship forever. The friendship between the three is renewed by the end of the novel. Once their friendship is reestablished, Gistan helps Joe get a better job at a hotel. The hotel's clientele are so wealthy that they are able to tip the workers with paper money—a fact that helps Violet and Joe financially.

Golden Gray Golden Gray is Vera Louise's mixed-race son. Vera Louise Gray conceives the boy while, during her youth, she has an affair with African-American Henry LesTroy. Following her parents' discovery of her pregnancy, Vera Louise Gray is disowned by her family. Although they cast her off, they supply the woman with enough money for her to live comfortably for the remainder of her life away from them and from her home. Vera Louise takes their money and the woman who has functioned as her MAMMY, True Belle, and relocates to Baltimore where she gives birth to her son whom she names Golden Gray because of his appearance.

Ignorant of his parentage until he is 18, Golden believes he is Vera Louise's protégé rather than her son. He is raised by Vera Louise and True Belle.

The women dote on him and make him feel as if he is the most important person in the world. The two women name him for his hair, which is golden and curls in tendrils around the boy's neck. True Belle tells him that pretty hair can never be too long. True Belle, Vera Louise's slave, is Golden Gray's first love. Golden Gray is proficient at two things: reining in his horse and playing the piano.

Golden Gray learns the truth about his parentage when Vera Louise finally tells him the story of his life. Capable of conceiving of life only in chivalric terms, he decides that his sole course of action is to go and confront the man who is his father in order to defend his mother's honor. Golden Gray leaves Baltimore, his home, Vera Louise, and True Belle, and goes out into the world on a confused and misguided quest for revenge and justice. Golden Gray cannot reconcile with his self-image—the reality that he is black. He has always looked down on people that he considered to be black and as a result is in the only turmoil he has ever had to face as he tries to understand who he is as the illegitimate son of a black man.

Golden Gray sets off on an ill-conceived journey designed to assuage his discomfort and to revenge his mother. He sets off with all of the trappings of the chivalric hero—velvet jacket, carriage, and horse. While on his quest, Golden Gray happens upon a young, naked, and pregnant black woman who, when she sees him, knocks herself out by running into a tree. The chivalric hero, ironically, is not pleased by his discovery of a damsel in distress. Golden Gray puts the woman, ultimately known as Wild, in his carriage only with the greatest of reluctance. Although Golden Gray has cast himself in the role of chivalric hero, the youth is more concerned about his clothes than Wild's well-being.

When Golden Gray finally arrives at his destination, the home of Henry LesTroy, he is uncertain how to proceed. Again, his concerns and priorities demonstrate a marked disregard for the life of Wild and her unborn child. Eventually, he settles the woman, without ceremony or concern, on Henry LesTroy's bed.

When LesTroy finally returns from his hunting trip he confronts Golden Gray, who he thinks is white, about his intrusive presence in his house.

Golden Gray tells LesTroy that he is his son and the two proceed to have an encounter, the outcome of which the reader does not have access to and does not fully experience.

The only other account of Golden Gray in *Jazz* occurs through both Joe and Violet's recollections of the enigmatic man. Violet learns about Golden through the stories told to her by her grandmother, Vera Louise Gray's slave, True Belle. When True Belle leaves Vera Louise after news of the downfall of her daughter Rose Dear, she returns to her family after her long exile to care for her grandchildren, one of whom is Violet. True Belle is enamored of the young Golden Gray who has been under her primary care since his birth. She transfers her adoration of the boy to her granddaughter, Violet. The stories of Golden Gray make Violet feel inadequate and unattractive. The stories of Golden Gray's hair may be the source of Violet's adult occupation as a hair dresser. True Belle's stories are at the nexus of Violet's feelings of loss and inadequacy, feelings that are particularly acute following the death of Violet's mother by suicide. Rose Dear, Violet's mother, kills herself by drowning herself in the family well and that loss, interspersed with True Belle's stories of Golden Gray, sets Violet on a path of low self-esteem that eventually contributes to the decay of her marriage to Joe.

Likewise, Joe is also plagued by the legacy of Golden Gray. Joe is adopted as a child by the Williams family, which raises him as their own He ultimately recognizes, however, that he is an orphan. This recognition makes him long and search for his mother, who, he learns from rumor, might be Wild. As he searches for Wild, he finds traces of Golden Gray.

Harlon Ricks Harlon Ricks is the owner of the farm where Violet and Joe work when they first meet in Virginia. Joe and Violet live at Harlon Ricks's place when they first marry. Ricks sells the land to Clayton Bede who proves even more exploitative.

Helen Moore One of the letters Malvonne's miscreant nephew Sweetness (William Younger) steals and Malvonne finds is addressed to Helen Moore.

Henry LesTroy (Lestory, Hunter's Hunter)
Henry LesTroy is the black man Vera Louise Gray has an affair with. Until Golden Gray arrives at his house, he never knows he has a son. He is out hunting when Golden comes to seek revenge against the man he learns is his father. LesTroy is a legendary hunter and is sometimes called Hunter's Hunter. He helps the pregnant woman, Wild, give birth and, when Joe comes of age, teaches her son how to hunt. After Joe moves to the city, he recalls this first teacher as a man who could remember things clearly and who would express the truth.

Honor Honor is Patty's boy. He is the first to see Golden Gray at Henry LesTroy's house. Honor tends animals for Henry LesTroy when he is hunting. Although he is a child, he knows better than Golden Gray how to care for the injured and laboring Wild. He is compassionate and exhibits a large degree of common sense. Honor is startled when he first discovers Golden Gray in Henry LesTroy's home and believes that Golden Gray is a white man.

Hot Steam Hot Steam is the female writer of a letter to Mr. M. Sage. The letter is one of those stolen by Malvonne's delinquent nephew Sweetness. The letter is so spicy that Malvonne is conflicted about sending it on and fostering what she sees as the couple's sinfulness.

Hunter's Hunter See Henry LesTroy

Joe Trace Joe Trace is Violet's husband. Shortly after his birth he is abandoned by his mother, a woman called Wild. Following his abandonment at birth by Wild, Joe is raised by Rhoda and Frank Williams. Rhoda tells him that his mother disappeared without a trace, so, with the misapprehension of a child, he assumes he is the trace in the sentence. So when he is asked at school what his name is, he tells the teacher that his name is Joseph and then he adds the last name Trace, thinking that trace is his last name. Joe is given the name Joseph by the Williamses.

As a boy, Joe's first job is cleaning fish. Before leaving Virginia to relocate to New York, Joe is a hunter. One night while sleeping in a tree, he falls out of a tree landing onto the ground beside Violet. This nocturnal fall is how the two first meet.

After marrying Violet, the two begin working a part of the property Harlon Ricks owned that is later turned over to Clayton Bede. Bede establishes a SHARECROPPING relationship that keeps all of his workers in his debt and ensures that they remain that way. As a consequence, Joe leaves to work in the sawmills for five years. He also works for a while laying rail. Then, he decides to buy some land of his own, but loses the land to whites who steal it from him. Eventually Joe gives up on the idea of remaining in the land that he knows so well and that he loves to hunt. Joe decides to leave Virginia with Violet after a fire decimates his hometown. Joe loves the woods, so it shocks everyone that he knows when he takes Violet to the city.

Joe has eyes that are two different colors—one that is said to look inside the hearts and minds of other people and another that lets people look inside of him. He does not want to become a father when he marries Violet, but he has a way with children. While in the city some of the jobs he has include cleaning fish, waiting tables, and working hotels. Once, he is almost killed in a riot.

He moves north from Vesper County, Virginia, with Violet in 1906. While living in the city, Joe and Violet grow estranged and stop communicating with each other. Violet begins to act peculiarly and stops connecting with her husband. After their marriage disintegrates, he begins having an affair with Dorcas whom he later kills. The loss of Joe's mother early in his life is profoundly connected to his attraction to Dorcas and his hunt for satisfaction and understanding.

Joe Trace is a diligent boyfriend and suitor and always brings Dorcas gifts. He is a door-to-door salesman for Cleopatra cosmetic products and he sells soaps and perfumes for the company. He talks a neighborhood busybody, Malvonne, into letting him rent a room from her in exchange for money, products, and fixing up the place. Joe is the kind of man whom everyone trusts.

Although Joe's attraction to Dorcas is inexplicable to those outside of their relationship, Joe Trace is moved, literally and metaphorically, by Dorcas' innocence, freedom, youth, and sweetness. While

Dorcas paints Joe's fingernails, they experience a metaphoric orgasm, implying that their connection is more than merely physical. Although he does not realize it until later, his hunger for the young girl is really about his yearning for his mother. When Dorcas leaves Joe, he feels the same pain of abandonment he experienced earlier as a result of not knowing his mother and feeling discarded.

Joe does not handle Dorcas's breakup with him well. He responds in the only way that he knows how, as a hunter. He goes searching for Dorcas even after she repeatedly asks him to leave her alone. Joe even offers to leave Violet for Dorcas. Eventually, he kills the girl at a rent party. After he kills Dorcas, he sits at the window in his apartment and cries for months. Clearly, Joe mourns something other than his action and his lost love. Joe, like both Violet and Dorcas, grieves for his lost mother.

Eventually, he and Violet reconcile and grow close again. At the end of the novel, he is working at a speakeasy so he can spend his days with Violet. The two have an older, more settled love that can sustain them and that helps to heal the wounds of the past and their unfulfilled and impossible longings.

King King is Golden Gray's female cat.

L. Henderson Woodward L. Henderson Woodward is Helen Moore's father.

Lila Spencer Among the letters that Sweetness steals and opens, Malvonne discovers Lila Spenser's application to law school. Missing is the $1 bill that was originally enclosed to pay for Lila Spenser's application fee. Malvonne worries about this theft and sends the money that Sweetness stole along with the application.

Little Caesar See SWEETNESS

Malvonne Edwards Malvonne Edwards is the upstairs neighbor of Joe and Violet who rents a room in her apartment so that Joe can have a love nest for his affair with Dorcas. She lives alone and fulfills her emotional and psychological needs with other people's stories. She cleans offices in the evenings. The room that she rents to Joe belonged to her nephew William Younger, also known as Sweetness, before he moved west. Malvonne was the caretaker for her nephew since he was seven. After her nephew moves out, she discovers that the boy was a thief and that he has stolen several bags of mail. She tries to fulfill the wishes contained in the letters William stole.

Martin   Martin is Dorcas's dance partner at her first party. He had been in elocution class with her, but was told to leave after the first day as the instructor believed that he would not be successful in mastering the nuances of standard English. Martin's dismissal from the elocution class is a commentary on the assimilationist aspirations of the African-American middle class.

May   May is True Belle's daughter, Rose Dear's sister, and Violet's aunt. As a young girl, she loses her mother's presence and care when True Belle is forced to relocate to Baltimore with Vera Louise when it is discovered that Vera Louise is pregnant with Henry LesTroy's child. May is 10 when her mother leaves for Baltimore. She remains in the care of her father and her aunt, True Belle's sister.

Miss Ransom   Miss Ransom is a client of Joe's. Joe leaves Miss Ransom's house just before he goes to Alice Manfred's for the first time and meets Dorcas.

Mr. M. Sage (Daddy)   Mr. M. Sage is the intended recipient of a letter from an unnamed woman. The letter is in the mail bag that Sweetness steals and whose contents Malvonne attempts to resend. The letter to Mr. M. Sage is overtly sexual and makes Malvonne uncomfortable. The prospect of sending the sexual letter presents Malvonne with a conflict of interest. If she sends it, she feels she will be endorsing a relationship she views as inappropriate. Malvonne compromises with herself and sends the letter along with a cautionary note and an inspirational article.

Narrator   The narrator of *Jazz* says she wants a long-term love like an old couple—a love that can be public. The narrator intervenes throughout the novel and shapes the story to her whim. She is, perhaps, the definition of the unreliable narrator. She cannot be believed or trusted with the story and is often incorrect about the motivations of the characters.

Neola Miller   Neola Miller and her sister take care of young children while the childrens' parents are at work. Neola reads Psalms to the children in her care. She has one working arm. Her fiance left her when she was a young woman and afterward, according to the stories she tells to the children, her left arm that had the engagement ring on it froze and curled up. She often tells the children stories about good behavior. She believes that these morality tales will help to control their actions when they are adults and prevent them from facing a situation like the one in which she finds herself.

parrot   After she tries to cut Dorcas's face at the funeral, Violet puts her parrot outside in the cold to fly or freeze. The parrot says "love you" and remains on the stoop for several days before, eventually, flying off to an uncertain end.

Philly   Philly is the baby boy Violet may have tried to kidnap. When she is caught walking down the street with the infant, Violet says she is merely taking the baby for a walk. Most of the crowd, annoyed by Philly's sister's carelessness, is inclined to believe Violet, especially since she leaves her hairdressing supplies by the carriage on the sidewalk. Some who witness the incident, however, feel that Violet is trying to steal the baby.

Philly's sister   Philly's sister leaves her baby brother, Philly, in his carriage and asks Violet to watch him as she runs inside to retrieve the record, "Trombone Blues." Most of the crowd who witness the event condemn her as irresponsible and blame her for leaving the child in the care of a stranger for no good reason.

Rhoda Williams   Rhoda Williams agrees to adopt Joe when his own mother, Wild, refuses to care for him. Rhoda breast-feeds the infant Joe along with her own biological child, Victory. The two boys grow up to form a bond closer than that of most brothers.

When Joe grows up and asks about his biological mother, Wild, Rhoda tells him that the woman disappeared without a trace, so, with the misapprehension of a child, he assumes he is the trace in the sentence and adopts Trace as a last name.

Rose Dear   Rose Dear is Violet's mother and True Belle's daughter. When Vera Louise becomes pregnant with Henry LesTroy's child, True Belle is forced to leave her family, including her daughter, Rose Dear, to go to live in Baltimore with Golden Gray and Vera Louise. Rose Dear is eight when her mother leaves for Baltimore. She remains in the care of her father and her aunt, True Belle's sister.

As an adult, Rose Dear has four children, one of whom is Violet. When, in her husband's absence, white men come to threaten her and repossess her furniture, they knock Rose Dear out of a chair although she is sitting in it at the time. Rose Dear never seems to recover from that fall. She and her family are dispossessed from her sharecropper's hut and forced to move out. After learning of her daughter's predicament, True Belle leaves Vera Louise in Baltimore and returns to her family. After her mother comes to stay with the family, Rose Dear jumps in a well and kills herself.

Sheila   Sheila is Malvonne's cousin. When Joe goes to Alice Manfred's during the Civic Daughters meeting and accidentally meets Dorcas for the first time, he goes there with the intention of delivering Sheila's order to her and collecting payment.

Stuck   Stuck is a friend of Joe's. When Joe has problems with Violet and later with Dorcas, he cannot talk with his friend about it. When Joe kills the girl, Stuck comes by with Gistan to tell him that they cannot play cards with Joe anymore. Their friendship is renewed by the end of the novel.

Sweetness (William Younger, Little Caesar)   William Younger, better known by the ironic nickname of Sweetness, is the nephew of Malvonne and is raised by her from the age of seven. Believing that it is cool, William changes his name to Little Caesar. Malvonne still calls him Sweetness. After he leaves town, Malvonne discovers that he is a petty thief who has robbed at least one mailbox. Sweetness leaves Harlem headed to a city whose name ends in "o." Malvonne tries to right the boy's misdeeds by going through the letters he stole and replacing and resending the money the boy took out of them.

True Belle   True Belle is the grandmother of Violet and the mother of Rose Dear and May. She has to leave her two daughters, Rose Dear and May, as well as her husband, under the care of her sister when she is forced to go with Vera Louise Gray to Baltimore. True Belle is a slave in the Gray household and is responsible for Vera Louise's care as a child and young girl. Having no choice, True Belle goes with Vera Louise to Baltimore after Vera Louise's family disowns her when she becomes pregnant with a black man's (Henry LesTroy) child. True Belle spoils the resulting child, Golden Gray, and dotes on the boy, but does not tell him that Vera Louise is his mother. She is particularly taken with his long, curly blonde hair. True Belle often smiles at Golden because she knows all along whom his father is and she seems bemused by the situation.

After the Civil War, True Belle transitions from being a slave to servant. Vera Louise begins to pay True Belle for her labors. True Belle leaves her job with Vera Louise in Baltimore when she learns that things are not well for her daughter, Rose Dear. Significantly, Golden Gray has already left Baltimore before True Belle makes the decision to return to her family.

After Rose Dear's suicide, True Belle raises her four grandchildren, including Violet. True Belle lives with Violet and her sisters 11 years before she dies, which is enough time to see her son-in-law return four times and for her to make six quilts and 13 shifts. It is also long enough for her stories of Golden Gray to affect Violet and for the young girl to think less of herself by comparison. Violet's career choices, mid-life crisis, and low sense of self-worth derive from the legacy of True Belle's Golden Gray stories.

Vera Louise Gray   Vera Louise Gray raises and adores a blond boy, Golden Gray, as her protégé who is actually her own bi-racial child. Vera Louise is the daughter of Colonel Gray, a slave master and plantation owner. She has a sexual encounter with Henry LesTroy, an African-American man, which results in her pregnancy. As a result Vera Louise is disowned by her family and they give her a great deal of money to leave town. Vera Louise gives birth to a son named Golden Gray.

Following the Grays' disowning of their daughter, Vera Louise moves with True Belle to Baltimore where they raise Golden Gray together. Vera Louise keeps largely to herself, reads, and explains to acquaintances that Golden Gray is an adopted protégé. The two women spoil and overindulge Golden Gray. Vera Louise never tells LesTroy, Golden Gray's father, about the boy and does not tell the boy about his parentage until he is 18.

Victory Williams   Victory Williams is one of Rhoda and Frank Williams's sons. He is three months older than Joe and the two are raised like brothers after the Williamses decide to adopt Joe. Victory thinks that his parents will be upset when they find out that Joe gave himself the last name Trace instead of Williams when asked about his last name in school. Victory hunts with Joe—they are both picked out to become hunting men by Hunter's Hunter, Henry LesTroy.

Violet's father   As a result of threats of vigilante violence against him, Violet's father does not live with his wife, Rose Dear, and their children. Because of circumstances never made completely clear in the novel, it is dangerous for Violet's father to return to his family. As a result, he visits the family periodically. When he arrives, he is always bearing gifts for everyone, but is not able to provide the continuous support they need to survive. His absence is a source of grief and longing for Rose Dear and may contribute to her mental decline and eventual suicide. Violet thinks of her father as a dashing character who brings presents to her and to her sisters but who never is a constant presence in their lives. After Rose Dear's death, Violet's father comes again, bearing gifts. Not knowing about his wife's death, he brings her a pillow she will never use. He visits periodically over the next several years and then is never heard from again. After she moves to the city, Violet wonders if he is still alive.

Violet Trace   When *Jazz* begins, Violet is a 50-year-old resident of Harlem described as "skinny . . . but still good looking." Violet is a freelance hairdresser who is unable to resolve her feelings about an affair her husband, Joe Trace, has had with a young woman named Dorcas. When Dorcas ends the relationship, Joe fatally shoots her at a rent party. Violet realizes that the shooting is evidence of her husband's adoration of his lover. Violet longs for this kind of love and her desire leads her to peculiar acts such as trying to stab Dorcas's body during the girl's open casket funeral, sitting down in the middle of a busy Harlem street, trying, possibly, to kidnap an unattended baby, and releasing her pet parrot into the New York winter air because she cannot stand its repetition of the phrase "I love you." These acts earn her the nickname Violent in her Harlem neighborhood.

Violet becomes obsessed with Dorcas. She wants to know everything about Dorcas so she can discover why her husband loved the girl with such intensity. She begins visiting Dorcas's guardian and aunt, Alice Manfred, and she even keeps a picture of Dorcas on her mantel. Violet's obsession feeds Joe's and the two become caught in a cycle of self-destruction that is rooted in their pasts. Some of the troubling events in Violet's childhood include the suicide of her mother, Rose Dear, and the influence of her grandmother's stories. Violet's grandmother, True Belle, returns to Vesper County from Baltimore to take care of Violet and her siblings upon learning of Rose Dear's death. When True Belle leaves Baltimore, she abandons the service of her white mistress, Vera Louise Gray, and Vera Louise's mixed race son, Golden Gray.

In addition to her two miscarriages, another of Violet's unresolved problems is her inability to attain the kind of adoration her grandmother, True Belle, expressed when telling stories about Golden Gray. Eventually, both Joe and Violet find resolution of their marital discord through their shared grief and through their interactions with Dorcas's friend Felice. The couple begins listening to music again and even purchases another bird that they revive with their songs.

A flashback midway through the novel reveals a young Violet in 1906 as she travels 15 miles from her birthplace in Vesper County, a small, fictional African-American community in Virginia, to pick cotton as an itinerant worker. Although strong, Violet is not a good cotton picker. While working, she meets Joe, her future husband. The two first connect when Joe, sleeping in a walnut tree, literally falls on Violet. After this encounter, Violet never returns home. The narrator describes Joe and Violet as "dancing" into New York City and Harlem as they ride the train north from Virginia. Their dancing evokes the rhythms of the city and alludes to the title of the novel. When the couple arrives in Harlem, they feel at home, as if they have finally found a place to belong. Joe and Violet represent the thousands of anonymous African Americans who migrated from the South to the North in search of economic opportunities and freedom from racial oppression and violence.

Walter Walter is Felice's father. He works in a place called Tuxedo and when he comes for brief periods to the city he likes to sleep and to be waited on by the women in his life. He also relishes reading newspapers. Later in the novel, he gets a job working as a PULLMAN PORTER.

Wild Wild is Joe Trace's mother. Golden Gray discovers her, pregnant by the side of the road, as he travels to find his father, Henry LesTroy. When Wild sees Golden Gray, she flees from him and runs headlong into a tree, knocking herself unconscious. Golden Gray is disturbed by the woman and does not want to put her into his carriage, but, ironically, feels he is too chivalrous to leave her by the side of the road. Golden Gray puts the naked, pregnant Wild into his carriage and drives with her to Henry LesTroy's. When he gets to the house, he places the woman on the bed, only after caring for his horse.

After giving birth to Joe, Wild is taken care of by Hunter's Hunter, Henry LesTroy. Wild will not touch or tend to her child, Joe, who was given to the Williamses to raise. Joe, the child of the wild woman, needs to be nursed by another woman, Rhoda Williams, in order to stave off impending death. Wild's refusal to nurse her child may be an indication of her symbolic rejection of motherhood.

When he becomes an adult, Joe searches for his mother in the woods. There are legends about

Wild. Wild is said to disturb the minds of the men cutting cane and to cause women to lose their unborn babies. Joe finds traces of Wild in a cave in the woods but never sees the woman herself.

William Younger See SWEETNESS

Winsome Clark Mrs. Winsome Clark is the author of one of the letters that William Younger (Sweetness) stole from a mailbox. Her husband was working on the Panama Canal. She and her children are in a bad living situation and plan to return to their home in Barbados.

FURTHER READING

Hardack, Richard. "'A Music Seeking Its Words': Double-Timing and Double-Consciousness in Toni Morrison's *Jazz*," *Callaloo* 18 (1995): 451–471.

Jones, Gayl. *Liberating Voices: Oral Tradition in African American Literature*. Cambridge: Harvard University Press, 1991.

Loris, Michelle C. "Self and Mutuality: Romantic Love, Desire, Race, and Gender in Toni Morrison's *Jazz*," *Sacred Heart University Review* 14, nos. 1–2 (1993–94): 53–62.

Mbalia, Doretha Drummond. "Women Who Run with Wild: The Need for Sisterhoods in *Jazz*," *Modern Fiction Studies* 39 (1993): 623–646.

Treherne, Matthew. "Figuring In, Figuring Out: Narration and Negotiation in Toni Morrison's *Jazz*," *Narrative* 11, no. 2 (May 2003): 199–213.

Van Der Zee, James. *The Harlem Book of the Dead*. Dobbs Ferry, N.Y.: Morgan and Morgan, 1978.

Yeldho, Joe V. "Toni Morrison's Depiction of the City in Jazz," *Notes on Contemporary Literature* 36 (January 2006): 14–16.

Love (2003)

INTRODUCTION

Love is Toni Morrison's eighth published novel. It received mixed reviews after its publication, and to date the novel does not enjoy the same reputation as some of Morrison's earlier works. *Love* is another chronicle in Morrison's continuing exploration of the lives, communities, and histories of African Americans. The story specifically questions the meanings of love for post–CIVIL RIGHTS MOVEMENT African-American communities. The novel has as its center the pre-integration gathering site of Cosey's Hotel and Resort, a beach escape for middle-class African Americans. This site becomes the locale for both the very particular conflict between the novel's main characters, Heed and Christine Cosey, as well as a stage for exploration of the larger issues of assimilationism versus nationalism, class conflicts, and sexism as the affect African Americans.

SYNOPSIS

Love begins with a compelling first line "The women's legs are open, so I hum" (3). The voice belongs to the novel's narrator, later identified as L. L speaks in this opening chapter about her despair about the novel's present day in which she finds women lacking in self-respect. She says that there is much to be said by not talking—that listening is as essential as talking. The narrator says that she used to be able to make critical points when necessary, but now she is resigned to humming. Through her hum, L dispenses her observations that women today, especially the women of Up Beach, the coastal community where she is from, are hurt and that this hurt makes them wild and predatory.

L tells about the actions of some of those women and a mysterious entity called Police-heads. While relating the history of the Police-heads, L begins to tell the narrative of the main setting of *Love,* the memory and ruin of the most popular vacation spot for black people during the immediate post–World War II era, Cosey's Hotel and Resort.

The fictional Cosey's Hotel and Resort drew African-American vacationers from around the United States to its welcoming doors to hear live JAZZ and rhythm and blues. When the hotel closes, Bill Cosey, the owner and proprietor of Cosey's Hotel, relocates to Monarch Street in the town of Silk. The community of Up Beach no longer exists in the form it did when Cosey's was open because the community is now underwater due to hurricane Agnes.

There is some controversy with respect to the characters' understandings of why Cosey's Resort closes. According to L, Bill Cosey believed that the hotel and resort failed because of the smell from a local cannery that filled the hotel. Cosey's daughter-in-law May believed, before she died, that the freedoms brought about by the Civil Rights movement were responsible for the hotel's demise. L believes that the closure occurred for other, undisclosed reasons.

The African-American residents of Up Beach were visited with a series of misfortunes that changed the realities of their community forever. Many residents of the Up Beach community moved into the second-rate community of Oceanside, which evolved into a superficial and hollow community without the connectivity and vitality of Up Beach.

Not much remains of Up Beach and of the Cosey Hotel and Resort, except the shell of the building, ravaged by the salt water and by the sea licking at its threshold. Bill Cosey's legacy exists in the long-standing hatred between the two survivors in his family, his granddaughter, Christine, and his wife, Heed. The two women remain, long after his passing, in the house that he built on Monarch Street in Silk, hoping against hope for each other's demise and remaining alive to ensure the other's destruction and failure to be the sole inheritor of Cosey's estate.

L ends the first chapter on a note of concern for the Cosey women, Heed and Christine. L states that she is worried about the two women, hell-bent as they are upon each other's destruction. She also notes her concern about a young woman, who at this point remains nameless, who has recently taken up residence at One Monarch Street. L's description of the woman brings the chapter full circle as the nameless girl seems to be one of the hurt and exposed women L ruminates upon at the chapter's inception. Reminiscent of the narrator in *Jazz,* L says that the story is all she has and that she needs a morality tale about the ability of morally loose women to destroy upstanding men.

1 – Portrait
The first chapter of the novel begins with the arrival of Junior Viviane in Silk on an unprecedentedly cold

afternoon. As she arrives, she encounters Sandler Gibbons. Junior asks Sandler for directions to One Monarch Street, the home of Christine and Heed Cosey. Sandler is taken aback by the girl's hair, which he feels is wild, and by her scanty dress. He gives the young woman the directions she requests and tells her that the house is so big there is no way that she can miss it. Junior continues on her way, leaving Sandler to reflect upon the encounter.

When Vida, Sandler's wife, arrives home along with their grandson Romen, Sandler tells them about Junior and about her strange mission to the Cosey house. The conversation veers toward the topic of Bill Cosey and his death. Vida reveals her long-held belief that the man died after being poisoned. Although they have different interpretations about what happened to Cosey, Sandler has fond memories of Up Beach and of the physical beauty of the place. Vida sees the cannery in particular as a locale of enforced labor and feels that Bill Cosey rescued the community from that fate. The two do not seem to notice the bruises on their grandson's knuckles that he massages as he washes his hands after dinner.

Junior, at this point in the novel called the girl, finds the house and says that she has come in search of a job after seeing the ad that Heed Cosey placed in the newspaper. Heed's ad requests the services of a companion. After being suspiciously directed up to Heed's quarters on the second floor of the house by Christine, Junior speaks with and is hired by Heed.

During the interview, Junior notices several oddities about her soon-to-be employer. Although Heed has food that Christine cooks for her, she does not eat. She also notices that Heed's hands are deformed from some unknown ailment. After Junior eats the dinner intended for Heed, she falls into the first restful sleep she has had in many years.

While asleep, she dreams and feels safe. The sleep is similar to that she had during her first days at a youth detention facility, called Correctional. At Correctional when she had scary dreams about snakes, a mysterious stranger would appear in her dream and would protect her from the snakes. Junior associates her feelings of safety and comfort

with the protection she imagined acquiring from the man in her dreams and then—significantly—connects and conflates the stranger of her dreams with the portrait of Bill Cosey hanging in Heed's room and begins, that night, a fantasy or supernatural relationship with the man.

2 – Friend

Chapter two begins as Vida irons her uniform for her present-day job as a hospital aide and reflects on her experiences working at Cosey's Hotel and Resort. Vida remembers Cosey's motto, "the best good time," and how that motto was made real through Bill Cosey's magnanimous personality. Vida remembers the romance of the place—the sensual experience of good food, wonderful music, and a beautiful natural setting—and the way that the feeling of it all was enhanced by Bill Cosey and his impeccable memory and intuition regarding the needs as well as the whims of his guests.

By the time Vida's child, Dolly, Romen's mother, is born in 1962, the inn has lost most of its magic. Vida remembers the fight that Christine and Heed had at Bill Cosey's funeral and L's intervention. At the funeral, Christine pulled a knife against Heed. L quits Cosey's the very day of the funeral and left the resort without her things. Although Heed tried to run Cosey's Hotel and Resort after her husband's death, the resort never recovered from his and L's absence and from the substitution of recorded music for live musicians.

Although Vida's job keeps the family comfortable, she misses the work that she did at Cosey's. Vida remembers the resort as a kind of sanctuary from the violence and disrespect experienced by African Americans. Vida is still plagued by the question of what happened to the resort. She remembers Bill Cosey's loss of interest in the resort before his death. She also recalls the arrogant immaturity that alienated Heed from those who might have been able to help her after Cosey died. Vida also recalls that May, Bill Cosey's daughter-in-law, is a kleptomaniac. Vida wonders if perhaps the woman's perpetual thieving contributed to the inn's decline, but then decides that May could not have been the source of the inn's downfall. She also refuses to believe that Bill Cosey's death was accidental. Although others speculate that Cosey might have had syphilis or that he simply died of old age, Vida believes that she saw the water he drank at lunch shortly before he died. She is convinced that the water appeared cloudy and that Cosey was poisoned.

Sandler's report of meeting a young girl headed toward the Cosey house makes Vida curious about the woman. She believes that the girl must be Heed's relative since Heed comes from a large family. Vida decides that she will satisfy her curiosity by asking Romen to find out the new girl's identity.

Sandler recognizes that his wife realizes that he is attracted to the young girl. As Sandler adjusts the heat on the house, he speculates that, given her attire, Junior must be from somewhere north and be accustomed to the cold. Like his wife, Sandler decides that he will ask Romen to find out who the girl is and what business she has with the Cosey women.

Sandler's efforts to heat his insubstantial Oceanside house are nearly futile. His thoughts reveal his nostalgia for Up Beach and for the feeling of the place, so lacking in the Oceanside community. He particularly misses the beach and its landscape at night, with the moon that seems to belong to him. His meeting with Junior reminds him of the relationship he once shared with the moon over Up Beach.

Sandler had a less positive relationship with Cosey than Vida. The men fished together for years and the charismatic and enigmatic aura that the man held for most of the community did not affect Sandler. Sandler knows that Cosey does not mix with local people and turns people away from the hotel that he does not feel are suitable clientele. Sandler had been impressed with the hotel and the man when he was a boy, but once he has the opportunity to spend time with the man, he realizes his flaws, which include frequent drinking and womanizing. Bill Cosey complains to Sandler that women are everywhere in his life, and Sandler senses that Cosey's involvement with the women in his life makes him deeply confused and unhappy.

Although Sandler tells Cosey that he has the community's respect, Cosey is disappointed, knowing that Sandler's answer lacks the complexity of the truth. Then Cosey reveals to Sandler some

of the source of his anguish. Cosey speaks of the unexpected death of his son Billy Boy, and the way that the experience shook the man to his core and changed his perceptions. Cosey also speaks of the disadvantages of life as a black person.

After many fishing trips, Cosey eventually persuades Sandler to leave his job at the cannery, but Sandler returns to his old job after spending a few months at Cosey's working as a waiter. The men continue to fish together, but Sandler never really feels close to the man despite this intimacy. In time, Sandler grows to realize that Cosey's money makes him impulsive, insecure, and childish.

Giving up on his attempts to warm the house, Sandler reflects upon his retirement from his job as a mall security guard. Retirement makes him feel as if he is losing his mental edge and sharpness. He seems to dwell increasingly in the past. As he enters the kitchen, he takes Vida into his arms and begins to dance with her.

The next scene finds Romen reflecting upon the reasons that he has been crying. He remembers the hands of a girl six of his friends gang-raped and wonders why he was not able to commit the same violent violation of the girl as had the other boys. Having watched the other boys rape the girl, Romen was supposed to rape her next. Inexplicably, he unties the knot that binds the girl's hands and carries her out of the bedroom where the rapes took place.

Rather than becoming a hero for his actions, Romen is ostracized by his peers. Three days after the incident, the boys who were there beat him up. This fight is the source of the bruises that are on Romen's hands at the beginning of the novel.

Romen believes that now the authentic Romen has emerged, and he is not pleased that his real self would not rape Faye. The real Romen cries in his bed alone and confused by the turn of events.

3 – Stranger

The third chapter details the background of Silk's newest arrival, Junior Viviane, who comes from a place called the Settlement. The residents of the Settlement are referred to as rurals. The Settlement seems to attract negative attention from those in authority and develops a reputation as a backward and stagnant community.

The rural, stereotypically country community emerges from the closure of a jute mill. Former employees that can relocate do; those who cannot become residents of the Settlement, consisting of disempowered, poor, and uneducated black and white people. Junior is a descendant of one of those individuals. Junior's mother, Vivian, wanted to name her baby girl right after her birth, but is so exhausted by the labor she sleeps for three days after the delivery; Vivian's husband, Ethan Payne Jr., takes to calling the child Junior after himself. He may be motivated to do so because neither Junior nor her four brothers are fathered by Ethan Payne Jr. He leaves the family shortly thereafter.

Junior likes attending school and finds it a reprieve from her home life. Junior longs for her absent and unknown father. That longing sets up her later desire for a mythical mysterious man. Junior is alienated at school as the girls from other communities are not interested in communicating with children from the Settlement. Junior finds a friend in a boy named Peter Paul Fortas. Peter is 11, and he is more interested in exploring the contours of Junior's imagination than in discriminating against her because of her origins. The two are sensitive to each other's feelings and exchange small gifts. One of those gifts proves the downfall of their innocent friendship.

One Christmas, Junior gives Peter a young cottonmouth snake. He gives Junior a box of crayons. The gifts cause a great deal of consternation among the adults in Junior's world. Junior's miscreant uncles, demand, for no apparent reason, that she get the snake back from her friend. Junior refuses to do so and runs away from her uncles. When her uncles eventually catch up with Junior in their pickup truck, they run over her foot with their truck, permanently maiming the girl.

Junior runs away from the Settlement forever at the age of 11. After running away, Junior is arrested for stealing a G.I. Joe Doll and is sent to a detention center called Correctional. At Correctional, the officials rename her Junior Smith. She believes that her experiences at Correctional prepare her for working for Heed Cosey.

The morning after her arrival at the Cosey house, Junior encounters Romen for the first time.

Earlier that morning, Heed shows the girl a photograph from Heed's wedding to Bill Cosey. Heed wears a wedding gown that is much too large for her and Junior notices that Bill Cosey does not look at his bride in the photo. Junior sees Romen from Heed's window.

When Junior first encounters Romen, she asks him if he is having sex with the old women. The question startles and delights Romen. It restores his sense of self-esteem. Junior suggests that there are plenty of places in the house for her and Romen to have sex.

The chapter concludes with more of L's observations and commentary. L says that there is a difference between relationships that are based upon sex rather than on something more profound and insightful. She claims that love cannot be spectacle—the natural world outlaws that kind of display with its inherent beauty.

L says that her appreciation of the natural world may come from her birth during a storm. Her mother goes into labor while outside hanging laundry, forcing the woman and L's father to deliver their newborn outdoors in the pouring rain. L connects her watery birth with her first sighting of Bill Cosey, years later, as the man stands in the sea holding his first wife, Julia, in his arms. This scene between the two lovers seems to L be an example of true love. L's retelling of the scene evokes her own feelings of affection for Bill Cosey. She says that memory of the scene sparks her desire to apply for a job at Cosey's Hotel and Resort nine years after the incident.

L also talks about her job as a cook at Maceo's Cafeteria. Although the establishment belongs to Maceo, L claims that it really belongs to her. After cooking at Cosey's for almost 50 years, L leaves the resort the day of the man's funeral. She earns a living doing laundry for a while and then takes another job cooking at Maceo's. After a time, L is unable to stand to cook, in part from having to walk to work. In order to keep her services, Maceo agrees to pick her up and take her home each day. He also gets her a counter-high chair on wheels that enables her to cook while sitting down.

L says that no one alive remembers her real name. She also has been forgotten. She also says, mysteriously, that she "glides" now. Junior is one of the girls who comes into Maceo's. L describes the lust that Junior generates in the young boys who frequent the restaurant. Junior reminds L of a woman named Celestial whom, L suggests, Bill Cosey knew as well. Cosey deeply loved his first wife Julia who lost respect for her husband when she learned where the man acquired his wealth. According to L, Cosey's father, Daniel Robert Cosey, was a police informant and worked in that capacity, betraying the African-American community for 52 years. The white people of Silk called him Danny Boy, but the black people who knew or knew of him called him Dark, as suggested by the conflation of his initials. Dark left his son, Bill Cosey, nearly $115,000 when he died. Disapproving of his father's choice of profession, Bill Cosey lives his life trying to regain the approval of the community Dark alienated.

Julia's family was exploited by people like Bill Cosey's father and she was horrified when she learned the source of her husband's money and was unable to continue to express her affection toward her husband. Julia gives birth to Bill Cosey's only son, Billy Boy, and dies when the child is 12.

4 – Benefactor
The fourth chapter begins with Heed bathing. She is terrified by the thought that she could fall and drown. She wants to ask Junior to help her dye her graying hair. Heed's inability to care for herself in these simple ways stems from her deformed hands.

Heed is concerned that she might not be able to get the assistance she requires from the girl because of Junior's preoccupation with Romen. Heed sees the first encounter between the two from her window. In spite of her concern, she thinks that if Romen is involved with Junior, he will be more willing to stay at One Monarch Street longer hours to work. Heed reflects also upon the fights between her and Christine. The fighting between the two women begins with Christine's theft from Heed of a bag of diamond engagement rings Bill Cosey won in a card game. After she steals them, Christine wears the rings.

Christine shares the ire her mother, May, felt at Heed for marrying Bill Cosey. Heed comes from a poor, Up Beach family that is marginally literate.

Both May and Christine feel that, as a result, the girl is unworthy of marriage to the man they adore. Although she also cannot read, Heed compensates for the deficit with her phenomenal memory.

Heed remembers overhearing a conversation some of the hotel guests had about why Bill Cosey might have married her. They make fun of her appearance, particularly of her hair and her skin color. The conversation hurts her into the present day. In spite of these setbacks, at Bill Cosey's (whom she calls Papa) insistence, Heed learns how to run the hotel. L is a salvation for Heed and often rescues her from the cruelties inflicted by May and Christine.

As Heed takes her bath, she reflects on Papa's tenderness as he introduced her to sexuality by opening her legs to the sea. She also remembers the first time she met Christine when the two were little girls. She also recalls Papa's infidelity.

Christine leaves One Monarch Street to consult with a lawyer. Christine is trying to sue Heed for sole ownership of Cosey's estate. The only will ever found of Bill Cosey's is some scribbling L says she found on a menu. Another such menu is found a year later that appears to clarify that Bill Cosey intended to leave his fortune to Heed.

Christine's departure on her quest leads Heed to reflections about Christine's mother, May. May, Billy Boy's wife, loses touch with reality as she is confronted with the ideological contradictions of the civil rights era. She begins to feel that the movement is dangerous and represents a serious threat. She begins to feel that Cosey's Hotel is the only sanctuary against the violence perpetrated against African Americans. In her paranoia, May begins to steal and hide things she thinks are valuable. One day, May walks into the kitchen, preparing to hoard more booty just as Heed, arguing with L, is burned on the hand by a stray splash of hot oil.

When remembering the scene previously, Heed had focused on the pain of the burn. This time, however, she wonders if the box that May was carrying, which eventually ended up in the attic, contained menus from 1964 or 1965 upon which Heed hopes to get Junior to forge a draft of Bill Cosey's will.

Christine's journey to her lawyer's office takes her down Route 12, a path that she has taken many times before when leaving Silk. Her trip reminds her of another car, the car of her former lover, Dr. Rio. When she finds herself replaced after a three-year relationship with the married Dr. Rio, Christine destroys the man's Cadillac. Christine believes that her relationship with Dr. Rio was her last chance at having a relationship. Unceremoniously, Dr. Rio removes her from the apartment he set her up in and takes back all of the gifts he has given her. Christine ends up living in a building filled with prostitutes and owned by a kind-hearted woman named Manila. From Manila's, Christine returns for the last time to Silk.

As she drives, Christine reflects on her many departures from Silk down the same road. When she was 13, she tried to run away and was gone less than half a day. At 17, her attempt to run away was also unsuccessful. Her last departure from Silk occurred in 1971. Christine returned home from that departure to Silk to take care of her mother May. When she returns, the hatred between Heed and Christine is as sharp as when Christine left, and Christine genuinely fears Heed.

Christine's reverie is interrupted by the sudden appearance of a turtle in the middle of the road. Trying to avoid the turtle, she hits another one. Looking behind her for the turtles, eventually she sees both of them heading for the shelter of the trees. Christine, filled with murderous rage for Heed, is glad not to have killed the turtles.

Arriving at her lawyer's office, Christine receives a less than warm reception from her attorney, Gwendolyn East. Gwendolyn East believes that the 1958 menu will can be invalidated in court and encourages Christine's ambitions. Junior's arrival makes Christine nervous and certain that Heed is trying to strengthen her claim that Bill Cosey's leaving the house to his "sweet Cosey child" meant that he wanted to leave his house to his wife.

Christine mistrusts all people associated with the law and its enforcement. She has been arrested five times and all of her arrests were connected to the relationships she has had with various men.

Christine also reflects on her departure from Silk in 1947 at 16 years old. She mistakenly goes to Manila's boarding house, not knowing that, although not entirely intended for prostitutes, the

house allows them to operate within its doors. Her first evening in the house, she meets her soon-to-be husband, Ernie Paul. The man comes to Manila's looking for a prostitute and instead discovers Christine. Charmed with the girl, he asks her to dinner and, shortly thereafter, to become his wife.

Gwendolyn East patiently points out to Christine that Heed has not as yet excluded her from access to Cosey's resources. Gwendolyn tells her that the designation of the estate is entirely in Heed's hands, information that makes Christine very angry. She reiterates that she is the only surviving blood relative of Bill Cosey and therefore is the rightful heir. She ends the session with the lawyer by shouting an expletive at her, calling her stupid, and firing her from the case.

The novel shifts to the omniscient narrator and to a once-upon-a-time tone as it reveals some of the story of Christine's childhood. The narrator describes Christine's bedroom and her girlhood hairdo, but of particular interest is Christine's best friend.

The story continues when the little girl—Christine—has to move to another bedroom. She is told that she has to relocate for her own good but is given no other explanation. In her frustration about the move, the little girl runs away. Eventually she is discovered by a policeman and returned to her home at the hotel. When she returns, she is allowed to return to the room, but her mother locks her in the room at night in order to ensure her safety. The little girl does not know or understand why she is imprisoned in this way and does not comprehend the dangers from which her mother feels she needs protection.

Eventually the little girl is sent away from her home. Throughout all of her ordeal, the little girl is proud of her ability to contain her tears. The narrator also explains that the little girl's mother slaps her hard across the face when she is returned to the hotel. She finds some refuge under L's bed, but then is sent away to boarding school at Maple Valley School.

Christine's mother, May, is a vociferous, if unintelligible, advocate for the rights of African-American people and frequently writes letters to newspapers. These letters cause Christine a great deal of embarrassment. She does not fit in at Maple Valley School and her feelings of alienation contribute to her general sense of abandonment.

The narration continues, providing background information on May. May comes from a poor family and her insecurity about the changes brought about by the Civil Rights movement derives from her history. May comes to believe that she and those she loves are in danger from the changes in the world. May's anxieties appear extreme to those around her. May always wears an army helmet and even attempts to wear it to Bill Cosey's funeral. L dissuades her from wearing the helmet to the funeral, but May brings the helmet to the service with her just in case. These memories make Christine regretful about the fact that her life has become a series of tasks she performs in an attempt to stake her claim on her grandfather's estate.

Before Christine returns at the end of May's life, Heed wants to have May, her long-sworn enemy, committed to an institution. L forbids her from doing so. The fact that Heed does not put May in an institution is a testimony to the power of L's influence. Heed is infuriated by the discovery in Bill Cosey's menu will that, apparently, the man left the hotel to May.

It is this anger as well as Christine's long-standing fury at Heed that fuels the public fight between the two women at Bill Cosey's funeral. Christine threatens Heed with a knife. When she does so, L pins Christine's hand behind her, preventing the woman from stabbing Heed. L stops both women in their tracks with her threat to tell on them. It is unclear whether L threatens Heed or Christine, or both of the women. Also unknown is the information that L possesses that seems to have such an impact on the women's behavior. Nonetheless, L's words contain and control both Christine and Heed—at least until after the funeral.

The fight between Christine and Heed at Cosey's funeral appears undignified and disrespectful to the community. The event lowers the stature of the women in the community. May especially feels that Heed is an intruder from whom her daughter needs protection. May writes to Christine while Christine is away from Silk that Heed is attempting to find a way to have her institutionalized. According to

May, Heed tries everything she can think of to ensure that the woman is discredited and declared unfit to live an independent life, but, while L is still at Cosey's Hotel and Resort, Heed is unable to carry through on her plans. After L's departure and Billy Cosey's death, Heed has too many problems of her own, including the deformation of her hands, to pursue her plans to commit May. Reflecting upon this, Christine determines to put Heed away in an institution.

The novel shifts back to L's narration. L declares that the sea is her lover. She says that the ocean knows when to move and when to be still and that the sea is always true.

Although she is young when she first meets Cosey, she takes on the responsibility for caring after Bill and his son Billy Boy following the death of Cosey's first wife, Julia. As such, L is a firsthand witness to the relationship between the father and son. L describes the relationship as devoted. She says that all of the love that Bill Cosey had for Julia, belongs to the boy following her death. Billy Boy is a sweet and loving child who happily pleases his father. Bill Cosey is determined that his son not be anything like his own father, Daniel Robert Cosey, Dark.

Billy Boy chooses May as his wife and May devotes herself to the care of Bill Cosey's Hotel. L talks of the way that she and May work collaboratively in the kitchen of the hotel, and Billy Boy works as the bartender and at booking the musicians. After L takes over the kitchen responsibilities, May is the administrative core of the hotel. According to L, things went well when the hotel was run by the two women and that the environment became difficult only with the introduction of Heed and Christine. L also refers to May's response to EMMETT TILL's death in 1955. The death of the boy sends May into a panic that catalyzes her tendency to steal things and to prepare for a siege against the hotel and the people she loves.

L sees the origins of the ruin of the hotel in Bill Cosey's marriage to Heed. L says that Bill Cosey stole Heed from Christine. L thinks that, perhaps, Bill Cosey's choice of bride might have been predicated upon his desire for more children after Billy Boy's death; however, Heed never provides him with any offspring. L also reveals that, although Cosey is faithful to Heed for a while after their marriage, he eventually returns to his mistress, perhaps the love of his life, Celestial.

L remembers one night seeing Bill Cosey walking home despondently. Then she sees him meet up with a woman who walks into the sea at night without fear, which L admires and remembers. The beautiful woman then let out a sound that L wanted to match with her own voice. Although L does not approve of Celestial's profession as a prostitute, she understands that the woman comes from a context where that profession was normal. She also implies that the two, Celestial and Bill Cosey, love each other—even in death.

L ends this chapter as she began with further reflection upon the sea and its magical qualities. She says that she watches him—her lover, the sea—every night from the abandoned hotel. She says that the song of the sea is that of a tenor.

5 – Lover

Chapter five begins with Sandler and Vida Gibbons's concerns about the change in the demeanor of their grandson, Romen. They sense that the boy has begun a relationship. They do not want to believe that the relationship is sexual.

Remembering his own sexual maturation, Sandler wants to help the boy retain his confident masculinity. Sandler believes that the boy could either become sexually repressed or overly aggressive with women if he is not able to develop his own organic sense of himself as a sexual being. Sandler fears the boy becoming a man like Bill Cosey whose sexuality becomes a sign of his confusion and insecurity. Sandler speculates that Bill Cosey married Heed because the man believed that he could mold the young girl into becoming the kind of woman he imagined he wanted. Instead, Cosey's boat became a site for his numerous affairs.

Sandler is amenable to the relationship that develops between him and Bill Cosey in part because Sandler's own father moved up north. Although Bill Cosey is no father-figure, Sandler's father's absence may make him miss the occasional company of older men. On one of the fishing trips, Sandler asks Bill Cosey about his own father. Cosey says that he hated his father and that he was glad when the man died on Christmas Day.

Sandler remembers also his discomfort while on some of the fishing trips with Bill Cosey. During the trip that particularly bothered the young Sandler, Cosey's boat is filled with middle-aged white men, a fact that makes Sandler as uncomfortable as does the presence of the rich African-American men also present. But the real problem for Sandler is the delusion that the dynamic on the boat represents. He feels that the artificial power relationships on the boat—where women are in control and white men defer to blacks—are insulting and disconcerting. There is one exception to the artificial environment Bill Cosey fosters on his fishing trips, the love interest of his life, Celestial. Cosey tells Sandier that he cannot live without the woman and that having her in his life makes his life tolerable. Sandler knows that Cosey's love for Celestial generates the look in Cosey's eye in the photograph that is the source for the portrait hanging over Heed's bed. The hunger in Bill Cosey's gaze and his firsthand knowledge of the obsessive love that generates it makes Sandier cautious about his approach toward his grandson's newfound sexuality.

Vida cannot figure out how Romen has time to develop a relationship since he is always either at school, at work, or performing tasks that she and Sandler have assigned. Vida does not want the boy to develop a disease or get a girl pregnant and wants to find out immediately who the girl is. Sandler feels that they might be able to wait until the boy's parents return for Christmas. The conversation sparks lust in Sandler.

Romen feels empowered by Junior and all she represents. The boy is only 14 years old and is having sex with a woman he finds appealing who is four or five years older. The two seem to have an equal desire for sex and he has never felt better about himself. Romen has distinguished himself from his gang-raping peers. His masculinity is defined by the desire that he and Junior share and not by imposing force or coercion. The boys who tormented Romen after the rape recognize the change in his demeanor and stop bothering him.

During school, Romen has a hard time concentrating because of his thoughts of Junior and of the pleasure that her body brings. Romen wants to remember everything about his love and her body. His desire for her is urgent and ever-present. They have sex everywhere they can think of, from a phone booth to the back seat of the Cosey car.

While Junior develops her relationship with Romen and the confidence of her new employers, she also has a private affair with her imagined projection of Bill Cosey. Based on her interaction with his portrait, Junior creates a whole fantasy life with the man. Calling him Good Man, Junior seeks his approval for her actions and feels he is watching her from afar. The circumstance that Junior finds herself in at the Cosey house is the best situation she has ever had in her life. The new environment makes her reflect upon the past and upon her abrupt departure from Correctional, the institution she was placed in when, as a young girl, she stole a G.I. JOE doll.

When Junior is at Correctional, there is an administrator who is interested in her sexually. When Junior is scheduled to leave the institution because she has reached 18, the predatory administrator is the one with whom she has her Exit Conference. During the Exit Conference the Administrator sits on the railing. As he does so, he pushes Junior's head down to his crotch and begins to undo his belt buckle. Junior grabs the backs of his legs and throws the man over his balcony. Although another administrator sees that the man has his fly open when he lands on the ground, he lies in order to protect his colleague. The others who run the institution choose not to believe Junior's story. The group of administrators responsible for making disciplinary decisions at Correctional, side with the molesting Administrator and send Junior to prison. Junior believes that her Good Man was overseeing the turn-of-fate that brought her to Silk and to the Cosey women.

As previously mentioned, Junior's Good Man first appears to her as a part of her fantasy and dream life. In these visions, Junior is protected and held by this man. Seeing the portrait of Bill Cosey that hangs above Heed's bed allows Good Man to come to life for Junior. Part of her motivation for being such an attentive employee to Heed stems from her desire to see Bill Cosey's portrait as much

as possible. She also finds that Bill Cosey's closet and the feel of his things, as well as the lingering remnants of his scent, delight her and convince her of his present-day existence.

She cannot believe her good fortune when not only does Good Man become more tangible than ever, but also she has a real live boyfriend, Romen. Junior also figures that she can manipulate the Cosey women into doing and becoming exactly what she wants and needs. Junior learns the women's secrets and feels that she understands their motivations. As a self-perceived master of manipulation, Junior feels totally in control of the situation and her life for the very first time.

6 – Husband

The beginning of chapter six finds Junior dyeing Heed's hair. While Heed has her hair done by the girl, the older woman talks away about events she remembers. The barber's chair that Heed sits in while Junior does her hair was the one that Bill Cosey bought after Billy boy died. It was the chair that they both used to sit in to get their hair cut. Heed tells Junior that while Bill sat in the chair, he would instruct Heed about how to take care of his personal grooming. She also speaks of her insecurities as a result of her identity as a girl from Up Beach.

As Junior blows Heed's hair dry following the removal of the dye, Heed continues her story, telling Junior about Bill Cosey's relocating the family to Silk and that their arrival in the town marked the presence of the first African Americans to live there. Even in 1945, not one white resident protested because of Bill Cosey's status in the community and because of his money. The building of the house and its acceptance by the white residents of Silk sparked a celebration at the resort that lasted all summer. Heed also tells Junior that, as Bill Cosey's wife, she was not allowed to go into the kitchen to help cook, a memory that brings Heed obvious delight.

Heed grows silent as she remembers two other celebrations held at the hotel in close proximity to the enormous one held during the summer of 1945. In 1947, the hotel hosted a combination birthday and graduation party for Christine, who had not been home in four years. In 1943, Christine was sent to boarding school at Maple Valley School. When Christine returns, her appearance is slick and she has very little to say to anyone except Heed, whom she continually antagonizes. Heed, in her impatience with the situation, hurls a water glass at Bill Cosey, who proceeds to throw his wife onto his lap and to spank her in front of May and Christine who are both more than delighted to witness the humiliation of their enemy.

Returning to the present, Heed avoids a question from Junior about her family of origin. Heed dismisses the question with a wave. Junior, identifying with Heed's reluctance to discuss her family, says that she understands and tries to avoid talking about her family as well. They both remember sleeping on the floor at their birth homes.

These revelations make Heed believe that it is the commonality of their situations that first attracted her to Junior and made Heed trust the girl. When Heed marries Bill Cosey, she loses her family, and the Coseys, despite their expressed hostility, become her only family. The bitterness begins when Christine resentfully rejects Heed's friendship. May, also horrified by the marriage and worried for her daughter, scorns Heed rather than taking out her ire on Bill Cosey.

When Heed first marries Bill Cosey, she takes to wearing the clothing she sees on the elegant women at the hotel. These clothes are ridiculous on Heed who does not realize how ludicrous she looks. Bill Cosey, or Papa, as she calls him, simply lets her buy whatever she wants while they are on their honeymoon. When Heed returns, she wants to share her experiences with her friend Christine and is met with a cold and indifferent gaze. Before the marriage, the two shared even their own language, a way of communicating that only the two of them understand. Christine uses it to tell Heed that she has been bought and is now a slave. Christine is sent to Maple Valley School less than two weeks later, leaving Heed alone in a house of adults.

Junior tells Heed that she did not ever meet her father and the untruth that the man was killed in Vietnam. Junior wonders if she should get married since it seems to have been such a helpful event in Heed's life. Junior says to Heed that it was a

good thing that her husband left her the big house that she lives in and a great deal of money. Heed remembers that, after 1947, Bill Cosey never told her that he loved her and that when he died, she was bereft at knowing that she would never hear it again. Feeling that she can trust the girl, she makes Junior her co-conspirator. She tells Junior that she needs some documents that can be found in the attic of the Cosey Hotel and that she wants the girl to take her there so that they can find them.

When next Junior seeks out her Good Man, she cannot find him. She is not sure that he approves of her assistance in taking Heed out to the hotel. While waiting for Christine to leave so she can take Heed out to the hotel, Junior engages Christine in conversation. Christine, trying to enact her plan, tells Junior that Heed is mentally unstable. She also tells Junior that Heed is her grandmother. Confused, Junior asks if the two women are not the same age. Christine tells her that she is actually older than Heed by almost a year. Junior quickly does the math and figures out that Heed was 11 when she married Bill Cosey. Christine tells Junior of her friendship with Heed and how that relationship was ruined suddenly by her grandfather's lustful affection for her same-aged friend. Christine sees the people in her life as entirely responsible for the way that her life has turned out. She holds Bill Cosey, her mother, and L accountable, but her deepest ire is reserved for Heed whom she cannot and will not forgive. Christine is sad and lonely about her life.

Christine wonders why everything did not turn out differently—the way she had intended. She remembers her return from Maple Valley School and her intentions to be well-behaved and not to antagonize Heed. She also thinks of the spanking Bill Cosey gave Heed and how happy it made her, especially when she, her grandfather, and her mother left the house after dinner to go dancing, leaving Heed embarrassed and alone in the house. Upon their return, they found a sack of smoking sugar left by L in order to put out a fire set by Heed on Christine's bed.

Following the incident and much to Christine's hurt and surprise, Bill Cosey asks that she be sent away for a couple of weeks until things settle down.

Although May questions why Christine is the one who should leave, Bill Cosey insists, stating that Heed is his wife, not Christine. It is this favoritism and injustice that sends Christine out into the world, determined never to see Cosey's Hotel and Resort or her grandfather alive again.

The chapter ends with L's reflections on her conversations with May. When May begins to let fear control everything about her existence, L tells her that her problem is a preoccupation with death. L believes that May's behavior is explicable when she understands her efforts as an attempt to thwart the inevitability of death.

L believes that, as a result of May's convictions, Heed's arrival on the scene, indeed the girl's very existence, represented all that May feared. Heed's marriage to Bill Cosey seems to be concrete evidence of impending downfall. L knows that May was not always brutal, unforgiving, and vindictive. She remembers when May first married Billy Boy and was a humble and sweet, self-effacing young woman who wanted nothing more than to be helpful.

May encouraged Billy Boy to take on more responsibility with the hotel and to become more of a force in the operations of the establishment. After Billy Boy's death, May turned over the responsibility for raising Christine to L who, in her mourning for Billy Boy, was more than happy to take over care of his daughter. May devotes herself to the care and prosperity of the hotel for the next seven years until Cosey abruptly informs his daughter-in-law, and the mother of his only grandchild, that he is going to marry her daughter's only friend.

Heed's status as an Up Beach resident adds to May's hatred and fear of the girl. May is appalled that Wilber and Surry Johnson, Heed's parents, are so willing to give up their daughter for marriage at the age of 11 to Bill Cosey. She also believes that the Johnsons are not protective of their children's innocence and that the girls are already sexually active.

The excuse that Bill Cosey uses in order to explain his behavior when questioned is that he wants more children in the wake of the death of his son Billy Boy. May and L do not believe that he is telling the truth with this excuse. The women think that Cosey simply is attracted to the girl. L thinks that part of Cosey's motivation for marrying the 11-year-old best friend of his granddaughter is his desire to continue to enact a kind of revenge on his father even though the man is long dead.

L states that it is her feeling that everyone has a family member who, like Dark, casts a long shadow on all of his or her descendants. These individuals spread dysfunction like disease, rendering stronger and more capable those who survive their presence, but impairing with bitterness and hate those very survivors. The problem, as L notes, is that interfamily hatred and revenge is never unidirectional; it inevitably and permanently deforms and ultimately destroys the individual perpetrating and harboring the malice.

L mentions that she told Bill Cosey that he was wrong to hit Heed and that, if he ever repeated his actions, she would leave Cosey's forever. Bill Cosey tells L that he was wrong. L remembers that, after Cosey spanked Heed, she heard Heed moving around and then smelled smoke. L puts a sack of sugar on Christine's bed to make sure that the fire Heed set on the mattress is out.

Although L is sure that the girl set the fire, Heed never admits her actions. L cannot figure out why Heed takes out her frustration and anger on Christine and not on Bill Cosey. L also notes that Bill Cosey is not visibly upset when he learns what Heed has done. In spite of her eventual dependence upon Heed, May feels that she has achieved revenge because the girl has to care for her after May is no longer able to care for herself and Christine is gone.

When Christine returns to care for May, Heed grudgingly allows her to stay. May is not pleased with her daughter's return to care for her and the two do not get along. L even feels that Christine's presence may have hastened her mother's eventual demise. After a year under Christine's care, May dies. L says that the woman dies with a smile on her face. After May's death, Heed and Christine resume their fight, not realizing that both of them are victims of other people's manipulations.

7 – Guardian

Sandler and Vida Gibbons continue to disagree about the way to proceed with their worries about Romen's sexual activity. The couple has discovered that Romen's partner is Junior. Knowledge of the identity of their grandson's lover has made them more, not less, anxious. Vida is particularly concerned since she does not know anything about the girl or her people. Sandler feels that talking to Romen is futile. He feels that whatever the boy will do is up to him since he is already involved with the girl. Sandler also sees the flaws in Vida's argument about the Cosey women and feels that it is wrong for her, like everyone else, to blame Heed for her marriage at 11 to a 52-year-old man when, of course, Cosey is the one responsible for the entire debacle. Heed is disliked because of her family and because people are jealous of her marriage. It is easier to blame a defenseless girl than to hold Bill Cosey accountable.

Sandler recalls seeing Heed when he went to the Cosey mansion to ask if the women might have some work for Romen to do. Heed invites Sandler in and politely entertains him. Sandler believes that Heed's long-term kindness to him might stem from her knowledge of his friendship with Bill Cosey. Bill Cosey told Sandler that he waited until a year after the marriage to sleep with Heed in deference to her age. This information makes Sandler sympathetic toward Heed and understanding of the idiosyncrasies that others find so unforgivable. Even though Bill Cosey is unfaithful to Heed, Sandler remembers him talking about her respectfully and with a measure of awe. Sandler, in an effort to avoid disillusioning Vida about Bill Cosey, does not share the man's conversations with her.

Sandler and Vida arrange a time when he and Romen can be alone together so that Sandler can talk to the boy. Watching the men in her family drive away, Vida remembers an incident that occurred while she was working at Cosey's Hotel and Resort, when a young person showed disrespect to Bill Cosey.

In Vida's memory of the event, a crowd gathers in front of Cosey's Hotel and Resort. Bill Cosey arrives at the crowd and a young man throws a bucket of excrement on him. Rather than react, Bill Cosey moves through the crowd greeting those that he knows by name. Then he cordially says goodbye and leaves the crowd in confusion about what happened. Bill Cosey seems to meet the protesters who come demanding his land respectfully

and thus defuses their anger and dismantles the seeming divergence of their positions.

Vida believes that Romen fundamentally has a generous and caring nature, but that the boy, as evidenced by his current choices, is a bit misguided and adrift at the moment. Vida is confident that the talk between Sandler and the boy will set things right again.

The couple has arranged for Romen to accompany his grandfather while the man delivers plates of food to those in the church who are unable to cook for themselves because they are ill or enfeebled. Sandler thinks of his own experience as a young man and cannot remember ever having a conversation with his own father or grandfather that was not a command. Sandler is certain that he does not want to repeat that behavior with Romen. Sandler asks his grandson if Junior is pregnant. Romen tells his grandfather that the girl is not pregnant. When Sandler asks Romen what he and Junior do together, Romen tells Sandler about the couple's trip out to the ruins of Cosey's Hotel and Resort. Romen admits to his grandfather that he and Junior went there to have sex.

Romen remembers going up to the attic with Junior. In the attic the two begin to have sex when the floorboards of the old building begin to give way. This danger makes the couple more excited. At that point, Romen bites Junior's nipple. This memory shames Romen and he tells his grandfather that Junior likes very physical sex. This revelation distracts Sandler and the man stops at a green light. Startled, Sandler then drives through the intersection with the light red. Sandler asks his grandson a question about the nature of the sex without passing judgment. This expression of openness frees Romen to tell his grandfather about the conflict the boy has been experiencing.

Romen is confused about Junior's desire for sex that is interwoven with pain. Romen is uncomfortable with his role as someone who inflicts pain in the process of providing pleasure even though he also is aware that the experience is exciting for him as well. Romen is conflicted by his feelings of repulsion when he nearly raped Pretty-Faye and is trying to understand the connection between that experience and the sex he has with Junior.

Again, Sandler listens to what the boy is saying without making a judgment about it. He repeats what the boy tells him and advises him to listen to his own instincts. Sandler informs the boy that those feelings are the most reliable he has. Sandler says that a lucky man finds a woman who is able to take care of him, provide good sex, and be a good companion. He says that if a woman does not meet his needs, he should not stay with her and should be certain to move on before it is too late to do so. Romen's thoughts about abusing Junior and about his perceived control over the girl seem to undercut Sandler's optimism about their talk.

Junior thinks of her Good Man and about his taste. She wonders what kind of an environment he would create, what would make him comfortable. She also wonders about the relationship between Bill Cosey, her Good Man, and the women in the house. Junior does not think that Heed really loved the man. Junior also thinks that Christine hates Bill Cosey, her grandfather.

Junior remembers that she was only 11 when she ran away from the Settlement. In her estimation, Bill Cosey rescued Heed rather than robbing the girl of her childhood. She imagines that Bill Cosey would have rescued her from all of the abuse and suffering she experienced as a young girl.

She believes that Good Man can see what is going on with her at all times and believes that the man can see when she and Romen have sex. She says that she feels Good Man, everywhere. She also mentions that whatever Heed wants her to do at Cosey's Hotel and Resort, she knows that will have devastating consequences for Christine. Then she thinks that in the long run, both of the women will lose. She just wants to ensure that, even if both women destroy each other, she ends up triumphant.

8 – Father

As Christine drives out to Cosey's Hotel and Resort in pursuit of Junior and Heed, she remembers a friend, Anna Krieg, she had as a young woman when she lived in Germany with her then-husband Ernie Holder. When Christine returned from a hike with Anna Krieg, she found Ernie Holder in bed, having sex with the wife of a staff sergeant.

She feels superior to Ernie and cannot understand how the man could possibly cheat on her. In response to Ernie's affair, Christine leaves her husband immediately, but discovers that she has no place to return to from Germany. Christine calls her mother, May, to ask if she can come back to Silk; May's response, while characteristically vague, discourages Christine.

Christine settles for a time in Idlewild, New Jersey. She begins work as a waitress and eventually begins to cook for the restaurant. She has several relationships with married men until she meets a man named Fruit with whom she begins a long-term relationship.

Christine and Fruit end up having a nine-year relationship. Fruit seems to help Christine to see her family more clearly and to put them into perspective. Fruit is a nationalist and fervent admirer of MALCOLM X. Christine travels with Fruit across the country participating in the activism of the CIVIL RIGHTS MOVEMENT. Christine still feels that the time she spent with Fruit was, perhaps, the most meaningful time of her life.

The relationship with Fruit seems like it could last, but it does not. After Christine has her seventh abortion, she believes that she sees part of the fetus of her aborted infant. The experience unsettles Christine even though she has not wanted to become a mother. Shortly thereafter, Bill Cosey dies and Christine returns to Silk for his funeral.

A 17-year-old, who is a member of the group of activists Fruit and Christine belong to, is raped by another member of the group. Christine is disturbed by the nonchalance of Fruit's reaction to the event and the fact that he even blames the woman for the rape. Fruit does not believe that the man who committed the rape should be confronted, claiming that the perpetrator is essential to the overall success of their cause. Although Christine does not leave Fruit over the event, her perceptions of him begin to erode their bond. Christine remembers her former lover as her last friend.

The final break between the two occurs as a result of Christine's return to Silk for Bill Cosey's funeral. After the funeral and the fight with Heed, crippled by her own self-doubts, Christine loses confidence in her self-worth. As a result of her sense of despondency, the relationship between her and Fruit ends amicably. Christine believes that Fruit would have been sad to learn of her degrading relationship with Dr. Rio and her desperate return to and fight for the home that she fervently claims as her possession.

Christine continues her drive toward the hotel to find Heed and Junior. It has been many years since Christine last drove down the road toward Cosey's Resort and Hotel. During that last trip, Christine was dressed like a celebrity in a beautiful rhinestone dress. She remembers that her mother was in the car, riding in the backseat, and that her grandfather was driving and talking about his desire to purchase a new car. Christine and May enjoy the feeling of victory they believe they have experienced after Bill Cosey's spanking of Heed at the dinner immediately preceding the drive. Christine and May delighted in the knowledge that Heed did not come to Christine's birthday/graduation party.

Christine remembers arriving at her party at the hotel and feeling beautiful and refined as the band plays music just for her. As the party continues, she, and everyone in attendance, notice with shock Heed's sudden appearance and dance with an unnamed man who is dressed in a green zoot suit. Bill Cosey, seeing the couple dancing, stands up. The crowd parts and the band stops playing music as he looks at his wife, Heed.

As Christine approaches the formerly glorious hotel, she thinks she begins to hear the ocean. Since she is not yet close enough for the sound of the surf to reach her, it is probably the sound of her own pulse beating in her ears. Christine has high blood pressure and the excitement and stress of chasing Junior and Heed is taxing for the older woman. Christine wonders why she trusted Junior. Christine realizes that trusting the girl was a mistake.

When Christine arrives at the hotel, it is extremely dark. Christine's suspicions about Heed and Junior's activities are validated by her sighting of a car in the driveway of the abandoned structure. Once back in the hotel, Christine identifies with the sadness and loss experienced by her childhood self. Christine has these thoughts as she climbs the steps to the attic and reaches for the door.

The narrative shifts back in time to Heed and Junior's journey out to the hotel. Junior offers to go out to the hotel by herself and save the older woman the trip. The idea of going out to the hotel with Heed unnerves Junior. The girl's unease stems in part from the seeming abandonment of Good Man. Feeling that his absence is a bad sign, Junior tries to persuade Heed to postpone their journey.

Heed ignores the girl's questions and, like Christine, the journey out to the resort sends Heed into a reverie about the past. Heed remembers being 28 years old and watching the hotel guests during the period of its decline. She then thinks back to the year 1958 and to a man, Knox Sinclair, who visited the hotel following the drowning death of his brother. When he arrives, he is overwhelmed by grief. Heed identifies with the man's pain and reaches out to console him.

Following that initial interaction, Heed helps the man unceasingly in his tasks and also begins to have an affair with Knox. Heed has never been with a man who wants her for herself and she finds the experience exhilarating. The two lovers make promises to each other that they will continue their relationship. Heed decides that she will leave Papa and run away with Knox Sinclair.

Once Knox returns home to Indiana with his dead brother, Heed never hears from him again. Frantic with concern and fear, Heed calls the man's home. His mother answers the phone each of the seven times Heed calls and tells her that he is not available. Finally, Knox's mother tells her not to call back and that she and her son are in mourning.

Heed is devastated by what she feels is the man's betrayal until she discovers that she is pregnant and is delighted by the discovery. Heed has believed that she is the cause of Bill Cosey and her childlessness, but with her pregnancy, she discovers that it is him and not her who is the source of their infertility. Heed suffers a miscarriage, but for 11 months refuses to believe that she is not pregnant. During that time she gains weight and imagines her breasts swelling. Eventually, L slaps her and tells her to stop imagining what is not to be. The community mocks her and Heed falls into a deep depression from which she emerges thin again. Although she has no way to know this for sure, Heed believes that the child she conceived with Knox Sinclair was a boy. She also feels that had the child lived, she would not have had the life she ends up with and that she would not be sneaking off to Cosey's Hotel and Resort with a girl who is almost a stranger.

When Junior and Heed arrive at the hotel, Heed lets them in with her key, but notices the damage that Junior and Romen did earlier with their break-in through the hotel's window. Heed tells Junior that they are looking for a particular box. While the two are searching for the box, they both experience the mysterious smell of baking cinnamon rolls. When they find the box, Heed discovers the menus she expected that May left there. The dates on the menus they discover say 1964. This date works for Heed's plan to have Junior write a new will that is later than the one that has "for my sweet Cosey child" on it. She plans to ask Junior to write on the menu that she, Heed Cosey, is the sole inheritor of the Cosey estate.

Heed starts to proceed with the plan and to tell Junior what to write on the menu when she discovers that the girl brought a ball-point pen, not a fountain pen. Junior then argues with Heed, telling her that people did use ball-point pens in 1964. Heed angrily informs Junior that Bill Cosey would never use a ball-point pen. Junior persuades Heed, telling her that using a ball-point pen will lend authenticity to the document. In her broken English, Heed tells Junior to write that everything in the estate should be left to Heed as Bill Cosey's wife and that, in case of her death, the remainder of the estate should pass on to Heed's sister, Solitude. Junior does as Heed requests. She has studied Bill Cosey so much that she can imitate the man's handwriting flawlessly. As the two enact Heed's plan, Heed hears a noise she believes is Christine. The sound frightens Heed, who begins to search the attic for something with which to defend herself against Christine's wrath. Junior tells Heed not to be concerned because the girl believes that she can beat up Christine. Heed knows better and tells Junior so.

When Christine enters the room, Junior starts to tell her that she and Heed are looking up some information for the book Heed is supposedly writing.

In an ambigious reaction, Junior pulls the carpet on the floor where Heed is walking, causing the woman to fall. The old building cannot withstand the weight of Heed's slight body and the woman falls through the boards of the attic to the floor below.

With Heed's fall, Christine experiences all of the loss and devastation she has felt with each and every incident of abandonment in her life. Christine's hatred for Heed transforms immediately. When she sees her childhood friend plunge through the attic floor, Christine's only response is to run to her side and see if she can help. What she discovers is the love and adoration the two shared as children, which was lost when Bill Cosey intervened in the young girls' genuine love for each other. The two women witness Junior as she extinguishes the light in the attic and runs off outside. When she reaches outdoors, Junior gets into the car and drives off, leaving the injured Heed and the newly caring Christine alone in the dark of the abandoned hotel. The women do not react to Junior's departure, In fact they do not seem to care at all that the girl has left them in such a predicament.

Junior excuses her behavior, leaving Heed and Christine alone in the house, by saying to herself that the "cinnamon-ny" smell of the baking bread in the house was too strong for her to stay. She also believes that her Good Man was not there in the house and that he will be amused by her actions. She decides that she will say that the reason she left the house was to get help if either Christine or Heed live. If they do not, she figures that she will not have to say anything and that people will believe that the women killed each other.

At the house, Junior discovers that Christine left in such a hurry that she did not even shut the door to the house or turn off the oven on the lamb she was cooking. Junior walks around the house looking for her Good Man. She believes she finds her Good Man in Heed's room in the portrait of Bill Cosey hanging above Heed's bed.

Romen arrives at the house in search of Junior. Junior leads the surprised Romen upstairs to have sex. When he asks about the Cosey women, Junior lies about their whereabouts. Junior and Romen play and take a bath in Heed's tub. The couple have sex in Heed's bed.

Afterward Romen asks Junior again where the Cosey women are and she tells them that the women are at the hotel. Surprised, Romen inquires what the women are doing there at night and Junior tells him the truth. Romen cannot believe that Junior left the women there. Junior tries unsuccessfully to lure Romen back to bed and tells him to turn out the light.

9 – Phantom

Back at Cosey's, Christine and Heed are assessing the situation as well as their newly rediscovered affection for each other. Heed refuses to examine the broken places in her body. Christine covers Heed with an old blanket she finds and goes to scour the abandoned hotel for something to ease Heed's agony. Christine knows that the medicine she seeks could be available anywhere in the hotel because of her mother's propensity to hide supplies. While Christine searches, in Heed's agony, the details of the room stand out and she thinks back on the way that she believed that she was home when she first came to the resort.

Christine returns with the objects she has discovered hidden in the old building. There is, among May's scavenged treasures, a candle that Christine lights. She has also found pain relief powders for Heed as well as a can of pineapples that Christine hopes contains enough juice for Heed to swallow the medicine. Christine opens the can with a nail and then helps Heed to swallow the powder with the juice.

The women find themselves isolated in a present that seems to make both their pasts and any futures they may have irrelevant. The two begin a conversation about everything they have been thinking and feeling in the years since their last real conversations as girls. What they do believe they have in common is that each of them has been bought and sold by others and, when they managed to get themselves free, they sold themselves. While the two converse, Christine looks inside a dresser and finds her childhood bathing suit. The women wonder at the tiny size of the suit and think back on the little Christine who used to inhabit it. Heed's suit is not in the drawer.

Heed asks Christine if she was ever a prostitute. Christine tells her that she never was. Heed says that she was a prostitute when she was sold to Bill Cosey. Christine disagrees, saying that Heed had no choice. Heed replies that she feels she is responsible for what happened to her because she wanted Bill Cosey's attentions after he chose her for his wife. Heed also reveals that Boss Silk is the reason that Bill Cosey began losing money. Heed tells Christine that Bill Cosey had to pay Chief Silk money for years in order to keep the hotel open and to have a liquor license. The two were not friends. Cosey was at the mercy of the Silks, who extracted money from him illegally. When Cosey's money began to run low, Boss Silk, Chief Silk's son, lent Bill Cosey money in small increments.

The women also remember a secret saying they used to share with each other, the words "Hey Celestial." Christine and Heed begin to use the phrase when they are 10 and are playing together on the beach. The two hear someone else call out the phrase. The woman, Celestial, the recipient of the call, is mysterious and beautiful to the girls. Christine remembers that May tells the girls to stay away from Celestial without explaining to them why. The girl's construct Celestial as fearless and they use the woman's name to represent courage.

Heed also recalls the secret language, idagay, the girls created with they were children. She tells Christine how devastating it was to her when Christine, angry at not being allowed to try on Heed's wedding ring, calls Heed a slave in idagay. Both women begin to point their anger and lifelong frustrations away from each other and toward the source of their problems, Bill Cosey.

Heed also reveals that the novel's narrator, L, died years before while she was cooking at Maceo's. They both admit that they miss L and recognize that they have spent their entire lives defined by Bill Cosey and by the long shadow of his actions.

The narrative shifts to the past and to the source of the rift between Heed and Christine. The two best friends play in their favorite spot on the beach. Heed returns to the hotel because the girls have forgotten to bring their jacks outside. Christine waits for her with the rest of their supplies. Heed retrieves the missing jacks, but runs into Bill Cosey before she can get back to Christine.

At first, Heed is too embarrassed and intimidated to speak to Bill Cosey. He asks her who she is and then Bill Cosey touches Heed's nipples in a sexual way. After Cosey stops touching her and leaves, Heed tries to run back to Christine, but feels confused and guilty at the feelings that Cosey's touch creates in her young body.

As she runs away, she encounters May. May chastises the child for running and makes her help carry dirty laundry to the washroom. By the time Heed returns to the spot where she left Christine waiting, the girl has left. Eventually, Heed finds Christine, but Christine has a stain on her bathing suit and will not look at Heed. Despite these occurrences, the two continue with their picnic without speaking at first, but something has changed irreparably. Although Christine does not mention it, Heed believes that Christine saw what happened between her and Bill Cosey. Heed blames herself for what happens and thinks that something in her causes Bill Cosey to react the way he does. What Heed did not realize was that Christine went to find her friend. When Christine got to her room, she found her grandfather there masturbating. The sight confuses her and makes the girl vomit.

Neither girl explains to the other what they have experienced. They are both unsure about what has happened and are guilty about their feelings of sexual excitement. Christine's room is forever haunted by the memory of what she saw her grandfather doing there. The girls both feel responsible for and sullied by the experiences they have separately with Bill Cosey.

The narrative returns to the present day and to Heed's suffering in the wake of her terrible fall. Christine gives Heed more of the pain relief powder and tries to reassure her. Christine finds a bag of jacks and throws them on the floor to play, only to find that there are not enough left. There are only five jacks in the bag. Christine uses the rings she stole from Heed when she returned for Bill Cosey's funeral as the other five jack pieces. Heed recalls hearing that Bill Cosey paid her father $200 in exchange for their marriage. Heed tells Christine that she was excited to marry Bill Cosey because she thought it would allow her to live with Christine. Heed also tells Christine about her affair with Knox Sinclair.

The two continue sharing memories that flow from them like poems. They both are deeply sorrowful about what Bill Cosey took from them and also about the time they wasted hating instead of loving and nurturing each other. Finally, they express their love for each other.

Romen arrives at the Cosey Hotel and Resort and finds the two women with the beam of his flashlight. By the time he arrives at the hotel, Heed has died. Romen leaves Junior at the Cosey mansion and remembers his grandfather's talk and the advice that Sandler gave him about taking care to choose the right kind of woman.

Junior remains at the Cosey mansion distraught at Romen's departure. Junior finds herself bereft at the thought that he might think negatively of her actions. She also finds herself feeling regretful and sorry for something she has done for the first time in her life.

Lost, Junior wanders around the Cosey mansion. Junior feels abandoned by both Romen and Good Man. She eats pieces of the burned lamb that Christine left in the oven. Even after eating, Junior remains ill at ease.

Back at the ruins of the Cosey Hotel and Resort, Romen gets the women out of the building. He picks up both Christine and Heed and puts them in the car. Christine asks Romen if Junior has run away again and he tells her that the girl is still at the house.

As the day dawns, Christine, Romen, and the dead Heed arrive back at One Monarch Street. As Romen carries Christine into the house and the kitchen, Junior comes in pretending that she has been concerned and trying to help. Christine ignores the girl's lies and tells her to shut herself into L's old room. Junior, without resistance, does Christine's bidding. Christine then asks Romen to lock the door, which he does. Christine then tells Romen to call an ambulance for her and for him to take Heed to the mortuary, but before he does, Christine expresses her sincere gratitude to the boy.

After Romen leaves, Christine begins a posthumous conversation with Heed about Junior and what should happen with the girl. Christine imagines that Junior is trying to escape and Heed tells her that the girl is not. Christine recognizes Junior's rootlessness and it makes her sympathetic. Heed suggests that, with certain understandings and conditions, Junior might be allowed to remain at One Monarch Street. The women seem to identify with the girl and with her problems. Christine and Heed will treat her with compassion—the compassion, love, and understanding that neither woman experienced themselves. Romen drives slowly with Heed through Silk and toward the mortuary. When he looks back at the house, it appears ominous, with storm clouds overhead shading all of the windows except one, which reflects the morning sun like a wink.

Love ends as it begins with L's reflections on the contemporary moment and on the question of love. L begins the novel's final monologue by recalling seeing Christine as a little girl. She remembers the girl sitting alone, pretending that she has a friend. Heed, playing in the waves, comes by where Christine is sitting. Heed does not have a bathing suit and walks past Christine while wearing an oversized shirt. Lonely, Heed also has an imaginary friend.

According to L, when Christine sees Heed, she offers the little girl some of the ice cream she is eating and both Christine and Heed replace their imaginary friends with each other. L says that the childhood love that the girls share is pure and forthright—unselfish. L says that adults underestimate the significance and strength of these relationships since she contends that adults nearly always overestimate the importance of their own relationships with their children. L thinks that a parent's love will always be second in a child's heart to their first love of another child. L maintains that if the children meet before they have fully formed their individual selves or if they become attached when something is askew in their other relationships, the friendship, a first love, can bond the children forever. L believes that the early love shared between Heed and Christine is such a relationship.

L maintains that relationships like the one that Heed and Christine developed originally are rare. L says that she is an expert on the topic of love and reveals that love is her name. L feels that the power

of childhood love is such that, if interfered with, it can make adulthood a horror and destroy the capacity for mental and emotional health. L states that the fault for Heed and Christine's wasted lives and energies lies primarily with two adults in their lives, May and Bill Cosey.

L also speculates on Junior, wondering what Bill Cosey's assessment of the girl would have been had the man made Junior's acquaintance while alive. L remains critical of contemporary women, finding them duplicitous and lewd. L returns to her ruminations on Bill Cosey, feeling that the problem with the man came from his relationship with his father, Dark. L believes that Cosey was flawed, but not uniquely or even unusually so. Then L reveals that, although she is forgiving of the man, she had to stop his behavior and was responsible for doing so.

L reveals that none of the menus established as Bill Cosey's last will and testament were written by the man. L says that she wrote the wills herself. It turns out that Bill Cosey did write a will, and in that document he left all of his property to the love of his life, Celestial. Cosey also remembered Sandler Gibbons in the will, leaving him a fishing boat, but gave nothing to either his wife, Heed, or to his only surviving blood relative, Christine. L writes the fake will because she is certain that Celestial would have destroyed the hotel. Although Bill Cosey claimed to love the woman, he did not acknowledge her and never asked her to come to the hotel and be his legitimate lover, certainly not his wife. L feels that she had no choice but to rescue May, Christine, and Heed from Bill Cosey's lack of compassion and concern by making sure that the legitimate will was never found. L fatally poisoned Bill Cosey and admits that she gave Bill Cosey the poison found in the foxglove plant because she thought that he was unable to do what was required in order for things to function within the kingdom he had created and was beginning to destroy.

L says that the scar that used to trace Celestial's neck from ear to ear has vanished with time and death. L states that she and Celestial are the only souls who travel to Bill Cosey's grave to pay their respects. When L has seen Celestial at Cosey's grave, the woman seems at peace as she sits there and sings to him. While Celestial, dressed in red, sings, L sits with her and listens to the yearning songs the woman sings to her lover. L, having her own complicated feelings about Bill Cosey, sometimes cannot sit quietly but joins in with Celestial and hums.

CRITICAL COMMENTARY

The Beloved Community

Toni Morrison's last four published novels—*Beloved, Jazz, Paradise,* and *Love*—each, in one way or another, ask about the possibility for the establishment of a BELOVED COMMUNITY. The Beloved Community is a philosophical construct originated by JOSIAH ROYCE in the early 20th century and espoused and popularized by MARTIN LUTHER KING JR. during the Civil Rights movement of the 1960s. According to Dr. King, the Beloved Community can emerge following the changes brought about by non-violent direct action. Non-violent direct action, influenced by the legacy of Mohandas Gandhi, was the primary strategy King and his followers used to bring about a change in the relationship between oppressed African Americans and segregationist and discriminatory whites. Non-violent direct action is designed to create a crisis that will shame the oppressor into recognizing the immorality of their actions and altering the dynamic of their relationship with the oppressed group. Once that recognition has occurred, then a new relationship can emerge between the two groups. It is at this point that Dr. King believed that the formation of a Beloved Community would be possible.

In his conception, the Beloved Community is not a utopian ideal. King believed that a community could be established where the inevitable conflicts of human interaction could be resolved by negotiation and compromise rather than through retaliation and revenge. Love is the essential ingredient in the success of the Beloved Community. Each individual within the community must use love in their interactions with each other in order to generate the compassion necessary to coexist.

With her novel, *Love,* Toni Morrison explores the question of whether a group of individuals, coexisting with love at their center, can form a Beloved Community. Like WILLIAM FAULKNER's

Addie Bundren in his novel *As I Lay Dying* (1930), Bill Cosey is at the center of and influences and informs the actions and thoughts of all the characters in the book. The other central character that impacts all of the characters' lives is the mysterious L or, perhaps, Love. Through these two characters in *Love,* Morrison ponders the possibilities, potentialities, and pitfalls of the Beloved Community.

Bill Cosey

The specter of Bill Cosey forms the axis of the narrative of *Love.* Although the man himself does not ever have any first-person appearance in the novel, he is the nexus of its energy and action. It is Bill Cosey's vision that allows for the creation of Cosey's Resort and Hotel. The hotel becomes a space where Bill Cosey imagines that the persecuted African-American community can find sanctuary—music, dance, food, and safety—from the persistent problems of racism and exclusion that it faces in the outside world. Cosey purchases the hotel from a white man who is down on his luck as a result of the Depression. The economic catastrophe of the Depression does not affect Cosey because the money that his father, Dark Cosey, left him is not invested in the stock market and remains unaffected by the plunge in its value; however, ironically, the taint of Dark's money is ultimately the source of the failure of the resort.

Bill Cosey never forgives his father for what he perceives is a betrayal of the black community. Daniel Robert Cosey's work as a police informant makes him a traitor in his son's eyes, but rather than wrestling with his father's choices and coming to some resolution of the conflict, as is suggested by the basic premises of the Beloved Community, Bill Cosey embraces the conflict with his father and proceeds to define himself in opposition to his father well after his father's death. In so doing, Bill Cosey determines that he will do and be everything of which his father would not have approved.

In making this choice, Bill Cosey does not deal with his father, the oppressor in the situation, with compassion and forgiveness, as mandated as a prerequisite to the formation of a Beloved Community. Rather, Bill Cosey makes the choice to live the rest of his life as a revenge narrative in a vain attempt to right the wrongs of his father—where

Dark is prudish and reserved, Cosey is bold and brazen. Because of these choices, the Cosey Hotel and Resort cannot become a community defined by love and equality.

The question of equality is a particular block to the formation of the community Cosey wants to create. The Beloved Community is grounded in a subversion of individual needs and desires to the demands and requirements of the larger group. Because Bill Cosey chooses to retaliate against his father rather than forgive him, all of his subsequent actions are necessarily individualistic and self-serving and, as such, ultimately self-destructive. Bill Cosey is elitist and, in the establishment of his hotel, is exclusive and exclusionary.

From the beginning, the hotel caters to and allows the admission only of middle- and upper-class African Americans. With this inequality, Bill Cosey replicates the economic hierarchies of the oppressive dominant culture. Without economic justice, the formation of Beloved Community and the realization of Bill Cosey's dream is not possible. Bill Cosey's exclusivity infects the dream he has of creating a haven. Cosey's Hotel and Resort ends up replicating the hierarchies of the dominant culture and is brought to its inevitable end by its reliance on a belief in its own superiority. What Cosey's attempted replication of the Beloved Community lacks is dedication to the employment of love and forgiveness as primary tools for conflict resolution.

L, Love

If the character L's name is in fact love, then the centrality of her role in the novel and in the question of whether the creation of a Beloved Community is possible becomes more apparent. L reveals that her name actually is love when she says that her, "name is the subject of FIRST CORINTHIANS, Chapter 13" (199). Comprehension of the dynamics of the failure of Cosey's dream can be found in that most famous biblical passage on love, First Corinthians, Chapter 13, and his relationship to the character L. The Beloved Community is dependent upon agape love, love that is forgiving, self-effacing, and generous, the kind of love that is defined in Corinthians. Similarly, the success and health of the Cosey Hotel and Resort is

dependent upon the presence of L. The character L seems perfectly described by the writings on love in Corinthians. "Love does not delight in evil but rejoices with the truth. It always protects, always trusts, always hopes, always perseveres" (13: 6–7). L plays a central role in the novel as its truth teller. L knows what actually has happened and her perspective corrects the misperceptions and erroneous judgments made by the novel's other characters.

L is the central force and voice in the novel *Love* in her role as the core sustaining presence in the Cosey Hotel. Love is the cook at the Cosey Hotel. She is at the heart of the hotel's success in its heyday. Not only does she prepare the sustenance that the guests consume and return to the resort for year after year, but she helps to bring about reconciliation when there is conflict in the hotel's community.

In the beginning of the resort's life, L is attracted to the potential she sees for love to thrive. When L is a child, she sees Bill Cosey and his first wife, Julia, touching each other in what she perceives is a profoundly loving way. "She lifted an arm, touched his shoulder. He turned her to his chest and carried her ashore. I believed then it was the sunlight that brought those tears to my eyes—not the sight of all that tenderness coming out of the sea. Nine years later, when I heard he was looking for house help, I ran all the way to his door" (63). L, love, is attracted to and enters the world of the Cosey Resort and Hotel because of the genuine love, if immature and romantic, that Cosey has for his first wife. L begins her work in the community of the hotel caring for the sick Julia and for the couple's much-loved son, Billy Boy.

Despite L's presence, the world that Cosey attempts to create with his hotel lacks sustainable love in part because of its roots in Dark's betrayal of the community of Silk. When Julia learns about the source of her husband's money, Dark's many years of collusion as a police informant providing information to incriminate blacks, she falls ill and her marriage to Bill Cosey suffers as a result. After the loss of love in the relationship, all else dies including Julia and, later, Billy Boy. "Where there are prophecies, they will cease; where there are tongues, they will be stilled; where there is knowledge, it will pass away" (13: 8). Julia's inability to tolerate her knowledge of the source of Bill Cosey's inheritance contributes to her demise and to the destruction of Cosey's Beloved Community.

Cosey then turns to another woman, Celestial, a prostitute, to love. Cosey's refusal to acknowledge publicly the woman he loves leads to the devaluing of that love and to the demise of the hotel and the potential of the Beloved Community. Celestial is a vague character in *Love,* known through the observations of others who see her as beautiful, magnetic, powerful, brave, and self-reliant. Bill Cosey betrays Celestial and his love for her by refusing to acknowledge their relationship publicly. L believes that Cosey makes the choice to love Celestial as a result of his life-long determination to defy and to undo the legacy of his father. In fact, had Cosey married Celestial, he would have been in harmony with the precepts of the Beloved Community and of agape love—acceptance, inclusion, and equality. Although Cosey spends his whole life trying to defy his father's legacy, with his choices—his refusal to marry Celestial, the woman he loves, and to bring her into the hotel—Cosey reinforces his father's betrayal and sense of hierarchy and dooms his Beloved Community to failure. Just as Cosey's first wife destroys the love the couple shares with her inability to reconcile herself to her husband's history, Cosey himself does not acknowledge the woman he loves because of her familial inheritance, her work as a prostitute.

The destruction of the resort, like the destruction of Cosey himself occurs because of this failure of heart. Cosey dies when L poisons him with the herb foxglove. The leaves of the foxglove plant contain digitalis, which, when consumed in substantial quantities, causes heart failure. Cosey dies of a broken heart. L poisons him when she learns that in his will he leaves the resort and all of his money to Celestial. This act is not only a thoughtless discarding of Cosey's relationships with his family—his second wife, daughter-in-law, and granddaughter—it is also a betrayal of the relationship with Celestial since, although he leaves the resort to Celestial, he does not acknowledge their love while he is alive. He has to die, from a broken heart, if you will, in order for her to be accepted

as his beloved. Cosey's death at the hands of love demonstrates the admonition in First Corinthians, "If I speak in the tongues of men and of angels, but have not love, I am only a resounding gong or a clanging cymbal. If I have the gift of prophecy and can fathom all mysteries and all knowledge, and if I have a faith that can move mountains, but have not love, I am nothing. If I give all I possess to the poor and surrender my body to the flames, but have not love, I gain nothing." Cosey's action is too much, too late and love, L, kills him and protects the Cosey women, disallowing Bill Cosey's intended inheritance to Celestial and the chance for Cosey's to become an inclusive loving community.

Even before his death, Cosey acts in ways that will ensure the destruction of the hotel. Rather than marrying Celestial, Cosey chooses to marry his granddaughter's 11-year-old friend, Heed-the-Night Johnson. This decision is purely selfish and lustful. Cosey seeks a love interest that he can control, mold into the kind of woman he wants her to be. This act can be understood as another way of Cosey trying to defy his father, but again First Corinthians provides an instructive answer to explain his behavior. "When I was a child, I talked like a child, I thought like a child, I reasoned like a child. When I became a man, I put childish ways behind me" (13: 11). Cosey acts childishly, exploiting the Johnson family by essentially purchasing his bride Heed, molesting the child and robbing her of her innocence, and separating Heed and Christine from each other and from their pure and passionate first love of each other. After he realizes that Heed will never be the woman he wants and that the couple will not have children together, Cosey stops telling Heed that he loves her and engages in sexual liaisons with other women. The signal that love is gone from the couple's peculiar marriage occurs when Cosey forbids Heed, as the lady of the house, from cooking in the kitchen with L. This separation from L leaves Heed essentially orphaned and particularly unloved.

After Cosey marries Heed and destroys her relationship with Christine and permanently poisons May against the child, he ruins any chance for success that his hotel may have had. Rather than operating out of love, Cosey sets up contention in his house and family. From that point on, Christine and Heed act in direct opposition to the description of love in Corinthians. "Love is patient, love is kind. It does not envy, it does not boast, it is not proud. It is not rude, it is not self-seeking, it is not easily angered, it keeps no record of wrongs" (13: 4–6). Christine and Heed spend years of their lives abusing each other and holding on to the bitterness of their perceived wrongs.

Christine has an opportunity to purge herself of the legacy bestowed upon her and Heed when she leaves Silk and, after some time away, becomes involved with the activism of the Civil Rights movement. While involved with the movement and with a man named Fruit, she begins to see the possibilities of life undefined by the memory of what she perceives are the wrongs done to her by Heed. She believes that the community that she joins is more legitimate than the one she grew up in. Unfortunately, she simply exchanges her focus on Bill Cosey, shared by all the women in Cosey's hotel, for adoration of and obedience to Fruit. Christine recognizes the failure of the relationship and of the group when a female member is raped and the male member who raped the girl is not held accountable. After entering into another destructive relationship with a man named Dr. Rio, Christine returns home to nurse her mother and to resume her fight with Heed.

Another woman, Junior, who, as a result of her life history has little experience with love, enters the life of the two rivals and quite unintentionally enables the two to have an authentic reunion and to allow for the reemergence of love as the foundation for their relationship in the way that it was when they were girls. Heed lures Junior into her plans to forge a new menu will in order that she can possess the remains of Cosey's Beloved Community. Junior, who confuses sex for love, visits the Cosey Hotel and Resort with Romen for sexual adventures, and eventually agrees to take Heed back to the hotel and to the attic to look for the menus Heed believes May might have hidden in the attic. During the excursion, Christine discovers the women in the attic. When Junior pulls a rug out from under Heed causing her to fall through the floor, Christine remembers the profound love that

she had for her childhood friend that was destroyed by the lust and self-absorbed inconsideration of Bill Cosey.

After the women are abandoned in the ruins of the hotel by Junior, they discuss the "record of wrongs" they have kept on each other and embrace each other with compassion, in their last hours together resuming the loving partnership they once shared. The presence of love, L, is suggested by the sudden and pervasive smell of baking cinnamon rolls that surrounds the women. The smell recalls the sweet, if temporary, extinction of hostilities between Heed and Christine that L enacts when she throws a sack of sugar on Christine's bed after Heed sets it on fire. L's intervention is tangible and palpable.

What the women revive is the sense of fellowship and recognition that occurs when two individuals love each other unselfishly. The love the women recall and renew is spoken of in First Corinthians: "Now we see but a poor reflection as in a mirror; then we shall see face to face. Now I know in part; then I shall know fully, even as I am fully known" (13: 12). The fall that Heed makes through the floor of the attic of the hotel has the opposite effect of the fall from innocence that the girls experience when Bill Cosey molests and then marries Heed and Christine witnesses her grandfather masturbating. They return to the language they created as children, idagay, and reclaim themselves in the loving eyes of each other.

The innocent embrace and acceptance of Christine and Heed's relationship is similar to that shared by Junior in her loving friendship with Peter Paul Fortas, another relationship that is destroyed by the intervention of misguided adults. With the renewal of their love, Christine and Heed form their own Beloved Community and each can say that she "know[s] fully, even as [she is] fully known" (13: 12). Although Heed dies during the night, the women are able to continue their relationship. Confirmation of their transformation occurs when Christine returns to their home, One Monarch, and does not react to the delinquent and negligent Junior with wrath. Instead the women decide to treat her with the compassionate, understanding love that they never received when they were her age. Additionally, they lock her in L, love's old rooms. Heed and Christine, in spite of Heed's death, will engage with each other with agape love, a love that eluded Bill Cosey and whose absence or departure is at the core of the failure of his resort, his Beloved Community.

Love is a complex examination of the centrality of love to individual, relational, and communal well-being. Bill Cosey's inability to transcend the impact of the loveless relationship his father, Dark, has with him and with the black community, dooms to failure all of his efforts to redeem his family's legacy and to become a positive and accepted member of the community. L's love is central to Bill Cosey's enterprise. When she leaves, when love is no longer at the center of the energy of the place, nothing remains but a hopeful, faithful, but empty shell.

SOME IMPORTANT THEMES AND SYMBOLS IN *LOVE*

The Power and Purity of First Love
At the end of the novel, L speaks of the power of pure love, the love between children who have not learned to process and categorize the world in terms of difference. This open acceptance allows for a powerful and formative love that has profound impact on the development of identity and upon all future relationships. Such relationships allow the children in them to place an adoring and affirming mirror before their eyes. If the relationships are allowed to flourish, the children may develop a sense of well-being, grounded in the confidence of being seen and understood. If this first pure love is interrupted, the children may be traumatized and may come to understand the world as an emotionally unsafe, isolating place.

Before the interference of Bill Cosey and May, Heed and Christine have a relationship that helps both of them to heal each other's pain, to stimulate each other's imagination, and to affirm for each of them a fundamental faith in the world. After Cosey's introduction of sexuality to the girls, in the form of his molestation of Heed and Christine's observation of his masturbation, the girls' relationship becomes bitter and vicious. Both women spend the better part of their lives trying to soothe the pain that the end of their friendship caused by

trying to hurt the other. Their reconciliation at the novel's end reinforces and resurrects the power of the original relationship.

Junior and Peter Paul Fortas have a similar experience when they are children. The two lonely and perceptive children find joy in sharing their genuine interests with each other. They feel heard and seen by each other and are therefore validated. This first love is pure and sincere and the children's acceptance of each other is affirmed by their presents to each other. Peter Paul Fortas gives Junior a box of crayons and Junior gives him a snake. The children are delighted with the presents and the way that the gifts support what they have learned about themselves in the eyes of the adoring other. Like Heed and Christine, this relationship is disrupted by the misguided interference of adults. The loss of her relationship with Peter Paul Fortas has a long-term impact upon Junior and her adult choices. Her maimed foot is a tangible and permanent reminder of her loss.

Sexuality and Violence
The novel begins with L's thoughts about the state of women's lives. She reports that contemporary women are shameless and lack self-respect because of the traumas they have experienced that have made them tough rather than brave. Throughout the novel, sexuality is linked with violence.

Perhaps most graphically, the gang rape of Pretty-Faye highlights the novel's linking of sexuality and violence. Pretty-Faye apparently was attending a party with friends when she becomes the victim of a gang rape. Just before participating in the rape of the girl, Romen unties the girl's hands and carries her to her friends. This act earns him the disgust and anger of his peers, who beat him up and exclude him from their group. Romen does not understand his actions himself. He is uncertain about what causes him to rescue the girl. Something in his character refuses to allow him to participate in this violent coming-of-age rite and he is able to show compassion, a kind of humane love for the victim of this rape rather than enacting violence.

The question of the connection between rape and violence occurs again when Romen becomes sexually involved with Junior. When he and Junior have sex he learns that Junior likes violent sex and derives pleasure from having someone inflict pain. Romen is troubled by these experiences and particularly by the knowledge that there is a part of him that enjoys inflicting the pain, although he is not comfortable with his feelings.

Junior has had to defend herself against violently imposed sex. While she is at a correctional institution, an administrator tries to force her to perform oral sex. She retaliates by pushing the man off of the balcony. Junior learns from this experience that she will not be believed or defended when she tells the truth about her sexual victimization.

Heed is too young to define Bill Cosey's molestation of her as a violent act. Rather than defending herself, Heed believes that she has done something wrong. For the rest of her life she is ashamed of the feelings that Bill Cosey's molestation induce. Her perceptions of her sexuality are distorted as a result of this early violence.

The Personal Costs of Racism

Throughout *Love*, there are many characters whose lives are distorted by the impact of racism on their personal development and choices. The individual in the novel perhaps most affected by the impacts of racism is May. May is terrified of what she perceives as the vulnerability of African Americans. She believes that African Americans imperil themselves by making demands for equality and she is always arming herself and preparing for the attack against her and her family that she always believes is coming. As a result of her fear of racist violence, May loses the ability to live fully and to experience her life. She is alienated and ignored, insulted by those who come into contact with her and she is out of touch with reality.

Hands

As with many of Morrison's works, hands are a central symbol in the novel *Love*. In *Love* hands take on many different significances and are an important representation of the connections and disconnections human beings have with each other. Romen's hands are bruised as he washes them in preparation for dinner. Although she does not mention this fact to her grandson, the bruises disturb Vida and make her worry that Romen is involved in destructive

behavior. In fact Romen's knuckles become bruised when he defends himself against the attack of the boys who raped Pretty-Faye.

When Romen tries to understand his actions, his rescue of the girl, what occurs to him is the memory of her hands. Somehow, the sight of Pretty-Faye's hands restores her humanity to Romen. She is no longer merely a sexual object to be consumed. Romen's identification with Pretty-Faye's hands reminds him that she is a person and motivates his rescue.

As a young bride, Heed is burned on the hand as she scolds L while she is cooking. Heed's negative interactions with L cause her pain. As Heed ages, her hands become more and more useless as she is stricken with a debilitating degenerative condition. As a result of this condition, Heed cannot care for herself. Her impaired hands emphasize her relative helplessness and powerlessness. This infirmity begins when Heed conflicts with love, L.

On her fingers, Christine wears multiple wedding rings that were won by her grandfather in a card game. When Cosey dies, Christine wants to place the rings on her grandfather's hands as he lies in his coffin, but is prevented from doing so by Heed. Christine wears the rings as a vengeful act until, after Heed's fall through the attic floor, she takes off the rings and uses them as jacks. The rings regain their worth as a sign of the value of the innocent love shared by the girls during their childhood.

One of the mythologies Bill Cosey maintains about his son Billy Boy is his elaborated story of the boy's rescue of a young girl on the beach in front of Cosey's Hotel and Resort. According to Cosey, a young girl, while fishing, gets a homemade hook stuck in her face. The brave and compassionate Billy Boy deftly uses his hands to remove the hook from the girl and brings her into the hotel for care. Bill Cosey tells this story about his son as evidence of Billy Boy's moral character and generosity.

Perhaps most graphically, during Bill Cosey's funeral, Christine, knife in hand, goes after Heed. Christine is still so angry at her lost friend that she seems to threaten to use her hands to kill Heed. This act is prevented only because of L's intervention between the women.

CHARACTERS

Administrator, the The Administrator is the counselor at Correctional who attempts to molest Junior during her exit interview. Having reached maturity, Junior is about to be released from Correctional when her plans are changed due to the misdeeds of the Administrator. Described as nearly 30 years old and as wearing a too-wide red tie, the Administrator acts inappropriately toward Junior during the interview, touching her and, eventually, exposing himself for her to perform oral sex. Rather than succumb to his advances, Junior tosses the man over his balcony. The other officials at Correctional believe the Administrator's version of the story rather than Junior's and, as a result of his lies, they send Junior to prison rather than releasing her as scheduled.

Anna Krieg Anna Krieg is a young woman in her early twenties who befriends Christine while she is married to Ernie Holder. They meet each other while both are living on an army base in Germany and are married to young soldiers. Thinking back on her encounters with the woman, Christine assigns Anna Krieg a level of preparedness for unexpected situations that Christine envies and cannot seem to achieve. She recalls that Anna Krieg seems always prepared for contingencies while Christine feels often caught unawares. The women's bond is grounded in cooking and the commonalities that derive from the experience of living overseas and being married to men in the military. Anna Krieg's readiness is exemplified by her possession of hiking boots.

Christine remembers going on a hike with the woman. Christine, exhausted, cannot keep up and returns to her home earlier than expected. When she arrives at her home on the base, she discovers that her husband is having an affair. Ernie Holder is making love with the wife of a staff sergeant when Christine walks into the house.

Bill Cosey (Mr. William Cosey, Bill, Papa) Bill Cosey is at the center of the novel *Love*. He is the son of Daniel Robert Cosey, also known as Dark to the African-American community. Bill Cosey's relationship with his father is, perhaps, a root cause of the man's inability to function with or relate to other people throughout his life. Although superficially successful and amiable, Bill Cosey is at heart a selfish and unhappy man. The women in his life orbit him as if he is the sun and, although he instigates and demands their affection and attention, he does not live up to the responsibilities that kind of love requires.

Early in his life, Bill Cosey, devastated by the discovery of his father's occupation as an informant to the police about the activities of his own community, attempts to construct his own life in opposition to that of his father. Bill Cosey uses the considerable inheritance left to him by his father to build and support Cosey's Hotel and Resort. Bill Cosey tries to establish a place that will serve as a refuge for the African-American middle and upper classes against the psychological ravages of racism. He also is interested in creating a space that is under his control and where he is the sole person in command. The resort is, at first, very successful and makes Bill Cosey a respected and envied man in his community.

Bill Cosey cannot resolve his hatred of his father and that venomous infection affects each of his adult relationships. Bill Cosey's first wife, Julia loves him and gives birth to Cosey's only son, Billy Boy. Although Bill Cosey loves her, he is not faithful to his wife, Julia.

Julia falls ill after learning about the source of her husband's family money. She cannot reconcile herself to the betrayal of black people that the acquisition of the Cosey money required. Julia dies when Billy Boy is 12. Billy Boy is the light of his father's eyes. Bill Cosey takes the boy with him wherever he goes. Bill Cosey tells people of Billy Boy's exploits and accomplishments, frequently embellishing the truth when doing so.

After marrying a woman named May and, with her, having a daughter named Christine, Billy Boy dies unexpectedly at 22. His death is a life-changing devastation to Bill Cosey. Following the death of his son and wife, Bill Cosey seems to veer out of orbit and back into his obsessive attempt to be unlike his father.

Bill Cosey's inability to move beyond his self-construction as something other than his father leads him to engage in self-destructive behavior. Bill Cosey molests and then marries the 11-year-old best friend of his granddaughter Christine, leaving both his granddaughter, and his child bride, Heed-the-Night Johnson Cosey, bereft and emotionally infirm for life.

Bill Cosey is no more faithful to Heed than he was to Julia. The love of his life seems to be a prostitute named Celestial. When he writes out his will, Bill Cosey leaves everything except a fishing boat to Celestial. Bill Cosey goes on fishing trips with the white men who control the community, the black men who can afford to frequent his establishment, Celestial and her friends, and a young man named Sandler Gibbons, whom Bill Cosey befriends as a kind of replacement son. These fishing trips represent Bill Cosey's ultimately unsuccessful attempt to control the forces that threaten the stability of his hotel—his world.

The Cosey Hotel and Resort is located in Up Beach, an African-American beach community. Successful, Bill Cosey moves his family to Silk from Up Beach. Bill Cosey builds a house for his family with the original address of One Monarch Street. The house Cosey builds is said by Sandler Gibbons to be the size of a prison or a church. The Coseys are the first African Americans to locate in the all-white community of Silk, yet Bill Cosey is able to get them in there without trouble because of his ability to provide payoff money to the white leadership of the town, particularly to Police Chief Buddy Silk.

When Chief Buddy Silk dies, his son Boss Silk is not as willing to maintain the arrangement struck between his father and Bill Cosey. Boss Silk begins demanding more and more money from the man at a time when, because of the changes in segregation prohibitions, the resort begins to suffer from financial difficulties.

When L discovers that Bill Cosey will leave his whole fortune and all of his possessions, except for his fishing boat, to Celestial, she takes matters into her own hands. L thinks that Cosey goes too far when he plans in death to disregard the women in his life who depend on him—Heed, May, and Christine—and to acknowledge, finally, the love of his life, Celestial. In order to protect the women and to keep the hotel Cosey created from destruc-

tion, L fatally poisons Cosey with foxglove and destroys his will. L rewrites Cosey's will in the margins of a menu from 1958.

Although it remains open for a while after his death, Cosey blames the cannery smell for the decline of his resort. L, the cook at the resort and the novel's narrator, says that the resort failed for other reasons. Bill Cosey's portrait, which hangs over Heed's bed, reveals a handsome man who exudes a self-assurance and whose motto in life was "His pleasure was in pleasing." The question remains, pleasing whom?

Billy Boy Billy Boy is Bill Cosey's son. The boy is Bill Cosey's only son and is conceived with Cosey's first wife, Julia. Julia dies when Billy Boy is 12 years old. After the death of his mother, Billy Boy lives to please his father. He is around 22 when he dies unexpectedly from walking pneumonia in 1935. Billy Boy is the pride of his father's life and his death is devastating to the senior Cosey. When Billy Boy dies, Cosey buys the barbershop chair in which the two used to get their hair cut, sits in it and thinks about his dead son.

Billy Boy was married to May and is Christine's father. Billy Boy has gray eyes that he passes on to his daughter, Christine. The fact that Christine has her father's eyes, makes the girl's grandfather, Bill Cosey, wary of growing close to the girl. Billy Boy worked as a waiter and then, at May's insistence, as bartender and musician negotiator in the Cosey Hotel and Resort.

Bonita Bonita is a woman Bill Cosey calls to while he and Sandler are fishing. Presumably, Bonita is one of the many relatively anonymous women with whom Cosey has affairs.

Boss Silk Boss Silk is Chief Buddy Silk's son. When May tries to take up arms to defend herself, Boss Silk refuses to let her purchase a gun. According to the narrator, Boss Silk is very different from his father, Chief Buddy Silk, especially in terms of his dealings with the Coseys. Bill Cosey gives Chief Buddy Silk payoff money in exchange for the autonomous, hassle-free operation of Cosey's Resort and Hotel. Although exploitative, the relationship Bill

Cosey strikes with Chief Buddy Silk is not designed to destroy Bill Cosey, but to control the man. When his father dies, Boss Silk charges Bill Cosey exorbitant fees and lends Cosey money so that the fate of the hotel rests in Boss Silk's hands. The additional fees come at a time when the hotel is in decline and in dire economic straits to the extent that, when Cosey dies, the fate of the resort is in question. After Cosey's death, Heed turns the tables on Boss Silk by threatening to expose incriminating pictures of him and his father taken aboard Bill Cosey's boat. Through blackmailing Boss Silk, Heed temporarily gains control of the situation, although the resort is ultimately destined to close.

Bride Johnson   Bride Johnson is one of Heed's sisters. The Johnson girls have a reputation, warranted or not, of acting inappropriately sexually. The people in the community of Up Beach and Silk look down on the family and feel that all of the members of the family are less than desirable associates. Heed suffers throughout her marriage to Bill Cosey from the effects of her family's reputation.

Buddy Silk (Chief Silk)   Buddy Silk is the sheriff of Silk who is frequently invited to go fishing with Bill Cosey when Cosey is alive. Heed tells Junior that Chief Silk was Bill Cosey's best friend. According to the 1958 menu will, attributed to Bill Cosey but actually written by L, the man leaves Montenegro Coronas to Chief Silk.

Christine describes Chief Buddy Silk as gentle and respectful when he carries out his official duties. Chief Buddy Silk is the policeman who returns Christine to the Cosey Hotel following her attempt to run away after Bill Cosey's marriage to her best friend, Heed.

In actuality, the relationship between Bill Cosey and Chief Buddy Silk results from the complexities of racial negotiations and interactions between blacks and whites in the 1930s in the United States. In order to run his establishment and to have a liquor license, Bill Cosey has to nurture a relationship with the town's white authorities that will enable him to operate without interference. Chief Buddy Silk extorts money from Cosey in exchange for providing the man with a measure of autonomy

and security. Cosey also attempts to foster goodwill between himself, the sheriff, and other authorities in Silk by planning and managing parties on board his fishing boat that become lewd and deceptively friendly escapes.

Celestial   L says that Junior Viviane reminds her of Celestial. L speculates that the double "CC" engraved on the Cosey silverware might represent the initials of Bill Cosey's mistress, Celestial, if he had ever married the woman. Instead, Celestial is unable even to come to the hotel because of Bill Cosey's refusal to acknowledge his relationship with her publicly because of her status as a prostitute.

By all accounts, Celestial is overwhelmingly attractive even though she has a scar that embellishes her neck from ear to ear. Celestial comes from a family of prostitutes and Cosey seems to love her and needs to have her in his life until his death although he refuses to embrace her outside the secrecy that is the initial context for their affair. Bill Cosey is looking lovingly at Celestial in the portrait of him that used to hang in the hotel and now hangs in Heed's bedroom. Celestial leaves town after World War II.

Celestial is probably the love of Bill Cosey's life and accompanies him on some of his fishing trips with various town leaders. May tells Heed and Christine to stay away from Celestial and tells them that there is nothing that she will not do. After seeing Celestial as they play on the beach, Heed and Christine use the phrase "Hey, Celestial" to signify a bold act. They also name their playhouse, an abandoned rowboat, the Celestial Palace.

Toward the end of the novel, L reports seeing dead Celestial at Bill Cosey's grave. The woman appears dressed in red and the scar on her neck seems to have disappeared. Celestial sits on Cosey's tombstone and sings songs to him full of yearning and desire. Sometimes L joins her with a hum.

Chief Silk   See BUDDY SILK

Christine Cosey   Christine Cosey is the daughter of May and Billy Boy Cosey and the only grandchild of Bill Cosey. After Billy Boy's death when Christine is a very young girl, L takes over the responsibility for raising Christine from May, who is, at best, a disinterested mother. Christine never recovers from her feeling of abandonment when her father dies and later when her former best friend, Heed, through marriage, becomes her grandmother.

When Christine is 11, Bill Cosey molests her same-aged friend, Heed. Christine is five months older than Heed and has gray eyes that she inherits from her father Billy Boy. It is the similarity between her and her father's eyes that may explain Bill Cosey's emotional distance from the girl. Before the event that destroys their childhood friendship, Heed and Christine, as lonely children, form an intense relationship that is grounded in a pure love and need for each other. Rather than repenting from his sexual behavior toward Heed, Bill Cosey decides to marry the girl. Heed, formerly Christine's best friend, becomes the girl's grandmother. Additionally, on the same day that Bill Cosey molests Heed, Christine, unbeknownst to Bill Cosey, finds her grandfather masturbating in her bedroom. Witnessing Bill Cosey in this way traumatizes the child and literally makes her vomit. As an adult, Christine suffers from high blood pressure and low self-esteem as a consequence of this trauma and as a result of her grandfather's marriage to Heed, events that rob her prematurely of her girlhood and of her best friend. Christine and her mother May never get over Bill Cosey's marriage to Heed when Heed is 11 and Christine is 12.

Bill Cosey's marriage to Heed is the catalyst for Christine's attempt to run away from home when she is just a little girl. She is returned to the hotel by Chief Buddy Silk, Bill Cosey's supposed best friend. When she returns, her mother slaps her across the face. The slap is devastating to Christine and the girl hides for two days under L's bed after the event. After a brief time Christine is sent away to boarding school at a place called Maple Valley School. Christine does not fit in at the school and her experience there contributes to her overall sense of alienation and abandonment. Christine's mother, May, and her particularly peculiar and public expressions of racial outrage, are a real source of embarrassment for Christine while she is at Maple Valley School.

Understandably, Christine is unable to overcome the psychological impact of these events and takes out her anger and frustration on Heed rather than on her grandfather. Heed also bears some animosity toward Christine. Heed does not understand why Christine is angry with her and becomes hurt and resentful. When Christine is 16, she returns to home from school to celebrate her 16th birthday and her graduation from Maple Valley. After an argument between Heed and Christine, Bill Cosey spanks Heed in front of May and Christine. May and Christine delight in Heed's public humiliation and are pleased when, later that evening, Heed does not accompany them to the dance held in Christine's honor at the hotel. Heed, in an attempt to exact revenge on Christine, sets fire to Christine's bed. L puts out the mattress fire with a sack of sugar. After this event, Bill Cosey tries to send Christine, who has done nothing, away again. Infuriated, Christine enacts her revenge by refusing, for many years, to return to Silk.

In 1971, after an absence of 23 years, Christine returns to Silk for Bill Cosey's funeral. Christine steals diamond rings that Bill Cosey won in a poker game. After Heed does not allow Christine to put the rings on Cosey's fingers, Christine wears her grandfather's diamond rings. During the funeral, Christine, in fury and frustration, pulls out a knife to stab Heed. Heed and Christine fight until L intervenes.

While she is away from Silk, Christine has several relationships with different men. For a brief while, she is married to a military man named Ernie Holder. Christine travels with the man to his military assignment on a base in Germany. One day, while Christine is in Germany with her husband, she returns home unexpectedly early and finds Ernie Holder in bed with another woman. Christine leaves him immediately and returns to the States.

Upon her return to the United States, her lukewarm conversations with her mother persuade her not to return to Silk. She takes a job as a waitress and eventually becomes a cook. After having a series of affairs with married men, Christine meets a man called Fruit, with whom she has a relationship for nine years. Fruit is a nationalist activist and Christine becomes involved in the Civil Rights movement. The relationship between Christine and Fruit ends when the differences between the two become apparent to them both. The two part company amicably.

Later, Christine becomes a mistress to a physician named Dr. Rio. When she meets Dr. Rio, Christine believes that she is about to have the relationship for which she has yearned her entire life. After being discarded by the man when he tires of her, Christine returns home destitute. While Christine is away from Silk, she is arrested five times for different reasons; the final arrest is for destroying Dr. Rio's car. Christine believes that her relationship with the abusive and disregarding Dr. Rio stems from her unresolved and ambivalent feelings for her grandfather.

When Christine returns, she has with her only a Wal-Mart bag rather than the white Samsonite luggage she took with her when, previously, she departed from Silk. Christine returns to Silk without her luggage and broken in spirit. Christine comes back to care for May, her aging mother, and to claim the only meaningful possession she feels remains for her, her grandfather Bill Cosey's estate. Much to L's surprise, Heed, who remains in Silk and in the house on Monarch Street following Cosey's death, lets Christine return to the house and to take up residence there with her, although the two live as bitter and venomous enemies, united only in their hatred for one another. Christine becomes a good cook while away from Silk. Ironically, after May's death, she spends time cooking only for Heed who does not eat.

Christine and Heed hire Romen Gibbons to help them do the chores neither of them can manage. Later, Heed also hires Junior. She has a plan to ensure that Christine does not inherit any of Bill Cosey's fortune, even if Heed should die. Heed plans to use Junior to write another will for Bill Cosey that is more recent than the 1958 menu will and that definitively states that Bill Cosey left everything to his wife.

Christine is suspicious when Heed hires Junior and accelerates her own plans to outwit Heed. Christine has hired a lawyer, Gwendolyn East, to make the legal case that Christine, as Bill Cosey's only surviving blood relative, is the legitimate heir to his estate. Christine's plans backfire when she grows angry with Gwendolyn East and fires her outright.

One evening, Christine is livid when she discovers that Heed and Junior have left the house with-

out telling her where they are going. She follows them, guessing correctly that they have gone out to the hotel. When Christine arrives, she confronts the women in the attic. Seeing Christine, Heed tries to attack her with a pen and, when Junior pulls the carpet from under Heed's feet, Heed falls through the rotting wood of the attic and injures herself severely.

Christine's rage toward Heed dissipates entirely as she sees the injuries of her old friend. Christine runs to Heed's side and tries to help ease her pain. Junior drives off, leaving the women alone to reconcile nearly 40 years of hatred and misunderstanding. Through the night, the women talk and clarify that the problems they experienced were the result of May and Bill Cosey's meddling in their lives. The women rediscover the original love that they have for each other. Heed dies during the night.

Just before morning, Romen Gibbons drives out to the hotel and recovers the women and drives them to town. Even though Heed is dead, she and Christine seem able to communicate. They discuss what should be done with Junior and seem to decide that she deserves the compassion and intervention that they did not receive.

Daniel Robert Cosey (Danny Boy, Dark) Daniel Cosey is Bill Cosey's father and is miserly and greedy. When he dies, he leaves his family $114,000 from money that he earns as a police informant, providing the police with information about the goings-on in the black community. His life choices and self-interestedness haunt his son who designs his own life and identity in opposition to his father.

Julia, Bill Cosey's wife, is especially affected by knowledge of Daniel Robert Cosey's occupation. When Julia learns about the way that Bill Cosey's father made his fortune, the information has a profound effect upon her relationship with her husband, and may even be implicated in the woman's eventual illness and death. Daniel Patrick Cosey dies on Christmas Day, an event his son does not mourn; rather, Bill Cosey felt his father's death was, ironically, a kind of present.

Dolly Gibbons Dolly Gibbons is born in 1962 to Vida and Sandler Gibbons. She is in the army and her husband, Plaquemains, is in the merchant marine. They are both living and working away from home because there is no work in Silk. Their son, Romen, stays with Dolly's parents while Dolly and her husband are away.

Dr. Kenny Rio   Dr. Kenny Rio is the physician, a general practitioner, who takes Christine as his mistress and then discards her without warning or explanation. Christine is devastated by his abandonment and, trying to hurt the man the way that he hurts her, destroys his Cadillac. For all of her efforts, Christine ends up arrested and later discovers that Dr. Rio never even sees the car after her vandalism.

When he and Christine meet at the beginning of their three-year affair, Dr. Rio is almost 20 years older than she is. Dr. Rio is married and has a series of affairs with various women with whom he has brief and superficial relationships. Because of his money, Dr. Rio is able to supply the women he chooses as his mistresses with an apartment, clothes, and trips. He makes a point of giving each of his women a present of the plant dracaena and a bottle of the perfume White Shoulders.

When he breaks up with the women, he has already replaced them with a new mistress. He reclaims his gifts and never speaks with the women again. Christine cannot accept Dr. Rio's rejection and ends up forcibly evicted from the apartment he has provided for her during their affair. Christine comes to believe that she was susceptible to her relationship with Dr. Rio because of the foundationally problematic relationship she has with her grandfather, Bill Cosey.

Dr. Ralph   According to the 1958 menu will, Bill Cosey gives his boat, *Julia II,* to Dr. Ralph. The will found on the menu was not written by Bill Cosey, but by L. L writes the menu will to replace Bill Cosey's actual will, the will that L destroys in order to ensure that Heed, May, and Christine are not left penniless when Bill Cosey dies.

Dumb Tommy   According to the 1958 menu will, Bill Cosey leaves his record collection to Dumb Tommy. The will found on the menu was not writ-ten by Bill Cosey, but by L. L writes the menu will to replace Bill Cosey's actual will, the will that L destroys in order to ensure that Heed, May, and Christine are not left penniless when Bill Cosey dies.

Ernie Holder   Ernie Holder is Christine's only husband. She is married to the man for a brief period of time. Ernie Holder and Christine meet when he comes to Manila's boarding house in search of a prostitute and finds Christine there. Christine appears fresh and beautiful to Ernie and he is taken with the girl's appearance.

After their first date, the two decide to marry. The two of them do not know each other well and their relationship is doomed to fail. Christine marries Ernie Holder when she is 17. Ernie is irresponsible and gets the couple arrested at an illegally operated social club.

Following her private first class husband to an army base in Germany, Christine, for a while, enjoys her life as a military wife, making new friends and learning how to cook. After returning early from a hike, Christine finds her husband in bed with another woman and leaves him immediately. Christine returns to the United States while her husband remains overseas. After the end of her marriage, and perhaps because of the way that the marriage to Ernie ends, Christine has affairs with married men.

Ethan Payne Jr.   Ethan Payne Jr. is probably Junior Viviane's father. Ethan Payne Jr. has a relationship with Vivian, Junior's mother. The man may call his daughter Junior because she is the only one of Vivian's five children who is also his biological child.

Ethan Payne Jr. returns to his parent's house shortly after Junior's birth. Junior longs to meet him and fantasizes about her father's imagined return. Vivian, Junior's mother, tells the child that Ethan Payne Jr. may have joined the army. Junior's hunger for her father sets her up for her eventual imagined relationship with Bill Cosey. When speaking to Heed about her father, Junior tells her that the man died in Vietnam.

Freddie   Freddie is one of the boys who rapes Pretty-Faye. Unlike the other boys, Freddie is still willing to talk to Romen after the rape. The week following the incident, he brings Romen the leather jacket that he left in the bedroom where the rape took place; however, Freddie participates with the other boys when, three days after the rape, they all beat Romen up.

Fruit Fruit is the man with whom Christine has her longest and most successful relationship. Fruit is eight years younger than Christine and sleeps with other women while they are together. Christine rationalizes his behavior and comes to believe that fidelity is not necessarily desirable or possible.

Fruit is very neat in his appearance, liking crisply ironed shirts. The couple is known to their friends as Fruit and Chris. Fruit and Christine are together for nine years. Christine distributes the pamphlets he creates and makes his cause and convictions her own. Fruit helps Christine to understand her family narrative through his perspectives, which, although simplistic, seem to provide Christine with objectivity and context for a time.

The couple become activists and Christine transforms into a person who feels valued. Christine has her seventh abortion when she is with Fruit and imagines that she sees the child's profile in her shed blood. The couple's relationship begins to crumble when Fruit refuses to expel a fellow male worker from the organization he leads when Fruit learns that the man is responsible for the rape of a 17-year-old volunteer. Fruit believes that the man's contributions to the organization outweigh the seriousness and impact of his crime. In the wake of Fruit's obvious devaluation of women, Christine loses much of the self-esteem she has acquired while with Fruit. After nine years, the two end their relationship as friends.

Good Man, the Good Man is an entity who is born from Junior's dream life. Before she comes to One Monarch Street, the Good Man is a night and daydream persona who encourages and accompanies Junior. The Good Man is a protector, who looks a bit like G.I. Joe. When Junior imagines that Good Man is present, she feels safe and not quite as lonely as she does ordinarily.

When Junior arrives and moves into the Cosey house, and sees the portrait of Bill Cosey that hangs over Heed's bed, Junior comes to think of Bill Cosey as her Good Man. Junior feels that she senses the Good Man's presence at times throughout the house. She consults with him and feels that he watches over her. Just before Junior goes out to the hotel with Heed, she believes that Good Man leaves. Junior hopes for his return and despairs in his absence.

Gwendolyn East Gwendolyn East is the attorney Christine hires to take Bill Cosey's ambiguous 1958 menu will back to court. Christine wants to challenge the judge's original finding that "the sweet Cosey child" to whom the house is designated refers to Heed. Gwendolyn East is the daughter of an Up Beach cannery worker and encourages Christine to believe that her claim on her grandfather's estate has legal merit. The relationship between the two women ends badly when Christine loses patience with the woman, fires her, and then curses her out.

Heed-the-Night Johnson Cosey Heed-the-Night Johnson Cosey is Bill Cosey's second wife. In *Love's* present tense, Heed lives with Christine in Bill Cosey's house at One Monarch Street. Heed lives in the house fulfilling the role of bereaved widow and engaged in her long-term battle with Christine and false memories about the past. She has a picture of Bill Cosey hung over her bed.

At the beginning of the novel, Heed appears to Junior to be about 60 years old. Heed's hair is turning silver at the roots and one of the tasks she wants Junior to perform is to dye her hair and to help her get in and out of the tub. Heed is a small woman with gray eyes who likes to wear high heels. Heed has unnaturally acute hearing. Her hands are deformed and are increasingly dysfunctional. It is not clear what is wrong with Heed's hands. They seem to begin their decline following an accident where cooking oil splatters on them from L's stove. Heed's hands are also arthritic. She needs help to take care of herself and it is partly for this reason that she hires Junior.

Heed comes from a large family of five brothers and three sisters. The Johnson family has a bad reputation in the town of Silk. The family is not only impoverished, but also people suggest that the girls in the family are inappropriately and prematurely sexual. This rumor contributes to the lack of sympathy Heed receives when her parents allow Bill Cosey to marry the girl at the age of 11 in exchange for a small sum of money. Bill Cosey's interest in Heed emerges from her friendship with his granddaughter, Christine.

One day when Heed and Christine are playing, Bill Cosey intercepts the girl while she is alone. He touches her inappropriately, which begins his obsession with Heed and his desire to marry the girl. After he marries Heed, Bill Cosey teaches her how to run the hotel and, especially, how to take care of him.

Bill Cosey does not allow Heed's family to attend their wedding and tries to ensure that the girl severs contact with the Johnsons. Eventually, Heed is alienated from her family and comes to rely on Bill Cosey exclusively. Despite his possessiveness of Heed, Bill Cosey is not faithful to his second wife and does not respect her. One evening when celebrating Christine's 16th birthday party, Bill Cosey spanks his wife in front of Christine and May, much to their delight. Later the two women go with Bill Cosey to the hotel for a dance in Christine's honor. While they are away, Heed sets Christine's bed on fire. Heed then goes to the dance and tries to get revenge on her husband by dancing with another man.

Only once is Heed unfaithful to her husband. In 1958, a man, Knox Sinclair, visits the hotel to retrieve the body of his dead brother who has drowned in front of the hotel. Heed confronts the man and feels a bond with him as a result of having lost her own brothers in a drowning accident. In Knox Sinclair's arms, Heed finds the only genuine desire she will ever experience. She believes the man when he makes plans with her to run away and start a new life together, but when Knox returns home to Indiana, he never contacts Heed again. Heed is distraught until she learns that she is pregnant from the affair. Heed's only pregnancy ends in miscarriage. Heed falls into an 11-month period of denial when she believes that she is pregnant and refuses to accept that both the baby and the man are gone forever. Eventually, a conversa-

tion and slap from L return Heed to reality. She believes that the baby she lost was a boy and that, if the child had lived, her life would have had a very different outcome. She believes the child would have grown up to take care of her in her old age.

Cosey's sudden death, apparently without a formal will, fuels the feud between Heed and Christine. Heed takes care of May when she finally succumbs to madness and debilitation. Christine returns to Silk partly out of desperation and partly to take care of her mother. The two argue over Cosey's intentions and spend their time in the Cosey mansion fighting with each other. Heed conceives of the plan to fake a will written by Cosey. She hires Junior to enact this fraud.

When Heed and Junior travel out to the hotel to find a menu with a date on it that is later than the 1958 menu will, Heed falls through the rotting attic floor as Junior trips her to prevent Heed from attacking Christine with a pen. Junior, thinking only of herself, flees the scene, leaving the mortally wounded Heed to reflect with Christine about the past. The two exchange their views about what happened between them and come to the conclusion that they should have been angry not with each other but with the source of their conflict, Bill Cosey, the man they have spent their lives trying to love.

During the night at the hotel, Heed dies. Romen comes, just before morning, to rescue the women. He places Heed's body in the back of the car and later takes her to the mortuary. Despite her demise, Heed and Christine seem to continue the conversation they begin at the hotel. The two agree to try to help Junior in a way that no one helped them when they were girls.

Joy Johnson   Joy Johnson is one of Heed's brothers. The boy dies with his brother, Welcome Morning Johnson, when the boys are swimming in front of Cosey's Hotel and Resort. Bill Cosey pays for Joy and Welcome Morning's funeral.

Julia   Julia was Bill Cosey's first wife and the mother of his only child, Billy Boy. L fondly remembers witnessing Julia in Bill Cosey's arms as he carried his wife from the sea. The sight brings tears to the then five-year-old L's eyes. The scene between Julia and Bill Cosey comes to epitomize love for L. Although Bill Cosey loves Julia, he is not faithful to her and has affairs with many women, most significantly with the woman he seems to need most in his life, Celestial, the prostitute.

Julia is horrified by the knowledge that her husband's money comes from Daniel Cosey's betrayal of the black community through his work as a police informant. This knowledge about the source of her husband's money destroys their marriage and her health. Julia was haunted by the fear that her son would be like his grandfather. Julia dies as a young woman. Her son, Billy Boy, is only 12 when she dies.

Junior Viviane (Junior Smith, June)   Junior Viviane is a runaway whose arrival in Silk begins the novel. When she arrives in Silk, Junior is 18. She is hired by Heed after answering an ad Heed places in the newspaper for a companion. Junior lives with the Cosey women at One Monarch Street after Heed hires her, ostensibly, to help her write a book about her family. The real reason that Heed hires the girl is to help her to create a fake will to ensure that Christine will not inherit the Cosey house or fortune even after Heed's death.

Junior dresses in clothing that is more revealing than protective. Junior arrives in the midst of an unprecedented cold spell and snow storm. The girl, with her exposed body and wild hair, attracts the attention of many men including Sandler Gibbons and his grandson, Romen. Junior has hair that people notice because of its size and volume. She is said to look sweet and in need of care.

Junior comes from a community of people labeled "rurals." This group is an ungoverned, uneducated group of people marginalized by their poverty. Their children go to school at a government facility known as the Settlement. The community has its origins in the group of whites and blacks unable to move away after the closing of a jute factory that provided the community's only source of employment.

Junior was named by her mother Vivian's boyfriend, Ethan Payne Jr. The man may have called the girl Junior because he was not the father of any of Vivian's four older sons. Ethan Payne Jr.

leaves Vivian shortly after Junior's birth and, as a result, Junior spends a great deal of time longing for her father as she grows up. Until she is asked by a teacher at school, Junior never uses her last name and, as such, does not know what it is. She makes up a last name, Vivian, her mother's name. Later she adds the letter "e" to the end of her invented last name because she thinks that it makes the name more sophisticated.

Unlike many in her family and most in her community of origin, Junior is a good student and the girl enjoys attending school. Her sole friend in school is Peter Paul Fortas. Junior and Peter Paul Fortas enjoy each other's company and share a genuine and uncommon intellectual curiosity. They also share the experience of exclusion and alienation from their peers. When the two exchange Christmas presents—crayons for her, a snake for him—she gets in trouble at school and at home and runs away from the Settlement. Her uncles find her and run over her foot in their pickup truck. As a result, Junior's foot is left lame. She successfully and permanently runs away at 11.

Knox Sinclair   Knox Sinclair is a man who travels to Cosey's Resort after his brother drowns in a swimming accident at the hotel. Knox, who travels to the hotel from his home in Indiana, has an affair with Heed during the six days that he is at the Cosey Resort and Hotel. During the week Knox lives at the hotel, the two talk of going away together.

Naively, Heed believes that Knox's words are sincere and waits eagerly for him to call her after his return to Indiana. Not hearing from him after his departure, Heed calls Knox's house. Every time Heed calls Knox's house, his mother answers the phone and, after seven calls, the woman asks Heed not to call again.

Subsequently, Heed discovers that she is pregnant and, after a short time, suffers a miscarriage. Despite the miscarriage, Heed refuses to believe that she is not pregnant with Knox's child until, 11 months after the event, L slaps her in order to help the girl to face reality.

L   L is the narrator of *Love* who resigns herself to humming when she feels that her words have become futile. Ironically, she speaks frequently throughout the text and provides information about the novel's various characters and their interrelationships. L is obsessed with the questions that revolve around the meanings and expressions of love and ruminates on what she feels has been a denigration of the expression of love, particularly of women's expression of love, in the contemporary age. When L is a little girl of five years old, she sees Bill Cosey with his first wife, Julia, loving each other in the sea. L seems to be enamored with the image and depiction of love that she sees the couple expressing.

When L is 14, she becomes the cook at Cosey's Hotel and Resort and it is her cooking, in part, that makes the resort's reputation. Part of L's function at the hotel is to help to keep thing going, to maintain the peace. The biggest conflict in the Cosey family is between Christine and Heed, a conflict instigated by Bill Cosey and fanned by May. The women literally fight on many occasions. Most famously, L stops the fight between Christine and Heed at Bill Cosey's funeral. She quits the hotel the day of the funeral and moves into her mother's old beach shack. L causes Bill Cosey's death. When L discovers, by reading Bill Cosey's will, that the man plans to leave his family destitute and leave all of his worldly possessions and fortunes to his prostitute mistress, Celestial, L determines that Bill Cosey's wishes will never come to fruition. L poisons Bill Cosey by putting foxglove in the man's water at lunch. She also destroys his will and replaces it with notes on a menu dated 1958. The menu will is authenticated legally in spite of its ambiguity.

L was born late and in the middle of a storm and says that she moved from the water in her mother's womb to the water of the rain. After leaving Cosey's Hotel and working for a while as a washerwoman, she becomes the cook at Maceo's Café Ria where she reigns as a cook. L says that she is forgotten and says that no one wonders anymore what her name means—what the missing letters are. L's dialogues provide strong evidence that her name is love. L dies while cooking at Maceo's, but continues to haunt Silk. She particularly frequents Bill Cosey's grave where, occasionally, she joins in humming with Celestial's sad songs to Bill Cosey.

Lucas Breen Lucas Breen is a white boy who is said to be good at playing basketball and admired for his playing skills by the black boys with whom Romen plays ball.

Maceo Maceo is the owner of Café Ria, a small dining establishment in Silk where young people gather to discuss their love lives, but also, and more importantly, to eat the food that L cooks. The restaurant is located on Gladiator Street across from the Lamb of God Church. When L first takes the job cooking at Maceo's, her feet swell so much that she quits. In order to get her to come back to work, Maceo says he will pick L up for work and take her home each day and sets up a chair so that she can sit down and cook. L dies while cooking at Maceo's.

Like many men in Silk, Maceo finds Junior attractive and flirts with her whenever she comes into the café. Maceo has a wife and sons. One of his sons is Theo. Theo is one of the boys responsible for raping Pretty-Faye.

Manila Manila is named after her father's war exploits and runs a boarding house where women who need a space turn to go when they are abandoned. Some of the women who reside there are prostitutes, but the house is not a whore house. When Christine becomes destitute, Manila helps her to return to Silk.

May Cosey May is the youngest daughter of an itinerant preacher. She grows up in poverty and adds a loving and inclusive touch to the Cosey Hotel. May's life is controlled by fear and she tries, with all of her hoarding, to stave off, or at least prepare for, the barrenness of death. May's fearfulness begins in part with the death of her husband, Billy Boy, and is nurtured by her horror at Bill Cosey's marriage to Christine's playmate Heed when the girl is only 11 years old. May is married to Billy Boy, Bill Cosey's son, and becomes Bill Cosey's daughter-in-law and the mother of his grandchild, Christine. Bill Cosey disparages May by saying that she should have married his despised father, Daniel Robert Cosey, instead of his beloved son, Billy Boy.

Many people believe that May is mentally ill. She blames the Civil Rights movement—specifically, according to L, freedom—for the failure of Cosey's hotel. May is a kleptomaniac who steals perpetually from Bill Cosey and from the hotel. She steals items and objects that she feels will be useful in case of the emergency she believes is coming. She feels that the crisis will be brought about by African Americans demanding their rights.

May wears an army hat at all times and is paranoid that Civil Rights protesters are going to attack the Cosey resort. People begin to avoid her and she resorts to silence. She takes items and hides them in various places. The narrator states that May's problem is clarity—that her understanding of reality and the danger of living send her into an overt expression of defensiveness. Before May loses her ability to deal with the conflicting nature of reality she is, surprisingly, an effective and efficient caretaker of the hotel. According to the 1958 menu will written by L, Bill Cosey leaves the hotel to May, calling her Billy Boy's wife.

May dies on a beautiful morning with a smile on her face. She spends her final years in the care of her bitter enemy, Heed, until her daughter Christine's return. May is not as happy with Christine's return as might be expected. The two women, however, bond in the end over their hatred of Heed. After her reconciliation with Heed, Christine states that May was not a very effective or affectionate mother and that she cared more for Bill Cosey than Christine. May is a major catalyst of the conflict between Christine and Heed.

Meal Daddy According to the 1958 menu will written by L, Bill Cosey leaves his stickpins to Meal Daddy. There is some controversy about who the man is. Heed contends that Meal Daddy is the lead singer of a group called the Purple Tones. May disagrees with Heed saying that Meal Daddy is the imprisoned manager of the Fifth Street Strutters. Both women wonder whether a man in prison can inherit anything. Neither woman knows that the menu they argue over is a forgery.

Otis Rick Otis Rick is a Settlement resident, a Rural whose reputation remains a marker of the character of the Settlement community at large. At one point in his young life, young Otis Rick is said

to have had a fight with a child on the playground at school and, in the process of fighting the child, Rick is so vicious that, during the fight, he displaces the other child's eye from its socket. Following this event, Otis Rick is expelled from school. Teachers send notice of his expulsion home in a note, yet the boy continues to return to school. His return may signal that his parents do not know how to read. The principal pays a visit to the Rick home in order to ensure that the parents actually got the school's message. Little is known about the visit except for the fact that the principal is so anxious to depart the premises that he leaves the house on foot rather than in his car, which later is towed back to town.

Patty's Burgers After Romen rescues Pretty-Faye, the boys who rape her beat him up outside Patty's Burgers and then he throws up behind the restaurant.

Peter Paul Fortas (Pee Pee) Peter Paul Fortas is Junior Viviane's only school friend, perhaps her only childhood friend. The boy is the son of the manager of the bottling plant. Peter Paul and Junior become fast friends and explore with youthful enthusiasm the world they inhabit and that they mutually imagine. As bright children, the two have much in common. Their friendship is innocent and fast.

Peter Paul Fortas, like Junior, is a bit of an outcast at school and is teased with the nickname Pee Pee. Unlike the other children at District Ten School, Peter Paul does not care about Junior's home and her identity as a Rural. He simply enjoys her company.

One Christmas, the young boy gives Junior a box of crayons as a present. She gives him a baby cottonmouth snake that gets her into trouble at home. Inexplicably, Junior's uncles object to her present to Peter Paul Fortas. They demand that the girl get the snake back from the boy. Junior refuses. As a result of Junior's family's response to the gift exchange, Junior is hurt by her uncles and does not return to school, thus ending the friendship that had blossomed between her and Peter Paul.

Plaquemains Plaquemains is Romen's father and Dolly's husband. He has attended two years of college and is considered, by her parents, to be an appropriate match for Dolly. Both Vida and Sandler feel that Plaquemains is the best choice that Dolly can make among her peers. Like Dolly, Plaquemains joins the military because he cannot find appropriate work in Silk. He is away in the service and, for that reason, Vida and Sandler have his son, Romen, in their care.

Police-heads   The Police-heads are a group of mysterious fishlike creatures that the novel's narrator, L, describes during her monologue at the beginning of *Love*. These creatures appear when women and children commit acts that are described as shameful. The narrator knows about them from her mother's stories, but also hears of them appearing during the 1940s and 1950s when Cosey's resort is in its prime. At the end of the novel, L implies that the Police-heads may simply be another name for police officials who cause trouble. She says that Heed stands up to a Police-head, Boss Silk, when she turns the tables on the man. After his father dies, Boss Silk tries to exploit Cosey by demanding higher and higher fees from the man. When Cosey dies, Heed temporarily puts Boss Silk into check by blackmailing him with pictures from Bill Cosey's fishing trips.

Pretty-Faye (Faye, Faith)   Pretty-Faye is a woman who is gang-raped by a group of six boys Romen knows. Rather than raping her, Romen rescues the girl and carries her outside. Her friends follow them and then take Pretty-Faye home. Romen is moved by the sight of her hands tied up and helpless. She disappears from the novel after the rape.

Princess Starlight Johnson   Princess Starlight Johnson is one of Heed's sisters.

Righteous Spirit Johnson   Righteous Spirit Johnson is one of Heed's sisters. The girl and their other sister, Solitude, are the only two members of Heed's family allowed to witness, at a distance, Heed's marriage to Bill Cosey.

Romen Gibbon   Romen is Sandler and Vida Gibbons's grandson. The boy is 14 years old at the beginning of the novel. Vida and Sandler help raise the boy when their daughter and son-in-law join the military in the wake of the closing of the cannery at Up Beach. He has been living with Vida and Sandler for a month at the beginning of the novel. Romen also works doing yardwork and in that capacity he does occasional maintenance work for Heed and Christine Cosey. He is a virgin before he meets Junior. The first definitive act of his young life is the rescue of Pretty-Faye from rape. In the immediate wake of his rescue of Faye, Romen's social life deteriorates. He is ostracized and physically tormented by some of the boys at his school.

Sandler Gibbons   Sandler is the reliable and dependable husband of Vida and the grandfather of Romen. He does not stray far from his self-proscribed margins of propriety. Sandler Gibbons is the first person to encounter Junior upon her arrival in Silk. When he meets the girl, he is surprised, disturbed, and aroused by her appearance. At the novel's beginning, he is preoccupied with concern about his grandson's well-being. He is worried that the boy will get himself into trouble. He is a retired supervisor, works now as a security guard, and was one of Bill Cosey's best friends. Sandler believes that Cosey died of natural causes.

Sandler tells Bill Cosey that he misses his father. Sandler's father moves north to live with his daughter, Sandler's sister, after the death of Sandler's mother. The absence of his father may foster his willingness to spend time with Bill Cosey when the two develop a fishing partnership.

Solitude Johnson   Solitude Johnson is one of Heed's sisters. The girl, and their other sister, Righteous Spirit, are the only two members of Heed's family allowed to witness, at a distance, Heed's marriage to Bill Cosey.

Smart   Smart is one of the boys who rapes Pretty-Faye and beats Romen up three days after the boy refuses to participate in the rape and carries Pretty-Faye outside where her friends take her home. Smart and the other boys continue to harass Romen until Romen gets involved with Junior and no longer cares what the boys think.

Surrey Johnson   Surrey Johnson is Heed's mother. She and her husband Wilbur willingly give their daughter to Bill Cosey to marry when she is only 11. Once their sons, Welcome Morning and Joy, drown in front of Cosey's Hotel, the couple manipulates and exploits the situation to solicit sympathy and money from their neighbors.

Terry   Terry is a woman who befriends Junior and helps her out when she is living on the streets after her release from Correctional.

Theo   Theo is one of the boys who rapes Pretty-Faye and beats Romen up three days after the boy refuses to participate in the rape and carries Pretty-Faye outside where her friends take her home. Theo sneers at Romen whenever he sees him after the incident. Theo calls Romen the worst word in the world. After his rescue of Pretty-Faye, Theo and the rest of the boys excommunicate Romen from their company. Theo works at his father Maceo's café.

Uncles, the   The Uncles are Junior's mother's brothers who torment Junior. They are miscreant teenagers who delight in causing trouble. When Junior gives her only friend, Peter Paul Fortas, a baby cottonmouth snake as a Christmas present, the uncles, for no reason other than to cause trouble, demand that she get the snake back from the boy and bring it home. When she refuses, the uncles chase her through the woods. When they catch up with her, they run over her foot with their pickup truck. The accident leaves her foot permanently maimed.

Vida Gibbons   Vida Gibbons is the wife of Sandler Gibbons and the grandmother of Romen. Romen lives with Sandler and Vida while his parents are away serving in the military. She worries about the boy and his involvements as well as his relationship with her husband and his grandfather, Sandler. Vida works outside the home as a hospital aide and also has primary responsibility for the domestic tasks in her home even though her husband, a retired security guard, is at home all day. Vida used to work for Cosey at Cosey's Hotel and Resort.

Vida works for Bill Cosey at the first job for which she needs to wear panty hose and a good dress. Vida worked as a receptionist at Cosey's hotel and felt that her job there was the most satisfying job she had. While working at Cosey's. Vida Gibbons calms a visitor, who happens to be the lady friend of a well-known musician, who thinks L's steak tastes like conch. L says she is hurt by the visitor's comment. Vida believes correctly that Bill Cosey was murdered, poisoned.

Vivian   Vivian is Junior Viviane's mother. The woman misses naming her child because, when she sleeps for nearly three days following the birth of her daughter, Ethan Payne Jr. begins calling her Junior, perhaps because Vivian's four older sons are not his. Vivian tells her daughter that the girl's father, Ethan Payne Jr., may have joined the army when the girl asks longingly about his whereabouts.

When the uncles, her brothers, chase after Junior on Christmas morning, in their futile attempt to get Junior to return the snake, Vivian calls after them to leave the girl alone. She does not run after the girl though.

Vosh   Vosh is an old man, a Rural, who is said to wander the valley naked, holding his genitals and singing hymns. Junior's uncles threaten to give the girl to him if she does not retrieve the snake she gave Peter Paul for a Christmas present.

Welcome Morning Johnson   Welcome Morning Johnson is one of Heed's brothers. The boy and his brother, Joy, die when swimming in front of Cosey's Hotel and Resort. Bill Cosey pays for Welcome Morning and Joy's funeral.

Wilber Johnson   Wilber Johnson is Heed's father. He and his wife Surry willingly give their daughter to Bill Cosey to marry when she is only 11. Once their sons, Welcome Morning and Joy, drown in front of Cosey's Hotel, the couple manipulate and exploit the situation to solicit sympathy and money from their neighbors.

FURTHER READING

Asim, Jabari. "Toni Morrison Composes a *Love Supreme*," *Crisis (The New)* 110 (November/December 2003): 44.

Birne, Eleanor. "Drip Feed," *London Review of Books* 26 (August 19, 2004): 23.

Campbell, James. "Dark and Light in the Territory," *Texas Literary Studies.* 5250 (November 14, 2003): 21–22.

Davis, Thulani. "Not Beloved," *Nation* 20 (December 15, 2003): 30–32.

Grossman, Lev. "Love and the Laureate," *Time* 162 (November 3, 2003): 75.

Hengen, Nicholas. *"Love," Virginia Quarterly Review* 80 (Spring 2004): 259.

Houser, Gordon. *"Love," Christian Century* 25 (December 13, 2003): 48–49.

Kakutani, Michiko. "Family Secrets, Feuding Women," *New York Times* 153 (November 31, 2003): E37–E46.

Kang, Nancy. "To Love and Be Loved," *Callaloo* 26, no. 3 (Summer 2003): 836–355.

Mantel, Hilary. "Ghost Writer," *New Statesman* 132 (December 8, 2003): 50–51.

McDowell, Deborah E. "Philosophy of the Heart," *Women's Review of Books* 21 (December 2003).

Miller, Laura. "The Last Resort," *New York Times Book Review* 153 (November 2, 2003): 10.

Minzeheimer, Bob. "Morrison's 'Love' Is What it's All About," *USA Today*, September 30, 2003.

Pinkney, Darryl. "Hate," *New York Review of Books* 50 (December 4, 2003): 18–21.

Roynon, Tessa. *"Love," European Journal of American Culture* 23 (2004): 236–238.

Smith, Candace. *"Love," Booklist* 12 (February 15, 2004): 1,081.

Smith, Stuart E. *Love, Library Journal* 128 (December 15, 2003): 99.

Paradise (1998)

Paradise is the final work of Morrison's trilogy on the question of love in its myriad forms and the way that love is abused and/or fulfilled. The state and status of love relationships determines not only the course of individual and familial interactions, but can affect and charter the direction and health of whole communities.

Paradise tells the story of lost women who find themselves at the edge of an all-black town called Ruby. The members of the town, as descendants of historical outcasts, might find common connections with the women who find themselves living in the Convent just beyond Ruby's limits. Instead, the town leaders, enmeshed in fear of change and of the world outside of Ruby, see the women as threatening. They are so shaken by the women's presence and potential influence that they attempt to kill them rather than grapple with the realities of inevitable change.

SYNOPSIS

Ruby

Morrison's novel *Paradise* begins with the murder of a white woman whose identity is not revealed. In fact, the mystery of the woman's specific identity is never clearly resolved throughout the novel, except for the information that the murdered woman lived with four other women in the Convent—a former embezzler's home, then former school. Nine men from the town of Ruby stalk the four women who have taken up residence inside the Convent walls. As the men enter the Convent, it is cold even though it is an early July day in 1976.

The men divide up to search for the four women. In the kitchen, one man finds a pot boiling on the stove. He reflects that the reason the men have come to the Convent is to protect their town, Ruby. Ruby is the second of two towns founded by Ruby's leading families. The original town, Haven, was established by the Old Fathers in 1889 and, after Haven falls on hard times and fails, the town's leaders relocate and form the town of Ruby. The men hunting in the Convent want to ensure that the mistakes of Haven are not repeated in Ruby. Seeing a pitcher of milk on the kitchen table, the man drinks half of it before noticing that it contains the herb WINTERGREEN.

Two other men walk the upper floor of the Convent. They encounter two names on doors, SEN-ECA and Divine. Entering into these rooms and the corresponding bathrooms does not reveal the women. The men searching the rooms expect to find their worst imaginings of what women can be, women unlike the women they have known their whole lives who they consider to be virtuous and wholesome.

Although the Convent predates Ruby, the men who invade the place believe that the survival of Ruby matters above all else. When inexplicable and strange events start to happen in Ruby—the birth of four special needs children in one family, too many cases of sexual diseases, and general misbehavior—the men blame everything on the women living at the Convent and decide that the women must be destroyed in any way possible. The men searching in the basement of the Convent have no more success in finding the women than do their companions.

The two men examining the basement are identical twins and know the story of the founding of Haven and Ruby by heart: Leaving Mississippi, a group of 158 freedmen find no town on their journey that will welcome them. As they search for a home, they are rejected repeatedly, most painfully by other black people. One of the first acts of the Old Fathers, the original patriarchs of the community, is to build a community cooking and gathering spot called the Oven. They also chisel a phrase on the Oven that is supposed to help to inspire and redeem the people.

When Haven begins to fail and people begin to leave, these twins along with a select group of the others who remain in the Haven decide to try to reestablish the vision of the Old Fathers in a new location. They break down the Oven and head Out There in hopes of getting a second chance. They settle in Oklahoma and form the town of Ruby in 1949. The town is named after the twins' sister, Ruby, who dies shortly after the group arrives in their new home in Oklahoma.

Outside of the Convent, the women are running. The men see them. The sun is beginning to rise as the men raise their guns and fire at the women. They believe that they are doing the only thing available to them to ensure the future of Ruby.

Mavis

The Mavis chapter begins in 1968 with Mavis Albright being interviewed by a journalist about the death of her twin babies, Merle and Perle, who died in her husband's treasured green Cadillac outside of a grocery store. Mavis was in the store when the twins died. The interview takes place as Mavis sits in her living room with her other children, Frankie, Billy James, and Sal. As Mavis speaks with the reporter, Sal pinches her mother's waist.

That night, Mavis escapes from the house and her abusive husband, Frank, and the children that cause her so much torment. Mavis fears that her children are trying to end her life. Mavis escapes to her mother's house and tells her mother, Birdie Goodroe, that she thinks her children are trying to kill her. Mavis leaves her mother's house within a week once she overhears her mother telling Frank to drive up and get her. Mavis heads for California.

As Mavis drives, she picks up other women who are hitchhiking so that she does not have to drive by herself. The last hitchhiker Mavis picks up is Bennie, who sings that whole time they are together. After Bennie leaves, stealing Mavis's raincoat and boots, Mavis is terrified at the isolation she experiences and starts to imagine that she sees Frank. Mavis pulls off the highway and runs out of gas. Walking along the same road, Mavis comes to Convent door.

At the Convent, Mavis meets Connie, whose full name is Consolata Sosa. Connie lives at the Convent with Mother, who used to be the Mother Superior of the Convent and is now ailing and bed-ridden. Mavis tells Connie that she is going to California. Instead, Mavis stays at the Convent and Connie puts her to work shelling pecans. Soane Morgan, one of the women of Ruby, arrives at the Convent to buy pecans. Soane takes Mavis to get some gas for her car and then a young boy drives Mavis out to her car. Mavis drives back to the Convent and ends up staying there almost continuously for two years.

When she returns to the Convent after getting gas for her car, Connie asks Mavis for help with the ailing Mother. Mother asks Mavis about her children. Although the house has no electricity, there is a mysterious light in Mother's room that seems to come from the woman herself. Mavis is one of the women present when the men arrive at the Convent with guns.

Grace

The chapter begins with the story of K.D. and Arnette. K.D. is the son of Ruby, the woman for whom the town is named and the nephew of Steward and Deacon Morgan. Arnette is the daughter of Arnold Fleetwood. The young people's fathers are meeting because Arnette is pregnant with K.D.'s child. On the way to the Fleetwood house, K.D. sees Gigi, who has just arrived in Ruby for the first time, and the young man does not ignore his attraction to her.

Jeff and Sweetie Fleetwood and their four children, all of whom have serious deformities and illnesses, also live in the house. The men all gather to discuss what will happen between K.D. and Arnette. Deek and Steward offer to pay the girl's way though college. The Fleetwoods agree.

Before she arrives at Ruby, Gigi has a boyfriend named Mikey. Mikey tells Gigi a story of a statue of a black couple making love that he heard was in a town called Wish, Arizona. Mikey is arrested and sends Gigi a message that she thinks asks her to meet him in the town of Wish on April 15. Gigi tries to find the town but cannot locate it. When she cannot find the town, she calls her grandfather and tells him that she is coming home.

On the bus trip to her grandfather's house, a stranger named Dice tells Gigi about Ruby, and she decides to go there instead. Once she gets to Ruby, she realizes that there is nothing there that she is looking for, and she starts walking down the road out of town. While she walks, Roger Best offers her a ride thinking she is headed down to the Convent. Gigi realizes that she is in a hearse when Roger stops at the Convent to pick up Mother's body. Gigi goes into the house and starts to eat some of the food people have brought to Connie since Mother died.

Gigi sees Connie and Connie asks her to stay so that Gigi can watch things while Connie sleeps. Connie says she has not slept in 17 days. Gigi stays as Roger drives off with Mother's body. Gigi walks around the Convent and discovers that it used to be an embezzler's mansion. The place is huge and filled with obscene embellishments that the nuns who eventually possess the house tried to erase. By the time Gigi returns to Connie's presence, Connie

wakes up and asks the girl her name. Gigi says that her given name is Grace. She decides to stay at the Convent. K.D., having heard that Gigi was staying there, drives out to the Convent and takes her for a ride.

Mavis, who has been gone for a month, returns to the Convent to find Gigi living there and Mother dead. When Mavis pulls up in the Cadillac, Gigi is outside sunning herself in the nude. Mavis resents Gigi's presence and wants her to leave. Their animosity is temporarily stilled by the arrival of another outcast woman who says she has been raped.

Seneca

The chapter begins with the story of the lives of Dovey and Steward Morgan. Dovey and her sister, Soane, marry the twin brothers—and New Fathers of Ruby—Deacon and Steward Morgan. The couples are, like the rest of the town, engaged in an argument about the meaning of the words the Old Fathers engraved on the Oven. Some people believe that the words say "Be the furrow of his brow," while others believe that the words are "Beware the furrow of his brow." The difference between the interpretations reflects a growing split in the town between active and passive strategies for survival.

Dovey has a mysterious, occasional visitor whose arrival was once precipitated by the sudden appearance of a huge flock of butterflies. The man says that he lives nearby and although Dovey knows everyone in Ruby, she does not know him. Dovey is checking on an empty house that she and Steward own, and the man asks if she minds if he walks through the yard. She says that it is fine if he wants to traverse the yard and, saying goodbye, the man leaves as quickly as he came.

Dovey sees the man fairly regularly and speaks with him about the things she considers insignificant and does not share with anyone else. Dovey has fixed up the backyard garden of the house and hopes that the man, whom she calls her Friend, will come by for a visit.

Steward is defined by the stories he has heard his whole life about the search for Haven made by the original Fathers. The difficulty of that quest and his belief that homelessness and rejection are always a real possibility keeps him rigidly adherent to the status quo and inflexible in his outlook. One of the stories tells of Steward's grandfather, Zechariah, called Big Papa, and how the group of ex-slaves was refused admission to a town outside Fairly, Oklahoma. Steward's grandfather, Big Papa, has a vision and hears footsteps; from that point on, the group follows the footsteps until they arrive at the place where they establish Haven.

Stuart's sister-in-law, Soane, married to his brother Deacon, also reflects on the past and the death of her sons, Scout and Easter. Although she loves her husband, Deacon, she sees that he, like his brother, makes his life more difficult though his inflexibility. She also worries about what she perceives as his lack of compassion.

Deacon indulges his vanity by driving his ostentatious car every day to make the less-than-a-mile trip to work. His love of his car may come from the memory of traveling with his father and brother in 1932 on a car trip. They visited many towns, but the one thing that remains in Deacon's memory is a well-off community and a group of beautiful women they saw there. In order to get the ladies' attention, the twins, Deacon and Steward, fall off of the railing on which they sit. The boys remember the beautiful ladies and their pastel dresses for the rest of their lives. When their sister, Ruby, dies upon their arrival in the new town, Deacon and Steward strike a deal with God about death. No one dies within the town of Ruby's limits. The twins believe that the death of their sister Ruby has paid the price for them all.

Watching Deacon as he circles the bank, Anna Flood is annoyed by the man's sense of ownership. She discusses this irritation with Richard Misner, one of the town's ministers, who urges her to be patient. She remembers asking Steward once what it felt like to be a twin, and he says to her that it makes him feel better than other people. Anna left Ruby for sometime and then returned. When she returns, two issues make her the subject of gossip: her relationship with Misner and her unstraightened hair. Anna runs the grocery store begun by her father, Ace.

One winter day, a white family pulls up in front of the town in their car. They ask for directions and if there is a doctor who can see their sick baby.

There is no doctor in town, but Anna offers the man and his wife coffee and volunteers to get them some aspirin from the drugstore. Several people in the store warn the couple about traveling farther since there is a blizzard coming, but the couple continues on their journey. On the same day, Deacon and Misner see Sweetie Fleetwood walking down the road. This is unusual because the woman is always in her house tending her four disabled children.

Sweetie does indeed walk down the road toward the Convent and is also seen by SENECA, who jumps out of the truck she is hitchhiking in to walk with her. Seneca identifies with the stricken look on Sweetie's face because she has had her own share of trauma. When Seneca is five years old, she is abandoned by the woman, Jean, who she thinks is her sister, but is actually her mother. Seneca believes that Jean has left because of Seneca's misbehavior, so the child tries to do everything her sister told her to so that she will come back. She finds a letter, written in lipstick, that she cannot read and carries it with her for the rest of her life.

Seneca saves Sweetie by turning her around and going back toward the Convent rather than continuing down the empty road in the cold. Sweetie believes that the women in the Convent are demons and fears and mistrusts all of the help that they give her. Sweetie has a fever and hallucinates throughout her time in the Convent. In the night Sweetie thinks she hears a baby cry, and the sound angers her because her own children do not cry. In the morning, her husband comes to find her. She tells him that the Convent women kidnapped her and made her stay with them.

SENECA stays with the Convent women and becomes the mediator between Gigi and Mavis. In addition to escaping her childhood abandonment, Seneca also runs away from her imprisoned and abusive boyfriend, Eddie. After making a promised visit to Eddie's mother, Seneca accepts a proposition from a rich woman, Norma Keene Fox, to be a concubine for three weeks. After that humiliation, Seneca travels around on the backs of trucks until she sees Sweetie walking away from town and jumps off to join her.

Divine

The Divine section of *Paradise* begins with a set of dueling sermons delivered by Ruby's two ministers, Pulliam and Misner, at the wedding of Arnette and K.D. Pulliam, in his sermon, presents an angry and wrathful God to the congregation, while Misner holds up the cross trying to emphasize what Christianity has to offer—the intersection between the human and the divine on equal terms in the person and sacrifice of Jesus. Billie Delia, Arnette's best friend, remembers during the wedding how much she used to enjoy riding horses and that, as a very small child, she unwittingly pulled down her panties before reaching up to be placed on the horse's back. This act labels her and alienates her from the town from the time she is a child. Billie Delia, although she is a virgin, is labeled as a wild girl. Billie Delia knows that the wedding is not a good idea because K.D. lacks the maturity and character to be a good partner to Arnette. In fact, Arnette comes out to the Convent on her wedding night looking for the baby she conceived with K.D. and gave birth to at the Convent.

As Soane Morgan sits in the pews, she dreads the wedding reception because she has made the mistake of inviting the women who live at the Convent to the wedding reception. The women arrive, inappropriately dressed by Ruby standards. The women play loud music and dance outside of Soane's house. Anna believes that the women, unintentionally, save the wedding by distracting everyone from the minister's conflict and from the real problems that the couple and the town face.

Misner berates himself for allowing Pulliam to anger him. He ponders what it is about this town that gets to him. He believes that the residents of Ruby have become reliant on the stories of their ancestors' bravery to the extent that they do not act courageously themselves. He arrives at the reception just as the Convent women are asked to leave. Gigi and Mavis fight each other all the way home from the reception.

There is a new woman with the Convent women, Pallas Truelove. Pallas, a privileged and neglected girl, runs away from home with Carlos, the maintenance man from her high school. Pallas and Carlos go to her mother, Dee Dee. Dee Dee is an artist and her given name is Divine.

Patricia

Patricia Best is working on a project to write the history of the families of Ruby. She figures that there are nine central families of Ruby—Blackhorse, Morgan, Poole, Fleetwood, Beauchamp, Cato, Flood, and two DuPres families. About 158 people made the original journey from Fairly, Oklahoma, to Haven. The group is defined by the rejection they experience at the hands of other blacks who find them too dark-skinned to join them. These nine families are called the 8-rock families after a deep level in the coal mines where rich coal comes from. These nine families form the core of both Haven and Ruby. Pat also discovers the source of her own alienation from the people of Ruby. Her mother, Delia, was a light-skinned black and, as such, threatened the homogeneity of the community. Finally, Pat believes that the secret pact that the Morgans make with God is that, if they do not mix 8-rock blood, no one in Ruby will die. Pat eventually abandons her quest for the exact history and burns her papers.

Consolata

After Mother dies, Consolata gives in to a kind of desperation that drives her to drink. At 54, she tires of her role as the leader of the outcast women. Consolata has her own painful history. She was originally brought to the United States by Mary Magna, known to Connie as Mother, when she was kidnapped from the streets of Brazil at nine years old. Mary Magna brings Consolata along with her to her new assignment teaching at a Native American girls' school. Consolata works as a servant in the school and devotes herself to Mary Magna and God.

When Connie is nearly 40, she has an affair with Deacon Morgan. The two fall completely in love and have an all-consuming relationship that exceeds their ability to control their actions. The affair comes to an end when Consolata, overcome with passion, bites Deacon. Her gesture frightens him, and he ends their encounter. Although Consolata is desolate, she recovers and resumes her former life.

Lone DuPres teaches Consolata that she has supernatural gifts. Consolata has the ability to bring people back from the dead. Connie uses her powers to restore Soane and Deacon's son, Scout, to life after he is fatally injured in an accident. Later, he is killed in Vietnam. Consolata also uses her powers to keep Mary Magna alive well after the time she would have died naturally. When she finally allows Mary Magna to die, Connie is left without a focus or purpose.

In the midst of her drunken decline, Consolata receives a visitation from an unknown stranger who looks like her and helps to restore her faith and sense of purpose. She tells the women that they can go elsewhere or do as she tells them. What she tells them is the way to embrace the cruel realities of their lives and to move on—to live. After their work with Connie, the women residing at the Convent are restored to their own possibilities.

Lone

Lone is the community midwife and the woman who teaches Consolata about her powers. Lone is less and less in demand as the people of Ruby begin to rely more and more on the medical establishment and on hospitals for delivery of their children. K.D. and Arnette, for example, do not go to Lone for delivery of their son.

Lone knows that the women of the Convent are in trouble and goes out to warn them that the men of Ruby are coming to kill them. She warns the other women of the town about what the men are planning, and they head out to the Convent. Lone's efforts are too late, and the men, lead by Deacon and Steward, shoot the women of the Convent. Deacon and Steward's wives, the sisters Soane and Dovey, are permanently estranged as a result of their different responses to their husbands' actions. Roger Best goes to the Convent to look for the women's bodies, and he finds no sign of them anywhere. The Cadillac, too, has disappeared.

Save-Marie

Sweetie and Jeff Fleetwood's youngest child, Save-Marie, dies, becoming the first person to die in Ruby since Ruby Morgan Smith's death. Anna Flood and Richard Misner are out of town when the Convent women are murdered, and, when they return, they try to piece the truth together from the myriad stories they are told. Deacon and Steward, like their wives, have different responses to what has hap-

pened. Deacon feels isolated and responsible and, after taking a barefoot walk through town, speaks to Misner about his guilt. Steward is defensive and feels justified in his actions. Anna and Richard go out to the Convent to try to discover what happened. Richard asks Anna to marry him. When they are in the garden of the Convent, they both see something. One sees a door. The other sees a window.

The Convent women are seen at the various locations and with the people that were the source of their pain. The women seem to forgive their transgressors and drive off in the green Cadillac. The final scene finds Consolata on a beach, strewn with debris, in the arms of a mother GODDESS, Piedade, awaiting the arrival of a ship.

CRITICAL COMMENTARY

Fundamentally, *Paradise* is an exploration of the impact of and desire for control of human behavior. Each of the central conflicts of the novel involves the issue of control and who wields it. One of the most contested issues in human interaction involves the question of what is right and what is wrong and who will create those definitions. All cultural institutions rely on one definition or another in order to address this most fundamental question. These definitions guide the creation of social order and, frequently, an idealized version of social order becomes a definition of paradise that is understood by the members of a community as a goal.

The novel, *Paradise*, challenges the traditional ideal of paradise as a centralized, conforming, ordered, and perfect space by placing the formation of such a place in a specific historical space and time. The mass exodus of African Americans from the South in the wake of the Civil War created a time in which African Americans could, hypothetically, have some control over their destiny. For some African Americans, this impulse led to the founding of ALL-BLACK TOWNS. This moment in history and this opportunity are the setting and motivation for the characters and communities in *Paradise*. There are many questions of control that form the core of the text. The question in the novel seems to split between the use of control that leads to creation and the abuse of control that brings about destruction.

The social order that creates a hierarchy based on the dominance of men is often referred to as patriarchy. The brutality of patriarchy manifests in Toni Morrison's *Paradise* as the men of Ruby invade the Convent and attempt to disrupt the restorative experiences of the women who have found solace—home—within its cool dark sanctuary. The men of Ruby who convene at the Convent door cannot abide the rejuvenation they sense within. The women's independence and autonomy seems dangerous and threatening to the men of Ruby since the women's authority does not come from them. Because the men cannot control the women's actions, the men of Ruby believe that the women must be destroyed.

Within the Convent, after her transformation following the visitation by the man in the cowboy hat, Consolata offers the women sanctuary and love. The discovery of pleasure brings salvation to the Convent women in *Paradise*. By understanding the community they have formed as a paradise, the Convent women create that paradise. Once they accept that there is no perfect place other than the one they can imagine and form, the women cease their wandering and begin to find peace where they are and, most importantly, with whom they are. The women's redemption emerges from the telling of their collective narratives, and by their communion with each other, generated by Connie's careful compassion. Connie's cooking represents her healing impulses. She wants to feed the women's bodies and psyches with literal and symbolic nutrients.

In her kitchen Connie prepares healthy and sensual food for the women, most particularly apples. The apples are an important symbol as they represent the knowledge forbidden to Adam and Eve in the garden of Eden. With her baked apples, Connie rewrites biblical narrative. Rather than prohibiting the acquisition of knowledge, Connie's nutritional gift of apples encourages the women of the Convent to know. What the women need to relearn is their own lives. Connie has the women trace their bodies on the cellar floor in tangible forms so that they can rewrite their own stories. Each of the women who arrive at the Convent has been brutalized and traumatized by her experiences in the world. Connie tries to teach the women to go back into their own pain so that they can honestly confront the fear and despair that the pain has created. By acknowledging the complete narrative of their experiences, the women are able to accept the realities of their lives honestly, without the impulse to control anything that is beyond their capacity.

The fluidity of sweet, warm apples both attracts and repels the men of Ruby who raid the convent. Their incompatible and competing desires are particularly evident in their actions as they enter the Convent. As the men invade the Convent, one of them, we are not told which one, stops and "lifts the pitcher of milk. He sniffs it first and then, the pistol in his right hand, he uses his left to raise the pitcher to his mouth, taking such long measured swallows the milk is half gone by the time he smells the wintergreen" (7). The destructive, phallic power of the gun must be set aside, albeit temporarily, in order to consume the sustenance, the women's milk.

Shortly before the men arrive to kill them, the women participate in a spontaneous ritual that celebrates the arrival of long-awaited rain as well as their newfound self awareness.

> There are great rivers in the world and on their banks and the edges of oceans children thrill to water. In places where rain is light, the thrill is almost erotic. But those sensations bow to the rapture of holy women dancing in hot sweet rain. They would have laughed, had enchantment not been so deep. (283)

The rain mirrors the balm of the women's narrative community, the balm that will allow the women to recover from injury, perhaps, as *Paradise*'s ending may suggest, even to transcend death. The women's wintergreen smell sends the hunter back to his task of envisioning the women as prey. He fails, however, to realize the irony of his consumption of sustenance, milk, which derives from the very source he seeks to destroy. With this action, the hunter becomes the archetype of patriarchy and illustrates its limitations, its hunger, and its self-destructiveness as a result of the desire to control women.

Another major conflict in *Paradise* is philosophical. The townspeople argue about whether the message on the oven built by the Old Fathers and carried to Ruby by the New Fathers reads "be the furrow of His brow" or "beware the furrow of his brow." Each message has a significantly different connotation and reverberates with the questions circulating in African-American communities following the CIVIL RIGHTS MOVEMENT of the 1960s.

"Beware the furrow of His brow" is a phrase associated in the novel with the traditions and histories of both Haven and Ruby. The exodus of the approximately 81 original freedmen from Mississippi and Louisiana is akin to the exodus of the Israelites from Egypt and seems rooted in the Old Testament depictions of God as an angry and vengeful deity who must be appeased. When this idea is adopted as the controlling social narrative, communities emerge in which the compliance of all members to a centrally held set of beliefs is critical.

When the group of wanderers tries to find a home in which they are able to exercise some control over their destinies, they believe that they are leaving behind violence, exclusion, and subordination. The group's status as second-class citizens comes from definitions of race that emerged with the evolution of slavery. As slavery became a formal, legalized institution in American life, the association between race and status or worth was an integral tool. As blackness became nearly equal to enslavement, African Americans lost their legal status and therefore their claim to basic human rights. After emancipation, in 1890 the group heads west, hoping to find a place where they can reclaim the humanity and equal status they have been denied, even after the end of slavery.

Three defining events occur for the group as they head west and become the narrative core of their future community in Haven and later in Ruby. When the patriarch of the group, Zechariah Morgan, is still living in the South, he is called Coffee. He and his identical brother, Tea, have a confrontation with white men who demand that the two black men dance or face physical harm. Tea dances as the men request, while Coffee refuses and is shot in the foot, and permanently injured. This event causes an irreparable rift between the brothers because Coffee judges his brother and refuses to forgive him for his choice. This story becomes

a centerpiece for the residents of Haven and Ruby and is fundamental to the establishment of their belief that there is only one way to approach and to ensure their survival. This singular thinking is similar to the dictatorial approach to control outlined in the Old Testament. In that text, there are laws and the laws must not be broken if one is to survive. Similarly, as a result of Coffee's (renamed Zechariah) story, the people of Haven and Ruby and their descendants internalize the idea that there is one way to deal with the potential devastation and violence of racism and that is to resist overtly. They become inflexible and unbending in their belief that there is only one way to be. The argument can be made that Tea made the wiser choice of the twins. Although he temporarily sacrifices his dignity, he does not permanently disable himself. The impact of Coffee's choice manifests itself during the journey when he, as the leader, has to be carried on a board at the end of the group and also when the group arrives at Fairly, Oklahoma, and Zechariah's inability to stand keeps him from joining the group to ask if the African-American residents of Fairly are willing to accept the group in its town.

The events in Fairly, Oklahoma, become the second defining event/story to determine the actions of the community. The encounter that comes to be known as the Disallowing is devastating to the group as it forces them to confront the reality that they are not only excluded and considered undesirable by whites but also that other African Americans threaten the group's search for control over their status. This exclusion by lighter-skinned blacks leads the group to the conclusion that no one outside of their community can be trusted. Ironically and defensively they adopt the same position as the residents of Fairly when they determine that no outsiders can be included in their community. The story of the Disallowing preserves for generations the idea that the residents of Ruby are somehow better than others. Rather than isolating the event and interpreting the Disallowing as the action of a group of misguided individuals, they come to believe that anyone who is not one of their own, who is not 8-rock pure, is dangerous and should not be allowed access to life in either the town of Haven or Ruby.

The third event/narrative is the story of the founding of Haven itself. Although the story of Big Papa and his conjuring of the walking man is presented in *Paradise* as if it is fact, the story is recreated from Steward's memory. There are many significances and possible interpretations of the tale, but the elements that are central to Steward foreground the singular vision of Zechariah. Like Old Testament prophets, he becomes the sole voice of authority because he, and his son Rector by association, are the only two adults who see the walking man. Thus the rest of the group are put into the position of following faithfully the vision of the patriarch. The exodus from the South in this story occurs successfully only because of the wisdom and supernatural abilities of Zechariah rather than as a communal effort. This story establishes the community's reliance on a single leader for its governance and future rather than on the collective will of the group.

As a result of these foundational stories, "Beware the Furrow of His brow" becomes for the residents of Haven and Ruby a representation of their worldview. As a result of these events and their repeated retelling, the residents endorse the perspective that there is only one way to operate in a racist world, that they are superior to other African Americans and must be exclusive in order to maintain the purity of that superiority, and finally, that their survival depends on reliance on a singular male perspective that functions as the intercessor between the people and the divine order. The admonition "Beware the Furrow of His brow" is a way of repeating these lessons and assuring, like the Ten Commandments, that salvation and survival depends upon compliance with these core beliefs derived from the ancient story of the towns' foundings.

However threatening this warning is, over time and with generational distance from the events recounted in these narratives, the young and progressive residents of Ruby want to revisit the static tales and words and to become active participants in the creation of meaning in their own community. In the spirit of the assertions of the Black Power movement circulating during the meeting about the Oven, some of the young people suggest that the message on the Oven should more

accurately be understood as "Be the Furrow of His Brow." To those advocating the change, the new understanding of the message of the Oven allows each member of the community to be a participant in the power symbolized by the divine. In this vision, more akin to that of the New Testament, the community as a whole is divine. The individual relationship with the divine is no longer parental, commanding, and controlling. Rather, the individual has both the right and the responsibility to act in a way to bring about, to create a social order. The image of the furrow shifts from disapproval to intense engagement, even thoughtfulness. It also plays with the meanings of the word furrow. With the phrase "Beware the Furrow of His brow," furrow seems to refer to the scowl on a deity's face, as if he is disapproving. The phrase "Be the Furrow of His Brow" seems to suggest other possible definitions of the word furrow. Perhaps the second phrase points toward the possibility of becoming like a furrow in the earth, the trench plowed that opens the ground so that it may contain seeds. This idea allows for active interactions with the divine and holds the possibility of growth from whatever might spring from the fertile brow.

The reinterpretation of the Oven offends the elder men of the town because it shakes their confidence about their control of Ruby's central narrative. The threatened change is but one of the incidents that signal for the men a radical and dangerous shift in their ability to adhere to the lessons they have absorbed from the stories of their fathers. The tension between the two possible interpretations of the words on the Oven manifests during the wedding of K.D. and Arnette Fleetwood Smith. Reverend Senior Pulliam delivers a sermon that reinforces the position of the elders of Ruby as he paints a portrait of a vengeful and angry God who looks damningly upon people as his unworthy servants. Reverend Richard Misner reacts with an action that embraces the message behind the New Testament perspective offered by the phrase "Be the Furrow of His Brow." Misner raises the cross, the symbol of forgiveness and compassion, and holds it wordlessly in front of the congregation.

The elders are resistant to the message Misner has to offer and, as a result of their stubborn refusal

to consider other possibilities and other definitions of reality, they find themselves at the Convent attacking and attempting to kill the women
who reside there, the women they feel represent
everything that cannot, but must be, controlled.
Paradise is a complex novel that can be overwhelming because of its ambition and its dedication to
presenting two communities in as much detail as
possible. One character, Patricia Best, attempts
to possess the narrative of the residents of Ruby
by charting out the details of the relationships
between the residents in order to piece together
the community's story. Readers may be tempted to
follow suit, but another, more fulfilling approach
is to focus on the issue of control and the connection between who creates and retells a community's
story and who possesses power over that community's way of being. The women of the Convent eventually learn and tell their own stories and so, from
the rigid, inflexible perspective of the patriarchs of
Ruby, represent a threat as they create a paradise
based upon an acceptance of the realities of their
lives and a forgiveness of those who have wronged
them in various ways.

It is no accident that the attack on the Convent
occurs during the month of the bicentennial of the
United States. Placing the attack on the Convent
at the same time as this much-celebrated anniversary draws attention to the possible relationship between the bicentennial and the issues raised
in the novel. The bicentennial celebration of the
founding of the United States was a time of great
public celebration coupled with the retelling of the
controlling narratives of the founding and evolution of the country. *Paradise* may point toward the
importance of questioning those narratives and to
considering who creates and perpetuates them.
Paradise suggests that without the tolerant coexis-
tence of different narratives, communities are destined to become violently defensive and ultimately,
perhaps, self-destructive.

SOME IMPORTANT THEMES AND SYMBOLS IN *PARADISE*

Darkness and Racial Meaning

In *Paradise,* Morrison often uses various unexpected comparisons to describe the skin color of
the residents of Haven and Ruby. Throughout the
novel, she uses night, coal, and wood among other
images to show readers her characters' skin color.
Her use of color imagery in this way may allow
readers to reconsider their understanding of racial
categories. The reinterpretation of the associations
of blackness is an example of one of the ways Morrison challenges her readers to consider language
and the way that its meanings can change.

Morrison calls Ruby's founding families 8-rocks,
referring to the eight original families, all of whom
have dark skin color. Pat Best, a mixed-race woman
with light skin, supposes that what bonds the 8-
rock families is the fact that they all have dark
skin and work to maintain that purity. The 8-rocks
deny the Best family the opportunity to become
one of them because Pat's father, Roger Best, married and bore children with a light-skinned woman,
Delia Best. Here Morrison reverses the traditional
belief of many black communities that the closer
the skin is to whiteness, the more valuable a person becomes. In Ruby, however, the authentic and
powerful members of the community have night-
colored skin.

Sister Mary Magna brings Consolata to the Convent because the nun falls in love with Consolata's
"sundown" skin. Morrison uses the movement of
the sun, of light fading into darkness, to describe
Consolata. Her skin color is between the extremes
of dark and light skin of the people of Ruby. This
difference may predict Consolata's exclusion from
and eventual destruction by the prominent men of
Ruby.

Darkness, in addition to its power as a racial
marker, is also a time for searching and wandering
in *Paradise*. Mavis leaves her abusive husband and
abandons her children during the night hours. The
original families of Ruby travel west in the darkness
in search of a place to establish their town. Steward
owns and rides with uncharacteristic joy a horse
named Night. The women of the Convent gather
at night to perform rituals of healing. At the novel's
end, several of the men of Ruby form a nighttime
posse to go to the Convent and kill the women who
reside there. The final image of the women after
the attack on the Convent is of them riding off in
the Cadillac toward the sunset.

Psychological Abuse and the Power of Language to Wound

Paradise reveals the potentially negative impacts of language. The ability of words to wound or even destroy the human spirit rivals the damaging consequences of physical abuse. An example of the pervasive destruction abusive language can inflict on a person can be found in the revelation of the character, Mavis Albright. Mavis is physically abused by her husband Frank for many years during their marriage. Although she recovers from these experiences, the damage done to her spirit takes much longer to heal than the physical wounds that occasionally require medical intervention.

While Mavis remains in her marriage, she is immobilized by indecision and self-hatred. Even after her escape from Frank, her marriage, and her children, Mavis carries with her the guilt of her role in the death of her twins. At the Convent, Mavis comes to terms with her children's death and forgives herself for the incident. In time, Mavis is able to achieve a sense of self-worth once she retrieves her story from the tyranny of her abusive husband and begins to create her own life with her own words.

The Destructive Power of Race-based Exclusion

The racism experienced by the forefathers of Ruby's citizens has far-reaching and catastrophic effects on the town and its inhabitants. The social and economic consequences of white racism drives the Old Fathers, the men who traveled from Mississippi to Oklahoma to found the town of Haven, away from their homes after the Civil War to the haven of an all-black community, only to be rejected by lighter-skinned blacks in the event that inscribed itself on the group's collective memory, the Disallowing.

The Disallowing has a profound effect on the forefathers and every generation after. Determined never to experience rejection again from either blacks or whites, the Old Fathers found their own community and consolidate their 8-rock blood. The experience of the Disallowing prompts the Old Fathers of Haven, and then the New Fathers of Ruby, to be as exclusionary as those who originally forbade them from joining their community. This tradition of exclusion becomes central to the social

order of Ruby, so much so that when Roger Best, one of the New Fathers, marries a woman who is not an 8-rock, he is excommunicated from the other New Fathers. The New Fathers give their time and energy to the preservation of their exclusionary status. In the process of self-preservation, the people of Ruby practice what they abhor in those who shunned them in the Disallowing.

The Oven

The Oven is a monument to the past for both the communities of Ruby and Haven. The structure reminds the communities of the struggles that they have endured as they tried to establish a home where they can be free. In spite of its rich heritage and historical significance, the Oven has negative associations for the younger generation of Ruby's townspeople. These young people experience the Oven as an oppressive and weighty symbol that they perceive as a kind of weight tying them to a past they believe they would like to move beyond.

The young people of Ruby do not fully understand how important the Oven is to the town. Some of the young people desecrate the Oven by painting a fist on the structure. They say that they desecrate the Oven in an attempt to change its meaning to something more expressive of the ways that they want to redefine Ruby. The argument about the message that was originally inscribed on the Oven reinforces the conflicts that the young people are having with the older members of the Ruby community.

CHARACTERS

8-rocks The 8-rocks are the nine founding families of Haven. They are very dark-skinned and are considered by the residents of Haven, and later of Ruby, to be pure-blooded. Patricia Best applies the name *8-rock* to the founding families of Ruby when she is writing the history and genealogies of the town's residents. The term *8-rock* refers to a deep, dark, rich layer of coal in a coal mine.

Aaron Poole Aaron Poole is the husband of Sally Blackhorse Poole. The couple has 13 children. Aaron Poole is one of Ruby's New Fathers, one of the men who lead the relocation of the town from

Haven to Ruby, Oklahoma. Poole owes Deacon Morgan money from a loan.

Able Flood Able Flood helps found the town of Haven with Big Daddy Morgan and is one of the Old Fathers, one of the men who made the exodus from the South to found the all-black town of Haven, Oklahoma. He is the father of Ace and the grandfather of Anna Flood.

Ace Flood Ace Flood is the son of Able Flood, the husband of Charity Flood, and the father of Anna Flood. Ace Flood is one of the New Fathers, one of the men who lead the relocation of some of the townspeople from Haven to Ruby, Oklahoma. Ace is the owner of the sundries store in Ruby. He is said to carry stock in his store that is of questionable quality, yet he charges his customers more than the goods are worth. As a result, the residents of Ruby often travel to the nearby town of Demby to purchase their goods. When Ace builds his store, he constructs it out of sandstone so it will last. After Ace dies while in a hospital in Demby, his daughter Anna takes over his store.

Alice Pulliam Alice Pulliam is Reverend Pulliam's wife. She is conventional and judgmental.

Anna Flood Anna Flood is the daughter of Ace and Charity Flood and the granddaughter of Able Flood. She is romantically involved with Reverend Richard Misner. For a while, she leaves Ruby and lives in Detroit. When she returns, she wears her hair in a natural style. Her hairstyle creates fervor in the town. Anna uses people's reactions to her hair as a gauge to evaluate their state of mind.

After the death of her father, Anna Flood returns to Ruby to run the family grocery store. At the store Anna sells pies and canned goods that she bakes herself. She also teaches typing. After she takes over her father's store, it prospers. Under her care, the store becomes a central gathering place for the community. Although Anna has doubts about becoming a preacher's wife, eventually she and Misner plan to marry. Together the couple has a vision of a window or a door that appears in the

field outside the Convent after the attack on its women residents by the men of Ruby.

Ansel Jury Ansel Jury is Fruit Jury's brother. The two boys are in the Christmas pageant. They are Solarine and Peace Jury's grandchildren.

Apollo Poole Apollo Poole is the son of Sally and Aaron Poole. He has 12 siblings. Apollo Poole is in love with Billie Delia and fights with his brother, Brood, for her attention. Eventually, the two call a truce.

Arapaho In the novel the Native American girls, who are sent by the government and the Catholic Church to the Convent to forget their native culture, are from the Arapaho tribe. At one time, the Convent served as a boarding school for native girls. The nuns who teach at the school attempt to replace the native knowledge of the girls with English and Catholicism.

Arnette Fleetwood Arnette Fleetwood is the daughter of Ace and Mable Fleetwood. Her brother is Jeff Fleetwood. Arnette Fleetwood is Billie Delia Best's best friend. Arnette is supposed to leave Ruby to attend college, but her plans go awry when at 14 she becomes pregnant with K.D. Smith's child. Arnette attempts unsuccessfully to abort her pregnancy. In desperation and despondency about the pregnancy, she wanders out to the Convent where she gives birth prematurely to a baby. Because of her abuse of her unborn child and her refusal to care for it after its birth, the child dies shortly after she abandons it at the Convent. Arnette does attend college. While there she writes K.D. more than 50 letters. She sends 12 of the letters, but stops mailing them after he does not write her back.

Four years after the death of their child, Arnette and K.D. marry. The evening after her wedding, Arnette again wanders out to the Convent looking for the baby she believes she left there. She accuses the women of the Convent of having taken her child.

Arnold Fleetwood (Fleet) Arnold Fleetwood is one of the New Fathers, one of the men who lead the relocation of the town from Haven to Ruby, Oklahoma. Arnold is married to Mable Fleetwood and he is the proud father of Arnette and Jefferson. Arnold Fleetwood is a businessman and is involved in a long-standing, competitive feud with Deacon and Steward Morgan. He owns a furniture store and is a part of the posse of men who go to the Convent to kill the women.

August Cato August Cato is married to Fawn Blackhorse Cato and is the father of William (Billy) Cato. August Cato is one of the Old Fathers, one of the men who made the exodus from the South to found the all-black town of Haven, Oklahoma. In a custom peculiar to the peoples of Haven and Ruby, August "takes over" Fawn Blackhorse after the premature death of her first husband. August is Fawn's great uncle. August Cato's age is the primary reason that the couple has only one child.

Beck Beck is Big Daddy Morgan's wife and the mother of Deacon and Steward. Beck is pregnant during the journey from Fairley, Oklahoma, to Haven.

Ben and Good Ben is one of Steward Morgan's hunting dogs. K.D. Smith takes care of his uncle's two dogs.

Bennie Bennie is one of the roadside girls Mavis picks up during her escape from her husband Frank following the death of the couple's infant twins. Bennie does not talk much, but she sings songs. Bennie says that she will not eat until she gets to a black town with good food. She is going to San Diego. She sets out on her own again one day while Mavis is in the bathroom while the two are traveling through Kansas. When Bennie leaves, she steals Mavis's raincoat and boots, but she does not steal her money. Bennie is the last girl that Mavis picks up before detouring to the Convent. After Bennie leaves her, Mavis misses the girl's songs and cannot bear the loneliness her absence creates.

Bernard Bernard is Eddie Turtle's dog. He gives Seneca instructions about how to care for the dog when she comes to visit him in jail.

Big Daddy Morgan Big Daddy's given name is Rector Morgan. He is the son of Zechariah and Mindy Morgan. He has seven children with Beck, of whom only four survive out of Haven: Ruby, Elder, and the twins, Deacon and Steward. In 1920, when Haven falls on desperate times, Big Daddy takes a 65-mile journey from Haven for supplies. While on this journey, Big Daddy finds a town with a "No Niggers" sign that horrifies him and reinforces his perspective on the dangers of the outside world. After his death, the people of Haven and Ruby remember him by saying that his bank failed, but he never did.

Big Papa Morgan See Zechariah

Billie Delia Cato Billie Delia Cato is the daughter of Patricia Best and Billy Cato. She is Arnette Fleetwood's best friend. The people of the town of Ruby ostracize Billie Delia because of an incident that happens when she is a little girl. Before riding Nathan DuPres's horse, Hard Goods, at three years old, Billie Delia pulls down her underpants. As a result, she is known as the fastest girl in town. Since she is a virgin, the label is completely inaccurate. The only people who are kind to her after the incident are Arnette Fleetwood and Dovey and Soane Morgan. Billie Delia is in love with both Brood and Apollo Poole. She decides that she cannot chose between the two brothers. Billie Delia helps Dovey clean up the backyard of the house on Saint Matthew's Street.

Billie Delia gets into a physical fight with her mother, Pat, after Pat refuses to believe that Billie Delia is not sexually active. Pat is overly invested in ensuring her daughter's positive reputation because of her own insecurities about the light skin color both she and Billie Delia inherit from Pat's mother, Delia. After the fight with her mother, Billie Delia seeks and finds sanctuary at the Convent for two weeks. While at the Convent, Billie Delia befriends the women who reside there. After her recovery at the Convent, Billie Delia disappears for some time and eventually finds a job working in a hospital in Demby. While working at the hospital, she befriends Pallas and tells the traumatized girl about the Convent. Billie Delia returns to Ruby to attend and be the maid of honor for Arnette and K.D. Smith's wedding.

Billy Cato (William Cato) Billy Cato is the son of August and Fawn Blackhorse Cato. He is Pat Best Cato's husband and the father of Billie Delia Cato. Billy Cato is one of the New Fathers, one of the men who lead the relocation of the town from Haven to Ruby, Oklahoma. Billy Cato is killed while serving in the Korean War. When he dies, his body is in so many pieces that he cannot be put together. The only recognizable item returned with Billy's body is a twisted and bent ring.

Billy James Albright Billy James Albright is Mavis and Frank Albright's son. He is the brother of Frankie and Sal and the deceased twins, Merle and Perle, Mavis and Frank's other children. During the visit between Mavis and Sal, Sal tells her mother that Billy James is keeping company with an unsavory crowd. Mavis promises her daughter that she will try to reconnect with Billy James.

Birdie Goodroe Birdie Goodroe is Mavis's mother. She lives in Paterson, New Jersey, and works at a preschool. Birdie is flippant when Frank calls looking for Mavis. She tells Mavis it would be safer if Mavis were to leave town. Birdie never liked Frank, but she tries to trap Mavis by secretly taking her keys and calling him. Later, after Mavis takes shelter at the Convent, Birdie tells Mavis that Frank has enlisted the police to issue a warrant for her arrest for the theft of the Cadillac and the probable murder of the twins.

Bitty Cato Blackhorse Bitty Cato Blackhorse is the daughter of Sterl and Honesty Jones Cato. Bitty is married to Peter Blackhorse. Bitty and Fairy DuPres fight over what to name the orphan child, Lone, who Fairy finds during the journey to Haven. Bitty loses the squabble, and Fairy names the baby Lone. Bitty's given name is Friendship.

Booker DuPres Booker DuPres is the father of Pious DuPres.

Brood Poole Jr. Brood is the son of Sally and Aaron Poole. He has 12 siblings. Brood Poole is in love with Billie Delia and fights with his brother Apollo for her attention. Eventually, the two call a truce. Brood also plays the mouth organ.

Brood Poole Sr. Brood Poole Sr. is one of the Old Fathers, one of the men who make the journey from the South to Oklahoma to found the town of Haven. He is the father of Aaron and Wisdom Poole.

Caline Poole Caline Poole is one of the younger generation present at the meeting at the Oven. Caline is one of the young people of Ruby who petition the adults to rename the Oven that was built by the Old Fathers and carried from Haven to Ruby by the New Fathers.

campfire men The campfire men are a band of men Big Daddy Morgan decides to talk with when he is alone in the woods during one of his journeys. The men warn him not to go into the nearby town. The men characterize the town as a breeding ground for immorality and as a haven for violent and exclusionary racists.

Carlos Carlos is Pallas Truelove's lover. When her Toyota will not start in the school parking lot, Carlos offers to help her and through that encounter, the two meet and become attracted to each other. Carlos is extraordinarily handsome. He is working at the school as a janitor, but his passion is sculpting. Carlos is much older than Pallas. The two run away together to Pallas's mother's home. Pallas's mother, Divine Truelove, is an artist. While at Divine's home, Carlos betrays Pallas when he begins an affair with her mother.

Carter Seawright Carter Seawright is one of the children of Ruby. He inadvertently steps on Patricia Best's foot after the Christmas pageant.

Catherine Blackhorse Jury Catherine Blackhorse Jury is Harper Jury's second wife and Kate Jury Golightly's mother. Catherine is one of the women of Ruby who tries to help Delia Best while she is struggling in childbirth, but Catherine cannot drive. Harper is so worried about Catherine committing adultery that he develops nervous indigestion.

Celeste Blackhorse Celeste Blackhorse is Drum Blackhorse's wife. Sally Blackhorse is her sister. Celeste is pregnant during the journey from Fairly,

Oklahoma, to Haven. During the journey, Celeste takes the food offered to the group during the Disallowing and distributes it to the women and children, even though Drum and Zechariah forbid her to do so. Celeste is Soane and Dovey Morgan's grandmother. When Patricia Best tries to chart the genealogy of the community, she cannot discover Celeste's maiden name.

Charity Flood   Charity Flood is Ace Flood's wife and Anna Flood's mother. Charity Flood also tries to help Delia when she is having trouble during labor.

Charmaine   Charmaine is the girl Sally Albright tells her mother, Mavis, that she is going to live with.

Chaste Cary   Chaste Cary is one of the four youngest Cary girls who participate in Ruby's Christmas pageant.

Che   Che is the name Gigi gives Arnette and K.D.'s stillborn baby. Arnette delivers the premature infant at the Convent after numerous abortion attempts. The child dies shortly thereafter.

Clarissa   Clarissa is a wayward girl who lives at the Convent while Consolata is involved in her affair with Deacon. Clarissa and her friend, Penny, help Consolata to hide her affair. Clarissa and Penny want to escape from the Convent. The girls ask Consolata for money to help with their escape. Eventually, Consolata relents and gives the girls the money. Penny and Clarissa are the last two of the Native American girls at the Convent. After their escape, they send the money back to Connie using fictional names.

Coffee Smith (Private Smith)   Coffee Smith is Ruby Morgan Smith's husband and the father of K.D. He is an army buddy of Deacon and Steward. Coffee Smith is killed while serving in World War II.

Consolata Sosa (Connie)   At the heart and center of the Convent is the orphan Consolata. When *Paradise* begins, Consolata is the last remaining resident of the Convent who enters while it is still a residence for nuns. Consolata, also known as Connie, has light brown skin, straight braided hair, and

unusual green eyes. At nine years old she arrives at the Convent after the mother superior, Mary Magna, kidnaps her from the streets of Brazil. With a few brief and infrequent exceptions, Consolata remains at the Convent for the rest of her life. While working as a house servant at the Convent, she loses her native language and identity.

The one break in the monotony of her years as the Convent servant occurs in the form of an intense, but brief, romantic, and sexual affair with one of the most prominent men of Ruby, Deacon "Deek" Morgan, who is married to Soane Morgan. The affair ends because of Deek's guilt, which is sparked when, in the midst of passionate lovemaking, Consolata bites him. After the incident Deacon begins to view Connie as dangerous and as someone with the potential to devour him. Accordingly, he ends the affair. The loss of her only love leaves Connie bereft. Shortly after the end of the affair with Deacon, his wife, Soane Morgan, walks out to the Convent in winter to confront Connie. Soane says that she will abort the child she is carrying if the affair between Connie and Deacon does not end. Although Soane is bluffing, she loses the child she is carrying through a miscarriage.

One of the women of Ruby, Lone DuPres, encourages the middle-aged Connie to develop her supernatural abilities to heal and to resurrect, abilities that Connie is unaware she possesses. Connie uses these gifts on several occasions during the novel. Consolata calls her gift Practicing. Most frequently she uses it to sustain the life of her surrogate mother, Mary Magna. Later, Connie uses her supernatural talents to return Deek and Soane's son, Scout, to life after he suffers a fatal car accident. Subsequently, Connie and Soane become friends.

Eventually, the Convent closes and Mary Magna dies. Connie then becomes the sole resident of the Convent until, gradually, it becomes home to four lost women, each seeking refuge from a deeply troubled life. At the time the women begin to arrive, Connie is despondent over Mary Magna's death and has nearly lost her sight and her ability to withstand light, which forces her to don sunglasses and to spend most of her time in the darkness of the Convent's cellar.

After passively accepting the conflicts and bad behavior of the Convent's new residents and spurred by the arrival of a mysterious stranger known as the Man, Connie gathers the women, and her spiritual and emotional resources, in order to bring transformation into her own life as well as into the lives of the outcast women. She gives the women an ultimatum: to follow her rules or leave. They all remain at the Convent and begin to embark on paths of healing under Connie's guidance.

When the men of Ruby attack the Convent and attempt to kill the women who reside there, Steward, Deacon's twin brother, shoots Connie in the head. She appears again at the novel's end, however, with a GODDESS FIGURE named Piedade, who frequented Connie's childhood dreams and who was the subject of the many stories she shares with the women of the Convent.

crazy woman   Inappropriately, crazy woman calls for private parts of her anatomy and sings obscene versions of Christmas carols while riding on a public escalator in a shopping mall. She is dressed erratically, with dazzle and clunk and with lots of makeup and chunky jewelry. She looks cheap and her panty hose are full of runs. Pallas is unnerved by her encounter with the woman.

David   David is Mrs. Norma Keene Fox's chauffeur. He is trolling at the bus station for his employer when he discovers and propositions Seneca. Seneca, desperate, accepts the man's offer.

Deacon Morgan (Deek)   Deacon Morgan is the son of Rector (Big Daddy) and Beck Morgan and is Steward Morgan's identical twin. His other siblings are Elder and Ruby Morgan. Deacon is one of the New Fathers, one of the men who lead the relocation of the town from Haven to Ruby, Oklahoma. Until the incident at the Convent, Deacon feels that being a twin makes him feel complete. He smokes Te Amo cigars and is physically smooth and agile. Deacon is the more subtle of the twins. Deacon runs Ruby's bank. Every day, he drives his meticulously clean black Oldsmobile three quarters of a mile through the town of Ruby to his job.

When he is 29 years old, Deacon has a passionate affair with Consolata. He ends the relationship after Consolata bites him and draws blood. After his

sons Easter and Scout are killed in Vietnam, Deacon asks Roger Best to inspect his sons' remains to ensure that all of the parts are black before burying the boys. During the invasion of the Convent, Deacon tries to prevent Steward from shooting Connie, but is unsuccessful. After the shooting, Deacon no longer feels close or connected to Steward. After a barefoot walk though town, Deacon begins to confide all of his confusion and deeply buried complexities to Reverend Richard Misner.

Dee Dee Truelove   See DIVINE TRUELOVE

Deed Sands   Deed Sands is a resident of Ruby and one of the men who participates in the attack on the women who live in the Convent.

Deeper Poole   Deeper is the son of Sally and Aaron Poole. He has 12 siblings. Originally, Aaron wants to name his son Deep, but compromises with his wife and names the boy Deeper.

Delia Best   Delia Best is Roger Best's wife and Patricia Best's mother. Delia and Roger meet while he is away from Haven, serving in World War I. Delia lives in Tennessee and the two first encounter each other at an AME Zion picnic held for black servicemen. From the affair that commences, Delia becomes pregnant with the couple's daughter, Patricia. After the war, Roger sends for and marries Delia. The relationship and marriage is not approved of by Roger's parents, Fulton and Olive Best, or by the community of Haven and, later, of Ruby.

The source of the disapproval that Roger and Delia experience is Delia's skin color. Delia is light-skinned, so much so that she can often pass for white. As a result of her skin color, she is not accepted by the Ruby community. In spite of this exclusion, the people of Ruby use her to get supplies from segregated stores but many of the men refuse to help her while she is in childbirth. As a result, when she gives birth to Faustine, Patricia's sister, Delia dies in childbirth. The baby, Faustine, dies as well. Delia dies while Roger is at his mortuary school graduation. When Roger returns from his graduation, Delia becomes his first mortuary customer. Roger never recovers from the loss of his wife.

Delia's daughter and granddaughter, Patricia and Billie Delia, inherit Delia's light skin color and, as a result, are also considered outsiders in Ruby.

Destry Beauchamp Destry Beauchamp is the son of Luther and Helen Beauchamp and the brother of Royal and Vane Beauchamp. He speaks at the meeting at the Oven saying that no ex-slave would tell anyone to beware. Destry is one of the young people of Ruby who petition the adults to rename the Oven that was built by the Old Fathers and carried from Haven to Ruby by the New Fathers.

Dice Dice is the man Gigi befriends on the train. He is short, almost dwarf-like. Gigi notices that he does not wear polyester. He has gold seeds that he wears around his neck. Gigi and Dice tell stories to each other. One of the stories Dice tells Gigi is about Ruby, rhubarb pie, and the two trees intertwined next to the water. His story is so intriguing that she decides to go there.

Dina Poole Dina is the youngest daughter of Sally and Aaron Poole. She has 12 siblings. Dina Poole is in the Christmas pageant with her brother. Dina is one of Pat's students and tells Pat about one of her brother's visits to Billie Delia in Demby.

Divine Divine is the name given to Pallas's baby. The child's name is written in capital letters above one of the bedroom doors upstairs in the Convent. When the men come to invade the Convent and to attack the women, Connie has the baby downstairs in the cellar with her and decides to leave him on the cot when she hears the noise of the men entering the house. After she is shot in the head by Steward, Connie's last words are about the infant. Soane misunderstands her words. Later when Roger goes to the house to retrieve the women's bodies, the bodies are gone, as is the baby.

Divine Truelove (Dee Dee) Divine is Pallas's mother and Milton Truelove's ex-wife. She is an artist. Dee Dee is the name that she uses. Dee Dee lives in Mehita, New Mexico. When Pallas runs away from her father's house with Carlos, the janitor from her high school, she runs to her mother's house. At first when Dee Dee sees her daughter, she smothers her in hugs and kisses. After some time, Dee Dee betrays Pallas by becoming sexually involved with Carlos.

Dovey Morgan Dovey Morgan is the daughter of Thomas and Missy Rivers Blackhorse. She is also Steward Morgan's wife and Soane Morgan's sister. Dovey often stays by herself in town in the house that Steward owns and rents. Dovey has a friend, imaginary or not, who visits her sometimes. She is a curious woman and has many questions about the controversy over the words on the Oven. Dovey is a character that seems to be yearning for something more in her life. Her husband, Steward, loves her very much and has a hard time staying away from her while she is in town. He would prefer that Dovey stay with him on their ranch. Dovey is close to her sister, Soane, until Steward shoots Consolata during the attack on the Convent. After the attack, Dovey sides with her husband and positions herself against the women of the Convent.

Drew and Harriet Person Drew and Harriet Person are the parents of James who is in the town play.

Drum Blackhorse Drum Blackhorse is one of the Old Fathers who takes part in the journey from the South to Haven. Drum is married to Celeste Blackhorse. Celeste Blackhorse is the sister of Sally Blackhorse. Drum Blackhorse is the father of Thomas and Peter Blackhorse. Thomas and Drum lead the processional of refugees from the South to Haven.

Dusty (Sandra) Dusty's given name is Sandra. She is the first hitchhiker that Mavis picks up. She talks nonstop for 32 miles. Dusty keeps and wears the dog tags of six men she knew from high school who died in Vietnam. Dusty is traveling to her friend's house in Columbus, Ohio.

Easter Morgan Easter Morgan is the son of Deacon and Soane Morgan and the brother of Scout Morgan. Easter is killed while serving in Vietnam.

Eddie Turtle Eddie Turtle is Seneca's boyfriend. Eddie is in prison. While he is incarcerated, he asks

Seneca for shoes and a Bible. In spite of Seneca's attempts to cater to Eddie's desires, he is concerned only about his dogs, Sophie and Bernard. Eddie asks Seneca to visit his mother, a request she fulfills. Eddie Turtle is imprisoned because he drives over a child and leaves the scene.

Edward Sands Edward Sands is one of the New Fathers, those who traveled from Haven to Ruby.

Elder Morgan Elder Morgan is the son of Zechariah and Mindy Morgan and brother of Steward, Deacon, and Ruby Morgan. He is married to Susannah Morgan. The couple has seven children. Elder Morgan has a life-changing experience while in New York, after returning from military service in World War I in 1919. Elder Morgan sees two white men beating an African-American girl Morgan believes is a streetwalker. Defending the woman, Elder gets in a fistfight with the men. He never quite gets over the impact of that incident. He is uncertain about his defense of the woman in light of what he perceives and judges as her promiscuous sexuality. Steward sympathizes with the white men's disrupted violence toward the woman because she is a prostitute.

After the attack, Elder insists that his army uniform remain tattered and torn. Elder dies as a relatively young man, leaving his wife Susannah to raise their six living children. Four of the seven children survive into adulthood. When he dies, Elder leaves instructions that he be buried in his tattered uniform. Steward and Deacon comply with his wishes even though Susannah objects.

Susannah and Elder's children leave Ruby and return only for occasional visits. As a result, Deacon does not consider Elder's children to be legitimate Morgan heirs.

Ella Morgan Ella Morgan is one of the children of Zechariah and Mindy Morgan. She and her sisters, Loving and Selanie, gather pink yarrow to place on Lone's mother's grave.

embezzler, the The embezzler builds the building that later becomes the Convent. He is paranoid about discovery of his illegal activities, so he builds his dwelling with all the windows facing north. The house is decorated with profane objects. The embezzler builds the house in the shape of an ammo cartridge. Eventually he is arrested by a northern law man whom the embezzler invites to his first and only party.

Esther (Miss Esther) Esther is Fleet Fleetwood's mother-in-law. After the death of Ruby Morgan, Miss Esther chooses the name Ruby for the town. Miss Esther could not read when she felt the letters on the Oven, but claims to remember the original lettering on the Oven as "Beware the Furrow of His Brow." Esther is five at the time she feels the letters on the Oven.

Esther Fleetwood Esther Fleetwood is one of Jeff and Sweetie Beauchamp Fleetwood's sick children. The child is named for her great-grandmother Miss Esther.

Ethan Blackhorse Ethan Blackhorse is Drum Blackhorse's youngest brother. Ethan may have had a sexual relationship out of marriage with a woman named Solace. He has a line drawn through his name in the Blackhorse Bible.

Fairy DuPres Fairy DuPres is one of the migrants from Haven. During the migration, 15-year-old Fairy DuPres rescues Lone, names her, and raises the girl as her own. Fairy serves as the midwife in Haven and later in Ruby. Lone learns the craft of midwifery from Fairy. Fairy dies on the way back to Ruby after a trip to Haven.

Faustine Faustine is the baby girl of Roger and Delia Best. The child dies while Delia is in labor.

Fawn Blackhorse Fawn Blackhorse is Billy Cato's mother and August Cato's wife. In the words of Fairy DuPres and Patricia Best Cato, Fawn is "taken over" by August when Fawn's husband dies. August is Fawn's great uncle.

Fleet Fleetwood See ARNOLD FLEETWOOD

Frances Poole DuPres Frances DuPres is the wife of Sut DuPres.

Frank Albright Frank Albright is Mavis's husband. His erratic moods and abusive behaviors keep Mavis on edge. He is quite possessive of his Cadillac, which Mavis steals when she runs away. Frank rapes Mavis, seems to be an alcoholic, and is mentally and physically abusive.

Frankie Albright Frankie Albright is Mavis's eldest son, named after her husband, Frank. When Sally and Mavis meet at the diner after the attack at the Convent, Sally tells her mother that Frankie is doing alright. Mavis tells Sal that she will contact Frankie and his brother, Billy James.

Friend Friend is Dovey's visitor at the house on Saint Matthew's Street. He appears to Dovey to be about 20 years younger than she is. He listens to Dovey as if he is interested in everything Dovey says. Dovey looks forward to his visits. Dovey's friend stops visiting after the attack at the Convent.

Fruit Jury Fruit Jury is Ansel Jury's brother. The two boys are in the Christmas pageant. They are Solarine and Peace Jury's grandchildren.

Fulton Best Fulton Best is Olive Best's husband and Roger Best's father. The couple's other children die during the influenza epidemic of 1919. He is an 8-rock and an Old Father, one of the men who make the journey from the South to Oklahoma to found the town of Haven. When the group finds the orphan Lone and takes the baby with them, Fulton Best fashions a cross to place on the grave that the men dig for Lone's mother's body.

Gigi Gibson See GRACE

Good Good is one of Steward Morgan's hunting dogs. K.D. takes care of his uncle's two dogs and writes songs for Good.

Governor Morgan Governor Morgan is one of the children of Zechariah and Mindy Morgan.

Grace Gibson (Gigi) Grace is a misfit and runaway from the San Francisco Bay area. She is the daughter of a convicted killer, Manley Gibson, who is on death row. She grew up uncertain of the identity of her mother. Gigi is prone to screaming fits and she takes drugs. Grace has a consciousness and has been involved in Civil Rights activities. She finds her way to the Convent after taking a ride with Roger Best from town. Roger is driving to the Convent to pick up the body of Mary Magna. Gigi stays at the Convent and in the vicinity of Ruby after Connie asks her to stay while she sleeps. After arriving in Ruby, she has a four-year affair with K.D. Smith. Gigi's grandfather, the man she calls Granddaddy, is from Alcorn, Mississippi. She has a habit of sunbathing nude.

Before arriving in Ruby, Grace spends a great deal of time searching for a rock formation in the desert that looks like two people perpetually making love in a town called Wish, Arizona. Mikey Rood is Grace's ex-lover and she gets the story of the rock formation from his unreliable ramblings. She learns about Ruby from a man named Dice whom she meets on the bus while looking for Wish, Arizona, and the rock formation.

Grace is sarcastic and promiscuous. Although she searches for the perfect place to be, she cannot seem to find her paradise. After she settles in with the women of the Convent, she grows close to Seneca. She and Mavis, though, hate each other with an intense passion until all of the women are redeemed by the reformed Consolata.

Granddaddy Granddaddy is Grace's grandfather. During phone calls from his granddaughter, Granddaddy expresses concern about her safety and urges her to come home to him in Alcorn, Mississippi. Her tells Grace about the assassinations that have taken place during her absence and encourages her to abandon her activism.

Hard Goods Hard Goods is the winning horse, owned by Nathan DuPres, that K.D. Smith rides during a race held during the celebration of Ruby's founding. Hard Goods is the horse that three-year-old Billie Delia Best tries to ride without her panties.

Harper Jury Harper Jury is the father of Menus Jury and Katherine (Kate) Golightly Jury. Harper is married twice. Harper believes that his first wife, Martha Stone Jury, the mother of Menus, has an affair. Harper remarries Catherine Jury who becomes the mother of his daughter, Kate Jury. He owns the town drugstore. He is one of the New Fathers, one of the men who lead the relocation of the town from Haven to Ruby, Oklahoma. Harper is responsible for the maintenance and repair of the star each year for Ruby's annual Christmas pageant. Harper Jury owns the drug store in Ruby. Harper Jury is a part of the posse of men who go to the Convent to kill the women.

Harry   Harry is a boy who lives at one of the foster homes where Seneca resides for a time. Harry molests Seneca and is the catalyst for the beginning of her habit of masochistic self-abuse by cutting herself. The habit of cutting begins when Seneca associates Harry's rape of her with a scratch she receives during his attack.

Helen Beauchamp (Ren)   Helen Beauchamp is Luther Beaucamp's wife and Royal, Destry, and Vane Beauchamp's mother.

Honesty Jones Cato   Honesty Jones is Sterl Cato's wife and Bitty Cato's mother. Honesty originally names her daughter, Bitty, Friendship.

Hope Cary   Hope Cary is one of the four of the youngest Cary girls who participate in Ruby's Christmas pageant.

Hurston Poole   Hurston is the son of Sally and Aaron Poole. He has 12 siblings. Hurston Poole is one of the younger generation at the meeting at the Oven. Hurston is one of the young people of Ruby who petition the adults to rename the Oven that was built by the Old Fathers and carried from Haven to Ruby by the New Fathers.

Indian woman   The Indian woman and the Indian boys pick up Pallas on the side of the road after she is raped by a gang of boys. The Indians feed her and take her to a church. Later the woman returns for Pallas and takes her to a clinic because she has an intuitive feeling that Pallas has been the victim of violence.

Ivlin   When Patricia Best tries to chart the genealogy of the community, she cannot discover Ivlin's maiden name.

Jack   Jack is Jean's, Seneca's mother, husband.

James Person   James Person is the son of Drew and Harriet Person. James is one of the children who participate in Ruby's Christmas pageant.

Jean   Seneca believes that Jean is her older sister. In fact, Jean is her mother. When Seneca is a small child, Jean abandons her without explanation. Jean leaves the five-year-old Seneca a note written in red lipstick. Seneca keeps the note with her even into her adulthood. After the attack at the Convent, Seneca encounters Jean at a football game. Seneca seems unaware of Jean's identity and Jean does not realize until it is too late that Seneca is in fact her lost child.

Jefferson Fleetwood (Jeff)   Jefferson Fleetwood is the son of Arnold and Mable Fleetwood and husband of Sweetie. All of the children he has with Sweetie are sick. Jeff defends his sister Arnette during the meeting with the Morgans. Before Arnette's wedding to K.D., Jeff takes to carrying a gun. Jeff is heir to his father Arnold's furniture store. He is also a Vietnam veteran. Jeff Fleetwood is a part of the posse of men who go to the Convent to kill the women.

Jerome Truelove   Jerome Truelove is the son of Divine and Milton Truelove and Pallas Truelove's brother.

Joanne Truelove   Joanne Truelove is Milton Truelove's second wife and Pallas Truelove's stepmother.

Joe-Thomas Poole   Joe-Thomas Poole is the son of Aaron and Sally Poole. He is one of the children of Ruby who participate in the annual Christmas pageant.

John Seawright   John Seawright is one of the New Fathers, one of the men who lead the relocation of the town from Haven to Ruby, Oklahoma.

July　July is the clerk/secretary at the Morgan's Bank. He was best friends with Easter and Scout Morgan and is with the boys when Scout Morgan dies in an automobile accident and is resurrected by Connie.

June　June is the journalist who comes to interview Mavis Albright after her twins, Merle and Perle, suffocate in the back seat of the Cadillac. During the interview, June wears new white high heels. She appears objective and sympathetic, but tends toward implicit disapproval. June is manipulative. She befriends Mavis only so that she can conduct the interview.

Jupe Cato　During the Disallowing, Jupe Cato refuses to accept the charity of the community in Fairly, Oklahoma, that refuses to allow the group to join their community. The residents of Fairly are light-skinned blacks and do not want the dark-skinned travelers to join their numbers.

Juvenal DuPres　Juvenal DuPres is the father of Nathan and an Old Father, one of the men who lead the journey from the South to Oklahoma to found the town of Haven.

Kate Jury Golightly (Katherine)　Kate Jury Golightly is Catherine and Harper Jury's daughter. She marries early because of her father's obsessive vigilance. She plays the organ at Arnette and K.D. Smith's wedding and directs the children's singing during the Christmas pageant. Kate is one of the younger generation of Ruby women and is a friend of Anna Flood. The two women scrub the fist off of the Oven. Kate helps Anna to shape her hair. They also share a laugh at Alice Pulliam during the reception for K.D. and Arnette's wedding.

K.D. Smith (Coffee Smith)　K.D. Smith is the son of Ruby Morgan and Coffee Smith. Coffee Smith is an army buddy of K.D.'s uncles, Steward and Deacon Morgan. K.D. is the last person in the Morgan family line. His given name is Coffee, but he goes by K.D., which is short for Kentucky Derby, a name he earns as a child after winning a horse race held at the celebration of Ruby's founding. He looks like a Morgan/Blackhorse mix. K.D. has a sexual relationship with Arnette that results in Arnette's pregnancy when she is 14 years old. He does not want to take responsibility for his unborn child. He slaps Arnette and creates quite a fuss, which leads to a meeting between the Fleetwoods and Morgans.

When Gigi arrives in town, K.D. has an affair with her that continues for four years. K.D. also propositions Billie Delia twice. When Gigi finally rejects K.D., he asks Arnette to become his wife. His proposal occurs four years after her still-born pregnancy. K.D. and Arnette have an uncomfortable wedding that serves as a platform for the primary ministers of Ruby to weigh in on the community's conflicts. After they are married, K.D. and Arnette have a son.

Although limited in many ways, K.D. is good at brushing and nurturing his uncle Steward's hunting dogs. He especially loves Steward's dog, Good, and writes a song about the animal. K.D. is selfish and immature, spoiled by his family's money and status. K.D. is a part of the posse of men who go to the Convent to kill the women.

Leon Fox　Leon Fox is Norma Keene Fox's husband.

Lily Cary　Lily is Reverend Cary's wife. The couple is known for their duets.

Linda DuPres　Linda Dupres is Pious DuPres's daughter. She is one of the children who participate in the annual Ruby Christmas pageant.

Linda Sands　Linda Sands is Lorcas Sand's sister. The siblings are members of the younger generation who attend the meeting at the Oven. Linda is one of the young people of Ruby who petition the adults to rename the Oven that was built by the Old Fathers and carried from Haven to Ruby by the New Fathers.

Little Mirth　Little Mirth is one of the younger generation of Ruby who follow the teaching of MARTIN LUTHER KING, JR. Little Mirth is one of the young people of Ruby who petition the adults to rename the Oven that was built by the Old Fathers and carried from Haven to Ruby by the New Fathers.

Lone DuPres Lone DuPres is one of the babies stolen/rescued during the trip from Haven to Ruby. The baby Lone is discovered by Fairy DuPres and Missy Rivers. After discovering that the infant Lone's mother has died and that the baby has been existing for sometime alone, Fairy DuPres insists on taking the orphan infant along with the group. Fairy takes on Lone as her surrogate mother. Lone learns midwifery from Fairy, who is the first midwife in Haven and, later, in Ruby.

In Ruby, during her later years, Lone is hurt that many of the younger generation, like Arnette Fleetwood, will not use her services. The Fleetwoods seem to blame Lone for the health problems with Jeff and Sweetie's kids. Lone learns accidentally about the plot against the women at the Convent and drives out to warn them about the impending attack. The women do not heed her warnings and so Lone tries to get other residents of Ruby involved to prevent the attack. Lone's efforts are delayed by her impaired car and the group that she gathers arrives too late to prevent the shootings. In the wake of the attack and the women's subsequent disappearance, Lone is one of the few people willing to tell the truth about what happened at the Convent.

Lorcas Sands Lorcas Sands is the son of Payne Sands. He is Linda Sand's brother. The siblings are members of the younger generation at the meeting at the Oven. Lorcas is one of the young people of Ruby who petition the adults to rename the Oven that was built by the Old Fathers and carried from Haven to Ruby by the New Fathers.

Lovely Cary Lovely Cary is one of the four youngest Cary girls who participate in Ruby's Christmas pageant.

Loving Morgan Loving Morgan is one of the children of Zechariah and Mindy Morgan. She and her sisters, Ella and Selanie, gather pink yarrow to place on Lone's mother's grave.

Luther Beauchamp Luther Beauchamp is the brother of Sweetie Beauchamp Fleetwood and the husband of Helen (Ren) Beauchamp. The couple are the parents of Royal, Destry, and Vane Beauchamp. He is one of the New Fathers, one of the

men who lead the relocation of the town from Haven to Ruby, Oklahoma.

Mable Fleetwood Mable Fleetwood is the daughter of Miss Esther. She is Arnold Fleetwood's wife and the mother of Jefferson and Arnette. She is a proud woman. She is more jovial with Reverend Misner than with anyone else. Mable Fleetwood takes turns with Sweetie taking care of Sweetie and Jeff's sick children.

Mama Greer Mama Greer is one of Seneca's foster mothers.

Man behind the counter The man behind the counter in the train dining car charges Gigi for ice even when she does not actually get any in her cup.

Manley Gibson Manley Gibson is Gigi's father. He is a convicted fellow on death row until he receives a reprieve. After the attack on the Convent, Manley Gibson has a visit from Gigi. Manley gives Gigi a necklace that she throws away. Some critics have read the relationship between Manley and Gigi as incestuous.

Martha Stone Jury Martha Stone is Harper Jury's first wife and Menus Jury's mother. Harper believes that she betrays him by having an affair.

Mary Magna (Mother, Mother Superior) Mary Magna is a Catholic nun who eventually becomes the Mother Superior at the Convent. She kidnaps Consolata from the streets of Brazil along with two other street children. Mary Magna becomes enamored of Consolata. She leaves the other two children in Brazil and brings Connie with her to her new assignment in Oklahoma. Mary Magna helps raise Connie at the Convent. Mary Magna lives in the Convent until she dies. Consolata prolongs Mary Magna's life by using her powers to resurrect the woman. Mary Magna has a strange, unexplained light surrounding her as she lies in her bed. In her delirium, she rambles incoherently, switching from Latin to English. She dies looking very pale and without color in her eyes. Connie says that Mary Magna's eyes originally were blue. When

Mary Magna dies, upon her request, her body is shipped to Lake Superior. After Mary Magna's death, Consolata is inconsolable and despondent.

Mavis Goodroe Albright Mavis Albright is the first woman to arrive at the Convent after the school closes. Mavis is on the run from Maryland after having escaped from an abusive marriage. The catalyst for Mavis's departure is the death of her infant twins and her belief that her other children are trying to kill her. Mavis leaves her babies, Merle and Pearl, in her car during the summer while she goes grocery shopping; when she is in the store, the babies suffocate. After the death of the babies, Mavis steals her husband's prize possession, his mint green 1965 Cadillac and she runs away from him and from her children, Sal, Frankie, and Billy James.

After making a brief stop at her mother's home, Mavis takes off for Los Angeles. She takes panties, aspirin, money, and gas from her mother's house. As she drives cross-county, Mavis picks up hitchhiking girls who are standing along the roadside. She wants the girls to help pay for gas. Mavis grows attached to one of the girls, Bennie. While traveling west, Mavis accidentally arrives at the Convent after running out of gas. She lives at the Convent for long stretches, interrupted by periodic road trips. Mavis is haunted by what she believes are the ghosts of her dead twins. Mavis loves Consolata, but she never quite gets along with Gigi. Gigi thinks that Mavis is sexless. Mavis's fights with Gigi make her feel liberated and exhilarated. Like the other Convent residents, eventually she finds consolation and affirmation through Consolata's healing wisdom.

Melinda DuPres Melinda DuPres is Pious DuPres's wife. Pious sends her for help after Lone tells him about the plan for the attack on the Convent.

Menus Jury Menus Jury is the son of Martha Stone Jury and Harper Jury. Harper Jury believes that Martha Stone has an affair and as a result, their marriage ends. Harper remarries Catherine Jury. Harper seems to hold his belief in Martha's infidelity against Menus. He does not let his son forget his mother's flaws.

Menus Jury serves time in Vietnam. After his tour, he drinks heavily every weekend upon returning to Ruby. Menus creates a great deal of controversy when he brings a light-skinned woman home from Virginia as his bride. As a result of this relationship that the New Fathers understand as a breach of the rules of Ruby, Menus has to give up his home.

After his return from Vietnam, Menus cuts hair in the back of Ace's Grocery on Saturdays after Anna takes over the store. During a particularly bad period, Menus Jury goes to the Convent drunk and the women take care of him and clean him up. Despite their kindness, Menus Jury is part of the group that goes out to the Convent to gun the women down.

Merle and Perle Albright Merle and Pearl Albright are the twin babies that Mavis leaves in the mint green Cadillac while she goes into the grocery store to get hot dogs for her husband and the babies' father, Frank. The boy and girl twins suffocate in the Cadillac. After Mavis arrives at the Convent, she thinks that the infants haunt the place. She experiences them as lost, laughing babies who grow with time.

Michael Seawright Michael Seawright is Timothy Seawright's grandson and is one of the children who participate in the Ruby Christmas pageant.

Mickey Rood Mickey is Gigi's ex-lover. He tells Gigi (Grace) about a rock formation located in Wish, Arizona, of a couple who look like they are having sex. Mickey is with Gigi in Oakland, California. Mickey is sentenced to 90 days in jail after his arrest in the wake of a riot.

Milton Truelove Milton Truelove is Pallas Truelove's father and Divine Truelove's former husband. Milton Truelove works as a talent scout for young performers. Pallas runs away with Carlos from the home she shares with Milton and her brother Jerome. Pallas begins to reconnect with Milton during her stay at the Convent.

Mindy Flood Morgan (Miss Mindy) Mindy Flood Morgan is Zechariah Morgan's wife and Rector Morgan's mother. She is pregnant during the journey from Fairley, Oklahoma, to Haven. Miss Mindy is Deacon and Steward's grandmother and Anna Flood's great aunt.

Ming Fleetwood Ming Fleetwood is one of Sweetie and Jeff Fleetwood's sick children. Jeff insists on naming the child Ming after his return from Vietnam.

Mirth Mirth is Elder Morgan's eldest daughter and the wife of Nathan DuPres.

Miss Esther See ESTHER

Missy Rivers Blackhorse Missy Rivers is the wife of Thomas Blackhorse and the mother of Soane and Dovey. Her name is a sort of joke, a pun on Mississippi River. She and Fairy DuPres are responsible for finding and saving Lone while on the journey from the South to Haven.

Moss DuPres Moss DuPres is one of the New Fathers, one of the men who lead the relocation of the town from Haven to Ruby, Oklahoma.

Mrs. Turtle Mrs. Turtle is the mother of Eddie Turtle, Seneca's boyfriend. Mrs. Turtle is a vegetarian who eats a strict diet. After he is imprisoned, Eddie asks Seneca to visit his mother and to ask her to cash her savings bonds and send the money to him. During Seneca's visit, Mrs. Turtle refuses to cash her savings bonds given to her by her husband. Mrs. Turtle refuses to support her son because of the nature of the crime he commits. After Seneca leaves Mrs. Turtle's house, she returns to ask Eddie's mother if she can use her phone to make a call. From outside the door, Seneca hears Mrs. Turtle crying about her son. Mrs. Turtle lives in Wichita, Kansas.

Nathan DuPres Nathan DuPres is the son of Juvenal DuPres. He is believed to be the oldest occupant of Ruby. Nathan is one of the New Fathers, one of the men who lead the relocation of the town from Haven to Ruby, Oklahoma. Nathan DuPres delivers the opening remarks at the annual Christmas pageant. The remarks consist of an anecdote, which is an incoherent recollection from his life and from a dream he has had. The tale is of a vision or dream involving an encounter with an Indian in a cotton field. Nathan DuPres loses all of his children in the tornado of 1922. His wife, Mirth, also dies in Haven, which is why he decides to leaves for Ruby. After the group relocates to Haven, Nathan tries to teach the children to ride horses, a necessary skill in his estimation.

Nathan owns a horse named Hard Goods. Billie Delia especially enjoys the rides, deriving from them a three-year old's innocent sexual pleasure. The revelation of that pleasure forever and erroneously brands Billie Delia as promiscuous. Nathan is a member of the posse that guns down the women at the Convent.

New Fathers, the The New Fathers are the men who journey with their families from Haven to establish the new town of Ruby. They are Ossie Beauchamp, Roger Best, William Cato, Moss DuPres, Nathan DuPres, Arnold Fleetwood, Ace Flood, Harper Jury, Deacon Morgan, Steward Morgan, Sargeant Person, Aaron Poole, Edward Sands, and John Seawright.

Night Night is the horse Steward rides in the dark early morning so that he can think.

nineteen negro ladies, the The nineteen negro ladies are women that Deacon and Steward admire for their beautiful skin. The women wear light materials that are mostly white in color. Some of the women wear salmon and yellow. When Steward and Deacon see them, the women are in the process of having their picture taken. The two boys fall off the fence they are sitting on in order to get the women's attention. The twins encounter the ladies when they go on a trip with their father to examine other all-black towns. Deacon and Steward are attracted to the women's light skin but reject their memory of the women because of the Disallowing and their negative associations with light-skinned African Americans.

Noah Fleetwood Noah Fleetwood is one of Sweetie and Jeff Fleetwood's sick children.

Norma Keene Fox Through her chauffer, David, Norma Keene Fox propositions Seneca under the guise of hiring the girl to do secretarial work for her while her husband, Mr. Leon Fox, is out of town. Norma Keene Fox has champagne-colored hair and has a son at Rice University. She is originally from the East and is now living in Wichita, Kansas. She calls Seneca Sweet Thing and never asks her name. Norma Keene Fox toys with Seneca for three weeks and then pays Seneca $500.00 and gives her some old clothes in return for her services.

Old Fathers   The Old Fathers are the original founders of Haven who led the exodus from the South to Oklahoma. Some of the Old Fathers are Drum Blackhorse; Zechariah Morgan; Able Flood; August Cato; Brood Poole, Sr.; Juvenal DuPres; and Booker DuPres.

Olive Best   Olive Best is Fulton Best's wife and Roger Best's mother. The couple's other children die during the influenza epidemic of 1919. Both she and Fulton are disappointed when Roger marries Delia who is not only an outsider, but is light-skinned. When Patricia Best tries to chart the genealogy of the community, she cannot discover Olive's maiden name.

Ossie Beauchamp   Ossie Beauchamp is one of the New Fathers, one of the men who lead the relocation of the town from Haven to Ruby, Oklahoma. He organizes a race to celebrate the naming of the first road in Ruby. He has a two-year-old and a four-year-old horse at the time of the celebration that he thinks are pretty as brides.

Pallas Truelove   Pallas Truelove is a rich girl who falls in love with Carlos, the janitor at her high school. Pallas Truelove has been pudgy as a child and is able to lose weight while dating Carlos. With Carlos she runs away from the home where she lives with her dad, Milton Truelove, to her mother Divine Truelove's home in Mehita, New Mexico. While Pallas and Carlos are at Divine's house, Divine and Carlos begin an affair and Pallas runs away. While she is on the run, a group of boys chase her and may have raped her. Pallas escapes from the boys by hiding in a swampy lake. While she hides, she is frightened by the possibility of discovery by the boys and by the

possible presence of unseen creatures in the water. Eventually, she gets a ride with a group of Indians, one of whom is a compassionate older woman.

Billie Delia finds Pallas at the hospital after the Indian woman drops her off there. The Indian woman is the first person to think that Pallas is pregnant. From the hospital, at Billie Delia's urging, Pallas makes her way to the Convent. Pallas is sick to her stomach during her first few weeks at the Convent, and, eventually, shows signs of her pregnancy and gives birth to a son. The baby is named Divine. Consolata helps Pallas to recover from her trauma and, after the shooting at the Convent, Pallas becomes a warrior with the other women. Her mother, Divine, sees Pallas at her home with the baby, retrieving shoes that she left at the house.

Pansy   When Patricia Best tries to chart the genealogy of the community, she cannot discover Pansy's maiden name.

Pastor Simon Cary   See SIMON CARY

Patricia Best Cato (Pat, Patsy)   Patricia is the daughter of Delia and Roger Best. Patricia's mother, Delia, dies while giving birth to a breach baby. Delia is light-skinned and the stigma of her skin color causes her to be ostracized by most of the members of the Ruby community. Patricia inherits her mother's skin color and also feels alienated from the community. Pat's house is next to the Ruby school.

Patricia is married to Billy Cato for a brief time before he is killed while serving in the military. The people of Ruby call her by her maiden name because her marriage is so short. Patricia runs the local school in Ruby and is the mother of Billie Delia. Patricia craves baking soda when she is pregnant with her daughter. She is romantically interested in Reverend Richard Misner, but the feeling is not returned. She creates a town genealogy to try to document the relationships of the inhabitants of Haven and Ruby, which she eventually destroys. Patricia and Billie Delia have a terrible fight during which Patricia gets so mad at her daughter, she almost kills her with an iron. Pat believes erroneously that her daughter is promiscuous. After the fight, Patricia and Billie Delia remain estranged.

Payne Sands   Payne Sands is the father of Linda and Lorcas Sands, two of the children in Ruby's Christmas pageant.

Peace Jury   Peace Jury is Solarine Jury's husband and the son of Harper Jury.

Peg   Peg lives in the same town as Mavis, but Mavis does not really know her well. Mavis drives by Peg's house when she is running away from her husband Frank after the death of the twins Merle and Pearl. Peg grows Rose of Sharon in her front yard and Peg's house represents Mavis's ideal of home. Peg cries at the funeral of the twins.

Penelope Person Poole   Penelope Person Poole is Sargeant and Priscilla Person's daughter. She is married to Wisdom Poole. When Lone is searching for people to help her avert the attack on the women at the Convent, she considers Penelope, but decides not to ask her since she is the daughter and the wife of two of the perpetrators.

Penny   Penny is a wayward girl who lives at the Convent while Consolata is involved in her affair with Deacon. Penny and her friend, Clarissa, help Consolata to hide her affair. As the last students at the Convent, Clarissa and Penny want to escape and have some role in determining their own destiny. The girls ask Consolata for money to help with their escape. After much coaxing, Connie gives the girls the money they request. After their escape, they send the money back to Connie using fictional names.

Peter Blackhorse   Peter Blackhorse is the son of Drum Blackhorse and the brother of Thomas and Sally. Peter Blackhorse is married to Bitty Cato Blackhorse. They are Fawn Blackhorse Cato's parents and Billy Cato's grandparents.

photographer, the   The photographer accompanies June when the journalist comes to interview Mavis after she leaves her twins, Merle and Pearl, in the Cadillac and they suffocate. The photographer takes more pictures of the car than of the family. In contrast to June, he is nonjudgmental and polite.

pick-up truck driver   The pick-up truck driver and his wife are driving past Ruby when they encounter Sweetie during her nearly unconscious walk from the town to the Convent. Although they stop, Sweetie does not accept their offer of assistance. Unbeknownst to them, Seneca has been hiding in the back of the pick-up. Seneca gets off the truck when she sees Sweetie.

Piedade   Piedade is the goddess figure in the stories Consolata tells. According to these tales, Piedade does not speak, she just sings. She appears with Consolata at the end of the novel sitting on a trash-strewn beach. She may be Consolata's mother.

Pious DuPres   Pious DuPres is Booker DuPres's son, Melinda DuPres's husband, and the father of Linda DuPres and another daughter. He is the nephew of Juvenal DuPres. After Lone tells him about the plan to attack the women of the Convent, Pious tries to intervene. He sends his wife, Melinda, to tell others and to get their help. After he learns what they have done, Pious scolds the men and tells them that they have brought shame on everyone.

Praise Compton   Praise Compton is one of the original migrants who travel from the South to Oklahoma to become one of the original members of the Haven community. Praise Compton tears her own clothes to cover baby Lone when the orphaned infant is discovered by Lone. After the Disallowing, Celeste Blackhorse gives Praise some of the food left for the group from the residents of Fairly, Oklahoma, to distribute to the other women and children.

Priscilla Person   Priscilla Person is Sargeant Person's wife and Penelope Person Poole's mother. The morning of the raid, Priscilla hears the men in her house and volunteers to cook the men breakfast. Not wanting her to overhear their plans, Sargeant sends her back to bed.

Private Smith   See Coffee Smith

Providence   Providence is the watchful housekeeper of Milton Truelove.

Pryor Morgan   Pryor Morgan is Zechariah and Mindy Morgan's son. He is also Big Daddy's brother and Deacon and Steward Morgan's uncle.

Pure Cary   Pure Cary is one of the four youngest Cary girls who participate in Ruby's Christmas pageant.

Queen Morgan   Queen Morgan is one of the children of Zechariah and Mindy Morgan.

Rector Morgan   See BIG DADDY MORGAN

Ren Beauchamp   See HELEN BEAUCHAMP

Reverend Richard Misner   Some of the more conservative residents of the controlled environment of Ruby view Richard Misner as a radical preacher. Misner is the Baptist minister at Mount Calvary. Always a mediator, Misner tries to help in the conflict between the Fleetwoods and the Morgans. He teaches black history at the school in Ruby in the afternoons. Misner values his interaction with and the perspectives of the young people of Ruby. He begins a small credit union. He has claustrophobia as a result of a jail stay he experiences following his participation in a Civil Rights protest. His willingness to embrace change and his Civil Rights activism mark him as dangerous in the estimation of the town fathers.

Reverend Senior Pulliam   Reverend Pulliam leads the Methodist congregation at New Zion. Pulliam is at philosophical odds with Reverend Richard Misner. Pulliam competes with Misner for the attention of the people of Ruby. He believes that the young people of Ruby are defaming a tradition in their interactions with the Oven and with their defiance of the traditional customs of the community. Pulliam delivers a bombastic sermon at K.D. and Arnette's wedding. Reverend Pulliam believes that the women residents of the Convent are offering food as a pagan sacrifice. He is a dark, wiry man with white hair and a very impressive physical presence. Pulliam enjoys the support of the town's fathers.

Richard Misner   See REVEREND RICHARD MISNER

Rita   Rita works with Billie Delia at the clinic where Billie Delia is employed as a nurse.

Roger Best   Roger Best is the son of Fulton and Olive Best and the husband of Delia Best. All of his brothers and sisters die during the influenza epidemic of 1919. His daughter and granddaughter are Patricia and Billie Delia Best. Roger Best drives the ambulance/hearse for the community of Ruby. Ruby's townspeople shun Roger Best because they do not approve of his wife. By marrying his wife, he becomes the first to violate the blood rule. Although he is one of the New Fathers, he is disallowed membership in the group because he marries a woman who is not from Ruby and whom the others consider too light-skinned to be accepted.

Best is the town embalmer, but he has no work since no one has died in Ruby since 1953. He dreams of being a doctor. He applies through the G. I. BILL to go to medical school but never is accepted. After abandoning his first dreams, Roger Best hopes to own a gas station. When Mary Magna dies, Roger goes out to the Convent to pick up Mary Magna's body. On the way out, he gives Gigi a ride. He leaves her there after Connie asks the girl to stay and watch while she sleeps. After the attack on the Convent, Roger Best is the person who discovers that there are no dead bodies there.

Royal Beauchamp (Roy)   Royal Beauchamp is the son of Luther and Helen Beauchamp and the brother of Destry and Vane Beauchamp. Royal is interested in Africa. Royal Beauchamp is at the meeting at the Oven and is scolded for talking back to his elders. Royal is one of the young people of Ruby who petition the adults to rename the Oven that was built by the Old Fathers and carried from Haven to Ruby by the New Fathers.

Ruby Morgan   Ruby Morgan is the person whom the town is named for. She is the baby sister of Deacon and Steward and the mother of K.D. Ruby falls ill on the journey from Haven to Ruby. She seems to recover after their arrival, but relapses. Deacon and Steward take her to Demby for medical attention, but the hospitals there will not treat her in their facilities. When she dies, her brothers learn that the personnel at the hospital were calling a veterinarian to care for their sister. Steward and Deacon remember their sister as a sweet and modest girl. Her death leaves the care of her son, K.D., in the hands of Deacon and Steward. After her death, Patricia Best believes that Steward and Deacon make a deal with God prohibiting death in the town as long as the residents keep the bloodlines pure and do not commit adultery. Miss Esther is the one who decides that the name of the new town should be Ruby.

Sal Albright (Sally) Sal is Mavis and Frank's daughter. During the interview June conducts with Mavis after the death of her twin infants, Sal digs her fingernails into her mother's side seeming to want to draw blood. Sal places Frank's razor on the table during dinner, a gesture Mavis interprets as life-threatening. Sal sits outside her mother's room and listens when her parents are having sex. The child genuinely frightens Mavis and this fear is a catalyst for Mavis's escape. Eventually, after the attack on the Convent, Mavis and Sal reunite in a diner. Sal no longer seems angry with her mother during the meeting.

Sally Blackhorse Poole Sally Blackhorse Poole is the daughter of Drum Blackhorse and the sister of Thomas and Peter. Sally Blackhorse Poole is also the wife of Aaron Poole. The couple has 13 children.

Sandra See DUSTY

Sargeant Person Sargeant Person is a local businessman and friend of Deacon and Steward. Sargeant Person is a New Father, one of the men who lead the relocation of the town from Haven to Ruby, Oklahoma. Sargeant Person is a part of the posse of men who go to the Convent to kill the women. He insists at the meeting at the Oven that the elders be respected. Sargeant Person owns a feed store. He leases land from the women of the Convent. After the attack and the women's disappearance, Sargeant is pleased that he will no longer have to pay them to use the land.

Save-Marie Fleetwood Save-Marie Fleetwood is Sweetie and Jeff Fleetwood's baby who dies.

Ruby holds its second funeral for the baby. Sweetie refuses to bury the baby on Morgan land. Richard Misner delivers a beautiful elegy for the baby—a declaration of hope and despair.

Selanie Morgan Selanie Morgan is one of the children of Zechariah and Mindy Morgan. She and her sisters, Ella and Loving, gather pink yarrow to place on Lone's mother's grave.

Seneca Seneca is abandoned by her mother, Jean, when she is only five years old. Seneca believes that Jean is her sister. Jean leaves the little girl alone in their apartment with only a note written in lipstick. Seneca thinks if she is good her sister will return. On the fourth day after Jean's departure, Seneca finally goes to the bread box where the Lorna Doones are stashed and finds the note. The desolate Seneca keeps the note with her for most of her adult life. She stashes the note in her shoe, even rescuing it from the garbage at times. As a result of the trauma of these incidents, Seneca cannot bear to see women cry.

After Jean leaves, Seneca is placed in foster care, which is where she develops the habit of cutting herself. This self-destructive behavior emerges as a response to the abuse she receives while in foster care. Seneca has a boyfriend named Eddie Turtle. Eddie Turtle is imprisoned and abusive. From prison he asks Seneca to bring him shoes and a Bible. Eddie tells her that the Bible she brings is too big. He lacks gratitude and asks only for more. He tells Seneca how to take care of his dogs and asks her to visit his mother, Mrs. Turtle, in Wichita, Kansas, in order to ask her to cash her savings bonds. Seneca travels to Wichita, but Mrs. Turtle will not cash the bonds.

In the Wichita bus station, Seneca is solicited by a woman, Mrs. Norma Fox, who pays her to be in her service for two weeks. After her time with Norma Fox, Seneca finds herself hitchhiking and stowing away in truck beds. While riding in the back of one such truck, she sees Sweetie Fleetwood walking toward the Convent. Sweetie's tears move Seneca to jump out of the truck and walk with Sweetie. While they walk, Seneca attempts to console Sweetie and keep her warm, although Sweetie seems not to notice any of her gestures. Seneca follows Sweetie all the way to the Convent, covering her with Mrs. Fox's serape. Seneca remains at the Convent. While there, Seneca tries to keep the peace between Mavis and Gigi. (For information on other significant definitions of Seneca, see Part III.)

Senior Pulliam   See REVEREND SENIOR PULLIAM

Scout Morgan   Scout Morgan is one of the sons of Mindy and Zechariah Morgan. His great-nephew is also named Scout Morgan.

Scout Morgan   Scout Morgan, named after his great uncle, is the son of Soane and Deacon Morgan and the brother of Easter Morgan. Scout is involved in a car accident while traveling home from an unapproved trip with Easter and the boys' friend July. After the accident, Consolata brings Scout back to life at Lone's request. As a result of her action, Connie earns Soane's lifelong gratitude. Later, Scout is killed while serving in Vietnam.

Shepard Morgan   Shepard Morgan is one of the children of Zechariah and Mindy Morgan.

Simon Cary (Pastor Simon Cary)   Simon Cary comes to Ruby at the end of the Korean War. He is the Pentecostal minister at the Church of the Holy Redeemer. Reverend Simon Cary is married to Lily Cary. The couple is known for their singing duets.

Sister Mary Elizabeth   Sister Mary Elizabeth is one of the Catholic sisters who teach the Arapaho girls English and Catholicism. The sisters try unsuccessfully to destroy all the evidence of the Embezzler and his lewd decorations in the mansion. After the Convent is closed as school, she leaves Oklahoma for a position in Indiana.

Sister Roberta   Sister Roberta is one of the four Catholic sisters who teach the Arapaho girls at the Convent English and Catholicism. Sister Roberta also teaches Connie to cook. The sisters try unsuccessfully to destroy all the evidence of the Embezzler and his lewd decorations in the mansion.

Soane Morgan   Soane Morgan is the daughter of Thomas and Missy Rivers Blackhorse. She is also Deacon Morgan's wife and Dovey Morgan's sister. Soane and Deacon are the parents of Easter and Scout. Soane is close friends with Consolata and with the other women at the Convent. The relationship with the women at the Convent begins after she learns that Deacon has had an affair with Consolata. Soane, while pregnant, goes to the Convent to warn Consolata to stay away from Deacon. Shortly after her walk to the Convent, Soane has a miscarriage. Later, she befriends Consolata after Connie uses her powers to save Soane's son Scout, after an automobile accident. Eventually both Easter and Scout are killed while serving in Vietnam. Soane keeps four unopened letters from her sons.

Soane Morgan takes Mavis to get gas when Mavis first arrives at the Convent. She brings Consolata sunglasses. Soane goes to the Convent to get hot peppers, which are the only things that her husband, Deek, can still taste. She also goes out to get the tonic that helps Soane to focus and relax after the death of her sons. Soane also gets pecans from the Convent. She makes more lace than she could ever use and prepares the quail that her husband hunts. After Arnette and K.D.'s wedding, Soane hosts their reception. Much to the dismay of the majority of the residents of Ruby, she invites the Convent women to the reception. After the shooting at the Convent and witnessing Steward shoot Connie in the forehead, Soane distances herself from her sister Dovey. The two women disagree about what happened and whether it was the right thing to do.

Solace Blackhorse   Solace Blackhorse is Ethan Blackhorse's wife. Patricia Best Cato believes that Ethan's name is crossed off in the Blackhorse family Bible because of infidelity in their marriage.

Solarine Jury   Solarine Jury is Peace Jury's wife and Harper Jury's daughter-in-law.

Sophie   Sophie is Eddie Turtle's dog. Eddie gives Seneca instructions about how to care for the dog while he is in prison.

Sorrow   When Patricia Best tries to chart the genealogy of the community, she cannot discover Sorrow's maiden name.

Spider Seawright Spider Seawright and his brother Timothy are at the Oven when the Convent girls arrive for Annette and K.D.'s wedding reception. They dance with the girls before the women are asked to leave.

Sterl Cato Sterl Cato is Bitty Cato Blackhorse's father. He has a peculiar relationship with Honesty Jones that is described as Sterl taking Honesty over after the death of Honesty's first husband. The couple's daughter, Bitty, is originally named Friendship.

Steven Seawright Steven Seawright is one of Thomas Seawright's grandsons. Steven is one of the children who participate in Ruby's annual Christmas pageant.

Steward Morgan Steward Morgan is the son of Rector (Big Daddy) Morgan and Beck Morgan and is Deacon Morgan's identical twin. Steward is one of the New Fathers, one of the men who lead the relocation of the town from Haven to Ruby, Oklahoma. His other siblings are Elder and Ruby Morgan. Steward is married to Dovey. Steward is a veteran and is the tougher, meaner brother. He hides his face when he prays and is known for his inflammatory remarks. He and his brother Deacon, along with eight other families, are the founders of Ruby. Steward is invested in trying to reinstate the spirit of Haven and in keeping the traditional order of the community intact.

Due to 20 years of chewing Blue Boy tobacco, his taste buds no longer function. He relies on Ace's Grocery to buy his Blue Boy. The only things that he likes to eat are the hot peppers from the Convent. From his childhood, Steward is known to be picky with his food. Steward cannot sleep without his wife next to him in bed. This reality becomes an issue because Dovey often stays in the house that they own in town rather than at the ranch Steward prefers. Throughout his life Steward has a habit of losing things every time he wins. He always has to have the last word. Steward rides his black horse, Night, early in the morning through his land at the ranch in order to think. Steward shoots Consolata in the forehead, even after Deacon says that he should not kill the woman, when the men from Ruby go to the Convent to attack the women.

Susannah Smith Morgan Susannah Smith Morgan is Elder's wife. The couple have seven children. Elder dies as a relatively young man, leaving his wife Susannah to raise their six living children. Four of the seven children survive into adulthood. Susannah and Elder's children leave Ruby and return only for occasional visits. As a result, Deacon does not consider Elder's children to be legitimate Morgan heirs.

Sut DuPres Sut DuPres is the husband of Frances DuPres.

Sweetie Beauchamp Fleetwood Sweetie Beauchamp Fleetwood is Luther Beauchamp's sister and is Jefferson Fleetwood's wife. All of the couple's four children are ill. Sweetie is quite serious, and leaves Richard Misner with the impression that she has an intimate relationship with God. Because of the incessant care her children need, Sweetie never seems to sleep and never leaves her house. In her desperation one night, she walks down the road all the way to the Convent without an overcoat because she just cannot handle life with her children any more. While Sweetie walks down the road, Seneca, who is hitching a ride in the back of a truck, sees Sweetie and jumps off of the back of the truck to help. When the two arrive at the Convent, Sweetie rejects the care the women offer. She swears that she hears babies crying in the house and she cannot understand why her children do not cry and are not as healthy as those she thinks she hears.

Tea Morgan Tea is Zechariah (Coffee) Morgan's twin brother. The two have an unresolved feud after Tea dances for white men who threaten the twins. Coffee does not dance. Coffee is shot in the foot as a result of his refusal and no longer considers Tea his brother. Tea's name is blotted out in the Morgan family Bible.

The Man The Man visits Consolata at the Convent. He wears a cowboy hat and sunglasses and looks like Consolata. He even has the same color eyes Connie's used to be. His visitation causes Consolata's epiphany and the complete transformation of her life.

Thomas Blackhorse   Thomas Blackhorse is the son of Drum Blackhorse and is the sibling of Peter and Sally Blackhorse. He is married to Missy Rivers. The couple are the parents of Soane and Dovey Blackhorse Morgan's father. Thomas Blackhorse is one of the Old Fathers, one of the men who make the journey from the South to found the town of Haven, Oklahoma. He and his father, Drum, lead the procession when the group migrates from the South.

Timothy Seawright   Timothy Seawright is the grandfather of Stephen and Michael Seawright.

Timothy Seawright Jr.   Spider Seawright and his brother Timothy are at the Oven when the Convent girls arrive for Annette and K.D.'s wedding reception. They dance with the girls before the Morgans ask them to leave.

Vane Beauchamp   Vane Beauchamp is the son of Helen and Luther Beauchamp and the brother of Destry and Royal Beauchamp.

walking man   The walking man is the man who appears to Big Papa (Zechariah) Morgan after his prayer vigil in the woods during the journey to Haven. Big Papa tells the wanderers to follow the man until they arrive at the land that will be Haven. The man wears a suit and carries a satchel. In addition to Big Papa, Rector (Big Daddy) Morgan sees the walking man twice, as do several young children.

white family, the   The white family consists of a man, a woman, and a baby. They are from Arkansas and stop briefly in Ruby asking for directions and medicine. Anna Flood and Richard Misner get the couple the medicine they request and advise them not to continue their travels until the impending snow storm has passed. Their baby is sick, but the wife refuses to get out of the car. The white family freezes in the blizzard because they do not heed the warnings of the townspeople. The car with their bodies remains undiscovered by anyone outside of Ruby. Some townspeople believe that the undiscovered dead whites represent a threat to the town's safety.

William Cato   See BILLY CATO

Wisdom Poole   Wisdom Poole is a resident of Ruby. He works as a farmer. Wisdom Poole is a part of the posse of men who go to the Convent to kill the women.

Zechariah Morgan (Kofi, Coffee, Big Papa)   Zechariah Morgan, otherwise known as Big Papa, is one of the Old Fathers, one of the men who make the journey from the South to found the town of Haven, Oklahoma. Coffee is his given name. Big Papa is married to Mindy Morgan. The couple are the parents of 14 children, nine of whom survive to adulthood: Pryor, Rector, Shepard, Ella, Loving, Selanie, Governor, Queen, and Scout. Big Papa is grandfather to Steward and Deacon Morgan.

Big Papa was originally named Coffee, possibly a variation on the African name Kofi. He has an identical twin named Tea. The brothers part ways after they are confronted by racist white men who demand that the two dance for their amusement. Tea complies and dances for the men. Coffee refuses and is shot in the foot as a result. When this injury happens, Coffee does not cry. After this event, Coffee no longer considers Tea his brother.

After the Civil War, Coffee holds office in Louisiana. He is thrown out of office under false charges. When he loses this position, he is unable to find a professional job. This lack of opportunity is partly what motivates him to gather a group of families and to head west to form their own town. He also changes his name to Zechariah.

Because Big Papa is unable to walk during the journey he is carried on a plank at the end of the procession. When the journey from the South to Haven seems at its lowest point, Big Papa goes to the woods to sit down and pray. After his prayer vigil, Big Papa sees a walking man. Big Papa's praying seems to conjure the appearance of the walking man. The walking man wears a suit and carries a satchel. In addition to Big Papa, the man is seen by Rector, Zechariah's son, twice and occasionally by young children. At Big Papa's insistence, the group follows the man until he leads them to the spot where Haven is built.

FURTHER READING

Bent, Geoffrey. "Less Than Divine: Toni Morrison's *Paradise*," *Southern Review* 35, no. 1 (Winter 1999): 145–150.

Cornier, Magali. "Re-Imagining Agency: Toni Morrison's *Paradise*," *African American Review* 36, no. 4 (Winter 2002): 643–662.

Dalsgard, Katrine. "The One All-Black Town Worth the Pain: (African) American Exceptionalism, Historical Narration, and the Critique of Nationhood in Toni Morrison's *Paradise*," *African American Review* 35, no. 2 (Summer 2001): 233–249.

Davidson, Rob. "Racial Stock and 8-Rocks: Communal Historiography in Toni Morrison's *Paradise*," *Twentieth Century Literature* 47, no. 3 (Fall 2001): 355–374.

Fraile-Marcos, Ana María. "Hybridizing the 'City upon a Hill' in Toni Morrison's *Paradise*," *MELUS* 28, no. 4 (Winter 2003): 3–34.

Kearly, Peter R. "Toni Morrison's *Paradise* and the Politics of Community," *Journal of American and Comparative Cultures* 23, no. 2 (Summer 2000): 9–17.

Krumholz, Linda J. "Reading and Insight in Toni Morrison's *Paradise*," *African American Review* 36, no 1 (Spring 2002): 21–35.

Page, Philip. "Furrowing All the Brows: Interpretation and the Transcendent in Toni Morrison's *Paradise*," *African American Review* 35, no. 4 (Winter 2001): 637–650.

Schur, Richard L. "Locating *Paradise* in the Post–Civil Rights Era: Toni Morrison and Critical Race Theory," *Contemporary Literature* 45, no. 2 (Summer 2004): 276–300.

Widdowson, Peter. "The American Dream Refashioned: History, Politics and Gender in Toni Morrison's *Paradise*," *Journal of American Studies* 35, no. 2 (August 2001): 313–326.

"Recitatif" (1983)

To date, Toni Morrison has published only one short story, "Recitatif." The short story first appeared in 1983 in an anthology of African-American women's writings. The collection, entitled *Confirmation*, was edited by Amiri and Amina Baraka. "Recitatif" is widely anthologized and regarded as an important component of Morrison's canon.

SYNOPSIS

The narrator of the story, Twyla, has been essentially abandoned at St. Bonaventure, or St. Bonny's, a shelter for children. The reason, says Twyla—who is eight when the story opens—is that her mother "like[s] to dance all night." At this shelter, Twyla meets another little girl, named Roberta. The narrative implies that one girl is white and the other, black, but she never clarifies which girl is of which race. That determination is left to the reader.

The two girls share a room and become good friends. Unfortunately, their mothers are not as compatible. When they visit, Roberta's mother—a large religious woman with a Bible in hand—snubs Twyla's mom, who becomes bitter, calling the other woman an expletive.

Roberta is eventually the first to leave the shelter, and the two girls lose touch. Years later, Twyla is working at a Howard Johnson's when her old roommate shows up with two men "smothered in head and facial hair." Roberta herself wears a lot of makeup. Twyla is excited, but when she reintroduces herself, Roberta seems uninterested, even dismissive. She tells Twyla that her boyfriend has an appointment with Jimi Hendrix on the west coast, but Twyla does not even know who Hendrix is. The conversation ends with Twyla feeling insulted. The two again lose touch.

Some years later, Twyla is married to a man from Newburgh, New York, a town where half the population is on welfare; the more well-to-do people—many of whom work for IBM—live outside of town. While visiting a fancy new supermarket for these rich folk, Twyla again runs into Roberta, who now lives in a nearby upper-class community and has four boys, all stepchildren. Twyla herself has a son. Roberta is obviously living well. Outside the store, Twyla sees that her old roommate arrives at the grocery in a limousine, complete with a chauffeur.

The two seem to reconnect, like old times at the shelter, and they reminisce, but Twyla asks Roberta about the snub at the Howard Johnson's. Roberta is not sure herself why she acted that way. By way of explanation, Roberta says, "Oh, Twyla, you know how it was in those days: black-white. You know how everything was." This time they promise to stay in touch.

That fall, Newburgh is divided over a racial controversy as a plan to integrate schools through busing becomes public knowledge. Twyla never really feels the racial antagonisms until she sees how much anger there is over the issue. Then, from her car, she sees her old friend, Roberta, picketing with a sign that reads "MOTHERS HAVE RIGHTS TOO!" Twyla can't understand why Roberta does not want her sons bused to other schools. Worse, Roberta only watches while the other angry mothers start to rock Twyla's car in protest. The police finally come over to break up the crowd.

Roberta is defensive about her picketing. "Maybe I am different now, Twyla," she admits. But she then recalls how, back in the shelter, Twyla once "kicked a poor old black lady when she was on the ground." But Twyla does not remember that the old lady, whose name was Maggie, was black, but only that she was a mute and could not scream for help when she was attacked. The two friends do not remember the events in the same way.

The next day, Twyla joins a counter-demonstration. With Roberta on the anti-bussing line, and Twyla on the pro-bussing line, the two women see each other from across the street, day after day, and their protests become a more personal and angry conversation between them. These protests eventually end when the schools are integrated.

A few years later, Twyla is still bothered by the accusation that she kicked an old black woman. She wonders if she could she be wrong and if Maggie actually was black. Then she remembers that she never kicked Maggie, black or white. Twyla concludes that Roberta remembered the incident incorrectly.

Finally, one Christmas, Twyla and Roberta have another reunion in a restaurant, and Roberta admits that she herself was not sure if Maggie was black or not. More importantly, she admits that Twyla did not kick the woman. She does not want Twyla to feel guilty about something she did not do. No sooner does Roberta make this revelation than she breaks down and starts to cry for the old woman and wonders about Maggie's fate.

CRITICAL COMMENTARY

The title of Morrison's lone short story has sparked much critical speculation on its significance. *Recitatif* is the French form of the word "recitative." A recitative is a musical term that refers to a segment of an opera that is sung in a way that resembles speech. The recitative is generally a solo that helps the plot to progress. It usually does not have a great deal of detail in terms of the music. The short story is a kind of solo performance for Twyla. It is also a recital, a rendition of memorized information. As with many of Morrison's other works, memory is not consistent and yet it provides the key to the central connection between the narrative's main characters, Twyla Benson and Roberta Fisk Norton.

Morrison's only published short story bears many of the characteristics of her longer works. Primarily the tale examines a friendship between two young girls whose coming of age is complicated by their uncertain relationships with their mothers. Although the girls' mothers abandon them for different reasons, the absence of a consistent, dependable maternal presence in their lives has a similar impact on both girls. Their profound feelings of loss and isolation lead them to seek sanctuary with each other in spite of their differences. "Recitatif" emphasizes one of Morrison's primary themes, the assertion that shared emotional experiences, although often profoundly distorted by perceptions of difference, are the most accurate and solid foundation available for authentic human connection.

The story hides this reality beneath layers of insignificant, yet determinative details, descriptions that often foreground and mark interactions between individuals. When Twyla and Roberta first meet, Twyla expects that Roberta is not a person with whom she should associate because of the racial difference between the two girls. Twyla has learned from her dancing mother that the differences between she and Roberta are the most crucial sources of information available to determine the nature of their relationship. Twyla learns through her interactions with Roberta that the similarities the two girls share—their vulnerability, their experience of abandonment, their lack of academic success, their loneliness—are much more profound and are better predictors of the way that they will be able to relate to each other.

Significantly the story also engages the reader in the same dilemma. The details provided about Roberta and Twyla, their mothers, and their economic status have meaning for the reader only because of the reader's own associations. Whether Twyla's mother Mary's love of dancing, for example, indicates that she is black or white is dependant upon the meanings and connotations dancing has in the reader's experience. Throughout the story, Morrison scatters information about Twyla and Roberta that proves inconclusive in terms of firmly determining the women's racial identities. The ambiguity of these details suggests that what is essential about the women, in fact about all people, is the nature of their relationship and their emotional connection with each other rather than the categories of difference that too often become the primary determining factor in human interactions.

There is a telling line in the middle of the story when both Roberta and Twyla say to each other "I wonder what made me think you were different." This line has an important and complex set of meanings. The women say this to each other in the middle of the conflict over busing in Newburgh. What they mean is that they thought that they were in agreement about what is right and what is wrong about the proposed solution to racial inequalities. The two women believe that their shared experiences should guarantee that they have common opinions. What they both fail to understand is the irony of their statement. Although they have shared life experiences and have a profound connection, they have different perceptions of what is right and wrong in the ensuing "racial strife." These differences are still not as important as the connection they share—a connection grounded in the honest sharing and communication the women generated between themselves as girls. They are not in fact substantially different. What makes them think that they are different is the world in which they live that places a premium on superficial differences as the fundamental markers of identity. The past that the girls share and their common experiences of loss at a critical point in their development unite the girls in profound ways that far outweigh the superficial distinctions that divide them.

One of those losses, the psychological motherlessness of both Twyla and Roberta, helps to explain their retrospective concern about and obsession with Maggie. Maggie is the cook at St. Bonaventure, the woman who cannot speak and, possibly, cannot hear. While Twyla and Roberta are at the orphanage, they witness the big girls attack Maggie after the woman falls in the orchard. Throughout "Recitatif," different versions of the incident surface. Although the details of the event are recounted differently, the women's obsession with Maggie indicates their fearful identification with her both as a maternal figure—as the cook, she provides the sustenance the girls consume while at the orphanage—and as a possible foreshadow of their own fate. Maggie is the disrespected and unheard old woman who appears frequently in Morrison's works. Only after Twyla and Roberta mature do they recognize the woman's potential significance and that her fate is inevitably connected with their own. The final question of the narrative, "whatever happened to Maggie" is the same as Roberta asking Twyla, "what will happen to us both," perhaps even, "what will happen to any of us?"

CHARACTERS

Bad girls (gar girls) The bad girls are the older girls at St. Bonaventure. Twyla and Roberta are afraid of the older girls because the big girls tease them and, occasionally, beat them up. Twyla and Roberta call the big girls gar girls after Roberta misunderstands and mishears the word gargoyle in civics class. The gar girls dance and smoke in the orchard.

Big Bozo (Mrs. Itkin) Twyla and Roberta call Mrs. Itkin, the woman who supervises them at St. Bonny's, Big Bozo. Twyla and Roberta's mutual dislike of Big Bozo is a source of their bonding with each other. The girls are not fond of Mrs. Itkin because she is distant and remote, if competent.

James Benson James Benson is Twyla Benson's husband. Twyla finds comfort in her relationship with James. James comes from a different background from Twyla. His family is united and close and has deep roots in their community. When Twyla is an adult, she and James live in Newburgh, James's hometown. James works as a fireman.

Joseph Benson Joseph Benson is Twyla and James Benson's son. Joseph is involved in the busing dispute in Newburgh. Joseph's involvement motivates Twyla's participation in the debate about busing.

Kenneth Norton Kenneth Norton is Roberta's wealthy husband. He is a widower with four children.

Maggie Maggie is an important figure in the early lives of Twyla and Roberta. Maggie is a kitchen worker at St. Bonny's while the girls are there. Maggie has physical challenges and is unable to speak.

While the girls are at St. Bonny's Maggie, according to Twyla, has a mishap and falls. When Twyla and Roberta remember this event, the women have different memories of what happens after Maggie falls. In Twyla's recall of the event, she remembers the girls at the orphanage laughing at Maggie after she falls. She also insists that neither she, nor Roberta help Maggie. Roberta remembers the event differently. Roberta identifies Maggie as African American. Twyla does not remember Maggie as black and says that both she and Twyla kick Maggie sometime after her fall. Later, Roberta revises her memories, and tells Twyla that the two felt inclined to kick Maggie, but did not actually follow through on their desires. Maggie and the girls' different memories of her become a source of controversy between the women.

Mary Mary is Twyla's mother. Mary is not a conscientious mother. In fact her daughter Twyla tells Roberta that she has been left at St. Bonnie's because her mother likes to dance into the early hours of the morning. Mary is easy-going and warm, but she does not provide her daughter with the care that she needs. She is described as physically attractive.

Roberta Fisk Norton When Roberta and Twyla are at St. Bonny's the girls form a fast friendship based on their similar emotional needs. Roberta finds herself at the shelter because her mother is ill. Her mother is very religious and serious. After the girls leave St. Bonny's, their meetings over the years are uncertain and superficial. Roberta has married and has four stepsons. When she and Twyla reconnect, their conflict centers around their different memories of Maggie, what happened to her, and Maggie's racial identity.

Roberta's mother Roberta's mother is ill and her incapacitation does not allow her to raise her daughter. Roberta's mother occasionally brings food to her daughter when she comes to visit. Roberta's mother is extremely religious and has with her at all times a large Bible. Roberta does not approve of Twyla's mother, Mary, but like Mary, she also is an inadequate mother to her child.

Twyla Benson Twyla Benson is the narrator of "Recitatif." She finds herself in St. Bonny's because her mother is self-absorbed and more concerned with her own needs and pleasures than those of her daughter. While she is at St. Bonny's, she develops a close friendship with another girl, Roberta.

As an adult, Twyla lives in Newburgh, New York, marries, and has a son. Occasionally through the years she encounters Roberta and the meetings with her old friend are conflicted because of the women's different memories of their shared past. Even as an adult, Twyla dreams of the orchard at St. Bonaventure.

BIBLIOGRAPHY

Hardy, Sarah Madsen. "'Recitatif': Maggie as Metaphor," *Short Stories for Students*. Vol. 5. Edited by Marie Rose Napier Kowski. Detroit: Gale, 1988. Available online. URL: http://www.enotes.com/recitatif/21689. Accessed on September 19, 2006.

Goldstein-Shirley, David. "Race and Response: Toni Morrison's 'Recitatif,'" *Short Story* 5 (Spring 1997): 77–86.

Morrison, Toni. "Recitatif." In *Confirmation: An Anthology of African American Women*, edited by Imamu Amiri Baraka and Amina Baraka. New York: Morrow, 1983.

Song of Solomon (1977)

Like Morrison's first two novels, *The Bluest Eye* and *Sula*, *Song of Solomon* is a coming of age story. Unlike her first two novels, *Song of Solomon* centrally is the saga of a young man. In fact, *Song of Solomon* is the first of Morrison's novels to have a male as a primary protagonist.

Song of Solomon draws on diverse mythological traditions, particularly biblical, Greco-Roman, and African to create a uniquely African-American narrative. The story requires the reader to participate in order to piece together the seemingly incompatible elements of the story to make a sensible and meaningful whole.

Milkman, the primary character in *Song of Solomon,* is a self-absorbed, petulant, and rootless man who begins a self-interested quest for financial gain and ends up discovering the story of his family. Through the process of learning about his history, Milkman matures, learns responsibility, transcends his own selfishness, and creates a meaningful existence for himself embedded in an embrace of his family history. *Song of Solomon* won the National Book Critics Circle Award in 1977. Morrison credits the success of *Song of Solomon* with her self-identification as a writer.

SYNOPSIS
Part I

Chapter 1

Song of Solomon begins with the story of the suicide of Robert Smith, the town's African-American life insurance agent. The man posts a note on the door of his home two days before he plans to leap off the roof of the hospital on blue silk wings he has constructed for himself. The note asks for forgiveness and states Smith's love for the entire community. Although the townspeople come to watch, no one intervenes in advance to stop Smith from his public demise.

In addition to introducing the story of Robert Smith, the first chapter demonstrates the subversive agency of the town's African-American community. The town calls a particular street Doctor Street because the only black doctor in town used to live there. The town authorities want the street to be called by its official name, Mains Avenue, and not Doctor Street. The community defies authority by calling the place Not Doctor Street.

The daughter of the doctor who used to live on the street, Ruth Dead, is present at Robert Smith's leap from Mercy Hospital. Ruth has her daughters First CORINTHIANS and Magdalene, called Lena, at her side. Mesmerized by the scene, the girls drop the red velvet rose petals they spend their days

making. Ruth is pregnant with her last child and only son, Macon Dead, who will be named after her husband, Macon Dead. After his birth, Ruth's son Macon is more popularly known as Milkman. Milkman is born shortly after Robert Smith's jump. Also present as the insurance salesman attempts to fly is Milkman's aunt, his father's sister, Pilate Dead, who tells Ruth that Milkman is about to be born.

The novel begins with this evocative and sensuous winter scene. With the snow, the blue wings, and the red petals, Morrison suggests that this is fundamentally an American story. As Robert Smith sways in the wind on the roof of the hospital, Pilate sings a song that seems to narrate the scene. Although Pilate does not know it, the song contains the primary story of the novel: the story of Milkman and the Deads.

Eventually Robert Smith jumps off the roof and his inability to fly marks the consciousness of Milkman as he is born the next morning. Although some people feel that Milkman has some supernatural qualities, others find him uninteresting. Milkman arrives in a family that is deeply unhappy and terrorized by its patriarch, Macon Dead. Macon is mean and verbally vicious to Ruth, for whom he has no respect. He criticizes everything about her, from her attempts to decorate to her cooking.

Seeking affection and affirmation, Ruth breastfeeds her son long past the time that he requires her direct sustenance. Macon's helper, Freddie, witnesses Ruth breastfeeding the boy and christens him with the name that he retains for the rest of his life, Milkman. Although he does not know the source of the name, Milkman's father, Macon, hates it and sees it as an example of a problematic naming tradition in his family. His own father chose Pilate's name in a random selection from the Bible. Because Macon Sr. could not read, the midwife explained to him that the name referred to the Pilate who was responsible for Christ's killing. Macon Sr., bitter about the death of his wife during childbirth, keeps the name for his daughter.

The family name, Macon Dead, was also acquired by chance. An intoxicated Yankee soldier puts all of the information for Milkman's grandfather in the wrong blanks, leaving the family with the last name as Dead and the first name as Macon rather than his place of origin. In that inglorious way, the first Macon Dead receives his name and passes it down to his son, who, despite his disdain for it, likewise bestows it upon his own son, Milkman.

Macon Dead Jr.'s entire identity and sense of self-worth are built upon his possessions. Through ownership, Macon feels he has control of the world and that he has security. It is that sense of security that gives him the courage to ask Dr. Foster for permission to marry his daughter, Ruth. She appeals to Macon because of her status as the doctor's daughter.

Not only does Macon show a lack of empathy and compassion to his family, but he also has no mercy for his tenants when they fall on hard times and are unable to pay their rent. One of his tenants, Mrs. Bains, comes to ask for an extension on the rent, and he simply repeats the date that the money is due. Mrs. Bains's grandson, Guitar, who eventually becomes Milkman's best friend, witnesses Macon's disregard, and his eventual bitterness toward Milkman's father and the Deads has its roots in that exchange.

Another tenant of Macon's, named Porter, gets drunk and threatens to kill himself or someone else if he cannot find someone to have sex with. Macon is entirely unconcerned with any of the details of the situation. Knowing that Porter just got paid, all Macon wants is the rent money Porter owes him.

Macon's character stands in stark contrast to that of his sister, Pilate. The two siblings value completely different aspects of the world. To make money, Pilate sells wine to the community. She lives simply in a one-story house without electricity. Pilate's character is epitomized by the absence of her navel. Pilate comes into the world of her own agency and lives without dependency on others. Although Macon witnesses Pilate's birth, which occurs after their mother's death in childbirth, he disregards and devalues precisely what is unique about his sister.

As Macon walks home at the end of the chapter, he passes Pilate's house and he loiters as he hears her singing by candlelight with her daughter, Reba, and her granddaughter Hagar as she gently stirs the contents of a pot.

Chapter 2

Macon likes to display his possessions, including his family and his car, so on Sundays they go for rides

so that he can display his wealth to the community. While out on the ride, the young Milkman has to urinate. He carelessly pees on his sister Magdalene, called Lena. The incident repeats symbolically over and over again in Milkman's relationship with his sisters and with his family in general.

Although Macon tries to prevent Pilate and Milkman from developing a relationship, the boy seeks out the aunt he has heard so much about. During the first meeting between Pilate and her nephew, Milkman is enchanted by her presence. She gives Milkman and his friend Guitar a soft-boiled egg, and she tells them the story of her father, Milkman's grandfather, Macon Dead Sr. She tells Milkman about how he was murdered for his land and that she and his father, Macon Jr., were left orphaned and wandering around in the woods. She also shares her encounters with her father after his death. He visits Pilate frequently and speaks to her.

While at Pilate's, Milkman also meets his cousin Hagar and begins a lustful infatuation with her that lasts for many years. They also meet Reba, Pilate's daughter and Hagar's mother. Reba's most notable characteristic is that she is lucky. Without trying, she wins things. The boys witness that all is not perfect with Pilate and her family when Hagar says that she has not always had all that she needs emotionally. The three women continue to enchant the boys as they break into song.

Macon is greatly displeased with his son's association with Pilate, yet Milkman's encounter causes him to reflect on the past and to share some of that history with Milkman. He tells Milkman about his father's land in Montour County and of the farm they called Lincoln's Heaven. He also tells Milkman more about his parents and their meeting on a wagon headed north right after the end of the Civil War.

In spite of his reverie, Macon still warns Milkman to stay away from Pilate. He tells him the story of the snake that, although nurtured and fed, kills the man who cares for him. When the man questions the snake about why, the snake says that the man always knew that she was a snake. This cautionary tale is meant to warn Milkman away from Pilate. Macon also says that he is going to teach Milkman about work and about some practical skills.

Chapter 3

In spite of Macon's efforts, Milkman continues to visit Pilate. He also works with his father and spends time with his friend Guitar. During one of their roams about town, Guitar tells Milkman that he is not able to eat sweets because they remind him of his father's fatal accident in a sawmill. The sawmill owner's wife gave Guitar and his siblings a candy called Divinity, and ever since that time, sweets make Guitar ill.

Guitar is Milkman's bridge to a community that, because of his father, sees him as an outsider. As he grows, Milkman notices a physical abnormality—one of his legs is longer than the other. He is self-conscious about what he views as a deformity and expends a great deal of effort trying to disguise his leg. He also spends a great deal of energy trying to distinguish himself physically from Macon. All of this effort at identity formation is external and superficial, and Milkman spends no time developing an interior life, a self.

One act Milkman perpetrates that makes him feel as if he is a man is the evening he hits his father, presumably to protect his mother. Following Milkman's assault, Macon tells his son the reasons he feels justified in hitting Ruth. He tells Milkman that he believes that the relationship between Ruth and her own father was unnatural. Macon claims that when the doctor died, he found Ruth naked in bed with his corpse, sucking on the fingers of his body.

After his father's revelation, Milkman goes for a walk to reflect on what he has been told. As he walks he remembers the incident that earned him his name, Freddy's observation of Ruth breastfeeding him when he was past the age to need his mother's milk. This memory makes his father's story seem more credible.

Milkman finds himself at Tommy's Barbershop. When he walks in, the men are listening intently to a radio broadcast detailing the murder of EMMETT TILL. The men in the shop debate the situation and what they believe the outcome will be, given the racism of the time. Guitar and Milkman leave the barbershop and head for a bar named Mary's where Milkman tells Guitar the story of his fight with his father. Trying to be empathetic, Guitar tells Milkman the story of accidentally killing a doe when hunting. Milkman and Guitar connect their situations with Emmett Till; eventually, with nothing resolved, they end the evening.

Chapter 4

Milkman grows tired of his escapades with Hagar and decides to end the relationship. In the beginning, Hagar is in control of the relationship and Milkman is hungry for her. As the years progress, Milkman begins to lose interest in his cousin and, rather than speaking to her face to face, he writes her a note expressing his appreciation for the years they have spent together. The note deranges Hagar and causes her to respond violently in a desperate attempt to get Milkman's attention.

Milkman also begins to feel a strain in his relationship with Guitar. Guitar begins to get serious about the realities of racial conflict and violence and Milkman is too self-involved to care about anything that is not immediately affecting him. Guitar accuses Milkman of being aimless. Freddie warns Milkman that Guitar has found an outlet for his frustration through membership in an organization. Thinking Freddie drunk, Milkman does not believe him.

Chapter 5

Tired of running from Hagar's monthly attempts to kill him, Milkman decides to confront his fear of her and of death. The night he expects Hagar, he goes to Guitar's apartment in a half-hearted effort to hide.

The two get into a heated discussion about what is important and what they need to value in their lives. They do not agree. Guitar, however, concedes to let Milkman spend the night in his apartment. Alone, Guitar awaits Hagar's impending, potentially murderous arrival.

While he waits, he thinks about the trip he took following his mother. Seeing her going out at an uncharacteristically late hour, he decides to go often her and see what she is doing. Milkman discovers that his mother travels to a nearby town, Fairfield Heights, where her father is buried. She spends the night at the cemetery on his grave. When she learns that she has been discovered, Ruth tells Milkman her side of the story.

Ruth tries to explain to Milkman her childhood isolation. She says that the doctor is the only person who cares about her existence, who is interested enough in her to be curious about her activities. She accuses Macon of trying to kill her father and the unborn Milkman. She maintains that Pilate's guidance was the only force that allowed Milkman to survive his trials and to be born. When asked, Ruth tells Milkman that she was not naked with her father. She says she was in her slip and kissed her father's fingers as the only part of him not ravaged by disease. Milkman also asks her about breastfeeding him too long. She says that her only intention was to guide him and to hope for the best for him.

Milkman's reverie is broken by the sound of Hagar's approach. She has been trying to attack Milkman once a month since she received his letter ending their relationship. Hagar is incompetent in her attempts to kill Milkman because she really does not want him to die. When she reaches the inside of Guitar's apartment, she raises the butcher knife she carries up above her head and brings it down on Milkman's collar bone. When she raises the knife again, she finds she cannot move her arms.

Milkman feels he has achieved the victory he sought. With no compassion for this woman, his cousin, who loves him so madly, Milkman utters an obscene suggestion for Hagar to plunge the knife into her genitals. In this decisive moment, Hagar despairingly gives up her monthly hunts.

Ruth learns of Hagar's attempts to kill her son from Freddie and she is reminded of the other time Milkman's life was threatened, when his father wanted to kill him before he was even born. After the doctor's death, Macon stops having sex with Ruth. Pilate and Ruth conspire to get Macon to make love to her so that she can have another child. Macon is furious about Ruth's pregnancy and tries to kill his unborn son. Ruth and Pilate together protect the child from Macon.

So when Ruth learns of Hagar's attempts to murder her son, she again turns to Pilate for help. At Pilate's house, she has a confrontation with Hagar in which they both declare their importance in Milkman's life. Pilate interrupts to remind them that Milkman cares for neither of them. Pilate shares with Ruth some of the history of her father

and of her travels after she and Macon go separate ways following the murder of their father.

Pilate headed for Virginia because she remembered that Virginia is the state her dead mother was from. Pilate finds herself with a preacher's family who takes her in, but she has to leave when the wife discovers the preacher fondling her. With only a geography book she acquired during her stay with the preacher's family, Pilate ventures out again on her own. This time she stays with a group of migrant workers and is nurtured by a root woman. While with this group, she takes a lover who casually mentions to the others that she has no navel. They ask her to leave, and Pilate learns that her stomach is different from everyone else's in the world.

After several other rejections, Pilate learns to keep her stomach hidden. She ends up on an island off the coast of Virginia where she meets another lover. She becomes pregnant and gives birth to Reba. While she recovers from the delivery, her dead father comes to her. She finds the visit comforting and decides to follow what she believes is his advice and sing. The singing cheers her, along with her father's other admonition that cryptically advises her that there is always responsibility when a person leaves a situation. Pilate believes that her father means that she needs to return to the cave where she and Macon went after he was murdered and retrieve the body of the man she and Macon killed there. She does this and carries the body around with her for the rest of her life.

Restless, Pilate leaves the island with Reba and wanders from place to place for the next 20 years and decides, because she thinks it will be good for her granddaughter Hagar, to find Macon and settle down near family. Although Macon does not welcome her arrival, Pilate stays because she thinks she can be of some help to Ruth.

Chapter 6

The chapter begins with Milkman and Guitar's discussion of Hagar as they sit in Mary's Place. Guitar recalls that, when he returned to his apartment after her final confrontation with Milkman, he finds her standing in the same position she was in when Milkman left. Guitar asks Milkman what he did to Hagar, and Milkman takes no responsibility for her emotional state. Milkman confronts Guitar about his newfound secrecy and asks if Guitar trusts him. Guitar tells Milkman that he is not sure he can trust Milkman.

Eventually deciding that he can trust his friend, Guitar tells Milkman of his involvement in an organization called the Seven Days. Guitar explains that the Seven Days states as its purpose retribution for racially based injustice. The group consists of seven men. Their function is to make certain that if a crime is committed against a black person and goes unpunished, they will commit the same crime against a white person to even the score. Guitar explains to Milkman his belief that whites are unnatural and violent. Milkman tries to counter Guitar's arguments but is unsuccessful. Guitar reveals that he is the Sunday man, responsible for replicating all racist violent acts that go unpunished and originally happen on Sunday.

Chapter 7

Milkman senses his inertia and pleads with his father to be able to travel for a year, to go and do something on his own. As they discuss the situation, Milkman inadvertently mentions Pilate's green bag—the one that, unknown to Milkman, contains human remains. When Macon learns of the bag, he immediately believes that it contains money and he tells Milkman the rest of the story of the days following his father's death:

Following the witness of their father's murder, the children run to the home of the midwife who delivered them, Circe. She takes them in without her employer's knowledge. The children—Pilate and Macon—are in danger because they can identify the men who killed their father. While the children stay with Circe, Pilate pierces her ear and makes an earring of her mother's snuffbox, the only item the children take from their home. In the box, she places the piece of paper from the Bible where her father wrote her name. They stay with Circe for two weeks and then decide to set out on their own.

At first the children are delighted to be out in the open air and free. Then they notice a man who looks like their father following them at various points in their journey. He appears to be there no matter which direction the children go. At night

they find a cave and move toward its mouth. The man stands there and beckons to them to come into the cave. They follow the man who they believe is their father.

In the morning, Macon wakes and goes to find a place to defecate. As he returns to the cave, he happens upon a white man who had been sleeping in the cave. In his terror, Macon kills the man and covers him with a blanket. He then examines the man's things and finds gold. The children argue about whether they should take the gold. Pilate argues that it does not belong to them and that taking the gold will make them more of a target for the people who are looking for them. The children fight and, eventually, go their separate ways. Macon always believes that Pilate takes the gold.

After hearing from Milkman that Pilate has a green sack hanging in her home, Macon feels that his long-term suspicion has been confirmed. Macon is certain that Pilate has the gold. In order to motivate Milkman, he assures him that if he gets the gold, he will let him go on the trip that he wishes to go on and that he will give his son half of the money.

Chapter 8

The chapter begins shortly after the 1963 attack on the Sixteenth Street Bethel Baptist Church in Birmingham, Alabama. As the Sunday man, Guitar becomes responsible for replicating the event. As such, he is in desperate need of money. So when Milkman approaches him about robbing Pilate he is more than eager to participate. Preparing for the task renews the bonds between Guitar and Milkman that had grown strained.

When the boys muse about what they will spend their money on, Guitar thinks of things for other people, while Milkman only dreams of buying things he wants for himself. On the other hand, Milkman is reluctant to rob his aunt and feels guilty about taking from a woman who has been so generous toward him. Guitar inspires him with a speech that encourages him to embrace and live his life. Milkman then begins to understand what it might be like to have a self, a personhood based on his own action and thought.

Guitar and Milkman go to Pilate's house on a night when the air, inexplicably, smells like ginger.

They cut the sack down from its moorings and walk out the door. Pilate, who of course is aware of what the boys are doing, wonders what they want with the green sack.

Chapter 9

Chapter nine begins with the story of the now-adult Corinthians Dead. The college-educated woman says that she finds work as a secretary and personal assistant for the state poet laureate, Michael-Mary Graham, when in reality she works as her maid. While riding the bus to work, she is drawn into a courtship with Porter.

Although he is content for a while to have a furtive, secret relationship with Corinthians, eventually, after her repeated refusals to go to his room, Porter recognizes that she is ashamed of him and decides to end the relationship. Corinthians, recognizing that the relationship means a great deal to her, fights to keep him and agrees to go to his room. As Corinthians sneaks back into her father's house, she overhears Macon and Milkman arguing.

Corinthians's brother and father are arguing about the outcome of Milkman and Guitar's robbery of Pilate. Guitar and Milkman are picked up by the police after they leave Pilate's house. They discover in the police station that the green bag contains bones and rocks, not gold. Macon refuses to accept the reality of his son's vulnerability—that his money and reputation will not prevent his son from being harassed by the police. He wants to blame the trouble on Guitar and the fact that he is poor.

In fact, the whole situation is salvaged by a combination of Macon's money and Pilate's willingness to perform for the policemen the stereotypes that they already believe. When Pilate arrives at the police station seeming like a witless, superstitious MAMMY, the police are amused and see the entire episode as comic rather than as threatening.

Macon still will not let go of the idea that acquiring the gold is a possibility. He tells Milkman that the gold must still be in the cave. As Milkman reflects on the evening, he marvels at Pilate's craft, worries about Guitar's transformation into someone filled with hate, and, by association, figures out that Corinthians's Porter is a member of the Seven Days.

Milkman's next several days are spent in an alcoholic haze. He drinks rather than confronting the meanings of his act. His sister Magdalene, called Lena, confronts him and points out his ineffectual and parasitic relationship with his family. She reveals to him the results of his casual report to Macon of the relationship between Porter and CORINTHIANS: Macon ends the relationship and Corinthians is devastated. Magdalene called Lena tells Milkman that his passive abuse must stop and that he should leave. Milkman decides to take her advice.

Part II

Chapter 10

After taking his first flight and then a bus, Milkman begins his adventure away from home by visiting the home where Macon and Pilate ran to after the murder of their father. When Milkman arrives in Danville, Pennsylvania, for the first time in his life he is in a community where they know his family. He feels a sense of belonging and connection that he has never had before. He also gets a more generous, broader portrait of his father.

At the house, Milkman is shocked to discover the woman Milkman and Pilate sought when they ran there so many years ago, Circe. Whether Circe is alive or a ghost is unclear. She tells the story of her work with the owners of the house, the Butlers. She claims to have overseen the demise of the family and that she will remain in the house until everything is utterly destroyed.

Milkman learns many important details of his family's story from his encounter with Circe. Two of the most important details are Milkman's discovery that the men who killed his grandfather took his body to the cave to hide it after the body floated up out of a shallow grave and that his grandfather's name before the drunken Yankees' rechristening was Jake.

Milkman walks to the cave and finds that the gold is not there. The hunt has him energized, however, and so he decides to continue to look for the lost gold and leaves Danville on a bus headed for Virginia.

Chapter 11

In Virginia, Milkman looks for a town that he eventually learns is called Shalimar. He also discovers that Guitar is looking for him. His friend leaves Milkman a cryptic and ominous message about days (a reference to Guitar's association with the Seven Days) that Milkman recognizes as a threat.

The difference between Milkman's way of functioning in the world and the mores of the town get him in trouble with the men in the town. He gets in a fight because he unintentionally offends the people by not getting to know them before he requests information and favors. After the fight with a young man named Saul, some of the older men of the town ask him if he would like to join them to go hunting. Finally, feeling somewhat accepted, Milkman agrees to go with the men.

As they walk through the woods, Milkman has a kind of initiation ritual. He has to communicate with the other men to follow what is happening. They are used to the woods and the arduous distance and Milkman is no match for them. He stops to rest and realizes that all of the props that he has used to support him his whole life, his money, his name, mean nothing out here. In the woods, with these men, he only has himself on which to depend. He also notes that there are other ways to communicate than the ones with which he is familiar. The language of the hunt is the language of survival, communicating necessary information rather than relying on systems of meaning that do not ultimately have relevance.

In the midst of his reflections, Milkman is interrupted by a wire pulled around his neck by Guitar. His oldest friend tries to kill him. Startled by the approaching men who have treed a bobcat, Guitar runs away. Milkman uses his own, newly acquired resources to join the men and help them to kill the bobcat. The encounter in the woods is critical to Milkman's development. For the first time in his life he has a genuine connection to others that is based on experience and not on hierarchy. The men like him for who he is and Milkman begins to like himself more. He also loses his limp.

The next morning, Milkman awakes eager to find out more about his family's story. He learns that his grandmother, Sing, may have been a playmate of one of the older ladies in town, Susan Byrd. He spends the night with a woman named Sweet, a woman whose care and attention he appreciates

and who he wants to nourish and care for, an experience he has not had before.

Chapter 12

Milkman begins the day by visiting Susan Byrd and asking if she has any information about his grandmother Sing. Susan tells him the story of Sing Byrd, but the information she has about her does not match the story Milkman knows. As he walks back to town from Susan Byrd's, he runs into Guitar. Guitar accuses him of taking the gold from the cave and then sending it somewhere. Despite Milkman's denials, Guitar does not believe him. The hatred that is at the heart of the Seven Days infects Guitar and distorts his judgment. He tells Milkman that he is going to kill him after the gold he believes Milkman has shipped arrives.

Milkman returns to Sweet's that night and he dreams of flying. While he is at the general store, he overhears some children in the town playing a game that tells the story of his family. Although he has heard it many times, he finally has both the knowledge to understand its meaning and the ears to hear. He also experiences empathy and regret for the first time in his life. Milkman understands more about the way his father behaves and about his mother's pain. He also regrets his treatment of Hagar and acknowledges his participation in her downfall. He realizes that Hagar's craziness made him a celebrity and made him seem more desirable and manly.

Chapter 13

The novel shifts back north and to Hagar's story. After Milkman's rejection, Hagar desperately tries to understand the reasons Milkman does not love her. She lies in bed until Pilate gives her a compact. When Hagar sees her reflection, she thinks that her appearance is the reason for Milkman's rejection. She decides that the solution is to go shopping for new clothes, cosmetics, and a new hairdo. It begins to rain, and Hagar's bags and her temporary recovery begin to disintegrate. Hagar cannot recover from Milkman's rejection and, eventually, dies of a broken heart.

Ruth insists that Macon pay for the funeral. Reluctantly he does so. The funeral is filled with Pilate and Reba's singing. The two women sing for mercy. Pilate proclaims that her lost granddaughter was dearly loved.

Chapter 14

In Shalimar, unaware of the events that have transpired at home, Milkman returns to Susan Byrd's house to ask her some more questions about the story that he is piecing together. He discovers that Susan Byrd simply did not want to tell the story of Sing in front of her nosy friend Grace. He learns that his great-grandmother and grandfather grew up together and that his grandfather is one of the flying Africans, the group of enslaved Africans who were said to be able to fly. Solomon, Milkman's great-grandfather is the man of the legend. Milkman's grandfather, Jake, is said to be the only one of Solomon's 21 children that he tries to take with him when he flies off.

Chapter 15

Milkman returns to Michigan energized by his knowledge that he comes from a family that can fly and has a real story. He cannot wait to see Pilate and Macon and to tell them about what he has learned about their family. He goes to Pilate's house first and she greets him by breaking a green bottle over his head and knocking him unconscious. When he regains consciousness, he realizes that something must be wrong with Hagar. Eventually he learns of her death, and Milkman finally acknowledges his responsibility for her life and death. Pilate gives him a box of the dead girl's hair as a way of accepting the burden of his failure.

Milkman tells Pilate that it is her father's bones she has been carrying all of those years. He also tells her that her father's ghost was not telling her to sing but was calling to Pilate's mother, Sing. Pilate and Milkman return to Shalimar to bury Jake. After the twilight burial, Guitar fatally shoots Pilate. Milkman's transformation into responsible adulthood is complete as he sings to Pilate the family song as she passes into death.

After Pilate dies, Milkman faces Guitar and offers him his life. The novel does not specify what the particular details are of the final encounter between Guitar and Milkman. What ultimately matters is that Milkman values himself and his family narrative enough to relinquish the illusion of control that prevents human beings from living, from flying with the currents of time and change.

CRITICAL COMMENTARY

One of the many long-lasting impacts of the slave trade and the subsequent dispersal of Africans throughout the countries of the Western Hemisphere was the erosion of a positive collective identity. The importance of a personal sense of history is particularly evident for African Americans given their involuntary severance from their heritage coupled with the inherent difficulties of minority life.

Song of Solomon highlights the personal and community impacts of the erasure of the histories of marginalized people. Through reclamation of his family's lost history, the novel's central male protagonist, Milkman Dead, becomes self-affirming and discovers his own worth with the assistance his aunt, Pilate Dead. In order to become self-affirming Milkman Dead must reconstruct his ancestral narrative and relinquish his selfishness and materialism. Through Milkman's evolution, Morrison demonstrates the negative effects of the inability to construct an individual identity that is grounded in a historical foundation.

Milkman Dead is a character without rootedness. He is unable to progress spiritually or emotionally until he acknowledges, recognizes, and reclaims his connection to the past. Milkman's search demonstrates the need for African Americans to maintain or to reestablish continuity with the past in order to create the sense of identity necessary for healthy survival. Milkman is able to become self-affirming and to access a balanced identity when he rediscovers and acknowledges his family's legacy.

Before delineating the individual struggle Milkman undergoes in his search for his uniquely African-American narrative, it is important to examine the ways in which Morrison demonstrates his need for such a structure. Through self-conscious manipulation of certain biblical referents Morrison demonstrates their inability to provide a meaningful foundation for either Milkman or for his aunt, Pilate Dead.

Many sociological studies affirm the necessity of a relevant narrative for the successful development of individual identity. Connecting symbolically with a larger narrative provides a way to validate the significance of individual existence. The underlying narrative of a society functions as a common denominator and point of reference for the members of that group. In other words, the general ritual or narrative of a society is what provides an individual with personal and communal motivations.

Without a significant narrative, life can become meaningless. The situation is compounded when an individual, like Milkman Dead, is a member of a minority group, and, perhaps, excluded from the narrative structures of the dominant culture. As a result of the dissipation of a relevant cultural mythology, *Song of Solomon* suggests that African Americans must validate their individual existences by personally reconnecting with their particular past. Accordingly, Morrison emphasizes the fundamental, intrinsic importance of a larger relevant narrative to the formation of individual identity and structures her novel around the protagonist's simultaneous acquisition of self-affirmation and his ancestral/racial narrative. Utilizing the larger narratives of Western society, particularly biblical mythologies, Morrison reveals their failure to satisfy the need to uncover an ethnically relevant story. Biblical reference points become a guide to Milkman's discovery of a personal, unique, and particularly African-American narrative.

The opening scene of the novel graphically illustrates the loss of meaning in the fictional African-American community in which *Song of Solomon* is set. During this once-upon-a-time establishing scene occur both a suicide and a birth. From its beginning, *Song of Solomon* establishes life and death as parts of a cycle rather than as opposites. The drama of both the birth and the death that occur in this scene are enhanced by equally disconcerting sensory data: red velvet rose petals falling against white snow, blue silk wings, and a haunting song. All of these elements, particularly the color images, suggest an American story but, like the scattered rose petals, the parts lack unity and coherent meaning. They need a narrative framework to coalesce the pieces into a discernible whole.

Comprehension and assimilation of these pieces is the quest of Milkman Dead and also the way in which Morrison demonstrates the inability of traditional narratives to provide a completely satisfying base of meaning for her characters. Morrison particularly emphasizes the inadequacy of the biblical narrative through her use of naming. Early on, the novel establishes the inadequacy of the Bible as a lone source of information when Pilate's brother, Macon Dead, questions the accuracy of the narrative from which his family selects its names. He thinks that the names they have chosen at random from the Bible provide him with no useful knowledge of himself or of his family. Macon Dead longs for a relevant narrative from which he can derive a meaningful sense of self. Instead, he settles for the inadequate story he has inherited and relinquishes any possibility of true self-knowledge.

Unlike her brother, Pilate Dead embraces the past and her ancestors as a dynamic and useful source of information. Although Pilate does not fully understand the information she possesses, including the various nuanced meanings of her name, she appreciates that the information she has, even if incomprehensible, has value and worth. Like her biblical predecessor, Pontius Pilate, Pilate is largely unaware of the significance of her actions. Pilate, like her biblical namesake, functions as a blind catalyst for her nephew's redemption. She is unaware that she acts as a guide, but, nonetheless she provides Milkman Dead with the means to transcend his own limitations and narrowed vision through her unintentional revelation of what she knows of the Dead family narrative.

Although these similarities exist between Pilate and Pontius Pilate, it is the differences between the biblical definition and the essence of her character that expose Pilate's need for another narrative structure from which to derive meaning. For example, unlike Pontius Pilate, Pilate's actions are not destructive despite her lack of knowledge. Pilate was named when her father,

> confused and melancholy over his wife's death in child-birth, had thumbed through the Bible, and since he could not read a word, chose a group of letters that seemed to him strong and handsome; saw in them a large figure that looked like a tree hanging in some princely but protective way over a row of smaller trees. (18)

Perhaps if Macon Dead had been aware of another, more pertinent narrative source than the Bible, he could have chosen a name out of that tradition, a name that embodied the tenacity, nurturance, royalty, and connection with nature that he found appealing in the physical appearance of the word Pilate. Without such a narrative to depend on, Macon Dead is forced to remove himself even further from his own heritage and to select blindly a name from the stories of others.

Interestingly, Macon is not unaware of the Western connotations associated with his daughter's name. When the midwife examines Macon's choice of names she objects and explains the name is:

> 'Not like no riverboat pilot. Like a Christ-killing Pilate. . . . Ya don't want to
> give this motherless child the name of the man who killed Jesus, do you?'
> 'I asked Jesus to save my wife.'
> 'Careful, Macon.'
> 'I asked him all night long.'
> 'He give you your baby.'
> 'Yes. He did. Baby name Pilate.' (19)

Macon's naming of Pilate becomes a conscious rejection, a defiance of the Christian narrative within which he finds himself confined. Pilate's name, though randomly chosen, becomes a symbol of his defiant anger toward Christ who had not saved his wife, Pilate's mother. As such, Macon's choice of Pilate's name is a rejection of, and perhaps an attempt to rewrite, the biblical story.

This history of the origin of Pilate's name foreshadows her role as author of her own tale. Pilate's life is lived in defiance of traditional definitions of womanhood. Her birth from a dead mother and her maturation without a navel reinforces her metaphysical and psychological independence. Pilate is "fluky" about her name (19). Recognizing its significance, she wears a brass box earring in her ear that contains a scrap of paper with her name written on it. In this way the name remains attached to her person only by a thin band of gold. This pervasive but superficial connection demonstrates that a person's name is but one element in the definition of his or her identity. This quest for a personally, culturally, and historically apt identity that is rooted in a narrative that provides context and meaning is central to *Song of Solomon* and is the primary quest of Pilate's nephew, Milkman.

Milkman does ultimately unravel the family narrative and this victory gives some true significance to both his and Pilate's lives. During the climactic ending to the novel, Pilate yanks the name-bearing earring out of her ear to use it as a marker for her father's grave. Shortly after Pilate removes her earring, she is fatally shot. As she lies dying, her nephew renames her as he sings for her the narrative of their ancestors.

This scene, like the opening scene of the novel, is both a death and a rebirth. Pilate is baptized in her own blood, reborn/renamed from within her own tradition. She dies as Sugargirl. Sugargirl becomes an African-American personification of universal love, a singing tribute to the power of the recovery of a significant narrative. Milkman's singing of his family's song brings the novel full circle and demonstrates the necessity of the African-American narrative it unfolds.

The title of the novel *Song of Solomon* also affirms the fundamental interrelatedness between narrative and identity. The title is, in part, an allusion to the biblical book of the same name. Although there are many interpretation of the biblical SONG OF SOLOMON, one of them suggests that the story tells about the power of love over the magnetic attraction of material goods. It is the biblical emphasis on the transformative power of love that Morrison retains and incorporates into the African-American narrative that is at the heart of the novel *Song of Solomon*.

The biblical *Song of Solomon* is a love story. Chapter 1, verse 6 in the biblical *Song of Solomon* reads:

> Look not upon me because I am black,
> because the sun hath looked upon me:'
> My mother's children were angry with me;
> they made me the keeper of the vineyards;
> but mine own vineyards I have not kept.

This verse can be applied to the African experience of enslavement and as such demonstrates the role of "keeper of the vineyard" of other people's narratives that has been forced upon African Americans.

The statement "mine own vineyards I have not kept" indicates the loss of tradition and relevant narrative that occurred as a result of slavery.

The opening scene of the novel *Song of Solomon* is illusive when one attempts to understand it from an uninformed, a contextual perspective. Immediately the death and the birth that occur are seen as opposing entities. As such the events are confusing and seemingly unconnected. After completing the novel, however, and discovering a different narrative through which to comprehend the opening scene, the pieces, particularly the connection between the birth and the death, become comprehensible and fall into an intelligible pattern. In this opening scene, Morrison collapses opposing distinctions and synthesizes these elements into the creation of a new story. Through rediscovery and comprehension of an appropriate, relevant, alternative meaning-giving past, the pieces of the lives of these African-American characters take on a contiguous shape, the wholeness and unity of a newly stitched quilt constructed from pieces of an ethnically and culturally relevant narrative.

Toni Morrison's *Song of Solomon* demonstrates the need for connection with a personally relevant belief system in order to become self-affirming and to empower oneself to overcome oppression. Morrison establishes that the Bible is not, by itself, an appropriate meaning-giving source for Milkman Dead or any of the African-American characters in the novel. As an alternative, she offers the song of Solomon, a narrative grounded in the actual histories of the novel's characters.

Like so many mythological figures, by attaining flight, Milkman transcends both his humanity and his mortality and attains god-like stature. With this action he conflates the past, the present, and the future, and knits the narrative strands of the novel together. Milkman's search for identity involves recognizing and overcoming his dependence and emotional isolation through assimilation of his familial narrative. At the end of the novel, he is finally adult: capable and loving. Through her exposition of Milkman's transformation, Morrison firmly establishes the centrality of ancestral narrative and of the achievement of individual self-affirmation and an authentic identity within her fictional universe.

SOME IMPORTANT THEMES AND SYMBOLS IN *SONG OF SOLOMON*

Dependence v. Independence

From the beginning of *Song of Solomon*, Milkman needs to overcome both his dependence on and emotional isolation from others. The pivotal first scene of the novel demonstrates the secondhand way in which Milkman participates in the various events of his life. His very birth occurs as a result of someone else's action. Milkman's mother, Ruth Dead, witnesses Robert Smith's suicide, the man's failed attempt to fly on manmade wings from the roof of Mercy Hospital. The witnessing of this event brings about the early arrival of Ruth's son, Macon Jr., who soon acquires the nickname he is known by for the remainder of his life, Milkman Dead. Milkman's birth represents one of the symptomatic difficulties in his personality—his near-pathological dependence. Until he becomes autonomous through an understanding of his past he is parasitically tied to the others in his life.

Milkman's lack of interest in his own life is directly attributable to the absence of a relevant narrative. Until Milkman develops self-interest through a connection with his past, his ability to develop a positive identity is seriously handicapped. Throughout his childhood Milkman develops his unhealthy dependence on others. This characteristic of Milkman's leads to acquisition of his nickname, yet another indicator of Milkman's dependency. The traditional meaning of the name milkman is of a man who delivers to others a natural, essential, life-sustaining substance. The name as linked with *Song of Solomon*'s protagonist, however, emphasizes the boy's failure to nurture others. He is indeed a dead milkman, incapable of existing on his own, much less of enriching and nurturing the lives of those around him. The negative connotations of the name indicate Milkman's parasitical dependence on his family and his refusal to grow up and to be responsible for his own nurturance. On the other hand, the name may foreshadow Milkman's future role as a carrier of milk—the story of his family as he progresses and transforms.

The actual incident that results in Milkman's label also emphasizes his extensive dependence on others. The influence of his mother becomes a major deterrent to Milkman's autonomy. In order to satisfy her unfulfilled sexual and emotional needs, Ruth Dead breast-feeds Milkman long after it is necessary. Milkman, until this time known as Macon Jr., is no longer interested in breast-feeding, but Ruth persists until she is discovered in the act by her husband's assistant, Freddie.

Ruth Dead's abuse of her son causes him both immediate and long-term damage. The example Ruth sets for Milkman encourages him to think of people in terms of what they can do for him and begins a pattern of selfish dependence on those around him until he discovers meaning for himself through comprehension and assimilation of his family's history.

In order to fulfill his sexual needs, Milkman has a long relationship with his cousin Hagar. In this relationship he also exhibits his characteristic selfishness. His only interest in Hagar is sexual. This focus is established during his first encounter with the girl when he, ignoring her magical personality, falls in love with her behind. Throughout the course of their long relationship, Milkman insists upon positioning Hagar as a receptacle for his sexual desire. Milkman's lack of emotional connection with Hagar becomes especially apparent when he ends their long relationship with a letter. Milkman's letter illustrates his absolute disregard for Hagar when she, crazed by his rejection, attempts to kill him. The attempts on his life frighten Milkman but never cause him to reflect upon the pain he has caused Hagar or even to try to talk to her about their situation. He simply continues, albeit uneasily, in the egocentric orbit he has inhabited his entire life.

Flight

Song of Solomon borrows its central narrative, the story of Milkman's flying great-grandfather from an African-American folktale often referred to as the myth of the "Flying Africans." This folktale is thought to have been a survival of the slave trade, originating in West Africa and changing in focus and meaning with the experience of the slave trade. The tale of the flying Africans has many versions but generally involves a central mystical figure, sometimes an elder, who has firsthand knowledge of Africa and/or of African folkways. When the situation of enslavement becomes intolerable, the individual shares his or her knowledge and gives the group the insight necessary to fly back and return to Africa, away from oppression and exploitation.

This folktale provides an essential thematic frame for Morrison's *Song of Solomon*. Throughout the novel, images of flight abound. The first pages of the text introduce the theme of flight with Robert Smith's suicide note where he tells his community the date and time that he will fly from the roof of the hospital. Smith's attempted flight and failed wings begins the quest of Milkman Dead for wings of his own.

From the flying figurine on the hood of his father's Packard, to the peacock that he and Guitar observe, to the homonym of Pilate's name, "pilot," the novel resonates with all of the possible nuances and implications of the word and the idea of flight. Not only is the literal act of flight and the desire to achieve it a powerful, connecting theme in the narrative, but also flight, defined as the movement of people with an urgent need to escape their present circumstance, is key to the novel's concerns.

At the heart of the narrative Milkman eventually unravels is the trauma of the Middle Passage and the involuntary severance from Africa. The desire to return to that illusory, imagined home is the motivation for Solomon's flight. Sing and Macon Dead I meet on a wagon as they flee the South in an attempt to begin anew in the North. When that dream is destroyed by the greed and brutality of whites hungry to profit from their father's hard work, Pilate and Macon must flee for their lives from the only home they have known. Separated for years, their rift culminates in Milkman's flight back South at Lena's bitter urging.

Perhaps the most dramatic flight in the novel occurs at the end when Milkman, in the wake of Pilate's death, finally recognizes his own power and comes to value his life enough to be willing to lose it. Milkman's leap off the cliff and toward the murderous Guitar is left unresolved in the text because, whether he lives or dies, Milkman has learned to fly. He has transcended the banality of his existence and has gained the courage to embrace his own power and is, finally, fully alive.

The exploration of the dimensions of African-American flight in *Song of Solomon* is balanced and critical. The novel always takes stock of what and who is left behind, who is damaged by the departure of those seeking freedom through escape. With Solomon's departure, Ryna, his love, is left inconsolable, forever wailing in the gulch. In a moment of ironic erasure, Macon, formerly Jake, loses his entire identity and the marking that connects him with his past when he and Sing register with the FREEDMAN'S BUREAU and the drunken soldier mistakenly, yet officially renames him. When Pilate and Macon II run away from their father's land, Macon murders the old prospector, and misunderstandings about this incident forever separate the formerly close siblings. Like Ryna, both Milkman's emotional and then his physical departure from Hagar leave her inconsolable. Her value and personhood is irrelevant to Milkman when he sets off on his journey. Her subsequent death is the first consequence for which Milkman acknowledges his culpability. This acceptance is central to Milkman's soaring personal triumph at the end of the novel.

Nationalism v. Assimilation

Arguably, there have been two main philosophical points of view articulated by politicians, intellectuals, and artists about the most promising solution for the complex, often treacherous situation many African Americans face in the United States. In the early decades of the 19th century, radical writers such as David Walker advocated for racial separatism and black nation-building as a solution for what he believed were intractable race-based inequalities in American culture. Frederick Douglass and others maintained that racial equality and true integration could occur if the United States would honestly and without bias adhere to the principles articulated in its own founding documents, such as the Declaration of Independence. These two philosophical strains are apparent in the more contemporary assertions of African-American leaders MALCOLM X and MARTIN LUTHER KING JR. Their ideas and the controversy over the differences in the solutions for which these two

men were martyred were a major focus of African-American concern during the years *Song of Solomon* encompasses.

Macon II and Guitar represent extreme adaptations of assimilation and nationalism, respectively. Milkman is torn between these two most significant men in his life and is ambivalent about who to adopt as a role model. Macon Dead is defined by his adherence to capitalism and to his belief that by acquiring wealth, property, and status, he can ensure his safety and that of his family, while keeping at bay the circumstances that befell his father. Macon is deeply concerned with appearances. He marries Ruth Foster because she is the daughter of the town's most prominent African-American professional. Macon understands success in traditional American terms and believes in meritocracy, the idea that if you work hard, irrespective of your identity, you will ultimately succeed. This passion for assimilation leads him to heartless acts, as when he threatens Guitar's grandmother with eviction because she is late with the rent.

This encounter with Macon imprints itself upon the young Guitar who is a witness to Macon's mercilessness. This revelation leads him to the conclusion that materialism is akin to conformity to the same structures in the dominant culture that encourage racism. For Guitar, wealthy blacks are distanced from most African Americans and are in allegiance with the forces of oppression. Guitar's fundamental concern for African Americans is one element that differentiates him from Milkman and is the root of his eventual murderous mistrust of his best friend.

Throughout the course of their relationship, Milkman's conversations with his best friend Guitar always center on Milkman's immediate concerns whereas Guitar is most frequently focused upon larger issues that impact the entire black community. Whenever Guitar discusses something of interest to himself, Milkman ignores or changes the subject. Milkman skates on the surface of this relationship and never explores its depths, yet he illustrates his physical dependence on it by his use of Guitar's apartment for his sexual adventures.

Guitar's membership in the vigilante organization the Seven Days seems to indict the extremes of nationalism in the same way that Macon Dead's life exposes the limitations of complete adherence to assimilation. As the novel unfolds, readers learn that Robert Smith's suicide at the book's beginning is brought about, in part, from the isolation imposed by his membership in the Seven Days. The irony of the organization is that in spite of its proclamation of love for the African-American community it has pledged to protect, the Days have adopted the same brutality and inhumanity of those who perpetuate violence against them. Their rigidity and strategy of raw revenge robs the members of the organization of the very community they want to protect. This extremism ultimately leads Guitar to attempt to murder his best friend.

Through the flaws of Macon Dead and Guitar, *Song of Solomon* asks readers to consider the cost of blind adherence to ideological positions on both ends of the spectrum. Milkman eventually discerns that both the paths outlined by Macon and by Guitar lead to a closing down of individuality and possibility. After his evolutionary quest, Milkman's potential emergence may represent another possibility between the extremes of nationalism and assimilation.

CHARACTERS

Anna Djvorak Anna Djvorak is a Catholic Hungarian woman who had been one of Dr. Foster's patients while he was practicing. Because Ruth is Dr. Foster's daughter, Anna Djvorak invites Ruth to her daughter's wedding. Anna Djvorak is indebted to Dr. Foster because she believes that his medical advice, not to send her son Ricky to a sanitarium, saved the boy's life. Contrary to the opinions of most medical experts in 1903, Dr. Foster advised Mrs. Djvorak to give her son cod liver oil, rest, and eat healthy foods. After the doctor's death, Anna Djvorak extends her gratitude to his daughter, Ruth. Ruth embarrasses herself at the wedding by taking communion even though she is not Catholic.

Butlers The Butlers are the family that Circe works for as a slave and then as a servant. The Butlers are also the ones responsible for Macon Dead I's death and the loss of his land.

Calvin Breakstone Calvin Breakstone is one of the men who take Milkman on a hunting trip at night while he is in Shalimar. Calvin takes the lead in the hunt and shines the light that all of the men follow through the darkness. Calvin is the one who discovers the bobcat and explains to Milkman the sound that comes from Ryna's Gulch. He tells Milkman that the legend of Ryna maintains that she was so heartbroken at the flight of her husband, Solomon, that she lost her mind and that she could be heard screaming even after her death. Although Milkman is 20 years younger than Breakstone, he has a hard time keeping up with the fitter man. It is Calvin who, during the hunt, demonstrates communication between man and animal in a primal form that Milkman was unaware existed.

Circe Circe is an old, mysterious black woman who takes Pilate and Macon in after their father is shot and hides them in the Butlers' house, the very people who had killed him and the family for whom she works. Circe is a midwife who delivered both Pilate and Macon as well as almost everybody else in their community. Circe is present at Pilate's birth when the children's mother, Sing, dies.

While the children hide in the Butlers' house, Circe brings Pilate cherry jam on white toast, which makes the girl, accustomed to fresh and wholesome food, cry. When Pilate wants to make an earring out of the little brass box that belonged to Pilate and Macon's mother, Sing, Circe goes to the blacksmith, Reverend Cooper's father, and has him fasten a gold wire to the box. After inserting the piece of paper from the family Bible in the gold box, Pilate pierces her ear with the soldered gold wire and does not take off the earring until the very end of her life.

Circe helps Macon and Pilate for two weeks after their father is killed. Then the children run away. Inexplicably, she is still living in the Butlers' house when Milkman returns decades later on his quest for the lost gold. Characterized as a witch, Circe helps Milkman on his quest. In her extremely old age, she also outlives the Butlers, the racist white family she works for, and is determined to stay in the late Butlers' mansion with their Weimaraner dogs to watch it crumble. When Milkman comes to visit her, Circe gives him information about his family. For example, she tells him that his grandmother, Sing Dead, made his grandfather, Macon, keep the erroneous name the Union soldier gave him, Macon Dead, and that his original name was Jake. (For information on the mythological Circe, see Part III.)

Crowell Byrd (Crow Byrd)   Crowell Byrd is the father of Susan Byrd and the husband of Mary Byrd. His sister was Sing Byrd.

Dr. Foster   Dr. Foster is Ruth's father and a respected doctor, so respected that the African-American residents of the town call the street where he lives, Mains Avenue, Doctor Street. After town officials protest the impromptu renaming, the black community slyly calls the street Not Doctor Street.

Dr. Foster is well-off and elitist and is obsessed with skin-color consciousness. He treats dark-skinned blacks, including his son-in-law, Macon Dead, as inferiors. Dr. Foster has an odd relationship with his daughter that has unexplained and uncomfortable sexual overtones. Dr. Foster assumes behaviors that get him accused of acting white by blacks in his community; ironically enough, he literally turns white at the end of his life when an illness causes him to be pale, bloated, and weak.

The major cause for the break between Macon and Ruth is Macon's belief that there was some kind of attraction or behavior between Ruth and her father that had sexual dimensions. Macon objected strongly to the doctor delivering the couple's daughters, First Corinthians and Magdalene, called Lena. Macon believes that he sees Ruth kneeling, or lying, beside the doctor's dead body. After this event, Macon can never again look at his wife without disgust. Another source of Macon's resentment toward his father-in-law is the fact that Dr. Foster would not lend Macon money to buy property near the railroad.

Dr. Foster dies an awful death. He loses his vitality and strength. Macon believes that his death is due to an overdose of ether.

Dr. Singleton   Dr. Singleton is a professional in town who, according to Corinthians, can afford to buy a house on the lake in addition to his main home.

Elizabeth Butler   Elizabeth Butler is the last remaining member of the Butler family. She has no children. Some of the members of the black Danville community believe that her death is a kind of karmic retribution for the murder of Macon Dead and the theft of his land. She is the one who raised the Weimaraner dogs that Circe eventually allows to destroy the house. She kills herself because the family fortune is gone.

Emmett Till   Emmett Till was a young African-American boy who was tortured to death in 1953 in Sunflower County, Mississippi, because he was accused of whistling at a white woman. In the novel, a crowd of men gather in the black barbershop when the news of his murder comes over the radio. Each of the men reacts differently to the news of Till's lynching. Freddie says it is stupid for a black man to do what Till was accused of in the South and expect to get away with it. Others argue that black men cannot be men in the South.

In the midst of debate, Empire State stands silent and thoughtful. Later, the novel reveals that Empire State is one of the Seven Days and that he has killed a white man in retaliation for Till's murder. By reexamining the scene in the barbershop, it becomes apparent which of the speakers present are in the Days and which are not. (For more information about Emmett Till, see Part III.)

Empire State   Empire State is a possibly mute man who works at the barber shop. Although many people believe that he is mentally impaired, Empire State's issues come from his response to the discovery of his wife in bed with another black man. Empire State met his wife, who was white, in France during World War I. They lived together happily for six years until he discovered that she loved and was attracted to all black men, not just him. Guitar hides Empire State when police believe that he killed a white boy.

Esther Cooper   See MRS. COOPER

Father Padrew   Father Padrew is a Catholic priest who tells Ruth that only Catholics take communion after she takes communion during the wedding of Anna Djvorak's daughter.

Feather   Feather is the owner of the pool hall on Tenth Street. The pool hall is in the middle of a seedy, shady area of town. Feather is a short and stout man with thinning curly hair. Feather does not want Milkman in his pool hall because he is underage and, mostly, because he is Macon's son.

First Corinthians Dead (Corinthians, Corrie)
First Corinthians Dead is Ruth's second daughter. First Corinthians is one year younger than Lena, and is not as interested in making velvet roses as her sister. Corinthians goes away and spends three years in college, at Bryn Mawr, including a junior year in France before returning to live with her family. She is trained to become a genteel wife. Both she and her mother are shocked that she never receives a marriage proposal. The professional men in her community find her too complacent and elitist to be fully desirable.

Perhaps because she has seen more of the world, First Corinthians is more restless than her sister Lena, and, as she grows older, she begins to feel that she will rot away in her father's house. When she is 42, Corinthians becomes depressed about her life, and decides to get out of the house by taking a job.

She finds a position as a maid to a white woman poet, Michael-Mary Graham, who encourages her to learn to type. Corinthians becomes almost a secretary to the woman. Embarrassed by her status, she and Ruth tell people that she has become an amanuensis.

On the bus home from work one day she meets a man, Henry Porter, who courts her patiently until she accepts him and begins a relationship. Her brother, Milkman, eventually intervenes in the relationship by telling their father about the relationship. Neither Milkman nor Macon feels that Porter is good enough for First Corinthians. Milkman feels this way not only because Porter comes from the Southside, but also because he knows that the man is part of a group of vigilante-style killers, the Seven Days.

Corinthians, after college and time abroad, is still naive as a teenager; however, eventually she

decides for herself that she wants a relationship with Porter and has sex with him at his apartment. Ironically, Porter lives in a group of houses owned by her father. Corinthians's mother and father tell her that she is too good for Porter and she herself wrestles with this notion. She dates Porter and, eventually, after confronting her father, moves out of her parents' house and in with Porter.

Freddie   Freddie is the town gossip and Macon's handyman. He has gold teeth that he flashes with his frequent smile. He discovers Ruth breastfeeding Milkman when Freddie feels that the boy is too old. Following his discovery, Freddie gives the toddler his nickname, Milkman. Freddie tells Macon about Robert Smith's suicide and Porter's drunken outburst. Freddie also knows about the Seven Days and informs Milkman and Macon about the organization.

Freddie was born in Jacksonville, Florida, and does not reveal, or perhaps does not know, his actual age. His mother died shortly after his birth and his father died two months before Freddie was born. Freddie was raised in jail because that is where black orphans were placed at the time. Freddie is abandoned by the black community from which he comes because of the way his mother dies. According to Freddie, she was killed by ghosts. Freddie also has had his own encounters with the supernatural world.

Fred Garnet   Fred Garnet is one of the residents of Danville. He gives Milkman a ride to town after Milkman misses Nephew's noon pickup during his visit to the Butlers' and to his grandfather's stolen farmland. Garnet is insulted when Milkman tries to pay him for a coke he has offered. Milkman does not yet understand the concept of just being neighborly and doing something for someone else out of kindness.

Grace Long   Grace Long is a friend of Susan Byrd's. She is at Susan Byrd's home when Milkman comes to visit the first time. Susan Byrd does not tell Milkman what she knows about his grandmother, Sing, because she does not want to talk in front of Grace Long. Grace Long is a schoolteacher at the normal school. She puts a note with her address on it in the cookies she sends home with Milkman. She also takes his watch.

Guitar Bains Guitar is the cat-eyed child the Mercy Hospital nurse orders to get the guard as Robert Smith leaps from the hospital roof in the opening scene of the novel. Guitar grows up to be best friends with Milkman Dead, who happens to be the baby whose mother went into labor the day Mr. Smith jumped.

Guitar's father dies in an accident in the saw-mill where he works. The man is sliced in half lengthwise. He is buried with the two halves of himself facing each other. Following the accident, Guitar's mother gratefully accepts $40 as compensation. The white wife of the factory owner offers Guitar and his brother some candy, divinity, in the wake of the accident, and his mother buys Guitar and his siblings peppermint candy on the day of his father's funeral with the money she received from the factory owner. From that point on, Guitar cannot abide sweets.

After the accident, Guitar's mother has a break-down and abandons her family. Guitar's grand-mother, Mrs. Bains, moves in with Guitar and his siblings to take care of the children. When Guitar is a small boy, his grandmother, Mrs. Bains, goes to see Macon Dead to ask him for an extension on the rent the family owes. Macon refuses. This encounter has a profound impact on Guitar's perceptions of the world.

Guitar wins Milkman's loyalty and affection early by saying his nickname, Milkman, in such a way that it sounds cool, rather than derisive. Because he is five years older than Milkman, Guitar is the leader of the two and has great influence on Milkman. Guitar takes Milkman to see Pilate for the first time.

When both men are in their thirties, Guitar's new seriousness and fault-finding with Milkman contributes to Milkman's feeling that things need to change in his life. Although Guitar is right that Macon's life was self-absorbed, his obsession with Milkman's flaws may blind him to careful consideration of his own flaws. Guitar reacts much differently than Milkman as a result of his experience with racism. Guitar joins the group the Seven Days and devotes himself to their cause— enacting vigilante justice. Guitar is the Sunday man in the Seven Days. As an adult he works in an auto plant.

Eventually Guitar becomes so consumed with the abstract ideal of justice embodied by the Seven Days that he tries to kill Milkman thinking that his best friend has betrayed him. He succeeds in killing Pilate and he and Milkman have a final confrontation at the end of the novel.

Guitar's mother and father Guitar's father worked at a saw mill and was cut in half lengthwise by a saw in an accident. After his death, the owner of the saw mill comes to see Guitar's mother and gives her $40 to compensate for his death. Her smiling manner when she thanks the factory owner, sickens the young Guitar. He associates his sickness with the candy, divinity, that the foreman's wife gives to Guitar and his siblings and to the candy canes his mother buys each of the children on the day of their father's funeral, but the real cause of Guitar's nausea is his mother's willingness to love the man responsible for cutting his father in half. This early instance of witnessing a black person willing to forsake her own dignity to curry favor with a white person is formative in Guitar's life and helps to determine his future actions. Shortly after the accident, Guitar's mother has a breakdown and abandons her family. Guitar's grandmother, Mrs. Bains, moves in with Guitar and his siblings.

Hagar Dead Hagar is Reba's daughter and Pilate's granddaughter, although the relationship between Hagar and Pilate is more like that of mother and daughter. Milkman is attracted to Hagar and is said to fall in love with her behind. Although she is about five years his senior, Hagar also falls in love with Milkman, her cousin, and dates him for years until he harshly and unfeelingly ends the relationship. Hagar cannot handle Milkman's rejection. She tries repeatedly to kill him, doubts her own looks, hair, and self-worth, and eventually dies from a broken heart after going on a shopping frenzy while Milkman is away.

When Pilate forces Milkman to confront his responsibility for Hagar's demise, he eventually accepts his culpability for her death and carries around her hair in a box—symbolic of her insecurities, but also of their connection.

Heddy Byrd Heddy Byrd is Sing Byrd's mother. She has skin color issues and does not like her children playing with dark-skinned blacks. She is an Indian woman. After Solomon flies off, dropping Jake, Heddy takes care of the abandoned infant. Heddy never married and her children have different fathers.

Hospital Tommy Hospital Tommy owns the barber shop with Railroad Tommy. He speaks in elevated and formal language. In spite of cataracts, Hospital Tommy is in good shape for a man of his age. Hospital Tommy is a member of the Seven Days.

Jake (Macon Dead I) Jake is Macon and Pilate's father and Sing's husband. Jake and Sing meet on a wagon headed north. Jake receives his new name when a drunken Union soldier mixes up the information on a survey form, confusing Jake's place of birth with his first name. Jake and Sing acquire land in Pennsylvania and try to settle there and begin their family. Their plans are disrupted when Sing dies giving birth to Pilate and corrupt whites steal the land from Jake, in spite of his determination to defend himself, his land, and his family.

Macon and Pilate remember their father sitting on a fence for five days when the Butlers try to steal his land. The thieves eventually shoot him five feet in the air. The mob buries his body and, when it resurfaces in a rainstorm, they throw the body into the cave Pilate and Macon hide in when they run away. Unknowingly, Pilate carries the bones of her father around for years thinking they belong to the white man Macon kills in the cave.

After his death, Jake visits Pilate. Repeatedly he says to her "Sing. Sing." Pilate thinks that he is telling her to sing. In fact, the ghost is just repeating the name of his wife, Sing Byrd.

John John is one of Susan Byrd's cousins who decides to pass as white.

King Walker King Walker is the owner of an old unused service station where the hunters meet before taking Milkman off to hunt at night. King Walker does not look like his name. He is an older man who used to play baseball in the Black Leagues. He lends Milkman some clothes to wear on the hunt and helps him with his chaffing feet.

Lilah Lilah is one of Susan Byrd's cousins who decides to pass as white.

Lilly Lilly is the owner of Lilly's Beauty Parlor. She is known for doing a light press that lasts.

Luther Solomon Luther Solomon is one of the men who take Milkman off on a hunting trip at night in the dark while he is in Shalimar. Luther Solomon is not related to the Mr. Solomon who owns the store where Milkman gets into a fight.

Macon Dead I See JAKE

Macon Dead II Macon Dead is the son of Macon and Sing Dead and the brother of Pilate. Macon witnesses his mother die while giving birth to Pilate. Later, he and his sister witness their father's murder. Orphaned, the two seek shelter with Circe, the community midwife, and then set out on their own.

When they encounter a white man in a cave on their father's land, Macon kills him. Pilate and Macon quarrel and then separate. Macon believes that Pilate takes the gold that was in the white man's possession. The two do not see each other again for many years.

Macon settles in the North and begins to establish a business in real estate. Many in the community dislike Macon for being cold and unfeeling. Macon is forever changed by witnessing the murder of his father. After that, he resolves that the only security in the world for a black man is money and property.

Macon spends his life acquiring the possessions he feels will keep him safe and immune from racism. He marries the woman in town, Ruth Foster, who has the most status and spends the rest of his life despising her. Eventually, Ruth and Macon have three children, First Corinthians, Magdalene, called Lena, and Macon III, better known as Milkman. Although Macon feels duped into his son's conception, he tries to connect with Milkman by teaching him how to work. He never lets Milkman be himself though and always tries to impose his vision of the world on his son.

Macon is also alienated from and embarrassed by his sister, Pilate, whose moral center is completely alien to him. Pilate cares for Macon but realizes that the only way to maintain any vestige of a family connection is through Macon's son, Milkman. As Milkman grows and unravels the family story, Macon seems to come to terms with his past, although his relationship with Ruth does not improve nor does he reconcile with Pilate.

Macon Dead III (Milkman)   There is a profound connection between the birth of Macon Dead III, otherwise known as Milkman, and the death of Robert Smith in the opening scene of the novel. Milkman is the child of Macon and Ruth Dead. Ruth goes into labor as Robert Smith begins to fly from the roof of the hospital. Forever the child's life is informed by the idea of flight.

While a young man, Milkman is hampered by his metaphorical inability to fly and is warped by his parent's dysfunctions. His birth occurs only because his aunt, Pilate, decides that the Deads need a male heir. Pilate is instrumental in temporarily restoring the sex life between Macon and Ruth so that Ruth can conceive. When Macon learns of Ruth's pregnancy, he is furious and tries to cause her to lose the baby. Pilate helps Ruth to save her pregnancy. Macon is largely uninterested in his son until he is an adolescent.

Ruth, Milkman's mother, is pathologically needy and uses her son to fulfill her emotional hunger. The proof of her unfulfilled desires manifests itself in her extended breast-feeding of Milkman, which she prolongs, not for the good of her child, but because the act brings her a great deal of pleasure. Freddie, an employee of Macon, witnesses Ruth feeding her son and christens him Milkman, a name he holds for the remainder of his life.

While growing up, Milkman is self-absorbed and frustrated. His parents' ill-will toward each other poisons the atmosphere of his home and Milkman is not encouraged to consider or to bond with his sisters. His primary outlet as a boy is his friendship with Guitar, an older, charismatic young man who befriends Milkman and teaches him much of what he knows of the world. Guitar takes Milkman to meet his aunt, Pilate, and the younger boy's world is never the same again.

Pilate shows Milkman another way of being. She is not obsessed with possessions or appearance like her brother, and thus she provides for Milkman an alternative perspective, one that he will draw on as he matures. Macon becomes alarmed when he learns of his son's involvement with Pilate and draws Milkman into his business endeavors.

At this time in his life, Milkman is particularly selfish, unsympathetic, and immature. After having a sexual relationship with Hagar, his cousin, he breaks off the relationship by leaving her a note. This treatment sends Hagar into a kind of insanity and she begins to attempt to kill Milkman one time each month. Milkman's eventual confrontation with her is as cruel as his thoughtless breakup and ends, after some time, in Hagar's death.

In an attempt to assert his masculinity, Milkman hits his father. Although the premise for the act is the defense of his mother, Milkman really hits his father because he is trying to assert his authority. Macon responds to his son's assault by telling Milkman about his suspicions about an incestuous relationship between Ruth and Dr. Foster. Milkman then remembers Freddie's discovery of Ruth's extended breastfeeding and his own feelings of shame, which seem to confirm Macon's story. Later he confronts his mother about the information he uncovers from his father and she tells him that there was nothing untoward about her relationship with her father.

Inadvertently, Milkman tells his father about a green sack that hangs in Pilate's house. Macon then tells Milkman of the experiences he and Pilate had after their father was killed. He tells his son about the white man he killed and the gold that the man had. Macon believes that the bag in Pilate's house must be the gold from the cave. Macon, Milkman, and Guitar conceive a plan to steal the gold. The plan fails when they all discover that the bag contains bones. Macon becomes obsessed with finding the gold and Milkman decides to return to his father's birth home to try to find it. Guitar wants Milkman to find the gold so that he can pay for his activities with the Seven Days.

Milkman embarks on a quest to find the gold and this leads to his discovery of identity and self. Milkman's entire character is revealed by his name. He begins with a parasitic relationship with everyone in his life, particularly his immediate family. After he gains some autonomy, Milkman grows into the other meaning of his name, as someone capable of delivering and providing sustenance to his community.

He unravels his family's story and, although he is unable to unravel all of the harm he has caused, he learns to fly with the knowledge that he comes from powerful people and also that only through the willing acceptance of death does a person really and fully live.

Magdalene (called Lena) Dead   Magdalene (called Lena) Dead is Ruth and Macon's oldest daughter. She is 13 years old when her brother Macon is born. Lena is the one who conceives the idea for her and her sister, First Corinthians, to make red velvet roses to sell to Gerhardt's department store. This inane activity occupies a great deal of her time for much of her life.

Lena never marries and stays at home with her parents. Much of her time is spent, also, in caring for her younger brother, though she seldom talks with him. The two have no relationship. When Milkman interferes with First Corinthians's relationship with her lover, Henry Porter, Lena finally tells her brother what she thinks of him—that he is completely self-absorbed and abusive.

Lena's desire to make velvet flowers is symptomatic of her relative powerlessness throughout the novel, with the exception of her uncharacteristic stand against Milkman. During that exchange, Lena claims that Milkman has urinated on the women of the family his whole life. Milkman leaves on his journey south shortly after her devastating analysis.

Marcelline   Marcelline is a hairdresser who works in Lilly's shop. When Hagar comes into the shop frantic and hysterical, Marcelline agrees to do

Hagar's hair partly because she is afraid of Hagar. Hagar never returns to keep the appointment.

Mercy Hospital nurse   During the opening scene of the novel an unidentified white nurse who works at Mercy Hospital emerges from the building during the chaos caused by Robert Smith's imminent suicide and arrogantly tries to take control of the situation. She addresses Mrs. Bains, Guitar's grandmother, abrasively and instructs her to send one of her children to get the hospital guard. When Mrs. Bains tells the nurse the name of the child, Guitar, the nurse looks at her as if she is addle-brained. The nurse then addresses Guitar directly and, without saying please, orders him to run and get the guard.

The nurse punctuates her orders to the boy by making pushing motions with her hands, as one might shoo away birds. She provides one example in this novel of white people treating black people with less than common courtesy, as if courtesy was not thought of or called for.

Michael-Mary Graham   After abandoning her hopes of marriage, First Corinthians gets a job working for Michael-Mary Graham. Ruth tells her friends that Corinthians is working as Michael-Mary Graham's amanuensis, although in reality Corinthians works as the woman's maid.

Michael-Mary Graham is a pretentious poet who never realizes that Corinthians is actually better educated and more widely traveled than she is. Michael-Mary Graham fancies herself liberal and progressive, although she is quite provincial and racist. The woman imagines herself a great artist and her inherited wealth allows her to perpetuate her fantasy. Although Michael-Mary Graham's poetry is trite and predictable, she finds success as a published poet, wins awards for her writing, and serves as the state poet laureate.

Milkman   See MACON DEAD III

Miss Mary   Miss Mary is a barmaid and part-owner of a bar/lounge in town, one of several that operate in the area called the Blood Bank. Mary's bar is known by her name. She is described as attractive, but garish. Prostitutes frequent and work in her bar, as well as ordinary housewives. The space is a kind of sanctuary for all who seek validation and community.

Moon Moon is a man who helps to hold and disarm Hagar during one of her attacks against Milkman. Moon and Guitar hold Hagar as she threatens Milkman with a Carlson skinning knife in a neighborhood bar.

Mrs. Bains Mrs. Bains is initially described as the stout grandmother standing outside Mercy Hospital when Robert Smith tries to fly from the roof on his blue wings. She is Guitar's grandmother who raises him, his brother, and his two sisters after his father's accident in the sawmill and after his mother's subsequent abandonment.

When Guitar's mother leaves, his grandmother comes to live in the house that his mother has been renting from Macon Dead. Mrs. Bains does not have the money to feed her grandchildren and pay Macon the rent. When finances become difficult, Mrs. Bains goes to Macon to ask for help. In spite of the extenuating circumstances, Macon has no sympathy for the woman's situation and gives her only a couple of days to pay, telling her that if she does not come up with the past due rent, she will have to move out. Mrs. Bains tells her grandchildren, "A nigger in business is a terrible thing to see, a terrible, terrible thing to see," and this pronouncement seems to make a deep impression on them, particularly on the young, cat-eyed Guitar.

Mrs. Cooper (Esther Cooper) Mrs. Cooper is Reverend Cooper's wife. The couple live in Danville, Pennsylvania. She brings Milkman and the Reverend rye whiskey when Milkman visits. The day Milkman goes to visit Circe, Mrs. Cooper makes a huge country breakfast that he does not eat.

Mr. Solomon Mr. Solomon is the owner of the store in Shalimar where Milkman manages to alienate everybody by seeming to be better-off than they are and by being inconsiderate of their feelings. Mr. Solomon is light-skinned and has red hair that is turning white. He gives Milkman the information

that lets Milkman know that Guitar is looking for him and that Guitar is upset with Milkman.

Nephew Nephew is the 13-year-old nephew of Reverend Cooper. He is called Nephew since he is the Coopers' only nephew. Nephew drives Milkman out to Circe's house. He does not have much to say, but is very curious about Milkman's clothing. The Coopers send him to the bus station to pick up Milkman's suitcase.

Milkman asks Nephew to return at noon to the spot where he drops him off. The boy leaves Milkman at Circe's around nine in the morning.

Nero Brown Nero Brown is a man who is in the barbershop when the conversation about the death of EMMETT TILL occurs. He is cynical about the possibility of any kind of retribution. He is also a member of the Seven Days.

Omar Omar is one of the men who take Milkman on a hunting trip at night while he is in Shalimar. While Milkman sits against a tree, worn-out and resting, he comes to see his past behavior for the self-involved immaturity it has been. He begins to gain an appreciation for what it means to be a man in nature without all the trappings that money can buy to help him out. He begins to feel a connection to the other men he is with who can count only on the same things he can right then—what he was born with and what he has learned to use. It is a time of looking at himself without rationalization and accepting himself as a man, and of accepting others along with himself. Omar becomes the male elder Milkman has needed but has not had access to at this point in his life.

Pilate Dead In the initial scene of the novel, Pilate Dead is the singer in the crowd standing in the snow waiting for Robert Smith to jump to his death. She sings a song about a man flying away, which echoes the note Mr. Smith left on his house saying he was going to "fly away on his own wings."

Pilate Dead is the daughter of the deceased Sing and Macon Dead. As children she and her brother, also named Macon, escape from the people who killed their father and stole their land. The two become separated, and, until they are adults and Pilate seeks out her brother, they lead totally separate lives.

Pilate chooses a different way to reason and to live after their father's murder than Macon does. As a result, there is little chance that the brother and sister can ever understand each other. Because she is so different from her brother, Pilate and Macon remain estranged.

In spite of, or perhaps because of, those differences, she helps Ruth to conceive and to carry her baby, Milkman, to full-term. As the novel opens, Pilate is the sister-in-law of the pregnant Ruth Foster Dead and the aunt of the two girls, First Corinthians and Magdalene, called Lena, who try to collect the scattered rose petals. Later, Pilate gets to know her nephew, Milkman, the boy whose existence she engineered. Milkman is a young teenager and, at that point, Pilate begins to have an influence in his life that grows more profound as Milkman begins his own search for his identity.

Although Pilate is certainly different from almost everyone else—she is idiosyncratic and ragged and a bootlegger—she is wise and beautiful and loving in her own unique way. Pilate is born after her mother's death, pushing out of the womb herself. As such, she has no navel and is a much more spiritual person than her brother.

After witnessing her father's death, she sees him in visions for most of the rest of her life. She is a midwife and healer. She possesses psychic and supernatural abilities. She is a witch figure and magical. She seems to embody the spiritual strength of her family as exemplified by her grandfather Solomon's ability to fly. Pilate is a deeply loving person as her father had been. Macon's sister is strong, places value on family, and is always chewing on things. She is Milkman's pilot in life, helping him to develop and grow. She also will do anything for her daughter and granddaughter.

When she and Macon run away from their home after their father is murdered, Pilate gets Circe to make an earring from her mother's snuff box. Pilate puts her name, written by her father on a piece of brown paper, into the earring and wears it for the rest of her life until she rips it out, at the end of the novel, to place it on her father's grave. She does

this in her family's homeland after she and Milkman bury Jake's bones. Immediately after she rips the earring out of her ear and figuratively unnames herself, she is shot and killed by Guitar. Her final words are a wish to have had the opportunity to love more people.

Porter (Henry Porter) Henry Porter is a member of the Seven Days who, like Robert Smith, is greatly emotionally affected by his membership in the organization and has a very public episode of distress on the roof of his apartment. When Porter has his breakdown, he drunkenly sits in his apartment window and urinates, waves a shotgun, and calls for a woman. During this episode, Macon confronts him to ensure that the nearly suicidal man pays his rent.

Porter papers the walls of the apartment he rents from Macon with old calendars, beginning with one dated 1939. He eventually courts and develops a relationship with Macon's daughter, First Corinthians and, after several years, moves in with her, though her parents disapprove of his class status. In retaliation for his relationship with First Corinthians, Macon evicts Porter and has his wages garnished. Porter becomes dependent on the Seven Days for financial assistance during this time.

Railroad Tommy Railroad Tommy owns a barbershop with Hospital Tommy. Railroad Tommy tells Guitar and Milkman all of the things they will never have because they are black men. Railroad Tommy is a member of the Seven Days.

Reba Dead Reba, Pilate's daughter, likes to flirt with men, is lucky, and wins contests, and is always and unsuccessfully trying to please her daughter, Hagar. She is light-skinned with bad skin and has a habit of getting into abusive relationships.

Reba's boyfriend Pilate nearly kills Reba's unnamed boyfriend when she discovers that he has hit her daughter Reba. She allows him to live after he agrees to leave Reba alone.

Reverend Coles Reverend Coles, according to Corinthians, is one of the few African Americans in town who can afford to buy a house on the lake and also have a house in town.

Reverend Cooper When Milkman goes to Danville, Pennsylvania, to find the cave and the treasure, Reverend and Mrs. Cooper are the first people to welcome him. A couple of townspeople had taken a look at Milkman's three-piece suit and fancy shoes and had been cool toward him, but the Coopers treat him as a friend as soon as they hear his name and remember Macon and Pilate. The couple live on Stone Lane and Reverend Cooper is the A.M.E. Zion minister. Through his conversations with the Coopers, Milkman learns that Pilate's earring with her name in it was constructed by the Reverend's father, the town blacksmith.

All of the old men in the town come to the Coopers' house during the four days Milkman spends with them and tell stories about his father, aunt, grandfather, and grandmother and what had happened to them all. Milkman begins for the first time to appreciate the feeling of community—of having people and of belonging in a place. When the Coopers' car is fixed, their nephew drives Milkman out to see Circe at the Butlers' place.

Ricky Djvorak Ricky Djvorak is the son of Anna Djvorak. Dr. Foster saves his life from the fatal effects of childhood tuberculosis by prescribing bed rest, cod liver oil, and healthy foods, rather than a sanitarium.

Robert Smith Robert Smith is an insurance agent with the North Carolina Mutual Life Insurance Agency. The man jumps to his death from the roof of Mercy Hospital in 1931, an event that precedes the birth of the first African-American baby in that hospital, Milkman Dead. These two events are probably connected, as the narrator recounts that it must have been Mr. Smith's leap from the roof that made the hospital admit the woman who had gone into labor while seeing him prepare to jump. Smith's jump may happen in part as a result of his membership in the Seven Days. Robert Smith's "flight" at the novel's inception foreshadows Milkman's own jump at the novel's end and establishes the theme of flight that pervades the novel.

rootworker The rootworker is the woman who befriends Pilate when she is living with migrant workers in upstate New York. The woman shares with Pilate many of her secrets about natural cures and ways of being. Pilate has a relationship with a male relative of the rootworker. He discovers and shares with the group the fact that Pilate has no navel. When the group learns of her difference, they send her away.

Ruth Foster Dead Ruth Foster Dead is the black woman who at the beginning of the novel goes into labor, in the snow outside the hospital. Ruth is the daughter of the first black doctor in town, Dr. Foster. She was raised by her father after her mother's death and was completely devoted to him. She married the man he told her to marry, Macon Dead, even though she did not love him. She maintained a lifelong belief in her own superiority because she is her father's daughter, and never lets anyone else forget.

Her marriage with Macon becomes a battle of wills after Macon sees what he believes to be incestuous interactions between Ruth and her father as he is dying and even after he dies. Later, after her son Milkman learns of this source of his parents' marital discourse, he confronts his mother. Ruth replies that she is not strange, only small. Even as a grown woman she is completely defined by her father's understandings and expectations of her. Periodically she even travels miles to her father's grave and spends the night there. Even her love for her son is self-serving. She breastfeeds Milkman long after the time that he needs because the act brings her pleasure and makes her feel as if she has a purpose. Ruth is characterized as weak and lonely and lacks a center, a self.

Ryna Ryna is Solomon's woman and the mother of his 21 children. When he flies off, back to Africa, he leaves her crying inconsolably in a gulch.

Sam Sheppard Sam Sheppard is a man who, purportedly, murdered his wife with 27 hammer blows.

Saul Saul is the young man who starts a fight with Milkman in Mr. Solomon's store. Milkman insults Saul and the rest of the men in the store by flaunting his wealth and sophistication. Saul has a knife and Milkman has a broken bottle in a fight, but Milkman seems to come out the winner.

Seven Days The Seven Days are an organization, begun in 1920, that tries to balance out the injustices and violence experienced by African Americans by replicating the same atrocities against whites. The organization consists of seven men. They serve until they die, fall ill, or are no longer able to enact the objectives of the organization. Each man is responsible for a day of the week and is assigned to enact retribution for wrongs against blacks that occur on their day. The men cannot marry or have children. Guitar, Robert Smith, and Porter are members of the Seven Days. Before they exact their revenge, the members of the Seven Days say to their victims "your day has come."

Sing Byrd Dead (Singing Byrd) Sing Byrd is Pilate and Macon's mother and the sister of Crowell Byrd. Milkman finds out about her during his second visit to Susan Byrd. Pilate remembers the color of her mother's bonnet ribbon, but does not know her name until Milkman tells her the family story.

Circe tells Milkman that Sing Byrd is overly possessive and nervous. She also tells him that Sing and Macon met on a wagon going north after the Civil War. Sing was never a slave and was proud of the fact. She was mixed-race, partially Native American. Circe also tells Milkman that his grandmother was from Virginia.

Later, Milkman learns from Susan Byrd that Sing was traveling north on a wagon to Boston, Massachusetts, to attend a Quaker school.

Small Boy Small Boy is one of the men who take Milkman off on a hunting trip at night in Shalimar. The men tease Small Boy because he cannot read. While Milkman sits against a tree, worn-out and resting, he comes to see his past behavior for the self-involved immaturity it had been. He begins to gain an appreciation for what it means to be a man in nature without all the trappings that money can

buy to help him out. He begins to feel a connection to the other men he is with who can count only on the same things he can right then—what he was born with and what he has learned to use. It is a time of looking at himself without rationalization, understanding himself as a man, and learning acceptance of others.

Solomon (Shalimar) Solomon is the original flying African in Milkman's family. He is the father of 21 children and the husband of Ryna. When he flies back to Africa, he leaves Ryna crying in the gully and drops his son Jake, Milkman's grandfather, who he tried to take with him.

Susan Byrd Susan Byrd is related to Sing Byrd and, after some reluctance, tells Milkman the story of Sing and Jake. Susan, like most of the other members of her family, has skin color issues.

Sweet Sweet is a good and generous woman who nurtures Milkman. She takes him in after the hunt and tends to his wounds and the two make love. Through their interactions, Milkman learns that relationships between men and women can and should be reciprocal.

Uncle Billy Uncle Billy is Guitar's grandmother's (Mrs. Bains) brother. He moves from Florida after Guitar's father's death to help take care of Guitar and his siblings. Guitar dreams of having enough money to give his uncle material things to thank him for his support when he and his brother and sisters were orphaned.

Vernell Vernell is Omar's wife. She cooks breakfast for the men the morning after they return from the bobcat hunt. She tells Milkman that his grandmother Sing is from Shalimar. She remembers that her grandmother used to play with Sing when they were girls and that Sing was one of Heddy's daughters.

Walters Walters is a man who is in the barbershop when the conversation about the death of Emmett Till occurs. He is cynical about the possibility of any kind of retribution.

white man who works at the stationhouse
Milkman helps this old man load a heavy crate, an unusually kind thing for him to do. Later, this little act of kindness becomes important because Guitar sees it and thinks that Milkman was loading the gold he found in the cave. Of course, Milkman does not find any gold, but he cannot convince Guitar of that fact. Helping other people was so foreign to Milkman's nature that his best friend does not believe him when he tells the truth about what he has been doing.

white peacock Milkman and Guitar see the white peacock perched on the top of a used-car dealership when they are planning their robbery of Pilate's treasure. When Milkman asks why the bird cannot fly, Guitar tells him it is because the peacock's beautiful tail is too heavy and the tail is vanity. Guitar says that in order to fly, "you got to give up the shit that weighs you down."

Winnie Ruth Judd Winnie Ruth Judd is a white woman who, beginning in 1932, commits a series of violently bizarre murders and then is placed in an insane asylum. In 1955, the black residents of Southside say that Winnie Ruth escaped and that she has perpetrated some murders where the victims seem to be randomly selected. These murders are actually committed by the Seven Days.

Many people in the African-American community think that it is white madness to kill total strangers. They feel that black people will murder only people they know and only with some motivation and in the heat of passion. They do not think blacks kill someone in a coldly premeditated crime or kill total strangers. These beliefs underline the contrast between what black folks in the neighborhood believe and what some of them, the Seven Days, are actually doing. Winnie Judd becomes a source of story-telling and much bemusement.

FURTHER READING

Branch, Eleanor. "Through the Maze of Oedipal: Milkman's Search for Self in *Song of Solomon*," *Literature and Psychology* 41, nos. 1/2 (1995): 52–85.

Bryant, Cedric Gael. "Every Goodbye Ain't Gone: The Semiotics of Death, Mourning, and Closural Practice in Toni Morrison's *Song of Solomon*," *MELUS* 24, no. 3 (Fall 1999): 97–111.

Lee, Catherine Carr. "The South in Toni Morrison's *Song of Solomon*: Initiation, Healing, and Home," *Studies in the Literary Imagination* 31, no. 2 (Fall 1998): 109–124.

Murray, Rolland. "The Long Strut: *Song of Solomon* and the Emancipatory Limits of Black Patriarchy," *Callaloo* 22. no. 1 (Winter 1999): 121–134.

Rothberg, Michael. "Dead Letter Office: Conspiracy, Trauma, and *Song of Solomon*'s Posthumous Communication," *African American Review* 37, no. 4 (Winter 2003): 501–517.

Tidey, Ashley. "Limping or Flying? Psychoanalysis, Afrocentricism, and *Song of Solomon*," *College English* 63, no. 1 (September 2000): 48–71.

Sula (1974)

Sula is Toni Morrison's second published novel. Like *The Bluest Eye*, the novel is a story of two girls coming of age. As children, the two girls in question, Sula Peace and Nel Wright, function as two halves of a whole, often seeming to complete each other in opposition.

As they reach and achieve maturity, the differences in the girls' responses to the pressure to conform to the norms of their community separate them and split their bond, which is not reconciled until the end of the novel. *Sula* confronts issues of loyalty, family, assimilation, innocence, gender, and sexuality, but is at its heart an examination of the priorities that determine the character, quality, and relationships of a woman's lifetime.

SYNOPSIS

Part I

Sula begins with the story of an African-American neighborhood that once existed on the periphery of a town called Medallion. The story of the neighborhood unfolds years after it has ceased to exist. The neighborhood was called the Bottom because a white farmer, rather than give his freed slave the land he had been promised, lied to the man and told him that the land in the hills was more valuable.

The deceptive farmer called the land in the hills the bottom of heaven, and thus the neighborhood acquired its name.

"1919"

"1919" tells the story of the shell-shocked African-American soldier, known as SHADRACK, who returns from combat without any memory of who he is or where he comes from. This rootless man is haunted by his hands, which, in his delirium, continue to grow monstrously large every time he looks at them. After he is released, his perceptions of the out-of-control growth of his hands stop when he finally sees that his face, unlike that of the soldier he saw die in France, is still attached and intact. More than anything else, Shadrack fears death, and so, in an effort to contain his fears, he invents a holiday entitled National Suicide Day, the only day, according to his perceptions, on which death will occur. Through his belief that he has artificially controlled death, Shadrack is able to contain his fear and to begin a new life on the outskirts of the Bottom in a shack once owned by his grandfather. For sustenance, he sells fish to the people of the Bottom.

Shadrack celebrates National Suicide Day by holding a noose and ringing a cowbell and admonishing the townspeople that this is their one annual opportunity to kill themselves or each other. Although the people of the Bottom at first fear Shadrack and National Suicide Day, they grow accustomed to it and him. National Suicide Day, like Shadrack himself, becomes a point of reference in their lives.

"1920"

"1920" introduces the Wrights, Nel's family. Nel's mother, Helene Sabat Wright, is a Creole from New Orleans who spends her life escaping from the legacy of her mother's occupation as a prostitute. She marries a ship's cook, Wiley Wright, and moves to the Bottom where the people of the town admire her long hair and light skin. Helen keeps both her daughter and her house oppressively neat.

When Nel is 10 years old, Helene returns to New Orleans as her grandmother is dying. During the trip she is insulted by a white conductor who believes that she is trying to sit in the Whites Only car. Rather than respond with dignity, Helene smiles at the man's insults. Witnessing the event, Nel fears that she may have no more substance than her mother possesses. After the trip, meeting her grandmother, and attending her great-grandmother's funeral, Nel feels that she is a person separate from her mother for the first time. Although she does not know it at the time, the trip to the New Orleans funeral is the only one she ever takes out of the Bottom. The trip, however, does embolden her to make a new friend, Sula Peace.

"1921"

Unlike the Wrights, Sula lives in a house and with a family that is defined by its relative disorder and chaos. Unlike the traditional familial configuration the Wrights maintain, the Peaces are extended family consisting of the matriarch, Eva Peace, her daughter, Hannah Peace, her son, Plum, her granddaughter, Sula, as well as various and sundry boarders and visitors who occupy the house at various times. The house is teeming with human energy and activity.

The story of how the house came to be and how Eva acquired the resources to build her house at 7 Carpenter Road is shrouded in mystery: Abandoned by her husband, Boy Boy, and helpless to feed or protect her children, Eva leaves for a year and returns to the Bottom without a leg, but with all of the money she needs. Following a visit from her delinquent husband, Boy Boy, Eva determines to spend the rest of her life hating him for his abandonment.

Eva is generous with her house and her resources. When abandoned and neglected children arrive at her door, she always takes them in. In 1921, three such boys arrive at the Peace household. Eva names them all Dewey, and the boys start to resemble each other, eventually becoming indistinguishable. Another outcast, an alcoholic white mountain man that Eva calls TAR BABY, also comes to live at the Peace residence.

Both Hannah and Eva are nonchalant but interested in men. Sula learns from observation that men are fun but dispensable. Eva unintentionally confirms this point of view for her granddaughter when, in 1921, she sets Plum on fire in his sleep.

She sees herself as rescuing Plum from infantilization by allowing him to die as a man.

"1922"

Nel and Sula become fast friends as they grow older and both girls are drawn to the dreams of adolescence, fantasies of the opposite sex and of being loved. The girls' dreams of love are different though. Nel imagines herself a passive princess with an imaginary someone to share the details of her fantasy dress, bed, and flowers. Sula, on the other hand, imagines a beloved observing her as she rides with him on a horse. The differences in the dreams distinguish the girls, their experiences and expectations, as well as foreshadow their future choices.

The girls not only share dreams but also adventures as they pick their precarious paths toward adulthood. When the girls are hassled on the way home by Irish boys, Sula frightens the gang off by cutting off the tip of her own finger. On another summer day, just before the girls run off on an exploit, Sula overhears her mother saying that she loves Sula, but that she does not like her. This information hurts the child and changes her relationship with Hannah. The girls then run off to play and distract themselves by digging a hole deep in the earth with twigs. The girls stop when Nel's twig breaks and throw all of the detritus they can find into the hole, and then they refill the hole with earth.

Almost immediately, a little neighborhood boy, CHICKEN LITTLE, wanders by. The girls tease him and then, playfully, swing him around in a circle. When Sula accidentally lets go of the boy's hands, he falls into the river and drowns. Shadrack witnesses the event and, in language she does not understand, promises to keep her secret. Sula accidentally leaves the belt of her dress in Shadrack's shack.

The events that culminate in Chicken Little's death are a secret that Nel and Sula share as well. It is one of the key moments that the girls experience as they move from childhood to adulthood. The girls keep the secret throughout their lives.

"1923"

The occurrence of three strange events defines this chapter. The first instance that Eva finds out of sync is a question of Hannah. The second peculiar occurrence is a wind storm without lightning, thunder, or rain. The third event is Hannah's dream of a red wedding dress.

Hannah begins this chapter by asking her mother the question Eva finds so disturbing. Hannah asks Eva whether she ever loved her children. Eva is offended by the question and Hannah never gets the response she desires. Eva sees love as a pragmatic thing that you do, while Hannah wonders about Eva's feelings, which remain largely hidden and mysterious. Then Hannah asks Eva why she killed Plum. Eva tries to explain that Plum's addiction after the war had so impaired him that he is no longer able to function as an adult. As such, Eva feels that she had no choice but to relieve the man's suffering by ending his life.

Shortly thereafter, as Eva looks out her window while combing her hair, she sees Hannah on fire. Using the fastest method she can imagine, Eva breaks the glass in her window and leaps out trying to land on top of Hannah and save the life of her burning daughter. Eva misses Hannah, but survives the fall. Hannah dies as a result of her injuries. After her fall, as she lies on the ground, Eva sees Sula watching the scene. Eva believes that Sula is not moved to help her mother.

"1927"

This chapter begins with Nel's marriage to Jude Greene, an attractive, popular 20-year-old man. Jude believes that marriage to Nel will be the transition to manhood denied to him by racism. With the exception of her relationship with Sula, Nel has very little sense of herself and marries Jude because she believes he needs her. After the wedding, Sula leaves the Bottom for 10 years.

Part Two

"1937"

Sula returns to the Bottom during a time when the community experiences an abnormal proliferation of robins. The unnatural abundance of the birds becomes permanently associated with Sula's return in the mind of the community. The community needs to objectify evil and, as one who does not conform to their ideals of normalcy, Sula becomes the personification of all that is bad and wrong.

Even Eva criticizes Sula's lack of conformity and tells her that she needs to have children and that she needs a man. Sula says she is more interested in creating a self than in reproducing and decides that Eva needs to be placed in a nursing home. Later, she reveals to Nel that she has Eva committed because she is afraid of her.

In this chapter, Sula's return also profoundly impacts Nel's life. Sula casually sleeps with Jude. When they are discovered, Jude responds by leaving immediately. Nel blames Sula and begins to define her life in terms of Jude's absence from it. The fundamental difference between the two women becomes apparent. Nel cannot adapt to the change in her circumstances and sees the changeability of life as the source of the problem. This belief contrasts with Sula's earlier observation that hell is stasis, permanence without change. Without evaluating whether events are right or wrong, Sula's outlook is more in line with the reality of life's perpetual motion and transition.

Nel imagines her pain as a gray ball of fur that follows her, just out of sight. Its presence frightens her but becomes the defining reality of her life. Rather than moving beyond her loss, Nel chooses to try to freeze her life and to cling to the gray remains of the part of her life that has passed.

"1939"

In the wake of Eva's institutionalization and Jude's desertion of Nel, Sula becomes the town pariah. As a final transgression, the men of the town accuse Sula of sleeping with white men. Although this accusation is never substantiated, it is universally believed and is interpreted as the ultimate break between Sula and the community. Everything that happens that is negative in the Bottom becomes associated with Sula. Sula becomes the embodiment of evil and makes the people of the Bottom feel superior by comparison.

Interestingly, because there is some tangible presence to blame for all of their trials, the people of the Bottom are kinder and more compassionate toward each other after Sula's return. Sula is misunderstood. She is a woman who is sexually, psychologically, and culturally liberated in a time and space where there is no place for a free woman.

Even sexuality is for her not an act of union, but of self-affirmation. She does not need the traditional markers—wife, mother, lover—to define herself.

In spite of all her independence, Sula falls into a possessive love with A. Jacks, Albert Jacks. Jacks is attracted to her because he believes that she is self-possessed and independent enough to love him without controlling or trying to own him. Sula falls into the trap of trying to keep him—to make love that is fixed and unchanging. She forgets that nothing alive can ever be permanent. A. Jacks's absence when he leaves Sula sends her into an isolation and despair that manifests as illness.

"1940"

When Sula is dying, Nel comes to visit her. The visit allows Nel to feel superior and to act as if her motives are selfless. She gets Sula's medicine from the drugstore and then the two old friends talk about their lives. Sula stresses that even though she is dying alone, it is her choice that she does so—that freedom is not about escaping the inevitability of death but embracing that reality and fashioning it on her own terms. Sula makes a final speech to Nel about the need for breaking down oppositions and categories, something she has tried to do with her life. Then Sula asks Nel why she is so certain of her position as the good one, the right one, a question Nel is not able to answer. Sula dies and her first thought after realizing that she is dead is that she wants to share the experience with Nel.

"1941"

News of Sula's death is met with rejoicing in the Bottom. The people see it as a good omen. Their perceptions are reinforced when they hear rumors that blacks will be employed in constructing the tunnel that will allow easy passage of the river. The other news they view as a sign is the construction of an integrated nursing home that Eva will move to from the original dilapidated colored women's home where Sula leaves her.

After their hopefulness, the Bottom experiences a devastating ice storm that hurts them physically, psychologically, and economically and ruins their Thanksgiving. With Sula gone, the town has no one to blame for its misfortune and the inhabitants resume the behavior they had before Sula's return.

The narrative returns to Shadrack and reveals his slowly emerging awareness. He begins to feel lonely and to miss the company of others. He sees Sula's body and begins to comprehend that his solution to the problem of death, National Suicide Day, is ineffective. With a spirit of despair, Shadrack begins his marking of National Suicide Day 1941. The harsh weather the folks of the Bottom experienced following Sula's death breaks just before the new year. As a result, they are open to Shadrack's holiday in a way they have not been before.

Shadrack becomes a Pied Piper leading a large band of followers through the town and toward the river. When they get to the river, they see the excavation site for the tunnel, the tunnel they have not been allowed to work on because of racism. The joyous parade Shadrack begins transforms into an act of subversion as the people of the Bottom destroy the site of the tunnel construction. Some of them venture too far into the partially constructed tunnel and the structure collapses, killing many of them, including Mrs. Jackson, Tar Baby, Dessie, Ivy, and, possibly, the Deweys. While all of this happens, Shadrack stands on the adjacent hill ringing his bell.

"1965"

This concluding chapter of *Sula* provides the perspective of the 55-year-old Nel on the post–World War II Civil Rights–era Bottom. She reflects that much has changed and that the people, particularly the young people, are less vital, less powerful than the youth she remembers. Nel does not have another long-term relationship after Jude leaves. The Bottom also changes, with whites now interested in the land in the hills and blacks eager to move to the valley.

Nel visits Eva in the new integrated nursing home, Sunnydale. While Eva seems somewhat out of touch with reality, imagining, for example, that she is ironing, she asks Nel about Chicken Little and how she and Sula killed him. She also tells Nel that she and Sula are the same, echoing Sula's final question to Nel.

Nel leaves the nursing home disturbed and reflective. She recalls the events of Chicken Little's death and ponders her own experience in and cul-

pability for his death. She honestly admits that she enjoyed watching the boy slip from Sula's hand. She walks to the cemetery where the Peace family members are buried and sees the birth and death dates of each member of the family as a kind of incantation, a hope for a kind of serenity in the face of the realities of human existence. Nel understands what Sula represents to the community, an embodiment of all that they fear: change, difference, and, most importantly, themselves. Nel also recognizes her connection to Sula and that her relationship with her friend, not her marriage, is what she has been mourning all of the years since Jude left.

CRITICAL COMMENTARY

In *Sula*'s opening chapter, the narrator refers to the herb nightshade. Nightshade is a plant that has both medicinal and poisonous properties. As a symbol, its meaning may be either positive or negative, or even both simultaneously. Nightshade grows in the Bottom, the setting of the novel. The name of the Bottom comes from a deal between a slave master and the man he enslaves. The farmer does not wish to reward his slave with the best land, so he tells the man that the land up in the hills, the bottom land, is the best land, because it is the bottom of heaven. This definition, although intended to be malicious, calls into question the traditional definitions applied to various oppositions, such as good/bad and valuable/worthless. Both the nightshade and the name of the community, the Bottom, establish the core concerns of *Sula*. The novel addresses the question of the accuracy of traditional, socially agreed upon definitions. *Sula*, through its exploration of the relationship between its central characters, is a critique of oppositions—bottom and top, clean and dirty, ordered and disordered. The herb, nightshade, and the soil in which it is rooted, set the stage for the drama that unfolds in the novel, which centrally concerns the coming-of-age of two young girls.

At its core, *Sula* is the story of two friends, Sula Peace and Nel Wright. The girls come from two completely different homes. Sula Peace is the daughter of Hannah Peace and the granddaughter of Eva Peace. Sula's grandfather, Boy Boy, abandons the family when her mother is a small child, and Sula's father dies when Sula is young. As a result, Sula lives in a house dominated by women. From her observations of these women, Sula experiences life as a chaotic mix of different people in a house that has a random and eccentric design, one that mirrors the lifestyle of its inhabitants. As a result of her environment, Sula becomes a bold person, but she is uncertain about whether she is loved and about how to express affection for others.

On the other hand, Nel Wright, the child of Helene and Wiley Wright, lives in a meticulously ordered home. Her mother, Helene, is obsessed with ensuring that everything in the house is clean and in its proper place, and that desire extends to her daughter, Nel. Helene, through her insistence on perfection and on the importance of appearances, causes her daughter to feel inadequate and insecure. Nel internalizes an idealized notion of love, believing, along with many other young girls, that eventually she will be rescued from the tyranny of her mother's home by a gallant young man whose only objective is the guarantee of her happiness.

The friendship of the two girls brings into question the central issues of the novel, namely, who is right and who is not. Nel Wright's last name suggests this question and it is Nel who, through her experiences during her friendship with Sula, decides that she is the virtuous one. The community of the Bottom comes to agree with her conclusion.

The two girls draw from each other's strengths and supplement each other in such a way that their weaknesses are less significant as a result of their friendship. This mutual affirmation and reassurance continues until the two are involved with a life altering event, the accidental drowning of a little boy, Chicken Little. As with many literary texts that deal with the subject of coming-of-age, *Sula* reveals the girls' confrontation with the knowledge that brings about adulthood, particularly knowledge of sexuality and of death. In a climactic scene, Sula and Nel become familiar with both in a short period of time and, as a result, begin their divergent journeys into adulthood.

Just before the moment when Sula accidentally lets go of Chicken Little's hands and sends him spiraling toward the river and his death, she and Nel dig a hole in the earth and throw all that they can find into the space in the earth. There are many ways this action by Nel and Sula can be interpreted. This scene has been understood by some critics to refer to the girls emerging sexuality. Creating the deep hole in the earth seems to be an almost sensual experience for the girls until they begin to fill the hole they create with debris. The scene may suggest that, as a result of living in the era and the place in which they are coming of age, Sula and Nel's sexuality cannot develop in a way that would be wholesome and affirming for them both. Instead, their emerging womanhood is doomed to be polluted with all of the negative associations and definitions already assigned to it by the larger culture.

The impending separation between the two girls becomes apparent immediately after they fill the hole with debris. The girls do not talk to each other while they fill the hole together, and the activity fills the young girls with anxiety and tension, possibly predicting the eventual disintegration of their relationship. Because the accidental drowning of Chicken Little occurs immediately after the incident with the hole, there is an association for Nel and Sula between sexuality and death and their loss of innocence. This climactic moment results in their discarding what they perceive as waste, items that are, perhaps, symbolic of their lost innocence. Although Chicken Little's body is found and buried, the earth cannot contain his memory and its presence in Nel and Sula's lives. This event cements in Nel's mind the ideal that she is the morally superior of the two girls.

When the two reach young adulthood, their choices reinforce Nel's understanding of herself as good. In the time frame of the novel, the late 1920s, a woman was supposed to marry, settle down, and have children. This is the path Nel chooses as she marries Jude, an immature and unfulfilled man who believes that marriage will restore the manhood he feels deprived of as a result of racism. Nel's choice reinforces the norms of her community and is therefore sanctioned and defined as the right path. On the other hand, Sula chooses to spend her young adulthood in college and then traveling and exploring the country. When she returns to the Bottom after 10 years of absence, Sula represents an alternative to the traditional life of women and is therefore perceived as negative, the embodiment of evil. The town uses Sula and her behavior as a way of demonstrating its moral superiority.

Sula returns to the Bottom and to Nel with her definition of their friendship intact. The girls have always shared everything and so Sula believes that she can share Jude, Nel's husband. Jude and Sula have sex and Nel catches them during the act. Rather than trying to understand Sula's action in terms of the girls' lifelong friendship, Nel decides to judge the act in a way that supports her own understanding of herself as superior to Sula. Nel's assessment of the situation leads her to adopt martyrdom following the affair and Jude's abandonment of their marriage and children. After Jude leaves Nel, she has a feeling that reminds her of "mud and dead leaves" (107). This feeling connects Nel's response to Sula and Jude's affair with Chicken Little, his death and funeral, and her lost girlhood and innocence.

The negative associations the town holds of Sula are permanent, like dirt that cannot be washed away. She becomes the bottom of Medallion's moral hierarchy. She refuses to conform to the traditional expectations of women, such as caretaking, and places her grandmother in a home rather than nurse the woman herself. Sula is a woman out-of-sync with the time in which she lives. There is no place for her consistent refusal to obey the rules. Her lack of sexual inhibition is damning in the eyes of the town. One member of the community finds her independence intriguing and appealing. Sula's seeming self-possession attracts Ajax as it reminds him of his mother who is also a marginalized, yet powerful woman.

The relationship between Sula and Ajax is mutually satisfying until the experience of a love relationship with a man leads Sula to try to enter into a more conventional definition. This shift alienates Ajax and he leaves. In her desperation to keep Ajax, Sula characterizes him as water that needs to be mixed with loam to achieve stability. She is afraid, however, that she might instead make mud. This reference to mud is the nadir, or bottom, for Sula as, at that moment, she relinquishes her defining autonomy and independence and begins

a rapid decline upon Ajax's departure. As she lies on her deathbed Sula acknowledges her humanity and lack of shame as she tells Nel that she is unperturbed by her own dirt. At the end of her life, Sula comes to terms with her own humanity. Nel refuses to understand and characterizes Sula's behavior in Medallion, the affairs with various men in the town, the lost friendships, and the relationship with Eva, as dirty. She still needs to define Sula as the bottom so that she can remain superior.

Years later, after defining her existence around the fact of Jude's abandonment and Sula's betrayal, Nel has an epiphany. She realizes that the relationship between the two women should have been beyond evaluation through simple judgments of right and wrong. Instead, the women should have been able to love and nurture their friendship without the imposition of the expectations of the community. The gray ball that Nel feels dissipating when she recognizes this reality is the remnants of her decision after Chicken Little's death that the incident was Sula's fault. As Nel takes responsibility, not only for the boy's death, but also for her inability to forgive Sula's affair with Jude, she begins to mourn the one real connection in her life, her relationship with Sula. Preserving the relationship, she learns too late, was much more important than deciding who was right and who was wrong. Like the nightshade that flourishes in the Bottom, Nel's awareness is both devastating and healing. At the end of the novel she has the ability to experience her life without the limitations of judgment, but she also realizes the profundity of the loss of Sula.

SOME IMPORTANT THEMES AND SYMBOLS IN *SULA*

The Mystery of Shadrack

Sula both begins and ends with Shadrack. The entire second chapter of the book is devoted to this character and, yet, throughout the rest of the novel, although he is always around, he is on the outskirts of the narrative. Like his biblical namesake, Shadrack has survived the ravages of war, yet the scars of his experiences on the battleground leave him unable to communicate fully with others. Shadrack's psychic instability is rooted in the nonorganic world. When reconnected to the natural world or earth, he comes close to reassembling his fragmented psyche. When he exits the psychiatric hospital, the trees do not threaten him because they are embedded in the earth. Although his psyche seems fragmented, fundamentally he is rooted and senses essential truth.

Shadrack is alienated and isolated, yet is an integral member of the Bottom community. Shadrack understands the permanence of death and the destructive power human beings can render. His solution, National Suicide Day, is but a temporary containment of the inevitable, but from his perspective it eases the terror of the knowledge he has acquired. His annual ritual serves as a warning and reminder of the inevitabilities the residents of the Bottom face themselves, yet they do not understand the seriousness of the message delivered by a man they consider to be a familiar and harmless madman until the final National Suicide Day, when the realities Shadrack understands firsthand become tangible to the whole community. Shadrack's mysterious promise to Sula, "always," points toward his intimate understanding of the omnipresent reality of death.

The Sacrifices of Motherhood

Motherhood is a complicated and multidimensional experience as depicted throughout Morrison's canon, and *Sula* is no exception. Through the dilemmas of its characters, *Sula* asks the reader to consider the roles and responsibilities of motherhood. Rather than foregrounding a patriarch as the head of a family group, *Sula* exposes the particular dilemma of Eva, a single mother struggling to raise her children alone without resources. Although the exact nature of her sacrifice is not detailed, in her desperation, Eva abandons her children to the care of a generous neighbor. After some time, Eva returns to her children with money, but no leg. Eva's sacrifice obviously comes at great personal cost, but the ultimate value of her willing mutilation comes into question as her children become adults. Although they have material security, Eva's children have emotional and psychological damage.

Eva's son, Plum, returns from his service in the military addicted to heroin. After observing her son's addiction, convinced that he will not recover,

Eva takes his life by setting her son on fire. Eva does not feel that she kills her son but that she rescues him from a terrible fate.

Eva's daughter Hannah does not have the same interpretation of the events as her mother. Hannah does not understand her mother's actions as loving and asks Eva if she ever loved them. Eva does not understand what Hannah means by the question and responds with anger. Eva believes that her sacrifice speaks for itself and that she does not need to justify her love for her children. Nonetheless, Hannah clearly is uncertain about her mother's feelings.

Unwittingly, Hannah puts that love to the test when, shortly after the conversation about maternal love, she catches on fire while boiling water to wash clothes. Eva sees her daughter burning and leaps out of the window in an attempt to put out the fire by landing on her daughter. Eva does not reach the burning woman and Hannah dies from her injuries. Eva is badly hurt, but survives.

This question of what it means to be a mother also affects the next generation of the Peace family. Hannah herself has a tentative and uncertain relationship with her own daughter, Sula. Right before the death of Chicken Little, Sula overhears her mother talking to a friend. Hannah says of her daughter that she loves her but does not like her. This devastating revelation hurts Sula and adds permanent ambivalence to their interactions. When Hannah catches on fire, Sula watches her mother burn.

Sula's best friend Nel also has an uncertain relationship with her own mother, Helene Wright. Helene is the daughter of a prostitute. She is ashamed of her history and so tries to conform to what she understands as the proper way for a woman to behave. Helene imposes these expectations on her daughter, and grooms Nel for domesticity. Helene's need for respectability imposes on her daughter the ideal of romance rather than more practical information about self-awareness and personal development. Helene needs her daughter's life to vindicate the legacy of her mother's occupation. As a result, Nel enters into an unfulfilling marriage and wastes most of her adult life mourning its loss.

In turn, after her marriage fails, Nel turns to her children for emotional fulfillment they cannot provide. Her children are eager to escape into adulthood, away from her needy over-attentiveness.

Sula presents the complex sacrifices of motherhood without idealizing them. Each of the mothers in the text feels that she is doing what is necessary to provide for her child what she needs, and yet none of them succeed in passing on to their daughters what they actually need.

The Impacts of Shame

Throughout the novel, Sula is the primary focus of the town's various attempts to find a scapegoat to shame. Shame in the Bottom is expressed in relation to Sula. Shame is attributed by the weak-hearted to those who do not feel shame. The townspeople believe that their judgments of Sula will create in her a sense of shame. People in the community so associate her with what is wrong, that they refuse to look at her or to interact with her in the same way that they would with each other. Despite her many judgments, even Nel feels compassion for Sula's "shamed" eyes, but Sula's independence and freedom do not permit her to feel shame herself. Jude is also associated with shame in Nel's assessment. Jude does not seem ashamed himself, even when Nel witnesses his and Sula's affair. In fact, neither Jude nor Sula feel shame at that moment.

Nel is the only character in the novel who openly admits her own shame. She feels shame when Jude leaves her. Nel feels this shame because her status as a wife and mother is destroyed. Her inability to conform to the community's expectations causes Nel to feel ashamed.

Birds

Before Sula throws Chicken Little into the river, his cries of delight alarm the birds. When Sula returns to Medallion after 10 years' absence, robins and other birds overwhelm the town. The residents of Medallion perceive the presence of the birds, and by association, Sula, as a plague of biblical significance. Eva remarks that the unusual number of birds is a sign of Sula's return. The birds' departure creates a magical absence in Medallion, a delight in their non-being. This feeling Nel expresses lends ambiguity to the meaning and significance of Sula's return.

Night

Often the night seems to have a protective function for the residents of Medallion. Morrison compares Shadrack's desire to see his own face to moonlight sneaking under a window shade. Helene sews late into the night to make herself a dress of heavy velvet to wear for her return to the South. Nel makes the discovery of individual selfhood, separate from her mother, at night. Eva relieves Plum of his constipation during a late winter night.

Night also functions in the novel as a time of fear and destruction. When her children are young, Eva can find work only at night, which forces her to leave them alone. Eva burns Plum to death at night. A bargeman finds Chicken Little's body in the river at night.

Dirt

Sula and Nel's climactic digging in the earth before Sula's accidental flinging of Chicken Little into the river has sexual, possibly lesbian overtones. This climactic moment results in their discarding what they perceive as waste, items that are, perhaps, symbolic of their lost innocence during the scene that immediately precedes Chicken Little's death. Although Chicken Little's body is found and buried, the earth cannot contain his memory and its presence in Nel and Sula's lives. After Jude leaves Nel, she has a feeling that reminds her of "mud and dead leaves." This feeling is associated for Nel with Chicken Little, his death and funeral, and her lost girlhood and innocence. (107) Nel also associates mud with her characterization of the sexual relationship between Sula and Jude as dirty.

The Free Fall

In *Sula*, Morrison defines one of the central themes that repeat throughout her canon. After Jude leaves Nel, she closes off her life to possibility and clings to a past that can never be recovered. The narrator says that she becomes like an insect clinging to a wall to avoid the inevitable plummet to the bottom. The narrator suggests that, as the fall is inevitable, the more graceful and fulfilling thing to do would be to give into the free fall, the unavoidable end of life—death. This passage contains one of the first articulations of Morrison's ruminations on the difficult human reality of accepting death.

This passage suggests that, since one cannot avoid death, the best strategy is an artful acceptance of that truth and the full embrace of life, no matter how brief.

CHARACTERS

Ajax (A. Jacks, Albert Jacks) Ajax is an intelligent and attractively lazy man who loves women and treats them well. When Nel and Sula walk to Edna Finch's Mellow House for ice cream cones, they have to walk past the group of young men that hang around the businesses on Carpenter's Road. The young men in cream-colored trousers and lemon-yellow gabardines comment on the girls walking past, and the one who is best able to manipulate his language is Ajax. He is a beautiful young man, and the girls are delighted when he pays them the compliment of saying "pigmeat" as they walk by. Years later, Sula falls in love with him, and by the time of his departure, she has become possessive. This new desire for ownership seems to instigate the decline in her health that eventually leads to her death.

Sula proposes that women often fall in love with men and, when they do, find themselves desirous of possessing them, but Ajax does not want to be tied down. He has an affair with Sula because he is attracted to her independence and aloofness. Once she begins to fall in love with him, however, he leaves her.

As previously mentioned, Ajax, the man in the yellow gabardine pants, is an object of sexual desire for Sula from early age. Morrison characterizes him as gold. His name also suggests the similarly named Trojan warrior who was a good soldier but was also very arrogant. Ajax loves airplanes. He brings Sula milk, but she won't drink it; she just admires the bottles it comes in. He also is the only man who really talks to Sula. The mythological Ajax is like Ajax, Morrison's character, particularly with respect to his sexual prowess and to his ability to leave women easily. Ajax defends the helpless. He is reputed to shoot at Mr. Finley when he learns that the man shoots at his own dog.

The irony of his name manifests in the fact that his real name is Albert Jacks, A. Jacks, and that Sula never knows his real name until she finds his driver's license. Sula misses Ajax after he has left. Once she discovers that his real name is Albert Jacks, however, she seems to realize that she never could have loved him because she did not even know him.

Ajax's mother Ajax's mother is described as a beautiful, neglectful, toothless, evil CONJURE WOMAN who has seven sons that worship her and bring her the items she needs—the detritus of humanity—for her work, witchcraft. Her sons are open and respectful of women and they adore and admire her above, and perhaps to the exclusion of, all other women.

She ignores standards of beauty but, according to the narrator, if she took care of herself she would be a beautiful woman. She does not care about such superficial concerns as beauty. Ajax loves his mother and her independence deeply. It is Sula's similarity to his mother in this respect that initially attracts Ajax to her. Ajax's mother is an incarnation of the black, traditionally mystical conjure woman in African-American literature.

bargeman The white bargeman finds Chicken Little's body after Sula accidentally throws it into the river. When he finds the boy's body, he puts it in a sack for several days. He regrets having picked up the body because he does not want to return the two miles downriver to Medallion to find the family of the boy. The bargeman and the sheriff of the neighboring town give the body to the ferryman to return to Medallion.

bartender Nel has a brief relationship with a bartender at a hotel in Medallion, but the tryst does not develop into anything lasting.

Betty (Teapot's Mamma) Betty is the neglectful and irresponsible mother of a little boy named Teapot. The woman has a drinking problem and a reputation as a bad mother, until Sula returns to town and the town turns against her. When Teapot falls on Sula's stairs, the town believes Betty's story that Sula was responsible for the boy's accident, transforming Betty into a good mother. She does a little dance in celebration when she learns of Sula's death. After Sula's death, Betty returns to her original, neglectful patterns of mothering.

black soldiers on train The soldiers on the train are first sympathetic and then scornful of Helene when she smiles at the abusive and racist conductor. Nel is ashamed of her mother after seeing the looks in their eyes.

Boy Boy Boy Boy is Eva's husband. He leaves his wife and three children after five years of an unsatisfactory marriage in which he has been unfaithful and abusive. After a few years he returns to visit Eva. He arrives looking smug and prosperous rather than regretful. He has expensive city clothes and an easy, pleasant manner. The entire time he visits with Eva, he does not ask her about their children. His new city girlfriend waits outside for him.

After he leaves, Eva realizes that she will always hate Boy Boy and that this hatred will be her obsession in this life. At this point, Eva also begins to retreat into her bedroom and to live a reclusive life.

Boy Boy's name sets him up as an immature, irresponsible father who abandons his children to pursue his own boyish and selfish pleasures. He is nowhere near a match for Eva when it comes to responsibility and adulthood. Boy Boy may represent the losses inherent in the move toward the North and the city, as he leaves behind his family and heritage. Eva's response to his abandonment also may demonstrate that hatred, as much as love, can keep a person from moving forward in life.

Cecile Sabat Cecile Sabat is Helene's grandmother and the woman who raises her. Cecile rescues Helene from her mother Rochelle's brothel when Helene is a little girl. The description of the soft lights and colors in Sundown House where Rochelle lives and works compared with the restrictive religious conventions of Cecile's house makes Helene's rescue seem ambiguous.

Although it would not have been proper, Helene probably would have found more love and pleasure in the easygoing arms of her mother than she did in the strict embrace of her grandmother. This pos-

sibility illustrates another theme in *Sula*, the idea that what is thought of as right and proper behavior can be arbitrary and may not necessarily be the best course of action.

Cecile disapproves of her daughter's actions and instills in Helene a conservative outlook on life as well as shame about her past. Cecile raises Helene to be on guard always for signs of "her mother's wild blood." When Cecile's middle-aged nephew Wiley comes for a visit, Cecile marries Helen off to him to get her as far away from her mother's background as possible.

Chicken Little Chicken Little is the little child Sula throws into the water and who subsequently drowns. Sula does not intend to murder Chicken Little. She is merely playing with him when the accident happens. Before the accident, she helps him climb a tree and, when she unintentionally lets go of the boy, she is swinging him in circles for fun.

Neither Sula nor Nel tell anybody about Chicken Little's death because they are frightened of the ramifications. The boy is found by a bargeman three days after the accident and is unrecognizable by the time of the funeral. The events surrounding Chicken Little's death demonstrate the indifference with which the world treats the life and death of a young black boy.

This incident with Chicken Little occurs shortly after Sula overhears her mother saying she does not like her. This day seems pivotal in Sula's life because she is shocked to find out that she cannot count on her mother's love, and then she finds that she cannot count on herself either, since she accidentally killed someone. These revelations free her to the point where she has no center anymore and so she is left to invent herself.

Although Chicken Little's body is found and buried, the earth cannot contain his memory and its presence in Nel and Sula's lives.

China China is "the most rambunctious whore in town," whose death evokes more sympathy from the town than when Sula dies. She has a black son and a white son, neither of whom cares when they are told that their mother is dying. China is also a character in *The Bluest Eye*.

Conductor As Helene and Nel board the train for New Orleans and Helene's grandmother's funeral, the conductor questions Helene for walking through the white car. Although he is rude and abusive, Helene smiles at him. Nel sees her mother differently after that smile.

Cora Dessie gossips with Cora about Sula after seeing Shadrack tip his hat to her.

Dessie Dessie represents an average member of the Medallion community. She lives downstairs from her friend Ivy. Dessie is a Big Elk daughter and is therefore seen as an authority. Dessie says that she sees Shadrack tip an imaginary hat to Sula, which is proof of Sula's wickedness. She is the first to see Shadrack coming down the road on the last and fatal National Suicide Day. She laughs at his presence because she can see death approaching in the sunshine and feels unafraid. She, like many others, Tar Baby, the Deweys, dies in the tunnel that day. The people of Medallion argue about whether she was the first one to come out and join Shadrack.

Deweys Eva names three children that she takes in Dewey, although they are nothing alike. They are a year or two apart in age and, although they all have different skin and eye coloring, they grow to be so much the same in everyone's mind that no one can tell them apart.

Eva uses the term "dewey" as a generic word for them, effectively canceling their individualities. They differ in appearance, age, and temperament; however, the similarity of their names causes the boys to develop a deep and intense bond. Soon, no one can tell the three boys apart. They are mischievous and, although they grow older, they remain forever childlike. The mysterious trinity of characters with the name Dewey repeatedly drinks milk after they arrive at the Peace house. The Deweys' milk consumption may represent their status as orphans, motherless children who cannot find the nurturance they need in order to transcend childhood.

The Deweys demonstrate the power of naming and the resiliency of friendship. They are reborn when they move into Eva's house and are all considered the same age, as if nothing happened to them before they came to her house. The boys do not grow. They all remain 48 inches tall and are said to have gorgeous teeth. Although no one ever finds their bodies, the town assumes that they die in the tunnel on the last National Suicide Day.

Edna Finch Edna Finch is the owner of the Mellow House, Medallion's ice cream parlor.

Eva Peace Eva Peace is Sula's grandmother. Eva marries young and has three children, but after five years of marriage, her husband leaves. Her children are Hannah, Pearl, and Plum. The baby boy, Plum, quit having bowel movements as a baby at a time when Eva had no food left. Eva uses the last of her lard to lubricate her finger to unclog his bowels. This experience brings her to the realization that she has to do something drastic to get food for her children.

She is left without the means to support herself or her three children and, therefore, leaves them with a neighbor, Mrs. Suggs, for 18 months. When Eve returns, she comes back without one of her legs but with enough money to survive. Whether she sticks the leg under a train and is paid off by the train company or whether she sold it to a hospital for $10,000 never is definitively known.

Eva is a strong, proud, and beautiful woman despite the missing leg. She has many lovers and opens her house to all sorts of boarders, vagrants, and children. Eva kills her own child, Plum, after he returns from the war mentally disturbed and addicted to heroin. She douses him with kerosene and sets him on fire because she believes, metaphorically speaking, that he is trying to crawl back into her womb.

On the other hand, she nearly kills herself jumping out a window in an attempt to quench the flames that ultimately kill her other child Hannah. Eva does these things out of love for her children.

Sula puts Eva in a rest home because she feels threatened by her. The two women are independent, strong, and concerned with self-preservation. When they love or hate, they do so fiercely and deeply. The two women are too much alike to live amiably within the same household. Eva's love is the toughest of love. She is consistent and honest in the way she lives. Her name connects her to Eve, the first woman. She is the first and the last, the matriarch of the Peace women.

farmer Sarcastically described as a good white farmer, this man promises his slave freedom and a piece of bottom land if the slave will perform some very difficult chores for him. When the slave has completed the tasks, this farmer convinces the slave that the less-than-desirable hilltop land is really better because it is at the bottom of heaven and so the spot comes to be called the Bottom.

Great Aunt Cecile See CECILE SABAT

Hannah Peace Hannah is Eva's oldest child and Sula's mother. After her husband Rekus dies, Hannah has a string of lovers. She is free and easy with her sexuality because, like Eva, she likes maleness and men. She makes the men feel perfect as they are and she is therefore respected by her lovers. She has the attitude that making love to men is a pleasant but unremarkable activity and she does it whenever she feels the need or desire.

Hannah makes no demands at all of the men she loves—just accepts them as they are, so they bask and relax in her company. Sula adopts her mother's attitude and believes that men are to be enjoyed whenever she feels like it. This philosophy contributes to and explains Sula's ability as an adult to seduce Nel's husband, Jude.

Hannah, like Helene, is a distant mother. She is so preoccupied with her lovers and friends that she does not nurture or coddle Sula. Sula even overhears her mother say that she does not like her, although she loves her. The distance between mother and child allows Sula to watch, disinterested, as her mother burns to death.

Hannah is a diluted, more relaxed version of Eva. She teaches Sula her views on sex, but Sula takes them, along with everything else she learns from the women of her family, to a new and different level. Of the three women, Hannah has the weakest, most passive personality.

Helene Sabat Wright Helene is born to a Creole prostitute, Rochelle Sabat, but is raised by her grandmother, Cecile Sabat. After a short courtship, she marries Wiley Wright, a seaman and cousin who is absent for long periods of time due to his occupation as a seaman on the Great Lakes. After being married for nine years, Helene gives birth to her only child, Nel. Helene is a lot like Geraldine in *The Bluest Eye*. She is a proper, controlled African-American woman who feels superior to the rest of her community and enjoys controlling the "funkiness" in her daughter Nel.

Helene is embarrassed and ashamed of her own blackness, as evidenced by her ingratiating encounter with a white train conductor. This shame and embarrassment of her heritage is also symbolized by Helene's encounter with her mother, Rochelle Sabat, when Nel and Helene return to New Orleans after Cecile Sabat dies. Helene refuses to allow Nel to speak or learn Creole, her native language. Helene's oppressive wish to shed her poor black roots leads to Nel's ignorance of her own heritage and to the death of language. Nel's mother, upstanding and powerful in the community, well-mannered, conservative, and often emotionless, manages to suppress the desires of her daughter Nel.

Helene is described as an impressive woman who is convinced that she has the authority as social arbiter in Medallion. She holds sway both in her social and church activities and over her husband and daughter, whom she manipulates to suit herself.

Henri Martin Henri Martin is a resident of New Orleans and, apparently, a friend or acquaintance of Cecile Sabat. He writes a letter to Helen informing her about her grandmother's illness and urging Helene to return to New Orleans immediately.

Herrod Brothers, the The Herrod Brothers join Shadrack's parade on the last National Suicide Day.

Hester Hester is the daughter of one of Hannah's friends, Valentine or Patsy. In 1922, Hester is grown and out of the house and her mother says that she is not sure that she loves her daughter. Hannah replies with her feelings about loving but not liking Sula.

hovering gray ball, the   This ball appears to Nel, or would have appeared had she allowed herself to look at it. After the appearance of the gray ball, Nel finds she cannot allow herself to let out her personal howl of pain following the loss of Jude and her marriage. She feels the howl coming but it will not come. When she stands up, she believes that it is hovering just to the right of her in the air, just out of view.

It takes great effort for Nel not to look at the gray ball, so she is careful not to turn her head. The gray ball begins hovering in 1937, and it is not until 1965 that Nel is able to deal with the gray ball and all that it represents.

At the end of the book, a combination of events finally clarifies what the gray ball is. Nel visits with Eva who accuses her of Chicken Little's death and tells her that she and Sula were the same. Nel flees the woman and walks past the cemetery where Sula is buried and then, after she has been thinking back about her complicity in Chicken Little's death, SHADRACK passes by and reminds her of that day. Nel is finally able to let out her cry of pain, as she realizes the gray ball is the pain of her longing, not for Jude, but for Sula.

Irene   Irene is the owner of Irene's House of Cosmetology.

Ivy   Ivy lives upstairs from Dessie. Dessie says that Ivy is the only person she tells about witnessing Shadrack tip his hat to Sula. Dessie says that Shadrack's gesture is definitive proof that Sula is evil. Ivy dies on the last National Suicide Day when the river tunnel collapses.

Jake Freeman   Jake Freeman is one of the boys that Nel remembers as being beautiful in 1921. Jake has a brother, Paul Freeman.

John L.   John L. is a high school companion of Nel and Sula's who is rumored to have attempted to have sex with a woman's hip.

Jude Greene   Jude Greene is Nel's husband. Jude Greene works at the Hotel Medallion as a waiter to help out his parents and their seven other children.

Jude wants to work on the road crew, but they do not hire black workers. He really wants the job and all that it entails—the work clothes, the ability to say he built the road—the markers of masculinity in his world. It is his rage at not receiving the job and his determination to take on a man's role that inspires him to ask Nel to marry him. In his disappointment, he finds that Nel can comfort him as he believes a wife should, so he presses her to marry him. He wants someone to nurture him, care for him, and soothe his wounded pride. Nel's reluctance to marry is also an added incentive. Her reluctance makes the actual marriage seem like a conquest to Jude. Although Jude seems to Nel to be a model man at first, he cannot take the loss of manhood that racism precipitates. Eventually, Nel and Jude have three children together, two boys and a girl.

When Sula returns 10 years after their wedding, she seduces Jude. This act instigates the break in the women's friendship that is never repaired. Nel cannot understand why Sula sleeps with Jude, and Sula cannot understand why Nel makes such a big deal about a sexual act and why Nel does not forgive her. In the very long run, Jude is merely an obstacle in Sula and Nel's relationship. Sula feels she is doing Nel a favor by ruining her draining marriage, but it is only after Sula's death that Nel realizes this.

Laura   After Sula leaves Medallion, Laura cooks for Eva out of the goodness of her heart. When Sula returns, she sends Laura away because she says she does not belong in the house. Sula tells Nel that she believes that Laura is stealing things from Eva's house.

L.P.   L.P. is one of the boys that Nel remembers as being beautiful in 1921.

Mr. Buckland Reed   Mr. Buckland Reed points out to Eva that the Deweys are different ages when Eva decides to send them to school. He reminds Eva that the youngest Dewey is only four, but Eva sends the boys to school together anyway.

Mr. Finley   Mr. Finley is known for beating his dog. Ajax shoots at him for his meanness toward the animal. Indulging in his 13-year tradition of sucking chicken bones on his front porch, Mr. Finley chokes and dies when he looks up and sees Sula.

Mr. and Mrs. Hodges Mr. and Mrs. Hodges are the cemetery's gravediggers who assist with Sula's funeral. They also run a funeral parlor. Shadrack is cleaning leaves for the couple when he sees Sula's body. This sight sends him into despair and leads to the final National Suicide Day.

Mrs. Buckland Reed Mrs. Buckland Reed is a neighbor of the Peace family.

Mrs. Jackson When Eva has no money, Mrs. Jackson lets her have milk from her cow. Mrs. Jackson eats ice. She is also described as greedy as she continues to make preserves in 1923 when she still has stores of preserves from 1920.

Mrs. Reed Mrs. Reed is the woman who takes the Deweys to school and registers them all for kindergarten. She tells the teacher that they are all cousins, that they are all six years old, and that all of their names are Dewey King.

Mrs. Scott's twins Mrs. Scott's twins are two of the boys Nel remembers as being beautiful in 1921.

Nathan The otherwise undistinguished Nathan brings food to Sula when she is ill and near to death. He also gets her medicine and is the only one willing to care for her while she is an invalid. Nathan finds Sula's body after her death. He knows she is dead because her mouth is open.

Nel Wright Nel Wright is the daughter of Helene and Wiley Wright. As a child Nel resolves to leave Medallion and travel, but her trip to New Orleans for Cecil's funeral is the only time she ever leaves Medallion. Nel is changed by her trip to her great-grandmother's funeral. Her great-grandmother dies before they arrive. This trip is symbolic and sets up a frame for how the rest of the journeys in the story will work. It also sets up the dichotomies between North and South, life and death, truth and lies, and mothers and daughters.

Helene is not very visible for the rest of the novel, but she influences Nel and how Nel relates to Sula and the rest of the world. Nel has seen strange places and people, but most of all she has seen that her controlling mother is not the powerful figure Nel thought she was. After her return home, Nel realizes that she is not defined by her mother—that she is not just her parents' daughter, but that she is herself.

This sense of "Me-ness" she experiences prepares the way for her to act on her impulse to be friends with Sula Peace, whom she noticed at school but knew her mother would not approve of. After the trip, Nel knows that she has some control over herself and has the courage to initiate friendship with Sula, a friendship that her mother Helene comes to approve of eventually.

Nel becomes best friends with Sula Peace. They develop a profound and intense friendship. Nel is with Sula when Sula accidentally throws Chicken Little in the lake, causing him to drown. Neither girl panics and Nel stands steadfastly by her friend.

Nel eventually marries Jude, has children, and settles down in Medallion. After a few years, her marriage with Jude becomes oppressive and burdensome. This burden is somewhat relieved when Sula returns to Medallion and the two once again resume their friendship. This renewed friendship is abruptly cut short when Nel finds Sula and Jude in bed together. Jude leaves Nel and she has to find a job to support her family.

Not until long after Sula dies does Nel realize that it is not Jude she has been mourning all those years. It was her friend Sula. Unlike Sula, Nel is an example of a woman overly dependent on others, namely, a man, for her own satisfaction. She is representative of the woman who marries early, never leaves her home town, and never truly discovers her own wants, needs, ideas, and feelings.

Nel is supposedly the good member of the Nel and Sula partnership. The way that she is raised causes her to lose sight of her dreams of being her own person, traveling, and of having a self-defined identity. Together, Sula and Nel have a complete, well-rounded life. They lost parts of themselves when they lost each other.

nurse In the hospital where Shadrack is treated after returning shell-shocked from World War I, the male nurse is very unsympathetic to Shadrack's condition and insists that he feed himself. Shadrack cannot manage the task because he thinks his hands have begun to grow gigantic and out-of-control and he cannot take them out from under the covers.

Shadrack becomes violent and is put in a strait-jacket. Shadrack is so disoriented that he does not know who or what he is. A directive is issued that hospital space is needed, so Shadrack is dismissed from the army and from the hospital without having received the kind of treatment he needs to enable him to resume a normal life in society.

Old Willy Fields Old Willy Fields is an orderly who notices Eva bleeding unattended in the hospital and gets the dying woman help. Afterward, Willy boasts that he saved Eva's life. Eva did not want to be saved and curses Willy every day for the next 37 years.

Patsy Patsy and Valentine are Hannah's friends. Sula overhears them talking about motherhood and children and hears her mother tell them she loves Sula, but does not like her—a defining moment in Sula's maturation. Shortly after this revelation, Sula accidentally throws Chicken Little, and the innocence of childhood, into the river. After Sula becomes a grown woman and Hannah has died, Patsy turns against Sula and gossips, saying that Sula does not burp when she drinks beer.

Paul Freeman Paul Freeman is one of the boys that Nel remembers as being beautiful in 1921. He has a brother, Jake Freeman.

Pearl (Eva Peace) Pearl is Eva and Boy Boy's second oldest child, the one Eva names after herself. Pearl marries at 14 and moves to Flint, Michigan. She sends her mother whiny, uninteresting letters about her husband, children, and minor troubles and encloses $2.

Plum Peace (Ralph) Plum is Eva's youngest child. Eva's behavior toward Plum represents the extent of a mother's love. As a child, Plum suffers from severe constipation. Eva uses the last bit of food she has to soften her fingers as she inserts them in his rectum to physically remove the hard stools from his bowels.

After returning from World War I, Plum becomes addicted to drugs. He does not wash. He steals and he sleeps for days. Out of love for him and sympathy for his unhappiness, Eva holds him tight one last time and then sets him on fire. She loves him enough to try to save his life as a child and enough not to watch him waste his life as an adult.

police The police see Shadrack sitting next to the road and, making the assumption that he is drunk instead of sick, take him to jail. In the jail cell, Shadrack manages to see his own reflection in the toilet water and he begins to have some idea of who he is. The next day the sheriff reads his discharge papers from the army and arranges for someone to drop him off in Medallion.

Terrified by the unexpectedness of death and dying, Shadrack establishes National Suicide Day, January 3, as the day that everyone can kill either himself or someone else and get it all over with on the one day, thus removing the uncertainty from death and making it manageable in Shadrack's mind.

Ralph Peace See PLUM PEACE

Reba Reba joins in on Shadrack's parade on the last National Suicide Day.

Rekus Rekus is Sula's father. Described as a laughing man, he dies when Sula is three years old, leaving both Hannah and Sula alone. Sula grows up without a father and this childhood loneliness provides part of the basis for her friendship with Nel. Rekus is really significant only because he is absent and therefore the Peace house is comprised mostly of women.

Reverend Deal Reverend Deal is the religious and moral voice in Bottom. He denounces National Suicide Day and he delivers the moving sermon at Chicken Little's funeral.

Rochelle Sabat Rochelle Sabat is Helene's mother and a prostitute at the Sundown House in New Orleans. Cecile Sabat, Rochelle's mother, takes Helene from Rochelle because she feels that Rochelle's occupation makes her an unfit parent. Rochelle and Helene see each other, for the first time in many years, at Cecile's house before her funeral. Rochelle is dressed all in yellow, soft and smelling like gardenias. Nel finds her attractive and warm, yet the behavior between Rochelle and Helene is decidedly cool. Rochelle represents everything Helene wants to distance herself from— her poor, black, Creole heritage.

Rochelle seems free-spirited and affectionate. She seems to be like Sula and Hannah, which is why both Helene and Cecile do not wish to be associated with her. Interestingly, Nel finds her grandmother attractive and young-looking. Rochelle shows no discernible affection for her daughter, but holds her granddaughter tightly when she meets her.

Rudy Rudy is the child of either Valentine or Patsy. Rudy is wild with his mother, but behaves with his father. His mother says she will be glad when he is grown and gone, although she says she loves him.

sergeant During World War II, Nel has an affair with an unnamed sergeant. The relationship does not last.

Shadrack Shadrack is a young soldier who returns from combat in World War I psychologically scarred. He believes that his hands grow to a monstrous size whenever he looks at them. This belief symbolizes the lack of control Shadrack feels over his own body and the world around him. Although everything seems orderly on the outside—his hands do not really grow uncontrollably—on the inside he is a jumble of confused emotions and feelings.

Shadrack's psychic instability is rooted in the nonorganic world. When reconnected to the natural world or earth he comes close to reassembling his fragmented psyche. When he exits the psychiatric hospital, the trees do not threaten him because they are embedded in the earth.

The same is true of life. Although everything seems orderly and controlled, this is not always the case. Shadrack declares National Suicide Day on January 3rd of each year in order to control his fear of death. He figures that by devoting one day a year to death the "rest of the year would be safe and free." National Suicide Day reflects an important theme in Morrison's fiction, the necessity of accepting the inevitability of death in order to truly live life. National Suicide Day becomes a normal addition to life in Medallion. It is on this holiday that Shadrack inadvertently leads many Medallion residents to their deaths in the tunnel that holds the false hope of employment for the community.

Shadrack also witnesses Sula and Nel's involvement in Chicken Little's death. Although Sula was frightened by this knowledge throughout her life, Shadrack merely thought fondly of her as the one woman to visit his home. Cryptically, he says "Always" to her when she runs to his house. He keeps her purple and white belt with its liturgical colors. It is an encounter with Shadrack toward the end of the novel that brings about Nel's epiphany that Sula is the single most important person in her life. (For information on the biblical Shadrack, see Part III.)

sheriff The police see Shadrack sitting next to the road and, assuming that he is drunk instead of sick, take him to jail. In the jail cell, Shadrack manages to see his own reflection in the toilet water, and he begins to have some idea of who he is. The next day the sheriff reads his discharge papers from the army and arranges for someone to drop him off in Meridian.

Terrified by the unexpectedness of death and dying, Shadrack establishes National Suicide Day, January 3, as the day that everyone can kill either himself or someone else and get it all over with on the one day. For Shadrack, National Suicide Day removes the uncertainty from death and makes it manageable.

Shirley Shirley is a girl in Nel and Sula's graduating class who they think is sexually unappealing.

slave The slave in the story at the novel's beginning lets himself be fooled by the farmer into accepting the higher hilly land for payment. Later, when an African-American community grows up on the slave's land, they have to endure the problems of the slave's choice—the land is hard to work and rocky, the winds batter their homes, they receive the full brunt of winter and storms—while the white town of Medallion below is protected by the slope of the valley. The farmer tells the slave that the land is the bottom of heaven. In the long run, the land becomes valuable.

Suggs, the The Suggs are Eva Peace's neighbors. After Boy Boy leaves her, the Suggs and other members of the community provide her with the food, milk, and necessities she and the children need to survive. When the baby, Plum, gets constipated, Mrs. Suggs gives Eva castor oil. Eva leaves her children with the Suggs for 18 months and returns with the money and motivation she needs to raise her family. The Suggs represent the helpful and charitable nature of members within a self-sustaining community. Eva and her children could not have survived without their assistance.

Sula Mae Peace Sula lives in a large house belonging to her grandmother, Eva, along with her mother, Hannah, adopted little boys, and several assorted borders. The house is disorderly, reflecting in its physical characteristics the casually promiscuous attitudes of both Eva and Hannah, who enjoy maleness without apology.

Like Nel, Sula is an only child. The two girls have distinct upbringings. Nel is raised in a conventional household while Sula lives in a busy and hectic household, full of lodgers, alcoholics, and her mother and grandmother's lovers. These differences and their dissatisfaction with their lives is part of what draws the two girls together. Sula and Nel are such close friends that Sula cuts off the tip of her own finger trying to protect Nel from white bullies.

Even as a girl, Sula never fit into the Medallion community. The birthmark of a rose over her eye, her indifference to the opinions of others, her aloofness toward others besides Nel, sets her apart from the rest of Medallion society.

Sula accidentally throws Chicken Little into a river and watches her own mother burn to death. Sula seems primarily concerned with self-preservation but understands the inevitability of death. Sula

leaves Medallion after Nel marries, goes to college, lives in a city, and then returns many years later. Her return is accompanied by a plague of robins and is viewed by the community as an evil omen.

Sula places her grandmother in Sunnydale, a home for older people, and sleeps with many men, indifferently. She has a significant affair with Ajax, but after he leaves her, she loses her independence and self-assurance. In the wake of Ajax's departure, Sula contracts an undetermined fatal illness and dies. Her last thoughts are of Nel and the need to tell her that death does not hurt.

Sula is representative of an independent, strong, and proud black woman; however, her pride and her independence seem to leave her without enough empathy for other people and cause her ostracism from the community. A compromise between Nel's dependence and Sula's independence seems to be the novel's suggestion for achieving the right balance for a happy and full life.

Sula fears and, at times, despises both Hannah and Eva because of the way these two women influenced her. Sula stands and watches Hannah burn to death. She puts Eva in a nursing home. These two actions demonstrate her need for control. Her sexual relationships also show her as a demanding and dominant woman. Sula has a birthmark above one of her eyes that other people say looks like a rose, a copperhead, and Hannah's ashes, all in the same story.

Sula is disconnected from her mother and grandmother and seems genuinely attached only to Nel. She does not sleep with Nel's husband, Jude, to be malicious. She is merely curious about the man. She does not expect that the relationship with Jude will change her friendship with Nel.

After Sula dies, the people of Medallion do not come to wash and dress her body, as is the custom. Eventually, Nel calls the police and Sula's body is taken to the Hodges funeral home in a police van. After the funeral, the Hodges begin to bury Sula, and black members of the town come and sing "Shall We Gather At the River."

Tar Baby (Pretty Johnnie) Tar Baby is a boarder who lives in Eva's house. He is a beautiful and quiet man who never raises his voice. Eva is convinced that he is all white, but teasingly calls him

Tar Baby. The white policemen from the valley also believe that he is white. They physically abuse him for being a white man who chooses to live in a black community.

Tar Baby is a mountain boy. He lives as a recluse and is determined to drink himself to death. Although he is a drunk, he does not bother anyone and is therefore tolerated. Tar Baby has a beautiful singing voice and makes the women cry, especially when he sings "In the Sweet By and By." The people of Medallion do not think to try to help Tar Baby out of his depression and alcoholism. Tar Baby, like Shadrack, is obsessed with death but not willing to commit suicide. Significantly, he and the Deweys are the first ones to join Shadrack's National Suicide Day parade the year that the tragedy occurs. He dies that day when the shifting earth from the river tunnel project collapses. (For more information on the Tar Baby stereotype, see Part III.)

teacher The teacher is the Deweys' first instructor. She is annoyed that the boys are registered under the same name and the same age, but is sure that she will be able to distinguish them from each other. Much to her surprise, she confuses the boys and has trouble distinguishing them from each other.

Teapot The five-year-old son of an indifferent mother, Teapot knocks on Sula's door looking for bottles. After Sula denies his request, the boy accidentally falls down the steps. After this incident, his drunken and indifferent mother, Betty, exhibits motherly concern and love. She begins to feed him regular meals and nurture him. After Sula's death, however, he is soon neglected and beaten again by his mother. Teapot represents the vulnerability and dependence of a young child on parents. More importantly, he demonstrates the extent to which the Bottom needs Sula to have a benchmark for evil and bad behavior.

Teapot's Mamma (Betty) Betty is known as Teapot's Mamma because of her failure as a mother. After witnessing Teapot's fall down Sula's steps, however, she becomes devoted to her maternal duties. The imagined threat that Sula poses to her

son and the sympathy she receives from the community inspire her to drink less and provide for her son. After Sula's death, Teapot's Mamma returns to her drinking and to abusing Teapot. Teapot's Mamma demonstrates the beneficial influence Sula had upon the Medallion community because her difference provides the townspeople with inspiration to rally together and become better, more charitable people.

train depot lady and children Since there are no colored restrooms in the southern train depots, the train depot lady and her children show Helene and Nel how to pee in a field during their trip to New Orleans.

Uncle Paul Uncle Paul is the man who brings Kentucky Wonders, a kind of green beans, to Hannah for canning. He tells Hannah that he has two bushels of the beans for her, but he has not brought them to her by the time she and Eva are snapping the beans.

Valentine Patsy and Valentine are Hannah's friends. Sula overhears them talking about motherhood and children and hears her mother tell them she loves Sula, but doesn't like her—a defining moment in Sula's maturation. Shortly after this revelation, Sula accidentally throws Chicken Little and the innocence of childhood into the river. Valentine joins Shadrack's parade on the last National Suicide Day and dies that day when the shifting earth from the river tunnel project collapses.

Wiley Wright Wiley Wright is Nel's father and Helene's husband. He is a seaman and he is gone for long lengths of time. Wiley marries Helene, at the urging of his Great Aunt Cecile who is also Helene's grandmother. Although he is substantially older than her, Wiley Wright finds Helene well-mannered, powerful, and mature. It never seems to be an issue that the two are cousins. Wiley Wright works on a ship on the Great Lakes lines and travels for long stretches of time, but Helene is quite content in his absence, especially after her daughter is born. Wiley Wright does not play a large role in the novel or the lives of the women in his life.

FURTHER READING

Angelis, Rose De. "Morrison's *Sula*," *Explicator* 60, no. 3 (Spring 2002): 172–175.

Closser, Raleen. "Morrison's *Sula*," *Explicator* 63, no. 2 (Winter 2005): 111.

Cohen, Tom "Politics of the Pre-figural: *Sula*, Blackness, and the Precession of Trope," *Parallax* 8, no. 1 (January 2002): 5–17.

Galehouse, Maggie. "New World Woman: Toni Morrison's *Sula*," *Papers on Language and Literature* 35, no. 4 (Fall 1999): 339–363.

Mayberry, Susan Neal. "Something Other Than a Family Quarrel: The Beautiful Boys in Morrison's *Sula*," *African American Review* 37, no. 4 (Winter 2003): 517–534.

Miller, D. Quentin. "Making a Place for Fear: Toni Morrison's First Redefinition of Dante's Hell in *Sula*," *English Language Notes* 37, no. 3 (March 2000): 68–77.

Nissen, Axel. "Form Matters: Toni Morrison's *Sula* and the Ethics of Narrative," *Contemporary Literature* 40, no. 2 (Summer 1999): 263–286.

Novak, Phillip. "Circles and Circles of Sorrow: In the Wake of Morrison's *Sula*," *PMLA: Publications of the Modern Language Association of America* 114, no. 2 (March 1999): 184–194.

Thompson, Carlyle V. "Circles and Circles of Sorrow: Decapitation in Toni Morrison's *Sula*," *CLA Journal* 47, no. 2 (December 2003): 137–175.

Tar Baby (1981)

Tar Baby, Morrison's fourth novel, changes location from the geographical boundaries of the United States to the larger context of the Caribbean and Europe. In part, the novel is the story of two families, the Streets and the Childs, who are connected as employer and employee, but whose lives are interconnected as though they are family.

The novel brings together many oppositions, North and South, white and black, high and low culture, folk and institutionalized narrative in order to consider the value and merits of each. The focus of this coming together of different perspectives occurs with the courtship and breakup of the novel's central characters, Jadine Childs and Son Green. Their relationship prompts the reconsideration of the hierarchies that order and control the communities the characters inhabit.

The novel uses the mythic image of the TAR BABY to evoke the flaws of racial stereotyping and to suggest the stickiness of authenticity. The image of the Tar Baby suggests a false front, a substitute for reality that all of the characters either confront or embrace.

SYNOPSIS

1

The novel begins with one of the central characters, Son Green, as he emerges out of the sea from the ship where he has lived as a stowaway. His shoes, knotted to his belt, are his only possession. Son makes his way through the dark ocean water toward the shore and chooses a boat anchored there to find shelter for the night.

Son climbs on board unnoticed. There are two women aboard the ship, Jadine Childs and Margaret Street. He avoids discovery and finds himself traveling with them to the nearby island that Margaret Street calls home, the Isle des Chevaliers. The island is the retirement home of the Streets, Margaret and Valerian, who build a wonderful house, L'Arbe de la Croix, on the island and settle there after leaving their home in Philadelphia. Valerian Street builds a greenhouse near the main house so that he can have a controlled environment in which to raise the flowers he loves. He pipes classical music into the greenhouse while he is in there working on the imported flowers he grows.

The Streets bring to the island their two lifelong servants, Ondine and Sydney Childs, who attend to their needs and provide their meals. Valerian and Sydney carry on an extended conversation about a number of inanities, but a number of important facts weave themselves into the banter between the two men. Sydney mentions to Valerian that Margaret has said that the couple's son, Michael, is coming to the island for Christmas. Valerian tells Sydney that he does not believe that Michael will actually show up.

Margaret joins the conversation and it is apparent from the couple's interactions that their relationship is fraught with underlying tension that manifests itself in targeted pettiness. Jadine, the other woman on the boat, is an orphan who is adopted by her aunt and uncle, Ondine and Sydney. Jadine is a model living in Paris and is visiting her aunt and uncle for a few months on the island. She and Margaret, a former beauty queen, are more like friends than anything else. Jadine also functions as company for Margaret.

Sydney retreats to the kitchen, his wife's domain. The conversation between the two is mainly about Margaret and Valerian. Ondine takes it personally that Margaret does not eat the food that she prepared for her. They also speak about Michael, and Ondine expresses her certainty that he will not come for Christmas. Sydney accuses her of spoiling him. Ondine seems to hate Margaret, blames her for Michael's absence and calls her by the nickname, the Principal Beauty of Maine. The mean-spirited nickname comes from a newspaper describing her during her beauty pageant days. The two brighten up when Jadine comes into the kitchen and Ondine busies herself trying to find something for the girl to eat. As the conversation progresses, Ondine says to Jadine that she hopes that the girl never leaves them. Jadine does not reply.

While the three are in the kitchen, the Streets' helper, Yardman, appears at the door. Often he brings with him a woman who also helps with work at the Streets, whose name, Ondine and Sydney think, is Mary.

2

The chapter reveals the nighttime habits of the residents of L'Arbe de la Croix. Ondine and Sydney sleep well. Their bodies silently comfort and reassure each other. Valerian finds sleep elusive as he frequently sleeps during the day. He sleeps in a separate room from his wife, who hopes for peaceful sleep and good dreams. Sleep is not available to Jadine, who is awakened by a bad dream. The dream reminds her of an event that happened before she left Paris two months previously. She is in a grocery store purchasing great food for a party she throws for herself in celebration of being selected for the cover of *Elle* magazine. While she shops, she spots a statuesque black woman wearing a yellow dress. The woman, according to the stan-

dards that make Jadine beautiful, is too much—too dark, too heavy, too busty—and yet the woman has a majesty and mystique Jadine feels that she does not. People in the store are mesmerized by the woman, who chooses just three eggs from the case. Although the cashier tries to tell the woman that she cannot buy just three eggs, the woman ignores her, puts her money on the counter and leaves. The woman, before disappearing from sight, looks back at Jadine and then spits on the sidewalk.

What Jadine wants and does not get from the woman is respect. Then, as she looks sleeplessly out of her window, Jadine remembers the legend of the island. The legend states that there, on the other side of the island, one hundred horsemen ride. Jadine's sleeplessness comes in part from her attempt to make a decision about her relationship. She is not certain that the man she loves, Ryk, who is white, loves her or if he is in love with the idea of a black woman.

As Jadine finally falls asleep, Valerian wakes. Unlike Jadine's focus on the future, his gaze is fixed on the past. Valerian worked as the head of a family candy company. Valerian's father dies when Valerian is seven and his uncles take over the boy's future. They even name a candy after the boy. The candy sells only to a small market of African-American customers in Mississippi.

Valerian accepts the reins of the company, promising himself that he will retire at 65 and not become ineffectual. He enters an unhappy marriage and gets divorced. He then meets Margaret, who is on a float in her role as the winner of the Miss Maine beauty pageant. Valerian marries Margaret, and the two have a baby boy. He buys an island in preparation for the retirement he has always focused on throughout his career. He recognizes that Michael is not interested in the business. Valerian also accepts that he and Michael will never be close. Valerian misses the youth that he did not have after shouldering the adult responsibility for the family after his father's death.

As Margaret sleeps, the past also haunts her. The woman's life has been entirely defined by her beauty. Her looks isolate her from her family. Her red hair also distinguishes her and, although his fear is not justified, bothers her father. Her father worries that she might not be his child. Margaret grows up lonely and so her marriage, shortly after high school, is a hope for a new kind of connection. Valerian's life is too big for Margaret, and she has no tools to cope with the insecurities that the mansion, Valerian's wealth, and family generate. The one soft spot for Margaret in the early years of her marriage is her friendship with Ondine, a relationship Valerian soon terminates. The one outlet left to her is her son, Michael. Margaret tries to be a good mother to him but does not have the foundation to give him what he needs from a mother since she is too needy and insecure herself. Now that Michael is grown up, Margaret wants to go and live near him so that she can make up for her earlier failings.

3

Much of the action at the beginning of *Tar Baby* centers on the dinner table. At this particular meeting, Valerian seems hell bent on humiliating Margaret and pointing out her seeming inability to master the rules of the table. They also discuss the impending Christmas dinner, and Margaret assures Valerian that Michael is coming and that she has invited a poet, one of Michael's former teachers, as a surprise. Valerian believes that Margaret's plan is a terrible one, doomed to failure.

Jadine sits with the Valerians and watches uncomfortably as the couple pick at each other. The two continue fighting about Valerian's sister and other matters that disguise the larger issues the couple face. Jadine searches for a graceful exit and Sydney, when he enters, is disappointed that Ondine's carefully prepared soufflé has barely been touched.

Ultimately, the couple argue about Michael, and they blame each other for what they both feel is failed parenting. Valerian remembers coming home from work and finding Michael humming to himself while hiding under the sink. The song, Valerian remembers, was inconsolably sad. He also remembers that Margaret is inconsistent as a mother, sometimes interested and devoted and sometimes neglectful and abandoning. He experiences Michael's absence from their lives as a condemnation of their parenting.

Eventually Margaret and Jadine leave the table and, sometime later, they hear Margaret scream.

They all ask her what the problem is—Ondine impatiently—until Margaret reveals the source of her fear. The man Son, who without their knowing it, sailed with Margaret and Jadine to the island on the boat, has been hiding in Margaret's closet. When she sees him there, it triggers all of her fears, some real, some racialized and imaginary. In the midst of the conversation, Sydney comes downstairs with Son in front of him. Inexplicably, Valerian invites the man to have a drink.

4

The next morning finds Margaret longing for her original home for the first time. She is completely unhinged by the idea that her closet was violated by the presence of a man she sees as intolerable. She says that the only thing that keeps her from leaving the island that same day is the fact that Michael is coming for Christmas. She does not know what happened the night before—if her husband actually drank with the intruder or called the police. All she knows is that the man in her closet is a nightmare from her inventions of black men who lurk in the shadows with no other intention or purpose in life than to rape innocent white women.

Jadine reflects on the strange new man as she luxuriates in the black baby seal coat that was a present from Ryk. Ondine comes up to bring her some breakfast and asks whether she is going to marry him or not. Cryptically, Jadine tells her that the coat is only a present. Ondine tells Jadine that Valerian, rather than calling the police, allowed Son to spend the night. Jadine looks at the Christmas presents she bought for everyone and cannot seem to take off the coat. She recalls the dinner from the night before and thinks that Valerian is somehow comforted by her presence at the table. Sydney is beside himself and even drops something.

The next morning Ondine and Sydney talk seriously about their position and whether they should stay with the Streets, given what they perceive as Valerian's incredible lack of judgment. Sydney points out that Valerian lets the strange man sleep upstairs in the guest room when he and Ondine have always slept on the main floor. Ondine argues that Valerian is not as much of a racist as she feels most white men are. He tries to help ensure the couple's future by giving them stock instead of a present that would have less long-term value. Ondine advises Sydney to accept the situation so that he does not put them and their future in jeopardy. Ondine also believes that they will be safe as long as Jadine is there.

Although Son's presence in the house comes as a surprise to its inhabitants, the others who work at the house are aware that he has been hiding on the place. The man that the household calls Yardman is named Gideon, and he and Alma and Therese, the women who work with him at the house, have been wagering on how long the man would be able to stay on the place undiscovered. Therese believes that Son is a horseman of the legendary horsemen. She predicts that the situation will not turn out well for any of the blacks involved and that Son will end up dead.

Jadine still revels in her coat, and, as she does so, Son stands at her door giving her morning greetings. She notices his hair, which is locked, and sees it as wild. The two have a conversation. They talk about her modeling and Jadine focuses on her accomplishments that mark her profession and make her feel that she is successful. Jadine is patronizing and talks down to Son. She tells him about her position in the household. She says that she works for Valerian and tells him that the Streets put her through college. Son insults her by asking her if she has had to prostitute herself to get all of the things that she has been bragging about. She begins to hit him, and he threatens to throw her out of the window. Jadine tell him that if he rapes her, the men of the house will kill him. Son replies that he never thought of or intended to rape her and that she simply shares the fantasies of white women about black men wanting to rape them. Again she threatens to tell Valerian on him. Son reminds her not to forget to tell him that he smelled her. During their encounter, Son senses that she is attracted to him. Although she is angry with him, after he leaves, she acknowledges that there is something there that is disturbing and unsettling. When Jadine finally goes to talk with Valerian, she finds him laughing with Son in the greenhouse.

5

Jadine goes to tell Margaret what she has seen. During the exchange, Jadine calls Son a nigger, and Margaret agrees with her and repeats the term. Margaret wants to leave the island but is immobilized by her hope that Michael will actually show up for Christmas. Margaret and Jadine make plans and then retire to their rooms for the day. Their plans go awry. The next time that the women see Son he looks very different from the man they remember and invented.

Son uses Jadine's bathroom to shower and shave. During the shower, he thoroughly removes all of the excess that comes from being outside of the comforts of living and belonging inside. He thinks of his life outside, living as a shadow on the edges of other people's existences. While he is living on the outside, he dreams of a time when he lived in a place he called home, of learning to play the piano from Mrs. Tyler. Son does not follow the women home from the ship with the intention of stalking them or hiding out in the house. He merely seeks food and shelter, but while he waits to decide what he will do next, he finds himself obsessed with and, perhaps, beginning to love the beautiful black woman Jadine.

In the wake of Margaret's discovery of Son, Valerian retreats to the greenhouse. He reflects on his rationale for letting Son stay and realizes that his reasons are deeply embedded in his experience of Michael and his regrets about their relationship. In the back of his mind, he believes that if Michael had been present he would have been surprised at and pleased with his father. Valerian realizes that he has upset his servant Sydney. Even Valerian recognizes that Sydney and Ondine's ire at Valerian's acceptance of Son illustrates some real problems that the couple have in terms of their acceptance and internalization of race and class hierarchies and of their subordinate position within that order.

When Son visits Valerian in the greenhouse, Valerian agrees not to turn the man in to the authorities. He tells Son to get Sydney to give him some clothes. Son looks at one of Valerian's plants and plucks it with his fingers telling him that plants, like women, need to be shaken up every now and then. The men exchange jokes and are laughing with genuine rapport when Jadine comes to find Valerian in the greenhouse.

Son ventures into town with Gideon and Therese. Gideon, Therese, and Alma Estee gain some status in their community because of the visit of the American. Son is generous and listens patiently to their stories. Gideon has spent time in the United States and has stories of what he sees there. Therese finds each of his stories ammunition for her belief that the United States is a kind of macabre hell. Although things are not exactly as she imagines, Son cannot deny the beliefs that she holds. Gideon says that Therese, who is losing her sight, is one of the blind race on the island who lose their sight as they approach their 60s. They are said to be descendants of slaves who, upon seeing the island where they would be enslaved, went blind. Gideon also tells Son that Ondine does not know that Therese is the same woman who comes to the house each week. They believe that she is a different woman each time and have not taken the time or interest to discover differently. Gideon tells Son that he is welcome to stay with them.

When he returns to L'Arbe de la Croix, Son apologizes to Jadine for his earlier insult. Jadine asks him to apologize to Ondine and Sydney so that they can feel a bit better about what has happened. Son makes Jadine nervous because she is attracted to him and finds him, especially since he cleaned up, quite beautiful.

Son apologizes to Ondine and, during the conversation, says that he came back to the house to make things right with them before he leaves for good. Ondine asks about his family, and Son tells her that his mother is dead and that all of his family—his father and his sister—live in Florida and that he has been at sea for eight years and has not seen them in that time. When Sydney comes in, he is not as sympathetic and easily won over as Ondine seems to be. He does not trust Son and says he never will. Son says to the couple that he does not feel comfortable on the second floor. In a move of solidarity, Son asks them if he can eat with them in the kitchen.

Despite the interruption of Son's arrival, the house seems to recoup with everyone's effort to prepare for Christmas. Even Margaret is cajoled by the

thought that Michael might enjoy and be impressed by Son's company. She learns that Michael's poet professor has not picked up his ticket and, therefore, is probably not coming.

Son has deep ambivalences about the United States but realizes that the place is his home and that it is time that he returns. He remains on the island because he feels he cannot leave Jadine. He thinks that she has no feelings for him and tries to court her. He asks Jadine if she would like to have lunch with him and she agrees. Son tells Jadine that all he wants from his life is his original dime, the first money that he ever earned for cleaning a tub of sheep head. Son spends the money on five cigarettes and a Dr. Pepper. Son seeks the satisfaction and direct correlation between effort and reward inherent in the exchange. Son tells Jadine about his hometown, the ALL-BLACK TOWN of Eloe. He asks Jadine where she is from, and she replies that she has no home. She says she is a metropolitan woman, from the world's cities. Jadine asks him what his name is, and he tells her that people call him Son. She wants to know what he was named, and he tells her that the name he was given at birth was William Green. He also tells her that he has been running all of these eight years because he killed his wife Cheyenne when he found her in their house making love to another man. Then he tells her that he cannot hurt her because he loves her. Jadine rejects Son's statement. Despite her protestations, Jadine does indeed have feelings for Son, feelings she does not know how to handle. As they drive back to the house, they run out of gas. Jadine sends Son to the dock to get gas from the boat. Tired of waiting in the sun, Jadine seeks shelter under some trees and gets stuck in some mud. She has to hold onto a tree to keep from sinking in the muck and eventually gains solid ground. Her white skirt is stained black at the bottom. When she gets back to the house, she has a hard time removing the stuff from her legs.

Valerian apologizes to Margaret for not respecting her feelings. The two eagerly anticipate Michael's arrival. The Streets share the same bed for the first time in years.

Sydney and Ondine still are upset about Son's presence. They particularly worry about the man and Jadine after their lunch date. Ondine is also angered about Margaret wanting to come into her kitchen to cook Christmas dinner.

The Christmas dinner turns out to be a complete disaster. None of the invited guests, including Michael, arrive. While the entire household sits at the table, Valerian announces that he has fired Gideon and Therese (he knows her as Mary). Ondine and Son are angered when Valerian informs them that he has told the authorities about the theft from the house of the apples he imported from the States for Christmas. At that point, the evening disintegrates. Each of the couples divides into camps. Son accuses Valerian of not defending his wife. Valerian tells him to leave the house, and Son refuses. Ondine says that none of it would have happened if Margaret had not been in the kitchen and that she does not belong in the kitchen. She also says that Margaret is not a mother. Valerian fires Sydney and Ondine, but no one listens to him.

Margaret throws water in Ondine's face, and Ondine runs around the table and slaps Margaret. Ondine then reveals that Margaret abused Michael when he was a little boy by sticking pins in him and burning him. Sydney, Ondine, Jadine, and Son leave Margaret and Valerian at the table alone.

Son and Jadine discuss the night's events, and Jadine tells him that she is tired. She wants to go to sleep but she does not want anything sexual to happen between them. She also notices Son's hands for the first time and sees him and them as, perhaps, capable of holding her, of taking care of her. She asks him to reassure her that nothing will happen between them that night. Cryptically, Son tells her that stars in the sky do not twinkle, they throb. The throbbing becomes a euphemism for the sexual connection between Jadine and Son.

7

Son leaves the island two days after Christmas and goes to New York to wait for Jadine. Son finds the city disorienting and devoid of older people. In the two days following Christmas, Jadine and Son resolve to be together. When she arrives in the city, she has the opposite reaction from Son. She feels at home in the city and invigorated by its confines.

In New York, the two grow close and share everything with each other. It becomes clear,

although neither of them admits it, that there are serious differences between the two. Son has a hard time finding work in the city and does not like Jadine supporting him. On the other hand, Son makes Jadine feel as if she belongs and as if her parents are not dead. The two grow inseparable and their love seems like what each has been seeking. Although Jadine does not want to go, Son determines to take her to Eloe, the all-black town he is from. The two finally make arrangements to visit his hometown.

8

Ondine's Christmas revelation about Michael unmasks the couples at L'Arbe de la Croix. Margaret tries to explain to Valerian what happened. Eventually, she leaves Valerian sitting alone at the table. Sydney comes to him and tries to get him to go to bed, but he refuses. Then Sydney asks him if he plans to follow through on his threat to fire him and Ondine and Valerian says that he does not know. The revelation about Michael breaks Valerian and sends him into a deep depression.

Margaret continues to try to explain her abuse. She tells Valerian that she loves Michael. She talks of her feeling of inadequacy at the overwhelming demands of motherhood, that there was not enough self for her to be available to meet her infant son's needs. After some time, Margaret tells Valerian that she has spoken with Michael. Valerian is astonished, and Margaret tells him that she is sure that Michael has no permanent damage as a result of her abuse. Margaret asks him to hit her, and, although he says he will, he never does.

Margaret also speaks with Ondine. She says that she knows that Ondine loves Michael. She also tells her that it would have been better if she had told her secret. The two women apologize to each other. For the first time, Margaret learns that she and Ondine are the same age. She offers Ondine the possibility of becoming friends again as they grow old.

Valerian returns to his greenhouse. He accepts that he is partially responsible for what happened to Michael because he did not want to find out what was wrong with his son and did not take the time to get to know him. It had been easier for him to ignore the unease and unhappiness that was apparent in his son.

9

Jadine and Son travel to Eloe, and Jadine determines to document the trip with her camera. Son's reunion with his family and friends is joyous. Because of the town's strict sense of decorum, Son and Jadine cannot stay together at night as an unmarried couple. Son asks her to spend the night at his Aunt Rosa's house. Son hates the way that Jadine photographs rather than talks to his people. At one point, he snatches the camera out of her hand.

During one of the nights at Rosa's, Son comes to her, and the two spend the night together. Jadine awakes and finds the room filled with women from her life, including Therese, Ondine, Jadine's mother, and the woman in yellow from the grocery store in Paris. The women each reveal one of their breasts and haunt her until morning. Jadine is undone by what she believes she has seen and leaves Eloe without Son.

Although Son promises he will come the next day, he stays in Eloe more than a week without calling Jadine to tell her that he is going to stay longer. When he returns, things begin to unravel for the couple. They begin to fight emotionally and physically about what they need to do to have a future together. At one point, Son even dangles Jadine out of a window as he tells her that whatever she learned in school is of no value because it taught her nothing about herself or her people. She wants him to go to school and get a professional job. Eventually their arguments are too painful, too close to the marrow of each other's identity and Jadine leaves after giving Son his original dime. Son realizes that he still wants her in his life and goes to find her and to try to repair their relationship.

10

Jadine returns to the Streets' island retreat. When she gets there, she encounters Margaret cleaning out Valerian's closet. The couple seem to have arrived at a kind of peace in spite of the ugly truth at the heart of the marriage. Margaret is in control of the relationship now and, with Sydney's help, cares for Valerian as if he was a child.

Ondine and Jadine have a conversation about responsibility and loyalty. Ondine tells Jadine that respecting and caring for those who have taken care of her is essential, not for those people but for herself and her own character. Ondine equates this sense of responsibility with womanhood.

Sydney also recognizes that there is a change in Valerian. As he feeds Valerian dinner, Sydney recognizes that he, not Valerian, is in control. He will always take care of the man, but he will not let Valerian decide what happens. He will make the decisions while letting Valerian maintain the illusion of mastery.

Alma Estee is working at the airport and sees Jadine as she is leaving. The girl asks after Son. She tells Jadine that Therese believes Jadine has killed him. Jadine says good-bye to the girl, still calling her by the wrong name.

As Jadine takes off for Paris, the chapter ends with the story of the life of the queen ant. The queen mates once in life with a male ant she has created for that purpose. Everything else is work, no time for memory or dreams.

11

Son comes back to the island looking for Jadine. He returns to Gideon and Therese's. Therese is delighted to see him. Gideon tells him that Jadine has flown away and then advises him to leave her alone. Son decides to travel to L'Arbe de la Croix to ask for Jadine's address in Paris and then to follow her there. Therese agrees to row him out to the island. When they get there, he discovers that she has brought him to the other side of the island, the purported home of the blind horsemen. As he gets out of the boat, Therese advises him to go to the horsemen, telling him that they await his arrival. Son runs off. The last lines of the book repeat the lines from the TAR BABY story when B'rer Rabbit is finally free and runs toward his home.

CRITICAL COMMENTARY

Houses are central metaphors throughout Morrison's novels. The questions that emerge from the consideration of house and home as symbols are at the core of the novel *Tar Baby*. Interestingly, *Tar Baby* is the only one of Morrison's novels whose primary setting is outside of the United States. By placing the novel outside the geographic boundaries of the United States, yet having the central characters be American, Morrison extends issues of house and home beyond personal and community considerations and places them on a national and international plane.

The central characters of *Tar Baby* may be read as representing the race, class, and gender conflicts of the United States in particular, and more generally may represent the way that those conflicts appear in all human interactions. Symbolically, the house/home that Valerian erects on the Isle des Chevaliers is a kind of plantation and is maintained by racial hierarchies. *Tar Baby* exposes the limitations of the structures of race, class, and gender, the contemporary plantation, for both the architects and the residents, the masters and the slaves.

The house in *Tar Baby,* L'Arbe de la Croix (the tree of the cross), built by its master, Valerian Street, represents the history and legacy of European colonialists, the men who conquered and attempted to control the new world, represented in the novel by the island. From the beginning of the novel, the physical environment of the island is a vibrant character. That vitality is usurped and contained by the development instigated by Valerian and his desire to possess and control the land. Valerian purchases Isle des Chevaliers in order to own a space where, unlike his birthplace, he has complete dominion. Throughout his life, Valerian has been subjected to the will of his father and, after his father's death, his uncles and had no choice about his destiny. Although he accepts the decisions made for him by agreeing to become the proprietor of the family candy company, he resolves at age 39 to retire to his own pursuits by age 65. Isle des Chevaliers comes to represent for Valerian both freedom and power. The island provides an escape from the tyranny of expectation that dictates his life in Philadelphia.

Even though Sydney Childs is perpetually identifying himself as a Philadelphia Negro, after W. E. B. DuBois's book about middle-class blacks in the city, Valerian's identity as a native of Philadelphia provides even more illumination about the questions of freedom and oppression that

are the novel's central concerns. The history of the city of Philadelphia highlights the themes of the novel since the city provided the location for the founding fathers's creation of American racial hierarchies through their ratification of a Constitution that compromised the principles of individual freedom and equality with the existence and continuation of slavery. The creators and signers of the Constitution affirmed that slavery and inequality were compatible with the ideals of democracy. Morrison's character, Valerian Street, seems a clear descendant from and inheritor of that contradictory legacy.

Valerian's name emphasizes duality. According to the character's own self-description, he is named after the Roman emperor, Valerian. The emperor Valerian was largely unsuccessful and is perhaps best-known for his defeat and death at the hands of the Persians, who were considered by the Romans to be barbarians. So the name Valerian has the connotation both of authority and of humiliating conquest. The other meaning of the word "valerian" describes a root that was thought historically to induce strength and vigor, yet has properties that sedate and induce sleep. The medicinal qualities of valerian include relief for tension, anxiety, insomnia, emotional stress, intestinal colic, and rheumatoid disorders. These maladies seem to describe Valerian's ailments. Readers first encounter the character Valerian in *Tar Baby* as he complains about his health while eating his breakfast. Sydney, Valerian's black male servant, believes that Valerian has an ulcer, a possibility that Valerian denies vehemently. Readers also learn that Valerian is prone to putting medicine (cognac) in his morning coffee, that he has difficulty sleeping, and that he uses alcohol as a nightly sedative.

In the same way that the sun sets in the evening, Valerian Street is a man fading into old age. Morrison describes Valerian's eyes as nearing their twilight. Valerian's physical discomforts offer evidence of his overall disease and imbalance. The character Valerian is a study in contradiction. He is perpetually conflicted and, as such, his decision-making capacity, like that of his historical namesake, is ambiguous at best. For example, Valerian's decision to leave his hometown of Philadelphia for the Caribbean and Isle des Chevaliers might be understood either as nostalgia for the past, for a Philadelphia home that no longer exists, or as an overwhelming need to control his surroundings. Although Valerian states that he wishes to be in control and to be isolated in his created paradise, he sells parts of his private island and therefore dilutes his dominion.

Despite his desires, Valerian also is unable to direct even the most intimate of his interactions, his marriage to his wife, the former beauty queen, Margaret Lenore Lordi Street. Valerian's relationship with his wife is troubled and uncomfortable for them both. They sleep in separate beds. Their interactions are antagonistic and she seems to suffer from some sort of nervous condition that causes her to be forgetful. Together the Streets represent the instability and illusion of the authority of white privilege.

Despite the Streets' paradisiacal landscape, faithful servants, and wealth, neither of them is particularly happy and neither has any real control over the events that unfold in their home. Valerian, even as the supposed master of his house, is anxious and stressed. His attempt to establish dominance is an illusion and, ultimately, a failure. For example, Michael, Valerian and Margaret's son, bears the physical and psychological pain of Valerian's domination of people. Valerian is unaware of his wife's secret abuse of their son and thinks the boy weak, misunderstanding his son's pain and vulnerability for character flaw. Margaret's deference to her husband's position and symbolic authority cuts her off from her humanity. Valerian marries Margaret and values her because of her physical appearance. Because that objectification is a common denominator in all of her relationships, Margaret has no access to a meaningful inner life.

In a misguided and destructive attempt to connect with another living being, she ensures that someone will react to her by harming her son. She finds pleasure in harming Michael because he is helpless and her relationship with him is the one arena in which she exercises complete control. Margaret and Valerian Street illustrate the destructive impact of the intersection of power and identity. Without the labels conferred to them by

wealth and beauty, neither of them has any meaningful selfhood and, in fact, controls nothing of substance, including, as the novel reveals, life on Isle des Chevaliers.

The island becomes Valerian's imagined colony where he dreams that he will be able to control everything and everyone in a way he has been unable to accomplish in his hometown of Philadelphia. When the land is cleared to build Valerian's island paradise, there are negative repercussions. The detrimental effects of attempted conquest become apparent when the narrator reveals that, as a result of the development, a fetid swamp forms on what was once a pristine landscape. Valerian's imposition upon the natural landscape of the island parallels the slow destruction of the people who inhabit L'Arbe de la Croix.

Although the natural environment of the island changes in negative ways because of Valerian's intervention, this development is viewed by him and by many others as a civilizing process. Valerian embraces and embodies the idea that civilization begins after a geographical space and the people who inhabit that space are controlled and ordered according to the laws of the conquerors. Nearly all that exists naturally in the colonized space is dismantled, redirected, and harnessed. The necessity of civilization, as defined by the self-perceived virtues of those in power, becomes the primary tool used to justify exploitation and oppression.

Black Haitian laborers are employed to enact Valerian's plans. Although the clearing of Isle des Chevaliers could not have happened without them, they remain the invisible engine of Valerian's enterprise. Valerian's interactions with all of the black people in his life are predicated on his understanding of race as a hierarchal system that places him squarely on top and in control. Valerian's assumptions dictate his relationship with and sense of superiority to all of the black people in his life. Valerian's assumptions and actions mirror the colonial enterprise of nation building that has resulted in the domination of people who are racially marked as colored all over the world.

Evidence of his assumed power lies in interactions between Valerian and the blacks in his life. At L'Arbe de la Croix all of the work of maintaining the mansion is done by blacks. Yet, even within this division between white and black, there are additional levels of authority and power. Both Sydney and Ondine Childs, the black American servants, perceive themselves as superior to the black natives of the island. None of the Americans, including Ondine and Sydney, even know the names of the native blacks who work at the house. The native woman servants, Therese and Alma Estee, are known to all in the Street household by the generic name, Mary. Revealingly, Gideon, the Streets' handyman, is known to the inhabitants of L'Arbe de la Croix by a name that is associated with the work he provides for them, Yardman.

As their namelessness implies, these workers are denied individuality and, therefore, humanity. They are disposable as becomes evident when all three, Therese, Gideon, and Alma Estee, are dismissed from their duties after Valerian catches Gideon stealing apples. Their firing is ironic when one considers Valerian's appropriation of the island, its resources, and inhabitants for his pleasure. Valerian's response to Gideon and Alma Estee's theft affirms his sense of superiority and demonstrates his complete and unquestioned belief in his own authority and vision.

The apples that are the object of desire and the source of conflict suggest the apple that is the centerpiece of the biblical story of the garden of Eden. In the narrative in Genesis, Adam and Eve are cast out of Eden for defying God's power. As the self-appointed god on Isle des Chevaliers, Valerian casts Gideon, Therese, and Alma Estee out of the garden for defying his authority. Further irony exists in the fact that Gideon is stealing the apples for his celebration of Christmas and that Valerian, in spite of the holiday, has no compassion for or understanding of Gideon's motivations.

The Christmas holidays sit as background for the crucial scenes in the novel that unravel the power structures governing L'Arbe de la Croix and supplying Valerian with his authority. The sudden appearance of the character Son, who embodies all that is outside, dark, and alien in the Streets' imagination, dismantles all of the illusions of order and control. Son's emergence from the very heart of the house, Margaret's bedroom closet, challenges all of

the residents of L'Arbe de la Croix to reconsider their positions and to uncover the real dynamics that lie beneath the surface. From his initial interactions with the master of the mansion, Son's lack of deference and his disgust with Valerian's hypocrisy undermine Valerian's self-construction as the embodiment of civilization.

Valerian is dethroned, not by the natives that he seeks to control, or nature, but by his own lethal actions. Valerian's house/home becomes an extravagant self-constructed prison to which he is confined with his black servants who have long known that Valerian's power is no power at all, and with a liberated Margaret whose humanity emerges simultaneously with her insatiable need to detail for Valerian her motivations for abusing their son. Valerian never understands his culpability in his fall from power. Valerian's fate mirrors that of his namesake, the Roman emperor Valerian, who was tortured to death by people he felt were barbarians and then was stuffed in death and mounted in a mockery of his lost domination. For *Tar Baby*'s Valerian, the plantation is no longer home. The arrival of Son unmasks the illusion of L'Arbe de la Croix to reveal the end result of the colonizing experiment, the creation of a paradisiacal prison from which there is no exit.

While the master's house becomes a prison for the architect, the novel seems to suggest that its black, colonized residents are doomed to a perpetual state of homelessness. In the novel, each of the characters, Sydney, Ondine, Jadine, and Son and their relationship to Valerian provide a lens through which to examine the various and varying effects and impacts of exploitation and domination.

Adopted by Sydney and Ondine as a child and educated by Valerian, Jadine epitomizes the difficulty of finding both house and home. Jadine's education teaches her to dismiss aspects of black culture that would help her to negotiate the complexities of her life as an upwardly mobile black woman. Jadine is easily disarmed when she encounters what she perceives as "authentic" blackness, especially authentically black women. Modeling herself after Valerian, Jadine attempts to manipulate her environment and its inhabitants to suit her purposes. While she is attracted to Son, she rejects his sense of home as too limited, too provincial. Although Son's sense of home is romantic and not particularly progressive, it is home for him. Despite the unattractiveness and smallness of the physical structures that constitute Eloe, Son's home, he is able to find pleasure and love inside those constructions. The knowledge and proclamation that he is from Eloe is fundamental to Son's sense of self. Eloe is home, a community that knows and values him. Jadine has no such community and therefore feels homeless.

Sensing Jadine's homelessness, Son takes her to Eloe. Jadine's response to Eloe demonstrates her own anxiety about blackness, as well as her internalization of racial hierarchies. Jadine believes that she is fundamentally a more valuable person than the residents of Eloe. Though she photographs Eloe and its residents, Jadine is unable to see the value of the town or of its people. They always remain for her objects at the end of her lens. Although she is a black woman manipulating the camera, her gaze is the same as Valerian's would have been. She becomes like the photographers who have photographed her while she was modeling, who reduced her to nothing more than an image to be sold and bought.

Jadine misses the opportunity to understand the "ancient properties" of Eloe because she flees the town and its people. She flees Eloe when, at night, she thinks she sees black women bare their breasts to her. Jadine returns to New York, yet she does not possess a house in New York. While she is in the city, she searches for a domicile that she can inhabit and wanders through a series of subleases. Throughout the novel, she occupies other people's spaces only temporarily—she is perpetually the guest.

From his initial emergence from the depths of the night-darkened Caribbean seas, Son represents the idea of blackness that challenges the sensibilities of both the permanent and the temporary inhabitants of Valerian's house. Jadine leaves Valerian's house with Son hoping to change him into what she wants. Son resists Jadine's efforts violently and, eventually, Jadine chooses to flee from him and from New York because Son becomes abusive to her.

Son perceives Jadine's efforts to educate and change him, to colonize his blackness, as abusive as well. Valerian is most successful in colonizing Jadine because she believes that the education he provides makes her superior to others, especially to other blacks. She fails to realize what she loses in rejecting black people like Son, Ondine, and Sydney—an understanding of herself and a possible end to her perpetual hunger for belonging.

Son's dismissal of anything that is white is equally problematic. Son allows himself to become the shadow, the ever-present blackness that haunts Valerian's house, hiding in its closets, seeping into the fabric of sheets, curtains, and couches. After Valerian invites Son into the house without reservation, Jadine, Ondine, and Sydney are appalled and wonder if Valerian sees all blacks as the same. They want to be differentiated from Son. They have learned to believe in the hierarchies that place them in a superior position on the scale. Their anxiety emerges from a false sense of superiority they possess. Sydney and Ondine's understanding of themselves as Philadelphia Negroes and their characterization of Son as a primitive black illuminates the extent to which internalized racism destroys self-perception.

Valerian does not treat Son disrespectfully or distrustfully, rather, it is Jadine, Ondine, and Sydney who refer to him as a nigger and attempt to distance themselves from Son. Such distancing efforts serve no purpose in Valerian's house/home precisely because *it is* his.

Sydney, Ondine, and Jadine suffer from a false sense of power. While Sydney serves the master faithfully, he is not the master, and Ondine may own the kitchen, but it is not in her house. While Jadine is educated in and with the master's culture and values, she does not possess the anchor of home and thus does not own herself. Although Sydney and Ondine may attempt to make a home in Valerian's house, it is never a stable home because they will always be beholden to Valerian's power. Both Jadine and Son are unable to find a home together and end up apart and headed in opposite directions—Jadine on a flight to Europe and Son perhaps to ride with the blind horsemen for eternity.

Son and Jadine's failed effort to construct a home together provides little hope for either solution the two propose for escaping the impacts and legacy of the colonial project—for creating a house without hierarchy.

SOME IMPORTANT THEMES AND SYMBOLS IN *TAR BABY*

The Stickiness of Human Interactions

JOEL CHANDLER HARRIS's recordings and publications of African-American folktales included, perhaps most famously, "The Wonderful Tar Baby Story." The story tells about a crafty fox who seeks to ensnare a rabbit by creating a TAR BABY, a human-like figure covered with tar. When the rabbit greets the figure and she, of course, does not respond, he attacks her and gets stuck and provides a feast for the fox. In some versions, the rabbit has the last laugh when he tells the fox that a fate worse than being eaten by him would be to be thrown in the briar patch. The fox mean-spiritedly tosses the rabbit into the briar patch where the rabbit is able to extricate himself from the tar baby and run away to safety. The phrase Tar Baby also has a history as a derogatory slang term for African Americans. The tale and the stereotype provide a thematic frame for Morrison's novel *Tar Baby*.

There is no single answer to the question of which character functions as the tar baby in the novel, but the story depicts human interactions throughout by using sticky symbols as a common element. As suggested by the stereotype of the tar baby, race is, perhaps, the most tenaciously sticky of all of the factors that intervene in human interactions. Each of the characters is stuck, in one way or another to his or her own raced tar baby.

The candy business that is the source of Valerian Street's wealth is itself a gooey enterprise. Its scents waft over the neighborhood where Valerian's mother created the family business, saturating the memories of the residents with its sweetness, but because of its successful appeal, the candy and its residues separate Valerian and his family from their community of origin, depriving Valerian of a sense of home located in something other than the alienating trappings of wealth and privilege. Although Valerian, without question, roots his identity in his perception of himself as a white man, his unquestioned authority comes from his wealth and status, which, the novel reveals, derives in part from African Americans who purchase the products upon which the family business depends. When Valerian is born, his uncles honor the birth of the family's only male offspring by creating and naming a candy after the boy. The candy suffers from poor sales and remains popular only among African Americans in the South. As the novel unfolds, this candy becomes a connective thread between Valerian and Son, when Son reveals that, as a child, he used to eat the candy named for Valerian.

After his disruptive arrival at the house, Son makes the candy/stickiness association not only with Valerian, but also with Margaret. When he sees her sunning, Son notes that she looks like a marshmallow, melting and white in the heat. Margaret's behavior mirrors Son's vision of her. Margaret sits in the sun, yet she carefully avoids getting any color. She is the representation of the idealized white female beauty. Before the confrontation with Ondine over the Christmas dinner table, Margaret lacks substance and is incapable of providing sustenance. Ondine's exposure of Margaret's secret abuse of Michael reveals the lack of foundation behind the illusion Margaret has tried to create. Like the vision Valerian first has of her as the beautiful polar bear queen on the float, Margaret, throughout the majority of her marriage to Valerian, has worked to cultivate an appealing, insubstantial illusion.

Jadine's adherence to illusions that support her version of reality is also symbolized by a sticky symbol. As a result of Valerian's alterations to the landscape when he purchases the island, Isle des Chevaliers's pristine terrain transforms into a swamp. It is this sticky, smelly swamp that Jadine falls into after her first afternoon encounter with Son. Her misreading of the land causes her to fall into the swamp. Jadine sees a circle of trees that she wants to sketch and as she moves toward them, she falls into the muck. Jadine sinks in the insubstantial land because she does not see it for what it is. She stubbornly clings to what she imagines and envisions rather than discerning reality and, therefore, is unable to navigate what she does not control.

Significantly, when Jadine falls into the swamp, she loses the sketch book she is carrying that contains her portrait of Son. This loss foreshadows the ultimate failure of the couple's relationship as a result, in part, of Jadine's desire to construct Son through her vision rather than finding the ability to accept him as he is on his own terms.

Son, too, is symbolically immersed in various dark substances throughout the novel, but, unlike the other characters, he seems unencumbered by the stickiness that seems to trap the others. Son first appears in the novel as he dives into the sea at night from a ship. He uses the night to hide himself from the Streets as he lurks around their house, almost like a shadow. Before he meets her, Son watches Jadine in the darkness as she sleeps. As his relationship with Jadine develops, Son increasingly emerges from the night. Eventually, at the end of the novel, Son escapes the restrictions of the day, returns to the sea, and recedes into the darkness. The dark tar that traps the other characters seems, in some ways, a home, a familiar and fluid medium for Son.

The Search for Authenticity

One of the central themes of *Tar Baby* is the question of authenticity. When *Tar Baby* was published in 1981, many African-American writers and intellectuals were questioning the meanings of blackness as a racial identity in the post–Civil Rights era. During the CIVIL RIGHTS MOVEMENT, many activists attempted to define blackness in specific terms. These attempts were necessarily unsuccessful as no group of people can be adequately summarized by a list of characteristics. The effort to define people in these simplistic terms is sometimes referred to as essentialism. Essentialism is problematic because it can lead to a reduction of the complexities of human identity to simple qualities.

As some African Americans became upwardly mobile and became integrated into the dominant culture, some African-American intellectuals began to express concern about the potential loss of culture such changes might bring. The novel *Tar Baby* is in part Morrison's fictional examination of the questions raised by the changes brought about in African-American communities by the successes of the Civil Rights movement.

The novel begins with an epigraph that pays homage to the "ancient properties" of Morrison's female relatives and ancestors. By beginning the novel with this real-life reference point, Morrison roots the arguments of the novel in questions of authenticity in the actual lives of black people, specifically black women, that she knows. Although vaguely defined in several places in the novel, Morrison does not fall into the essentialist trap of defining her descriptive term, ancient properties, precisely. The character, Ondine, provides some illumination of the ancient properties of Morrison's authentic black woman when she says, "all you need is to feel a certain way, a certain careful way about people older than you are. . ." (281). Ondine tries to show Jadine that understanding and appreciating one's heritage and also one's responsibility to that heritage is paramount in her definition of what it means to be a black woman.

Other sections of the novel expand upon Ondine's foundation. When Jadine falls into the swamp, the narrator describes women hanging from the trees above Jadine's head. These women are confident about who they are and know their value. Their value is not measured in terms that are quantifiable. These women have value because they understand that their existence and that of the women they come from has been and remains critical to human survival. As such, they possess an intrinsic self-worth that is entirely unaffected by evaluation by anyone else.

Jadine, the quintessential motherless child, is the character who seems to have lost, or perhaps never acquired, an identity grounded in a dynamic and vital context. Somehow she lacks the genuine feeling of care and empathy that she should have developed for her surrogate parents Ondine and Sydney. Rather, her motivations originate, for the most part, in her deep fears and insecurities. Jadine's delight at Ryk's gift of the fur coat while she is residing on a Caribbean island is a perfect example of her desire to disguise her real self in the trappings of wealth and status. The coat represents the shield of material success Jadine feels will gird her from the difficulties of life. The choice that Jadine makes to situate her value in tangible terms places her in contrast with many other black women in the text and this difference generates further insecurity and removes her from associations that might have helped her to develop the community and sense of belonging for which she yearns.

Although Therese is barely acknowledged by Jadine, who refers to the woman as Mary, Therese is more aware of her value and has a more accurate understanding of the world than Jadine. Therese is essentially blind, yet sees through her intuitive/spiritual self. Beyond the age of potential pregnancy, Therese continues to lactate, which may suggest a kind of ever-lasting maternity. Therese's role as eternal maternal is particularly important to Son whose loss of his mother leaves him without access to the ancient properties of black motherhood. Therese also could have been instructive to Jadine as well had not Jadine held the woman beneath her notice.

Another character Jadine cannot seem to forget is the woman in yellow. The woman in yellow appears in a grocery store in Paris as Jadine shops for ingredients for a celebratory dinner for herself. The woman possesses a kind of regal elegance and beauty that is unappreciated by the traditional standards by which beauty is measured. In spite of this seeming deficit, the woman, incomprehensibly to Jadine, is completely mesmerizing and self-contained. Jadine feels slighted and judged by this woman and by the woman's assertive voluptuousness. The difference between the woman's self-presentation and Jadine's highlights the superficial and flimsy supports upon which Jadine has constructed her life and her self-esteem. Even though this encounter with the woman in yellow lasts but a few minutes, Jadine is haunted by the experience, for it has the power to expose the insubstantial architecture of her illusions.

In Eloe, Son's hometown, Jadine's deep-rooted anxieties reach a crisis. One night, while Son sleeps, Jadine imagines the woman in yellow and many of the other women in her life exposing their breasts at her in what she imagines is a kind of ceremony of derision. After this vision, Jadine feels she must leave Eloe and return to a setting that authenticates her, since her identity, seemingly, cannot withstand confrontation. Although she physically leaves Eloe, the images of the night women continue to plague Jadine. Their repeated appearances demonstrate her fear that she is somehow inauthentic and that she fails to measure up to the lives lived by these women.

Even though her search for an authentic self is most prominently articulated in the novel, other major characters also grapple with the questions that plague Jadine. When Valerian's father dies, the only help for the overwhelming grief that the boy feels is found through the wisdom of the washerwoman who knows that a mindless repetitive task can bring some meditative solace. This real labor, connected as it is to Valerian's first moments of self-awareness, is a state of grace, of authenticity that Valerian seeks for the rest of his life, including the construction of a replica of the washhouse from his childhood home on Isle des Chevaliers.

Valerian's wife Margaret comes to encounter her authentic self much later in life. After the Christmas dinner confrontation where Ondine reveals Margaret's secret abuse of Michael, Margaret begins to emerge from the façade she was born into and continues to assemble in her adulthood. Abandoning her role as the principal beauty, the revelations of Margaret's ugly truths free her to walk through her world as a person rather than as a symbol or object.

Son, too, has doubts at times about his identify and its authenticity. On their first outing together, Son reveals to Jadine some of the many aliases he has cultivated throughout the years. Although his identitylessness may seem to be freeing, it is this absence of self that sets Son on his plunge down into the sea and, ultimately, back to his home, Eloe. In Eloe, Son locates his center, but even that reunion is short-lived. When he looks at Jadine's photographs of Eloe that she leaves for him in their apartment, Eloe and its inhabitants appear small, insignificant, and unattractive to him. They no longer seem authentic. It may be that Son regains his compass and his authenticity at the end of the novel when he, presumably, runs of out of Therese's boat to join the blind horsemen.

Tar Baby engages questions about the definitions of authenticity and about how an individual may remain true to an authentic, personal and/or cultural self-definition. The novel can never completely sum up or definitively answer the philosophical questions it poses. As with most Morrison quandaries, the reader of *Tar Baby* is prompted to participate, to ponder his or her own possibilities instigated by the questions the narrative raises.

CHARACTERS

Aisha   Aisha is a friend of Jadine's who lives in New York. Jadine distinguishes between her friends, including Aisha, and the night women who haunts her while she is in Eloe.

Alicia   Alicia is one of the Buffalo great-aunts of Joseph Lenore, Margaret's father. Joseph is anxious for her and her sister, Celestina, to visit his family in order to prove that red hair runs in the family, yet to his dismay, when the aunts arrive, their formerly red hair has gone white with age.

Alma Estee   Alma Estee is a young girl who sometimes works with Gideon and Therese, and sometimes lives with them. She is very impressed with Son and asks him to fulfill her fondest wish by helping her get a wig from America. He does not do it.

Later, after Son and Jadine break up, Son sees Alma Estee again. She is wearing a terrible wig that he tries to remove from her head because he feels it makes her look ridiculous and that her natural hair is much more attractive. She sees Jadine before the glamorous model flees the island. Alma Estee later lies and tells Son that Jadine left the island with a man at her side. Alma probably is in love with Son. She is jealous of his relationship with Jadine.

Aunt Rosa   Aunt Rosa is Son's mother's sister. Aunt Rosa lets Jade stay in a small windowless room in her house. The room was formerly a porch that Rosa encloses herself. When she finds Jadine walking around naked in the middle of the night, she loans her a slip in which to sleep. Rosa's reaction makes Jadine feel obscene.

Beatrice   Beatrice is Soldier's beautiful daughter. Jadine takes pictures of her while she waits for Son. When Son sees Jadine's pictures later, he thinks that Beatrice no longer appears beautiful.

Betty   Betty is a friend of Jadine's who lives in New York. Betty experiments with bisexuality for six months, but returns to heterosexuality when she meets Son. Jadine distinguishes between her friends, including Betty, and the night women who haunt her while she is in Eloe.

B. J. Bridges   B. J. Bridges is a poet and Michael's former teacher. Margaret invites him to Christmas on the island as a gift for Michael. Bridges does not come because of a snowstorm. Valerian thinks that Bridges's poetry is insignificant.

blind race, the   The blind race are the descendants of slaves who went blind when they saw the island of Dominique. They were on a ship that sank and, according to legend, the blind slaves were carried by the current and tide to Isle des Chevaliers. The story maintains that the blind people hid from Frenchmen who came to return them to slavery and lived on the island, racing through the trees on the horses that had come ashore with them. They are said to see with the eyes of the mind instead of with their physical eyes. Gideon says that physical vision is not to be trusted.

Brants   The Brants are a family that live on the Isle des Chevaliers.

Broughtons   The Broughtons are a family that occasionally live on the Isle des Chevaliers.

Carl   Carl is the man who drives Son and Jadine from the bus depot to Eloe. Carl is amazed by the way Son and Jadine dress.

Celestina   Celestina is one of the Buffalo great-aunts of Joseph Lenore, Margaret's father. Joseph is anxious for her and her sister, Alicia, to visit in order to prove that red hair runs in the family. To his dismay, the aunts arrive with their formerly red hair turned white with age.

Cheyenne   Cheyenne is the girl Son marries after he returns to Eloe from the Vietnam War. He catches his wife sleeping with a teenager and drives his car into their house, killing her. When Son and Jadine visit Eloe, Soldier tells Jadine that Cheyenne had the best pussy in the state. Soldier's unkind words make Jadine jealous and threatened.

Cissy and Frank Cissy and Frank are Valerian's sister and brother-in-law. Margaret dislikes Cissy because she tells Margaret to take off the cross she wears on a necklace, saying that only whores wear crosses.

dark dogs with silver feet Dark dogs with silver feet are the imaginary dogs that Jadine envisions herself holding tightly reined. The dogs represent Jadine's natural desires, which she believes she has to keep always in check and subservient to her control and planning. If the dark dogs were unleashed, she would be swept away by something emotionally beyond her control.

Dawn Dawn is a friend of Jadine's in New York who lets Son and Jadine use her apartment while she is out of town. Jadine makes a distinction between Dawn and the night women who haunt her while she is in Eloe.

Drake See SOLDIER

Dr. Robert Michelin Dr. Robert Michelin is a French dentist who lives on the neighboring island of Queen of France. Valerian meets him when an abscessed tooth drives him to travel by boat and taxi to the dentist's house in the middle of the night. The dentist has been exiled from Algeria, and the two men are both elderly and in second marriages following disastrous first marriages; they have something in common, and a friendship develops between them. When the Streets entertain, which is seldom, Dr. Michelin is usually included.

Ellen Drake Ellen is Soldier's wife. Jadine finds it difficult to carry on a conversation with her. Son thinks she is pretty until he sees her in the picture Jadine takes while in Eloe.

Ernie Paul Ernie Paul is another friend of Son's. He has his own business in Montgomery, Alabama. He is coming to Eloe to see Son, so Son stays behind and sends Jade back to New York ahead of him. Son does not show up in New York until much later than he is supposed to. Since he has not called, Jade worries about him being in Eloe among the type of natural, motherly women that she does not feel that she is. It is Son's extended visit with Ernie Paul plus her own dreams of night women that set the stage for the tension between Jade and Son that leads to their breakup.

Felicite Felicite is one of Jadine's friends who lives in New York. Jadine distinguishes Felicite from the night women who haunt her while she is in Eloe.

Filipino houseboy The Filipino houseboy is the Streets' neighbor's servant. He steers the boat that takes Valerian to the dentist when the man has a terribly painful tooth abscess in the middle of the night.

Francine Green Francine is Son's sister, who is in a mental home in Jacksonville, Florida. Francine was a natural runner and one day, while she was out running, she was attacked by dogs who were tracking an escaped convict. This event begins Francine's mental decline.

Frank Green Frank is Son's brother, who is killed while serving in the military in Korea. He is married to Cissy and is Valerian's brother-in-law.

Franklin Green (Old Man) Franklin Green is Son's father. Franklin Green is nicknamed and called Old Man from the time he is seven years old. He has five children: Son, Horace, who lives in Gainesville, Frank G, who was killed in Korea, Francine, who lives in a mental home, and the baby girl, Porky, who attends Florida A and M on a track scholarship.

Old Man keeps in a cigar box, most of the money orders Son sends him over the eight years he is gone. He is very conservative and will not let Jadine stay with Son at his house because they are not married.

Frisco Frisco is the older man who pays Son a dime for his first gainful employment—cleaning a bucket full of fish. This dime is important to Son symbolically and becomes a bone of contention between him and Jadine.

Son values the five cigarettes and Dr. Pepper he buys with the dime. For him, those rewards represent working to earn the pleasures of life, but Jade thinks that Son lacks ambition for not wanting to make more money and for not desiring the power money would bring. When Frisco dies from working in a gas field, Son is unable to go to the funeral because he is on the run after killing his wife, Cheyenne.

George   George is the Streets' butler before Sydney. George tells young Valerian to stay away from the washerwoman because she drinks and because he believes that she tries to use the boy to do her work.

Gideon (Yardman)   Gideon is the black man who works around the Streets' property and runs errands for them. He kills the chickens for Ondine when she is not able to anymore. They call him Yardman, never bothering to learn his real name. Gideon befriends Son and tells him all about his life. He houses Son for a night after Son is discovered by the Streets. He cuts Son's hair and shows him around. While watching Gideon work one day for the Streets, Son is fascinated by Gideon's bare back.

Gideon lived in America for a while, worked at a hospital, and married a nurse to become a citizen. Gideon tells Son that America is a bad place to die. When Son and Jade want to go to the United States, Gideon loans Son his passport. Son later uses it to get unemployment benefits.

Gideon lives with Therese, and sometimes with Alma Estee. Gideon and Therese are fired after they are caught with Valerian's apples.

Grandmother Stadt   Grandmother Stadt is Valerian's grandmother, the candy queen, who used to make ollieballen for New Year. For Christmas dinner, Margaret cooks, since she thinks Michael is coming, and Valerian asks her to make ollieballen, which are similar to doughnuts.

Horace Green   Horace is Son's brother. He lives in Gainesville, Florida.

Jadine Childs (Jade)   Jadine is the other main character of the novel. She is an orphan of her family and of her own culture as well. She is in debt to Valerian, who gives her the money to get an education. In return she accepts many of his perspectives and assumptions as her own. She does not seem to care much about her own family either, even though she lives under the same roof with her Aunt Ondine and Uncle Sydney for a while. She never gives back to her aunt and uncle even though they offer her a place to stay and take care of her like she was their daughter. She does not eat with them or sleep downstairs with them.

Jadine is a very modern woman. She is a model and has lived in Europe and in New York City. She sleeps in the nude and has a white boyfriend named Ryk in Paris. She treasures a baby seal skin coat he has given her.

Son is in love with her and, before they meet, watches her as he hides in the house when she is asleep at night. Later, when the two go on a picnic, Jadine fall into a tar swamp, foreshadowing the fall she is about to make into her relationship with Son.

Later, after the couple relocate to New York, Jadine goes to Eloe with Son. She feels like an alien in that town. Everything in Eloe is foreign to her: the way the people talk, their strict morals—she cannot sleep with Son at night—and their perceptions of women as subordinate to men.

Very light-skinned and beautiful, Jade has been pampered and spoiled not only by her aunt and uncle, but also by the Streets. She is used to things falling into her lap. While in Paris, she is chosen for the cover of *Elle* magazine. As pretty and polished as she is, Jade is really not a kind or compassionate person. She has no genuine concern for Ondine and Sydney, or the Streets, and thinks almost exclusively about herself.

She is very smitten with Son but is unable to adapt to his more humble lifestyle and make a real commitment to him. In the end, it seems that she loves Son's looks and body, but is never in sync with his beliefs or personality. She abandons Son and her aunt and uncle when, at the novel's end, she returns to Paris.

Joseph Lordi   Joseph Lordi is Margaret's father. His daughter's red hair disturbs him and ruins his meals. He wonders if she is his child.

Leonora Lordi Leonora Lordi is Margaret's mother. Lenora is not bothered by her daughter's red hair or uncommon beauty.

Margaret Lenore Lordi Street (the Principal Beauty) Margaret Street is Valerian's wife, who at one time was Miss Maine. Ondine mockingly refers to her behind her back as the Principal Beauty of Maine. Valerian meets her when he sees her riding on a float in the Snow Carnival Parade, holding the paw of a giant fake polar bear. He falls in love with her instantly. She and Valerian do not communicate well and, at the beginning of the novel, are not even having sex.

Margaret is thought of by her husband as one of his prized possessions rather than as a human being. She travels back and forth between the island and their home in the United States, staying for extended periods of time in the United States without her husband so that she can see their grown son Michael as often as possible.

Margaret has bouts of confusion during which her perception is not to be relied on. She forgets words for objects and she sometimes cannot remember what to do with things—like not knowing what part of the fruit to eat or what to do with a finger bowl, to drink out of it or wash her hands.

Margaret is also pathologically needy. She abuses her son in order to control and dominate him and ends up alienating him in the process. The Streets' cook and housekeeper, Ondine, learns of Margaret's treatment of her son and keeps the secret of her employer's abusive motherhood until a stormy confrontation between the two reveals the truth to the entire household.

After her secret is revealed, Margaret seems freer to develop a self that is not rooted in her appearance. She also begins to connect with and take care of Valerian in a way that had never happened between the two. Margaret, interestingly, seems to shift the balance of power from Valerian to herself by the end of the novel.

Mary See THERESE MARIE

May Downing (Mama) May Downing is Soldier's mother.

Michael Street Michael Street is the 30-year-old son of Margaret and Valerian Street. Valerian does not really feel as if he knows Michael, but remembers him as he was at about two or three years of age. At that time Valerian would come home from work and find Michael huddled under the bathroom sink crooning to himself while Margaret stayed locked up in her room.

Michael is supposed to come for Christmas, but he has a history of not showing up for visits. He seems to have a social conscience and he urges Jadine to get involved in some kind of racial activism. Michael works for a Native American cause and, by the end of the novel, is accepted for graduate school at Berkeley. Michael never appears in the novel.

Miss Tyler As a child, Son played Miss Tyler's piano. At first his friends tease him about sleeping with Miss Tyler.

mulatto Mulatto is the term of reference used by the residents of L'Arbe de la Croix for the woman sent over by Dr. Michelin to do the work after Yardman (Gideon) and Mary (Therese) are fired for stealing apples.

night women The night women are a collection of the women that Jadine and Son know and who come to Jadine in a dream/vision while she is in Eloe, Florida. The women show her their eggs and breasts, threatening Jadine, but not Son. The dream makes Jadine feel inadequate and unworthy.

Nina Fong Nina Fong is the woman Ryk takes away for the weekend for a sexual rendezvous. Ryk is honest with Jadine about the incident, but she is still bothered by his infidelity.

Nommo NOMMO is a girl in New York City with a shaved head and nose ring. Son encounters her on the street. When Son first sees her, she is cursing out a man. She looks mean, but Son sees from her eyes that she is miserable inside and puts his arms around her and holds her until she cries. Nommo reminds Son of his sister. He takes her home to Jade, and they feed her with their last money. Later she steals the change from them and leaves.

Ondine Childs (Machete-hair) Ondine Childs is Sydney's wife and the Streets' cook. Ondine and Sydney have no children, but their niece Jadine comes to live with them as a girl when her parents both die. Ondine delights in mothering and loving the girl. Ondine is easily upset and requires Sydney to comfort and calm her. She has bad feet from a lifetime of standing on them and working in the kitchen.

She used to be able to kill the chickens, but now Yardman does it for her. When the Streets were first married, Ondine had a brief friendship with Margaret, but it did not last. She knows of Margaret's abuse of Michael, but she does not say anything until the Christmas dinner when Margaret makes all the food and Ondine feels displaced. Ondine has a ham and a pie ready if Margaret's meal fails. Ondine says her "crown" is Jadine. She wants Jadine to understand why she should want to care for her and Sydney as they grow older.

one hundred blind horsemen The one hundred blind horsemen supposedly ride on the other side of the hills of the Isle des Chevaliers, giving the island its name. The legend of the horsemen states that they lost their sight when they arrived on the shores of the island where they were to be enslaved. Margaret thinks there is only one rider. Son heads toward the alleged home of these mythical men at Therese's urgings when he gets out of her boat at the end of the novel.

Porky Green Porky, also referred to as the baby girl, is Son's youngest sister. She attends Florida Agricultural and Mechanical Institute on a track scholarship.

Raymond The night that Jadine leaves Son, she spends the night at her friend Raymond's before leaving the next day for Isle des Chevaliers.

Rosa Rosa was a friend of Son's grandmother. Together the two women built a cowshed. While Jadine and Son are in Eloe, they are not allowed to sleep together in Old Man's house because they are not married. Rosa offers Jadine her closed-in porch to sleep in and Jadine spends two hot and miserable

nights there. While she sleeps on the renovated porch, Jadine has her encounter with the night women.

Ryk Ryk is a white Frenchman who wishes to marry Jadine and sends her a sealskin coat as a gift at Christmas.

Sally Sarah Sadie Brown Sally Brown is Cheyenne's mother. Son is both shocked and grateful when Old Man tells him about Sally's death. Before she dies, Sally sleeps with a shotgun, waiting to exact her revenge on Son for killing Cheyenne. She is one of the night women who come to haunt Jadine in Eloe.

Solange Because she speaks French so well, Jadine places Margaret and Ondine's orders for food and other things from the United States with Solange.

Soldier (Drake) Soldier is Son's friend in Eloe who is so glad to see Son that he jumps up and down when Son returns. Soldier tells Jadine that Son does not like to be controlled by anyone.

Son (William Green, Herbert Robinson, Louis Stover) Son is one of the main characters of the novel. *Tar Baby* begins as Son jumps ship and swims to the Streets' boat that unknowingly takes him to the Isle des Chevaliers. Son hides out in the Streets' huge house, eating their food and sneaking around at night. He hides in Jadine's closet and then in Margaret's. Margaret discovers him there one night when she storms away from the dinner table after a fight with her husband, Valerian.

Unpredictably, Valerian treats him as a guest, inviting him to dine with the family at their table and to sleep upstairs in the guest bedroom, much to the disgust of the other members of the household. During the eight years preceding the novel's beginning, Son has held seven identities. He has unusual abilities, such as a gift for knowing how to make Valerian's flowers grow. Initially, for Valerian, Son is no more than an exotic being to amuse him rather than a person he is intimidated by.

While he hides in the darkness of the Street home, Son begins to fall in love with Jadine, but, at first, she is frightened of him. While at the house, Son becomes infatuated with Jadine. He watches her at night and tries to fill her mind with his dreams. After the confrontation between Ondine and Margaret at Christmas dinner, Son and Jadine leave for New York together and share an apartment. Son does not like the people there. He discovers that this is not the New York he has imagined: All the people are unrecognizable and unfamiliar to him, even the children.

Eventually, the couple return to Eloe, Son's hometown, for a visit. The differences between Jadine and Son are accentuated here and this visit to Son's home leads to their eventual breakup. But even at the end of the novel Son is trying to find Jadine and get her back.

Son and Jadine's relationship is doomed to failure from the beginning. Son is defined by his black heritage. He believes in the importance of understanding his culture. He realizes the importance of home and Eloe, the all-black town where he is from originally. He is also very concerned with his family and feels dedicated to them. He even sends his father (Old Man) money orders. On the other hand, he kills his first wife, Cheyenne, for sleeping with a 13-year old boy by driving through the house when the two lovers are inside.

Jadine does not feel in debt to Ondine or Sydney and usually does not write letters to them or let them know where she is staying. She believes there is prestige in an education and having a high-paying job. Because of these fundamental differences Son and Jadine try to change each other, which only forces them apart.

When their relationship falls apart, Jadine leaves Son. The novel concludes with him looking for her. Son is always looking to rescue people, especially Jadine. He is also looking for what he believes is authentic truth. Perhaps at the novel's end, while he is climbing up the rocks on the far end of the island, Son realizes and accepts his cultural heritage, much like Milkman's ambiguous leap into the air at the end of *Song of Solomon*. Son also may choose, with the help of Therese, to become one of the blind horsemen, racing through the rainforest.

Stacey   Stacey is Valerian's niece, the daughter of Cissy and Frank.

Sydney Childs   Sydney Childs is the Streets' butler, who has been with the Street family since before Margaret and Valerian were married about 30 years prior to the present time of the novel. Sydney is a black man from Philadelphia who is very knowledgeable about his employers' needs and prides himself on serving them impeccably.

He is very fond of his own wife, Ondine, and they are in much closer communication than the Streets. They share most things with each other, and he shows his tenderness by rubbing her sore feet when she is tired. Sydney does not have a lot of sympathy or empathy for the black people who are native to the island. He seems to feel superior to them, as a Philadelphia Negro, and does not even know the real names of the people who work at L'Arbe de la Croix—he and Ondine just call them by generic names.

Sydney advises Valerian about his health and holds a gun to Son's head when Margaret discovers him in the closet. He is disadvantaged because he does not own any property or very many belongings, but he has a sense of empowerment much stronger than either of the Streets. He is characterized often as noiseless when he serves the Streets.

Therese Marie (Therese Foucault, Mary)   Therese is Gideon's half-sister, the woman whom the Streets and the Childs refer to as Mary. She worked as a wet-nurse for many years because her breasts never stopped making milk, until the development of Enfamil put her out of business. She does the Streets' laundry, outside of the house in a separate wash shed. She does the laundry for the Streets by hand instead of using washing machines and dryers. The Streets and/or the Childs occasionally fire her and tell Gideon to get another woman to come instead, but he waits a while and then brings Therese back again. The residents at the Street house believe he is bringing a succession of women all named Mary—they do not see her clearly enough as a person to see that she is the same woman.

Therese's eyes are weak—she is going blind—and she has to move her head around to try to see things. Despite her eye problems, she is able to get around and work as if she has a supernatural means of seeing. Gideon teases her about being one of the blind race. Therese takes Son back to the Isle des Chevaliers at the end of the story, but she urges him to forget about Jadine and go to the men in the hills.

Valerian's first wife   Valerian's first wife is described by Valerian as an "unlovable shrew." Valerian is married to her for nine years; then the couple go through a prolonged and painful divorce. After she dies, Valerian believes that she visits him in his greenhouse at L'Arbe de la Croix.

Valerian Street   Valerian Street is a former candy businessman from Philadelphia who owns Isle des Chevaliers, where most of the story takes place. He spends time communicating with his dead ex-wife. He waits for the mail and never gets the message he is waiting for. He spends most of his time sitting in his greenhouse drinking wine and eating baked potatoes for lunch. Valerian never really recovers from the early death of his father and the sudden adulthood that is forced upon him as a result. Valerian's devotion to his family's candy business is sustained by his dreams of retiring to an island in the Caribbean. As soon as he retires, he relocates to Isle des Chevaliers permanently.

Margaret is Valerian's second wife. The two have a son named Michael. Valerian buys a chandelier in celebration when Margaret becomes pregnant with their son. After Ondine's revelations about Margaret's abuse of their son, Valerian gradually loses control of the island paradise he spent his life fanaticizing about creating.

washerwoman   The washerwoman does the wash for Valerian's family when he is a boy. She begins every conversation with Valerian by asking him "What your daddy doin' today?" When his father dies, Valerian reports "He's dead today" to the washerwoman. She then lets him wash the clothes, which he scrubs until his knuckles bleed. The washerwoman's actions allow Valerian to do something practical with his grief. She is the only one who lets the boy own his feelings. She is fired for her kindness.

Watts   The Watts are a family who occasionally live on the Isle des Chevaliers.

Willys   The Willys are a family who live on the Isle des Chevaliers. They often loan their boat and their jeep to the members of the Street household.

Winnie   Boom Winnie Boom is Drake's grandmother.

woman in canary yellow dress   The woman in the yellow robe is a tall, statuesque African black woman that Jadine encounters in a Paris grocery. The woman is full of dignity and has a natural grace and commands respect. She is dressed in bright yellow and, against store rules, purchases only three eggs. She seems to symbolize womanliness in a traditional role. Jadine is very impressed with her and is shocked when the woman looks her in the eye and spits, as if to belittle Jade's modern, chic, high-fashion persona.

FURTHER READING

Aithal, S. Krishnamoort. "Getting out of One's Skin and Being the Only Person: Toni Morrison's *Tar Baby*," *American Studies International* 34, no. 3 (October 1996): 76–86.

Emberley, Julia V. "A Historical Transposition: Toni Morrison's *Tar Baby* and Frantz Fanon's Post-enlightenment," *Modern Fiction Studies* 45, no. 2 (Summer 1999): 403–432.

Moffitt, Letitia L. "Finding the Door: Vision/Revision and Stereotype in Toni Morrison's *Tar Baby*," *Critique* 46, no. 1 (Fall 2004): 12–27.

Ryan, Judylyn S. "Contested Visions/Double-Vision in *Tar Baby*," *Modern Fiction Studies* 39, no. 3/4 (Fall/Winter 1993): 597–622.

CHILDREN'S BOOKS

The Ant or the Grasshopper? (Who's Got Game?) (with Slade Morrison, illustrated by Pascal Lemaitre) (2003)

The story features two main characters: the Ant, Kid A, and the Grasshopper, Foxy G. The two, Kid A and Foxy G, are best friends. The two spend the summer playing in the park. They play basketball. They swing and they especially love to sing together. After spending the season together, Kid A tells Foxy G that he has to get back to work. Foxy G stops him, claiming that Kid A has to hear the new song he has written. Foxy G has written an incredible song that others besides Kid A enjoy. Many others in the park gather round to listen to the fresh new sound that Foxy G produces.

After listening to and enjoying the sound, Kid A warns that in spite of Foxy G's talent, the warm summer is not going to last forever and that he and his friend must begin to prepare for the upcoming winter. Foxy G insists that he must continue to create and play his music. As a result, the two part ways.

Kid A begins a new industrious life—cleaning, shopping, and getting ready for winter and the coming cold. While Foxy G continues to create his music, Kid A works hard to prepare for winter. Hearing Foxy G's music in the background keeps Kid A motivated and working hard at his chores.

Meanwhile, Foxy G is living in a cardboard box at the park. Because of the cold, his wings—his instrument—begin to fall apart. Alone and freezing in his box, Foxy G cannot make his music. Desperate and alone, Foxy G leaves the park and heads into town for some assistance. He arrives at Kid A's door and asks if he can move in with him. Kid A scolds his friend and reminds him that he tried to warn him to prepare for the winter.

Foxy G is so despondent that he continues to beg his friend for help. As Kid A continues to criticize—even throwing a half-eaten doughnut hole at his former friend—Foxy G reminds Kid A that it was his music that helped Kid A to keep going when he was doing his work. With a dramatic

declaration, Foxy G says he is an artist and admonishes Kid A, saying that "Art *is* work. It just looks like play."

Kid A is still unconvinced and reminds his friend that he does not have what he needs to survive—such as food or shelter. Foxy G still maintains that the music—the art—is as important as what Kid A's efforts produce.

The story ends without a definitive conclusion, leaving the reader to decide who's got game—who is right and who is wrong.

BIBLIOGRAPHY

Morrison, Toni, and Slade Morrison. Illustrated by Pascal Lemaitre. *Who's Got Game: The Ant or the Grasshopper.* New York: Scribner, 2003.

The Big Box (with Slade Morrison, illustrated by Giselle Potter) (1999)

Three children—Patty, Mickey, and Liza Sue—are active, rambunctious children who cannot seem to be controlled by adults. One by one, these children are approached by the adults, who try to explain to them that they need to calm down if they are to be allowed the privilege of being free.

First, teachers approach Patty, who lives in a little white house with her parents. She does things like talking in the library and singing in class. The teachers explain to her that she has potential but that she is not living up to it. She will not get along in an adult world. She disagrees and tells them that she fulfills all her responsibilities—she folds her socks, washes her neck, and so forth—and so she sees no problem in her behavior. So the adults put her in a big brown box that actually has everything she needs to have fun—swings, slides, Barbie dolls—except her freedom.

Then grownup tenants approach Mickey, who lives in an apartment building. He does things like sit on the superintendent's Honda and holler in the hall. The tenants tell him he must behave, but Mickey says he does enough. He combs his hair and vacuums the rugs. But that is not enough for the tenants, who put him in a big brown box with lots of things to have fun with—like Matchbox cars and comic books—but it does not include Mickey's freedom.

Finally, grownup neighbors approach Liza, who lives in a farmhouse. She does things like let chickens keep their eggs and feed honey to the bees. So the neighbors tell her if she keeps all that up she will not get grownup approval. But she says she is already good enough. She does her fractions and bottle-feeds the lambs that are too small. But that is not enough for the neighbors, who put her in a big brown box. There, she has all sorts of fun things to keep herself busy—like a Bingo game and a movie camera with a film of a running brook—except she does not have her freedom.

And the question for all three children is this: "Who says they cannot handle their freedom?"

BIBLIOGRAPHY

Morrison, Toni, and Slade Morrison. Illustrations by Giselle Potter. *The Big Box*. New York: Jump at the Sun, 1999.

The Book of Mean People (with Slade Morrison, illustrated by Pascal Lemaitre) (2002)

The Book of Mean People follows a young bunny rabbit as he discovers all the different ways people can be mean. The book begins with an overview: Some mean people are tall, others are short, others shout, others whisper, and so forth.

Then the bunny gets specific. He presents all the mean people in his life—his family members, his teacher, babysitter, and so forth—and he shows how they are mean to him. "My grandparents are mean. My grandmother tells me to sit down. My grandfather tells me to sit up." In each case, he

expresses his confusion at what they want: "How can I sit down and sit up at the same time?"

In the end, no matter what mean people he faces, and no matter how confusing they may be because of their meanness, the bunny resolves that he is going to smile through it all.

BIBLIOGRAPHY

Morrison, Toni, and Slade Morrison. Illustrated by Pascal Lemaitre. *The Book of Mean People*. New York: Hyperion, 2002.

The Lion or the Mouse? (Who's Got Game?) (with Slade Morrison, illustrated by Pascal Lemaitre) (2003)

In a retelling of an *Aesop's Fables* tale, a lion struts around his kingdom, declaring to all who hear him that he is king, he is ferocious, all the other animals should be afraid of him, and he makes the laws.

In his ranting and roaming, the lion pushes through a bramble bush, and he gets a thorn in his paw. All those animals he had been scaring now refuse to help him. They walk right past him, gleeful that this lion king at last is hurting and cannot bother them.

It is only the humble mouse who dares approach the lion, and it only this mouse who finally removes the thorn from the lion's paw after the lion promises not to eat him. The lion is grateful and limps off to heal while the mouse returns to his own home.

The next day, the mouse feels empowered, like he himself is a lion. So now he goes around the countryside declaring that he is all-powerful and that all the other animals should be afraid of him. The problem is that none of the animals take him seriously. They laugh at him.

So the mouse goes to the lair of the lion to complain and wonder out loud why he cannot command the same respect as had the lion before the thorn. The lion tries to help the mouse. He dresses the mouse up as a lion. But the mouse only ends up looking comical, and the other animals continue to laugh at him.

Finally, the mouse decides to sit on the lion's throne as if this will elevate him. The lion leaves his lair to the mouse and roams the countryside. While the mouse continues to be a laughing stock, the lion has learned something about himself and all bullies: that bullies are not really so tough. They are really just too scared to be themselves.

BIBLIOGRAPHY

Morrison, Toni, and Slade Morrison. Illustrated by Pascal Lemaitre. *The Lion or the Mouse? (Who's Got Game?)*. New York: Scribner, 2003.

The Mirror or the Glass? (Who's Got Game?) (with Slade Morrison, illustrated by Pascal Lemaitre) (2007)

(Not released at time of publication.)

BIBLIOGRAPHY

Morrison, Toni, and Slade Morrison. Illustrated by Pascal Lemaitre. *The Mirror or the Glass? (Who's Got Game?)*. New York: Scribner, 2007.

The Poppy or the Snake? (Who's Got Game?) (with Slade Morrison) (2004)

Poppy is grandfather to Nate, a little boy who does not want to return to school in the fall. Nate thinks he is not able to be a good student, so Poppy offers him his "remembering boots." These are boots Poppy wears whenever he needs to remember, and he tells Nate the story behind these boots.

One day, Poppy is fishing, and when he returns to his truck, he finds a snake under one of the tires.

The snake begs Poppy to let him out from under the tire, but Poppy is nervous that the snake, which is poisonous, will bite him. The snake swears he will not do it. Poppy is reluctant, but the snake finally convinces him to move the truck forward. The snake is now free to move.

This liberation is not enough for the snake, who insists that he and Poppy are now friends. He wants Poppy to take him home, feed him, and take care of him. Poppy is a little suspicious, but then he is convinced that maybe they really are friends. He takes the snake home.

For a while it seems that the snake is sincere. He does not bite Poppy. Instead, they live together in Poppy's house as friends. Then, one morning, Poppy awakens to find that he was bitten in the night by the snake. He is angry at the snake and asks why he bit him. The snake has a simple answer: I am a snake. That is what snakes do.

Fortunately, Poppy had taken precautions and got snake serum so he wouldn't die. This adventure was a lesson to Poppy about knowing the true nature of those you meet. His boots always remind him of this lesson—since they are made of snakeskin.

BIBLIOGRAPHY

Morrison, Toni, and Slade Morrison. Illustrated by Pascal Lemaitre. *The Poppy or the Snake? (Who's Got Game?)*. New York: Scribner, 2004.

Remember: The Journey to School Integration (2004)

To commemorate the 50th anniversary of the *Brown v. The Board of Education of Topeka, Kansas* Supreme Court decision, which declared unconstitutional the legal practice of separate but equal established in the 1896 *Plessy v. Ferguson* Supreme Court decision, Morrison wrote and published the children's book *Remember: The Journey to School Integration*. Through a series of photographs, unnamed narrators tell the story of the landmark Supreme Court decision on *Brown v. Board of*

EDUCATION in 1954, which declared that separate schools for blacks and whites were "inherently unequal."

First, a young narrator tells what it is like to live as a black child in the JIM CROW South. She says she cannot go to school with white children. Her school, which is only for African-American children, is in very bad shape, not like the schools for white children. She must walk a long way to get to her school.

When the school is integrated, the narrator wonders what her new world will be like. The forced integration of schools is met with violence from angry white bigots. A young protestor, seen in a photo, is not even sure why he is protesting, except that he is doing it with his friends. Meanwhile, many white parents boycott the schools rather than have their children learn alongside black children, who do attend, but must walk through a gauntlet of angry protestors. Soldiers are there to protect the black children, but the soldiers are also scary.

Even when the white children start to attend again, it is uncomfortable for everyone—at least at first. They slowly start to discover that they—both black and white children—are not so different from each other. Meanwhile, the white parents continue to protest, and they yell at the black children, who are only trying to learn. The black children are afraid to attend school.

Unfortunately, the separation of African Americans and whites is not just in the schools. This segregation appears in all walks of life, even in separate drinking fountains and lunch counters. Blacks and many whites protest against this, and they are met with the same hostility from bigots. It is reassuring that good people unite, often under an important leader, like Rosa Parks or MARTIN LUTHER KING JR.

The children continue to attend school together, and they—both white and black—learn that there is nothing to be afraid of. In time, they can even become friends.

BIBLIOGRAPHY

Morrison, Toni. *Remember: The Journey to School Integration*. New York: Houghton Mifflin, 2004.

NONFICTION BOOKS

Baldwin, Collected Essays: Essays : Notes of a Native Son / Nobody Knows My Name / The Fire Next Time / No Name in the Street / The Devil Finds Work / Other Essays (written by James Baldwin, edited by Toni Morrison) (1998)

This collection of writings by JAMES BALDWIN was edited by Toni Morrison.

BIBLIOGRAPHY

Baldwin, James, and Toni Morrison. *James Baldwin: Collected Essays: Notes of a Native Son / Nobody Knows My Name / The Fire Next Time / No Name in the Street / The Devil Finds Work / Other Essays.* New York: Library of America, 1998.

Birth of Nation'hood: Gaze, Script, and Spectacle in the O. J. Simpson Case (edited with Claudia Brodsky Lacour) (1997)

Morrison edited this book, which is a collection of 12 essays by various writers on the subject of the O. J. SIMPSON murder trial. In her introduction to these essays—"The Official Story: Dead Men Golfing"—Morrison recounts Herman Melville's novella *Benito Cereno* (1856), in which a white sea captain is horrified at having been fooled by a Senegalese man, meant for the slave trade, who had transformed from an affable, servile man to a leader in murderous rebellion. Morrison sees an analogy in how Americans viewed what they saw as the transformation of O. J. Simpson from the telegenic and affable face on TV to the accused murderer of a white woman and a white man.

For Morrison, the trial was replete with time-worn representations of African-American men, especially the contradictory notions that they are—or are sup-

posed to be—servile and unthreatening, and yet can also be depicted as sexual predators, especially of white women. Simpson was cast into this role both within the trial and by the American media. Says Morrison, the media's "official story," which "obliterates any narrative that is counter to it," was not truly his legal guilt or innocence, but the playing out of the black man's stereotype in America's ongoing racial drama.

The media found a willing audience in their readers and viewers. Most whites, according to polls, believed Simpson guilty as charged, and most blacks, based on their history in this country, suspected foul play by the police; yet poll results can be ignored if they run counter to the "official story," such as the fact that the sizable minority of whites who believed that Simpson was innocent are often dismissed as "suffering from liberal paralysis."

Birth of Nation'hood brings together writers from various backgrounds and perspectives—black, white, male, female—to discuss Simpson, his trial, and America's racial narratives.

BIBLIOGRAPHY

Morrison, Toni, and Claudia Brodsky Lacour. *Birth of Nation'hood: Gaze, Script and Spectacle in the O. J. Simpson Case.* New York: Knopf Publishing Group, 1997.

The Black Book (compiled by Middleton Harris, edited by Toni Morrison) (1974)

Now out of print, Morrison's *The Black Book*, published in 1974, is a collection of photographs, music, artwork, letters, advertisements, newspaper articles, and other documents charting African-American history from early slavery to the second half of the 20th century. Middleton Harris compiled the material, and Toni Morrison edited it.

While working on this compendium Morrison ran across a 19th-century article about MARGARET GARNER, a runaway slave who killed her children rather than see them returned to slavery. This story became the basis for her novel *Beloved*.

BIBLIOGRAPHY

Morrison, Toni, ed. Compiled by Middleton Harris, et al. *The Black Book*. New York: Random House, 1974.

Case for Black Reparations (by Boris I. Bittker, edited by Toni Morrison) (1972)

This early treatment of the issue of reparations was written by law professor Boris I. Bittker and edited by Toni Morrison.

BIBLIOGRAPHY

Bittker, Boris I. *Case for Black Reparations*. New York: Random House, 1973.

Deep Sightings and Rescue Missions: Fiction, Essays, and Conversations (written by Toni Cade Bambara, edited by Toni Morrison) (1996)

As editor of this collection of essays and fiction by Toni Cade Bambara, Morrison first writes about the job of being an editor—". . . the restructuring, setting loose or nailing down; paragraphs, pages may need re-writing, sentences . . . may need to be deleted or recast . . ."—but she goes on to say that little of this was necessary for editing Bambara's fiction. Morrison invites the reader to appreciate Bambara's writing, where "her insights are multiple, her textures layered and her narrative trajectory implacable . . ." Morrison was greatly honored to edit Bambara's works when the author was alive, and editing this posthumous collection, says Morrison, "is a gift."

BIBLIOGRAPHY

Bambara, Toni Cade, and Toni Morrison ed. *Deep Sightings and Rescue Missions: Fiction, Essays and Conversations*. New York: Pantheon, 1996.

A Kind of Rapture (Robert Bergman, with an introduction by Toni Morrison) (1998)

Morrison introduces Robert Bergman's book of photographs with an essay called "The Fisherwoman." The essay recounts Morrison's odd encounter with an older woman in her neighborhood. The woman is fishing in a neighbor's yard and tells Morrison that she has the neighbor's permission to fish there anytime. Morrison proceeds to have an engaging conversation with the woman that sets up expectations about their future relationship. Morrison looks for the woman in the passing days, but she does not reappear. Eventually, Morrison asks the neighbor about the mysterious fisherwoman. She is surprised to learn that the neighbor has never made any such agreement with the older woman and has never seen her on her property. Morrison is disappointed that the woman will not return and in herself for projecting her desires and expectations onto the woman and the encounter. She surmises that the stranger is always the self, but that we do not allow the other to fully be individualized. Morrison ends by suggesting that Bergman's book has the potential to enable an authentic connection with the other.

BIBLIOGRAPHY

Bergman, Robert. *A Kind of Rapture*. New York: Pantheon, 1998.

Playing in the Dark: Whiteness and the Literary Imagination (1992)

In 1990, Morrison gave a series of three lectures at Harvard as part of the William E. Massey Lectures in the History of American Civilization, exploring the impact of constructions and understandings of blackness in the work of canonical, white American writers. Morrison later published these lectures as a book of essays, *Playing in the Dark: Whiteness and the Literary Imagination*.

In the first essay, "Black Matters," Morrison criticizes the lack of African and African-American literature in the American canon. In the second essay, "Romancing the Shadow," Morrison points out the contradiction of the New World as a place of freedom and new possibilities for some, but enslavement for others. In the third essay, "Disturbing Nurses and the Kindness of Sharks," Morrison discusses the rise of American Africanism in American literature.

Throughout these essays, Morrison contends that the condition of being white is treated by American writers—such as Melville, Cather, Poe, Twain, and Hemingway—as the standard condition for humanity. All else—such as roots in Africa—are a variance from the norm. Indeed, in presenting their white characters, American writers did little to acknowledge race. Morrison says that American literature and its protagonists should not be deracialized since the society is shaped so much by race, and many of American literature's common themes and assumptions—such as individualism, masculinity, and innocence—are responses to the presence of black characters. In fact, it was the early presence of African slaves that helped define who was American and who—was not. Thus, it is this presence of blacks that has shaped how Americans define themselves in society, and it is this presence that helps distinguish American literature from European.

BIBLIOGRAPHY

Morrison, Toni. *Playing in the Dark: Whiteness and the Literary Imagination.* Cambridge, Mass.: Harvard University Press, 1992.

Race-ing Justice, En-Gendering Power: Essays on Anita Hill, Clarence Thomas, and the Construction of Social Reality (edited by Toni Morrison) (1992)

Morrison edited this book, which is a collection of 18 essays by various writers on the subject of the testimony of Anita Hill at the Senate confirmation hearings for CLARENCE THOMAS for the U.S. Supreme Court. In her introduction to these essays, Morrison

reminds, or informs, the reader of the great debate that swirled around the nomination of Clarence Thomas, a judge who many thought was unsuited for a seat on the Court, not only because of his conservative positions but also because of the accusations of Anita Hill—a law professor—that Thomas had sexually harassed her when they both worked together at the Department of Energy and Equal Employment Opportunity Commission. Morrison says that the purpose of the book is to gather various perspectives on the hearings to help the reader explore the issues: ". . . one needs perspective, not attitudes; context, not anecdotes; analyses, not postures."

Morrison makes clear that so much of the discussion surrounding Thomas's confirmation included images and stereotypes of black men and black women, including issues that involved sex, personality, and even body types. Rather than focusing on the legal thinking of Thomas, the testimony of Anita Hill, a black woman, "simply produced an exchange of racial tropes" about both black men and black women.

Morrison sees in the Thomas hearings, and the discussions surrounding the hearings, cultural echoes of race that date back centuries and can be seen in DANIEL DEFOE's 18th-century novel *Robinson Crusoe*, where Friday's servile and uncivilized character presents an image of what whites expect from blacks. Says Morrison in her introduction, "both men [Friday and Thomas] . . . are condemned first to mimic, then to internalize and adore, but never to utter one single sentence understood to be beneficial to their original culture. . . ."

BIBLIOGRAPHY

Morrison, Toni. *Race-ing Justice, En-Gendering Power: Essays on Anita Hill, Clarence Thomas, and the Construction of Social Reality.* New York: Pantheon Books 1992.

Those Bones Are Not My Child (by Toni Cade Bambara, edited by Toni Morrison) (1999)

This novel by Toni Cade Bambara was edited by Toni Morrison after Toni Cade Bambara's death.

Those Bones Are Not My Child is set in Atlanta, Georgia, in the midst of the rash of child murders that occurred in the city in the late 1980s. Sundiata (Sonny), the son of the main character, Zala, disappears. The novel details Zala's search for her son and, in the process, uncovers the particular and peculiar nuances of race and racism in 20th-century America.

BIBLIOGRAPHY

Bambara, Toni, and Toni Morrison, ed. *Those Bones Are Not My Child.* New York: Pantheon, 1999.

To Die for the People: The Writings of Huey P. Newton (edited by Toni Morrison) (1995)

This collection of the writings of Black Panther Huey P. Newton was edited by Toni Morrison.

BIBLIOGRAPHY

Newton, Huey P., and Toni Morrison, ed. *To Die for the People.* New York: Writers and Readers Publisher, 1995.

Major Essays, Interviews, and Speeches

"Behind the Making of the Black Book" (1974)

With the publication of *The Black Book*, a collection of essays and pictures depicting moments in black history, Toni Morrison wrote an article for the journal *Black World* to explain her motivation in creating and editing the project. In her article, she says she sees too much of black history and culture being wrongly defined, either by whites or by misguided black youth. She sees the neighborhood drunk and pimp as signs of distorted solutions to living under the oppression of the dominant white society. Too many people, both black and white, have wrong impressions of black culture—that it is illiterate, that it adores white culture, and that there is some special, mysterious soul of black people rooted in the distant past. Morrison resents all of these attempts to define blacks beyond their actual culture and lived-history.

Morrison wants to fight the myth-making that she sees surrounding the struggle for black Americans to assert themselves in the white-dominated society. She feels that even the black-is-beautiful cry is a distraction. It may satisfy some needs—of both blacks and whites—but she feels that a culture's strengths should depend on what the people are, not on what they look like. She believes, "The concept of physical beauty as a virtue is one of the dumbest, most pernicious and destructive ideas of the Western world."

The Black Book is meant to address some of these issues by presenting blacks and black culture in much of its variety, showing black Americans as they have really lived their lives.

BIBLIOGRAPHY

Morrison, Toni. "Behind the Making of *The Black Book*." *Black World*, February 1974, 86–90.

"Clinton as the First Black President" (1998)

SYNOPSIS

After a summer in which she avoids watching, listening to, or reading most of the news media—preferring instead to get her news in "conversation, public eavesdropping, and word of mouth"—Morrison tentatively returns to catching up on current events to find that the big story is President Clinton's adultery. She is disappointed. "Serious as adultery is," she says, "it is not a national catastrophe." It is both a tired old story of adultery and also the stuff of high drama about presidential impeachment—at first seeming, she says sarcastically, similar to past presidential transgressions: "the suborning of federal agencies; the exchange of billion-dollar contracts for proof of indiscretion; the extermination of infants in illegal wars mounted and waged for money and power." But Clinton's adultery is not so serious as all that. It is "thinner stuff." It is "dangerously close to a story of no story at all." Morrison questions why Clinton's indiscretion so alarms the media, the Republicans, and the public—well, most of the public. She says that African-American men understand all too well. After all, Clinton is our first black president. Clinton, says Morrison, "displays almost every trope of blackness: single-parent household, born poor, working-class, saxophone-playing, McDonald's-and-junk-food-loving boy from Arkansas." Suffering impeachment charges, he is also experiencing a degradation that black men can relate to: that is, no matter how capable he is, no matter how far he has come, he will be put back in his place by other powers. The laws to attack Clinton seem tailored, or interpreted, to get him. The presidency is being stolen from us, says Morrison—and this is a fact most quickly recognized by black men. This brief, but well-known essay was published in the *New Yorker* magazine.

BIBLIOGRAPHY

Morrison, Toni. "Clinton as the First Black President." *New Yorker*, October 1998, 31–32.

The Dancing Mind: Speech upon Acceptance of the National Book Foundation Medal for Distinguished Contribution to American Letters (1996)

In her acceptance speech for receiving the National Book Foundation Medal for Distinguished Contribution to American Letters, Morrison speaks of the "dance of an open mind," which is to say the free exchange of ideas that can occur between the reader and writer. She thinks such an exchange is being threatened, and, to make her point, she offers two anecdotes.

The first is about a scholar who was very active in sports and school in his younger years but now finds, to his surprise, that he has a disability—that is, he has trouble simply sitting quietly in his room for hours with only his own thoughts and personal readings. He misses the forced engagement of non-stop activities that he had as a youngster.

The second story Morrison experienced herself. She attended a symposium that addressed politically persecuted writers from around the world, and during a panel discussion, one author broke down in tears as she asked the audience for help against the persecution of women writers who challenged her country's status quo. Morrison asked what she could do to help, and the author answered, "I don't know, but you have to try. There isn't anybody else."

In the first anecdote, Morrison sees a threat to the quiet act of reading and thinking in our overdrive society. In the second, she sees the danger to writing in societies that do not tolerate being challenged. Morrison combines the significances of both stories in her own life, as well as our society at large. She sees the importance of her ability to be alone for hours to read, think, and write and then to be able to publish without fear of being persecuted as the two parts necessary for a fully engaged, free, and dynamic culture. So Morrison asks her audience to join her in supporting this "dance of an open mind."

BIBLIOGRAPHY

Morrison, Toni. *The Dancing Mind: Speech upon Acceptance of the National Book Foundation Medal for Distinguished Contribution to American Letters.* New York: Knopf, 1996.

"The Dead of September 11" (2001)

"The Dead of September 11," written by Morrison in the days following the events of September 11, 2001, was first published in a commemorative edition of *Vanity Fair.* In her reflections on the terrorist attack on September 11, Morrison offers to speak directly to the dead, whose ancestry is rooted all over the globe. First she must set aside all her preconceived ideas about nations and what nations do, and for this she must cleanse her language of automatic descriptions. She feels she is limited in what she can say to the dead. She fears her language will be too limited. She can only offer "this thread thrown between your humanity and mine." Morrison wishes she could hold them as their souls make their journey.

BIBLIOGRAPHY

Toni Morrison. "The Dead of September 11." *Vanity Fair,* November 2001, 48–49.

"Home" (1998)

"Home," by Toni Morrison, was published in the collection *The House That Race Built* and is a reprint of a talk she gave at the *Race Matters* interdisciplinary conference held at Princeton University in 1994. Morrison starts by telling her audience about the empowerment that writing gives her to explore herself and her world, but she realizes that she is never fully in control of her stories because the issue of race must always inform them. "Whatever the forays of my imagination, the keeper, whose keys tinkled always within earshot, was race."

For her to explore how race has informed her writing, she pictures American society as a home.

This equation brings reality to her subject. The question of a society that is not driven by racial concerns does not have to be some fanciful utopia. The image of a home "domesticates" the issue, allows it to be something we can all enter and think about.

Morrison explains how, in *Beloved*, she had debated the novel's last word with her editor and a friend. Her original ending word—which she does not state here—was more racially and sexually charged, and dealt with the "estranged body, the legislated body, the violated, rejected, deprived body—," which spoke to Morrison about a kind of homelessness since she saw "the body as consummate home." In the end, she changed the word, and she expresses some regrets about doing that.

This debate over the endings of *Beloved* reveals Morrison's desire to deal with race in new and honest way, shorn of old assumptions and fantasies of a race-neutral society. It requires "a redesigned racial house." She then briefly expresses how her various novels have been her attempts as such a redesign.

She then calls for others, for society at large, to also explore its racial house, to finally let go of old language that says nothing new and that may even reinforce the inequities of a racial hierarchy. In the new racial world of her imagination and hope, differences are "prized but unprivileged." Morrison ends by describing her idea of a world "both snug and wide open, with a doorway never needing to be closed." This, for her, is home.

BIBLIOGRAPHY

Morrison, Toni. "Home." In *The House That Race Built: Original Essays by Toni Morrison, Angela Y. Davis, Cornel West, and Others on Black Americans and Politics in America Today*, edited by Wahneema Lubiano. New York: Vintage, 1998.

"How Can Values Be Taught in the University?" (2004)

In her lecture, Morrison asks if it is the place of universities to teach values, and answers her own question by saying it always has—from its roots in the church, which taught an ecclesiastical view of the world, to its transformed state as a mostly humanist institution that employs, or attempts to employ, reason.

Morrison points out that universities today already encourage an exploration of values through various initiatives, such as promoting volunteerism, public service, free speech, and the creation of institutes that focus on ethical questions. As the debate on separation of church and school continues (for instance, on the issue of school prayer), the question remains: What values to teach? The answer may be already decided, because values "seep" through whenever a teacher teaches, whether it be by her choice of readings or her emphases. "What I think and do is already inscribed on my teaching, my work," says Morrison.

Morrison adds that no one value need dominate in academia. She suggests a wide-ranging discussion of values, not just within a particular university but also among universities—an approach facilitated, perhaps, by the Internet. Regardless of how it is done, Morrison warns that the university must treat its responsibilities to teach values as an obligation, or else "some other regime or ménage of regimes will do it for us, in spite of us, and without us."

BIBLIOGRAPHY

Toni Morrison. "How Can Values Be Taught in the University?": A Lecture by Toni Morrison. Available on line. URL:http://www.umich.edu/~mqr/morrison. htm. Accessed on September 16, 2006.

"The Language Must Not Sweat" (an interview of Toni Morrison, by Thomas LeClair) (1981)

Shortly after the publication of Morrison's *Tar Baby*, LeClair interviewed Morrison in her office at Random House. Morrison explains what writing is for her, that it is a way of exploring her world, of problem-solving, as a way for her to think. With each successive novel, she has learned to more quickly recognize the path in the story, or the theme of the story, that she wishes to pursue.

One broad idea that she has learned to cultivate is what she calls "village literature," meaning stories that are intended to help define roles that people play in their immediate society and that help revive elements of a people's past that might have been lost through change of location—due to migration or enslavement—or to the passing decades, when an entire society might transform due to technology or other influence.

Because of her interest in writing "village literature," Morrison takes care to use language that has the energy of African Americans—that is, the energy of the people from her village. She wants the writing to be evocative but not forced. The language of her novels "must not sweat." As such, she does not want her novels to be described as poetic because she fears her writing might sound forced, perhaps too precious.

Morrison also explains her choices of characters. She is fascinated with the eccentric, partly because their personalities can often reflect the struggles and exuberances of a black community where "the rejects from the respectable white world" live more openly in their own village.

BIBLIOGRAPHY

Le Clair, Thomas. "A Conversation with Toni Morrison: 'The Language Must Not Sweat.'" *New Republic*, March 21, 1981, 26–27.

The Nobel Lecture in Literature, 1993 (1994)

On the occasion of accepting her Nobel Prize in literature, Morrison recounts a folk tale of an old, wise woman—possibly a GRIOT in this version—who is blind and confronted by children who wish to test her wisdom. One child holds a bird in his hand, and asks her if the bird is dead or alive. She cannot answer the question because she is blind, but she does respond: "I don't know whether the bird you are holding is dead or alive, but what I do know

is that it is in your hands." Thus, the wise woman turns the children's question from one in which they are testing her to one in which she places the responsibility for the bird's life in their hands.

In applying this story, Morrison reads the bird as language, and the old woman is a wise writer, who says that the children must see themselves as responsible writers, and their use of language—whether abusing it, keeping it alive, destroying it, using it to nefarious ends, or using it to good ends—is in their hands. Indeed, it is in all of our hands. As an example of irresponsible writing, and speaking, Morrison refers to "statist language," which censors and prevents newer explorations, a language that is "concerned only with maintaining the free range of its own narcotic narcissism, its own exclusivity and dominance." Morrison is particularly concerned with language when it is used to oppress. Often, statist language is used to keep a racial, ethnic, or economic class in power, just as surely as it might be used to keep in power an individual dictator. Morrison then turns the usual interpretation of the story of Babel in the Bible from regretful loss of unity to a tale of possibility, maintaining that comprehension of new language is a new way to see the world.

Morrison implores her listeners to embrace her conclusion that the current generation of writers and orators has a responsibility to explore with language, to create for those younger and yet unborn a way to see the world that opens vistas, not closes them. She imagines someone young confronting those who now control the language: "[Is there] No song, no literature, no poem full of vitamins, no history connected to experience that you can pass along to help us start strong? You are an adult. The old one, the wise one." The young want to be told stories that have meaning, an assurance that helps them find their own meaning when they begin to explore.

"We die," says Morrison. "That may be the meaning of life. But we do language. That may be the measure of our lives."

BIBLIOGRAPHY

Morrison, Toni. *The Nobel Lecture in Literature, 1993.* New York: Alfred A. Knopf. 1994.

The sculpture *The Gift,* by Dale Slavin, is located at the Lorain County Community College and features a phrase from Toni Morrison's Nobel acceptance speech: "We die. That may be the meaning of our lives. But we do language. That may be the measure of our lives." *(Photograph by Carmen R. Gillespie)*

"On the Backs of Blacks" (1993)

Morrison opens her essay by referring to a scene in an Elia Kazan movie in which a Greek immigrant, seeking the American dream, chases off an African-American competitor—they both shine shoes—and thus the Greek immigrant becomes, as Morrison puts it, "an entitled white." She suggests that it is only because of the presence of blacks—who are forced onto the lowest rung of the racial hierarchy—that the European immigrants could achieve the privileged status of white in America.

This encounter between the Greek immigrant and the African-American shoe-shiner is reflected in much of popular culture. Immigrants may vie with Americans generally for jobs, but they are most acutely put in competition with African Americans. Says Morrison, "the move into mainstream America [for immigrants] always means buying into the notion of American blacks as the real aliens."

After accessing the role of politicians and the media in promoting the notion of blacks-as-aliens, Morrison turns to examples from fiction, and she points to Pap, from Mark Twain's *Huckleberry Finn* (1884). Upon learning a black man can vote in Ohio, Pap says, "I'll never vote ag'in." Sounding embittered, Pap needs to have white privilege for him to feel like a true American.

As African Americans break down social barriers that had once distinguished them from white society—as the "old stereotypes fail to connote"—then stubborn talk of racial distinctions "is forced to invent new, increasingly mindless ones." Negotiating these inventions of race—whether refusing or accepting them—continues to be "the organizing principle of becoming an American."

BIBLIOGRAPHY

Morrison, Toni. "On the Backs of Blacks." *Time*, December 2, 1993, 57.

"The Pain of Being Black" (interview of Morrison by Bonnie Angelo) (1989)

Angelo's interview took place shortly after Morrison won the Pulitzer Prize for *Beloved.* In the interview, Morrison talks of her novel and of the brutalities of the slave trade upon Africans in Africa, on the voyage, and in the United States.

Several key points emerge in the interview. Morrison feels that bigotry against black Americans has served two purposes: It has been a distraction against recognizing the unfair class differences in this country, and it has united as Americans all other immigrants, who can claim to be white and therefore part of the mainstream simply because they are not black. She says that even Jews, who have participated as leaders in the CIVIL RIGHTS MOVEMENT, have become, in the

eyes of many African Americans, part of the white establishment. She also claims that many of the problems of being black in America appear entrenched because the society does not feel compelled to address them, such as the high unemployment rate among black teenagers in the inner city.

One issue Morrison addresses at length is single-mother homes within African-American communities. She says that the young black mothers—those in their mid-teens—are no younger than perhaps were their grandmothers or great-grandmothers when they had children. Morrison says that we need to support these young women, not criticize them, and that society must see to it that they can eventually engage in whatever careers they would like and are capable of achieving. If this effort requires giving them financial support, then society should do so. Assisting these young women, Morrison asserts, would be no more shameful an act than the rich succeeding either through inheritance or the "old-boy" network.

Ultimately, says Morrison, the solution to the racial divide in this country is education, both to draw attention to institutionalized racism and to remove the belief that African-American citizens of this country are the other.

BIBLIOGRAPHY

Morrison, Toni. "The Pain of Being Black." Interview with Bonnie Angelo in *Time*, May 22, 1989, 120–22.

"Rediscovering Black History" (1974)

Morrison begins this essay by recounting the struggle of many black leaders and organizations to remove stereotypes from the public arena: the black jockey lawn statues, the *Amos 'n Andy* (1951) TV program, and the story book *Little Black Sambo* (1899). Morrison believes these are misguided efforts. Indeed, she sees the black jockeys as reminders of the fact that many of the great jockeys before 1900 were black, and that *Amos 'n Andy* was not only funny but also trailblazing in getting black characters on television, and that *Little Black Sambo* was "the only joyful, non-caricatured black children's story in print." Morrison proposes that instead of devoting energy to removing such images, it would be more productive to instead work to fill out the picture of what black culture and history has been.

This is the reason for Morrison editing *The Black Book* (1974), a collection of posters, letters, newspapers, advertisements, movie frames, and other artifacts and memorabilia depicting the way black life was actually lived in all its variety. The book was often a heart-breaking project for Morrison because the book contains not only black culture but also elements of the larger white racist culture. For instance, within the collection was a letter by a white professor to W. E. B. DuBois, asking "whether the Negro sheds tears"—written in 1905. She says the collection also includes moments of grace between the races. "The Jewish hospital that opened its doors to the black wounded during the Civil War Draft Riots is as significant as Sydenham Hospital, which closed its doors to W. C. Handy's wife (she died on its steps)."

Morrison says the information in *The Black Book* renewed her pride as it recounts the many accomplishments of black Americans, and she also felt great joy at seeing black history depicted not by limited images but by the full range of the black American experience.

BIBLIOGRAPHY

Morrison, Toni. "Rediscovering Black History," *New York Times Magazine*, August 11, 1974, 14–24.

black churches, where people sometimes shout their support of what an individual is saying. She also appreciates many black autobiographies in which an individual's personal life can also represent much about the black community. The novel, too, Morrison believes, can play an important role in expressing the needs and spirit of a community. Morrison strives, therefore, to write something in which the reader can participate. She leaves out material in her prose so that the reader can fill in with his or her own imagination, in a kind of church shout. Morrison then explains that a particular quality of black culture she tries to incorporate in her novels is "the presence of the ancestor," which is an extension of the community. She believes such a presence, or lack of it, is a legitimate way to evaluate the literature of black writers. Using as examples the writings of Richard Wright, JAMES BALDWIN, and her own novels—such as *Song of Solomon* and *Sula*—Morrison makes the point that a writer should not be in opposition to her ancestors or community. The writer is of that community. Says Morrison, "If anything I do, in the way of writing novels (or whatever I write) is not about the village or the community or about you, then it is not about anything."

BIBLIOGRAPHY

Morrison, Toni. "Rootedness: The Ancestor as Foundation." In *Black Women Writers (1950–1980): A Critical Evaluation*, edited by Mari Evans. Garden City: Anchor, 1984.

"Rootedness: The Ancestor as Foundation" (1984)

Morrison begins by writing about the conflict between the public and private life of a writer, artist, or, for that matter, any person. She quickly explains that the conflict is not a problem, just a reality that these two modes exist and that they must be recognized, sometimes reconciled. She feels it is a shame that the individual no longer seems to represent the group but only herself, and she appreciates any situation where an individual does represent a larger community, such as one that can be found in many

"A Slow Walk of Trees (as Grandmother Would Say) Hopeless (as Grandfather Would Say)" (1974)

In discussing the state of race relations in America, Morrison begins by referring to her grandparents— John and Ardelia Wofford—who had very different predictions on the future of justice for blacks in America. In his youth and for all his 85 years, John, who had been cheated of land and of his ability to make a living through his carpentry, had little or no hope that American society would become a just one for blacks, while Ardelia, more religious and more patient, believed that life was improving for African Americans, if very slowly—hence, the title of the Morrison article. Ardelia noted the seasonal march of trees creeping up a hillside and saw in their slow ascent a generational improvement in the lives of African Americans.

Morrison points out that modern society has provided support for both of her grandparents' views. She still sees racist crimes against African Americans, but she also sees more black judges, politicians, and professionals. This dual view of racism was also reflected in Morrison's parents. Her mother tried to be patient in the face of insults, but her father felt fury. This duality is reflected in their children: their son, who was "emotionally lobotomized by the reformatories and mental institutions" and their daughter—Morrison herself—a Princeton professor.

Popular culture seems to provide evidence of improvement—for example, the images of blacks in a TV show like *The Jeffersons* or a movie like *Buck and the Preacher*—but Morrison questions how deep-rooted the changes are. She acknowledges the dramatic improvements African Americans have made in all areas of society but also sees many continued economic gaps between blacks and whites. She notes, too, that when blacks move into a white neighborhood, the whites flee.

In the end, Morrison feels the struggle of African Americans for equality does seem to be moving forward, though very slowly, like "a slow walk of trees."

BIBLIOGRAPHY

Morrison, Toni. "A Slow Walk of a Tree (as Grandmother Would Say), Hopeless (as Grandfather Would Say)." *New York Times Magazine,* July 4, 1976, 104.

"Toni Morrison, the Art of Fiction" (1993)

This interview of Toni Morrison was conducted by Elissa Schappell, with additional material from Claudia Brodsky Lacour. Morrison talks about her work habits such as getting up early and trying to get a large block of hours without interruption. Writing, for her, is a lifestyle. When asked if she always knew she would be a writer, she responds that she knew she would always be a reader. When she began writing her novels, it was because she wanted to read something that she had not read before. Asked when it was clear to her that she was indeed a writer, she answers, by the time she was writing *Song of Solomon.* Before that, given the external definitional limitations placed on her identity, it was difficult for her to envision herself a writer.

Morrison also speaks of her liberation when she became able to see herself not only as a writer but also as an individual, free to make her own choices, her own mistakes, and own explorations. She especially feels liberated from needing to model herself according to the expectations of men. ". . . I will never again trust my life, my future, to the whims of men, in companies [such as Random House, where she was an editor] or out. Never again will their judgment have anything to do with what I think I can do. That was the wonderful liberation of being divorced and having children."

Morrison speaks of the depiction of race by both white and black writers. She sees no problem with white writers depicting black characters, though some, such as FAULKNER, do it better than others. In her writing, she tries not to depict a black character by simply using the adjective black, but by what she or he says or does. When asked about whether she bases her characters on real people, Morrison says she does not. Writing fiction for her is a great liberating experience. She balances the creation of her characters by partly following them, but never letting them take control of her creative process—that is, never letting them stray from the novel's focus.

Morrison continues to speak of her craft as a writer, but she makes it clear she writes as an African American. She explains that white writers are not asked to give up their cultural heritage, whether that heritage is French, Russian, Irish, and so forth. "It's very important to me that my work be African American; if it assimilates into a different or larger pool, so much the better."

BIBLIOGRAPHY

Morrison, Toni. "The Art of Fiction CXXXIV," *Paris Review* 128 (1993): 83–125.

"What the Black Woman Thinks about Women's Lib" (1971)

Morrison begins this essay by noting distinctions in how black women and white women were perceived by society during the days before the feminist movement. Specifically, she remembers restroom signs in the JIM CROW South and notes that one room was for "White Ladies" while the other was for "Colored Women." The sign painters may have intended a compliment to white women—calling them ladies—but Morrison saw in the word the unflattering implication of helplessness and softness. Black females, meanwhile, were called women, implying a certain toughness and independence—traits extolled by feminists. Feminists see themselves as "women." In this way, black women were in the vanguard of feminism.

Morrison does not, however, see a natural alliance of black women and white women in the feminist movement. White women continue to play an elitist role, and they do not seem to see racism as an equal problem in the nation. In spite of this lack of acknowledgment, black women struggle not just as women in a male-dominated society but also as blacks in a white-dominated society.

Also, Morrison says that black women often do not have respect for white women, who she sees as too often playing the role of the "lady." As a result, black women are often frustrated by black men who choose relationships with white women. According to Morrison, black women often see these white women as inferior to themselves because they do not always see themselves as equals to men. She believes that these relationships appeal to many black men who are frustrated in a racist society. Black women become equally frustrated when their very strengths—toughness and independence—work against them with their own men.

BIBLIOGRAPHY

Morrison, Toni. "What the Black Woman Thinks about Women's Lib." *New York Times Magazine,* August 22, 1971, 14–15, 63–66.

Cinematic, Theatrical, Musical, Poetic, and Dance Productions

Beloved (film) (1998)

Directed by Jonathan Demme, *Beloved* was the film version of Morrison's Pulitzer Prize–winning novel of the same name. Set in Ohio after the Civil War, the story is about an ex-slave haunted by the guilt of having killed her daughter years before during an escape attempt rather than see her returned to slavery. The film was a favorite project of OPRAH WINFREY, who optioned the film rights to the book. She also played the leading role of Sethe, the ex-slave who had killed her daughter. Other leading actors in the movie are Danny Glover, playing Paul D; Thandie Newton, playing Beloved; Kimberly Elise, playing Denver; and Beah Richards, playing Baby Suggs. The film was produced by Winfrey's Harpo Film Productions in conjunction with Touchstone Pictures and Buena Vista Pictures. The screenplay was written by Akosua Busia, Richard LaGravenese, and Adam Brooks, and the score was composed by Rachel Portman. Released in 1998, the film received generally disappointing reviews and ticket sales.

BIBLIOGRAPHY

Beloved (1998). Buena Vista Pictures, DVD/VHS, 1998.

The Bluest Eye (play) (2005)

Adapted for the stage by Lydia Diamond, *The Bluest Eye* is based on Morrison's novel of the same name. It focuses on the story's central character, Pecola Breedlove, an 11-year-old girl in 1940s Ohio who thinks she will get love from her family and friends if only she had blue eyes. Directed by Hallie Gordon, the theatrical production received good reviews when it debuted in 2005 at Chicago's Steppenwolf Arts Exchange. In 2006, the theatrical version of *The Bluest Eye* premiered in New York.

BIBLIOGRAPHY

"The Bluest Eye." Steppenwolf. Available online. URL: http://www.steppenwolf.org/news/detail.aspx?id=106. Accessed on May 5, 2006.

Young, Harvey. "The Bluest Eye," *Theatre Journal* 57 (October 2005): 525–527.

Degga (1995)

Degga, a collaboration with BILL T. JONES and Max Roach, is a multimedia work involving spoken text, dance, and music. Meaning "to understand" in the Wolof language of Senegal, *Degga* was commissioned by Lincoln Center for its "Serious Fun Festival." Morrison wrote the text, the choreographer Bill T. Jones provided the dance, and percussionist Max Roach composed and arranged the music. Morrison's text included various vignettes, including a man in hiding, two elderly lovers, scenes from the city, and the profile of a slave. *Degga* blends moments of solo material by the three artists—readings, dance, drumming—with JAZZ-like interplay, or call-and-response, of their different media.

Dreaming Emmett (1986)

Dreaming Emmett is Toni Morrison's only play to date and is based on the murder of EMMETT TILL, a black 14-year-old killed in 1955 by Mississippi racists who accused him of whistling at a white woman. Till was beaten to death and his mutilated body was dumped in a river. The white men who allegedly killed him were eventually acquitted by an all-white jury. They confessed to the murder after their acquittal. Commissioned by the New York State Writers Institute at the State University of New York, Albany, *Dreaming Emmett* premiered in 1986 in Albany's Market Theater. The play's performance commemorated the first celebration of MARTIN LUTHER KING'S birthday as a national holiday.

The play is so far unpublished, and, indeed, no printed versions of *Dreaming Emmett* may exist because Morrison is reported to have destroyed all copies.

BIBLIOGRAPHY

Croyden, Margaret. "Morrison Tries Her Hand at Playwriting." *New York Times,* December 29, 1985.

URL:http://topics.nytimes.com/top/reference/timestopics/people/m/toni_morrison/index.html?offset=80&. Accessed on September 18, 2006.

Whitfield, Stephen J. "The Lynching of Emmett Till: A Documentary Narrative," *Southern Cultures* 9 (Winter 2003): 99–103.

Four Songs after poems by Toni Morrison, for Soprano, Cello and Piano (lyrics by Toni Morrison, music by ANDRE PREVIN) (1994)

Four Songs after Poems by Toni Morrison, for Soprano, Cello and Piano was composed by Andre Previn and premiered in concert in 1994. The songs were performed by Sylvia NcNair at Alice Tully Hall in New York. A review of the performance by Bernard Holland described the songs as a JAZZ-based conversation between voice and flute. The songs were recorded by Sylvia McNair on Previn's *From Ordinary Things*. They also appear on another recording entitled *Music From Lucerne* (2000).

BIBLIOGRAPHY

From Ordinary Things. (1997). Sony, CD, 1997.

Holland, Bernard. "Taking Music Beyond the Voice." *New York Times,* November 29, 1994. Available online. URL:http://query.nytimes.com/gst/fullpage.html?res=9E02EED71330F93AA15752C1A96295 8260). Accessed on September 9, 2006.

Music From Lucerne. (2000). Albany, CD, 2000.

Honey and Rue, A Song Cycle (lyrics by Toni Morrison, music by Andre Previn) (1995)

Honey and Rue is an art-song cycle with lyrics written by Toni Morrison and set to music by ANDRE PREVIN. Moved by Morrison's *The Bluest Eye*, the soprano

KATHLEEN BATTLE asked Morrison and Previn if they would collaborate on a song cycle for her, and they agreed. Commissioned by Carnegie Hall, the work premiered in 1992, with Battle singing.

The lyrics were the first that Morrison had written for an original score. They do not tell a particular story, she says, but use "images of yearning, satisfaction, resolution" [CD liner notes]. They are inspired by the struggles and searchings in the lives of women and of African Americans generally.

The cycle consists of six songs: "First I'll Try Love," a wistful reflection on something seemingly unattainable. "Whose House Is This?" is a depiction of alienation inspired by the African-American experience in American history. "The Town Is Lit" is a study in contrast between suburban comfort and city excitement. "Do You Know Him?" is an unaccompanied song addressing the identity of God. "I Am Not Seaworthy" is a dark reflection on drowning, inspired by the Middle Passage, and "Take My Mother Home" is a wish for self-sacrifice in the face of slavery.

Previn's music is scored for small orchestra and uses a free tonality that shifts in mood, according to Morrison's words, from dark and moody to light to playful. The music often uses the tonalities and rhythms of JAZZ, BLUES, and SPIRITUALS.

BIBLIOGRAPHY

Honey and Rue (1992). Deutsche Grammophon, CD, 1995.

Margaret Garner (lyrics by Toni Morrison, music by Richard Danielpour) (2005)

The opera *Margaret Garner* is based on Morrison's novel *Beloved*, which itself is based on the true events in the life of the opera's title character, a Kentucky slave in the 1850s who escaped to Ohio but, upon her recapture, killed her children rather than see them returned to slavery. Morrison wrote the opera's libretto, and RICHARD DANIELPOUR composed the music. The two-act opera has nearly

100 cast members, including two choruses: one for the slaves and one for the slave owners. Co-commissioned by the Michigan Opera Theatre, the CINCINNATI Opera, and the Opera Company of Philadelphia, *Margaret Garner* debuted on May 7, 2005, in Detroit, with mezzo-soprano Denyce Graves singing the lead role.

SYNOPSIS

Act 1

The story opens in 1856 at a property auction in Kentucky. Edward Gaines, standing among the bidders, is from the area, but he has been away for 20 years. When his family plantation, Maplewood, is brought onto the block, he interrupts the bidding and says that the plantation cannot be sold because it belonged to his dead brother. The other people have a hard time remembering him, but they accept his claim, so he takes possession of Maplewood. While signing the ownership papers, Gaines hears the singing of one of Maplewood's slaves, MARGARET GARNER. He recalls his childhood and grows wistful.

The Modern Medea, an 1867 oil on canvas painting by Kentucky artist Thomas Satterswhite Noble was inspired by the story of Margaret Garner's 1856 attempted murder of her children rather than have them returned to slavery. The painting is owned by Procter and Gamble Company and is on permanent display in the National Underground Railroad Freedom Center in Cincinnati, Ohio. *(Photograph by Carmen R. Gillespie)*

As the slaves of Maplewood return from the fields, Cilla—the mother-in-law of Margaret Garner—joins her son and daughter-in-law for supper. Their eating is interrupted when Maplewood's foreman, Casey, arrives with terrible news. Robert, Margaret's husband, has been sold to another plantation. Margaret is to remain at Maplewood.

Gaines hosts a marriage reception for his daughter, Caroline. Gaines and his new son-in-law, George, argue about the nature of love. Later, Caroline asks Margaret, now a servant in the Gaines house, for her views on love. The guests are horrified that Caroline should solicit a slave's opinion, and they leave. Gaines is also horrified and scolds Caroline. Later, he watches Margaret clean the parlor, and he forces himself on her.

Act 2

Margaret goes to Cilla's cabin to meet her husband, Robert, who is to visit from the plantation where he now lives. Robert is not there, but Margaret finds her mother-in-law packing and her own children missing. Cilla explains that Robert is planning an escape to Ohio. When he arrives, Robert confirms the news. This thrills Margaret, but she is upset that Cilla will not join them. Casey storms into the cabin, and this leads to a fight between him and Robert. It ends with Robert killing Casey. Robert and Margaret are now under even more pressure to escape. They flee and arrive at a shelter in Ohio. They are close to freedom, but Gaines catches up and captures Robert. Margaret fights back and witnesses Robert getting lynched. Unwilling to see her children returned to slavery, she murders them.

Margaret is returned to Kentucky, where she stands trial for the theft and destruction of another's property—that is, her own children. Caroline says that Margaret should not be charged with theft but with murder. She says the children are not property. They are human beings. The judges disagree. They sentence Margaret to be hanged for theft. Caroline begs her father to seek clemency for Margaret, and Gaines must choose between his daughter's respect and the morality of the times.

The next morning, Margaret ascends the scaffold. Gaines runs in with a legal document. The judges have granted Margaret clemency. She is on the gallows, with the rope around her neck, Margaret expresses her refusal to live as a slave. She gives herself her own freedom by hanging herself. The onlookers, both black and white, pray for their own repentance and for Margaret's soul.

BIBLIOGRAPHY

Loren Gary. "Breaking with Convention." Center for Public Leadership. Harvard University. Available online. URL: http://www.ksg.harvard.edu/leadership/compass/index.php?itemid=1006. Accessed on November 2, 2006.

"Margaret Garner: A New American Opera." Available online. URL: http://www.margaretgarner.org/mission.html. Accessed on June 5, 2006.

New Orleans: The Storyville Musical (book written by Toni Morrison, Donald McKayle, and Dorothea Freitag, music by Sidney Bechet and Jelly Roll Morton) (1984)

New Orleans takes place in 1917 in the city's Storyville district, which is credited for being the birthplace of JAZZ. Morrison wrote the lyrics, and co-wrote the book with Donald McKayle and Dorothea Freitag. Donald McKayle also directed and choreographed the musical. The score consists of music of the era, including works by Jelly Roll Morton, Scott Joplin, and Sidney Bechet. Additional music was composed by Dorothea Freitag. Geoffrey Holder designed the costumes. The musical was done as a six-week workshop at the Public Theater in New York. It also was a New York Festival script.

Poetry

Although Morrison is primarily a fiction writer and has claimed that she is not a poet, she has writ-

ten and published poetry professionally. Some of her poetry has proved the inspiration for classical composers ANDRE PREVIN, RICHARD DANIELPOUR, and Judith Weir who have used her words as the foundation for several of their musical creations. In the spring 2002 edition of the poetry journal *Ploughshares*, Morrison published four poems: "I Am Not Seaworthy," "The Lacemaker," "The Perfect Ease of Grain," and "The Town Is Lit." Morrison's poem "black crazies" appeared in *MS.* magazine in 2002. She also published a small book of poetry for charitable causes entitled *Five Poems* in the International Institute of Modern Letters Rainmaker Editions Series.

BIBLIOGRAPHY

Morrison, Toni. "black crazies." Ms. *Magazine*, Summer 2002, 95.

———. *Five Poems*. Rainmaker Editions. International Institute of Modern Letters. Berkeley, Calif.: Peter Koch Press, 2002.

———. "I Am Not Seaworthy," *Ploughshares* (Spring 2000): 105.

———. "The Lacemaker," *Ploughshares* (Spring 2000): 106.

———. "The Perfect Ease of Grain," *Ploughshares* (Spring 2000): 107.

———. "The Town Is Lit," *Ploughshares* (Spring 2000): 108.

Spirits in the Well (lyrics by Toni Morrison, music by Richard Danielpour) (1997)

Spirits in the Well is another collaboration between Toni Morrison and Richard Danielpour. After the successful performance of the piece *Sweet Talk: Four Songs on Text*, Danielpour asked Morrison to send him additional material. While Danielpour was attending the artists' retreat, Yaddo, he composed the music for *Spirits in the Well*.

BIBLIOGRAPHY

Richard Danielpour. *Spirits in the Well.* G. Schirmer Inc. Available online. URL: http://www.schirmer.com/default.aspx?TabId=2420&State_2874=2&workId_2874=27182. Accessed on September 17, 2006.

Sweet Talk: Four Songs on Text (lyrics by Toni Morrison, music by Richard Danielpour) (1996)

Sweet Talk: Four Songs on Text is the result of a collaboration between Morrison and the composer RICHARD DANIELPOUR in a Princeton University workshop series called the PRINCETON ATELIER. Created by Morrison and Robert Goheen, the workshop is meant to bring together creators from different fields, both within and outside the university's faculty, to work with each other and Princeton students.

Morrison herself worked with Danielpour, and the result was *Sweet Talk: Four Songs on Text,* which premiered at Carnegie Hall in 1997, with JESSYE NORMAN singing. Accompanied by piano, cello, and bass, the songs include "'I Am Not Prey," about a woman feeling safe in the country, "'Perfect Ease," which deals with the difference between bounty and excess, "Bliss," which explores the expressions of happiness, and "Faith," which explores immortality.

As of this printing, no recording has been made of *Sweet Talk.*

BIBLIOGRAPHY

Richard Danielpour. *Sweet Talk: Four Songs on Text.* G. Schirmer Inc. Available online. URL: http://www.schirmer.com/default.aspx?TabId=2420&State_2874=2&workId_2874=27185. Accessed on September 17, 2006.

This Thread (lyrics by Toni Morrison, composed by J. Mark Scearce)

After reading Toni Morrison's "The Dead of September 11," composer J. Mark Scearce used the piece as the foundation for his orchestral work entitled "This Thread." Scearce's work premiered on September 10 and 11, 2004, in Nashville, Tennessee.

BIBLIOGRAPHY

Benny Benton. North Carolina State University News Release. "NC State Composer Sets Music to Nobel-Laureate's 9/11 Text." Available online. URL: http://www.ncsu.edu/news/press_releases/04_09/244.htm. Accessed on September 21, 2006.

woman.life.song (lyrics by Toni Morrison, composed by Judith Weir) (2000)

woman.life.song was the brain child of Judith Aron, the former executive director of Carnegie Hall, who envisioned a song cycle about the life of a woman. Maya Angelou, Clarissa Pinkola Estes, and Toni Morrison agreed to write the lyrics and composer Judith Weir wrote the music for what became *woman.life.song,* a piece that traces the emotional and experiential nuances of a woman's lifespan. *woman.life.song* premiered on March 22, 2000, at Carnegie Hall with JESSYE NORMAN singing.

BIBLIOGRAPHY

"Judith Weir: woman.life.song." Chester Novello. Available on line. URL: http://www.chesternovello.com/Default.aspx?TabId=2432&State_3041=2&workId_3041=2764. Accessed on September 22, 2006.

Part III

Related People, Places, and Topics

abolition Activism in the United States around the issue of slavery was complex and took many different forms. Groups that believed in abolition often were in philosophical conflict and sometimes had divergent motivations for wanting to bring about the end of legalized slavery. Of course, the most active opponents of slavery were those individuals who were enslaved. Resistance to slavery took many forms, including suicide, work slow-down or stoppage, homicide, escape, sabotage, and rebellion and revolt. The most well-known slave rebellions in the American colonies and the United States are the New York City Slave Rebellion in 1712, the Stono Rebellion in 1739, Gabriele Prosser's Rebellion in 1800, Denmark Vesey's Uprising in 1822, and Nat Turner's Revolt in 1831.

The earliest religious group to oppose slavery in the American colonies was the Quakers. Also called the SOCIETY OF FRIENDS, this group was active in protesting slavery and in aiding and abetting those who attempted to escape from slavery. Another important early organization that worked toward the emancipation of slaves was the African Colonization Society, which was formed in 1816. This group did not believe that blacks were capable of becoming equal citizens in the country and, therefore, proposed that enslaved blacks be emancipated and then "returned" to Africa.

In 1833, the American Anti-Slavery Society was formed. The group began a campaign of educating the public about the evils of slavery. The group included African Americans who had escaped from slavery in its lectures and persuaded over 30,000 people to join its ranks. Well-known members of the American Anti-Slavery Society include William Lloyd Garrison, Frederick Douglass, Lydia Marie Childs, and Elizabeth Cady Stanton. Significantly, the American Anti-Slavery Society originally excluded women from its membership, but once women were allowed to participate in 1840, the organization became a major training ground for many of the women who eventually would become the leaders of the fight for women's suffrage.

No mention of abolition would be complete without discussion of John Brown. Brown established a base of activists, including several members of his own family, in Virginia. He then began to plan a raid on the federal arsenal at Harpers Ferry with the objective of using the arms to carry out an armed rebellion and instigate a slave revolt. Brown's 1859 raid was unsuccessful, but his legacy and subsequent martyrdom inspired continued abolition activism until the Civil War and the EMANCIPATION PROCLAMATION brought an official end to legalized slavery in the United States.

The Bodwins in *Beloved* (1987) are abolitionists as are some of the individuals and groups who rally around Sethe in the wake of the death of her baby girl.

BIBLIOGRAPHY

Adams, Alice Dana. *The Neglected Period of Anti-Slavery in America, 1808–1832.* Gloucester, Mass.: Peter Smith, 1964.

Aptheker, Herbert. *Abolitionism: A Revolutionary Movement.* Boston: Twayne, 1989.

———. *American Negro Slave Revolts.* New York: International Publishers, 1974.

Azevedo, Celia Maria Marinho de. *Abolitionism in the United States and Brazil: A Comparative Perspective.* New York: Garland, 1995.

Blackett, R. J. M. *Building an Anti-Slavery Wall: Black Americans in the Atlantic Abolitionist Movement, 1830–1860.* Baton Rouge: Louisiana State University Press, 1983.

Boyer, Richard O. *The Legend of John Brown: A Biography and a History.* New York: Knopf, 1973.

Buckmaster, Henrietta. *Let My People Go: The Story of the Underground Railroad and the Growth of the Abolition Movement.* Columbia: University of South Carolina Press, 1992.

Cheek, William F. *Black Resistance Before the Civil War.* Beverly Hills, Calif.: Glencoe Press, 1970.

Dillon, Merton. *The Abolitionists: Growth of a Dissenting Minority.* New York: Norton, 1974.

Fellman, Michael, and Lewis Perry, eds. *Antislavery Reconsidered: New Perspectives on the Abolitionists.* Baton Rouge: Louisiana State University Press, 1979.

Frey, Sylvia R. *Water from the Rock: Black Resistance in a Revolutionary Age.* Princeton, N.J.: Princeton University Press, 1991.

McPherson, James M. *The Abolitionist Legacy: From Reconstruction to the NAACP.* Princeton, N.J.: Princeton University Press, 1975.

Oates, Stephen B. *To Purge This Land with Blood: A Biography of John Brown.* Amherst: University of Massachusetts Press, 1970.

Perry, Lewis. *Radical Abolitionism: Anarchy and the Government of God in Antislavery Thought.* Knoxville: University of Tennessee Press, 1995.

Quarles, Benjamin. *Black Abolitionists.* New York: Oxford University Press, 1969.

Renehan, Edward J., Jr. *The Secret Six: The True Tale of the Men Who Conspired with John Brown.* New York: Crown, 1995.

Ripley, C. Peter. *Witness for Freedom: African American Voices on Race, Slavery, and Emancipation.* Chapel Hill: University of North Carolina Press, 1993.

Sanchez-Eppler, Karen. *Touching Liberty: Abolition, Feminism, and the Politics of the Body.* Berkeley: University of California Press, 1993.

Staudenraus, P. J. *The African Colonization Movement 1816–1865.* New York: Columbia University Press, 1961.

Stauffer, John. *The Black Hearts of Men: Radical Abolitionists and the Transformation of Race.* Cambridge, Mass.: Harvard University Press, 2002.

Sterling, Dorothy, ed. *Turning the World Upside Down: The Anti-Slavery Convention of American Women, Held in New York City, May 9–12, 1837.* New York: Feminist Press at City University of New York, 1987.

Stewart, James Brewer. *Holy Warriors: The Abolitionists and American Slavery.* 1976. 2d ed. New York: Hill and Wang, 1997.

———. *Joshua R. Giddings and the Tactics of Radical Politics.* Cleveland: Case Western Reserve University Press, 1970.

Yee, Shirley J. *Black Women Abolitionists: A Study in Activism, 1828–1860.* Knoxville: University of Tennessee Press, 1992.

Yellin, Jean Fagan, and John C. Van Horne. *The Abolitionist Sisterhood: Women's Political Culture in Antebellum America.* Ithaca, N.Y.: Cornell University Press, 1994.

Young, R. J. *Antebellum Black Activists: Race, Gender, and Self.* New York: Garland Publishers, 1996.

Afra American literary renaissance   The proliferation of writings by African-American women during the 1970s and 1980s—a literary profusion literary critic Joanne Braxton named the Afra American renaissance—was in part catalyzed by the shortcomings and sexisms of the Black Power movement, the public and political demonization of black women, and the rise of the black feminist movement at the end of the 1960s. Generally speaking, the writings of the renaissance urge reconsideration and rearticulation of the particular experiences of African-American women. Many of the authors of the Afra American renaissance, Alice Walker, TONI CADE BAMBARA, and Toni Morrison among others, challenge dominant constructions of black womanhood through their rewriting and recasting of stereotypes and flat portrayals of African-American women in literature.

By proposing and constructing a more well-rounded black and female image, these texts challenge the fundamentally patriarchal and racist ideologies of American society, undermine pervasive and persistent negative stereotypes of black women, and reflect the currency and influence of black feminist thinking.

BIBLIOGRAPHY

Braxton, Joanne, and Andree Nicola-McLaughlin. *Wild Women in the Whirlwind: Afra-American Culture and the Contemporary Literary Renaissance.* New Jersey: Rutgers University Press, 1990.

African-American club women   From the earliest period of American history, African-American women have been actively involved in the struggle for social, educational, and political equality and justice. The organized effort of groups of African-American women to achieve these aims is known as the African-American club women's movement.

Early black women's organizations focused on the strength of collectivity and advocated self-help. Two such organizations were the Colored Female Religious and Moral Society of Salem, Massachusetts, and the Daughters of Africa, in Philadelphia. Organized African-American women's activism gained momentum as black women participated in the struggle to end slavery. Activist organizers were women like SOJOURNER TRUTH who, while working within organizations that were predominantly white, advocated specifically for the particular concerns of African-American women. Out of the organizational lessons and premises of the ABOLITIONist movement emerged activism around women's rights. During the pivotal Women's Rights Conference held in Akron, Ohio, in 1851, Truth, delivering her well-known "Ain't I a Woman" speech, pointed out that the concerns of African-American women were not included in the general concerns articulated by the group.

African-American and white women who had discovered a common goal with the abolition of slavery began to part company over the issue of suffrage. Often white women activists were willing to argue for their right to obtain the vote rather than arguing for universal emancipation that would include black men and women. This split was the genesis of many African-American women's organizations that had as their main agenda the problems and concerns of black women.

For example, in the 1870s African-American women organized in struggle to end the practice of lynching, which had reached an appalling frequency. The efforts of Ida B. Wells Barnet were an important catalyst for the formation of African-American women's organizations that were specifically focused on the issue of lynching, as well as groups with other goals and aims.

Perhaps the most prominent of these organizations was the National Association of Colored Women, which was a coalition of over 100 clubs previously established by African-American women. The National Association of Colored Women began in 1896. The group was a consolidation of two older national groups, the Colored Women's League and the National Federation of African American Women. Some of the most prominent women in the ensuing Black Women's Club Movement were Anna Julia Cooper, Josephine St. Pierre Ruffin, Mary Church Terrell, and Mary McCloud Bethune.

At the turn of the century and beyond, the African-American club women's movement organized around issues of social justice and economic uplift. In the 1950s and '60s African-American women's organizations were centrally involved in the work of the CIVIL RIGHTS MOVEMENT. Experiences of exclusion and sexism during the fight for racial justice led to the emergence of a black woman's feminist movement. African-American women, academics and writers in particular, voiced concerns about their experiences of sexism in black organizations and racism in white organizations. The formation of African-American feminist organizations was a response. One of the most significant of these organizations was the National Black Feminist Organization, which began in New York in 1973. Another important group was the Boston-based Combahee River Collective, which began in Boston as a branch of the National Black Feminist Organization.

Toni Morrison's mother, Ramah Wofford, was involved in many clubs in her community in LORAIN, OHIO. Alice Manfred in *Jazz* (1993) can be considered a fictional version of an African-American club woman.

BIBLIOGRAPHY

Alexander, Amy. *Fifty Black Women Who Changed America.* Secaucus, N.J.: Carol Publishing Group. 1998.

Allen, Zita. *Black Women Leaders of the Civil Rights Movement.* Danbury, Conn.: Watts, 1996.

Anderson, Karen. *Changing Woman: A History of Racial Ethnic Women in Modern America.* New York: Oxford University Press, 1996.

Barnett, Bernice M. *Sisters in Struggle.* New York: Routledge, 1999.

Bobo, Jacqueline. *Black Women as Cultural Leaders.* New York: Columbia University Press, 1995.

Collins, Patricia H. *Fighting Words: Black Women and the Search for Justice.* Minneapolis: University of Minnesota Press, 1998.

Forbes, Ella. *African American Women during the Civil War.* New York: Garland Press, 1998.

Gordon, Ann D., et al. *African American Women and the Vote, 1837–1965.* Amherst: University of Massachusetts Press, 1997.

Hemmons, Willa M. *Black Women in the New World Order: Social Justice and the African American Female.* Westport, Conn.: Greenwood Press, 1996.

Hendricks, Wanda. *Gender, Race and Politics in the Midwest: Black Club Women in Illinois.* Bloomington: Indiana University Press, 1998.

Hine, Darlene Clark, and Kathleen Thompson. *A Shining Thread of Hope: The History of Black Women in America.* Des Plaines, Ill.: Broadway Books, 1998.

Hunter, Tera. *To Joy My Freedom: Southern Black Women's Lives and Labors after the Civil War.* Cambridge, Mass.: Harvard University Press, 1997.

Lemke-Santangelo, Gretchen. *Abiding Courage: African American Migrant Women and the East Bay Community.* Chapel Hill: University of North Carolina Press, 1996.

Pitre, Merline. *In Struggle against Jim Crow: Lulu B. White and the NAACP, 1900–1957.* College Station: Texas A and M University Press, 1999.

White, Deborah Gray. *Too Heavy a Load: Black Women in Defense of Themselves, 1894–1994.* New York: Norton, 1998.

African-American quilting   Scholarship on African-American quilting has blossomed since the 1980s. African-American quilts are understood as functional, artistic, and even textual. Theories about the aesthetics, traditions, and practices of African-American quilting are widely disputed and are the subject of scholarly controversy. Some scholars maintain that traditional African quilting and textile production was a great influence upon early African-American quilts. Although men were the major textile producers in West Africa, while enslaved, African-American women were the primary producers of quilts. Some scholars have noted patterns in early African-American quilts that suggest possible survivals from the Middle Passage and subsequent enslavement. There are observable patterns in these quilts that may connect them to some African aesthetic traditions. Some of those traditions include pattern improvisation, bright colors, asymmetrical design, and strip banding.

Of course, African-American quilters incorporated European styles and designs into their quilts; so African-American quilting, like so many other forms of African American art, is a synthesis of many different cultures and traditions. For that reason, it is difficult to define an African-American quilting tradition. Some scholars have posited that enslaved African Americans used quilts as texts, encoding in their various patterns messages, histories, and even maps of potential escape routes that they did not want their masters to be able to read or to understand. Others feel that such a thesis is unlikely.

Contemporarily, African Americans are actively involved in quilting as a hobby and as an art form. Contemporary African-American quilters produce traditional and experimental works using a variety of patterns, materials, and designs.

When Baby Suggs takes to her bed in *Beloved* (1987), she contemplates the squares of color in her quilt. Sethe's "bedding" dress in the same novel is quilted together. Pilate in *Song of Solomon* (1977) wears a quilt instead of a winter coat. True Belle from *Jazz* (1992) is also a quilter.

BIBLIOGRAPHY

Barry, A. "Quilting Has African Roots, a New Exhibition Suggests." *New York Times,* November 16, 1989, B8.

Benberry, Cuesta. "African American Quilts: Paradigms of Black Diversity," *The International Review
of African American Art* 12 (1995): 30–37.

———. *Always There: The African American Presence in American Quilts*. Louisville: Kentucky Quilt
Project, 1992.

Callahan, Nancy. *The Freedom Quilting Bee*. Tuscaloosa: University of Alabama Press, 1987.

Ferris, William. *Afro-American Folk Art and Crafts*.
Jackson: University Press of Mississippi, 1983.

Fry, G.-M. *Stitched from the Soul: Slave Quilts from the
Ante-Bellum South*. New York: Dutton Books and
The Museum of American Folk Art, 1990.

Grudin, Eva Ungar. *Stitching Memories: African American Story Quilts*. Williamstown, Mass.: Williams
College Museum of Art, 1989.

Harrison, C., and Paul Wood, eds. *Art in Theory 1900–
1990: An Anthology of Changing Ideas*. Oxford:
Blackwell Publishers, 1995.

Jeffries, R. "African Retentions in African American
Quilts and Artifacts," *International Review of African American Art* 11 (1994): 28–37.

Koplos, J. "Stitching Memories: African American
Story Quilts, Who'd a Thought It: Improvisation
in African American Quiltmaking," *Crafts, London
Crafts Council* 103 (1990): 49.

Leon, Eli. *Models in the Mind: African Prototypes in
American Patchwork*. Winston-Salem, N.C.: Winston-Salem State University, 1992.

———. *Who'd a Thought It: Improvisation in African
American Quiltmaking*. San Francisco: San Francisco Craft and Folk Art Museum, 1987.

Lyles, C. Y. "Redefining Cultural Roots: Diversity in
African American Quilts," *Surface Design Journal*
20 (Spring 1996): 13–14.

Picton, John, and John Mack. *African Textiles*. New
York: Harper and Row, 1989.

Tobin, Jacqueline L., and Raymond G. Dobard, Ph.D.
*Hidden in Plain View A Secret Story of Quilts and the
Underground Railroad*. New York: Anchor Books,
2000.

Wahlman, M. S. "Religious Symbolism in African-
American Quilts," *The Clarion* (Summer 1989):
36–44.

Watanabe, Y. "Afro-American Quilts," *Patchwork Quilt
Tsushin* 25 (July 1988): 12–17.

all-black towns Although most all-black towns
were established in the wake of the Civil War and
the mass exodus of freed African Americans from
the South, there were instances of African Americans forming towns that were inhabited primarily
by other African Americans as early as the 1830s.
There were hundreds of these towns, scattered
across the entire United States, including Alaska.
Most all-black towns, however, were formed in
the South, primarily in what is now the state of
Oklahoma. At the time, the area was called the
Indian Territory and was, according to treaty, in
the possession of various Native Americans. Often
the founders of these towns would obtain permission and land from Native Americans. Frequently
there were relationships between Native American enclaves and all-black towns, with intermarriage not uncommon. Although a few of them, like
Eatonville, Florida, home of author Zora Neale
Hurston, survive into the contemporary period,
most of these locales fell on hard times and the
towns disappeared.

Some of the most prominent of these towns were
Nicodemus in Kansas; Boley, Brooksville, Clearview,
Grayson, Langston, Lima, Redbird, Rentiesville,
Summit, Taft, Tatums, Tullahassee, and Vernon in
Oklahoma; as well as towns in other states such
as Dempsey, Alaska, and Parting Ways in Massachusetts, and Coit Mountain in New Hampshire.
The reasons for the creation of these towns varied.
Some of the towns were formed by emancipated
African Americans who sought the economic and
social solidarity that could be achieved by pool-
ing resources, skills, and strengths. Others did not
believe that they would be accepted into American
society and felt that their best chance for survival
existed by cultivating autonomy and self-sufficiency. The conditions freed African Americans
faced in the South were often perilous and life-
threatening. For some, all-black towns may have
represented sanctuary and a chance to escape pervasive racism.

The establishment of these all-black towns was
encouraged and supported by various individuals
who were motivated by combinations of altruism
and avarice. Men like Benjamin "Pap" Singleton
advertised for African Americans who had been

enslaved to leave the South and to relocate to Kansas and form towns there. Those who journeyed to Kansas were often referred to as EXODUSTERS, so called from Exodus, the Bible chapter that tells the story of the Hebrew exodus from Egypt.

Of the hundreds of all-black towns that were formed in the United States, very few remain. The all-black towns that did not survive met their demise as a result of many different factors, including changes brought about by JIM CROW laws, internecine struggles, and deliberate, sometimes violent destruction by whites eager to have the land. Later factors such as integration and the loss of economic viability impeded the sustainability of many of these towns. Many of the towns that survive are on the brink of extinction, with declining populations that are often in remote locations with few economic opportunities.

Son in *Tar Baby* (1981) is from the all-black town of Eloe. Toni Morrison's novel *Paradise* (1998) takes place in the all-black towns of Haven and Ruby.

BIBLIOGRAPHY

Crockett, Norman. *The Black Towns.* Lawrence: The Regents Press of Kansas, 1979.

Hamilton, Kenneth M. *Black Towns and Profit: Promotion and Development in the Trans-Appalachian West, 1877–1915.* Urbana: University of Illinois Press, 1991.

Johnson, Hannibal B. *Acres of Aspiration: The All Black Towns in Oklahoma.* Austin: Eakin Press, 2002.

Katz, W. *The Black West: A Documentary and Pictorial History of the African American Role in the Westward Expansion of the United States.* New York: Simon and Schuster, 1996.

Knight, T. *Sunset on Utopian Dreams: An Experiment of Black Separatism on the American Frontier.* Washington, D.C.: University Press of America, 1977.

Shepard, Bruce. "North to the Promised Land: Black Migration to the Canadian Plains," *Chronicles of Oklahoma* 66 (Fall 1988).

Tolson, A. *The Black Oklahomans: A History, 1541–1972.* New Orleans: Edwards Printing Company, 1974.

Wickett, M. *Contested Territory: Whites, Native Americans, and African Americans in Oklahoma, 1865–1907.* Baton Rouge: Louisiana State University Press, 2000.

A.M.E. (African Methodist Episcopal Church)

The African Methodist Episcopal Church is a branch of the American Methodist Church. The American Methodist Church emerged from the Methodist movement in England. In 1739, John Wesley began Methodism as a way of improving on Anglicanism. The movement gained strength and eventually became its own denomination. The founders of the Methodist Church realized that the future of the church was in the Americas and so they began their expansion into the colonies. Methodists rapidly spread the new denomination across the country and Methodism began to develop various branches. One of the main factions was the American Methodist Episcopal Church.

Although the American Methodist Church accepted African Americans as members and condemned slavery as an institution, African-American church members were forced to worship in segregation. In 1787, this segregation became unacceptable to a group of African Americans who were members of the St. George's Methodist Episcopal Church in Philadelphia, Pennsylvania. Refusing to endure the insult of segregated worship, a group of African Americans left the church and began the Free African Society. Eventually, the Free African Society splintered into two entities, the Episcopalians and the Methodist. In 1816, from the second group, the Methodists, emerged the African Methodist Episcopal Church under the leadership of Richard Allen.

The newly established denomination grew rapidly as churches were established in Philadelphia, New York, Boston, Pittsburgh, Baltimore, Washington, D.C., CINCINNATI, Chicago, and Detroit— major urban areas with significant populations of free African Americans. With the inception of the Civil War, the church found a new outlet for the activism that had been such a pivotal element in its foundation. As the Confederacy began to collapse, African Methodist Episcopal ministers worked within the slave states to convert former slaves. As a result, church membership grew exponentially and by 1880 had reached a new high of approximately 400,000 members. Due largely to the activities of one of its prominent bishops, Henry McNeal Turner, the African Methodist Episcopal Church gained significant converts in Africa, particularly in the countries of Sierra Leone, Liberia, and South Africa. In the 21st century the African Methodist Episcopal Church continues to be a vibrant African-American institution with an international membership of more than two million.

When Toni Morrison was a girl, the Woffords belonged to the Greater St. Matthews African Methodist Episcopal Church (A.M.E.) in LORAIN, OHIO. There are several A.M.E. ministers in Morrison's canon, including Reverend Cooper in *Song of Solomon* (1977) and Reverend Senior Pulliam in *Paradise* (1998). In *Tar Baby* (1981), Son also remembers the A.M.E. church in Eloe.

BIBLIOGRAPHY

Allen, Richard. *The Life Experience and Gospel Labors of the Rt. Rev. Richard Allen.* Nashville: Abingdon Press, 1960.

Broadway, Bill. "A Search for Meaning at AME Convocation," *Washington Post,* August 22, 1998, D7.

George, Carol V. R. *Segregated Sabbaths: Richard Allen and the Rise of Independent Black Churches, 1760–1840,* Oxford: Oxford University Press, 1973.

Klots, Steve. *Richard Allen.* New York: Chelsea House Publishers, 1991.

Melton, J. Gordon. "African Methodist Episcopal Church." *Encyclopedia of American Religions,* 5th ed. Detroit: Gale, 1996.

Atelier See PRINCETON ATELIER

Atwood, Margaret (1939–) Since the publication of her first novel, *The Edible Woman,* in 1969, Margaret Atwood has been one of the most well-known, influential, and acclaimed contemporary women writers in English. Atwood is Canadian and was born in Ottawa. Because of her father's occupation as an entomologist, Atwood and her family resided in many remote and isolated locations when she was a child. As a result, for the early years of her education, she was home-schooled by her parents. A successful student, Atwood continued her education into graduate school, eventually earning a master's degree from Radcliffe College.

She also began, but never completed, work toward a Ph.D. Atwood is married to author Graeme Gibson and the couple has one child, a daughter.

Although known primarily as a novelist, Atwood began her public writing career as a poet when, before her 21st birthday, she won the prestigious E. J. Pratt medal for her collection of poetry *Double Persephone* (1961). Atwood's best known work is her 1985 novel *The Handmaid's Tale.* The novel is a futuristic portrait of what could happen to a supposedly free nation when fundamentalism and patriarchy become the dominant paradigms. Atwood is a prolific writer, having published more than 30 novels, poetry and short story collections, and critical essays. She is the recipient of the Booker Prize, the Arthur C. Clarke Award, the Giller Prize, the Governor General's Award, and many other awards and honorary degrees. All of her works are grounded in a quest for equality and are elaborations on the dangers of injustice and intolerance.

Literary critics often compare the works of Atwood and Morrison.

BIBLIOGRAPHY

Atwood, Margaret. *Alias Grace.* New York: Doubleday, 1996.

———. *Cat's Eye.* New York: Doubleday, 1989.

———. *Double Persephone.* Toronto: Hawkshead Press, 1961.

———. *The Edible Woman.* New York: Atlantic Little-Brown, 1970.

———. *Good Bones.* New York: Doubleday, 1994.

———. *The Handmaid's Tale.* Boston: Houghton Mifflin, 1985.

———. *Margaret Atwood Poems 1965–1975.* New York: Virago Press Limited, 1991.

———. *The Robber Bride.* New York: Doubleday, 1993.

———. *Selected Poems II: Poems Selected and New, 1976–1986.* Oxford: Oxford University Press, 1986.

———. *Selected Poems 1966–1984.* Oxford: Oxford University Press, 1990.

———. *Wilderness Tips.* New York: Doubleday, 1991.

Bouson, J. Brooks. *Brutal Choreographies: Oppositional Strategies and Narrative Design in the Novels of Margaret Atwood.* Amherst: University of Massachusetts Press, 1993.

Davidson, Arnold and Cathy, eds. *The Art of Margaret Atwood: Essays In Criticism*. Toronto: House of Anansi Press, 1980.

Grace, Sherill, *Violent Duality: A Study of Margaret Atwood*. Montreal: Vehicule Press, 1980.

Hengen, Shannon. *Margaret Atwood's Power: Mirrors, Reflections and Images in Select Fiction and Poetry*. Toronto: Second Story, 1993.

Howells, Coral Ann. *Margaret Atwood*. New York: St. Martin's Press, 1996.

Ingersoll, Earl G., ed. *Margaret Atwood: Conversations*. Princeton, N.J.: Ontario Review Press, 1990.

McCombs, Judith, E. *Critical Essays on Margaret Atwood*. Boston: G. K. Hall, 1988.

Morey, Ann-Janine. "Margaret Atwood and Toni Morrison: Reflections on Postmodernism and the Study of Religion and Literature," *Journal of the American Academy of Religion* 60 (Autumn 1992): 493–513.

Rao, Eleonora. *Strategies for Identity: The Fiction of Margaret Atwood*. New York: Peter Land Publishing, 1994.

Staels, Hilda. *Margaret Atwood's Novels: A Study of Narrative Discourse*. Tübingen, Germany: Francke Verlag, 1995.

York, Lorraine M., ed. *Various Atwoods: Essays on the Later Poems, Short Fiction, and Novels*. Toronto: House of Anansi Press, 1995.

Austen, Jane (1775–1817) Jane Austen is one of the most important English novelists. Her novels are largely satirical. Jane Austen was unusual for a woman of her time in that she enjoyed the privilege of acquiring an advanced education. Jane Austen was born in Hampshire, England, in 1775 to the Rev. George Austen and Cassandra Leigh-Austen. The Austens had eight children of whom Jane was the seventh. As a very young girl, Jane became enamored of the art of writing and began to pursue it seriously.

In 1811, *Sense and Sensibility* became Austen's first published work. The popularity of the work guaranteed the publication of *Pride and Prejudice* in 1813 and *Mansfield Park* in 1814.

Although all of Austen's novels published during her lifetime were anonymously credited, the successful sales of her novels garnered a public following and a body of readers curious about her identity. During the next few years, perhaps encouraged by her success, Austen was incredibly productive. Beginning in 1814, Austen published a new novel every two years. *Mansfield Park* saw publication in 1814. The novel *Emma* appeared in print in 1816 and in 1818, the year after her death from Addison's disease, *Persuasion* and *Northanger Abbey*.

Austen had been ill repeatedly through the years. Addison's disease is a failure of the adrenal glands of the kidneys. At the time of Austen's death in 1817, the disease had not been identified and to this day remains incurable. Austen's posthumous publications saw the first acknowledgment of Austen's authorship of her writings. Contemporarily, Austen is considered to be one of the finest novelists to write in the English language.

Toni Morrison read and revered Jane Austen's writings as a young girl.

BIBLIOGRAPHY

Armstrong, Isobel. *Jane Austen, Mansfield Park*. London: Penguin, 1988.

Austen, Jane. *Mansfield Park*. 1814. New York: Dover Publications, 2001.

———. *Northanger Abbey*. 1803. Ontario: Broadview Literary Texts, 2002.

———. *Persuasion*. 1818. New York: Dover Publications, 1997.

———. *Pride and Prejudice*. 1813. London: Penguin, 1985.

———. *Selected Letters 1796–1817*. New York: Oxford University Press, 1985.

Austen-Leigh, William, Richard Arthur Austen-Leigh, and Deirdre LeFaye, eds. *Jane Austen: A Family Record*. New York: Simon and Schuster, 1989.

Bloom, Harold, ed. *Jane Austen*. New York: Chelsea House Publishers, 1986.

———, ed. *Jane Austen's Emma*. New York: Chelsea House Publishers, 1987.

———, ed. *Jane Austen's Mansfield Park*. New York: Chelsea House Publishers, 1987.

———, ed. *Jane Austen's Pride and Prejudice*. New York: Chelsea House Publishers, 1987.

Fergus, Jan S. *Jane Austen: A Literary Life*. New York: Macmillan, 1991.

Johnson, Claudia L. *Jane Austen: Women, Politics, and the Novel*. Chicago: University of Chicago Press, 1988.

Lauber, John. *Jane Austen*. Boston: Twayne, 1993.

B

Baldwin, James (1924–1987) Born in HARLEM, New York, to an impoverished family, James Baldwin developed into one of America's finest and most prolific writers. Baldwin's work bridges generic boundaries. Baldwin's relatively unhappy childhood was relieved by his frequent forays into the imaginative world of books. Baldwin credited reading and writing, both of which he did at a very early age, with providing him with options that allowed him to transcend, empathize with, share, and escape from the world in which he was born. During his life, he produced novels, essays, short stories, and children's literature. Generally Baldwin's work is concerned with the complexities of human interaction, particularly as these encounters are informed by the artificial, yet all-encompassing, categories of identity definition such as race, class, gender, nationality, religious affiliation, and sexual orientation.

Each of Baldwin's novels, from his landmark and defining first novel, *Go Tell It on the Mountain* (1953), to his final work on the Atlanta child murders, *The Evidence of Things Not Seen* (1985), offers his readers an unflinching examination of difficult and uncomfortable issues that reside in the heart of the conflict between American ideals and realities. *Go Tell It on the Mountain* is perhaps Baldwin's most autobiographical novel. Baldwin's first novel details the coming of age of a young African-American boy and the difficult negotiations the boy faces as the result of pressure from the various, sometimes conflicting, elements of his universe.

Baldwin was one of the first African-American writers to deal with homosexuality explicitly in fiction. Baldwin's second novel, *Giovanni's Room* (1966), is an investigation into the life of a homosexual white European man. Disturbed by American racism and racial violence, Baldwin relocated to Europe where he would spend much time on and off for the remainder of his life. Although he seemed to find life in Europe preferable to living in the United States, Baldwin was not naïve about the exoticism and racism African Americans experience in Europe. Baldwin's essays often investigate the questions raised by, and possible solutions to, oppression and inequity.

James Baldwin was the recipient of many awards during his career, including a Eugene F. Saxon Fellowship, a Rosenwald Fellowship, Guggenheim Fellowship, the MacDowell Colony Fellowship, and the French Legion of Honor. Baldwin also received several honorary degrees from several universities, including City University of New York and the University of Massachusetts. Baldwin lost a long battle with stomach cancer when he died at age 63 in France in 1987.

Toni Morrison edited a volume of Baldwin's work entitled, *James Baldwin: Collected Essays: Notes of a Native Son / Nobody Knows My Name / The Fire Next Time / No Name in the Street / The Devil Finds Work / Other Essays* (1998). Many critics have noted Baldwin's influence on Morrison's writings.

BIBLIOGRAPHY

Baldwin, James. *The Amen Corner.* New York: Dial, 1968.

———. *Another Country.* New York: Dial, 1962.

———. *Blues for Mr. Charlie.* New York: Dial, 1964.

———. *A Dialogue: James Baldwin and Nikki Giovanni.* Philadelphia: Lippincott, 1973.

———. *Evidence of Things Not Seen.* Henry Holt and Company, 1985.

———. *The Fire Next Time.* New York: Dial, 1963.

———. *Giovanni's Room.* New York: Dial, 1956.

———. *Going to Meet the Man.* New York: Dial, 1965.

———. *Go Tell It on the Mountain.* New York: Knopf, 1953.

———. *If Beale Street Could Talk.* New York: Dial, 1974.

———. *Jimmy's Blues: Selected Poems.* London: Joseph, 1983.

———. *Nobody Knows My Name: More Notes of a Native Son.* New York: Dial, 1961.

———. *Notes of a Native Son.* Boston: Beacon, 1955.

———. *Tell Me How Long the Train's Been Gone.* New York: Dial, 1968.

Baldwin, James, and Toni Morrison. *James Baldwin: Collected Essays: Notes of a Native Son / Nobody Knows My Name / The Fire Next Time / No Name in the Street / The Devil Finds Work / Other Essays.* New York: Library of America, 1998.

Burt, Nancy V., and Fred L. Standley, eds. *Critical Essays on James Baldwin.* Boston: G. K. Hall, 1988.

Campbell, James. *Talking at the Gates: A Life of James Baldwin.* New York: Penguin Books, 1991.

Eckman, Fern M. *The Furious Passage of James Baldwin.* New York: M. Evans, 1966.

Harris, Trudier. *Black Women in the Fiction of James Baldwin.* Knoxville: University of Tennessee Press, 1985.

Hatch, James V., and Ted Shine. eds. *Black Theatre U.S.A.: Plays by African Americans 1847 to Today.* New York: Free Press, 1996.

Kinnamon, Kenneth. *James Baldwin; A Collection of Critical Essays.* Englewood Cliffs, N.J.: Prentice Hall, 1974.

Leeming, David A. *James Baldwin: A Biography.* New York: Knopf, 1994.

Macebuh, Stanley. *James Baldwin; A Critical Study.* New York: Third Press, 1973.

Bambara, Toni Cade (Miltona Mirkin Cade, Toni Cade) (1939–1995) Among her many accomplishments, author Toni Cade Bambara is noted as one of the first African-American women to articulate feminist rhetoric in the wake of the CIVIL RIGHTS MOVEMENT. Bambara's work is a map of her commitment to equality and social change. Bambara, born Miltona Mirkin Cade in HARLEM, New York, changed her name to Toni at the ripe age of around five or six.

Always an excellent student, Bambara graduated at the age of 20 from Queen's College, began publishing fiction, and teaching. Bambara came of age during the turbulence of the late 1960s and found many outlets for her political, economic, and social concerns. She worked as a program director at Colony Settlement House. In 1970, Bambara edited the quintessential collection of African-American women's writing of its time. The anthology was entitled *The Black Woman.* This landmark volume was a critical threshold that ushered the particular concerns of African-American women into the national spotlight. Many women writers who had achieved or would achieve national prominence and acclaim were included in the text. Some of these writers were Paule Marshall, Audre Lorde, NIKKI GIOVANNI, and Alice Walker. With the publication of *The Black Woman* and *Gorilla, My Love* (1972), Bambara began to receive popular and critical attention for her writings. Following the aesthetics of the Black Arts Movement, Bambara's edited collections, as well as her own writings, reflect her belief that writing should serve a social and artistic purpose.

In 1977, Bambara released her second collection of short stories, *The Sea Birds Are Still Alive.* In the collection, Bambara remains consistently concerned with the lives of marginalized and disempowered women and children. Bambara began to connect the injustices she lived and wrote about with the larger geopolitical situations she learned about and observed firsthand during her travels overseas, particularly her trips to Cuba and to Vietnam. Bambara's first published novel, *The Salteaters,* appeared in 1980. The novel is a complex interrogation and integration of the conflicts arising out of the struggles of the Civil Rights and women's rights movements. The novel was an ambitious attempt to show that those divergences can be bridged and that they do not have to come at the expense of individual health and sanity. In 1987, Bambara published another novel, *If Blessing Comes*.

As she expanded her creative repertoire, Bambara became involved in filmmaking as a professor, writer, and producer. Bambara produced several documentary films that were critically acclaimed. At the age of 54, in 1993, Bambara was diagnosed with the cancer that eventually was the cause of her death in 1995. Following her death, two more of her works were published, *Deep Sightings and Rescue Missions: Fiction, Essays, and Conversations* (1995) and *Those Bones Are Not My Child* (1999), both edited by Toni Morrison.

BIBLIOGRAPHY

Bambara, Toni Cade. *The Black Woman; An Anthology.* New York: New American Library, 1970.

———. *Gorilla, My Love.* New York: Random House, 1972.

———. "Reading the Signs, Empowering the Eye: Daughters of the Dust and the Black Independent Cinema Movement." In *Black American Cinema,* edited by Manthia Diawara, 118–144. London: Routledge, 1993.

———. *The Salt Eaters.* New York: Random House, 1980.

———. *The Sea Birds Are Still Alive: Collected Stories.* New York: Random House, 1977.

Bambara, Toni Cade. *Deep Sightings and Rescue Missions: Fiction, Essays and Conversations,* edited by Toni Morrison. New York: Pantheon, 1996.

———. *Those Bones Are Not My Child,* edited by Toni Morrison. New York: Pantheon, 1999.

Butler-Evans, Elliott. *Race, Gender, and Desire: Narrative Strategies in the Fiction of Toni Cade Bambara, Toni Morrison, and Alice Walker.* Philadelphia: Temple University Press, 1989.

Byerman, Keith E. "Healing Arts: Folklore and the Female Self in Toni Cade Bambara's *The Salt Eaters,*" *Postscript* 5 (1988): 37–43.

Cartwright, Jerome. "Bambara's 'The Lesson,'" *Explicator* 47, no. 3 (Spring 1989): 61–63.

Collins, Janelle. "Generating Power: Fission, Fusion, and Post Modern Politics in Bambara's The Salt Eaters," *MELUS* 21, no. 2 (Summer 1996): 35–47.

Comfort, Mary. "Liberating Figures in Toni Cade Bambara's *Gorilla, My Love,*" *Studies in American Humor* 3, no. 5 (1998): 76–96.

———. "Bambara's 'Sweet Town,'" *Explicator* 54, no. 1 (Fall 1995): 51–54.

Diawara, Manthia, ed. *Black American Cinema.* New York: Routledge, 1993.

Gidley, Mick. "Reading Bambara's 'Raymond's Run,'" *English Language Notes* 28, no. 1 (September 1990): 67–72.

Griffin, Farah J. "Toni Cade Bambara: Free to Be Anywhere in the Universe," *Callaloo* 19, no. 2 (Spring 1996): 229–231.

Hargrove, Nancy D. "Youth in Toni Cade Bambara's *Gorilla, My Love,*" *Southern Quarterly* 22, no. 1 (Fall 1983): 81–99.

Kelley, Margot A. "'Damballah Is the First Law of Thermodynamics': Modes of Access to Toni Cade Bambara's *The Salt Eaters,*" *African American Review* 27, no. 3 (Fall 1993): 479–493.

Lyles, Lois F. "Time, Motion, Sound and Fury in *The Sea Birds Are Still Alive,*" *College Language Association Journal* 36, no. 2 (December 1992): 134–144.

Rosenberg, Ruth. "'You Took a Name That Made You Amiable to the Music': Toni Cade Bambara's *The Salt Eaters,*" *Literary Onomastics Studies* 12 (1985): 165–194.

Stanford, Ann F. "He Speaks for Whom? Inscription and Reinscription of Women in *Invisible Man* and *The Salt Eaters,*" *MELUS* 18, no. 2 (Summer 1992): 17–31.

Traylor, Eleanor W. "Music as Theme: The Jazz Mode in the Works of Toni Cade Bambara." In *Black Women Writers (1950–1980): A Critical Evaluation,* edited by Mari Evans, 58–74. Garden City, N.Y.: Anchor-Doubleday, 1984.

Battle, Kathleen (1948–   )   Kathleen Battle is a world-famous soprano opera singer whose voice has been revered at the same time that her reputation has often been publicly reviled. Like Toni Morrison, Kathleen Battle was born in a small industrial town in Ohio. As with many African Americans in Portsmith, Ohio, the Battles were a poor, working-class family who, with seven children, struggled to make ends meet. Kathleen was the youngest of the Battle children. The family was a musical one, with singing a frequent family event. Even as a young child, Kathleen distinguished herself with the beauty of her voice. After receiving much acclaim throughout her girlhood for her voice, Battle left Portsmith to pursue musical studies at the College Conservatory of Music at the University of CINCINNATI.

Battle began her professional training at the Conservancy in Cincinnati and majored in music education. Following her graduation from the Conservancy, Battle began teaching music and auditioning for professional roles in opera. While she was teaching, she won a role with the Cincinnati Opera to sing at the Italian Spoleto festival, which exposed Battle for the first time to the larger opera community and launched her career as a singer.

Soon thereafter, Battle began working with James Levine, who was then the principal conductor for the Metropolitan Opera. Levine became a mentor of sorts to Battle and, eventually, encouraged her to audition to become a member of the Metropolitan Opera company. After her successful audition in 1976, Battle quickly rose to national and international prominence, starring in premier roles in the world's best-known operas. Unlike many opera stars, Battle also had commercial appeal and her recordings frequently broke records for classical music sales. Battle became a personality and, as a celebrity, was able to generate ticket sales as well as critical accolades.

At the moment when Battle seemed most successful, stories began to surface about her being demanding and unprofessional behind the scenes. Eventually these rumors seemed to be substantiated when she was fired by the Metropolitan Opera in 1993.

Battle continues to perform in concert and to make recordings. Battle's recordings include the 1995 *Honey and Rue* song cycle, composed by ANDRE PREVIN, with lyrics by Toni Morrison. In addition to receiving several Grammy awards, Battle performed at the 1993 Clinton presidential inaugural festivities.

BIBLIOGRAPHY

Battle, Kathleen. *Carnegie Hall.* (1992). Deutsche Grammophon (USA), CD, 1992.

———. *Grace.* (1997). Sony Classical, CD, 1997.

———. *Honey and Rue.* (1992). Deutsche Grammophon (USA), 1995.

———. *So Many Stars.* (1995). Sony Classical, CD, 1995.

Kozinn, Allan. "Classical Music; A Weary Maestro Trudges Forward." *New York Times,* May 5, 1996, Section 2, 31.

———. "The Met Drops Kathleen Battle, Citing 'Unprofessional Actions.'" *New York Times,* February 8, 1994, Section A, 1.

———. "With Theatrics Stripped Away, A Diva Stakes All on Her Voice." *New York Times,* March 2, 1994, Section 2.

Mermelstein, David. "Television/Radio; Opening the Gates for Black Opera Singers." *New York Times,* February 13, 2000, Section 2, 35.

Patchett, Ann. "The Lives They Lived; The People's Diva." *New York Times,* December 29, 2002, Section 6, 47.

Pogrebin, Robin. "Met Chief Ready to Step Down after Long and Operatic Career." *New York Times,* February 10, 2004, Section A, 1.

Swan, Annalyn. "Battle Royal." *Vanity Fair,* May 1994.

Tommasini, Anthony. "Life after Met Goes on for Battle, Next Door." *New York Times,* December 16, 1995, Section 2.

"Toni Morrison to Read at the Philharmonic." *New York Times,* December 11, 1995, Section 2.

Van Gelder, Lawrence. "Footlights." *New York Times,* June 27, 2001, Section E, 1.

Beavers, Louise (1902–1962) Louise Beavers was an African-American film actress whose career spanned nearly four decades and included over 160 film and TV roles. Beginning with a small part in the silent *Gold Diggers* (1923) to her last movie, *The Facts of Life* (1960), which starred Bob Hope and Lucille Ball, Beavers's most common roles were those of a domestic—a cook, housekeeper, or maid—limited roles that were typical for a black actress during the years that she worked. In these roles, she often depicted the MAMMY figure: a controversial stereotype of a black woman domestic, or slave, who was heavy-set, warmhearted, sassy at times, folk-wise at other times, and who also came with a jolly laugh.

Perhaps her most important role was in the 1934 *Imitation of Life,* starring CLAUDETTE COLBERT, in which she played Delilah Johnson, whose light-skinned daughter, played by Fredi Washington, wanted to pass for white. It was the first time that a black woman's emotional story was told in an American movie. Though the film was considered progressive at the time, Beavers's role, nevertheless, was that of Colbert's maid; even as Colbert's character made a fortune from her maid's pancake recipe, Beavers's character remained content in a subservient position.

Between 1952 and 1953, Beavers starred in the TV show *Beulah,* playing the title role. She followed two other actresses who had played the part before her: Ethel Waters and Hattie McDaniel, and she was in turn followed by yet another actress, Amanda Randolph. Beulah was a maid.

Because few other parts other than a domestic—or Mammy—were open to her, Beavers, who was naturally thin, had to keep up her weight, and though she was originally from CINCINNATI, OHIO, had to develop a southern accent.

In the novel *Song of Solomon* (1977), when Milkman and Guitar are arrested after trying to steal the green bag from Pilate's house, Milkman describes Pilate's behavior in the police station as like that of BUTTERFLY MCQUEEN or Louise Beavers.

BIBLIOGRAPHY

Flamming, Douglas. *Bound for Freedom: Black Los Angeles in Jim Crow America.* Berkeley: University of California Press, 2005.

Beloved Community   The Beloved Community became a familiar and common term as the result of MARTIN LUTHER KING JR.'s use of it during the struggles of the CIVIL RIGHTS MOVEMENT. JOSIAH ROYCE is credited with originating and developing the influential idea of the Beloved Community in his development of absolute idealism as a philosophical concept in the United States. According to Royce, the Beloved Community derives from the collectivity of individuals who have organized their lives by adhering and acting in service to a central purpose. The challenge for the individual is to coordinate desires into a harmonious entity. This coordination creates a self. Each self constitutes a miniature Absolute. The Beloved Community can emerge when the micro Absolutes coalesce and work together. Royce believed that the emergence of the Beloved Community would bring about stability and peace among humanity.

Martin Luther King's version of the Beloved Community emerged from his embrace of the philosophy of nonviolent direct action as the primary tool in the struggle against oppression and discrimination. Through nonviolent direct action, the group that is experiencing oppression brings attention to the wrong being enacted upon them and therefore forces the oppressors to confront the immorality of their actions and, ideally, to correct and change their behavior. After a successful nonviolent intervention and transition, King believed that the emergence of the Beloved Community was the next step. The Beloved Community, in King's conception, was a group of different people coexisting with integrity and with love and mutual respect. Such a community, according to King, would be a realistic way for human beings to live together with a creative and compassionate mechanism for amicably resolving inevitable conflicts.

Morrison may allude to the Beloved Community in several of her novels, including *Beloved* (1987), *Paradise* (1998), and *Love* (2003).

BIBLIOGRAPHY

Carson, Clayborne, ed. *The Autobiography of Martin Luther King, Jr.* New York: Warner Books, 1998.

Carson, Clayborne, Susan Carson, Adrienne Clay, Virginia Shadron, Kieran Taylor, eds. *The Papers of Martin Luther King, Jr.,* Volume IV: *Birth of a New Age, December 1955–December 1956.* Berkeley: University of California Press, 2000.

Dekar, Paul A. *Creating the Beloved Community: A Journey with the Fellowship of Reconciliation.* New York: Pandora Books, 2005.

Dyson, Michael Eric. *I May Not Get There with You.* New York: The Free Press, 2000.

King, Martin Luther, Jr. *Where Do We Go from Here: Chaos or Community?* Boston: Beacon Press, 1967.

King Center, the. *The Beloved Community.* "Welcome to The Beloved Community." Available online. www.thekingcenter.org/prog/bc/index.html. Accessed July 13, 2005.

Ling, Peter J. *Martin Luther King, Jr.* London: Routledge, 2002.

Bid Whist Bid Whist is a variation of the card game Whist, a game played in many versions in many countries throughout the world. The origins of the game are a mater of controversy, with some scholars contending that the game began in England, while others believe it originated in Turkey. The first written guide to the game of Whist in English is found in Edmond Hoyle's 1742, *A Short Treatise on the Game of Whist.* After gaining popularity in England, versions of the game proliferated in Europe. The game migrated to what would become the United States with the British migration west. In addition to generating variations such as Bid Whist, the well-known game of Bridge is thought also to derive from Whist.

Bid Whist is played primarily by African Americans and is thought to have originated with African-American Civil War soldiers. By the turn of the century, the game had gained popularity among PULLMAN PORTERS who probably were responsible for the terminology of the game, which has a directional orientation. Bid Whist uses a traditional set of 52 cards without jokers. There are four players in the game who work in pairs as partners and sit across the table from each other. In each round, the lead player sets the suit. Players must play that suit if they have that card. If they do not, they may play any card. The highest card of the original suit wins the hand, unless someone plays a trump card. In that case, the highest trump wins. The winning pair is the set of partners with the most successful bids.

Bid Whist is a game that traditionally is associated with strategy and trash talking. Often there is as much wit involved in a game as there is card playing. With the advent of other entertainment distractions, Bid Whist is not as popular as it once was. There are individuals and groups dedicated to ensuring the game's survival in African-American communities.

Morrison has her characters playing or referring to Bid Whist in several of her novels, including *Sula* (1973), *Tar Baby* (1981), and *Jazz* (1992).

BIBLIOGRAPHY

Andrews, Joseph B. *The Complete Win at Whist.* New York: Bonus Books, 2000.

"History of Bid Whist." Available online. URL: www.bidwhist.com/help/195.htm. Accessed February 8, 2006.

Morrison, Greg, and Yannick Rice Lamb. *Rise and Fly: Tall Tales and Mostly True Rules of Bid Whist.* New York: Three Rivers Press, 2005.

Black Aesthetic In his 1968 article, "The Black Arts Movement," Larry Neal articulated his version of the foundational principles of the Black Aesthetic. According to Neal, the function of black art is to conflate ethics and aesthetics, political action and artistic creation. In literary terms, the Black Aesthetic was one of the central artistic objectives of the writings produced during the BLACK ARTS MOVEMENT. The Black Aesthetic was defined by several architects, including Houston Baker, Larry Neal, Hoyt Fuller, and Addison Gayle. Although there are many different components of the various definitions of Black Aesthetics, fundamentally the Black Aesthetic of the 1960s asserted that art produced by African Americans should, in addition to artistic concerns, address and help to transform the political, social, and economic problems faced by African-American communities.

According to the precepts of the Black Aesthetic, the value of art could be measured by the extent to which it expressed the realities of African-American communities and helped those communities to advance. The writers articulating the principles of the Black Aesthetic also felt that there were particular characteristics that could be assigned to blackness and therefore a work deserved merit to the extent to which it could be described as black.

An important aspect of the Black Aesthetic was the reclamation of definitions of blackness. For centuries blackness had been associated with negative ideas such as ugliness, dishonor, and evil. Neal, Fuller, and others attempted to reclaim the word and redefine black as beautiful. This redefinition of blackness included a reexamination of the history of African Americans and Africans and an affirmation of what that history represents. There was a sense of mission among the Black Aestheticians. They believed there was a truth, an essential quality of blackness and black people, that had been lost and could be recaptured by art that understood and valued the essential quality that had been erased by the legacy of slavery and racism.

The Black Aesthetic insists on affirming the connection between a black present and past through art. This connection would catalyze a revolution in thought that would lead to a revolution in action. The revolution would usher in a world of black power and control over the destiny of black people. Black Aesthetic theory, even as expressed by the artists themselves, did not necessarily contain or confine the literature produced in its name.

Although Morrison's works are not examples of the Black Aesthetic, she was influenced by the artists whose works are defined by its principles.

BIBLIOGRAPHY

Baker, Houston A., Jr. *Afro-American Poetics, Revisions of Harlem and the Black Aesthetic.* Madison: University of Wisconsin Press, 1988.

———. *Blues, Ideology, and Afro-American Literature: A Vernacular Theory.* Chicago: University of Chicago Press, 1984.

Cruse, Harold. *The Crisis of the Negro Intellectual.* New York: Morrow, 1967.

———. "Rebellion or Revolution?" *Liberator* 4, no. 1 (1964): 14–16.

Fuller, Hoyt. "Towards a Black Aesthetic." In *The Black Aesthetic,* edited by Addison Gayle, 3–12. Garden City, N.Y.: Doubleday. 1971.

Gayle, Addison. *The Black Aesthetic.* Garden City, N.Y.: Doubleday, 1971.

Henderson, Stephen. *Understanding the New Black Poetry: Black Speech and Black Music as Poetic References.* New York: William Morrow, 1973.

Jones, LeRoi "Black Art." Newark, N.J.: Jihad Productions, 1967.

Karenga, Maulana Ron. "Black Cultural Nationalism." In *The Black Aesthetic,* edited by Addison Gayle. Garden City, N.Y.: Doubleday, 1971.

Neal, Larry. "Any Day Now: Black Art and Black Liberation," *Ebony* 24 (1969): 54–58.

———. "The Black Arts Movement," The *Drama Review* 12, no. 4 (1968): 29–39.

———. "The Black Writer's Role," *Liberator* 6, no. 6 (1966): 7–9.

———. "The Cultural Front," *Liberator* 5, no. 6 (1965): 26–27.

———. *Visions of a Liberated Future.* St. Paul, Minn.: Thunder's Mouth Press, 1989.

Scot-Heron, Gil. "The Revolution Will Not Be Televised." *The Revolution Will Not Be Televised.* New York: BMG Music, 1988.

Black Arts Movement The Black Arts movement, in literary terms, consists of the writings produced approximately between the years of 1965 and 1965 that produced works that affirmed many of the precepts of the BLACK AESTHETIC. The artists of the Black Arts Movement, generally speaking, embraced the precepts of the Black Power movement and wrote art that attempted to catalyze both collective affirmation and political action.

The phrase Black Power was popularized during the CIVIL RIGHTS MOVEMENT, in 1966, when Stokely Carmichael, chairman of the Student Non-Violent Coordinating Committee (SNCC), began to advocate for Black Power rather than nonviolent direct action as a strategy to achieve equality. This shift caused a rift between SNCC and the other organizations, such as SCLC, involved in the civil rights struggle. As advocated by Carmichael and SNCC, Black Power called for self-defense, affirmation of black people, and eradication of white domination.

Artistically speaking, LeRoi Jones, who changed his name to Amiri Baraka in 1967, is often named as the artistic founder of the Black Arts Movement. In 1965, in the wake of the assassination of MALCOLM X, Jones founded the Black Arts Repertory Theatre. The theatre became a haven for young writers eager to use drama as an accessible means of social statement and transformation. The Black Arts Repertory Theatre, along with other organizations such as Umbra, began to produce poetry and plays that were primarily performative in nature with the intention of reaching people in the community who might not otherwise be attracted to literature.

In addition to Baraka, other important voices in the articulation of Black Arts Movement theory were Askia Toure, Larry Neal, Hoyt Fuller, and Maulana

Karenga. Some of the artists associated with the movement were Ed Bullins, GWENDOLYN BROOKS, Eldridge Cleaver, Jayne Cortez, Harold Cruse, Mari Evans, Hoyt Fuller, NIKKI GIOVANNI, Lorraine Hansberry, Gil-Scott Heron, Maulana Ron Karenga, Etheridge Knight, Adrienne Kennedy, Haki R. Madhubuti, Larry Neal, Dudley Randall, Ishmael Reed, SONIA SANCHEZ, Ntozake Shange, Quincy Troupe, and John Alfred Williams. These artists found public voice for their publications in new publication venues created and designated for black writers, in journals and publishing houses such as *Journal of Black Poetry, Black Scholar, Negro Digest, Lotus Press, Broadside Press,* and *Third World Press.* Another important vehicle for the dissemination of Black Arts movement writers was anthologies. Some of the most significant collections were *Black Fire* (1968), *New Black Voices* (1972), *The Black Woman* (1970), and *Understanding the New Black Poetry* (1970).

Despite its rhetorical commitment to the production of art inseparably connected to the elimination of oppression experienced by black people, the gender oppression of black women was not acknowledged by the primary architects of the Black Arts Movement as germane to the struggle against racial oppression. The movement has also been considered by some as homophobic and racially exclusive. By the mid-1970s, African-American writers associated with the Black Arts Movement began to work in other directions and to experiment with other forms, but the lasting impact of the movement remains, especially in terms of the integration of African-American studies into the academy and African-American literature into the mainstream publishing establishment.

Although Morrison has not been a direct participant in the Black Arts Movement, she was influenced by the artists whose works are defined by its principles.

BIBLIOGRAPHY

Chapman, Abraham, ed. *New Black Voices.* New York: New American Library, 1972.

Fuller, Charles H. "Black Writing Is Socio-Creative Art," *Liberator* 7, no. 4 (1967): 8–10.

———. "Black Writing: Release from Object," *Liberator* 7, no. 9 (1967): 17.

Henderson, Stephen. *Understanding the New Black Poetry: Black Speech and Black Music as Poetic References.* New York: William Morrow, 1973.

Henderson, Stephen E., and Mercer Cook. *The Militant Black Writer in Africa and the United States.* Madison: University of Wisconsin Press, 1969.

Jones, LeRoi. "The Black Arts Repertory Theatre School," *Liberator* 5, no. 4 (1965): 21.

Jones, LeRoi, and Larry Neal. *Black Fire: An Anthology of Afro-American Writing.* New York: Morrow, 1968.

Neal, Larry. "Any Day Now: Black Art and Black Liberation," *Ebony* 24 (1969): 54–58.

———. "The Black Arts Movement," *The Drama Review* 12, no. 4 (1968): 29–39.

———. "The Black Writer's Role," *Liberator* 6, no. 6 (1966): 7–9.

———. "The Cultural Front," *Liberator* 5, no. 6 (1965): 26–27.

———. *Visions of a Liberated Future: Black Arts Movement Writings.* New York: Thunder's Mouth Press, 1989.

Smith, David Lionel. "The Black Arts Movement and Its Critics," *American Literary History* 3 (Spring 1991): 98–110.

Thompson, Julius E. *Dudley Randall, Broadside Press, and the Black Arts Movement in Detroit 1960–1995.* New York: McFarland, 1998.

Toure, Askia Muhammad. "Black Magic!" *Journal of Black Poetry* 1 (Fall 1968): 63–64.

Ya Salaam, Kalamu. *Magic of Juju: An Appreciation of the Black Arts Movement.* Chicago: Third World Press, 2001.

Black Panther Party   The Black Panther Party was a political and social party that was formed in Oakland, California, in 1966 by a group of African Americans who felt that the objectives and tactics of the CIVIL RIGHTS MOVEMENT, with its emphasis on nonviolent direct action, were misguided and no longer effective. The primary founders and leaders of the Panther Party were Huey P. Newton and Bobby Seale. The two men and the other members of the Party began the organization with the founding principles of self-determination and self-defense for African Americans who sought liberation. Unlike the primary strategies of the Civil Rights movement, the

Panthers felt that violence was a viable solution for the achievement of black autonomy and freedom. The aims and objectives of the party were articulated in a 10-point platform that called for black autonomy and self-sufficiency. In order to accomplish their goal of self-sufficiency, party members developed programs that would address the needs of the community and wean them from economic and psychological dependence on the government.

Both Huey P. Newton and Bobby Seale became involved in legal conflicts with the police, with Newton charged with murdering a policeman and Seale indicted for political conspiracy. Neither was convicted of the crimes of which they were charged. Later investigations and documentation demonstrated that many of the legal problems encountered by the Black Panthers, particularly the murder of Panther member Fred Hampton in 1969, were the result of orchestrated interference and framing by agencies of the federal government, including the Central Intelligence Agency and Federal Bureau of Investigation.

By the early 1970s, internal struggles combined with external pressures to rend apart the foundations of the organization. Newton became heavily involved in drugs and Seale eventually left the party. The Black Panther Party was an important and influential group whose articulation of self-determination was an important component in the struggle for African-American equality and justice. The New Black Panther Party, begun in 1998, is a distinct organization from the original.

Toni Morrison edited a volume containing the writings of Huey P. Newton, entitled *To Die for the People: The Writings of Huey P. Newton* (1995).

BIBLIOGRAPHY

Anthony, Earl. *Picking Up the Gun; A Report on the Black Panthers.* New York: Dial Press, 1970.

Brown, Elaine. *A Taste of Power: A Black Woman's Story.* New York: Anchor Books, 1993.

Churchill, Ward, and Jim Vanderwall. *Agents of Repression: The FBI's Secret Wars against the Black Panther Party and the American Indian Movement.* Boston, Mass.: South End Press, 1988.

Cleaver, Eldridge. *Soul on Ice.* New York: McGraw-Hill, 1967.

Cleaver, Kathleen, and George N. Katsiaficas, eds. *Liberation, Imagination, and the Black Panther Party: A New Look at the Panthers and Their Legacy.* New York: Routledge, 2001.

Foner, Philip S., ed. *The Black Panthers Speak.* Philadelphia: Lippincott, 1970.

Haskins, James. *Power to the People: The Rise and Fall of the Black Panther Party.* New York: Simon and Schuster Books for Young Readers, 1997.

Marine, Gene. *The Black Panthers.* New York: New American Library, 1969.

Newton, Huey P. *A Huey P. Newton Reader.* New York: Seven Stories Press, 2002.

———. *Revolutionary Suicide.* New York: Harcourt Brace Jovanovich, 1973.

Newton, Huey P. *To Die for the People,* edited by Toni Morrison. New York: Writers and Readers Publisher, 1995.

Seale, Bobby. *Seize the Time: The Story of the Black Panther Party and Huey P. Newton.* New York: Random House, 1970.

Van Peebles, Mario, Ula Y. Taylor, J. Tarika Lewis, and Melvin Van Peebles. *Panther: The Pictorial History of the Black Panthers and the Story behind the Film.* New York: Newmarket Press, 1995.

blues, the   The music known as the blues was originally an African-American art form that expressed the joys and heartbreaks in the wide range of African-American experiences. Although there are a number of forms, the primary, classic form of the blues is the 12-bar structure where the first two lines of each stanza are the same and then the third is a response to the first two. The structure of the blues is thought to derive from the African and African-American practice of communication and exchange between audience and performer known as call and response. This structure contributed to the originality and the improvisation of the blues as a form of expression. Ironically, singing the blues is supposed to have the effect of lifting the singer's mood and relieving his or her sadness. Although blues is primarily sung, there are blues instrumentalists as well, with piano, drums, harmonica, and guitar the most significant blues instruments.

Most scholars agree that the blues began as an art form after the Civil War. The form is thought to be a hybrid of the African-American work song and the SPIRITUAL. The blues are thought to have originated in the Mississippi Delta region of the southern United States, but also to have deep roots in Georgia and Texas. One of the first singers popularly associated with the blues was Huddy Ledbelly who was one of the first 19th-century celebrities of the genre. One of the first popular blues songs was W. C. Handy's "Memphis Blues."

In the 1920s the first blues recordings appeared by such luminaries as Ma Rainey, BESSIE SMITH, Mamie Smith, and Ida Cox. The blues are said to have moved north with African Americans in the GREAT MIGRATION and by the 1930s and 1940s, the heart of the blues was in the urban North, particularly in the midwestern mecca of Chicago.

The blues has been highly influential in the development of contemporary popular music, from rock to jazz. Many of the most popular rock musicians, including the Beatles and the Rolling Stones, name the blues and blues musicians as their primary source of inspiration.

The blues are often cited by literary critics as a primary influence in Morrison's novels.

BIBLIOGRAPHY

Charters, Samuel B. *The Bluesmakers.* New York: Da Capo, 1991.

———. *The Roots of the Blues.* Salem, N.H.: Marion Boyars, 1981.

Cohn, Lawrence. *Nothing but the Blues: the Music and the Musicians.* New York: Abbeville, 1993.

Davis, Angela Yvonne. *Blues Legacies and Black Feminism: Gertrude "Ma" Rainey, Bessie Smith, and Billie Holiday.* New York: Pantheon Books, 1998.

Davis, Francis. *The History of the Blues.* New York: Hyperion, 1995.

Epstein, Dana. *Sinful Tunes and Spirituals: Black Folk Music to the Civil War.* Urbana: University of Illinois Press, 1977.

Erlewine, Michael, ed. *All Music Guide to the Blues.* San Francisco: Miller Freeman, 1996.

Harrison, Daphne Duval. *Black Pearls: Blues Queens of the 1920s.* New Brunswick, N.J.: Rutgers University Press, 1988.

Herzhaft, Gerand. *Encyclopedia of the Blues.* Fayetteville: University of Arkansas Press, 1992.

Jones, Leroi. *Blues People: Negro Music in White America.* New York: Morrow, 1963.

Keil, Charles. *Urban Blues.* Chicago: University of Chicago Press, 1966.

Leadbitter, Mike, ed. *Nothing but the Blues.* New York: Hanover Books, 1971.

Lomax, Alan. *The Land Where the Blues Began.* New York: Pantheon Books, 1993.

McKee, Margaret, and Fred Chisenhall. *Beale Black and Blue: Life and Music on Black America's Main Street.* New Orleans: Louisiana State University Press, 1981.

Moses, Cat. "The Blues Aesthetic in Toni Morrison's *The Bluest Eye,*" *African American Review* 33, no. 4 (Winter 1999): 623.

Oliver, Paul. *Blues Fell This Morning: Meaning in the Blues.* Cambridge: Cambridge University Press, 1990.

Palmer, Robert. *Deep Blues.* New York: Penguin, 1981.

Rubenstein, Roberta. "Singing the Blues/Reclaiming Jazz: Toni Morrison and Cultural Morning," *Mosaic* 31, no. 2 (June 1998): 147–164.

Sackheim, Eric, ed. *The Blues Line: A Collection of Blues Lyrics.* New York: Ecco Press, 1993.

Santelli, Robert. *The Best of the Blues: The 101 Essential Albums.* New York: Penguin, 1997.

Southern, Eileen. *Music of Black Americans: A History,* 3rd ed. New York: W.W. Norton, 1997.

Welding, Pete, and Toby Byron. *Bluesland.* New York: Dutton, 1991.

Woods, Clyde Adrian. *Development Arrested: The Blues and Plantation Power in the Mississippi Delta.* London: Verso, 1998.

Brooks, Gwendolyn (1917–2000) Although she was known primarily as a poet, Gwendolyn Brooks also wrote novels, essays, and children's literature. She was one of the most highly regarded American literary figures of the 20th century. Her birthplace, Topeka, Kansas, was not the location Brooks called home. For most of her life, Brooks lived in Chicago, Illinois. The experiences she had in that city colored all of her writing.

From a very early age, Brooks was drawn to writing and saw language as fundamental to her existence. Brooks's parents, Keziah Wims Brooks and David Anderson Brooks, encouraged their daughter and her younger brother, Raymond, to pursue education and the fine arts, including writing and music. Despite this affirmation from home, Brooks faced both discrimination from whites and exclusion from some blacks as a result of her class and her color. Reading and writing provided a sanctuary for Brooks from the insults and injuries of everyday life as a dark-skinned African-American girl.

Early in her adolescence, Brooks began to publish her poetry and, after finishing high school, completed an associate degree in English. In 1939, Brooks married Henry Blakely. The next year the couple gave birth to their first child, Henry. A daughter, Nora, was born in 1951. Brooks had a life-altering experience when she became a protégé of Inez Cunningham Stark who ran a series of poetry workshops for African-American writers. From these workshops, Brooks honed her poetic craftsmanship, continued publishing, and began to have a reputation in the Chicago area. Her first book of poetry, *A Street in Bronzeville,* was published in 1945 and received a great deal of positive critical reception. *A Street in Bronzeville* launched Brooks's career and established her as an important emerging voice in American letters, which was, at the time, a nearly unprecedented achievement for an African American.

With the publication of her next book of poems, *Annie Allen* (1949), Brooks's literary reputation was set. Not only did *Annie Allen* receive critical acclaim, but also, as a result of the publication, Brooks became the first African American to win the coveted Pulitzer Prize in literature. In 1953, Brooks published her only novel, *Maud Martha.* As Brooks's career progressed, she became increasingly intrigued with the more experimental forms of writing introduced and promoted by those espousing the BLACK AESTHETIC. She began to transform her understanding of the purpose of her writing to one that focused on the conditions and realities of African-American communities and to their liberation.

Her poetry became more reliant on free verse and less willing to conform to the expectations of the literary establishment. Her subjects shifted to a more direct examination of African-American urban life. In a show of solidarity with the quest for black self-sufficiency, Brooks left her publisher, Harper and Row, and signed with the black-owned Broadside Press. In 1968, Brooks was appointed as poet laureate of Illinois and received many literary awards throughout her career, including the National Book Foundation Award for Distinguished Contribution to American Letters. During her career, Brooks published more than 20 books of poetry. Gwendolyn Brooks died in December 2000 of cancer. The Gwendolyn Brooks Center for Creative Writing and Black Literature at Chicago State University, founded by Haki Madhubuti, continues to support her legacy and her commitment to nurturing young writers.

Many contemporary writers and artists, including Toni Morrison, cite Gwendolyn Brooks as an important influence on their work.

BIBLIOGRAPHY

Bloom, Harold, ed. Philadelphia: Chelsea House, 2000.

Brooks, Gwendolyn. *A Street in Bronzeville.* New York: Harper, 1945.

———. *Annie Allen.* New York: Harper, 1949.

———. *The Bean Eaters.* New York: Harper, 1960.

———. *Bronzeville Boys and Girls.* New York: Harper, 1956.

———. *In the Mecca.* New York: Harper, 1968.

———. *Maud Martha.* New York: Harper, 1953.

———. *Report from Part One.* Detroit: Broadside, 1972.

———. *Report from Part Two.* Chicago: Third World, 1995.

———. *Primer for Blacks.* Chicago: Brooks, 1980.

Gayles, Gloria Wade, ed. *Conversations with Gwendolyn Brooks.* Jackson: University Press of Mississippi, 2003.

Kent, George E. *A Life of Gwendolyn Brooks.* Lexington: University Press of Kentucky, 1990.

Madhubuti, Haki R., ed. *Say That the River Turns: The Impact of Gwendolyn Brooks.* Chicago: Third World Press, 1987.

Melhem, D. H. *Gwendolyn Brooks: Poetry and the Heroic Voice.* Lexington: University Press of Kentucky, 1987.

Mootry, Maria K., and Gary Smith, eds. *A Life Distilled: Gwendolyn Brooks, Her Poetry and Fiction.* Urbana: University of Illinois Press, 1987.

Shaw, Harry B. *Gwendolyn Brooks.* Boston: Twayne, 1980.

Wright, Stephen Caldwell. *The Chicago Collective: Poems for and Inspired by Gwendolyn Brooks.* Sanford, Fla.: Christopher-Burghardt, 1990.

———. *On Gwendolyn Brooks: Reliant Contemplation.* Ann Arbor: University of Michigan Press, 1996.

Brown v. The Board of Education of Topeka, Kansas

This landmark 1954 Supreme Court case was the culmination of many years of legal effort to end the practice of segregation legitimated with the 1896 Supreme Court decision PLESSY V. FERGUSON. The *Plessy* decision arose as a result of the defense of Homer Plessy who was accused by officials of the East Louisiana Railroad of violating a Louisiana law that mandated that railroads provide separate accommodations on all of the passenger trains that traveled through the state. The law, passed in Louisiana in 1890, mandated that passengers who were found sitting in the "wrong" compartment would be fined $25 or could spend 20 days in jail.

Homer Plessy sat in the white section of a railroad car and was jailed as a result. Plessy was found to be in violation of the law. Unwilling to accept this injustice, and the fundamental violation of the Thirteenth and Fourteenth Amendments to the U.S. Constitution that the Louisiana law represented, Plessy attempted to assert his rights in court. In 1896, the Supreme Court heard the case, *Plessy v. Ferguson,* and found that Plessy was in violation of the Louisiana law. The Court made its decision with an eight to one ruling that asserted that there was a difference between the equality guaranteed by the Thirteenth Amendment and Fourteenth Amendments and the separation or distinction between the races mandated by the Louisiana law. In other words, the Court asserted that social and political equality could be considered as separate conditions. With this ruling, the Court established the legality and constitutionality of separate but equal.

From the date of the *Plessy* decision, African Americans began the struggle to overturn this legal obstacle. The National Organization for the Advancement of Colored People (NAACP) was one of the many organizations whose political, economic, and legal energies were directed to overcoming the precedent established by the *Plessy* decision. These efforts culminated in 1952 with the presentation of the *Brown v. The Board of Education* case to the U.S. Supreme Court by NAACP lawyer Thurgood Marshall. The argument in the Brown case was a conglomerate of several cases from Delaware, Kansas, South Carolina, and Delaware. The specifics of the case *Brown v. The Board of Education of Topeka, Kansas* involved a fifth-grade girl, Linda Brown, and her legal inability to attend an all-white elementary school close to her residence that had better facilities and funding than the black school that she attended. Linda Brown's father, Oliver Brown, is the Brown named as the litigant in the *Brown* case. The *Brown* case was representative of the others, all of which involved the issue of the inequality of segregated public education. The Brown argument entailed demonstrating that separate was not equal.

The Supreme Court heard the case, but did not give its decision until nearly two years later. The Court, headed by Chief Justice Earl Warren, finally gave its decision on May 17, 1954. In a unanimous decision, the justices found the *Plessy v. Ferguson* decision in violation of the Constitution and declared that the segregation of public schools was also unconstitutional. The decision was a major step forward in the fight for civil rights that African Americans had been actively pursuing since emancipation. The decision was controversial and met with resistance throughout the South. The case provided the legal justification for the federal government's intervention in the state of Arkansas's resistance to the integration of Central High School in Little Rock. The public school system in Prince Edward County, Virginia, closed rather than desegregate. The issue of school desegregation, catalyzed by the *Brown* decision, provided the legal basis for the strategies and actions of those individuals and organizations involved in the CIVIL RIGHTS MOVEMENT of the 1950s and 1960s.

In 2004, Toni Morrison published a book for young readers reflecting on the consequences of the *Brown* decision entitled *Remember: The Journey to School Integration.* The book marked the 50th anniversary of the *Brown* decision and won the 2005 Coretta Scott King Author Award.

BIBLIOGRAPHY

Bates, Daisy. *The Long Shadow of Little Rock, A Memoir.* New York: David McKay, 1962.

Beals, Melba Pattillo. *Warriors Don't Cry: A Searing Memoir of the Battle to Integrate Little Rock's Central High.* New York: Pocket Books, 1994.

Cottrol, Robert, Raymond T. Diamond, Leland B. Ware, and Leland Ware. *Brown v. Board of Education: Caste, Culture, and the Constitution.* Lawrence: University Press of Kansas, 2003.

Friedman, Leon, ed. *Argument: The Complete Oral Argument before the Supreme Court in Brown v. Board of Education of Topeka, 1952–1955.* New York: Chelsea House, 1969.

Greenberg, Jack. *Crusaders in the Courts: How a Dedicated Band of Lawyers Fought for the Civil Rights Revolution.* New York: Basic Books, 1994.

Kluger, Richard. *Simple Justice: The History of Brown v. Board of Education and Black America's Struggle for Equality.* New York: Knopf, 1976.

Margo, Robert. *Accounting for Racial Differences in School Attendance in the American South, 1900: The Role of Separate-But-Equal.* Cambridge, Mass.: National Bureau of Economic Research, 1987.

———. *Race and Schooling in the South, 1880–1950: An Economic History.* Chicago: University of Chicago Press, 1990.

———. *Segregated Schools and the Mobility Hypothesis: A Model of Local Government Discrimination.* Cambridge: National Bureau of Economic Research, 1990.

———. *The Competitive Dynamics of Racial Exclusion: Employment Segregation in the South, 1900–1950.* Cambridge: National Bureau of Economic Research, 1990.

———. *The Decline in Black Teenage Labor Force Participation in the South, 1900–1970: The Role of Schooling.* Cambridge: National Bureau of Economic Research, 1991.

Martin, Waldo E., Jr. *Brown v. Board of Education: A Brief History with Documents.* Boston: Bedford/St. Martin's, 1998.

McGee, Leo, and Robert Boone, eds. *The Black Rural Landowner? Endangered Species: Social, Political, and Economic Implications.* Westport, Conn.: Greenwood Press, 1979.

Morrison, Toni. *Remember: The Journey to School Integration.* Boston: Houghton Mifflin, 2004.

Orfield, Gary, and Susan E. Eaton. *Dismantling Desegregation: The Quiet Reversal of Brown v. Board of Education.* New York: New Press, 1996.

Patterson, James T. *Brown v. Board of Education: A Civil Rights Milestone and Its Troubled Legacy.* Oxford and New York: Oxford University Press, 2001.

Smith, Bob. *They Closed Their Schools: Prince Edward County, Virginia, 1951–1964.* Chapel Hill: University of North Carolina Press, 1965.

Tackach, James. *Brown v. Board of Education.* San Diego: Lucent Books, 1998.

Tushnet, Mark V. *The NAACP Legal Strategy against Segregated Education, 1925–1950.* Chapel Hill: University of North Carolina Press, 1987.

Wolters, Raymond. *The Burden of Brown: Thirty Years of School Desegregation.* Knoxville: University of Tennessee Press, 1984.

Caliban Caliban is the name of Shakespeare's servant/beast character in the play *The Tempest* (1611). *The Tempest* takes place on an island that is under the control of an exiled king, Prospero. Caliban, the son of the hag Sycorax, is the only native inhabitant of the island to appear in the play.

Caliban has a vexed relationship with his master, Prospero. He claims that Prospero stole the island from him and that the land is rightfully his. He and the characters Stefano and Trinculo plot unsuccessfully to murder Prospero. Caliban is often understood as a foil to Prospero's other servant, Ariel, who is said to be of the air and who willingly obeys Prospero's commands. At the end of the play, Caliban seems to be humiliated and back in Prospero's complete control and command.

Because of his status as a slave and his claims to be the rightful owner of the land, Caliban has been read allegorically as a representation of the enslaved workers of the New World—Africans and Native Americans—who were in a similar position to that of Caliban in *The Tempest*.

The character of Caliban has had particular theoretical potency for postcolonial writers in the Caribbean. In 1969, Aime Cesaire wrote *A Tempest* a response to the Shakespearian play; it repositions Caliban as a dignified and oppressed individual who demands of Prospero the return of what is rightly his and an end to the exploitation he has experienced at Prospero's hands.

In 1971, Cuban literary and cultural critic Roberto Fernandez Retamar wrote a seminal essay, entitled "Caliban: Notes toward a Discussion of Culture in Our America," in which Caliban figures as a symbol of both the oppression and resistance experienced and manifested by Caribbean peoples. Caliban has become an important symbol of both colonial tyranny and postcolonial quests for autonomy and identity. Some literary critics suggest that Son, one of Morrison's central characters in *Tar Baby* (1981), alludes to Caliban.

BIBLIOGRAPHY

Cartelli, Thomas. "After the Tempest: Shakespeare, Postcoloniality, and Michele Cliff's New, New World Miranda," *Contemporary Literature* 36 (Spring 1995): 82–102.

Césaire, Aimé. *A Tempest.* New York: Editions du Seuil, 1992.

Retamar, Roberto Fernandez. "Caliban: Notes toward a Discussion of Culture in Our America." In *Caliban and Other Essays.* Minneapolis: University of Minnesota Press, 1989.

Rodó, José Enrique. *Ariel.* Cambridge: Cambridge University Press, 1967.

Cane (1923)   See JEAN TOOMER

Catherine the Great (Sophia Augusta Frederica, Ekaterina Alexeevna, Catherine II) (1729–1796) Although she is best known as a monarch in Russia, Catherine the Great was actually born into a German royal family. When she was born in 1729, the area now known as Poland was then German.

Her birth name was Sophia Augusta Frederica. At the age of 15, Sophia was betrothed to the heir to the Russian throne and moved to St. Petersburg to meet and marry her new husband.

At the time of her marriage, Sophia converted to the Russian Orthodox religion and consequently took the name Ekaterina, Catherine. Although she was quite young, Catherine was deeply invested in acquiring knowledge and became intellectually and politically astute, mainly through reading and writing, so much so that in 1762, at age 33, she had garnered enough support and resources to overthrow her husband, Peter III, who had become emperor the year before. Catherine became one of the most successful monarchs in Russian history. Catherine's reign worked primarily because she enjoyed the support of the aristocracy at the expense of the impoverished classes. In spite of this discrimination against the poor, Catherine did work to increase educational opportunities and expanded Russian territory through war.

In 1796, Catherine died rather suddenly of a stroke. She was succeeded on the throne by her son, Paul I. Toni Morrison references Catherine the Great in her novel, *Tar Baby* (1981). While he examines a photospread she is in, Jadine tells Son that she is wearing earrings that belonged to Catherine the Great.

BIBLIOGRAPHY

Alexander, T. *Catherine the Great: Life and Legend.* Oxford: Oxford University Press, 1989.

Catherine the Great. The Memoirs of Catherine the Great, tr. Moira Budberg. London: Hamish Hamilton, 1955.

de Madariaga, Isabel. *Catherine the Great: A Short History.* New Haven, Conn.: Yale University Press, 1991.

———. *Politics and Culture in Eighteenth Century Russia.* New York: Longmans, 1998.

———. *Russia in the Age of Catherine the Great.* London: Phoenix Press, 2002.

Leonard, Carol S. *Reform and Regicide: the Reign of Peter III of Russia.* Bloomington: Indiana University Press, 1992.

Raeff, Marc, ed. *Catherine the Great, A Profile.* New York: Hill and Wang, 1972.

Reddaway, W. E. *Documents of Catherine the Great.* Cambridge: Cambridge University Press, 1931.

chain gang Following the Civil War, groups of prisoners were often involuntarily forced to work while imprisoned. These groups of prisoners were frequently chained together while they worked and were therefore called chain gangs. African Americans were frequently the individuals who were forced to work on chain gangs; many of these individual were also wrongly imprisoned. Because of the prevalence of African Americans who were used for their free labor on chain gangs, as well as the large percentage of those prisoners who were imprisoned even though they had committed no crime, the chain gangs are understood by some historians to be an extension of slavery. African Americans who were in the SHARECROPPING system also frequently became imprisoned and ended up as captives on chain gangs. The sharecropping system required that African Americans work the land and produce an unrealistic profit. When they were unable to meet the impossible goal set for them by the landowner or employer, sometimes their debt was criminalized and the individuals would be sent to jail and then made to work on chain gangs as punishment.

Labor from prisoners on chain gangs was largely responsible for the construction of the highways and railroads of the United States, particularly in the South. Investigative reports during the 1950s and 1960s brought public attention to the abuses of chain gang labor and, as a result, the practice receded from large-scale implementation. Even though chain gangs do not exist on the scale they did in the past, during the last 20 years there has been a resurgence in the practice of using prisoners for labor.

In *Beloved* (1987), Paul D is sold to a chain gang after he tries to escape from Sweet Home.

BIBLIOGRAPHY

Booker, Christopher B. *I Will Wear No Chain!: A Social History of African-American Males.* Westport, Conn.: Praeger Publishers, 2000.

Burley, Lynn M. "History Repeats Itself in the Resurrection of Prisoner Chain Gangs: Alabama's Experience Raises Eighth Amendment Concerns," *Law and Inequality* 15, no. 127 (Winter 1997).

Burns, Robert E. *I Am a Fugitive from the Georgia Chain Gang.* New York: Vanguard, 1932.

Burns, Vincent Godfrey. *The Man Who Broke a Thousand Chains; The Story of Social Reformation of the Prisons of the South.* Washington, D.C.: Acropolis Books, 1968.

"Continuing Cruelties in the Convict Chain Gangs and Camps of the Southern United States." London: Howard Association, 1901.

Gorman, Tessa M. "Back on the Chain Gang: Why the Eighth Amendment and the History of Slavery Proscribe the Resurgence of Chain Gangs," *California Law Review* 85, no. 441 (March 1997).

Mancini, Matthew J. *One Dies, Get Another: Convict Leasing in the American South, 1866–1928.* Columbia: University of South Carolina Press, 1996.

Morris, Norval, and David J. Rothman. *The Oxford History of the Prison: The Practice of Punishment in Western Society.* Oxford: Oxford University Press, 1995.

Mosely, Walter. *Workin' on the Chain Gang: Shaking Off the Dead Hand of History.* New York: Ballantine Books, 2000.

Rustin, Bayard. "Twenty-Two Days on a Chain Gang." In *Down the Line: The Collected Writings of Bayard Rustin.* Chicago: Quadrangle Books, 1971.

Spivak, John L. *Georgia Nigger.* Montclair, N.J.: Patterson Smith, 1969.

***Chicago Defender,* the**   African-American newspapers, newspapers that were largely written and produced by African Americans for a mostly African-American audience, were an essential and influential community institution in the United States. One of the most influential of these papers was the *Chicago Defender,* based in Chicago, Illinois. The paper began its circulation in 1905 and was headed by Robert S. Abbott. Abbott did not shy away from controversial and forthright exposés of the realities of racism in the United States. From the beginning the *Defender* covered lynchings, riots, and the brutality that was the norm for African Americans at the beginning of the century, particularly in the South. The paper began to have a wide circulation in the South and was one of the catalysts of the mass migration of African Americans from the South to the North, known as the GREAT MIGRATION.

The *Chicago Defender* reached its peak circulation around mid-century. One of its lasting influences was its support of African-American artists. Several writers got their start or cultivated a wide reading audience because of their publication in the paper. Two well-known African-American writers who appeared in the *Defender* were Gwendolyn Brooks and Langston Hughes. Although its circulation is greatly reduced, the *Chicago Defender* is still being published in 2006.

BIBLIOGRAPHY

Best, Wallace. "*The Chicago Defender* and the Realignment of Black Chicago," *Chicago History* 24 (1995): 4–21.

DeSantis, Alan D. *Selling the American Dream: The Chicago Defender and the Great Migration of 1915–1919.* Bloomington: Indiana University Press, 1993.

Grossman, James R. "Blowing the Trumpet: *The Chicago Defender* and the Black Migration during World War I," *Illinois Historical Journal* 78 (1986): 82–96.

Kornweibel, Theodore, Jr. "'The Most Dangerous of all Negro Journals': Federal Efforts to Suppress *The Chicago Defender* during World War I," *American Journalism* 11 (1994): 154–168.

Perry, Earnest L., Jr. "A Common Purpose: The Negro Newspaper Publishers Association's Fight for Equality during World War II," *American Journalism* 19 (2000): 31–43.

Stovall, Mary E. "*The Chicago Defender* in the Progressive Era," *Illinois Historical Journal* 83 (1990): 159–172.

Strother, T. Ella. "The Black Image in the *Chicago 'Defender,'* 1905–1975," *Journalism History* 4 (1977–78): 137–141, 156.

Chicken Little   There are many versions of this tale, whose origins are unclear, but the basic story is as follows: Chicken Little is the children's tale of a small chick who is struck on her head by a falling acorn and concludes that the sky is falling. She rushes off to tell the king, and, along the way, she warns others with the refrain "The sky is falling!" Everyone she meets—including such animals as Henny Penny, Goosey Loosey, and Lucky Ducky—panics and joins her to tell the king. But one animal does not believe it: Foxy Woxy, who tries to lure them all to his den with the promise of a short cut to the king. His real intention is to eat them all. There are many versions to the ending. In one, for instance, the animals are eaten, in another, one animal warns the others, and in still another they are saved at the last minute by the king's hunting dogs, who scare Foxy Woxy out of the realm.

The character of Chicken Little has worked itself into a culture reference for a person who becomes unduly afraid of something that is actually harmless, while perhaps ignoring a true danger. Another moral of the story is to beware of those people—in the form of the fox—who would take advantage of mass hysteria. Chicken Little is a dismissive term, used to either calm fears, insult the concerned party, or both. The refrain "the sky is falling" is similarly used in this dismissive fashion. The story has appeared many times in books, movies, and television.

In *Sula* (1973), the character, Chicken Little, is a young boy who is accidentally drowned in the river when Sula inadvertently lets go of his hands while she swings him in circles.

chitterlings   During slavery, most African Americans were limited in their basic sustenance, including their food supply. Frequently those who were enslaved were provided with only the remnants of the food supply. Often the staples they were provided were molasses and the offal of the meat, specifically the parts of the pig that the whites would not generally eat—ears, feet, bones, intestines, stomach, and anything else that could be scavenged. The creativity of African Americans materialized with the transformation of these scraps into not only edible, but also delicious cuisine that would come to be called soul food.

The dish known as chitterlings was among the most well-known specialties of soul food. Chitterlings are made from pig's intestines. Before the dish is prepared, the intestines are carefully cleaned. They are soaked and rinsed several times until it is certain that all debris has been removed. Traditionally the intestines are then boiled until they are soft. After they are boiled, chitterlings then are stewed along with other ingredients and seasonings or fried in a flour and seasoning batter. The consumption of chitterlings has decreased with time as discoveries about the potential health risks of eating high-fat foods have become more apparent. Chitterlings and soul food, however, remain an important component of African-American culture as well as a reminder of the creative responses of African Americans to the deprivations imposed upon them by slavery.

Chitterlings are a meal in Morrison's *The Bluest Eye* (1970).

BIBLIOGRAPHY

Beoku-Betts, Josephine A. "We Got Our Way of Cooking Things: Women, Food, and Preservation of Cultural Identity among the Gullah," *Gender and Society* 9 (1995): 535–555.

Booth, Sally Smith. *Hung, Strung, and Potted: A History of Eating in Colonial America.* New York: Clarkson N. Potter, 1971.

Brown, L. K., and K. Mussell, eds. *Ethnic and Regional Foodways in the United States: The Performance of Group Identity.* Knoxville: University of Tennessee Press, 1995.

Burke, Cathryn Boyd, and Susan P. Raia. *Soul and Traditional Southern Food Practices, Customs, and Holidays.* Chicago: American Dietetic Association, 1995.

Burns, LaMont. *Down Home Southern Cooking.* New York: Doubleday and Company, 1987.

Dirks, R. T., and N. Duran. "African American Dietary Patterns at the Beginning of the 20th Century," *Journal of Nutrition* 131 (2000): 1,881–1,889.

Harris, Jessica. *Iron Pots and Wooden Spoons: Africa's Gift to the New World Cooking.* New York: Simon and Schuster, 1999.

Hilliard, Sam B. "Hogmeat and Cornpone: Foodways in the Antebellum South." In *Material Life in America 1600–1860,* edited by Robert Blair St. George, 311–328. Boston: Northeastern University Press, 1988.

Wilson, C. R., and W. Ferris. *The Encyclopedia of Southern Culture.* Chapel Hill: University of North Carolina Press, 1989.

Witt, Doris. *Black Hunger: Food and the Politics of U.S. Identity.* Oxford: Oxford University Press, 1999.

———. *Black Hunger: Soul Food and America.* Minneapolis: University of Minnesota Press, 2004.

Chopin, Kate (1851–1904)   Kate Chopin is one of the most revered of American writers. Although she was born in St. Louis, Missouri, she is associated with the South and is claimed as a southern writer.

She married her husband, Oscar Chopin, when she was 19 years old. Her husband died in 1882 of what was then called swamp fever, and at that time she returned to her home in St. Louis, Missouri, with her six children from her marriage.

Unlike many writers, Chopin did not begin to write until well into her adulthood. Chopin published her first poem in 1889. Much of her writing concerns the lives of women and her novels and short stories were often an implicit critique of the limitations placed on women's lives by the traditional roles imposed upon them. Much of her writing has as its central locale Louisiana and the South. Eventually, doubting her abilities, Chopin stopped writing altogether, but during her 10 years or so as a creative writer, Chopin produced some classic works of American fiction, including her novel, *The Awakening* (1899), and many short stories.

Chopin died in 1904 of a brain hemorrhage at the age of 53. Chopin's work fell into obscurity until her writings received new appreciation and recognition in the wake of the renaissance of interest in women's literature that happened as a result of the feminist movement of the 1960s and 1970s. Morrison analyzes Chopin's work in her literary critical book, *Playing in the Dark* (1992).

BIBLIOGRAPHY

Barker, Deborah E. "The Awakening of Female Artistry." In *Kate Chopin Reconsidered: Beyond the Bayou,* edited by Lynda S. Boren and Sara de Saussure Davis, 61–79. Baton Rouge: Louisiana State University Press, 1992.

Bauer, Margaret D. "Armand Aubigny, Still Passing After All These Years: The Narrative Voice and Historical Context of 'Desiree's Baby.'" In *Critical Essays on Kate Chopin,* edited by Alice Hall Petry, 161–183. New York: G. K. Hall, 1996.

Bloom, Harold, ed. *Kate Chopin.* New York: Chelsea House, 1987.

Boren, Lynda S., and Sara Davis. eds. *Kate Chopin Reconsidered: Beyond the Bayou.* Baton Rouge: Louisiana State University Press, 1992.

Chopin, Kate. *At Fault.* St. Louis: Nixon-Jones Publishing, 1890.

———. *The Awakening.* Chicago and New York: Herbert S. Stone, 1899.

———. *The Complete Works of Kate Chopin,* edited by Per Seyersted. Baton Rouge: Louisiana State University Press, 1969.

Dyer, Joyce. *The Awakening: A Novel of Beginnings.* New York: Twayne, 1993.

Ewell, Barbara C. "Making Places: Kate Chopin and the Art of Fiction," *Louisiana Literature: A Review of Literature and Humanities* 11, no.1 (Spring 1994): 157–171.

Ficke, Thomas H., and Eva Gold eds. "Kate Chopin, Race, and Ethnicity," *Louisiana Literature: A Review of Literature and Humanities* 14, no. 2 (Fall 1997): 95–125.

Foy, Roslyn Reso. "Chopin's 'Desiree's Baby.'" *Explicator* 49 (Summer 1991): 222–223.

Koloski, Bernard. *Kate Chopin: A Study of the Short Fiction.* New York: Twayne, 1996.

Martin, Wendy, ed. *New Essays on The Awakening.* New York: Cambridge, 1988.

Morrison, Toni. *Playing in the Dark: Whiteness and the Literary Imagination.* Cambridge, Mass.: Harvard University Press, 1992.

Petry, Alice Hall, ed. *Critical Essays on Kate Chopin.* New York: G. K. Hall, 1996.

Platizky, Roger. "Chopin's *The Awakening,*" *Explicator* 53 (Winter 1995): 99–102.

Seyersted, Per. *Kate Chopin. A Critical Biography.* Baton Rouge: Louisiana State University Press, 1969.

Showalter, Elaine. *Sister's Choice: Tradition and Change in American Women's Writing.* Oxford: Oxford University Press, 1991.

Simons, Karen. "Kate Chopin on the Nature of Things," *Mississippi Quarterly* 51, no. 2 (Spring 1998): 243–252.

Skaggs, Peggy. *Kate Chopin.* Boston: Twayne, 1985.

Springer, Marlene. *Edith Wharton and Kate Chopin: A Reference Guide.* Boston: G. K. Hall, 1976.

Taylor, Helen. *Gender, Race, and Region in the Writings of Grace King, Ruth McEnery Stuart, and Kate Chopin.* Baton Rouge: Louisiana State University Press, 1989.

Thomas, Heather Kirk. "Kate Chopin's Scribbling Women and the American Literary Marketplace,"

Studies in American Fiction 23 (Spring 1995): 19–34.

Toth, Emily. *Kate Chopin*. New York: Morrow, 1990.

Tuttleton, James W. "A Solitary Soul: The Career of Kate Chopin," *The New Criterion* 9, no. 9 (April 1991): 12–17.

Walker, Nancy, ed. *The Awakening: Kate Chopin*. Boston: Bedford Books of St. Martin's Press, 1993.

Cincinnati, Ohio   The city of Cincinnati, Ohio, was founded in 1788. At the time of its founding, it was called Losantville. The name of the city was changed to Cincinnati in 1790. Cincinnati had its largest period of growth at the height of the steamship era when steamboats became the primary form of interstate transportation early in the 19th century.

In addition to its prominence as a port for the steamship industry, Cincinnati was an important location for hog slaughtering, packing, and transportation. The river also became a porous boundary for escaping slaves trying to cross from the slave state of Kentucky to the free state of Ohio. For this reason, Cincinnati became a center of ABOLITIONist activity and a major hub for the system of escape from slavery known as the UNDERGROUND RAILROAD. Harriet Beecher Stowe's father, Lyman Beecher, relocated from New England to Cincinnati when he was appointed to a position at the Lane Theological Seminary. After Harriet Beecher Stowe moved to the city in 1832, her exposure to and involvement in the abolitionist movement led her to write *Uncle Tom's Cabin* (1852) as a work designed to garner support for the movement.

The location on the Ohio River where Margaret Garner, the real-life inspiration for the character Sethe in *Beloved,* is believed to have escaped from slavery in Kentucky to freedom in Ohio in January of 1856. It is the current location of the John A. Roebling Suspension Bridge. *(Photograph by Carmen R. Gillespie)*

MARGARET GARNER, the real-life inspiration for Morrison's Sethe in *Beloved* (1987), escaped from Boone County, Kentucky, to Cincinnati in 1856. Her subsequent trial was held in Cincinnati.

Today Cincinnati is a thriving metropolitan area and, after Cleveland, is the second largest city in Ohio.

BIBLIOGRAPHY

Architecture and Construction of Cincinnati: A Guide to Buildings, Designers and Builders. Cincinnati, Ohio: Architectural Foundation of Cincinnati, 1987.

Austerlitz, Emanuel H. *Cincinnati, From 1800 to 1875, A Condensed History of Cincinnati.* Cincinnati, Ohio: Bloch, 1875.

Clubbe, John. *Cincinnati Observed: Architecture and History.* Columbus: Ohio State University Press, 1992.

Dabney, Wendell Phillip. *Cincinnati's Colored Citizens: Historical, Sociological and Biographical.* New York: Negro Universities Press, 1926.

Wimberg, Robert J. *Cincinnati Over-the-Rhine.* Cincinnati: The Ohio Book Store, 1987.

Circe   In Greek mythology, Circe is the daughter of the sun god Helios and the sea nymph Perseis. The characteristics given to Circe vary with the sources of the references to her. She has been described alternately as a GODDESS, a nymph, and as an immortal sorceress. Nearly all accounts of Circe cast her as the inhabitant of an island, Aeaea, which is located variously by different authors off the eastern coast of Italy or on the promontory of Circeii in Latinum, south of Rome.

According to scholars, as a mythological figure Circe may be a survival from the religions of pre-Hellenic matriarchal societies. In these cultures, women, because of their role as child-bearers, were associated with the mysteries of life and death and the natural climatic cycles of regeneration and decay. There are at least three significant references to Circe in Greek mythology. Circe appears in the tale of Scylla, the legend of Jason and the Golden Fleece, and in the quest of Odysseus. In the Scylla narrative, Circe falls in love with a minor sea god, Glanaus. This god approaches Circe on her island and she believes that he comes to her with the intention of declaring his love for her. Glanaus's purpose in going to Circe's island, however, is to request from her a love potion so that he can use it to seduce the sea nymph Scylla. Glanaus's request outrages Circe and she reacts by making him a potion that, instead of seducing Scylla, transforms her into a malicious beast.

During his quest for the Golden Fleece, Jason seduces Circe's niece, the sorceress Medea. With Medea's assistance, Jason steals the Golden Fleece and murders Medea's father, Apsyntus, Circe's brother. Jason and Medea then come to Circe's island to request forgiveness and absolution for Medea. Circe grants their request; however, the couple does not tell Circe the whole truth about their deeds. When she learns the truth, she drives them from the island.

Lost in his journeying, Odysseus and his men happen upon Circe's island, Aeaea. Depending on the version of the story, Circe transforms Odysseus's men into beasts or stones. Odysseus avoids Circe's spell because of the protective power of a herb given to him by Hermes, the son of Zeus. Eventually, Circe frees the men from her spells after falling in love with Odysseus. Odysseus remains with Circe on Aeaea for five years. In a later version of the story, following Odysseus's death, his wife Penelope and his son Telemachus come to Aeaea. Circe gives them both immortality and Telemachus marries Circe.

As these stories suggest, Circe seems to be an ancient symbol of the powerful woman. This figure may have become threatening in stories that come from a male-dominated culture in which strong women are often portrayed as evil. In spite of the probable change in the characteristics of Circe, her original significance as a figure that can control and manipulate the forces of life and death is still present in the stories about her that survive. Morrison creates a southern and African-American Circe with her character of the same name in *Song of Solomon* (1977).

BIBLIOGRAPHY

Aurbach, Erich. *Mimesis: The Representation of Reality in Western Literature.* Princeton, N.J.: Princeton University Press, 1953.

Camps, W. A. *An Introduction to Homer.* Oxford: Clarendon Press, 1980.

Homer. *The Odyssey of Homer,* translated by Richmond Lattimore. New York: Harper and Row, 1975.

Yarnall, Judith. *Transformations of Circe: The History of an Enchantress.* Urbana: University of Illinois Press, 1994.

Civil Rights movement The Civil Rights movement in the United States was the struggle for African Americans to achieve equality and citizenship as provided for white males in the Declaration of Independence and the Constitution. Throughout African-American history there have been two major strains of thought regarding the nature of what the African-American struggle for equality consisted of, how that battle was to be waged, and what the ultimate objective or prize would be. These two major intellectual and political beliefs, known generally by the labels integrationism and separatism, were held by individuals who, for the most part, adhered to the notions that the solutions to the African-American problem could be achieved either through fighting for the right to assimilate and integrate into American society or through strengthening African-American communities from within and developing them as separate communities, largely independent from American society as a whole.

The Civil Rights movement of the late 1950s and early to mid-1960s was largely based upon the integrationist school of thought elaborated by men and women such as Frederick Douglass, Anna Julia Cooper, Frances Ellen Watkins Harper, W. E. B. DuBois, Walter White, Septima Clark, Diane Nash and MARTIN LUTHER KING JR.

The black church through slavery and up through the first half of the 20th century was the stronghold and organizing center of the African-American community. Although legally begun by various experts within African-American political organizations such as the NAACP in the early decades of the 20th century, the Civil Rights movement of the 1950s and '60s took place largely through the actions and support of black Christian churches. The main strategy of the Civil Rights movement was to confront racist and segregationist laws and practices with nonviolent direct action. This strategy manifested in boycotts, sit-ins, and other nonviolent protests that forced confrontation and examination of the practice of JIM CROW segregation in public life, housing, schooling, and voting practices.

In the mid- to late 1960s, there occurred a major schism in the Civil Rights movement between those who favored integration and those younger people who abandoned the principles of the early movement in favor of nationalism, separatism, communism, or socialism, in other words, for a multiplicity of ideologies.

This ideological split in the intellectual and activist community marked the beginning of the disintegration of integrationism and nonviolent direct action as the dominant strategic tool of the Civil Rights movement. The actions of the individuals involved in the Civil Rights movement brought about the 1954 Supreme Court decision BROWN V. THE BOARD OF EDUCATION, which rendered illegal segregated schooling, and various voting rights acts, the 1961 Interstate Commerce Commission's ban on segregation in pubic transportation, and the Civil Rights Act of 1964.

Morrison's works are centrally concerned with the issues of the Civil Rights movement.

BIBLIOGRAPHY

Anderson, Carol. *Eyes off the Prize: The United Nations and the African-American Struggle for Human Rights, 1944–1955.* Cambridge, U.K.: Cambridge University Press, 2003.

Blake, John. *Children of the Movement.* Chicago: Lawrence Hill Books, 2004.

Bloom, Jack M. *Class, Race, and the Civil Rights Movement.* Bloomington: Indiana University Press, 1987.

Borstelmann, Thomas. *The Cold War and the Color Line: American Race Relations in the Global Arena.* Cambridge, Mass.: Harvard University Press, 2003.

Branch, Taylor. *Parting the Waters: America in the King Years, 1954–1963.* New York: Simon and Schuster, 1988.

———. *Pillar of Fire. America in the King Years, 1963–1965.* New York: Simon and Schuster, 1998.

Campbell, Clarice. *Civil Rights Chronicle: Letters from the South.* Oxford: University Press of Mississippi, 1997.

Chafe, William Henfy. *Civilities and Civil Rights: Greensboro, North Carolina and the Struggle for Freedom.* Oxford: Oxford University Press, 1990.

Davis, Townsend. *Weary Feet, Rested Souls: A Guided History of the Civil Rights Movement.* New York: W. W. Norton, 1998.

Dierenfield, Bruce J. *The Civil Rights Movement.* White Plains, N.Y.: Longman, 2004.

Dudziak, Mary L. *Cold War Civil Rights: Race and the Image of American Democracy.* Princeton, N.J.: Princeton University Press, 2002.

Eskew, Glenn T. *But for Birmingham: The Local and National Movements in the Civil Rights Struggle.* Chapel Hill: University of North Carolina Press, 1997.

Eubanks, W. Ralph. *Ever Is a Long Time: A Journey into Mississippi's Dark Past: A Memoir.* New York: Basic Books, 2003.

Friedland, Michael B. *Lift Up Your Voice Like a Trumpet: White Clergy and the Civil Rights and Antiwar Movements, 1954–1973.* Chapel Hill: University of North Carolina Press, 1998.

Gaillard, Frye. *Cradle of Freedom: Alabama and the Movement That Changed America.* Tuscaloosa: University of Alabama Press, 2004.

Grant, Joanne. *Ella Baker: Freedom Bound.* Hoboken, N.J.: John Wiley and Sons, 1998.

Halberstam, David. *The Children.* New York: Random House, 1998.

Hansen, Drew D. *Dream: Martin Luther King, Jr. and the Speech That Inspired a Nation.* New York: HarperCollins, 2003.

Higham, John. *Civil Rights and Social Wrongs: Black-White Relations since World War II.* University Park: Pennsylvania State University Press, 1997.

Hill, Lance. *Deacons for Defense: Armed Resistance and the Civil Rights Movement.* Chapel Hill: University of North Carolina Press, 2004.

Honigsberg, Peter. *Crossing Border Street: A Civil Rights Memoir.* Berkeley: University of California Press, 2000.

Huckaby, Elizabeth. *Crisis at Central High, Little Rock, 1957–58.* Baton Rouge: Louisiana State University Press, 1980.

Lawson, Steven, and Charles Payne. *Debating the Civil Rights Movement: 1945–1968.* New York: Rowman and Littlefield, 1998.

Lee, Chana Kai. *For Freedom's Sake: The Life of Fannie Lou Hamer.* Champagne: University of Illinois Press, 2000.

Levy, Peter. *Civil War on Race Street: The Civil Rights Movement in Cambridge, Maryland.* Gainesville: University Press of Florida, 2003.

Litwack, Leon F. *Trouble in Mind: Black Southerners in the Age of Jim Crow.* New York: Alfred A. Knopf, 1998.

Manis, Andrew Michael. *A Fire You Can't Put Out: The Civil Rights Life of Birmingham's Reverend Fred Shuttlesworth.* Tuscaloosa: University of Alabama Press, 1999.

McKnight, Gerald D. *The Last Crusade: Martin Luther King, Jr., the F.B.I., and the People's Campaign.* Boulder, Colo.: Westview Press, 1998.

Moody, Anne. *Coming of Age in Mississippi.* New York: Dell, 1975.

Postgrove, Carol. *Divided Minds: Intellectuals and the Civil Rights Movement.* New York: Norton, 2001.

Ransby, Barbara. *Ella Baker and the Black Freedom Movement: A Radical Democratic Vision.* Chapel Hill: University of North Carolina Press, 2003.

Shakoor, Jordana Y. *Civil Rights Childhood.* Oxford: University Press of Mississippi, 1999.

Webb, Clive. *Fight against Fear: Southern Jews and Black Civil Rights.* Athens: University of Georgia Press, 2001.

Weisbrot, Robert. *Freedom Bound: A History of America's Civil Rights Movement.* New York: Plume, 1990.

Wexler, Sanford. *An Eyewitness History of the Civil Rights Movement.* New York: Facts On File, 1999.

Williams, Juan. *Eyes on the Prize: America's Civil Rights Years, 1954–65.* New York: Viking Press, 1987.

Young, Andrew. *An Easy Burden.* New York: HarperCollins, 1996.

Clabber Girl baking powder lady Clabber Girl baking powder has been a baking product since 1879, when the new powder was touted as faster and more consistent than other leavening agents of the time. Introduction of Clabber Girl baking powder made the Hulman family, owners of the process, wealthy.

On the original label was an image of a woman churning milk. Clabber is sour milk, though milk was not an ingredient in the baking powder. In 1923, a new label depicted a young woman holding a plate of biscuits while an elderly woman plucks a goose, children watch, and a kitten stalks a feather and a broken toy horse. The key feature of the label is the Clabber Girl herself, a young blonde girl, sometimes shown alone eating a biscuit or offering a tray of biscuits made with the baking powder.

In the 1930s, the Hulman family conducted a major advertising campaign to promote their product. Based in Terre Haute, Indiana, they sent salesmen across the country, nailing signs to roadside posts and knocking on the doors of homes to speak to the lady of the house. Despite the Great DEPRESSION, Clabber Girl sales rose to become a national brand.

In *Sula* (1973), Sula has a dream/hallucination about the Clabber Girl.

Cliff, Michelle (1946–   )   Michelle Cliff is an important contemporary writer whose writings expose the complex intersections of race, gender, sexuality, and colonialism. Cliff was born on the Caribbean island of Jamaica. Cliff's mother was a member of a black Jamaican family that was in a position of relative privilege as a result of the island's skin-color and class hierarchies.

When Cliff was a young girl, her family moved to the United States. Cliff and her family returned to Jamaica in 1956 to launch her father's ultimately unsuccessful ambition to begin his own business on the island. Eventually the family returned to the United States.

Cliff completed high school and college in the United States and then continued her studies on the graduate level in Europe. While in Europe, Cliff began to explore and acknowledge her identities as a black person and as a lesbian. When she came out as a lesbian, Cliff was estranged from her family.

When Cliff returned to the United States she worked as an editor and began to publish her own works, particularly poetry. Cliff continues to publish, focusing in recent years mainly on prose and fiction. While Toni Morrison worked at Random House, she was Cliff's editor. Cliff has held a number of teaching positions at various colleges and universities and shares her life with poet Adrienne Rich.

BIBLIOGRAPHY

Cartelli, Thomas. "After the Tempest: Shakespeare, Postcoloniality, and Michelle Cliff's New, New World Miranda," *Contemporary Literature* 36 (1995): 82–102.

Cliff, Michelle. *Abeng.* New York: Penguin, 1985.
———. *Bodies of Water.* New York: Dutton, 1990.
———. "History as Fiction, Fiction as History," *Ploughshares* 20 (1994): 196–202.
———. *Free Enterprise.* New York: Dutton, 1993.
———. *No Telephone to Heaven.* New York: Dutton, 1987.

Edmondson, Belinda. "Race, Writing, and the Politics of (Re)Writing History: An Analysis of the Novels of Michelle Cliff," *Callaloo* 16 (1993): 180–191.

Raiskin, Judith. "Inverts and Hybrids: Lesbian Rewritings of Sexual and Racial Identities." In *The Lesbian Postmodern,* edited by Laura Doan, 156–172. New York: Columbia University Press, 1994.
———. "The Art of History: An Interview with Michelle Cliff," *Kenyon Review* 15, no. 1 (1993): 57–71.

Schwartz, Meryl F. "An Interview with Michelle Cliff," *Contemporary Literature* 34, no. 4 (1993): 595–619.

Clifton, Lucille Sales (1936–   )   Lucille Clifton is one of the most prolific African-American poets. Clifton has been writing and publishing poetry for more than 30 years. Clifton was born in New York in 1936 to a working-class family that emphasized learning, particularly reading and writing. As a result of her parents' emphases and influences, Clifton completed high school and entered college at Howard University in Washington, D.C. While she was at Howard, she met her future husband, Fred Clifton. She also made the acquaintance of other fellow students who would become writers—Toni Morrison, who was known in her Howard days as Chloe Wofford, and the writer Amiri Baraka, who was known in his Howard days as LeRoi Jones. While at Howard, Clifton majored in drama.

After graduating from college, Clifton worked as a poet and as an actor. Clifton's first book of poems to be published was entitled *Good Times.* *Good Times* was published in 1969 to much critical acclaim. In addition to her poetry, Clifton began writing works of fiction for children. Clifton has published more than 20 children's books as well as more than 10 collections of poetry. When Toni Morrison was working at Random House, she worked with Clifton as her editor.

Clifton's personal life has been marked by many losses of friends and family, including the untimely deaths of her mother, husband, and daughter. Clifton herself has had numerous bouts of cancer and yet continues to write and to teach. She has been a finalist for the Pulitzer Prize in poetry and has served as the poet laureate for the state of Maryland.

BIBLIOGRAPHY

Clifton, Lucille. *Amifika.* New York: Dutton, 1977.

———. *An Ordinary Woman.* New York: Random House 1974.

———. *Everett Anderson's Nine Month Long.* New York: Henry Holt, 1978.

———. *The Book of Light.* Port Townsend, Wash.: Copper Canyon Press, 1993.

———. *The Boy Who Didn't Believe in Spring.* New York: Dutton, 1973.

———. *My Friend Jacob.* New York: Dutton, 1980.

———. *Three Wishes.* New York: Viking Press, 1976.

Bryant, Thema. "A Conversation with Lucille Clifton," *SAGE: A Scholarly Journal on Black Women* 2, no. 1 (Spring 1985): 52.

Holladay, Hilary. "'I Am Not Grown Away from You': Lucille Clifton's Elegies for Her Mother," *CLA Journal* 42, no. 4 (June 1999): 430–444.

———. "Song of Herself: Lucille Clifton's Poems about Womanhood." In *The Furious Flowering of African American Poetry,* edited by Joanne V. Gabbin. Charlottesville: University Press of Virginia, 1999.

Hull, Akasha. "In Her Own Images: Lucille Clifton and the Bible." In *Dwelling in Possibility: Women Poets and Critics on Poetry,* edited by Yopie Prins and Maeera Shreiber, 273–295. Ithaca, N.Y.: Cornell University Press, 1997

Johnson, Joyce. "The Theme of Celebration in Lucille Clifton's Poetry," *Pacific Coast Philology* 18, no. 1–2 (November 1983): 70–76.

Kallet, Marilyn. "Doing What You Will Do: An Interview with Lucille Clifton." In *Sleeping with One Eye Open: Women Writers and the Art of Survival,* edited by Marilyn Kallet and Judith O. Cofer, 80–81. Athens: University of Georgia Press, 1999.

Lazer, Hank. "Blackness Blessed: The Writings of Lucille Clifton." *Southern Review* 25, no. 3 (Summer 1989): 760–770.

Madhubuti, Haki. "Lucille Clifton: Warm Water, Greased Legs, and Dangerous Poetry." The *Black Women Writers (1950–1980): A Critical Evaluation,* edited by Mari Evans, 150–160. Garden City, N.Y.: Anchor-Doubleday, 1984.

Mance, Ajuan M. "Re-Locating the Black Female Subject: The Landscape of the Body in the Poems of Lucille Clifton." In *Recovering the Black Female Body: Self-Representations by African American Women,* edited by Michael Bennett and Vanessa D. Dickerson, 123–140. New Brunswick, N.J.: Rutgers University Press, 2001.

McCluskey, Audrey T. "Tell the Good News: A View of the Works of Lucille Clifton." In *Black Women Writers (1950–1980): A Critical Evaluation,* edited by Mari Evans, 139–149. Garden City, N.Y.: Anchor-Doubleday, 1984.

Ostriker, Alicia. "Kin and Kin: The Poetry of Lucille Clifton," *American Poetry Review* 22, no. 6 (November–December 1993): 41–48.

Rowell, Charles H. "An Interview with Lucille Clifton," *Callaloo* 22, no. 1 (Winter 1999): 56–72.

Rushing, Andrea B. "Lucille Clifton: A Changing Voice for Changing Times." In *Coming to Light: American Women Poets in the Twentieth Century,* edited by Diane W. Middlebrook and Marilyn Yalom, 214–222. Ann Arbor: University of Michigan Press, 1985.

Wall, Cheryl A. "Sifting Legacies in Lucille Clifton's Generations," *Contemporary Literature* 40, no. 4 (Winter 1999): 552–574.

White, Mark B. "Sharing the Living Light: Rhetorical, Poetic, and Social Identity in Lucille Clifton," *CLA Journal* 40, no. 3 (March 1997): 288–304.

Clotel; or, The President's Daughter: A Narrative of Slave Life in the United States (1854)

Published in 1854, *Clotel,* the first novel written by an African American, tells the fictionalized story of Clotel, a young slave girl fathered by Thomas Jefferson. *Clotel* was written by William Wells Brown.

Although the novel's protagonist is the president's daughter, due to laws dictating that children follow the condition of their mother, Clotel is a slave. Throughout the text she attempts to free herself and eventually escapes to Washington, D.C. Discovered by slave catchers, she flees the tentative sanctuary of the city and is trapped by the slave catchers on a bridge traversing the Potomac River. Spanning the river, the bridge polarizes Virginia and Washington, black and white, slavery and freedom. Given the choice between the Washington, D.C., side of the bridge and the awaiting slave catchers on the Virginia side and the inevitable return to slavery, Clotel jumps into the river, finding her only escape in the arms of death. Clotel's struggle is the embodiment of double-consciousness as she literally battles her dual identities as American and African American in her fight for liberty. Textually, Washington, D.C., represents the potential freedom she is entitled to and yet is denied solely because of her racial identity. Clotel is an important literary antecedent for African-American writers, including Toni Morrison.

BIBLIOGRAPHY

Brown, William Wells. *Clotel, or The President's Daughter.* New York: University Books Title, 1969.

———. *Narrative of William W. Brown, a Fugitive Slave.* Reading, Mass.: Addison, 1969.

Fabi, Giulia. "The 'Unguarded Expressions of the Feelings of the Negroes': Gender, Slave Resistance, and William Wells Brown's Revisions of *Clotel*," *African-American Review* 27, no. 4 (Winter 1993): 639–654.

Jackson, Blyden. "The First Negro Novelist." In Blyden Jackson, *A History of Afro-American Literature, Vol. 1,* 326–332. Baton Rouge: Louisiana State University Press, 1989.

Lewis, Richard O. "Literary Conventions in the Novels of William Wells Brown," *College Language Association Journal* 29, no. 2 (December 1985): 129–156.

Rosselot, Gerald S. "*Clotel,* a Black Romance," *College Language Association Journal* 23 (1980): 296–302.

Simson, Rennie. "Christianity: Hypocrisy and Honesty in the Afro American Novel of the Mid 19th Century," *University of Dayton Review* 15, no. 3 (Spring 1982): 11–16.

Yellin, Jean F. "Preface." In *Clotel, or, the President's Daughter,* by William Wells Brown. New York: Arno Press, 1969.

Colbert, Claudette (Lily Claudette Chauchoin)
(1903–1996)   From the 1920s to the 1980s the actress known as Claudette Colbert made more than 60 Hollywood films. Born in Paris, France, to a wealthy family, Colbert's birth name was Lily Claudette Chauchoin. When Colbert was a girl, her family relocated to the United States. After completing high school, Lily decided to pursue a career as an artist and studied at the Art Student's School.

When Lily was cast in her first professional play, she abandoned her art, changed her name to Claudette Colbert, and pursued acting full-time. Beginning as an actress on Broadway, Colbert earned progressively more significant roles and garnered more acclaim. In the 1920s she began to receive attention as a film actress, and a string of successful films convinced her to abandon Broadway for Hollywood. Colbert enjoyed a successful career, winning an Academy Award for the 1934 film *It Happened One Night.*

In the late 1950s, as her film career began to wane, Colbert returned to Broadway and made some television appearances. Her last feature film was the 1961 movie, *Parrish.* Colbert is mostly remembered for her contribution to the film genre of the screwball comedy.

In later years, Claudette Colbert spent most of her time in Speightstown, Barbados, in her home, Bellerive, which she owned for 30 years until her death there in 1996. While living in Barbados, she often invited celebrity friends to the island as her guests. Two of her most famous visitors were Nancy and Ronald Reagan.

Toni Morrison references Claudette Colbert in her novel *The Bluest Eye* (1970).

BIBLIOGRAPHY

Quirk, Lawrence J. *Claudette Colbert: An Illustrated Biography.* New York: Random House, 1985.

Collins, Addie Mae (1949–1963)   In 1963, the
CIVIL RIGHTS MOVEMENT was, in many ways, reaching a peak. In August, the leaders and organizations

primarily involved with civil rights protests organized the well-publicized March on Washington. Shortly afterward, in September of 1963, KU KLUX KLAN members in Birmingham, Alabama, committed the terrorist act of bombing a church, specifically the African American 16th Street Baptist Church, which in 1963 was the largest black Baptist church in Birmingham.

On Sunday morning, at the time that the Klan had chosen to bomb the church, services were about to begin. Four teenage girls who served in the church as ushers, Addie Mae Collins, Denise McNair, Cynthia Wesley, and Carole Robertson, were in the basement of the church preparing for the service. Members of the Ku Klux Klan had placed 15 sticks of dynamite under the church stairwell, near the basement where the girls were. When the dynamite exploded, all four of the girls were killed. Twenty other church members were seriously injured.

Addie Mae Collins was only 14 years old when she and her friends were murdered. Her parents, Alice and Oscar Collins, were the parents of six children in addition to Addie. There was outrage nationally and internationally in response to the murder of the four girls. Their death trained a spotlight on the devastating realities of racism and racially motivated terrorism in the United States.

In the initial aftermath of the crime, astonishingly, no one was charged. It took more than a decade, and a change in the social and political climate, of the United States before one of the Klan members, Robert Chambliss, was accused, tried, and finally convicted of first-degree murder. Chambliss began serving his sentence when he was convicted in 1977 and remained in prison until his death in 1985.

Two other men were eventually convicted of the murders of the four girls killed in 1963. In 2001 Thomas Blanton, like Chambliss, was found guilty of murder. He received a life sentence as did his fellow Klan member, Bobby Cherry, in 2002. Cherry died in prison in 2004. None of the convicted men ever acknowledged their guilt.

In *Song of Solomon* (1977), as the Sunday man in the Seven Days, Guitar Bains is supposed to avenge the deaths of the four girls killed in the 16th Street Baptist Church bombing. *Paradise* also alludes to the bombing.

BIBLIOGRAPHY

4 Little Girls. Dir. Spike Lee. HBO Studios, 1999.

Cobbs, Elizabeth H., and Petric J. Smith. *Long Time Coming: An Insider's Story of the Birmingham Church Bombing That Rocked the World.* Birmingham, Ala.: Crane Hill, 1994.

Eskew, Glenn T. *But for Birmingham: The Local and National Movements in the Civil Rights Struggle.* Chapel Hill: University of North Carolina Press, 1997.

Fallin, Wilson. *The African American Church in Birmingham, Alabama, 1815–1963: A Shelter in the Storm.* New York: Garland Publishing, 1997.

Sikora, Frank. *Until Justice Rolls Down.* Tuscaloosa: University of Alabama Press, 1991.

Sims, Patsy. *The Klan.* Lexington: University Press of Kentucky, 1996.

Theoharis, Athan G., and John Stuart Cox. *The Boss: J. Edgar Hoover and the Great American Inquisition.* Philadelphia: Temple University Press, 1988.

Tolnay, Stewart, and E. M. Beck. *A Festival of Violence.* Chicago: University of Illinois Press, 1992.

Wade, Wyn Craig. *The Fiery Cross: The Ku Klux Klan in America.* New York: Simon and Schuster, 1987.

Colored Ladies of Delaware, Ohio, the   The Colored Ladies of Delaware, Ohio are mentioned twice in Toni Morrison's *Beloved.* The group is said in the novel to assist in the effort to free Sethe after her attempt to murder her children rather than have them returned to slavery. In the article, "'The Colored Ladies of Delaware, Ohio,'" Anne Bower and Diane Silleck try to discover if this reference has any historical basis. Their efforts uncover that Morrison elaborated the women's group from a reference found in Herbert Aptheker's *A Documentary History of the Negro People in the United States* (1951) to a petition submitted to the Ohio Convention of Negro Men from the Ladies' Anti-Slavery Society of Delaware, Ohio.

BIBLIOGRAPHY

Aptheker, Herb. *A Documentary History of the Negro People in the United States.* New York: Citadel Press, 1951.

Bower, Anne, and Diane Silleck. "'The Colored Ladies of Delaware, Ohio' in Toni Morrison's *Beloved*,"

Obsidian: Black Literature in Review 12 (Spring–Summer and Fall–Winter 1997): 156–173.

colored only   In the wake of the Civil War, there was a backlash against African-American emancipation and the African-American quest for full participation in American democracy through acquisition of equal access to public facilities, education, and voting rights. As a result, those resistant to African-American equality instituted various measures designed to ensure black subordination. These measures took the form of legislation, vigilante terrorism, and institutionalized segregation. The Supreme Court case, PLESSY V. FERGUSON, was critical to the evolution of segregation. The Court decision legalized the racial separation of schools, public facilities, and public transportation. This separation of the races was often marked by signs that became the symbols of segregation. These signs were used to designate which facilities were exclusively white and which were for African Americans. During the time of segregation, African Americans were often called colored people, and so the signs indicating black facilities most frequently read "colored only." Correspondingly, the signs for white people would read "whites only." The southern United States was littered with these signs. The signs were gradually removed as those fighting against segregation were able to dismantle institutionalized racial separation through civil rights legislation passed in the 1960s and 1970s.

Contemporarily, and ironically, authentic "colored only" and "white only" signs are quite valuable. There is increasing interest in African-American memorabilia by both African-American and white collectors. Representations of the racism of the United States, such as MAMMY dolls, lawn jockeys, and "colored only" signs are frequent components of antique and vintage collectibles sales and auctions.

In *Sula* (1973), Nel Wright encounters "Colored Only" signs and the corresponding realities of segregation when her mother, Helene Wright, accidentally enters the "Whites Only" car on the train.

BIBLIOGRAPHY

Andrews, Kenneth T. *Freedom Is a Constant Struggle: The Mississippi Civil Rights Movement and Its Legacy.* Chicago: University of Chicago Press, 2004.

Beals, Melba Patillo. *Warriors Don't Cry: A Searing Memoir of the Battle to Integrate Little Rock's Central High.* New York: Pocket Books, 1994.

Belfrage, Sally. *Freedom Summer.* New York: Viking Press, 1965.

Buster, Larry V. *The Art and History of Black Memorabilia: We Never Fade.* New York: Clarkson Potter, 2000.

Citton, Thad, James H. Conrad, and Richard Orton. *Freedom Colonies: Independent Black Texans in the Time of Jim Crow.* Austin: University of Texas Press, 2005.

Cole, Thomas R. *No Color Is My Kind: The Life of Eldreway Stearns and the Integration of Houston.* Austin: University of Texas Press, 1997.

Emilio, John D. *The Civil Rights Struggle: Leaders in Profile.* New York: Facts On File, 1979.

Erenrich, Susan. *Freedom Is a Constant Struggle: An Anthology of the Mississippi Civil Rights Movement.* Montgomery, Ala.: Black Belt Press, 1999.

Eskew, Glen. *But for Birmingham: The Local and National Movements in the Civil Rights Struggle.* Chapel Hill: University of North Carolina Press, 1996.

Fairclough, Adam. *Better Day Coming: Blacks and Equality, 1890–2000.* New York: Penguin, 2002.

Halberstam, David. *The Children.* New York: Fawcett Book Group, 1999.

Hale, Elizabeth. *Making Whiteness: The Culture of Segregation in the South, 1890–1940.* New York: Random House, 1999.

Jonas, Gilbert. *Freedom's Sword: The NAACP and the Struggle against Racism in America, 1909–1969.* Abingdon, Oxfordshire: Taylor and Francis, 2004.

Kilpatrick, James Jackson. *The Southern Case for School Segregation.* New York: Crowell-Collier Press, 1962.

Klarman, Michael J. *From Jim Crow to Civil Rights: The Supreme Court and the Struggle for Racial Equality.* Oxford: Oxford University Press, 2003.

Kramer, Edward G., ed. *An Annotated Bibliography of Housing and School Segregation Articles and Documents with Additional Material for Research.* Monticello, Ill.: Vance Bibliographies, 1980.

Loewen, Jamew W. *Sundown Towns: A Hidden Dimension of Segregation in America.* New York: New Press, 2005.

McWhortor, Diane. *Carry Me Home: Birmingham, Alabama, Climactic Battle of the Civil Rights Revolution.* New York: Simon and Schuster, 2001.

Parsons, Sara. *From Southern Wrongs to Civil Rights: The Memoir of a White Civil Rights Activist.* Tuscaloosa: University of Alabama Press, 2000.

Segregation in Education, Law and Legislation: A Bibliography. Monticello, Ill.: Vance Bibliographies, 1986.

Smith, Douglas. *Managing White Supremacy: Race, Politics, and Citizenship in Jim Crow Virginia.* Chapel Hill: University of North Carolina Press, 2002.

Smith, James Wesley. *The Strange Way of Truth.* New York: Vantage Press, 1968.

Stanton, Mary. *From Selma to Sorrow: Life and Death of Viola Liuzzo.* Athens: University of Georgia Press, 2000.

Theoharis, Jeanne, and Komozi Woodars, eds. *Freedom North: Black Freedom Struggles Outside the South, 1940–1980.* New York: Macmillan, 2003.

———. *Groundwork: Local Black Freedom Movements in America.* New York: New York University Press, 2005.

Williams, Juan. *Eyes on the Prize: America's Civil Rights Years, 1954–1965.* New York: Viking, 1987.

Coltrane, John (1926–1967) John Coltrane is one of the best-known and respected JAZZ musicians. He is known for his innovations as a composer and jazz saxophonist. Coltrane was a native of North Carolina. His father, also named John Coltrane, was a musician and Coltrane grew up influenced by his father's playing.

He spent his formative years in the South before moving north to Philadelphia in his late teens following the deaths of his grandfather, father, and uncle and his mother's relocation to New Jersey. Although he received very little formal education in music, Coltrane played throughout high school and began to pick up professional gigs. During World War II, Coltrane served in the navy for a year. In 1946, while still in the navy, he made his first recording.

After the war, Coltrane worked as a saxophonist for a variety of well-known bands, including those of Dizzy Gillespie, Earl Bostic, and Johnny Hodges. Coltrane's most productive and influential years were spent following the beginning of his collaboration with Miles Davis in 1955. During the 1950s, Coltrane also played with another giant of jazz music, Theolonius Monk.

Unfortunately, Coltrane also developed an addiction to heroin that began to interfere with his performance. His addiction made him unreliable and obscured his abilities. As a result, in 1956 Miles Davis fired him from his group. This dismissal was a wake-up call for Coltrane who decided to enact his own recovery from his drug addiction. Coltrane had his family lock him in his room as he withdrew from heroin completely alone.

This experience brought about a transformation in Coltrane. Afterward, he pursued his music passionately. Again he worked with Thelonius Monk and, eventually, reunited with Miles Davis. During this period, Coltrane delved into experimental reformulations of jazz and of the saxophone. Due to creative and temperamental differences, in 1960 Davis and Coltrane again parted ways. Coltrane then formed his own group.

Coltrane's innovations were controversial and remain so into the contemporary period. He was the creator of the sub-genre of jazz called free jazz. Coltrane's reliance on long improvisational solos was applauded by some and scorned by others. Nevertheless, his playing was unique and brought about a reinvention of, as well as increased interest in, jazz music. In 1967, John Coltrane died suddenly of liver cancer. He was 40 years old.

In an interview with Nellie McKay in the book *Conversations with Toni Morrison* (1994), Morrison makes the point that there are many different types of black writer. Just as John Coltrane does not sound like Louis Armstrong, but both are black, so her writing is distinct from other that of black writers (153).

BIBLIOGRAPHY

Budds, Michael J. *Jazz in the Sixties: The Expansion of Musical Resources and Techniques.* Iowa City: University of Iowa Press, 1990.

Cole, Bill. *John Coltrane.* 1976. New York: Da Capo, 1993.

Coltrane, John. *Interstellar Space* (1967). GRP/Impulse!, CD, 1991.

———. *Live in Japan* (1966). GRP/Impulse!, CD, 1991.

———. *The Major Works of John Coltrane* (1965). GRP/Impulse!, CD, 1992.

———. *Meditations.* MCA/Impulse!, Record, 1966.

———. *My Favorite Things.* Atlantic, Record, 1961.

———. *Newport '63* (1963). GRP/Impulse!, CD, 1993.

Fujioka, Yasuhiro, with Lewis Porter and Yoh-Ichi Hamada. *John Coltrane: A Discography and Musical Biography.* Metuchen, N.J.: Scarecrow, 1995.

McDonald, Michael Bruce. "Training the Nineties, Or the Present Relevance of John Coltrane's Music of Theophany and Negation," *African American Review* 29, no. 2 (1995): 275–282.

Nisenson, Eric. *Ascension: John Coltrane and His Quest.* New York: St. Martin's, 1993.

Simpkins, C. O. *Coltrane: A Biography.* Baltimore: Black Classic, 1989.

Taylor-Guthrie, Danille, ed. *Conversations with Toni Morrison.* Jackson: University Press of Mississippi, 1994.

Congress of Racial Equality   See CORE

conjure woman   When Africans arrived in the United States, the Caribbean, and South America, and were enslaved, they brought with them religious customs and traditions that they were often prohibited from practicing openly. Consequently, many African religious philosophies and practices were combined with Christian religions, particularly Catholicism, and created new systems of belief such as Vodun and Santeria. On the surface, these new religions resembled the religions of the slave holders and, therefore, allowed those who were enslaved to retain some of the elements of West African traditional religious practice.

In the belief systems that evolved in slave communities, frequently there were individuals to whom special powers were attributed. These individual men and women were said to be conjurers and purportedly were able to use supernatural powers and incantations to shift the dynamic of power from the slaveholder to the slave. Conjure men and women were often revered, and sometimes feared. Other slaves would go to them seeking solutions to problems and difficulties.

When African Americans began to publish literature, the conjure woman became an impor-

tant literary figure, most notably in the fiction of Charles Chestnutt. Like her real-life ancestor, literary conjure women frequently use knowledge, cunning, and community solidarity to subvert the power of an oppressor. The conjure woman as a literary trope enjoyed a renaissance with the proliferation of contemporary African-American women's writing. Critics have called many of Toni Morrison's characters conjure women, including Pilate Dead from *Song of Solomon* (1977), Sula and Ajax's mother from *Sula* (1970), and Baby Suggs from *Beloved* (1987).

BIBLIOGRAPHY

Ammons, Elizabeth, and Annette White-Parks. *Trick-sterism in Turn-of-the-Century American Literature: A Multicultural Perspective.* Hanover and London: University Press of New England, 1994.

Tucker, Lindsey. "Recovering the Conjure Woman: Texts and Contexts in Gloria Naylor's *Mama Day,*" *African American Review* 28, no. 2 (1994): 173–188.

CORE (Congress of Racial Equality)   The Congress of Racial Equality (CORE) was an early civil rights organization founded in Chicago, at the University of Chicago, in 1942. In the beginning the membership of the organization was mostly white and middle class. Several of the original members of CORE were also members of the older civil rights organization, the Fellowship of Reconciliation (FOR). The organization was always integrated and was formed with the objective of implementing civil disobedience as modeled and defined by Henry David Thoreau and Mahatma Gandhi as a strategy for combating the inequalities experienced by African Americans in the United States. Members of CORE, such as Bayard Rustin, George Houser, Anna Murray, and James Farmer, became major figures in the CIVIL RIGHTS MOVEMENT of the 1950s and '60s.

One of the important early actions of CORE, which was implemented five years after the organization's founding in the spring of 1947, was called the Journey of Reconciliation. The members of CORE wanted to push the federal government to acknowledge that segregation in interstate travel was unconstitutional even though it was the practice throughout the southern United States. In order to accomplish this task, black and white members of CORE were assembled to travel together through the South, defying the segregation rules in the states they would pass through: Virginia, North Carolina, Tennessee, and Kentucky.

During the Journey of Reconciliation, CORE members faced physical violence and arrest. The most productive result of the journey was the national and international focus it brought to the injustices of segregation. The Journey of Reconciliation was the first of many CORE protests through nonviolent civil disobedience. These actions included more attempts to defy segregation in interstate transportation, voter registration drives, and sit-ins.

The fight against segregation in interstate transportation reached a climax with a series of actions called the Freedom Rides. Interracial riders went through the states that were most resistant to desegregation, Georgia, Alabama, Louisiana, and Mississippi. The riders again were met with violence, resistance, and arrest. The Freedom Rides continued until the federal government was forced, in 1961, to intervene and to declare segregation in interstate travel illegal.

CORE was one of the organizations responsible for organizing and implementing the 1963 March on Washington. Although his participation was relegated to behind the scenes status because he was a gay man, and therefore, at the time, thought to be a potential liability, many participants and historians have asserted that the March would not have happened without the efforts of CORE member Bayard Rustin.

CORE worked with the Student Non-Violent Coordinating Committee (SNCC), the Southern Leadership Conference (SCLC), and the National Association for the Advancement of Colored People (NAACP) to plan a voter registration drive and to encourage the growth of grassroots activism in Mississippi during the summer of 1964. This collaborative effort was known as Freedom Summer and focused its efforts on registering black people to vote and establishing freedom schools to provide education generally and also to teach organizing

techniques. The summer drew the participation of local residents, as well as that of volunteers from other states. During the summer, three young men involved in the work of Freedom Summer, James Chaney, Andrew Goodman, and Michael Schwener, were kidnapped and killed by local whites. Again, the publicity the event garnered brought essential attention to the conditions of life for blacks in the South and brought pressure to the federal government to pass legislation to support the efforts of CORE and the other groups working in the civil rights struggle. The most significant of these measures was the Voting Rights Act, passed in 1965. The act was designed to ensure that all American citizens, including African Americans, were guaranteed that they would not be discriminated against at the state or local level when they attempted to exercise their right to vote.

CORE continued throughout the 1960s and into the present day to advocate for racial equality. The organization has programs designed to continue to support its founding principles of the establishment of equality for all of the citizens of the United States and the world, irrespective of color.

In *Paradise* (1998), Christine, as a young girl, reads her mother May's notes about CORE and misunderstands, thinking that her mother is writing about a woman named Cora.

BIBLIOGRAPHY

Arsenault, Raymond. *Freedom Riders: 1961 and the Struggle for Racial Justice.* Oxford: Oxford University Press, 2006.

"Congress of Racial Equality." Available online. URL: www.core-online.org. Accessed on February 17, 2006.

Fairclough, Adam. *Better Day Coming: Blacks and Equality, 1890–2000.* New York: Penguin, 2002.

Farmer, James. *Lay Bare the Heart: An Autobiography of the Civil Rights Movement.* New York: Arbor House, 1985.

Houser, George M. *CORE: A Brief History.* Chicago: Congress of Racial Equality, 1949.

Interviews with Civil Rights Workers from the Congress of Racial Equality. (Stanford University Project South Oral History Collection) Glen Rock, N.J.: Microfilming Corp. of America, 1975.

Meier, August, and Elliot Rudwick. *CORE: A Study in the Civil Rights Movement, 1942–1968.* Chicago: University of Illinois Press, 1973.

The Papers of the Congress of Racial Equality. Glen Rock, N.J.: Microfilming Corp. of America, 1982.

Wink, Walter. *Peace Is the Way: Writings on Nonviolence from the Fellowship of Reconciliation.* New York: Orbis Books, 2000.

Corinthians   First and Second Corinthians are two books of the Christian Bible—two of the 14 chapters of the Bible known as the Pauline Epistles, the letters written by Paul to the people in the church at Corinth.

The city of Corinth is located off the Aegean coast of southern Greece. It was an essential hub for the largely sea-based transportation of the time, and in Corinth there were people of many different nationalities and experiences. As a port city, Corinth had a reputation as a city where sexual conduct often transgressed the boundaries of what was considered by many people of the time to be morally objectionable. In Paul's mission to spread Christianity, one of his primary targets was the city of Corinth because of its reputation and its size. He traveled to the city to establish a church there and was successful in his efforts.

After Paul's departure from Corinth he received word from a woman named Chloe and from others that the members of the church were not adhering to the principles that were fundamental to Paul's interpretation of Christian doctrine. While Paul was traveling and establishing churches, he went to the city of Ephesus where he wrote First Corinthians. The letter that would become First Corinthians was probably composed in A.D. 53.

In his letter, Paul addresses the moral crises the church was facing. He also answers questions they had addressed to him in an earlier letter. In First Corinthians Paul addresses the issues of incest, marriage, celibacy, divorce, idolatry, women's roles, and love. Paul's meditation on love and its significance in First Corinthians is one of the most well-known passages from the Bible.

Second Corinthians was composed in approximately 57 A.D. to try to correct the wrong direction Paul felt the church in Corinth had taken. After

his visit and as a result of the growth of the church, by the time Paul wrote Second Corinthians, the members of the church seemed to be conforming to Paul's expectations, but there were continuing problems. In Second Corinthians, Paul addresses the church of Corinth and attempts to clarify his role as the messenger of God's word.

Morrison refers particularly to First Corinthians with her character of the same name in *Song of Solomon* (1977). L also refers to Corinthians as the source of her name in *Love* (2003).

BIBLIOGRAPHY

Barclay, William. *The Letters to the Corinthians.* Philadelphia: Westminster Press, 1954.

Dunn, James, ed. *The Cambridge Companion to St. Paul.* Cambridge: Cambridge University Press, 2003.

Fee, Gordon. *The First Epistle to the Corinthians. The New International Commentary on the New Testament.* Grand Rapids, Mich.: William B. Eerdmans, 1987.

Fisk, Bruce N. *First Corinthians. Interpretation Bible Studies.* Louisville, Ky.: Geneva Press, 2000.

Hays, Richard B. *First Corinthians: Interpretation: A Bible Commentary for Teaching and Preaching.* Louisville, Ky.: John Knox Press, 1997.

Hughes, Robert B. *First Corinthians.* Chicago: Moody Press, 1985.

Kent, Homer A., Jr. *A Heart Opened Wide, Studies in 2 Corinthians.* Grand Rapids, Mich.: Baker Book House, 1982.

Morgan, G. Campbell. *The Corinthian Letters of Paul.* New York: Fleming H. Revell, 1946.

Morris, Leon. *The First Epistle of Paul to the Corinthians.* Grand Rapids, Mich.: William B. Eerdmans, 1985.

Tasker, R. V. G. *The Second Epistle of Paul to the Corinthians.* Grand Rapids, Mich.: William. B. Eerdmans, 1958.

Winter, Bruce W. *After Paul Left Corinth: The Influence of Secular Ethics and Social Change.* Grand Rapids, Mich.: Eerdmans, 2001.

crash of 1929   Beginning in March of 1929, there were signs that the 1920s boom of the New York Stock Exchange market was on perilous footing. The boom turned to bust in October of 1929 when, on the 24th, the market took a decided nosedive and the value of stocks plummeted perilously. On Tuesday the 29th, now called Black Tuesday, more than 16 million shares were traded, generating a massive sell-off and subsequent devaluing of the market.

These events are now called the Crash of 1929. From September of 1929 to July of 1932 the stocks in the New York Stock Exchange lost most of their value. This dramatic shift destroyed the fortunes of many millionaires and affected the lives of ordinary working people as well. The change in fortune resulted in the suicides of many. The market did not regain the levels it had attained in 1929 for a quarter of a century.

Many experts agree that the crash was probably caused by stock purchases made with credit rather than with cash, which ultimately resulted in bank failures and business closings. This chain of events was arguably a major catalyst for the Great DEPRESSION of the 1930s.

Morrison's characters in *The Bluest Eye* (1970), *Sula* (1973), *Song of Solomon* (1977), *Jazz* (1992), *Paradise* (1998), and *Love* (2003) are affected by the stock market crash.

BIBLIOGRAPHY

Bernstein, Michael A. *The Great Depression: Delayed Recovery and Economic Change in America, 1929–1939.* New York: Cambridge University Press, 1987.

Galbraith, John Kenneth. *The Great Crash, 1929,* 3rd ed. Boston: Houghton Mifflin, 1972.

Kindleberger, Charles Poor. *The World in Depression: 1929–1939.* Berkeley: University of California Press, 1973.

D

Danielpour, Richard (1956–) Composer Richard Danielpour is a native New Yorker who showed musical promise at a young age. Danielpour attended the New England Conservatory of Music and continued his music education at Juilliard. Danielpour has worked professionally and very successfully as a composer, becoming one of the most respected and in-demand contemporary composers.

Danielpour has received commissions from orchestras around the United States and holds an exclusive contract with the classical music division of Sony Music. He also works as an academic and has served on the faculty of the Manhattan School of Music since 1993. Some of Danielpour's best-known works are *Elegies* (2001) and *Celestial Night* (1999). Reviewers of his work often find that his music is grounded in the traditions of romanticism and that he is fundamentally American in his sensibilities, with his music heavily influenced by the American composers Aaron Copeland and George Gershwin. Included in Danielpour's many accomplishments are his collaborations with Toni Morrison. He wrote the music and she wrote the story and lyrics for the works *Sweet Talk: Four Songs on Text* (1997), *Spirits in the Well* (1997), and *Margaret Garner* (2005).

BIBLIOGRAPHY

Brown, Royal S. "An Interview with Richard Danielpour," *Fanfare* 5 (1996–97): 31–50.
Danielpour, Richard. *Celestial Night*. Sony Classical, CD, 1999.
———. *Concerto for Orchestra*. Sony Classical, CD, 1997.
———. *Elegies*. Sony Classical, CD, 2001.
———. *Quintet for Piano and Strings*, performed by Christopher O'Riley and the Chamber Music Society of Lincoln Center. Koch International Classics, CD, 1992.
———. "Quintet for Piano and Strings." Associated Music, Score, 1990.
McCutchan, Ann. "Richard Danielpour." In *The Muse That Sings: Composers Speak about the Creative Process*. New York: Oxford University Press, 1999.

Dante Alighieri (1265–1321) Born in Florence, Italy, Dante Alighieri is considered one of the masters of literature, particularly of poetry. According to most accounts, as a young child Dante saw from a distance and fell in love with a woman named Beatrice Portinari. Although the two apparently never actually conversed or spent any time together, Dante, in the chivalric tradition, internalized her as an ideal. Beatrice appears in many of Dante's works and was his muse even after her death. Both of Dante's parents died before he reached adulthood.

Dante married as a young man and had several children with his wife, Gemma Donati. As a result of his political affiliations, he was exiled from Florence. His family did not leave the city with him. While living in exile in northern Italy, Dante wrote his most well-known and acclaimed work, the epic poem, *The Divine Comedy* (1307–12).

The Divine Comedy is structured in three parts, "Inferno," "Purgatoria," and "Paradiso." The work consists of a total of 100 cantos. Written in terza rima, the poem's narrative traces the poet's first-person posthumous journey through each of these spaces. The Roman poet, Virgil, is Dante's guide through the first two sections of the poem. Beatrice, Dante's muse, leads the final leg of the journey into Paradiso where Dante joins St. Bernard and finally encounters God. Dante's work was an allegory of the human struggle to achieve salvation and became a template for many other such works.

Dante was accused posthumously of sympathizing with the Muslim physician and philosopher, Averroës, and his interpretations of Aristotle. As a result, Pope Leo X ordered some of Dante's works burned. In an effort to protect his remains, Franciscan monks hid his body.

Literary critics have discussed the influence of Dante in Morrison's works. Soaphead Church, a character in *The Bluest Eye* (1970), despises Dostoevsky and loves Dante.

BIBLIOGRAPHY

Anderson, William. *Dante the Maker.* London: Routledge and Kegan Paul, 1980.

Dante Alighieri. *The Divine Comedy.* New York: Doubleday, 1947. [1307–1312]

Ferrante, Joan. *The Political Vision of the "Divine Comedy."* Princeton, N.J.: Princeton University Press, 1984.

Hollander, Robert. *Dante: A Life in Works.* New Haven, Conn.: Yale University Press, 2001.

Jacoff, Rachel, ed. *The Cambridge Companion to Dante.* Cambridge: Cambridge University Press, 1993.

Lewis, R. W. B. *Dante. A Penguin Life.* New York: Penguin Putnam, 2001.

Miller, D. Quentin. "'Making a Place for Fear': Toni Morrison's First Redefinition of Dante's Hell in *Sula," English Language Notes* 37 (March 2000): 68–75.

Davis, Angela (1944–)   Born on January 26, 1944, into the pre–CIVIL RIGHTS MOVEMENT South, as a young child Angela Yvonne Davis, was heir to all of the racism and violence that an unrepentant Alabama had to offer. Although her parents, B. Frank and Sally Davis, were middle-class, professional African Americans, their class privilege could not protect their daughter from the realities of racial segregation and racially motivated violence. Davis's parents were activists and were involved in the Alabama Communist Party, so from a young age Davis learned that there were strategies to resist oppression.

Although Davis experienced the traumas of segregation, her family provided her with the resources she needed in order to thrive. The young Davis read voraciously and was a talented student; as such, she was ready for greater opportunities than the education system in Alabama could provide. At the age of 14, Davis went to New York City to attend the progressive and radical Elizabeth Irwin High School.

Following graduation, Davis pursued higher education at Brandeis University. She received a full scholarship to the institution and began her study of French, which became her eventual major. Davis spent the year 1963 overseas studying in Paris. While she was there, the Birmingham church bombing occurred. Davis had a personal acquaintance with the four girls who were murdered in the racially motivated terrorist act, and the incident had a profound impact on her. Davis graduated near the top of her class at Brandeis in 1965 and decided to pursue graduate school.

For her graduate work, Davis attended the University of California, San Diego. After finishing her master's degree, Davis returned to Germany and completed her Ph.D. from Humboldt University. While in graduate school, one focus of Davis's study was communism. Her advocacy of communism would lead to governmental scrutiny and eventually to her losing her first position as a professor.

Davis also became involved with the BLACK PANTHER PARTY. Her membership in the Panthers generated a false accusation by the FBI that she had provided the guns that members of the Panthers used in an attempt to free fellow Panthers member George Jackson.

Rather than surrendering to arrest for a crime she did not commit, Davis went into hiding. While she was a fugitive, Davis became a nationally and internationally known figure, gaining a tremendous sympathy for what was unjust persecution. In 1970, after two months under cover, Davis was arrested and imprisoned for a year and a half until her trial. When her trial was finally held, Davis was acquitted of all charges. Her time in prison increased her awareness of the inhumane circumstances in which most prisoners are held. Davis became and remains a passionate advocate of prison reform and prisoner's rights.

Davis is now a scholar and activist, writing books, articles, and essays. She is also a professor and politician. When Toni Morrison was an editor at Random House, she worked with Davis. Angela Davis ran for vice president of the United States in 1980. Currently she holds the position of University of California Presidential Chair and is a professor with the History of Consciousness Department at the University of California, Santa Cruz.

BIBLIOGRAPHY

Aptheker, Bettina. *The Morning Breaks: The Trial of Angela Davis*. New York: International Publishers, 1975.

Ashman, Charles R. *The People vs. Angela Davis*. New York: Pinnacle Books, 1972.

Davis, Angela Yvonne. *Angela Davis–An Autobiography*. New York: Random House, 1974.

———. *If They Come in the Morning: Voices of Resistance*. New York: Third Press, 1971.

———. *Women, Race and Class*. New York: Random House, 1981.

Major, Reginald. *Justice in the Round: The Trial of Angela Davis*. New York: Third Press, 1973.

Nadelson, Regina. *Who Is Angela Davis? The Biography of a Revolutionary*. New York: P. H. Wyden, 1972.

Parker, J. *Angela Davis: The Making of a Revolutionary*. New York: Arlington House, 1973.

Timothy, Mary. *Jury Woman: The Story of the Trial of Angela Y. Davis*. San Francisco: Glide Publications, 1975.

Defoe, Daniel (1660–1731) Daniel Defoe is one of the most well-known and respected early English writers. Born into a working-class family, as Daniel Foe, Defoe originally planned to follow his father's wishes and become a member of the clergy, but became a traveling merchant instead. Defoe married Mary Tuffley in 1684. Eventually the couple had seven children. Defoe added the "de" to his name because he felt that it was more distinguished.

After becoming involved in a rebellion, Defoe lost his trading business, but quickly rebounded and purchased a brick factory that quickly became successful. He began to write political tracts and, as a result, became a controversial figure; eventually he was incarcerated for publishing his opinions. Defoe turned to fiction and wrote the classic *The Life and Adventures of Robinson Crusoe*, published in 1719. The work remains his best-known, having been translated into many languages and read in countries all over the world.

Defoe got the story for *Robinson Crusoe* from the real-life narrative of the sailor Alexander Selkirk as told in the 1712 book, "*A Voyage Around the World*," written by Woodes Rogers. Defoe went on to write other literary classics—*Moll Flanders* (1722), *A Journal of the Plague Year* (1722), and *Captain Jack* (1722)—innovating the genre of the novel; before he died in 1731, he published more than 350 titles. His works remain among the most revered and widely read by an English writer. Contemporary literary critics, including Toni Morrison, have critiqued the novel, *Robinson Crusoe*, in terms of the relationship between Crusoe and the native on the island, Friday.

BIBLIOGRAPHY

Backscheider, Paula R. *Daniel Defoe*. Louisville: University Press of Kentucky, 1986.

Bell, Ian. *Defoe's Fiction*. London: Croom Helm, 1985.

Blewitt, David. *Defoe's Art of Fiction*. Toronto: University of Toronto Press, 1979.

Byrd, Max, ed. *Daniel Defoe: A Collection of Critical Essays*. Englewood Cliffs, N.J.: Prentice Hall, 1976.

Curtis, Laura Ann. *The Elusive Daniel Defoe*. London: Vision Press, 1984.

Defoe, Daniel. *A Journal of the Plague Year*, edited by Anthony Burgess. 1722. Harmondsworth, U.K.: Penguin Classics, 1966.

Earle, Peter. *The World of Defoe*. London: Weidenfeld and Nicolson, 1976.

Faller, Lincoln B. *Crime and Defoe: A New Kind of Writing*. Cambridge: Cambridge University Press, 1993.

de Gobineau, Joseph Arthur, comte (1816–1882)   Arthur de Gobineau was an influential French writer and diplomat who is best-known for his theories of human racial hierarchy. De Gobineau was born into a wealthy French family. As a young man he worked in the government and eventually was drawn to foreign service. De Gobineau served as a diplomat in Europe, Persia, and Brazil.

While overseas de Gobineau began to formulate theories about the racial distinctions among human beings. In his widely read book, *An Essay on the Inequality of the Human Races* (1853–55), de Gobineau delineated a structure of human hierarchy that attributed particular characteristics to different racial groups. De Gobineau theorized that the white or Aryan race was the superior group and was at the top of humanity in terms of intelligence, culture, and civilization. He was a particular advocate for the maintenance of "racial purity." De Gobineau's writings became the foundation for the theory of the Aryan master race and for the political manifestation of this theory with Adolf Hitler and the Third Reich. Although his theories have no scientific credibility in the contemporary world, at the time they were written, de Gobineau's ideas were thought to have merit.

In addition to his racial theorizing, de Gobineau also wrote novels and historical studies. He died in Italy in 1882. Morrison quotes de Gobineau in *The Bluest Eye* (1970) when the narrator of the novel explains the source of Soaphead Church's internalized racism.

BIBLIOGRAPHY

Corcos, A. *The Myth of Human Races.* East Lansing: Michigan State University Press, 1997.

de Gobineau, Arthur. *The Inequality of Human Races.* 1854. Los Angeles: Noontide Press, 1966.

Hankins, F. H. *The Racial Basis of Civilization: A Critique of the Nordic Doctrine.* New York: Knopf, 1925.

Hannaford, I. *Race: The History of an Idea in the West.* Baltimore, Md.: Johns Hopkins University Press, 1996.

Hitler, Adolph. *Mein Kampf.* 1927. Boston: Houghton Mifflin, 1999.

Jennings, H. S. *The Biological Basis of Human Nature.* New York: Norton, 1930.

Malik, K. *The Meaning of Race: Race, History and Culture in Western Society.* New York: New York University Press, 1996.

Mills, C. W. *The Racial Contract.* Ithaca, N.Y.: Cornell University Press, 1997.

Montagu, Ashley. *Man's Most Dangerous Myth.* Cleveland: World Publishing Co., 1964.

———. *The Idea of Race.* Lincoln: University of Nebraska Press, 1965.

Spencer, Jon Michael. "The Emancipation of the Negro and the Negro Spirituals from the Racialist Legacy of Arthur de Gobineau," *Canadian Review of American Studies* 24 (1994): 1–18.

Tucker, W. H. *The Science and Politics of Racial Research.* Urbana: University of Illinois Press, 1994.

Valette, Rebecca M. *Arthur de Gobineau and the Short Story.* Chapel Hill: University of North Carolina Press, 1969.

Young, R. J. C. *Colonial Desire: Hybridity in Theory, Culture and Race.* London: Routledge, 1995.

Demme, Jonathan (1944–   )   Jonathan Demme is a noted and popular film director and producer whose films are distinguished by their originality and development of character. Demme was born into a middle-class family in New York. Demme may have been influenced in his later choice to pursue a career in film by his mother, who was an actress.

Although Demme aspired to become a veterinarian, his experiences in college convinced him that his aptitude lay in other areas. After graduating from the University of Florida, he began writing film reviews and eventually began to work at film companies and to write. In 1970, Demme began working with filmmaker Roger Corman and began to write and direct films with him.

Demme moved on to creating his own films. His breakthrough movie was *Melvin and Howard* (1980). The film garnered Demme critical and commercial success. Over the next decade or so, Demme began to cultivate a reputation as a director of concert films and documentaries. His film *Silence of the Lambs* (1991), starring Jody Foster, was popular and highly acclaimed and earned Demme an Academy Award for best director. Other noted films by Demme include *Philadelphia* (1993), *Beloved* (1998), and *Heart of Gold* (2006).

The film *Beloved* was an adaptation of Toni Morrison's 1987 novel. The film, produced by and starring Oprah Winfrey, received mixed reviews and made a poor commercial showing.

BIBLIOGRAPHY

Bill, Michael, and Christina Banks, *What Goes Around Comes Around: The Films of Jonathan Demme.* Carbondale: Southern Illinois University Press, 1996.

Thompson, David, and Saskia Baron. "Demme on Demme." In *Projections: A Forum for Filmmakers,* edited by John Boorman and Walter Donahue. New York: Farrar Straus and Giroux, 1992.

depression, the (Great Depression)   The CRASH of the New York Stock Exchange in October of 1929 had a pervasive effect on the entire economy of the United States. After businesses began to fail, banks and other economic institutions began to suffer as well. As a result of the banks closing, many people lost all the money they had in the world. Subsequently, unemployment skyrocketed and eventually 25 percent of all Americans were unemployed. When Roosevelt defeated Hoover in the 1932 election, he initiated a new system of economic recovery he called the New Deal. Roosevelt's New Deal advocated for increased federal regulation and control of social and economic institutions as well as large federal programs to encourage employment and economic opportunity. The chief of these programs was the Works Progress Administration (WPA). The other major initiative was the formation of the Social Security Administration. The onset of World War II and U.S. involvement in the war following the attack on Pearl Harbor brought an end to the U.S. and world economic depressions.

Morrison's characters in *The Bluest Eye* (1970), *Sula* (1973), *Song of Solomon* (1977), *Jazz* (1992), *Paradise* (1998), and *Love* (2003) are affected by the stock market crash and subsequent Great Depression.

BIBLIOGRAPHY

Barlett, Donald, and James Steele. *America: What Went Wrong?* Kansas City: Andrews and McMeel, 1992.

Fox, James MacGregor. *Roosevelt: The Lion and the Fox.* New York: Konecky and Konecky, 1956.

Galbraith, John Kenneth. *The Great Crash: 1929.* Boston: Mariner Books, 1997.

Goldston, Robert. *The Great Depression The United States in the Thirties.* Indianapolis: Bobbs-Merrill, 1968.

Kennedy, David M. *Freedom from Fear: The American People in Depression and War, 1929–1945.* New York: Oxford University Press, 2001.

Kindleberger, Charles P. *The World in Depression, 1929–1939.* Berkeley: University of California Press, 1986.

Leuchtenburg, William E. *Franklin D. Roosevelt and the New Deal.* New York: Perennial, 1963.

McElvaine, Robert S. *The Great Depression.* New York: New York Times Books, 1984.

Nash, Gerald. *The Great Depression and World War II: Organizing America, 1933–1945.* New York: St. Martin Press, 1979.

Phillips, Kevin. *Boiling Point.* New York: HarperCollins, 1993.

———. *The Politics of Rich and Poor.* New York: Random House, 1990.

Schlesinger, Arthur M., Jr. *The Age of Roosevelt,* Volume I: *The Crisis of the Old Order, 1919–1933.* Boston: Mariner Books, 2003.

———. *The Age of Roosevelt,* Volume II: *The Coming of the New Deal, 1933–1935.* Boston: Mariner Books, 2003.

———. *The Age of Roosevelt,* Volume III: *The Politics of Upheaval, 1935–1936.* Boston: Mariner Books, 2003.

Watkins, T. H. *The Great Depression: America in the 1930s.* New York: Little, Brown, 1993.

Worster, Donald. *Dust Bowl: The Southern Plains in the 1930s.* New York: Oxford University Press, 1982.

Desdemona   Desdemona is a central character in William Shakespeare's tragedy *Othello* (1604, 1605). Othello is described as a Moor and has dark skin, while Desdemona is light-skinned. Desdemona is a central character in the play. She is Othello's wife and the daughter of Brabantio. Desdemona is a complex character who can be read as either self-assured and confident or demure and submissive, perhaps most accurately as both. Desdemona perpetually has to defend herself against her husband's obsessive jealousy. As a result of a plot by Othello's confidant, Iago, she loses the battle to retain her husband's confidence, and Othello kills her in a fit of jealous rage. As she is victimized by her husband, Desdemona forgives him for his unthinking act and declares that she has not been unfaithful.

Morrison's character Soaphead Church in *The Bluest Eye* (1970) is said to focus on Othello's love of Desdemona and her whiteness to the exclusion of other aspects of the play *Othello*.

BIBLIOGRAPHY

Shakespeare, William. *Othello*. 1604, 1605. Middlesex, U.K.: Penguin, 1970.

dichty   Dichty is a word derived from African-American vernacular that is used to refer either to individuals who have more money than most people residing in a community or to an individual who considers him or herself to be more valuable than all others with whom he or she comes into contact.

Dick and Jane Reader   The Dick and Jane Reader was a series of books created in the 1930s to help young children learn to read. First appearing in the *Elson-Gray Readers*, the adventures of Dick and Jane were created as an alternative to school readers that were heavily moralistic and drew their stories from the Bible, Shakespeare, and American legends. Dick and Jane quickly gained widespread use in school systems across the country and continued to be used as late as the 1970s. The recurring characters were a brother and sister named Dick and Jane. They had a younger sister named Sally and a dog named Spot. Their parents were simply called Father and Mother. The family lived in an apparently all-white suburb, and black characters did not appear in the stories until 1965, when an African-American family moved next door to Dick and Jane's house. The children of this family were named Mike, Pam, and Penny.

Created by Dr. William S. Gray, Zerna Sharp, and Harry B. Johnston, Dick and Jane built children's vocabularies and understanding of sentences by sight reading and repetition. A typical-sounding passage for a first-grade reader sounds like this: "Look Spot. Oh, look. Look and

see. Oh, see." The readers for each succeeding grade became increasingly more complex and were written to strict and specific standards so that the first-grade Dick and Jane used about 300 words, the third-grade reader, 1,000, and the sixth-grade reader, approximately 4,000.

Eventually, as studies showed that phonics was a better tool to teach children to read, the *Dick and Jane* readers fell into disuse. The books today have historic and nostalgic appeal. Original editions can fetch a high price and reissues of the books have been best-sellers, but at least one reissue came with a publisher's warning not to use the books to teach reading.

Morrison replicates the Dick and Jane books in the beginning of *The Bluest Eye* (1970). She critiques the presentation of the family in the narrative as normative and questions the damaging role that such foundational stories have on children who cannot identify with the portrait of life presented in the texts.

BIBLIOGRAPHY

Fun with Dick and Jane: A Commemorative Collection of Stories. San Francisco: Collins Publishers, 1996.

Dillinger, John (1903–1934)   America's most notorious bank robber was born in its heartland. Beginning life in Indiana, Dillinger's parents ran a store. Dillinger's mother died when he was a young child, and by the time he was 16 he had dropped out of school. Dillinger joined the navy in 1923, but was reported absent without leave in less than a year. At 20, he unsuccessfully tried domestic life, and entered into an unhappy union with Beryl Hovious. Dillinger continued his downward spiral as a troubled youth and was imprisoned after robbing a grocery store.

Dillinger remained incarcerated from 1924 until 1933. His wife divorced him in 1929; having no other experience or context to return to, he embarked on a life of crime, beginning one of the most notorious, if brief, crime sprees in American history. In a short time, Dillinger and his gang had robbed five banks. The robberies created a national reputation for Dillinger. Many saw him as a Robin Hood figure and began to cast him as an outlaw hero.

Dillinger continued his career of bank robbing and moved beyond the Midwest to the South and southwestern United States. Dillinger was captured and escaped several times, increasing interest in him as a folkloric character. He was listed by the FBI as Public Enemy Number One. After each escape, Dillinger continued to rob banks. Finally, he was captured by the FBI through information provided by a double-crossing girlfriend, Anna Sage. As he exited a movie theater, he was confronted by agents who shot him as he tried to escape. Dillinger died on the spot. His story is preserved in American popular culture through television, film, and books.

The prostitutes in *The Bluest Eye* (1970), Miss Marie and China, reference John Dillinger as Miss Marie fabricates for Pecola a story about her involvement in John Dillinger's capture. She claims to be the woman who turned him in to officials of the Federal Bureau of Investigation.

BIBLIOGRAPHY

Cromie, Robert Allen. *Dillinger, a Short and Violent Life.* New York: McGraw-Hill, 1962.

Gallagher, Basil. *The Life Story of John Dillinger and the Exploits of the "Terror Mob."* Indianapolis: Stevens Publishing Company, 1934.

Girardin, G. Russell. *Dillinger: The Untold Story.* Bloomington: Indiana University Press, 1994.

Toland, John. *The Dillinger Days.* New York: Random House, 1963.

Dorsey, Thomas (Georgia, Georgia Tom) (1899–1993)   Born in rural Georgia, Thomas Dorsey grew up enmeshed in the traditions and rituals of the Baptist church where he and his family were not only members, but where his father was often the preacher. When Dorsey was five, the family relocated to Atlanta.

In the city, Dorsey had access to the rich cultural life of the black South. He was particularly taken with the BLUES and began to play the piano by ear. In addition, Dorsey also learned to read music, a skill that would prove critical to his later life as a composer.

Like so many African Americans of his time, in 1916 Dorsey relocated north to the urban mecca of Chicago where he continued to pursue his music career. He also acquired an education in music when he attended the Chicago School of Composition and Arranging. While in Chicago, he acquired the name he would be known by professionally, Georgia or Georgia Tom.

As a result of his skill and experience, Dorsey was hired by Paramount Records. There his songs began to reach a wide audience and to be recorded by some of the most popular artists of the day. As a result of these associations, Dorsey met and went on tour with the famous blues singer, Ma Rainey.

As Dorsey's career accelerated he met and married his wife, Nettie Harper. While Dorsey continued performing and composing the popular music of the day, he also wrote and performed gospel music. This blending of two African-American musical traditions stimulated the roots of a new hybrid, rhythm and blues.

Thomas Dorsey's life was forever changed by the death of his young wife in 1932 during childbirth. The death of his infant son several days later sent Dorsey into a life-altering crisis in which he determined to spend his energies on creating gospel music. It was during this traumatic time that Dorsey composed the song he is best known for, "Precious Lord."

Dorsey threw his creative energies into directing the choir at one of Chicago's black landmarks, Pilgrim Baptist Church. Under his tutelage, many famous black gospel singers emerged, and some have attributed to Dorsey the birth of gospel music. Dorsey's beloved church and cultural landmark was completely destroyed by fire in 2006.

Dorsey lived a long and productive life and composed more than 400 songs before his death in 1993. His songs were recorded by singing legends such as Ma Rainey, Aretha Franklin, Elvis Presley, and Mahalia Jackson.

Pauline Breedlove in *The Bluest Eye* (1970) has a romantic fantasy that is associated with Thomas Dorsey's song "Precious Lord."

BIBLIOGRAPHY

Harris, Michael. *The Rise of the Gospel Blues: The Music of Thomas Andrew Dorsey.* Oxford, U.K.: Oxford University Press, 1992.

Reagon, Bernice Johnson, ed. *We'll Understand It Better By and By: Pioneering African American Gospel*

Composers. Washington, D.C.: Smithsonian Institution Press, 1992.

Smith, Ruth A. *The Life and Works of Thomas Andrew Dorsey: The Celebrated Pianist and Songwriter, Poetical and Pictorial.* Chicago: T. A. Dorsey, 1935.

Dostoevsky, Fyodor (1821–1867) Fyodor Dostoevsky is one of the most influential and respected 19th-century novelists. Dostoevsky was Russian and born into a professional family who valued education. His father was a physician.

He showed promise as a writer even from adolescence and had his first novel, *Poor Folk* (1846), published when he was 25. Dostoevsky became involved with a socialist group that was perceived as seditious and, as a result, he was sentenced to imprisonment until 1858. After he was released, Dostoevsky began writing in earnest and wrote perpetually. His most notable works, including *Crime and Punishment* (1866) and *The Brothers Karamazov* (1880), were written during this time period. *The Brothers Karamazov* was published posthumously. Dostoevsky also experienced personal tragedy, including the death of his brother and his first wife, as well as episodic epileptic seizures. In spite of these traumas, Dostoevsky continued to write.

By the time of his death in 1867, Dostoevsky was a literary and cultural hero. His work is notable for its investigation of the complexities of human psychology. In many ways, Dostoevsky laid a foundation for the trajectory the genre of the novel would take in the 20th century. Many authors, including Toni Morrison, count Dostoevsky as a profound influence on their work. Soaphead Church, a character in *The Bluest Eye* (1970), despises Dostoevsky and loves Dante.

BIBLIOGRAPHY

Dodd, W. J. *Kafka and Dostoyevsky: The Shaping of Influence.* New York: St. Martin's Press, 1992.

Frank, Joseph. *Dostoevsky: The Miraculous Years, 1865–1871.* Princeton, N.J: Princeton University Press, 1995.

Holquist, Michael. *Dostoevsky and the Novel.* Princeton, N.J.: Princeton University Press, 1977.

Kjetsaa, Geir. *Fyodor Dostoyevsky, A Writer's Life.* New York: Viking, 1987.

Leatherbarrow, William J. *Fedor Dostoevsky: A Reference Guide.* Boston: G. K. Hall, 1990.

Mochul'skii, K. *Dostoevsky: His Life and Work.* Princeton, N.J.: Princeton University Press, 1967.

Murav, Harriet. *Holy Foolishness: Dostoevsky's Novels and the Poetics of Cultural Critique.* Stanford, Calif.: Stanford University Press, 1992.

Simmons, Ernest Joseph. *Feodor Dostoevsky.* New York: Columbia University Press, 1969.

double consciousness Double consciousness is the construct set forth by W. E. B. DuBois in his classic work, *The Souls of Black Folk* (1903), which articulates DuBois's understanding of the racial struggle of African Americans. DuBois felt that African Americans, as a result of racism, discrimination, and exclusion, perpetually face the dilemma of trying to put together, to reconcile, the oppositions of their identity. By defining double consciousness, DuBois articulated the conflict inherent in being an American and yet not fully participating in the rights and privileges of that national designation because of the racial caste system. Dubois's metaphor continues to resonate today and is still used as a way of describing and theorizing the African-American condition.

At the turn of the last century, W. E. B. DuBois prophesied that the problem of the 20th century would be the problem of the color line. Narratives and histories of the 20th century reveal the power of the color line to fracture and polarize, to murder and destroy. Consider Dubois's task as he sat down to articulate literarily a narrative of African America in his 1903 *Souls of Black Folks.* Without hesitation, DuBois appropriated the role of storyteller and interpreter of his people's story. Although the solutions he presents in the text for the elevation of post–Civil War African America were hotly contested, his insightful analysis, particularly his definition of double consciousness, is still highly regarded today. Many literary critics, such as Denise Heinze in her book *The Dilemma of "Double-Consciousness": Toni Morrison's Novels,* employ double consciousness as a tool for understanding Morrison's canon.

BIBLIOGRAPHY

Baldwin, James. "A White Man's Guilt." In *Black on White: Black Writers on What It Means to Be White,* edited by David Roediger. New York: Schocken Books, 1998.

DuBois, W. E. B. *Dusk of Dawn: An Essay toward an Autobiography of a Race Concept.* New Brunswick, N.J., and London: Transaction Books, 1984.

———. *Darkwater: Voices from Within the Veil. The Oxford W. E. B. DuBois Reader.* Edited by Eric J. Sundquist. New York and Oxford: Oxford University Press, 1996.

———. *Souls of Black Folk.* 1903. New York: Signet, 1969.

———. *The Conservation of Races.* Washington, D.C.: American Negro Academy, 1897.

———. *Writings by W. E. B. DuBois in Periodicals Edited by Others.* Vol. 2. Edited by Herbert Aptheker. Millwood, N.Y.: Kraus-Thomson Organization Limited, 1982.

Fox, Frank W. "Washington, DuBois, and the Problem of Negro Two-ness," *Markham Review* 7 (1978): 21–25.

Heinze, Denise. *The Dilemma of "Double-Consciousness": Toni Morrison's Novels.* Athens: University of Georgia Press, 1993.

Jones, D. Marvin. "A Darkness Made Visible: Law, Metaphor, and the Racial Self." In *Critical White Studies: Looking behind the Mirror,* edited by Richard Delgado and Jean Stefancic. Philadelphia: Temple University Press, 1997.

dread locks Although dread-locked hair has an ancient history originating in Africa, contemporary references to dread locks derive from their proliferation on the Caribbean island of Jamaica in the 1950s when members of the Rastafarian religion began to wear their hair in twisted sections that, left uncombed, grew long. Dread locks refer to the specific ways some Rastafarians wear their hair for spiritual reasons. Locks are now a popular hairstyle worn by people of all nationalities and races. In Toni Morrison's *Tar Baby,* Son has locks when he first emerges from the sea. Toni Morrison herself wears her hair in long gray locks.

Dred Scott (1799–1858) Dred Scott was a slave of the American South who is known for having sued for his freedom before the United States Supreme Court. He based his bid on the fact that he had once lived in areas of the country where slavery was illegal. Scott lost the case and remained a slave.

Born in Virginia as a slave of the Peter Blow family, Scott was sold in 1830 to an army surgeon, Dr. John Emerson. Emerson took Scott to Illinois, which was a free state, and then, in 1836, to the Wisconsin Territory, where slavery was illegal according to the Missouri Compromise of 1820. There, Scott met and married Harriet Robinson, a slave owned by a justice of the peace. Scott never sued for his freedom in these northern free areas, where he had some legal standing to bid for his freedom, because he might have been unaware of his rights to do so.

Emerson eventually ended up in Louisiana, where he sent for Scott and Harriet. The couple returned, unaccompanied, to the South. It was not until Emerson died, in 1843, that Scott began to seek freedom for himself and his wife—first by offering to purchase it from Emerson's widow at the price valued for himself and his wife, $300. Mrs. Emerson refused.

Scott's attempt to sue for his freedom through the courts began in 1847. His case was built on the fact that he and Harriet had lived in a state and territory—Illinois and the Wisconsin Territory—where slavery was illegal. After a decade of appeals and court reversals—in which he gained and lost his freedom—his case was brought before the U.S. Supreme Court.

The makeup of the Court in 1856 did not seem to be in Scott's favor. Seven of the nine justices on the Court had been appointed by pro-slavery presidents from the South. Five of these seven were themselves from slave-holding families. In 1857, the Court decided against Scott. Chief Justice Roger B. Taney, who was a staunch supporter of slavery, wrote the majority opinion for the Court, which stated that all people of African ancestry—not only slaves but also those blacks who were free—were not citizens of the United States and so could not sue in federal court.

The decision also declared that the Missouri Compromise of 1820, which restricted slavery to certain territories, was unconstitutional and that the federal government did not have the right to prohibit slavery in these territories. The decision was well-received by southern slaveholders, but many northerners were outraged, and the decision influenced the nomination and subsequent election of Abraham Lincoln. This, in turn, led to the South's secession from the Union and the resultant Civil War.

Ironically, Dred Scott's last year was spent in freedom but not due to any court decision. The sons of Peter Blow, Scott's original owner, had been childhood friends of Scott. They helped pay for Scott's legal fees throughout the years, and when Scott lost his bid for freedom, they bought Scott and his wife and freed them. Scott died within a year of gaining his freedom.

Toni Morrison references the *Dred Scott* decision in her novel *Beloved* (1987).

BIBLIOGRAPHY

Brooke, John T. *Short Notes on the Dred Scott Case.* Cincinnati: Moore, Wilstach, Keys and Co., Printers, 1861.

Fehrenbacher, Don E. *The Dred Scott Case.* New York: Oxford University Press, 1978.

Hopkins, Vincent C. *Dred Scott's Case.* New York: Fordham University Press, 1951.

Kutler, Stanley I. *The Dred Scott Decision: Law or Politics?* Boston: Houghton Mifflin, 1967.

Stampp, Kenneth M. *America in 1857: A Nation on the Brink.* New York: Oxford University Press, 1990.

DuBois, W. E. B. (1868–1963)   W. E. B. DuBois was the influential editor of *The Crisis* from 1910 to 1934. He was also one of the most important cultural critics and political activists of the 20th century. DuBois was a New Englander born into a black upper-middle-class family. He excelled at school and entered Fisk University early. After graduation, he pursued graduate school at the University of Berlin and continued at Harvard. When DuBois graduated from Harvard in 1895, he was the first African American to earn a Ph.D. from that institution.

DuBois worked as an academic, serving on the faculty of Wilberforce University and at the University of Pennsylvania and Atlanta University. DuBois was also centrally concerned with the precarious situation African Americans found themselves in at the turn of the century, in the wake of the failures of Reconstruction. DuBois began to organize other politically minded, socially conscious intellectuals. One of these organizational meetings led to the formation of the Niagara Movement, which was a multi-racial coalition of activists dedicated to the achievement of civil rights.

The Niagara Movement was the root organization that led to the formation of the most important American civil rights organization, the National Association for the Advancement of Colored People (NAACP). The NAACP's journal, *The Crisis,* provided DuBois with a forum for expressing his political opinions, beliefs, and strategies for change. In addition to his work with the NAACP, DuBois continued to write important scholarly works and novels. His activism and scholarship led to unwarranted charges by the United States government. Although he was acquitted of the crimes against the state that he had been accused of, this indictment laid the groundwork for his belief that racial equality would never be achieved in the United States. As a result, in 1961, Dubois moved to Ghana where he would live out the remainder of his life. DuBois also embraced communism as a political philosophy.

DuBois grew to believe that African-American people could not achieve social equality by emulating white ideals—that equality could be achieved only by teaching black racial pride with an emphasis on an African cultural heritage.

BIBLIOGRAPHY

Andrews, William L. *Critical Essays on W. E. B. DuBois.* Boston: G. K. Hall, 1985.

Bell, Bernard W., Emily Grosholz, and James B. Stewart, eds. *W. E. B. DuBois on Race and Culture: Philosophy, Politics, and Poetics.* New York: Routledge, 1996.

Broderick, Francis L. *W. E. B. DuBois: Negro Leader in a Time of Crisis.* 1959.

Foner, Philip S, ed. *W. E. B. DuBois Speaks: Speeches and Addresses, 1890–1919.* New York: Pathfinder Press, 1966

Holloway, Jonathan S. "The Soul of W. E. B. DuBois," *American Quarterly* 49, no. 3 (September 1997): 603–615.

Lewis, David L. *W. E. B. DuBois: Biography of a Race, 1868–1919.* New York: Henry Holt, 1993.

Marable, Manning. *W. E. B. DuBois: Black Radical Democrat.* Boston: Twayne, 1986.

Rampersad, Arnold. *The Art and Imagination of W. E. B. DuBois.* Cambridge, Mass.: Harvard University Press, 1976.

———. "W. E. B. DuBois as a Man of Literature," *American Literature* 51 (1979): 50–68.

Rudwick, Elliott M. *W. E. B. DuBois, Voice of the Black Protest Movement.* Urbana: University of Illinois Press, 1982.

Sundquist, Eric J., ed. *The Oxford W. E. B. DuBois Reader.* New York: Oxford University Press, 1996.

Dunham, Katherine (1909–2006) The multi-talented artist Katherine Dunham excelled during her life in the fields of dance, choreography, and anthropology. Dunham was born in Joliet, Illinois. Due to early evidence of her prowess, Dunham received a scholarship to attend the University of Chicago where she eventually earned three degrees. While at the University of Chicago, Dunham pioneered the study of Caribbean and African dance forms. Dunham visited several Caribbean islands and brought important information about those traditions into the formal dance world. Her work introduced new ideas and concepts that had been previously unexamined.

Dunham created her own dance troupe as well as a dance methodology she called the Dunham Technique. She became known and was renowned worldwide. Dunham often did her own choreography and created commissioned works and music. She and her company were featured on Broadway and in Hollywood films.

Dunham's work and aesthetic challenged many of the racial stereotypes that prevail in the United States. Dunham used her work to fight against racism, sexism, and poverty. She also was an outspoken critic of U.S. policies toward Haiti and the Haitian people. She worked as a cultural adviser to the country of Senegal in Africa. Among the many honors accorded to her is the establishment of a museum dedicated to her life and art.

One of the women who visits Cosey's Resort in *Love* (2003) has trained with Katherine Dunham.

BIBLIOGRAPHY

Aschenbrenner, Joyce. *Katherine Dunham: Dancing a Life.* Champaign: University of Illinois Press, 2002.

———. *Katherine Dunham: Reflections on the Social and Political Contexts of Afro-American Dance.* New York: Congress on Research in Dance, 1981.

Beckford, Ruth. *Katherine Dunham: A Biography.* New York: Marcel Dekker, 1979.

Dominy, Jeannine. *Katherine Dunham: Dancer and Choreographer.* Chelsea House, 1992.

Dunham, Katherine. *A Touch of Innocence: A Memoir of Childhood.* Chicago: University of Chicago Press, 1994.

———. *Dances of Haiti.* Los Angeles: University of California Press, 1983.

———. *Island Possessed.* Garden City, N.Y.: Doubleday, 1969.

E

East St. Louis Race Riot   The East St. Louis Race Riot was not so much a riot as a white massacre of blacks, and it is considered the worst mass attack against blacks in the nation's history.

In the summer of 1917, as part of the war effort during World War I, many blacks were recruited to work in the aluminum and steel factories of East St. Louis, Illinois. Work in factories was partly what drew blacks to the North during the GREAT MIGRATION, and the presence of African Americans in East St. Louis was new. Local whites resented not only the jobs going to blacks but also the rumors that black men were fraternizing with white women at labor meetings and on the job. On May 28, in what turned out to be a precursor to the infamous riot, thousands of whites stormed black neighborhoods and attacked blacks on the street. No blacks were killed on this occasion, but white resentment remained high, along with fears that blacks were planning a counterattack. On July 1, as a result of a series of shootings involving a black man, rumors spread that a white man, possibly two white policemen, had been killed, and the next day thousands of whites returned to the black neighborhoods with even greater fury. In riots that lasted nearly a week, the whites burned sections of the neighborhoods, shot blacks escaping the flames, and lynched several more. White women also participated in the riot, attacking black women.

The Illinois National Guard did little to stop the violence, and, indeed, it was reported that many of the guardsmen helped the whites in attacking blacks. Accounts of the riot are filled with the brutalities of furious white men and women maiming and killing blacks. In the end, several whites and many dozens of African Americans were left dead.

BIBLIOGRAPHY

Rudwick, Elliot M. *Race Riot in East St. Louis.* Carbondale: Southern Illinois University Press, 1964.

Ellington, "Duke" Edward Kennedy (1899–1974)
The man who would ultimately be known as the world-famous musician Duke Ellington was born into a middle-class African-American family in Washington, D.C., at the turn of the century. Ellington had a wide exposure to the arts and culture and received a fine arts education at the Armstrong Manual Training School. Finding himself more interested in playing the piano, Ellington left high school to pursue a career in music.

Ellington began his music career by starting a band. The band was popular and was a favorite for parties and social engagements. The band also got exposure and developed an audience through radio engagements. After a time, he relocated in order to have greater access to the more extensive music venues of New York. Once in New York, Ellington and his band gained a national, and, eventually, international audience and following. Recording contracts followed as Ellington became known, not only as a musician and band leader, but also as a composer. Ellington became one of the most popular, respected, and innovative musicians of the 20th century. He died in 1974.

BIBLIOGRAPHY

Ellington, Duke. *Music Is My Mistress.* New York: Doubleday, 1973.
———. *Duke Ellington: Greatest Hits.* RCA Victor. Audiocassette. 1996.
———. *Sir Duke and Friends.* Ottenheimer Creations. CD. 1999.
Hasse, John Edward. *Beyond Category: The Life and Genius of Duke Ellington.* New York: Simon and Schuster, 1993.
Montgomery, Elizabeth R., and Paul Frame. *Duke Ellington: King of Jazz.* New York: Garrard, 1972.
Tucker, Mark, ed. *The Duke Ellington Reader.* New York: Oxford University Press, 1993.
Yanow, Scott. *Duke Ellington.* New York: Friedman/Fairfax, 1999.

Ellison, Ralph Waldo (1914–1994)   Although he published only one novel during his lifetime, *Invisible Man* (1952), he is counted as one of the most influential and significant writers of the 20th century. Ralph Ellison was born in Oklahoma City, Oklahoma, to a working-class family. When Ellison was a young man, his father was killed in an accident, leaving his mother to support Ellison and his brother on her own.

As a young man, Ellison was interested in music and played brass instruments, including the trumpet and saxophone. After graduating from high school, Ellison attended BOOKER T. WASHINGTON'S Tuskegee Institute in Tuskegee, Alabama. Ellison found Tuskegee's perspective on what education consists of to be limited, and he left to pursue other types of education. He was, at this time in his life, particularly drawn to the visual arts and relocated to New York to study sculpture.

While in the city, Ellison found himself surrounded by African-American literary luminaries such as Langston Hughes and Richard Wright. Wright especially became a mentor figure for Ellison. Around this time, the mid-1940s, Ellison began to write the work that would become *Invisible Man.*

When World War II began, Ellison joined the U.S. merchant marine. After the war, Ellison returned to his writing and *Invisible Man* was published in 1952. Ellison received widespread acclaim for his remarkable novel that follows his protagonist's literal and allegorical journey through the complex negotiations of African-American life.

One of the most frequently anthologized chapters of Ralph Ellison's *Invisible Man* is "The Battle Royal" within which the thematic foundations for the novel are outlined. One of these themes involves the politically and culturally derived tensions between black men and white women. In order to ensure that the Invisible Man knows his "place" in society the white town leaders tempt him with a nude white woman. The Invisible Man's confrontation with the paradox between his desire for this woman and the danger represented by her sexuality reveals the double-bind these encounters present to African-American men. The Invisible Man's reaction is conditioned by the ambivalent political cross-currents in which he unwittingly finds himself. From childhood he has been taught that even looking at a white woman can mean certain death, yet still he is inexorably drawn to gaze longingly upon the woman's naked frame.

After publication of *Invisible Man,* Ellison was in demand as a lecturer and he was offered various academic positions at major universities. Among the academic positions he held was an endowed chair at New York University. Ellison began work on a second novel that he never was able to complete during his lifetime. He did, however, publish collected volumes of essays and short stories. Ellison died in 1994, shortly after a diagnosis of pancreatic cancer.

Ellison's second novel, *Juneteenth* (1999), was published after his death and assembled from Ellison's notes by his literary executor, John Callahan. The novel has produced significant controversy and mixed reactions. Ellison has often been criticized for his optimism about the eventual resolution of race controversies in the United States. Toni Morrison's writings have often been compared with Ellison's and she counts him as one of her influences. Morrison was a supporter of Ellison's *Juneteenth* and participated in several promotional readings of the novel.

BIBLIOGRAPHY

Benston, Kimberly W., ed. *Speaking for You: The Vision of Ralph Ellison.* Washington, D.C.: Howard University Press, 1987.

Busby, Mark. *Ralph Ellison.* Boston: Twayne Publishers, 1991.

Callahan, John F., ed. *The Collected Essays of Ralph Ellison.* New York: Modern Library, 1995.

———. *Flying Home and Other Stories by Ralph Ellison.* New York: Random House, 1996.

Nadel, Alan. *Invisible Criticism: Ralph Ellison and the American Canon.* Iowa City: University of Iowa Press, 1988.

O'Meally, Robert G. *The Craft of Ralph Ellison.* Cambridge, Mass.: Harvard University Press, 1980.

O'Meally, Robert, ed. *New Essays on Invisible Man.* Cambridge, Mass.: Cambridge University Press, 1988.

Reilly, John M. *Twentieth Century Interpretations of Invisible Man; a Collection of Critical Essays.* Englewood Cliffs, N.J.: Prentice Hall, 1970.

Emancipation Proclamation   While the Emancipation Proclamation was the official decree eliminating slavery and freeing African Americans, the actual enactment of the Emancipation Proclamation did little to change the conditions of most of those who were enslaved.

Whether Lincoln had the constitutional authority to abolish slavery was a matter of tremendous controversy. The issue became a point of crisis as a result of slaves escaping to Union strongholds and being captured by Union troops as property during the Civil War. The question emerged as to whether these individuals could be held or should be returned as property. Although he did not support the policy, Lincoln did not insist that the escaped or captured slaves be returned. Lincoln stated that he believed in gradual and compensated emancipation.

Later, Lincoln enforced his position when he allowed General Henry Halleck to order that runaway slaves could not seek and would not find sanctuary with the Union army. Again Lincoln resisted freeing African Americans when he refused to allow another general, David Hunter, to free slaves in order to enlist them as soldiers. In response to this crisis, Lincoln emphatically stated his position about ABOLITION, maintaining that his concern was with the salvation of the Union and not with the abolition of slavery.

Eventually, as the necessity of enlisting blacks as soldiers in the war effort became apparent, Lincoln became persuaded that the president might have the power and authority to abolish slavery. Lincoln began to write drafts of the Emancipation Proclamation. After the Union victory at Antietam, Lincoln felt that he would have enough public support to issue the proclamation and he did so on September 22, 1862.

As issued, the proclamation went into effect the following January 1. It mandated that all those who were enslaved in states that were in rebellion by the New Year would be made free. Those enslaved in states that Union troops already occupied would not be freed by the Emancipation Proclamation.

The proclamation was signed into law on the promised day, January 1, 1863. In the version signed into law, there was a provision that allowed ex-slaves to enlist and serve in the Union army. As a result, African Americans became an active and important force in the Union army, with nearly 200,000 African-American soldiers serving in the Civil War.

Morrison's maternal grandfather, John Solomon Willis, told his family stories that he remembered of experiencing the Emancipation Proclamation as a young boy and being afraid of it because he did not know what it was or what it meant.

BIBLIOGRAPHY

Davis, David Brion. *The Emancipation Moment.* Gettysburg, Pa.: Gettysburg College, 1983.

Franklin, John Hope. *The Emancipation Proclamation.* Garden City, N.Y.: Anchor Books, 1965.

Klingaman, William K. *Abraham Lincoln and the Road to Emancipation, 1861–1865.* New York: Viking, 2001.

Thomas, Velma Maia. *Freedom's Children: The Journey from Emancipation into the Twentieth Century.* New York: Crown Publishers, 2000.

Eurydice   The legend of Eurydice is one of the best-known and most often adapted of the Greek myths. The story of Eurydice begins with Orpheus who was the son of the god Apollo. Orpheus is renowned for his musical abilities. With his lyre, he could charm the gods, humans, nature, and animals.

Orpheus was the love of Eurydice's life and the two married. Not long after the wedding, Eurydice, while running away from the advances of an untoward admirer, receives a fatal snake bite. Grieving for his lost wife, Orpheus wanders the land playing mournful tunes on his lyre. He wanders into the underworld and presents his case to the rulers of that realm, Hades and Persephone, in song. His songs move all of the inhabitants of the underworld.

Taking pity on the couple, Hades and Persephone grant Orpheus's request with one condition: Orpheus cannot turn to glance upon his bride until the two have completely exited from the land of the underworld. Orpheus and Eurydice begin their upward climb and, temporarily forgetting the conditions of the release. Orpheus looks behind to see if Eurydice is following. At that moment, Eurydice is forever consigned to the underworld and death.

Inconsolable, Orpheus wanders playing his lyre. In his grief, he does not care about his safety and he is killed, stoned to death by scorned women and ripped apart, limb by limb. The narrative ends happily, however, as he is reunited with Eurydice in death.

In *Tar Baby* (1981), Valerian Street corrects his wife, Margaret Street's, pronunciation of Eurydice.

BIBLIOGRAPHY

Locke, Liz. "Orpheus and Orphism: Cosmology and Sacrifice at the Boundary," *Folklore Forum* 28 (1997): 3–29.

Rose, H. J. *Handbook of Greek Mythology*. London: Methuen, 1928.

Exodusters   In the wake of the violent reprisals against African-American freedom that took place in the southern United States in the years following the Civil War, many African Americans chose to move to the North rather than remain in a seemingly impossible situation. Those who participated in the migration of African Americans to the West are often called Exodusters.

In the late 1870s Benjamin "Pap" Singleton, who had formerly been enslaved, began to persuade other formerly enslaved African Americans to move from the South to the American West, particularly to Kansas, where land was plentiful. The African Americans who took Singleton's advice are referred to as Exodusters after the biblical chapter of Exodus, which details the emergence of the oppressed Israelites into a better, even ideal, land.

Singleton attempted to establish settlements in Tennessee and, when that was unsuccessful, he moved on to acquire land in Kansas. After creating settlements in Kansas, Singleton sought to entice settlers to create towns at these sites. Singleton's enterprise was profitable for him. When the Exodusters took Singleton's advice about how and where to relocate, he charged them $5 for the information. The initial group of settlers generally found Kansas an improvement on the lives they had been living in the South; through them and through Singleton's campaign, word spread about the possibilities of Kansas. In 1879, during the peak of the Exoduster migration, more than 15,000 former slaves and free blacks made the journey to Kansas in search of a better life.

Although they are not Exodusters, the movement and motivations of the individuals who travel from the South to Oklahoma to found the town of Ruby in the novel *Paradise* (1998) resemble in some ways those of the Exodusters.

BIBLIOGRAPHY

Athearn, Robert G. "Black Exodus: The Migration of 1879," *The Prairie Scout* 3 (1975): 86–97.

———. *In Search of Canaan: Black Migration to Kansas, 1879–1880*. Lawrence: University Press of Kansas, 1978.

Painter, Nell Irvin. *Exodusters: Black Migration to Kansas after Reconstruction*. New York: Alfred A. Knopf, 1977.

———. "Millenarian Aspects of the Exodus to Kansas in 1879," *Journal of Social History* 9 (Spring 1976): 331–338.

Van Deusen, John G. "The Exodusters of 1879," *Journal of Negro History* 21 (April 1936): 111–129.

F

Father Divine, George Baker (1880?–1965)
The man who would eventually be known to the world as Father Divine was born George Baker in southern Georgia. As a young man, he became involved with a traveling preacher from whom, it is thought, he learned the techniques of public address that would serve him so well in later years. Baker struck out on his own and began to acquire his own admirers.

Baker relocated to Brooklyn, New York, as one of the thousands of African Americans migrating out of the South in 1914. Baker established a church on Long Island, New York, and he began to gather a significant following. He was known to his followers as Father Divine.

Because of the number of followers visiting his home, Divine was arrested in 1931 for disturbing the peace. This intervention by the police was believed by his followers to be racially motivated; as a result, they began a protest. Divine was sentenced to jail and fined. Shortly after handing down this sentence, the judge from the trial died. Divine's followers interpreted this event as a sign of Divine's supernatural powers. Publicity surrounding this event catapulted Divine into a larger public spotlight.

After serving his time, Divine relocated his church to HARLEM, the center of African-American life in the city at the time. His church grew exponentially. Divine attracted members through his programs of social uplift. He and his members purchased buildings and offered shelter to those who were homeless and unemployed.

Following his successes in New York, Divine relocated to Philadelphia where he and the headquarters of his church remained until his death. Divine's church is known as the Peace Mission. Members share possessions and expenses and pool all resources. Divine was said to be the messiah. His arrival was said to have been predicted in the Bible. His church is dedicated to black social, political, and moral uplift. Branches of the Peace Mission continue to exist in diminished form in New York, New Jersey, Pennsylvania, and California.

At the beginning of *Song of Solomon* (1977), the scene framing Robert Smith's suicide is compared to the dramatic entrances characteristic of Father Divine.

BIBLIOGRAPHY

Burnham, Kenneth. *God Comes to America: Father Divine and the Peace Mission Movement*. Boston: Lambeth Press, 1979.

Harris, Sarah. *Father Divine*. New York: Collier Books, 1971.

Parker, Robert Allerton. *The Incredible Messiah; the Deification of Father Divine*. Boston: Little, Brown, 1937.

Watts, Jill. *God, Harlem, U.S.A.: The Father Divine Story*. Berkeley: University of California Press, 1992.

Weisbrot, Robert. *Father Divine and the Struggle for Racial Equality*. Chicago: University of Illinois Press, 1983.

Faubus, Orval (1910–1994) Six-time governor of Arkansas during the critical years of the CIVIL RIGHTS MOVEMENT, Faubus was born in the state to a family that was much more liberal than he proved to be in later years. After attending college and training to teach, Faubus became involved in politics. As his political activism increased, Faubus became more and more conservative, particularly with respect to issues of integration.

Faubus first ran for governor of Arkansas in 1954, the same year that the United States Supreme Court outlawed segregation of public facilities with its ruling on the BROWN V. BOARD OF EDUCATION decision. Following his successful campaign, Faubus was originally responsible for desegregating some public facilities. When his actions began to lose public support, Faubus began to take a hard line against desegregation.

The year 1957 was critical in his history as a governor when his actions to prevent desegregation and to regain his popularity led to a confrontation between the state of Arkansas and the federal government. A group of African American students in Little Rock, Arkansas, known as the Little Rock Nine, were set to enroll in Little Rock High School. Faubus and residents of Little Rock prevented the students from enrolling by using harassment and violence.

This resistance by the highest official of the state forced federal officials, particularly President Eisenhower, to take action to enforce the decisions of the Supreme Court and the law of the land. Eisenhower was forced to send in military troops to ensure that the students could enroll and could safely attend Little Rock High School. The children were enrolled. Among the state's anti-desegregation advocates, Faubus became a hero and remained the governor of Arkansas for the next 12 years.

Eventually, public sentiment began to change and, after his defeat, Faubus never won elected office again. Faubus died in 1994 and is remembered as a symbol of southern hostility toward and resistance to racial integration.

When the men in Tommy's Barbershop in *Song of Solomon* (1977) discuss various instances of racial violence, they mention Orval Faubus as an adversary.

BIBLIOGRAPHY

Faubus, Orval Eugene. *Down from the Hills.* New York: Pioneer Press, 1980.

Reed, Roy. *Faubus: The Life and Times of an American Prodigal.* Fayetteville: University of Arkansas Press, 1997.

Rowland, Walter E. *Faubus, Arkansas and Education.* Conway, Ark.: River Road Press, 1989.

Vaughn, Curtis M. *Faubus' Folly: The Story of Segregation.* New York: Vantage Press, 1959.

Faulkner, William (1897–1962) Faulkner was born in the southern American city of New Albany, Mississippi. His family had deep roots in the aristocracy of Mississippi, but the family had nearly depleted its fortune by the time William was born. When he was a boy of five, the family relocated to Oxford, Mississippi. Although he was not known as a model student, Faulkner began writing as a boy. As a young man, he was particularly interested in writing poetry.

During World War I, Faulkner served in the Canadian and British Royal Air Forces. After the war, he returned to Mississippi, attended classes for a time at the University of Mississippi, and held odd jobs at a bookstore and as a writer for a newspaper. He began to write seriously, and in 1926 he had his first novel, *Soldier's Pay*, published. This novel was the first in a series of novels about a fictional Mississippi locale called Yaknapatawpha County, loosely based on Faulkner's own memories and perceptions of his home.

Faulkner's novels are concerned with the perceived disintegration of order in the world and, in particular, in the South. The characters generally emerge from or revolve around the narratives of three fictional families, the Compson, Sartoris, and Snopes families. The most acclaimed of his novels include *The Sound and the Fury* (1929), *Sanctuary* (1931), *Requiem For a Nun* (1951), *Light in August* (1932), *Absalom, Absalom!* (1936), *The Hamlet* (1940), *Intruder in the Dust* (1948), *The Town* (1957), *The Mansion* (1959), and *The Reivers* (1962).

Faulkner is one of the most influential and innovative writers of the 20th century. Faulkner was awarded the 1949 Nobel Prize in literature. Many critics mark the similarities between the subjects and styles of Toni Morrison and William Faulkner. She is but one of many important writers who cites Faulkner as a central influence; she wrote her master's thesis on suicide and alienation in the novels of Faulkner and Virginia Woolf. In 1962, Faulkner died of a heart attack.

BIBLIOGRAPHY

Brooks, Cleanth. *William Faulkner: First Encounters.* New Haven, Conn.: Yale University Press, 1983.

————. *William Faulkner: Toward Yoknapatawpha and Beyond.* Baton Rouge: Louisiana State University Press, 1978.

————. *William Faulkner: The Yoknapatawpha Country.* Baton Rouge: Louisiana State University Press, 1963.

Carey, Glenn O., ed. *Faulkner, the Unappeased Imagination: A Collection of Critical Essays.* Troy, N.Y.: Whitston, 1980.

Chabrier, Gwendolyn. *Faulkner's Families: A Southern Saga.* New York: Gordian, 1993.

Clarke, Deborah. *Robbing the Mother: Women in Faulkner.* Jackson: University Press of Mississippi, 1994.

Davis, Thadious M. *Faulkner's "Negro": Art and the Southern Context.* Baton Rouge: Louisiana State University Press, 1983.

Dowling, David. *William Faulkner.* New York: St. Martin's, 1989.

Doyle, Don H. *Faulkner's County: The Historical Roots of Yoknapatawpha.* Chapel Hill: University of North Carolina Press, 2001.

Duvall, John N. *Faulkner's Marginal Couple: Invisible, Outlaw, and Unspeakable Communities.* Austin: University of Texas Press, 1990.

Faulkner, William. *A Fable.* New York: Random House, 1954.

————. *Absalom, Absalom!* New York: Random House, 1936.

————. *As I Lay Dying.* New York: J. Cape and H. Smith, 1930.

————. *Go Down, Moses, and Other Stories.* New York: Random House, 1942.

————. *The Hamlet.* New York: Random House, 1940.

————. *Intruder in the Dust.* New York: Random House, 1948.

————. *Light in August.* New York: H. Smith and R. Haas, 1932.

————. *The Mansion.* New York: Random House, 1959.

————. *Pylon.* New York: H. Smith and R. Haas, 1935.

————. *The Reivers, a Reminiscence.* New York: Random House, 1962.

————. *Requiem for a Nun.* New York: Random House, 1951.

————. *Sanctuary.* New York: J. Cape and H. Smith, 1931.

————. *The Sound and the Fury.* New York: J. Cape and H. Smith, 1929.

————. *The Town.* New York: Random House, 1957.

————. *The Unvanquished.* New York: Random House, 1938.

————. *The Wild Palms.* New York: Random House, 1939.

————. *William Faulkner's Speech of Acceptance upon the Award of the Nobel Prize for Literature, Delivered in Stockholm on the Tenth of December, 1950.* New York: Chatto and Windus, 1951.

Ford, Dan, ed. *Heir and Prototype: Original and Derived Characterizations in Faulkner.* Conway: University of Central Arkansas Press, 1988.

Fowler, Doreen. *Faulkner: The Return of the Repressed.* Charlottesville: University Press of Virginia, 1997.

Fels-Naptha   In its trademark red and green label, Fels-Naptha, created by the Dial Soap company, was a bar soap used for laundry detergent. The primary claim made for the effectiveness of the soap was the combination of soap and naptha, a solvent derived from plant extracts. The company claimed that the soap smelled fresh and would leave clothes pure white and without a residue.

Fels Naptha is used for cleaning in Morrison's *The Bluest Eye* (1970).

for colored girls who have considered suicide when the rainbow is enuf   With Ntozake Shange's publication of the choreopoem *for colored girls who have considered suicide when the rainbow is enuf* (1975), the renaissance in contemporary African-American women's writing reached a Broadway audience. Through its various monologues, the choreopoem documents the struggles of seven anonymous black women as they attempt to live their lives in an environment fraught with racism, sexism, and poverty.

for colored girls who have considered suicide when the rainbow is enuf reflects the time in which Ntozake Shange wrote and performed the choreopoem. By the late 1970s, the dissatisfaction and exclusion African-American women experienced within both the CIVIL RIGHTS and women's movements led to the establishment of organizations dealing specifically with the concerns of African-American women. Shange's choreopoem mirrors the development of African-American feminist coalitions in the larger society. Although the women in the choreopoem are, to some extent, distinct from each other, it is only through their collective efforts that they are able to expiate their pain and to become self-affirming.

Although often seen as disparate selections of poetry and prose, Shange's *for colored girls* is in fact a tightly structured coming-of-age story. Through her seven women characters, Shange documents a journey from innocence to experience that leads to figurative death and then to spiritual rebirth. Although the seven anonymous women in the play, identified only by their colors, appear as individuals in the choreopoem, on a figurative level they represent black womanhood in its diversity.

The many shades and hues of the African-American woman converge most distinctly in the central character, appropriately named lady in brown. Although this character, clad in the color of earth and of African-American women, appears only briefly at the beginning, middle and end of the choreopoem, she serves both as a frame and as its narrator. Within the dialogue of the lady in brown, the path these women take from subjection to survival unfolds. Shange's work shares an important cultural moment with Morrison's emergence as a major American writer overlapping with Shange's success.

BIBLIOGRAPHY

Elder, Arlene. "Sassafras, Cypress, and Indigo: Ntozake Shange's Neo Slave/Blues Narrative," *African American Review* 26 (1992): 99–107.

Lester, Neal A. "At the Heart of Shange's Feminism: An Interview," *Black American Literature Forum* 24 (1990): 717–730.

———. *Ntozake Shange: A Critical Study of the Plays.* New York: Garland, 1995.

Shange, Ntozake. *A Daughter's Geography.* New York: St. Martin's Press, 1983.

———. *Betsy Brown.* New York: St. Martin's Press, 1985.

———. *for colored girls who have considered suicide/ When the Rainbow is Enuf.* New York: Macmillan, 1975.

———. *From Okra to Greens.* New York: St. Martin's Press, 1984.

———. *Liliane: Resurrection of the Daughter.* New York: St. Martin's Press, 1994.

———. *Nappy Edges.* New York: St. Martin's Press, 1978.

———. *Sassafras, Cypress, and Indigo.* New York: St. Martin's Press, 1982.

———. *Riding the Edge in Texas: Word Paintings.* New York: St. Martin's Press, 1987.

———. *The Love Space Demands: A Continuing Saga.* New York: St. Martin's Press, 1991.

Forsythe, William (1949–)   William Forsythe is an experimental artist and choreographer with an international reputation for innovative explorations of dance and the symbolic meanings of the movements of the human body. Forsythe, a native New Yorker, studied dance at Jacksonville University and the Joffrey Ballet School.

Forsythe acquired his reputation as one of the premier innovators in contemporary dance, particularly in ballet, in Europe, where he was a dancer and resident choreographer at the Stuttgard Ballet. Forsythe has conceived of ballet as a kind of language through which a unique understanding of human communication can emerge. In 1984, he began a 20-year tenure with the Frankfurt Ballet.

Forsythe formed his own company, The Forsythe Company, in 2004. In recent years, his work has become more experimental and interdisciplinary, as incorporating film and other media.

William Forsythe and Toni Morrison have collaborated on several projects, including Morrison's *Foreigner's Home* exhibition at the Louvre in November of 2003 and Morrison's *Art Is Otherwise* festival at the Baryshnikov Arts Center in New York.

Freedman's Bureau (The Bureau of Refugees, Freedmen and Abandoned Lands)   In 1865, the War Department established the agency known commonly as the Freedman's Bureau. The agency was charged with organizing, cataloging, and assisting formerly enslaved African Americans as they transitioned from slavery to freedom. Throughout its existence, one man, former Union general Oliver O. Howard, led the Freedman's Bureau as its commissioner. The bureau was created to develop relief, educational, employment, economic, justice, and relocation programs. Secondarily, the agency was also in charge of reallocating lands that had been confiscated as a result of the Civil War.

Many scholars attest that the most significant accomplishment of the Freedman's Bureau was the establishment of public schools in the South. More than 1,000 elementary schools were founded by the bureau and bureau officials were involved in the formation of black colleges and universities. Although it never lived up to its well-known 40 acres and a mule claim, the bureau did redistribute some land to approximately 3,000 former slaves. This land was mostly reclaimed after the former Confederates were given back the land they held before the Civil War.

Bureau records are increasingly valued as a unique source of information about those African Americans whose lives were in flux as a result of their change in status and the difficulties of the Reconstruction era. As the compromises of Reconstruction eroded, public support for freed African Americans and political and financial support for the Freedman's Bureau waned as well. By 1872, the bureau was eliminated by Congress.

In *Song of Solomon* (1977), Jake gets his new name, Macon Dead, from a drunken Union soldier when he registers with the Freedman's Bureau.

BIBLIOGRAPHY

Bently, George R. *A History of the Freedmen's Bureau.* Philadelphia: University of Pennsylvania, 1955.

Donald, Henderson H. *The Negro Freedman.* New York: Henry Schuman, 1952.

Foner, Eric. *A Short History of Reconstruction.* New York: Harper and Row, 1990.

Lawson, Bill E., and Howard McGary. *Between Slavery and Freedom.* Bloomington: Indiana University Press, 1992.

Peirce, Paul Skeels. *The Freedmen's Bureau.* New York: Haskell House Publishers, 1971.

Fugitive Slave Law   In 1850, the Congress of the United States ratified an agreement that would come to be called the Compromise of 1850. The compromise that the Congress reached admitted the new states of California and Texas to the United States, with California admitted as a free state and Texas as a slaveholding state. The compromise also eliminated the slave trade in Washington, D.C. One of the laws included in the compromise was the Fugitive Slave Act. The act enabled slaveholders to reclaim African Americans who had run away on the basis of the word of the slaveholder. Proof of "ownership" was no longer required. The act also introduced harsh penalties for those who were caught aiding or assisting individuals who had run away from slavery.

These laws were met with much resistance. ABOLITIONists and others feared that any free black would be subject to kidnap and enslavement. The law catalyzed activism and increased the number of people assisting and utilizing the UNDERGROUND RAILROAD, a network of safe harbors for those running away from slavery. The law may also have been a major factor in the social and political events leading up to the Civil War.

Sethe and her family are affected by the Fugitive Slave law when schoolteacher comes to recapture them after they escape from Sweet Home in *Beloved* (1987)

BIBLIOGRAPHY

Campbell, Stanley W. *The Slave Catchers: Enforcement of the Fugitive Slave Law, 1850–1860.* Chapel Hill: University of North Carolina Press, 1968.

Finkleman, Paul, ed. *Fugitive Slaves, Articles on American Slavery.* New York: Garland Publishing, 1989.

Franklin, John Hope, and Loren Schweninger. *Runaway Slaves: Rebels on the Plantation.* New York: Oxford University Press, 1999.

Gara, Larry. *The Liberty Line: The Legend of the Underground Railroad.* Lexington: University of Kentucky Press, 1961.

Gordon, Asa H. "The Struggle of the Negro Slaves for Physical Freedom," *Journal of Negro History* 13 (January 1928): 22–35.

Hadden, Sally E. *Slave Patrols: Law and Violence in Virginia and the Carolinas.* Cambridge, Mass.: Harvard University Press, 2001.

Harrold, Stanley. "Freeing the Weems Family: A New Look at the Underground Railroad," *Civil War History* 42 (December 1996): 289–306.

Litwack, Leon. *North of Slavery: The Negro in the Free States, 1790–1860.* Chicago: University of Chicago Press, 1961.

Wilson, Carol. *Freedom at Risk: The Kidnapping of Free Blacks in America, 1780–1865.* Lexington: University of Kentucky Press, 1994.

G

gandy dancer The name "gandy dancer" derives from a manufacturer of railroad lining tools, the Gandy Manufacturing Company. The mostly African American crews who were responsible for placing and repairing the railroad track lines came to be called Gandy dancers. They worked in crews that numbered around 10 men. There was a rhythm connected with the work of laying the lines, and the crew chief would call the beats out to keep the crew together. The men invented work songs and worded chants in order to make the work more interesting and to correspond with the kind of work that was being performed. The work was long and exhausting, but the men, and particularly the lead man, kept his crew together and motivated through his music and their collective Gandy dance. This cultural response to the oppressive work situation borrowed from the African-American tradition of call and response. During the depression, some of the work songs were recorded by folklorists and anthropologists working for the Works Progress Administration (WPA). The Smithsonian has collected them on several recordings.

In *The Bluest Eye* (1970), there is a reference to gandy dancers.

BIBLIOGRAPHY

Bainbridge, Russ. *Life of a Gandy Dancer.* New York: Carleton Press, 1993.

Classic Railroad Songs from Smithsonian Folkways. Smithsonian Folkways. CD. 2006.

Lomax, Alan. *Negro Work Songs and Calls.* Rounder Select. CD. 1999.

Garbo, Greta (1905–1990) The youngest of her parents' children, Greta Garbo was born into an economically struggling family in Sweden. After her father's untimely death in 1919, the family's fortunes declined further and Garbo had to go to work. As an attractive young girl, one of the jobs Garbo held was as an advertising model for print and film. Through her film work, she was noticed and her life as an actress began.

Garbo attended acting school at the Royal Dramatic Theatre. She appeared in Swedish and German films, and eventually was able to get a contract at the American mega-studio, Metro-Goldwyn-Mayer (MGM). After signing with MGM, Garbo became a movie star. Although she began, and achieved fame as a silent movie star, Garbo was able to succeed in sound films as well.

After making dozens of successful films, Garbo stopped acting in the movies in 1941. She earned an Academy Award in 1954 for lifetime achievement in film. She had become internationally famous and an icon of beauty and glamour.

Garbo spent the final decades of her life out of the public eye in New York. In recent years, scholars have confirmed that Garbo was bisexual and a closeted lesbian.

Mr. Henry of *The Bluest Eye* (1970) calls Frieda and Claudia MacTeer by the pet names of Greta Garbo and Ginger Rogers.

BIBLIOGRAPHY

Corliss, Richard. *Greta Garbo*. New York: Pyramid Publication, 1974.

Paris, Barry. *Garbo*. Minneapolis: University of Minnesota Press, 2002.

Vickers, Hugo. *Loving Garbo, The Story of Greta Garbo, Cecil Beaton and Mercedes de Acosta*. London: Pimlico, 1995.

Viera, Mark A. *Greta Garbo, A Cinematic Legacy*. New York: Harry N. Abrams, 2005.

Garner, Margaret (1833–1858) When Toni Morrison created the fictional character of Sethe for her novel *Beloved* (1989), the story of Sethe and her children was loosely based on the actual story of Margaret Garner, a Kentucky woman who tried to escape slavery with her children in 1856.

Margaret Garner was born in Kentucky. At the time of her birth, she was enslaved by the Gaines family. Historians believe that Garner's father was white because the census records state that Garner was mulatto, although her parents were recorded as black. When Margaret was 15, she married Robert Garner. Robert Garner was enslaved on a neighboring farm and was frequently hired out. Between 1850 and 1855, Margaret gave birth to four children, Thomas, Samuel, Mary, and Pricilla. The paternity of these children is the subject of much debate. There is circumstantial evidence that the children's father might have been Margaret's owner, Archibald Gaines.

Richwood Presbyterian Church, where Margaret Garner attended services as a slave. The story of Margaret Garner was the inspiration for Morrison's fictional character Sethe in *Beloved*. *(Photograph by Carmen R. Gillespie)*

This mural commemorating Margaret Garner and her family's 1856 escape from Kentucky to Ohio is painted near the spot where the family is thought to have crossed the Ohio River. The mural was painted on the Covington Kentucky Flood Wall by artist Robert Dafford. *(Photograph by Carmen R. Gillespie)*

Margaret Garner was pregnant with a fifth child when she and her husband Robert, and Robert's parents, decided to make an escape during the cold winter of 1856 when the Ohio River was frozen over. Nine others enslaved in the area made the escape with the Garners. The family traveled from the Garner and Gaines farms by horse-driven sleighs. Robert left the horses in a livery stable in Kentucky and the family and the other nine escapees made their way across the frozen Ohio. Those escaping with the Garners went another way and were successful in their escape, the Garners fled to the home of a relative, Joseph Kite, Margaret's cousin.

Kite went to ABOLITIONist and UNDERGROUND RAILROAD conductor Levi Coffin to get advice about what the fugitives should do next. Coffin advised that the family should go to the west side of CINCINNATI. He told Kite that he would meet the Garners there and help them on their way to Canada.

The family never made it there. They were still at Kite's house when they were discovered. Both Margaret and Robert fought to defend their family. Robert engaged in an armed struggle with his family's captors, firing shots at those who wished to re-enslave him and his family. Margaret decided that death was preferable to allowing her children to be returned to slavery. Although she was trying to kill all of her children, only Mary died.

Margaret and Robert were arrested and made to stand trial. The Garners' capture made national news and added to the controversy over slavery. Eventually, Margaret, Robert, and Pricilla were returned to Kentucky and to slavery. They were declared property.

In March, the family was sold and were traveling south on a ship called *The Lewis* when the ship was in an accident. Margaret was nearly drowned and the baby girl, Pricilla, died in the accident. According to contemporary newspaper accounts, the family was sold first to owners in New Orleans and then in Mississippi. Margaret died of typhoid fever in 1858. The last account of the boys has them residing on a small farm in Vicksburg, Mississippi. In 1863, Robert joined the Union army. He lived to see the end of the Civil War, became a free man, and returned to Cincinnati.

The saga of Margaret Garner and her desperate attempt to free her family was a major catalyst for abolitionist activism; as a result of Morrison's fictional retelling of her story in *Beloved*, Margaret Garner's tale has been returned to public and scholarly awareness. In addition to her re-creation of the Margaret Garner story in *Beloved*, Morrison wrote the libretto for an opera about Margaret Garner's life, entitled *Margaret Garner*. The opera, which premiered in 2005, was composed by RICHARD DANIELPOUR.

BIBLIOGRAPHY

Carby, Hazel. "Ideologies of Black Folk: The Historical Novel of Slavery." In *Slavery and the Literary Imagination*, edited by Deborah McDowell and Arnold Rampersad, 177–198. Baltimore: Johns Hopkins University Press, 1989.

Coffin, Levi. *Reminiscences of Levi Coffin, the Reputed President of the Underground Railroad*. Cincinnati, Ohio: Robert Clarke and Co., 1876.

Collins, Patricia Hill. *Fighting Words: Black Women and the Search for Justice*. Minneapolis: University of Minnesota Press, 1998.

Henderson, Mae. "Toni Morrison's *Beloved*: Re-membering the Body as Historical Text." In *Comparative American Identities: Race, Sex, and Nationality in the Modern Text*, edited by Hortense Spillers, 62–86. New York: Routledge, 1991.

Krumholz, Linda. "The Ghosts of Slavery: Historical Recovery in Toni Morrison's *Beloved*," *African American Review* 3, no. 26 (1992): 395–408.

May, Samuel J. "Margaret Garner and Seven Others." In *Toni Morrison's Beloved: A Casebook*, edited by William L. Andrews and Nellie Y. McKay, 25–36. New York: Oxford University Press, 1999.

Mobley, Marilyn Sanders. "A Different Remembering: Memory, History, and Meaning in Toni Morrison's *Beloved*." In *Modern Critical Interpretations: Beloved*, edited by Harold Bloom, 17–25. Philadelphia: Chelsea House Publishers, 1999.

Oliver, Stephanie Stokes. "The Search for My Beloved Margaret Garner." *Essence*. February 2006. Available online. URL: http://www.essence.com/essence/themix/artsandculture/0,16109,1149639,00.html. Accessed on September 19, 2006.

Reinhardt, Mark. "Who Speaks for Margaret Garner?: Slavery, Silence, and the Politics of Ventriloquism," *Mississippi Quarterly* 29 (Autumn 2002): 81–119.

Winter, Kari. *Subjects of Slavery, Agents of Change: Women and Power in Gothic Novels and Slave Narratives, 1790–1865*. Athens: University of Georgia Press, 1992.

Wisenburger, Steven. *Modern Medea: A Family Story of Slavery and Child-Murder from the Old South*. New York: Hill and Wang, 1998.

Garvey, Marcus (1887–1940) Although he was born in the Caribbean, on the island of Jamaica, Marcus Garvey became one of the most influential figures in African-American history. Although Garvey left formal schooling at a young age, he became active in local politics. He was particularly concerned with workers' rights.

Like so many Jamaicans of the time, Garvey sought economic opportunities in England. Garvey continued his political activism while in England and became associated with anticolonial movements whose objective was the attainment of independence for England's colonies.

Garvey returned to Jamaica, and in 1914 began the organization he would forever be associated with, the United Negro Improvement Association (UNIA). The organization was dedicated to the development of black autonomy and self-sufficiency through the building of black-owned and -controlled social, political, and economic institutions. He aligned himself with the intellectual traditions and arguments of black nationalism.

In 1916, Garvey immigrated to the United States and took his organization and his hopes for black progress with him. By 1917, Garvey had established his organization in the United States and by 1919, the organization boasted a membership that included more than two million.

Garvey felt that blacks needed to have control of their own lands in order to achieve true independence and autonomy and, to that end, he proposed a back-to-Africa plan that involved mass emigration of black Americans from the United States to lands in Africa he proposed to purchase. With the proceeds gathered from UNIA members, Garvey began to enact his plan by purchasing a shipping line that would serve as the primary means of transportation from the United States to Africa.

Garvey's plans ultimately failed as a result of financial mismanagement. He was jailed on fraud charges, and, ultimately he was deported by the federal government. Some scholars maintain that Garvey was falsely accused and wrongly convicted.

Garvey never gave up on his ambitions and was involved in unsuccessful attempts to reinvigorate his organization and to bring about social and political change. He died in England in 1940. His widow, Amy Jacques Garvey, carried on his legacy and continued his campaign after Garvey's death.

Marcus Garvey's United Negro Improvement Association (UNIA) is referenced in Morrison's novel *Jazz* (1992).

BIBLIOGRAPHY

Bair, Barbara, and Robert A. Hill. *Marcus Garvey: Life and Lessons.* Berkeley: University of California Press, 1987.

Clarke, John Henrik, ed. *Marcus Garvey and the Vision of Africa.* New York: Vintage Books, 1974.

Cronon, Edmund David. *Black Moses: The Story of Marcus Garvey and The Universal Negro Improvement Association.* Madison: University of Wisconsin Press, 1969.

Garvey, Amy-Jacques. *The Philosophy and Opinions of Marcus Garvey.* Dover, Mass.: Majority Press, 1986.

Hill, Robert A., ed. *Marcus Garvey, Life and Lessons: A Centennial Companion to the Marcus Garvey and Universal Negro Improvement Association Papers.* Berkeley: University of California Press, 1987.

Lewis, Rupert, and Bryan, Patrick, eds. *Garvey: His Work and Impact.* Mona, Jamaica: Institute of Social and Economic Research, 1988.

Manoedi, M. Korete. *Garvey and Africa.* New York: New York Age Press, 1922.

Martin, Tony. *Race First: The Ideological and Organizational Struggle of Marcus Garvey and the Universal Negro Improvement Association.* Westport, Conn.: Greenwood Press, 1976.

———. *Literary Garveyism: Garvey, Black Arts, and the Harlem Renaissance.* Dover, Mass.: Majority Press, 1983.

———. *African Fundamentalism: A Literary and Cultural Anthology of Garvey's Harlem Renaissance.* Dover, Mass.: Majority Press, 1983.

———. *Marcus Garvey: Hero.* Dover, Mass.: Majority Press, 1983.

———. *The Pan-African Connection: From Slavery to Garvey and Beyond.* Dover, Mass.: Majority Press, 1983.

———. *The Poetical Works of Marcus Garvey.* Dover, Mass.: Majority Press, 1983.

Smith-Irvin, Jeannette. *Marcus Garvey's Footsoldiers of the Universal Negro Improvement Association.* Trenton, N.J.: Africa World Press, 1989.

Stein, Judith. *The World of Marcus Garvey: Race and Class in Modern Society.* Baton Rouge: Louisiana State University Press, 1986.

Gibbon, Edward (1737–1794)   Edward Gibbon was an 18th-century British historian best known for his epic work, *The History of the Decline and Fall of the Roman Empire* (1776). The work covers Roman history from the second century A.D. to the fall of Constantinople in 1453.

Born in London to a wealthy Tory member of Parliament, Gibbon was educated at Westminster and Magdalen College, Oxford. He later spent several years in Switzerland, after which he settled down in his father's household, where he could devote much of his time to his writing. Between 1774 and 1783, Gibbon himself sat in the House of Commons.

At one-and-a-half-million words, *The Decline and Fall of the Roman Empire* is one of the longest histories written by a single person and is considered a classic of historical research and writing. It is noted for its thoroughness, accuracy, and ornate prose style. Gibbon attributed much of Rome's decline to the rise of Christianity, the invasions of the Teutonic tribes, and the spread of Islam. He also considered Rome's decline to be the result of moral decadence from within the empire itself. A cynic all his life, Gibbon considered history "little more than the register of the crimes, follies and misfortunes of mankind."

In *The Bluest Eye* (1970), Soaphead Church is attracted to the more bitter aspects of Gibbon's writings rather than his empathy.

BIBLIOGRAPHY

Carnochan, W. B. *Gibbon's Solitude: The Inward World of the Historian.* Stanford, Calif.: Stanford University Press, 1987.

Craddick, Patricia, and Margaret Craddick Huff. *Edward Gibbon: A Reference Guide.* Boston: G. K. Hall, 1987.

De Beer, Gavin. *Gibbon and His World.* London: Thames and Hudson, 1967.

Gibbon, Edward. *The History of the Decline and Fall of the Roman Empire.* 1776. New York: Penguin, 2000.

Pocock, G. A. *Barbarism and Religion: The Enlightenments of Edward Gibbon, 1737–1764.* Cambridge, U.K.: Cambridge University Press, 2000.

Porter, Roy. *Edward Gibbon: Making History.* London: Weidenfeld and Nicolson, 1988.

G.I. Bill (General Infantry Bill of Rights, Servicemen's Readjustment Act)   Because of the economic difficulties encountered by veterans returning from World War I, there was public and political pressure to develop a comprehensive program of support to assist veterans and to ensure their long-term well-being as compensation for their service to their country. Toward the end of World War II, in response to the anticipated needs of returning servicemen, Congress passed the General Infantry Bill of Rights, more frequently called the G.I. Bill. The legislation was designed to assist returning veterans. The program entitled veterans to receive money to cover the expenses of higher education and included funds to support them while they were in school.

The bill also included provisions for home loans and medical care, as well as other aspects of financial maintenance the veterans might require. The G.I. Bill was instrumental in securing the economic well-being of thousands of veterans and proved to be a creative stimulus for the economy generally. It dramatically increased attendance at institutions of higher education and led to upward mobility for the veterans and their families. Another major benefit was the low-interest home loans that allowed veterans to purchase homes that might otherwise have been inaccessible.

In *Love* (2003), the mood at Cosey's Resort and Hotel is amplified during Christine Cosey's 16th birthday/graduation party as the future feels secured by the postwar prosperity made possible in part by the G.I. Bill.

BIBLIOGRAPHY

Gubin, E. K. *Veteran's Handbook for Veterans of World War II and Their Dependents, Including an Explanation of the G.I. Bill of Rights.* Washington, D.C.: Army Times, 1945.

Kandel, Isaac Leon. *The Impact of the War upon Higher Education.* Chapel Hill: University of North Carolina Press, 1948.

Olson, Keith W. *The G.I. Bill, the Veterans, and the Colleges.* Lexington: University Press of Kentucky, 1974.

Ross, Davis R. B. *Preparing for Ulysses: Politics and Veterans during World War II.* New York: Columbia University Press, 1969.

G.I. Joe   In 1964, the toy company Hasbro introduced the iconographic toy, G.I. Joe, to the American public. The toy was modeled after the American soldier and became an instant hit. The original G.I. Joe was 11.5 inches tall and was uniquely flexible as a result of his 21 moving parts. G.I. Joe was marketed as a toy for boys. His military garb and rough appearance allowed him to transcend traditional gender biases and appeal to boys who might have been discouraged from playing with dolls.

Hasbro shifted G.I. Joe's image as a result of the controversies surrounding the Vietnam War. For several years, the G.I. Joe line transformed into adventurers rather than soldiers. Once the United States had ended its involvement in the Vietnam War, Hasbro reintroduced G.I. Joe as a fighting man. Since that time, the toy continues as a centerpiece in the Hasbro collection, but faces increased competition from high-tech toys. Since the 2004 40th anniversary of G.I. Joe's introduction, the toy has experienced a resurgence in growth.

In *Love* (2003), Junior goes to a facility for juvenile delinquents when she steals a G.I. Joe doll. She falls in love with the image and thinks that Bill Cosey looks like the doll.

BIBLIOGRAPHY

Cross, Gary. *Kids' Stuff: Toys and the Changing World of American Childhood.* Cambridge, Mass.: Harvard University Press, 1997.

Kline, Stephen. *Out of the Garden: Toys and Children's Culture in the Age of TV Marketing.* New York: Verso, 1993.

Giovanni, Nikki (1943–) From the publication of her first book *Black Feeling, Black Talk* in 1968, to *Quilting the Black-Eyed Pea* (2004), Giovanni's writing stands as artful and unflinching testimony to the complex realities of American life during the last 40 years. As a quilter of language and history, Giovanni's refusal to segregate American from African-American life grafts the artificial distinctions between the two. She dismantles the hierarchies that limit human possibility and potential. Her canon unquestionably proves that literature can be relevant and rigorous, political and poetic. Her work exemplifies that excellence in form is not the same thing as conformity or enslavement to convention.

In the tradition of Mamie Till, who held an open-casket funeral for her murdered and mutilated son, EMMETT in 1955, Giovanni's work often calls readers "to come and see" the devastating and grotesque results of racism, intolerance, and hatred,

and to reach toward other ways of being. Giovanni does not allow her reader to forget the past and uses that context as a lens through which to read the present.

Giovanni's work contains the narrative threads in the American story that link Sally Hemings, the enslaved mother of several of Thomas Jefferson's children, to the recent revelations of Essie Mae Washington-Williams, the black child of Strom Thurmond. Giovanni's insightful gaze asks us to ponder the national response to Janet Jackson's chest-baring Superbowl stunt in relation to the reaction Sojourner Truth received in 1858 when she exposed her breast in order to prove to an audience of suffragettes that she was a woman. Giovanni's work engages these issues, and provocatively and productively raises questions. Her use of language is scrupulous, yet thoughtful and graceful.

Although Giovanni was born in Tennessee, her parents' move shortly after her birth made Ohio her home. Giovanni was the precocious baby of her family and was very close to her older sister. Her parents provided a supportive and nurturing home for Giovanni and she grew up confident and self-assured. She graduated from high school early and enrolled at Fisk University.

This initial foray into higher education was unsuccessful and Giovanni dropped out for a time. When she returned to school in 1964, she was thrown into the activities of the student branch of the CIVIL RIGHTS MOVEMENT. Her activism evolved with her growing interest in the arts, particularly in writing.

After graduation, Giovanni continued her work as an activist/artist and began to publish and gain recognition for her poetry. Giovanni's reputation as a poet grew as she published prolifically. Giovanni became one of the most well-known poets of the BLACK ARTS MOVEMENT.

Giovanni has held numerous posts at various academic institutions and has received many awards for her work, which includes not only poetry, but also nonfiction prose, fiction, plays, children's literature, and autobiography. For more than 20 years, Giovanni has been a professor at Virginia Polytechnic Institute and State University. She has recovered from a bout with lung cancer and continues to teach, lecture, and perform around the country and internationally. Recently, Giovanni received national attention for her remarks in the wake of the shootings at Virginia Tech.

Both Morrison and Giovanni are African-American women writers from Ohio who came of age at roughly the same time. The women respect and influence each other. Giovanni writes about Morrison in her collection *Racism 101* (1994).

BIBLIOGRAPHY

Fowler, Virginia C., ed. *Conversations with Nikki Giovanni.* Jackson: University Press of Mississippi, 1992.

———. *Nikki Giovanni.* New York: Twayne, 1992.

Giovanni, Nikki. *Black Feeling, Black Talk, Black Judgment.* New York: W. Morrow, 1970.

———. *Cotton Candy on a Rainy Day.* New York: Morrow, 1978.

———. *A Dialogue by James Baldwin and Nikki Giovanni.* Philadelphia: Lippincott, 1973.

———. *Ego-tripping and Other Poems for Young People.* New York: L. Hill, 1974.

———. *Gemini: An Extended Autobiographical Statement on My First Twenty-five Years of Being a Black Poet.* Indianapolis: Bobbs-Merrill, 1972.

———. *The Genie in the Jar.* New York: H. Holt, 1996.

———. *Love Poems.* New York: Morrow, 1997.

———. *My House; Poems.* New York: Morrow, 1972.

———. *Racism 101.* New York: W. Morrow, 1994.

———. *Re:creation.* Detroit: Broadside Press, 1970.

———. *A Poetic Equation: Conversations between Nikki Giovanni and Margaret Walker.* Washington, D.C.: Howard University Press, 1974.

———. *The Selected Poems of Nikki Giovanni.* New York: William Morrow, 1996.

———. *The Women and the Men.* New York: Morrow, 1975.

———. *Those Who Ride the Night Winds.* New York: Morrow, 1983.

Gnostic Gospels According to leading scholars on the Gnostic Gospels, particularly Elaine Pagels, Muhammad Ali al-Samman, an Egyptian man, and several of his brothers were digging for fertilizer in the desert in late 1945 when they discovered an earthen jar. According to Ali al-Samman's own testimony, he and his brothers broke open the jar and found within 13 ancient books written on papyrus. Not realizing what he had discovered, he brought them home and several of them were burned as firewood. Ultimately, the majority of the remaining texts became the possession of the Egyptian government. One of the volumes, however, found its way to Europe and gained the attention of the religious scholar, Gilles Quispel. Quispel discovered that the volume contained several controversial and excluded biblical gospels, such as the Gospels of Thomas, Phillip, Truth, Egyptians, and James. These books revealed different and sometimes divergent portraits of Jesus and of his messages. All in all, the collection contained approximately 52 writings from the early Christian Church, some that challenged fundamental premises of the Old and New Testament. The epigraphs of *Jazz* (1992) and *Paradise* (1998) come from the Gnostic poem, *Thunder Perfect Mind.*

BIBLIOGRAPHY

Hoeller, Stephan A. *Gnosticism: New Light on the Ancient Tradition of Inner Knowing.* New York: Quest Books, 2002.

Holroyd, Stuart. *The Elements of Gnosticism.* Rockport, Mass.: Element Books, 1994.

Marvin Meyer, *The Gospel of Thomas: The Hidden Sayings of Jesus.* San Francisco: Harper, 1992.

Pagels, Elaine. *Beyond Belief: The Secret Gospel of Thomas.* New York: Random House, 2003.

———. *The Gnostic Gospels.* New York: Random House, 1978.

Seymor-Smith, Marvin. *Gnosticism: The Path of Inner Knowledge.* San Francisco: Harper, 1996.

Gobineau, Arthur Joseph, comte de See DE GOBINEAU, ARTHUR JOSEPH, COMTE

goddess figures (in literature by African-American women) The contemporary literary goddess figure in fiction written by African-American women emerges not only from social and literary histories but also from diasporic cultural roots. In addition to asserting a symbolic connection with the religious iconography of segments of west Africa, the goddess figure functions in many

African-American women's novels as an objective correlative for the successful struggle to achieve selfhood in a racist, sexist, and classist society. As these characters refuse to comply with the oppressor's limiting gaze, they open new definitional possibilities for black womanhood. Through their goddess figures, many of the writers of the AFRA AMERICAN LITERARY RENAISSANCE examine the complexities of "authentic," if mythological, black womanhood, the need for rethinking of imposed understandings of the black female self, and the possibilities and implications of personal and communal salvation for African-American women and their communities. By creating a mythology rife with images of goddess figures, some contemporary African-American women writers transcend the limitations of traditional stereotypes of African-American women by rewriting and re-creating black womanhood. Rather than barricading the creative energies of African-American women writers, these goddess figures mark an important paradigm shift. Like many mythological deities, Afra American goddess figures are powerful in their creative abilities and yet grounded by their humanity. The presence of goddess figures in contemporary African-American women's fiction represents a mythological inversion of the traditional denigration of black women in American society.

The emergence in contemporary fiction of a particularly African-American female iconography reflects a literary attempt to reassert power through the reclamation of control over images and representations. These fictional goddesses metaphorize the histories, humanity, power, pain, complexity, and creativity of black female subjectivity. Arguably, some goddess figures in Morrison's fiction might be Eva and/or Sula in *Sula* (1973), Pilate Dead in *Song of Solomon* (1977), the narrator in *Jazz* (1992), and Consolata and/or Piedade in *Paradise* (1998).

BIBLIOGRAPHY

Badejo, Diedre L. "The Goddess Osun as a Paradigm for Feminist Criticism," *SAGE* 7 (Summer 1989): 27–32.

Engelsman, Sabrina. *The Feminine Dimension of the Divine*. Oxford, U.K.: Oxford University Press, 1993.

Harris, Trudier. "This Disease Called Strength: Some Observations on the Compensating Construction of Black Female Character," *Callaloo*, 23 (May 1996): 14–38.

Grant, Ulysses S. (1822–1885)   Grant was a Union general during the American Civil War and the 18th president of the United States. In his military campaigns against southern forces, Grant is credited with turning the war in favor of the North.

Grant was born in Point Pleasant, Ohio, where his father worked as a tanner. At 17, Grant entered West Point, where he had an undistinguished career and graduated 21st in a class of 39. Between 1846 and 1848, he served in the Mexican War, where he was cited for bravery, but in 1854, having reached the rank of captain, he was forced to resign his commission due to his growing alcoholism. He returned to civilian life, where he tried several occupations, including farmer, real estate agent, and clerk in the leather shop owned by his father.

It was the Civil War that brought Grant back into the military. He began as a recruiter but worked his way up in rank and as commander of forces. His abilities in various military campaigns drew the attention of President Lincoln, who had been frustrated by his generals' reluctance to take on the forces of General ROBERT E. LEE. As general and then as Lincoln's general in chief, Grant went on to win critical battles that eventually won the war for the North.

In 1868, his national reputation as a war hero led Grant to win the first of two terms as president of the United States. Though his personal integrity was considered secure, his administration was plagued with scandal, and most historians consider his tenure as president to be weak.

A lifelong cigar smoker, Grant died in 1885 of throat cancer while writing his highly respected autobiography.

In *Song of Solomon* (1977), Macon I's cow on his farm, Lincoln's Heaven, is named Ulysses S. Grant.

BIBLIOGRAPHY

Fuller, J. F. C. *Grant and Lee, A Study in Personality and Generalship.* Bloomington: Indiana University Press, 1957.

Garland, Hamlin. *Ulysses S. Grant; His Life and Character.* New York: Doubleday and McClure, 1898.

Goldhurst, Richard. *Many Are the Hearts: The Agony and the Triumph of Ulysses S. Grant.* New York: Reader's Digest Press, 1975.

Grant, Jesse. *In The Days of My Father, General Grant.* New York: Harper, 1925.

Grant, Julia Dent. *Life Here and There.* New York: Harper, 1921.

————. *The Personal Memoirs of Julia Dent Grant (Mrs. Ulysses S. Grant).* New York: Putnam, 1975.

Grant, Ulysses S. *Letters to a Friend, General Grant's Letters to a Friend, 1861–1880.* New York: Crowell, 1897.

————. *The Papers of Ulysses S. Grant,* edited by John Y. Simon. Carbondale: Southern Illinois University Press, 1967.

————. *Personal Memoirs of U.S. Grant.* New York: Charles Webster, 1885.

————. *Ulysses S. Grant, Essays and Documents,* edited by David L. Wilson and John Y. Simon. Carbondale: Southern Illinois University Press, 1981.

Great Depression, the   See DEPRESSION

Great Migration, the   Following World War I, thousands of African Americans chose to leave the southern region of the United States to begin a new life in the North, a life they believed would offer greater opportunities, as well as increased freedom from racial and economic exploitation and injustice. The 25 years following World War I later became known as the Great Migration as a result of this mass exodus of African Americans from the South.

The Great Migration occurred roughly between the years 1910 and 1940. Northern African-American newspapers like the CHICAGO DEFENDER were active in encouraging southerners to relocate to northern cities. The Great Migration began as a result of reports of northern life pulling African Americans toward what they hoped would be a better life, as well as circumstances in the South pushing African Americans north.

A major factor pulling African Americans from their southern roots was the promise of decent paying jobs. During the war years, northern industries experienced a labor shortage. This need for workers was created by the void in the workforce due to the enlistment of white males in the military, the governmental restrictions on European immigration, and the general labor shortage stimulated by the demand for increased production.

Northern factories, mills, and workshops actively recruited southern African Americans. In order to entice African Americans to come north, industries ran ads in southern and black newspapers, offered train fares north, and promised to pay wages that were often more than twice the amount paid for labor in the South. In addition to economic advantages, African Americans were also motivated to move north by dreams of better educational opportunities and better working and living conditions.

There were other significant reasons that pushed African Americans out of the South. Primarily, JIM CROW laws, the set of evolving legal statutes that had created and enforced racial segregation in the southern United States, drastically blighted every aspect of life for African Americans. This system of racially based separation negatively affected the social, political, economic, and educational interactions and endeavors of southern African Americans. The less obviously oppressive racial climate of the North seemed to promise relief from second-class citizenship.

An additional brutal reality of life for southern African Americans was the grim reality of racial violence. Vigilante organizations such as the KU KLUX KLAN used violence in order to intimidate, threaten, and rob African Americans. These groups used terrorism, destruction of property, and lynchings. Historians estimate that between 1882 and 1930 more than 3,000 African Americans were lynched.

The Great Migration was a major historical and cultural event in American history. The city became a kind of mecca, or ideal promised land, where dreams could be achieved. The concentration of African-American communities in northern cities created new social and cultural identities in those locales. The Great Migration facilitated the cultural flowering known as the HARLEM RENAISSANCE. Morrison references the Great Migration and its impact in her work, most explicitly in *Jazz* (1992), with Joe and Violet's move from Virginia to New York. The migration also is integral to the Dead family narrative in *Song of Solomon* (1987). During the Great Migration, Georgia, South Carolina, Virginia, Alabama, and Mississippi experienced the greatest decline in their African-American populations, while New York, Illinois, Pennsylvania, Ohio, and Michigan had the greatest increases.

BIBLIOGRAPHY

Gottlieb, Peter. *Making Their Own Way. Southern Blacks' Migration to Pittsburgh, 1916–30.* Urbana: University of Illinois Press, 1987.

Grossman, James R. *Land of Hope: Chicago, Black Southerners, and the Great Migration.* Chicago: University of Chicago Press, 1989.

Henri, Florette. *Black Migration: Movement North, 1900–1920.* Garden City, N.Y.: Anchor Books, 1975.

Johnson, Charles S. *The Negro in Chicago: A Study of Race Relations and a Race Riot. Study Sponsored by Chicago Commission on Race Relations.* Chicago: University of Chicago Press, 1922.

Johnson, Daniel M., and Rex R. Campbell. *Black Migration in America: A Social Demographic History.* Durham, N.C.: Duke University Press, 1981.

Lemann, Nicholas. *The Promised Land: The Great Migration and How It Changed America.* New York: Knopf, 1991.

Lieberson, Stanley. "A Reconsideration of the Income Differences Found between Migrants and Northern-Born Blacks," *American Journal of Sociology* 83 (1978): 940–966.

———. *A Piece of the Pie: Blacks and Immigrants since 1880.* Berkeley and Los Angeles: University of California Press, 1980.

Lieberson, Stanley, and Christy A. Wilkinson. "A Comparison between Northern and Southern Blacks Residing in the North," *Demography* 13 (1976): 199–224.

Long, Larry, and Lynne R. Heltman. "Migration and Income Differences between Black and White Men in the North," *American Journal of Sociology* 80 (1975): 1,391–1,409.

Long, Larry H., and Kristen A. Hansen. "Trends in Return Migration to the South," *Demography* 12 (1974): 601–614.

Marks, Carole. *Farewell—We're Good and Gone: The Great Black Migration.* Bloomington: Indiana University Press, 1989.

Massy, Douglas S., and Nancy A. Denton. *American Apartheid.* Cambridge, Mass.: Harvard University Press, 1993.

Meier, August, and Elliott Rudwick. *From Plantation to Ghetto.* New York: Hill and Wang, 1976.

Mossell, Sadie Farmer. "The Standard of Living among One Hundred Negro Migrant Families in Philadelphia." *Annals of the American Academy of Political and Social Science* 97 (1921): 169–222.

Tolnay, Stewart E. "The Great Migration and Changes in the Northern Black Family, 1940 to 1990," *Social Forces* 75 (1997): 1,213–1,238.

———. "Migration Experience and Family Patterns in the Promised Land," *Journal of Family History* 23 (1998): 68–89.

———. "Educational Selection in the Migration of Southern Blacks, 1880–1990," *Social Forces* 77 (1998): 487–514.

Tolnay, Stewart E., and E. M. Beck. "Racial Violence and Black Migration in the American South, 1910 to 1930," *American Sociological Review* 57 (1992): 103–116.

griot   The term "griot" derives from West Africa, probably from the cultures of ancient Mali, and refers to an individual, usually a man but sometimes a woman, who becomes the voice of a family and/or community by memorizing and reciting the history of the group. Griots are performers and provide a critical and revered function in the cultures in which they are found. They are often perceived as intercessors in the divide between the living and their ancestors. Griots often have a rich musical tradition and become a repository for the arts of a community.

The griot figure appears frequently in the literature of the African diaspora. Some scholars maintain that Toni Morrison has griot figures in her novels. Pilate Dead from *Song of Solomon* (1977) may serve as an example. Griots are also sometimes referred to as djeli or jeli.

Guevara, Che, Ernesto Guevara (1928–1966) Although he is most often associated with the Cuban revolution, Che Guevara was an Argentinean by birth. As a young man Guevara trained to become a physician. Even while he was in school, Guevara was involved in political activism and was a participant in protests against the dictatorship of Juan Perón.

Disillusioned with Argentine politics, Guevara left his home country, relocating to several Central and South American countries. While living in Guatemala, Guevara began to study Marxism and became acquainted with several Cubans who advocated the overthrow of oppressive regimes. Guevara was forced to flee Guatemala when the government he supported fell.

In 1954, Guevara left Guatemala for Mexico. While he was in Mexico, Guevara met Fidel Castro. Together they planned to overthrow Cuba's Batista government. In November 1955, Castro and Guevara and their followers boarded the legendary boat *Granma* and invaded Cuba. By 1959, the revolution had succeeded and Castro and Guevara's forces gained control of the island.

After serving for several years in the government that Castro established in Cuba, Guevara decided to leave the regime and island in 1966. After traveling to Africa and leading a Cuban force in a conflict in the Congo, Guevara entered Bolivia under disguise in order to aid a revolutionary movement there. He was discovered and executed in 1967.

Che Guevara remains an international symbol of the fight for justice and human rights.

In *Paradise* (1998), the women in the Convent name Arnette Fleetwood Smith's abandoned dead baby Che. In *Love* (2003), in 1971, Christine Cosey dons a beret and military-style garb that is reminiscent of Che Guevara.

BIBLIOGRAPHY

Guevara, Ernesto Che. *Che Guevara Reader: Writings on Guerrilla Strategy, Politics and Revolution.* London: Ocean Press, 2003.

———. *Che Guevara on Global Justice.* London: Ocean Press, 2002.

———. *Che: Self Portrait.* London: Ocean Press, 2003.

———. *Guerrilla Warfare.* Lincoln: University of Nebraska, 1998.

———. *Reminiscences of the Cuban Revolutionary War: The Authorized and Revised Edition.* London: Ocean Press, 2005.

———. *The African Dream: The Diaries of the Revolutionary War in the Congo.* New York: Grove Press, 2001.

———. *The Motorcycle Diaries: Notes on a Latin American Journey.* London: Ocean Press, 2003.

Gypsies   The people commonly known as the Gypsies are thought to have originated in India. Their diaspora finds Gypsies living in nearly every country in the world. During the Middle Ages, the Gypsies began to arrive in Europe and were often revered and seen as exotic. They migrated to many European countries and were known as nomadic wanderers. They began to develop a negative reputation as they usually did not become fully integrated into the communities they frequented. They began to experience persecution. The Gypsies also migrated to parts of the Middle East, Asia, and Africa.

Beginning with the late 1400s, European countries began to forbid Gypsies to exist freely in their countries. Some even attempted to expel them altogether. Often, Gypsy communities were forced to live as peasants and to become laborers, even slaves.

Partially motivated by the hardships of life in Europe, the Gypsies began to migrate to the Americas. Migration continued as the United States became an independent country and a magnet for European immigration. There were a million or so people of Gypsy descent in the United States at the beginning of the new century.

Persecution against the Gypsies reached a peak during the Nazi regime, when more than 250,000 were murdered in concentration camps. Less than 10 million Gypsies remain in Europe today. There is a growing scholarly awareness of and interest in the unique nature of their language and culture and the need for its preservation.

Gypsies are mentioned in several of Morrison's novels as minor characters, including *The Bluest Eye* (1970) and *Song of Solomon* (1977).

BIBLIOGRAPHY

Fonseca, Isabel. *Bury Me Standing: The Gypsies and Their Journey.* New York: Alfred A. Knopf, 1995.

Nemeth, David J. *The Gypsy-American: An Ethnogeographic Study.* Lewiston, N.Y.: Edwin Mellen Press, 2002.

Okely, Judith. *The Traveler-Gypsies.* Cambridge: Cambridge University Press, 1983.

Sutherland, Anne. *Gypsies: The Hidden Americans.* New York: Free Press, 1975.

Sway, Marlene. *Familiar Strangers: Gypsy Life in America.* Urbana: University of Illinois Press, 1988.

Willems, Wim. *In Search of the True Gypsy: From Enlightenment to Final Solution.* London: Frank Cass Publishers, 1997.

H

Ham In Genesis 9, the story of Noah includes an account of his family. One of Noah's sons is named Ham. The narrative speaks of Noah becoming drunk and accuses Ham of telling his brothers, Shem and Japheth, about their father's condition and of encouraging them to look upon his nakedness. The story continues as Noah awakens and curses Ham, designating him to forever serve his brothers as an inferior.

Although there is no reference to Ham's subsequent racial identity, this passage has been used frequently in order to justify slavery, race-based hierarchies, and racial discrimination. The story of Ham figured prominently in the arguments in support of slavery in the United States.

In *Sula* (1973), when the white bargeman retrieves CHICKEN LITTLE's body from the river he makes a racial slur toward the people of Medallion by calling them Ham's children.

BIBLIOGRAPHY

Fredrickson, George M. *Racism: A Short History*. Princeton, N.J.: Princeton University Press, 2002.

Goldenberg, David M. *The Curse of Ham: Race and Slavery in Early Judaism, Christianity, and Islam*. Princeton, N.J.: Princeton University Press, 2005.

Haynes, Stephen R. *Noah's Curse: The Biblical Justification of American Slavery*. New York: Oxford University Press, 2002.

Hamlet When *Hamlet* begins King Hamlet has been dead for two months. He is mourned profusely by his son, Prince Hamlet, who is the play's central protagonist. Following the death of Hamlet's father, the king, Hamlet's uncle Claudius has ascended to the throne and assumed his brother's kingdom. In addition to becoming the new king, Claudius has also married his brother's wife, Hamlet's mother Gertrude.

The tone of the drama is infused with Hamlet's doubts and suspicions about his uncle. The young man is plagued with concern that his uncle may have intentionally murdered the king, Hamlet's father. Hamlet experiences shifting and intense emotions as he tries to discover the truth about what transpired between his father and his uncle.

There are reports of King Hamlet's appearance as a ghost. The ghost appears to Hamlet's friend Horatio. Following the encounter between Horatio and Hamlet, Hamlet sees the ghost of his father himself. The meeting between the dead father and his son occurs at midnight. During the meeting, King Hamlet tells his son that he indeed was murdered. King Hamlet reveals that his brother killed him by pouring a poisonous liquid into his ear. News of his father's murder outrages Hamlet who vows that he will ensure revenge.

The characters, particularly Claudius and Gertrude, begin to believe that Hamlet has become mad with grief for his father. The couple decide to enlist the help of Rosencrantz and Guildenstern to watch the young prince's behavior and to report anything suspicious to them. Hamlet's irrational and erratic behavior extends to the woman he has claimed to love, Ophelia, daughter of Polonius. His treatment of Ophelia causes her father Polonius to believe that Hamlet's behavior is rooted in the young man's deep love for his daughter. Polonius, who is notable for his verbose soliloquies, forbids his daughter from seeing or associating with Hamlet.

Hamlet, in an effort to prove his uncle's duplicity, arranges for a troupe of actors to simulate the story his father has told him about his recent and untimely death at the hands of his brother. Hamlet's plan fails to achieve its intended results, Claudius's confession of murder. In the wake of Claudius's angry response, Gertrude attempts to converse with her son and to persuade him that he is wrong about Claudius. While the two are engaged in conversation, Hamlet overhears Polonius spying on the conversation between him and his mother and, not knowing the identity of the predator, kills him with a sword-thrust through a curtain. thinking that he has killed Claudius.

Hamlet's murder of Polonius adds to the young man's sorrow. Claudius, fearing for his own life, sends his nephew on a journey to England with Rosencrantz and Guildenstern. Claudius plots with the two conspirators to arrange for Hamlet's murder once in England.

Polonius's son and Ophelia's brother, Laertes, returns from a journey to France, furious at his father's murder and vowing revenge. Grief at her father's death and Hamlet's distance, instigates Ophelia's death by drowning. The death of his sister serves only to fuel Laertes's rage at the absent Hamlet.

While on the way to England, Hamlet discovers the plot that Claudius, Rosencrantz, and Guildenstern have devised to bring about his untimely demise. Due to Hamlet's intervention, it is Rosencrantz and Guildenstern who become the victims in Claudius's scheme. Although he foils the original plan, Hamlet becomes the prey of a gang that kidnaps and ransoms the heir to the throne.

Claudius is forced to pay the ransom. Hamlet is returned and the wicked king tries yet again to end the life of his nephew. Claudius arranges for a duel to be held between Hamlet and Laertes. Utilizing poison once again to ensure his intended result, Claudius poisons not only the tip of Laertes's sword, but the victory cup as well, fearing that Hamlet might win the battle between the two men.

Unwittingly, Hamlet fights Laertes with the sword that Claudius has poisoned. In the midst of the duel, Gertrude drinks from the cup Claudius has poisoned. Although Hamlet wins the battle, both men are scratched with the poisoned tip of the sword. Gertrude, having drunk from the poisoned cup, cries out in her death throes, alerting Hamlet to what has occurred.

As he passes from life, Laertes acknowledges and exposes Claudius's plan. Hamlet, although near death himself, musters the strength to kill his uncle with the sword. Hamlet's true friend Horatio, overcome with horror and grief, wants to kill himself. Hamlet stops his friend and beseeches him to tell the story of all that has happened.

Shortly before Hamlet dies, Fortinbras arrives. Hamlet, with his final breath, requests that Fortinbras become the new monarch. Hamlet then dies and the play ends.

The narrator in *The Bluest Eye* (1970) describes Soaphead Church as identifying with Hamlet's negative characteristics—his abusiveness and his superficial political engagements—as opposed to other narratives that might be more fulfilling and would not reinforce Church's established flaws.

BIBLIOGRAPHY

Bevington, David M. *Twentieth Century Interpretations of Hamlet: A Collection of Critical Essays.* Englewood Cliffs, N.J.: Prentice Hall, 1968.

Bloom, Harold, ed. *Hamlet.* Major Literary Characters. New York : Chelsea House, 1990.

———. *Hamlet, Poem Unlimited.* New York: Riverhead Books, 2003.

———. *William Shakespeare's Hamlet.* Modern Critical Interpretations. New York: Chelsea House, 1986.

Bradley, A. C. *Shakespearean Tragedy: Hamlet, Othello, King Lear, Macbeth.* New York: Meridian Books, 1955.

Brown, John Russell. "Multiplicity of Meaning in the Last Moments of *Hamlet*," *Connotations* 2, no. 1 (1992): 16–33.

Clemen, W. H. "The Imagery of *Hamlet*." In *Shakespeare: Modern Essays in Criticism*, edited by Leonard F. Dean, 222–236. New York: Oxford University Press, 1957.

Dawson, Anthony B. *Hamlet*. Shakespeare in Performance. New York: St. Martin's Press, 1995.

Eckert, Charles W. *Focus on Shakespearean Films*. Englewood Cliffs, N.J.: Prentice Hall, 1972.

Eliot, T. S. "Hamlet and His Problems." In *The Sacred Wood*. London: Methuen, 1920.

Granville-Barker, Harley. *Prefaces to Shakespeare*. Princeton, N.J.: Princeton University Press, 1946–47.

Greenblatt, Stephen. *Hamlet in Purgatory*. Princeton, N.J.: Princeton University Press, 2001.

Jones, Ernest. *Hamlet and Oedipus*. Garden City, N.Y.: Doubleday, 1954.

Kerrigan, William. *Hamlet's Perfection*. Baltimore: Johns Hopkins University Press, 1994.

Knight, G. Wilson. *The Wheel of Fire: Interpretations of Shakespearean Tragedy, with Three New Essays*. London: Methuen, 1968.

Kott, Jan. "*Hamlet* of the Mid-Century." In *Shakespeare Our Contemporary*, translated by Boleslaw Taborski. Garden City, N.Y.: Doubleday, 1964.

Lavender, Andy. *Hamlet in Pieces: Shakespeare Reworked: Peter Brook, Robert LePage, Robert Wilson*. New York: Continuum, 2001.

Levin, Harry. *The Question of Hamlet*. Oxford: Oxford University Press, 1959.

Raven, Anton Adolph. *A Hamlet Bibliography and Reference Guide, 1877–1935*. Chicago: University of Chicago Press, 1936.

Robinson, Randal F. *Hamlet in the 1950s: An Annotated Bibliography*. New York: Garland, 1984.

Harlem   Harlem, like the rest of New York, was originally settled by the Dutch. The village of Harlem was called New Harlem when it was named in 1658. As with so many New York neighborhoods, Harlem began the transition from agricultural to urban with the construction of low-cost housing that attracted the new immigrants to the city, who began to arrive in large numbers from Europe in about 1845. From the beginning of the settlement of Harlem there was a substantial African-American population. In the late 1870s rail lines helped to integrate Harlem into the growing metropolis of Manhattan.

As real estate became scarcer in the city and therefore more valuable, Harlem began to attract residents who had more resources and who built more intricate and expensive homes in the neighborhood. When African Americans began to migrate from the South to New York, many settled in Harlem. At the turn of the century an overabundance of inexpensive housing made landlords inclined to rent to newly arriving African Americans. The community developed a reputation as a safe and affordable place for blacks in the city. The neighborhood was also home to substantial communities of Jewish, Italian, and Hispanic residents.

Harlem was also home to prominent and wealthy African Americans such as W. E. B. DuBois, Alain Locke, and Thurgood Marshall. The 1920s were a peak time for the neighborhood's property. During the '20s, African Americans migrated to Harlem in record numbers. The famous Cotton Club opened in 1923, and the cultural renaissance known as the HARLEM RENAISSANCE began with African-American artists flourishing and innovating in music, art, dance, and writing.

As a result of the national economic crisis brought about by the Depression, Harlem began a decline in the mid-1930s from which it did not recover until recent decades. Instead of its reputation as a black oasis and mecca, in the 1960s, 1970s, and into the 1980s, Harlem became a symbol of urban blight and a graphic representation of the complex issues that face African Americans.

Contemporarily, Harlem is enjoying a new economic resurgence. As Manhattan becomes an even more desirable locale, Harlem has benefited from rising real estate values. The gentrification of Harlem is not without controversy, and there are many efforts in place to ensure the historical continuity of the neighborhood. There is concern that low-income residents of the neighborhood may be dislocated by gentrification. Former president Bill Clinton's 2001 decision to place his office in Harlem is an indication of the improving fortunes of the community. Harlem is the setting for Morrison's novel *Jazz* (1992).

BIBLIOGRAPHY

Anderson, Jervis. *This Was Harlem*. New York: Farrar, Straus and Giroux, 1982.

Bontemps, Arna, ed. *The Harlem Renaissance Remembered.* New York: Dodd, Mead, 1972.

Harris, Middleton A. *The Black Book.* New York: Random House, 1974.

Hughes, Langston, and John Henrico Clarke, eds. *Harlem, a Community in Transition.* New York: Citadel Press, 1964.

Johnson, James Weldon. *Black Manhattan.* New York: Knopf, 1930.

Lewis, David Levering. *When Harlem Was in Vogue.* New York: Knopf, 1981.

Locke, Alain L., ed. *The New Negro.* New York: Atheneum, 1969.

Maynard, Aubre de L. *Surgeons to the Poor: The Harlem Hospital Story.* New York: Appleton-Century-Crofts, 1978.

McKay, Claude. *Harlem: Negro Metropolis.* New York: Harcourt Brace, 1940.

Osofky, Gilbert. *Harlem: The Making of a Ghetto. New York: 1890–1930.* New York: Harper, 1966.

Ottley, Roi, and William J. Weatherby, eds. *The Negro in New York: An Informal Social History, 1626–1940.* New York: Oceana, 1967.

Schoener, Allon. *Harlem on My Mind.* New York: Random House, 1968.

Van Der Zee, James, Owen Dodson, and Camille Billows. *The Harlem Book of the Dead.* Dobbs Ferry, N.Y.: Morgan and Morgan, 1978.

Woodson, Carter G. *The Mis-Education of the Negro.* Trenton, N.J.: Africa World Press, 1990.

Harlem Renaissance   New York was the most frequent destination of those African Americans fleeing the South in the exodus known as the GREAT MIGRATION. This surge in the African-American population and its concentration in HARLEM generated the artistic flourishing known as the Harlem Renaissance, a period of creative expression during the years 1923 to 1937.

Although most often associated with literary production, the artistry of the Harlem Renaissance included the genres of literature, film, music, theater, journalism, and politics. In each of these fields, various artists contributed unique and innovative creations. The philosophical articulations of the Renaissance were voiced by the writings of men such as W. E. B. DuBois, James Weldon Johnson,

Claude McKay, and Alain Locke. The dates of the Renaissance are a subject of debate but they generally extend from 1923 to 1937. During the decades of the 1920s and 1930s, African Americans made unique contributions to the various genres of the arts.

The Harlem Renaissance brought to the forefront of American culture and awareness the mores of African-American life and culture. Some of the literary themes and motifs particular to the Harlem Renaissance include the concept of DOUBLE CONSCIOUSNESS, the theme of alienation, the condition of marginalization, the notion of Africa as ancestral homeland, the questions about identity, the river as symbol, the BLUES as metaphor, the role of the marginalized artist in American society, the construction of beauty ideals, and the role of race in interpersonal relationships.

Frequently, Renaissance artists used the ideal of Africa as a mythical homeland as a focus of their work. Another central concept was the idea of the NEW NEGRO as articulated by Alain Locke. The era of the New Negro inaugurated a new sensibility and definition of Negro, or black, identity. MARCUS GARVEY's activism and ideology, particularly his focus on self-sufficiency, was also important to some of the artists of the Renaissance. This affirmation of black personhood would reemerge in the artistry of the BLACK ARTS MOVEMENT that reached fruition in the 1960s.

The stock market CRASH OF 1929 and the DEPRESSION were devastating to many of the artists of the Renaissance and to Harlem itself. The Renaissance began to disintegrate by the final years of the 1930s. The Harlem Renaissance is now recognized as one of the most prolific and important artistic periods in American history. The timeframe and location of Toni Morrison's novel *Jazz* (1992) are synonymous with the Harlem Renaissance.

BIBLIOGRAPHY

Anderson, Jervis. *This Was Harlem.* New York: Scribner, 1974.

Andrews, William. *Classic Fiction of the Harlem Renaissance.* New York: Oxford University Press, 1994.

Baker, Houston. *Modernism and the Harlem Renaissance.* Chicago: University of Chicago Press, 1987.

Bloom, Harold, ed. *Langston Hughes*. New York: Chelsea House, 1989.

Brown, Sterling Allen. *The Collected Poems*. New York: Harper and Row, 1980.

Cullen, Countee. *Caroling Dusk: An Anthology of Verse by Negro Poets*. New York: Harper and Row, 1955.

———. *Color*. New York: Harper and Brothers, 1925.

———. *My Soul's High Song*. New York: Doubleday, 1991.

DuBois, W. E. B. *The Souls of Black Folk*. 1903. Reprint, Millwood, N.Y.: Kraus-Thomson Organization, 1973.

Fauset, Jessie Redmon. *Plum Bun: A Novel without a Moral*. Boston: Beacon Press, 1990.

———. *There Is Confusion*. Boston: Northeastern University Press, 1989.

Honey, Maureen. *Shadowed Dreams: Women's Poetry of the Harlem Renaissance*. New Brunswick, N.J.: Rutgers University Press, 1989.

Huggins, Nathaniel. *Harlem Renaissance*. New York: Oxford University Press, 1976.

Hughes, Langston. *Selected Poems*. New York: Vintage Books, 1987.

———. *The Weary Blues*. New York: Knopf, 1926.

Hull, Gloria T. *Color, Sex, and Poetry: Three Women Writers of the Harlem Renaissance*. Bloomington: Indiana University Press, 1987.

Johnson, James Weldon. *God's Trombones: Seven Negro Sermons in Verse*. New York: Viking Press, 1980.

———. *The Autobiography of an Ex-Colored Man*. New York: Vintage Books, 1989.

———. *The Book of American Negro Poetry*. San Diego: Harcourt Brace Jovanovich, 1983.

Kellner, Bruce, ed. *The Harlem Renaissance: A Historical Dictionary for the Era*. Westport, Conn.: Greenwood Press, 1986.

Larsen, Nella. *Quicksand; and Passing*. New Brunswick, N.J.: Rutgers University Press, 1986.

Lewis, David. *When Harlem Was in Vogue*. New York: Knopf, 1981.

Locke, Alain. *The New Negro: An Interpretation*. 1925. Reprint, New York: Johnson Reprint Corp, 1968.

McKay, Claude. *Home to Harlem*. Chatham, N.J.: Chatham Bookseller, 1973.

Toomer, Jean. *Cane*. 1923. Reprint, New York: Liveright, 1993.

Van Vechten, Carl. *Nigger Heaven*. New York: A. Knopf, 1926.

Wintz, Cary D. *Black Culture and the Harlem Renaissance*. Houston: Rice University Press, 1988.

Harlow, Jean (1911–1937) Jean Harlow was one of the most successful film actresses of the 1930s. Known as the "Platinum Blonde," Harlow did not start out with critical acclaim. In fact, film critics often wrote quite harsh reviews of her acting ability. Her roles were designed to showcase her beauty—including her blonde hair—and audiences flocked to her films. These early films included *Hell's Angels* (1930), produced by Howard Hughes—who owned her contract—*Public Enemy* (1931), starring James Cagney, and *Platinum Blonde* (1931), costarring Loretta Young.

When Metro-Goldwyn-Mayer bought Harlow's contract from Hughes, Harlow began to get more interesting roles that showcased her comedic abilities. These films included *Red-Headed Woman* (1932), whose first draft was written by F. Scott Fitzgerald, and *Red Dust* (1932), costarring Clark Gable. By 1933—with the filming of *Dinner at Eight* and *Bombshell*—Harlow had become a superstar.

Today, film critics and fans generally consider the six movies she made with Clark Gable to be her best work. It was while working on her last film, *Saratoga* (1937), that Harlow was hospitalized with kidney failure; she died before the film was completed, at the age of 26.

In *The Bluest Eye* (1970), Mr. Henry calls Frieda and Claudia by movie star names such as Jean Harlow.

BIBLIOGRAPHY

Golden, Eve. *Platinum Girl: The Life and Legends of Jean Harlow*. New York: Abbeville Press, 1991.

Harris, Joel Chandler (1845 or 1848–1908) Joel Chandler Harris was an American folklorist who specialized in recreating the folktales of southern slaves. His best-known works were his appropriation of the Uncle Remus tales.

Harris was born in Eatonton, Georgia, and was raised by a single mother. He left school at 13 to become a printing apprentice at the newspaper of

Joseph Addison Turner, who also owned a plantation. It was on this plantation that Harris heard the slaves' African-based folktales that he would later use in his Uncle Remus tales.

Harris later became a journalist, working at various newspapers, eventually becoming an associate editor at the *Atlanta Constitution*. It was at this paper, in 1876, that he published his first Uncle Remus tales. Over the years, his stories were collected in several volumes, including *Uncle Remus: His Songs and His Sayings* (1880), *Nights with Uncle Remus* (1883), and *Uncle Remus and His Friends* (1892). Walt Disney's 1946 animated and live-action *Song of the South* was based on the Uncle Remus tales.

Uncle Remus was a fictionalized slave who narrated Harris's stories. He was a composite of slave storytellers whom Harris heard on Turner's plantation and whose dialect Harris tried to reproduce. A standard example of Harris's invention of black dialect can be seen in the following passage from "The Wonderful Tar Baby Story" in *Uncle Remus: His Songs and His Sayings*: "One day atter B'rer Rabbit fool 'im wid dat calamus root, B'rer Fox went ter wuk en got 'im some tar, en mix it wid some turkentime, en fix up a contrapshun w'at he call a Tar-Baby . . ." The slave folktales on which Harris's stories are based can be traced to the African oral tradition in which a popular character is the TRICKSTER, a sly being or animal who can outwit his foes. The trickster in Harris's writings is often represented by B'rer Rabbit. Morrison's novel *Tar Baby* (1981) alludes to the story of the Tar Baby.

BIBLIOGRAPHY

Bickley, R. Bruce. *Joel Chandler Harris*. Boston: Twayne Publishers, 1978.

Bickley, R. Bruce, Thomas H. English, and Karen L. Bickley, eds. *Joel Chandler Harris: A Reference Guide*. Boston: G. K. Hall, 1978.

Brasch, Walter M. *B'rer Rabbit, Uncle Remus, and the 'Cornfield Journalist': The Tale of Joel Chandler Harris*. Macon, Ga.: Mercer University Press, 2000.

Brookes, Stella B. *Joel Chandler Harris, Folklorist*. Athens: University of Georgia Press, 1950.

Cousins, Paul M. *Joel Chandler Harris; A Biography*. Baton Rouge: Louisiana State University Press, 1968.

Heatter, Gabriel (1890–1972)   Gabriel Heatter was a radio announcer during World War II. His signature opening, "There's good news tonight," became famous as a morale booster during even the darkest days of the war. A man who suffered great personal insecurities, Heatter presented to his listeners uplifting stories and bright spots in what might otherwise be considered bad news from the front. His work became a great influence on broadcast journalists who followed. Gabriel Heatter is referenced in Toni Morrison's novel *Sula* (1973).

BIBLIOGRAPHY

Heatter, Gabriel. *There's Good News Tonight*. New York: Doubleday, 1960.

hincty   Hincty is a vernacular word in American English, associated largely with the speech of African Americans. Its etymology is unknown. The first published record of the word hincty appears in the early decades of the 20th century, often in African-American fiction.

According to linguistic scholars, the primary meaning of the word is as a reference to someone who acts in a conceited way as a result of the perceived superiority of his or her station, appearance, or means. A second, less common usage describes a feeling and, consequently, the behavior a person would have if he or she believes that something is amiss with a person or situation.

Toni Morrison uses the word hincty in several of her novels, including *Jazz* (1992) and *Love* (2003).

BIBLIOGRAPHY

Dance, Daryl, ed. *Honey Hush: An Anthology of African American Women's Humor*. New York: Norton, 1998.

Jewell, T. L., ed. *The Black Woman's Gumbo Ya-Ya: Quotations by Black Women*. Berkeley, Calif.: Crossing Press, 1993.

Lanehart, S. L. *Sista, Speak!* Austin: University of Texas Press, 2002.

hog jowl A hog jowl is a term that refers to the meat taken for consumption from the jaw of a hog. This meat was left over after the prime cuts were taken and, therefore, became a staple of soul food, the cuisine creatively constructed by enslaved African Americans out of necessity. It was added to various meals in order to contribute flavor to an otherwise bland recipe. Dishes that might include hog jowls are collard greens, jambalaya, red beans and rice, and many others.

In *The Bluest Eye* (1970), the community contributes various items, including hog jowls, to make POT LIQUOR when Aunt Jimmy is ill.

hot comb According to scholars, metal combs intended for straightening curly hair were invented in France in the mid-19th century. The combs became popular with women of African descent throughout the diaspora. To straighten African-American hair with a hot comb, the hair is first thoroughly washed and dried. Oil is then applied to the hair to protect it from the potentially damaging effects of the heat. Traditionally, the metal comb was heated on a stove. Later, electric heaters were used; contemporarily hot combs are often electric.

The heated comb is run through the hair and the back of the comb is used to pull and straighten the hair with heat. The practice of straightening hair with a hot comb became routine in the United States. The practice was displaced with the introduction and improvement of chemical straightening products.

In *Jazz* (1992), Violet works straightening hair and uses a hot comb.

BIBLIOGRAPHY

Byrd, Ayana D., and Lori L. Tharps. *Hair Story: Untangling the Roots of Black Hair in America.* New York: St. Martin's Press, 2002.

I

Indian schools Before the arrival of Europeans in the Americas, Native Americans generally educated their young through example. By watching, imitating, and learning from elders, children began to understand the narratives, traditions, customs, and practices of the adults. In most instances, by experiencing life within a community, children would learn the rules, norms, customs, and skills and eventually come to perform their responsibilities within the group themselves.

During the repeated theft of Native lands that took place in the early 19th century, the federal government began to look toward programs of forced assimilation to control the children of the displaced and relocated Native Americans to prevent them from internalizing the Native traditions and beliefs. Government officials appointed Richard Pratt to become the architect of the federal "civilizing" programs that took the form of compulsory boarding schools.

The notorious school established by Pratt in 1879 was called the Carlisle Industrial Training School at Carlisle, Pennsylvania. The nefarious goal of the school was the indoctrination of Native children to white traditions, religions, values, and language and to eliminate the knowledge the children had acquired in their communities of origin. The Carlisle School became a model for enacting the government's plan to force the assimilation of

Indian children, a plan that had federal, private, and public support for nearly 50 years.

Students who were mandated to attend the Indian boarding schools were often subjected to terrible conditions—poor supplies, exposure to disease and cold, inferior nutrition, and psychological trauma. There were more than 25 Indian boarding schools established across the United States. Federally run Indian schools continued to exist until the late 1930s when awareness of their fundamental inhumanity caused a shift in public support.

In *Paradise* (1998), the Convent begins as an Indian school. The sisters tried to inculcate their girl students to Catholicism, the English language, and American mores.

BIBLIOGRAPHY

Adams, David Wallace. *Education for Extinction—American Indians and the Boarding School Experience 1875–1928*. Lawrence: University Press of Kansas, 1995.

Churchill, Ward. *Since Predator Came—Notes from the Struggle for American Indian Liberation*. Littleton, Colo.: Aigis Publications, 1995.

Coleman, Michael. *American Indian Children at School, 1850–1930*. Jackson: University Press of Mississippi, 1993.

Jaimes, M. Annette ed. *The State of Native America—Genocide, Colonization, and Resistance*. Boston: South End Press, 1992.

J

jazz Jazz is such a controversial subject that there is nothing clear that can be said of it in terms of the definition. Jazz is a musical form that arose in the African-American community, combining African rhythms, brought over by slaves, with European harmonic structures. A major component of jazz is the improvising of the musicians over set chord changes.

The beginnings of jazz can be traced to the second half of the 19th century and various musical forms current in the black community: black work songs, field shouts, sorrow songs, hymns, and SPIRITUALS. As a new and recognizable art form, jazz first gained prominence in New Orleans, from which it spread to northern cities such as Chicago, Kansas City, and New York City, and to the West Coast, with each location producing its own unique sound and experimentation.

Now recognized as one of the greatest artistic contributions to arise from the United States, jazz originally was not accepted by the wider, white community because of its association with black culture. White audiences and some black audience considered jazz to be lower-class and suggestive of loose morals. It was not until the 1930s, when Benny Goodman, a white clarinetist and band leader, performed jazz with black musicians—especially in his concerts at Carnegie Hall—that jazz started to become more "respectable" to white audiences.

The sound of jazz can vary greatly, but a few generalities can be made. First, a key influence in jazz is THE BLUES—a 12-bar music form based on the tonic, dominant, and subdominant chords. Jazz also emphasizes syncopations, where the rhythmic emphasis does not fall on the downbeat. In the melody line, jazz uses the "blue" notes—flattened thirds and sevenths in a chord. Throughout, a key feature of jazz is the improvising of the musicians. It is through the improvising that jazz musicians express themselves most personally and, in this way, hold an equal footing with the composer.

The resulting sound of jazz can express tragic, playful, dark, intellectual, upbeat, mournful, and indeed the whole range of human emotion. This emotional content has been presented in a great variety of ways, depending on the time period and the artist. Through the decades, different categories of jazz emerged as the art form developed.

Ragtime is a piano style that emphasizes syncopation and polyrhythms. Dixieland, or New Orleans jazz, is played with small brass bands emphasizing counterpoint above a steady beat. Swing uses a small wind orchestration. Bop revolts against traditional harmony, melody, and rhythm and is characterized by the flatted fifth, and an emphasis of harmony over melody. Progressive jazz emphasizes more laid-back harmonies. Hard-bop sounds more explosive in its rhythms and harmonies.

There are far more varieties and sounds of jazz. Often, composers and musicians blend, or fuse jazz with other musical traditions, such as classical music, rock, Latin, Afro beat, and so forth. Often jazz is purely instrumental. Other times it is sung, and many of America's greatest songs are songs inspired by jazz. Within a hundred years, jazz has emerged from being a grassroots folk music to an established art form to holding an enshrined position at the Lincoln Center for the Performing Arts.

Jazz is prominently featured in Morrison's work. Not only is it the title of her 1992 novel, but also the music of jazz is referenced in several other novels including *The Bluest Eye* (1970) and *Love* (2003).

BIBLIOGRAPHY

Arnaud, Gerald, and Jacques Chesnel. *Masters of Jazz.* Edinburgh: W. and R. Chambers, 1991.

Barlow, William. *Looking Up at Down: The Emergence of the Blues Culture.* Philadelphia: Temple University Press, 1989.

Bergreen, Laurence. *Louis Armstrong: An Extravagant Life.* New York: Broadway Books, 1997.

Charters, Samuel Barclay, IV. *Jazz: New Orleans 1885–1963: An Index to the Negro Musicians of New Orleans.* New York: Oak Publications, 1963.

Collier, James Lincoln. *The Making of Jazz: A Comprehensive History.* Boston: Houghton Mifflin, 1978.

Cook, Richard, and Brian Morton. *The Penguin Guide to Jazz on CD, LP and Cassette.* London: Penguin Books, 1992.

Dufty, William, and Billie Holiday. *The Lady Sings the Blues.* New York: Lancer Books, 1965.

Epstein, Dean J. *Sinful Tunes and Spirituals: Black Folk Music to the Civil War.* Urbana: University of Illinois Press, 1977.

Feather, Leonard. *The Encyclopedia of Jazz.* New York: Da Capo Press, 1960.

———. *The Jazz Years: Earwitness to an Era.* New York: Da Capo Press, 1987.

Fordham, John. *Jazz.* London: Dorling Kindersley, 1993.

Haskins, James. *Black Music in America: A History through Its People.* New York: Harper Trophy, 1987.

Hodier, Andre. *Toward Jazz.* New York: Grove Press, 1962.

Jones, Leroi. *Black Music.* New York: William Morrow, 1967.

Morgenstern, Dan. *Jazz People.* New York: Da Capo Press, 1993.

Porter, Lewis. *John Coltrane: His Life and Music.* Ann Arbor: University of Michigan Press, 1998.

Rosenthal, David. *Hard Bop: Jazz and Black Music 1955–1965.* New York: Oxford University Press, 1992.

Stearns, Marshall. *The Story of Jazz.* New York: Oxford University Press, 1956.

Ulanov, Barry. *A Handbook of Jazz.* New York: Viking Press, 1960.

Ward, Geoffrey C., and Ken Burns. *Jazz: A History of America's Music.* New York: Alfred A. Knopf, 2000.

Wexler, Jerry. *Rhythm and the Blues: A Life in American Music.* New York: St. Martin's Press, 1993.

jigs   Jig is a slur against African Americans. It is short for jigaboo, also a slur. Jigaboo is used by white racists, but it has also been used by lighter-skinned African Americans as a slur against very dark-skinned black people.

In *Tar Baby* (1981), a salesman for the Streets' candy business says that only *jigs* (meaning African Americans in the South) buy the candy Valerian's uncles named after Valerian when he was born.

Jim Crow   The term Jim Crow refers to both the laws that enforced racial segregation in the American South between 1877 and the 1950s and the resulting attitudes and lifestyle in the South, in which African Americans and whites could not mingle in most public arenas and blacks were forced into degrading and insulting social roles.

The name Jim Crow was derived from a stereotypical black character in a minstrel show. The segregation laws under Jim Crow were a reaction by southern whites against Reconstruction, which was introduced into the South after the Civil War. Many southern whites were angered and frightened by the freedoms granted to African Americans—almost all of them ex-slaves—under Reconstruction.

Unable to live in a society where blacks were their equals, the southern state legislatures began to pass laws that forced the two races apart and took back from blacks most of their rights as U.S. citizens. This meant blacks and whites had to be kept separate in such public spaces as street cars, restaurants, schools, hospitals, public toilets, boardinghouses, theaters, public parks, and so forth. Even sidewalks were often included. In some municipalities, blacks had to step aside to let whites pass. The separate facilities designated for African Americans were typically inferior to those for whites.

The Jim Crow laws led to daily insults and violations of African Americans. Because the message of Jim Crow was that whites were somehow superior to blacks, many whites felt free to take advantage of blacks. Black women could be raped by white men without legal recourse, black sharecroppers could be cheated of their money by white landlords, and even black shoppers could be publicly insulted by a white shopkeeper. At its worst, Jim Crow victimized blacks with white mob violence and lynchings.

A Supreme Court case that helped entrench Jim Crow was PLESSY V. FERGUSON. In 1892, Homer Plessy challenged the segregation laws on southern railroads by intentionally sitting in a whites-only car. His case was brought to the Supreme Court, which ruled that separate facilities for whites and blacks were constitutional.

It was not until after World War II that the constitutionality of Jim Crow was seriously challenged. In 1950, the Supreme Court ruled that the University of Texas had to admit an African-American man to its law school on the grounds that the state did not provide equal education for him. In 1954, the Supreme Court ruled in The BROWN V. BOARD OF EDUCATION OF TOPEKA, KANSAS, that separate facilities by race were unconstitutional.

African Americans and their white allies used boycotts, sit-ins, and court challenges to fight Jim Crow. In 1963, a march on Washington, D.C., against segregation drew over 200,000 people.

Southern whites often responded with violence to the gains made by blacks, and the federal government often had to send in troops to preserve order and protect blacks. Notable examples were at Little Rock, Arkansas, in 1957, Oxford, Mississippi, in 1962, and Selma, Alabama, in 1965.

The legal support for Jim Crow finally ended with a series of civil rights acts: the Civil Rights Act of 1964, the Voting Rights Act of 1965, and the Fair Housing Act of 1968.

Both sides of Toni Morrison's family fled the South to escape Jim Crow segregation. Her novels are informed by the history and legacy of Jim Crow in the United States.

BIBLIOGRAPHY

Chafe, William H., et al. *Remembering Jim Crow: African Americans Tell about Life in the Segregated South.* New York: New Press, 2001.

Chappell, David L. A *Stone of Hope. Prophetic Religion and the Death of Jim Crow.* Chapel Hill: University of North Carolina Press, 2003.

Conrad, Earl. *Jim Crow America.* New York: Duell, Sloan, and Pearce, 1947.

Dailey, Jane, et al. *Jumpin' Jim Crow: Southern Politics from Civil War to Civil Rights.* Princeton, N.J.: Princeton University Press, 2000.

Finkelman, Paul, ed. *The Age of Jim Crow: Segregation from the End of Reconstruction to the Great Depression.* New York: Garland Publishing, 1992.

Gellman, David Nathaniel. *Jim Crow New York: A Documentary History of Race and Citizenship, 1777–1877.* New York: New York University Press, 2003.

George, Charles. *Life under Jim Crow Laws.* San Diego, Calif.: Lucent Books, 2000.

Gilpin, Patrick J., and Charles S. Johnson. *Leadership beyond the Veil in the Age of Jim Crow.* Albany: State University of New York Press, 2003.

Kennedy, Stetson. *Jim Crow Guide to the U.S.A.: The Way It Was.* Boca Raton: Florida Atlantic University Press, 1990.

Klarman, Michael J. *From Jim Crow to Civil Rights: The Supreme Court and the Struggle for Racial Equality.* New York: Oxford University Press, 2004.

Litwack, Leon F. *Trouble in Mind: Black Southerners in the Age of Jim Crow.* New York: Knopf, 1999.

Packard, Jerrold M. *American Nightmare: The History of Jim Crow.* New York: St. Martin's Press, 2002.

Payne, Charles M. *Time Longer Than Rope: A Century of African American Activism.* New York: New York University Press, 2003.

Raper, Arthur Franklin. *The Tragedy of Lynching.* New York: Arno Press, 1969.

Smith, J. Douglas. *Managing White Supremacy: Race, Politics, and Citizenship in Jim Crow Virginia.* Chapel Hill: University of North Carolina Press, 2002.

Williams, Donnie, and Wayne Greenhaw. *The Thunder of Angels: The Montgomery Bus Boycott and the People Who Broke the Back of Jim Crow.* Chicago: Chicago Review Press, 2005.

Woodward, C. Vann. *The Strange Career of Jim Crow.* New York: Oxford University Press, 1955.

Wormser, Richard. *The Rise and Fall of Jim Crow.* New York: St. Martin's Press, 2003.

John Henry   Best-known through a famous ballad, John Henry was a 19th-century folk hero who worked as a steel-driving man on the railroads. In a contest with a steam-powered steel driver, Henry beat the machine only to die from his efforts.

There is debate among scholars on whether or not John Henry was based on a real person. The man, if he existed, was supposed to have been born a slave in Alabama in either the 1840s or 1850s. He was described as having grown to be six feet tall and 200 pounds, which was considered huge in those days.

Historically, the railroad companies employed thousands of men to cut through the American wilderness to make way for the tracks. Often, this meant blasting through mountains. To this end, the steel-driving men used heavy, two-handed hammers to pound metal stakes into the rock to create holes that were then filled with explosives. The steel-driving men had a competitor though: a new steam-powered drill that was faster.

In the story, the railroad was cutting through a mountain in West Virginia—some sources have the contest take place in Alabama—when the owner of the railroad bought one of the steam drills. Henry, fearing for the loss of his job, along with the jobs of thousands of his co-workers, challenged the inventor of the newfangled drill to a contest. With his foreman running the steam drill, Henry used two 20-pound hammers, one in each hand. He beat the engine but died of exhaustion or a burst heart. In modern versions of this story, Henry and the steam drill do not create holes into the ground for explosives but knock in railroad spikes to help lay the track.

Born during America's industrial revolution, the story of John Henry tells of the transition from traditional muscle power to the newer machine power. Some scholars and other interpreters say the story of John Henry—a working-class hero—warns of the capitalist drive to readily replace humans with machines for greater efficiency and profit. The story has also represented the plight of 19th-century African Americans who, after their manumission from slavery, were readily cast aside with no regard for their place in the new society.

In *Tar Baby* (1981), the narrator compares Son and other wandering men with John Henry.

BIBLIOGRAPHY

Coulander, Harold. *Negro Folk Music.* New York: Columbia University Press, 1963.

Johnson, Guy B. *John Henry: Tracking Down a Negro Legend.* Chapel Hill: University of North Carolina Press, 1929.

Killens, John Oliver. *A Man Ain't Nothin' but a Man: the Adventures of John Henry.* Boston: Little, Brown, 1975.

Porter, Jack Nusan. "John Henry and Mr. Goldberg: The Relationship between Blacks and Jews," *Journal of Ethnic Studies* 7 (Fall 1979): 73–86.

Tabscott, Robert. "John Henry The Story of a Steel-Driving Man," *Goldenseal Magazine* 22 (Summer 1996).

Williams, Brett. *John Henry: A Bio-bibliography.* Westport, Conn.: Greenwood Press, 1983.

Jones, Bill T. (1952–   )   Bill T. Jones is an American dancer and choreographer. As a gay African American, Jones has used both of these outsider roles to inform his dance, which is often highly charged, both racially and sexually. His long-time life partner, Arnie Zane, was also his dance partner from 1971 to 1988, when Zane died of Acquired Immune Deficiency Syndrome (AIDS). The two had formed the Bill T. Jones/Arnie Zane Dance Company in 1982. Jones himself is HIV-positive, and his dance pieces often reflect loss as subject matter. One of his best-known works is *Still/Here,* from 1994, which is a multimedia work that explores death and survival. That year, Jones received a MacArthur Fellowship.

Jones was born into a migrant worker family, and he spent his childhood traveling north and south each year with his parents, following the crop seasons. He began his studies in dance during the politically tumultuous 1960s at the State University of New York in Binghamton, where he met Arnie Zane.

In addition to creating dozens of dances for his own dance troupe, Jones has received commissions to choreograph for many other companies, including the Alvin Ailey American Dance Theater, the Boston Ballet, the Lyon Opera Ballet, the Berkshire Ballet, and the Berlin Opera Ballet. In 1995, Jones directed and performed in *Degga,* a collaborative work with Toni Morrison and Max Roach, the JAZZ drummer.

BIBLIOGRAPHY

Clarke, Mary. "Bill T. Jones/Arnie Zane Company," *Dancing Times* (July 1994): 997.

Desmond, Jane. *Dancing Desires: Choreographing Sexualities on and off Stage.* Madison: University of Wisconsin Press, 2001.

Gates, Henry, Jr. *Thirteen Ways of Looking at a Black Man.* New York: Random House, 1997.

Jones, Bill T. *Last Night on Earth.* New York: Pantheon, 1995.

Jones, Bill T., and Susan Kuklin. *Dance! With Bill T. Jones.* New York: Hyperion, 1998.

Kreemer, Connie. *Further Steps: Fifteen Choreographers on Modern Dance.* New York: Addison-Wesley, 1987.

Kuhn, Laura, and Thelma Golden. *Art Performs Life: Merce Cuningham/Meredith Monk/Bill T. Jones.* Minneapolis, Minn.: Walker Art Center, 1998.

Meisner, Nadine. "Bill T. Jones and Arnie Zane," *Dance and Dancers* (November 1982): 32–33.

Rubsam, Henning. "Bill T. Jones Introduces *Still/Here* to New York City," *Dance Magazine* (December 1994): 20–22.

Tegeder, Ulrich. "Bill T. Jones and Arnie Zane: Interview," *Ballet International* 7 (September 1984): 19–21.

Zimmer, Elizabeth. "Bill T. Jones/Arnie Zane and Company," *Dance Magazine* (May 1985): 20.

———. "An Advancing Army of Tenderness: Bill T. Jones and Arnie Zane Coming in from the Country," *On the Next Wave* 2, no. 3 (November 1984): 10–13.

Zimmer, Elizabeth, and Susan Quasha, eds. *Body against Body: the Dance and Other Collaborations of Bill T. Jones and Arnie Zane.* Tarrytown, N.Y.: Station Hill Press, 1989.

Jordan, June (1936–2002) Although June Jordan was born a New York native, her family was originally from Jamaica. Her parents, Granville and Mildred Jordan, created a home that was emotionally tumultuous and the young Jordan retreated from the frequent chaos of her home life into reading and writing. Jordan was an excellent student and thrived during her years at Millwood High School in Brooklyn and also while she was a student at the exclusive Northfield Mount Hermon School, a private boarding school in Northfield, Massachusetts. Following her triumphant high school experience, Jordan matriculated at Barnard College. During her years as an undergraduate, Jordan married and had a child, a son, Christopher. The marriage between Jordan and her husband, Michael Meyer, lasted less than 10 years.

Following the demise of her marriage, Jordan began to pursue writing professionally, a talent that she had nourished since childhood. Jordan's first published book of poetry, *Who Look at Me,* appeared in 1969, soon followed by her first novel, *His Own Where,* in 1971. Jordan's initial venture into fiction writing garnered a nomination for a National Book Award.

Despite her success as a fiction writer, Jordan primarily was a poet. She also published an autobiography, children's literature, and collections of essays. While Toni Morrison was an editor at Random House, she worked with Jordan. Jordan's writing was characterized by an unflinching commitment to social justice and to illuminating the creative strength of African Americans. Jordan was an author who enjoyed critical and popular success. In addition to her career as a writer, Jordan was an accomplished academic, holding positions at Sarah Lawrence College, Yale University, and, finally, at the University of California, Berkeley. In 2002, Jordan was a professor at Berkeley when she died of cancer. Over the course of her career, she published more than 25 books.

BIBLIOGRAPHY

Cliff, Michelle. "The Lover: June Jordan's Revolution," *Village Voice Literary Supplement* 126 (June 1994): 27–29.

Erickson, Peter. "The Love Poetry of June Jordan," *Callaloo* 9, no. 1 (Winter 1986): 221–234.

———. "Putting Her Life on the Line—The Poetry of June Jordan," *Hurricane Alice: A Feminist Quarterly* 7, no. 1–2 (Winter-Spring 1990): 4–5.

Harjo, Joy. "An Interview with June Jordan," *High Plains Literary Review* 3, no. 2 (Fall 1988): 60–76.

Jordan, June. *Affirmative Acts, New Political Essays.* New York: Doubleday, 1998.

———. "Black English: The Politics of Translation," *Library Journal* 98 (1973): 1,631–1,634.

———. *Civil Wars, Selected Essays, 1963–1980.* New York: Beacon Press, 1981.

———. *Directed by Desire: The Collected Poems of June Jordan.* Port Canyon, Wash.: Copper Canyon Press, 2005.

———. *Kissing God Goodbye, New Poems.* New York: Doubleday, 1997.

———. *Moving towards Home: Selected Political Essays.* London: Virago Press, 1989.

———. *New Days, Poems of Exile and Return.* New York: Emerson Hall, 1974.

———. *Soldier, A Poet's Childhood.* New York: Basic Books, 1999.

———. *Some of Us Did Not Die.* New York: Basic Books, 2002.

———. *Soulscript: Afro-American Poetry.* Garden City, N.Y.: Zenith, 1970.

———. *Technical Difficulties: New Political Essays.* New York: Pantheon Press, 1992.

———. "The Difficult Miracle of Black Poetry in America; Or, Something Like a Sonnet for Phillis Wheatley," *Massachusetts Review* 27, no. 2 (Summer 1986): 252–262.

———. *Things That I Do in the Dark, Selected Poems 1954–1977.* New York: Beacon Press, 1981.

Keating, AnaLouise. "The Intimate Distance of Desire: June Jordan's Bisexual Inflections," *Journal of Lesbian Studies* 4, no. 2 (2000): 81–93.

MacPhail, Scott. "June Jordan and the New Black Intellectuals," *African American Review* 33, no. 1 (Spring 1999): 57–71.

Joyce, James (1882–1941)

Joyce, James (1882–1941)   James Joyce is a celebrated Irish writer who is known for his critiques of the Catholic Church and of the traditions of Irish culture and family life. Joyce was born in Rathgar, Ireland, in 1882 to his father John Stanislaus and Mary Jane Murray Joyce. Joyce's father was a failed distiller and his mother was a pianist. Joyce's family life and early childhood made an indelible impression on him and was the subject of much of his writing. Joyce was the oldest of 10 children. Joyce attended Clonowes Wood College, a boarding school, as well as Belvedere College in Dublin. He was exceptionally bright, but disillusioned by what he saw as the hypocrisy of the priests who ran the Jesuit schools that the young Joyce attended. After graduation, James Joyce pursued his education at University College, also located in Dublin.

Curiously, Joyce did not live regularly in Ireland after his youth. Rather he chose to live elsewhere in Europe, returning home only periodically throughout his life. While still a young man, Joyce met the woman who would become his wife and the mother of his children, Nora Barnacle. The couple were married in 1931 and remained together for the remainder of their lives. The marriage came after many years of living together. The couple had two children together, a son, George, and a daughter, Lucia. The daughter, Lucia, had problems with mental illness that were a tremendous source of anxiety for both of her parents.

Joyce began his professional life as a writer in the genre of poetry. Joyce's first publication was a volume entitled *Chamber Music*, which appeared as a published volume in 1907. Although Joyce produced his famous collection of short stories, *The Dubliners*, shortly thereafter, he had a difficult time getting the collection published due to controversies over the content of the collection. The writings were so controversial that the collection was not published until 1914. Joyce's well-known novel, *Portrait of the Artist as a Young Man*, was written while he and his family lived in Switzerland and was published in its entirety in 1916. The novel remains Joyce's best-known work. The bildungsroman chronicles the coming of age of its creative and energetic young male protagonist in the often repressive and stifling environment of the Catholic Ireland so familiar to Joyce from his youth.

Literary critics often make comparisons between the works of Morrison and Joyce.

BIBLIOGRAPHY

Gifford, Don, and Robert J. Seidman. Ulysses *Annotated: Notes for James Joyce's* Ulysses. Berkeley: University of California Press, 1988.

Gilbert, Stuart. *James Joyce's* Ulysses: *A Study.* New York: Vintage Books, 1955.

Gillespie, Michael P. *James Joyce's Trieste Library.* Austin: University of Texas at Austin, 1986.

Gunn, Ian, and Alistair McCleery. *The Ulysses Pagefinder.* Edinburgh: Split Pea, 1988.

Hancock, Leslie. *Word Index to James Joyce's* Portrait. Carbondale: Southern Illinois University Press, 1967.

Hanley, Miles L. *Word Index to James Joyce's* Ulysses. Madison: University of Wisconsin Press, 1962.

Herring, Phillip F. *Joyce's Notes and Early Drafts for* Ulysses. *Selections from the Buffalo Collection.* Charlottesville: University of Virginia Press, 1977.

Herring, Phillip F., ed. *Joyce's* Ulysses *Notesheets in the British Museum.* Charlottesville: University of Virginia Press, 1972.

Hodgart, Matthew, and Mabel P. Worthington. *Song in the Works of James Joyce.* New York: Columbia University Press, 1959.

Jackson, John Wyse, and Bernard McGinley. *James Joyce's* Dubliners: *An Illustrated Edition with Annotations.* New York: St. Martin's Griffin, 1995.

Jahn, Manfred. "Postmodernists at Work on Joyce," *James Joyce Quarterly* 29, no. 4 (1992): 838–840.

Magalaner, Marvin, and Richard Kain, eds. *Joyce: The Man, the Works, the Reputation.* New York: New York University Press, 1956.

McCarthy, Jack. *Joyce's Dublin: A Walker's Guide to* Ulysses. Dublin, Ireland: Wolfhound Press, 1986.

Moseley, Virginia. *Joyce and the Bible.* De Kalb: Northern Illinois University Press, 1967.

Rice, Thomas Jackson. *James Joyce: A Guide to Research.* New York: Garland Publishing, 1982.

Scholes, Robert E., and Richard M. Kain, eds. *The Workshop of Daedalus: James Joyce and the Raw Materials for* Portrait. Evanston, Ill.: Northwestern University Press, 1965.

Schutte, William M. *Index of Recurrent Elements in James Joyce's* Ulysses. Carbondale: Southern Illinois University Press, 1982.

Spencer, Theodore, ed. *Stephen Hero: Part of the First Draft of* A Portrait of the Artist as a Young Man. London: New England Library, 1966.

Staley, Thomas F. *An Annotated Critical Bibliography of James Joyce.* New York: St. Martin's Press, 1989.

———. "James Joyce." In *Anglo-Irish Literature: A Review of Research,* edited by Richard J. Finneran, 366–425. New York: Modern Language Association, 1976.

Tindall, William York. *A Reader's Guide to James Joyce.* New York: Noonday Press, 1965.

juba   The juba was a dance of American slaves. It was danced into the 19th century and found throughout Dutch Guiana, the Caribbean, and the southern United States. The juba was a blend of the jig and clog—brought to the New World by Irish and Scottish indentured laborers—with West African step dances called "ring shouts."

The juba had a competitive element to it in which the dancers challenged one another with their rhythmic skills. In the dance, a circle of men formed around two other men who performed various steps in response to a rhythmic call and to the clapping of the encircling men. The juba is sometimes called the hambone. Juba can also refer to the use of supernatural power in order to subvert a powerful oppressor. The word "juba" is used in this context to describe Sixo's power in *Beloved* (1987).

Juneteenth   Juneteenth is the celebration, generally held annually on June 19th, commemorating the end of slavery in the United States. The end of slavery happened officially in the United States with enactment of the EMANCIPATION PROCLAMATION on January 1, 1863. The news of emancipation, however, took much longer to affect those who remained enslaved in the South after the proclamation became law. Those enslaved in Galveston, Texas, for example, did not hear about emancipation until the arrival of Union soldiers on June 19, 1865. That news sparked the first celebration of Juneteenth.

Contemporary Juneteenth celebrations vary from educational programs, to picnics, to historical reenactments, to parades. There are several groups working to make Juneteenth a national holiday.

Juneteenth (1995) is also the name of RALPH ELLISON's final novel. *Juneteenth* is Ellison's fictional rumination on the condition of post-*Brown* America. The protagonists of the novel, the African-American itinerant preacher Hickman and his estranged protégé and foster child, the white-appearing Bliss, are the foci of the novel. Their fraught relationship becomes allegorically aligned with the country's racial struggles. The novel is a collaborative telling of subjective narrative history as recounted by both Hickman and Bliss. The question that looms over the text is the central concern that emerges for the United States after the BROWN decision: Can whites and blacks coexist as equal participants in this experiment with democracy? The narratives surrounding the creation of the novel *Juneteenth* are, perhaps, as complicated at the text itself. Ralph Ellison, author of the much acclaimed *Invisible Man* (1952), began writing *Juneteenth* in 1954, the same year as the *Brown* decision. The novel went through many permutations while Ellison was alive, and the final manuscript he produced was over 2,000 pages. His literary executor, John Callahan, assembled the text of *Juneteenth* without instructions from Ellison, following Ellison's death. This posthumous collaboration has been the subject of much discussion and criticism in the wake of the novel's publication.

Toni Morrison has been a supporter of the novel and even helped to promote it by giving several readings of the text at bookstores.

BIBLIOGRAPHY

Abernerty, Francis Edward, ed. *Juneteenth Texas: Essays in African-American Folklore (Publications of the Texas Folklore Society)*. Denton: University of North Texas Press, 1996.

Barrett, Anna Pearl. *Juneteenth!: Celebrating Freedom in Texas*. Austin, Tex.: Eakin Press, 1999.

Branch, Muriel Miller. *Juneteenth: Freedom Day*. New York: Cobblehill/Dutton Books, 1998.

Ellison, Ralph. *Juneteenth: A Novel*. New York: Random House, 1999.

———. *Invisible Man*. New York: Vintage, 1995.

Wesley, Valerie Wilson. *Freedom's Gift: A Juneteenth Story*. New York: Simon and Schuster Books for Young Readers, 1997.

Wiggins, William H. *O Freedom!: Afro-American Emancipation Celebrations*. Knoxville: University of Tennessee Press, 1987.

K

keeping room The keeping room was the single room in colonial American houses. This was the space where the family cooked, ate, and worked on their individual projects. The central object in the room was the fireplace, typically very large, which was used both to cook meals and to keep the house warm. At night, the adults and the babies slept in this room while older children slept in a loft or attic, reached by ladder.

In *Beloved* (1987), 124 Bluestone Road has a keeping room. The room serves as a retreat for Denver and Beloved and is the site where Beloved and Paul D consummate their relationship.

King, Martin Luther, Jr. (1929–1968) Martin Luther King Jr. was the most prominent civil rights leader in the United States during the 1950s and 1960s. As a major part of the movement to finally end racial segregation after World War II, King believed integration could best be accomplished through nonviolence. Much of the success of the CIVIL RIGHTS MOVEMENT is credited to King's nonviolent protests and marches.

Born in Atlanta, Georgia, King was the son and grandson of Baptist ministers and attended segregated schools in the then JIM CROW South in Atlanta, Georgia. He was himself ordained in the ministry in 1954, becoming pastor of a church in Montgomery, Alabama. The following year, he received his doctorate in theology from Boston University. It was at Boston that he met and married Coretta Scott, who was to become his ally in the fight for civil rights.

One of his first efforts to win civil rights for African Americans was leading a boycott to end Montgomery's racial segregation on public transportation. This boycott began when Rosa Parks refused to give up her seat to a white man on a public bus. During this boycott, tensions became so high that King's house was firebombed, but the protest ended with a Supreme Court decision that the segregation was unconstitutional.

In 1957, King became president of the Southern Christian Leadership Conference (SCLC), which furthered the use of nonviolence to achieve civil rights for African Americans. A great influence on his organization, as well as on King himself, were the civil disobedience tactics of Mahatma Gandhi and that leader's successful movement to push British colonizers out of India.

In 1960, King became co-pastor with his father of Ebenezer Baptist Church in Atlanta, Georgia. There, he was jailed for protesting against racial segregation at a lunch counter. John F. Kennedy, then a candidate for president, obtained his release.

In 1963, while again jailed—this time for his protests in Birmingham, Alabama—he wrote his "Letter from a Birmingham Jail," which was a response to white Alabama clergymen who said that the struggle for civil rights should be fought solely in the courts, not in the streets. King responded that civil rights for African Americans would not occur without the highly public civil disobedience that he espoused. As Gandhi believed before him, civil disobedience was justified when confronting unjust laws. King also explained in his letter that African Americans should not be expected to wait any longer for their civil rights.

In 1963, King helped organize the March on Washington, which drew over 200,000 people to protest segregation and became a major influence on the Civil Rights Act of 1964 and Voting Rights Act of 1965. It was at this march that he delivered his speech, "I Have a Dream," which spoke to his vision of an America free of bigotry, where people "will not be judged by the color of their skin but by the content of their character."

In 1964, he won the Nobel Peace Prize. At 35, he was the prize's youngest recipient. Soon after, his protest actions were made not only on behalf of African Americans but also for all people who were disenfranchised. He also began to speak out against the Vietnam War.

King was in Memphis, Tennessee, to support a strike by sanitation workers when he was assassinated. He is the only non-president of the United States to have his birthday celebrated as a national holiday.

Morrison references King and the Civil Rights movement throughout her novels, and she mentions King specifically in several, including *Paradise* (1998) and *Love* (2003).

BIBLIOGRAPHY

King, Coretta Scott. *My Life with Martin Luther King, Jr.* New York: Holt, Rinehart and Winston, 1969.

King, Martin Luther, Jr. *Stride toward Freedom: The Montgomery Story.* New York: Harper Perennial Library, 1958.

———. *A Testament of Hope: The Essential Writings of Martin Luther King, Jr.,* edited by James Melvin Washington. San Francisco: Harper, 1986.

———. *The Trumpet of Conscience.* New York: Harper and Row, 1967.

———. *Why We Can't Wait.* New York: Harper and Row, 1963.

Garrow, David J. *Bearing the Cross: Martin Luther King, Jr., and the Southern Leadership Conference.* New York: Morrow, 1986.

Lewis, David L. *King, a Critical Biography.* Urbana: University of Illinois Press, 1978.

Lokos, Lionel. *House Divided; The Life and Legacy of Martin Luther King.* New Rochelle, N.Y.: Arlington House, 1968.

Oates, Stephen B. *Let the Trumpet Sound.* New York: Harper and Row, 1982.

Ku Klux Klan   The Ku Klux Klan is a group of organizations loosely linked together. The Ku Klux Klan promotes racism, anti-Semitism, anti-immigration, and, in past decades, anti-Catholicism in order to create an American society that is ruled by the concept of white supremacy.

The Klan has had two major incarnations. In 1866, after the Civil War in Pulaski, Tennessee, it originated as a reactionary and violent response to Reconstruction. Originally intended as a social club for six ex-Confederate officers, the Klan quickly transformed into a terrorist organization. Feeling threatened by newly freed African Americans, the Klan's members started using intimidation, shootings, and lynchings of black Americans in an attempt to restore the social hierarchy in which whites were superior to blacks. The Klan also targeted "carpetbaggers" from the North and local Republicans—with thousands of murders against these two groups—but the Klan's main goals, most of which were successful at the time, were to restrict or eliminate black education, economic advancement, voting rights, and their right to bear arms. As part of their terrorism, the Klan's members dressed in sheets and pointy-headed hoods to cover bodies and faces. The organization went into decline partly because some southern politicians and other elites abandoned the group, but it was eventually destroyed in the early 1870s by President GRANT's aggressive use of the Civil Rights Act of 1871.

The Ku Klux Klan reappeared in 1915 with no formal connection to its earlier namesake but with the same goals. Its rebirth was spurred by a number of factors, including the influx of immigrants into the United States, the lynching of Leo Frank, a Jewish man accused of the rape and murder of a white girl, and most dramatically by the film *Birth of a Nation* (1915), which glorified the earlier Klan, and whose factual content was endorsed by President Woodrow Wilson, who said of the film, "It is like writing history with lightning, and my only regret is that it is all so terribly true." The new Klan preached racism, anti-Semitism, anti-Catholicism, and nativism. Many local chapters of the Klan participated in the same terrorist activities of shootings and lynchings as its earlier namesake. At its height, in the 1920s, the Klan had almost five million members in both the South and the North.

Over the decades, the Klan kept losing influence and members, first due to a scandal in which a Grand Dragon of the Klan was convicted of the bizarre rape and murder of a woman in the 1930s, and later by the Klan's association with Nazi sympathizers during World War II. Finally, with the expansion of the CIVIL RIGHTS MOVEMENT after the war, in which civil rights organizations actively took on the Klan, the total membership of all the loosely knit Klan groups shrank to a couple thousand, which is its current approximate total. Morrison references the Klan in several novels, including *Beloved* (1987) and *Song of Solomon* (1977).

BIBLIOGRAPHY

Alexander, Charles. *The Ku Klux Klan in the Southwest.* Lexington: University Press of Kentucky, 1925.

Goldberg, David. *Disconnected America: The U.S. in the 1920s.* Baltimore: Johns Hopkins University Press, 1999.

Jackson, Kenneth. *The Ku Klux Klan in the City.* New York: Oxford University Press, 1957.

Mecklin, John. *The Ku Klux Klan: A Study of the American Mind.* New York: Russell and Russell, 1923.

L

Lake Erie   Lake Erie is the southernmost of the five Great Lakes on the United States–Canada border. It is bounded in the north by Canada's Ontario province and in the south by the states of Michigan, Ohio, Pennsylvania, and New York. At 241 miles across and 57 miles north to south, with an average depth of 62 feet, Erie is the smallest of the Great Lakes. It therefore warms rapidly in spring and summer and can freeze over in winter. The land around Erie is intensively farmed, and its shoreline is the most densely populated of the Great Lakes. Erie is fed by the Detroit River from Lake Huron and Lake St. Clair (not one of the Great Lakes) and drains via the Niagara River, which passes over Niagara Falls on its way to Lake Ontario. In the 19th century, several towns and cities on Lake Erie were major destination points of the UNDERGROUND RAILROAD.

For Toni Morrison, as a childhood resident of LORAIN, OHIO, Lake Erie featured prominently in her real and imaginative landscapes. The lake is featured in *The Bluest Eye* (1970) and *Song of Solomon* (1977).

Lake Erie, as seen from the shores of Lorain, Ohio, Morrison's hometown. Lake Erie and the particular psychological and cultural impact of the Great Lakes on midwesterners are a focus of some of Toni Morrison's work. *(Photograph by Carmen R. Gillespie)*

BIBLIOGRAPHY

Great Lakes Atlas, Environment Canada and U.S. Environmental Protection Agency, 1995.

land-grant colleges   A land-grant college is a U.S. institution of higher learning that was created when it received federal land in the 19th century. The goal of Congress was to create institutions throughout the United States that focused on agriculture, the mechanic arts, and military tactics, but that would also provide a traditional education in higher learning to more Americans, especially in the working class.

Called the Land Grant College Act of 1862, or the Morrill Act—after the Vermont congressman who sponsored it—the act granted each state 30,000 acres of federal land for each of that state's congressional seats. The states were free to use the money in whatever way would further the goal of Congress, which meant they could create new schools or contribute to schools they already had.

The Second Morrill Act, in 1890, provided additional endowments for the land-grant colleges, but it prohibited giving the money to states that used race in their admissions policy, which denied blacks access to the colleges. In a compromise, however, the act did allow states to provide a separate land-grant institution to African Americans. The land-grant institutions that were designated for blacks in the then-segregated South came to be called the 1890 land-grants.

A similar compromise in the act existed for Native Americans, and the 29 tribal colleges are sometimes called the 1994 land-grants, institutions after the National Agricultural Research, Extension and Teaching Act of 1994.

Morrison references land-grant colleges when she describes women like Geraldine, in *The Bluest Eye* (1970), who are crippled by their desire for upward mobility.

BIBLIOGRAPHY

Christy, Ralph D., and Lionel Williamson, eds. *A Century of Service: Land-Grant Colleges and Universities, 1890–1990.* New Brunswick, N.J.: Transaction Publishers, 1992.

Ohles, John F., and Shirley M. Ohles. *Public Colleges and Universities.* Westport, Conn.: Greenwood Press, 1986.

Lee, Robert E.   (1807–1870)   Lee was a general who led the Confederate forces during the American Civil War. Faced with the greater manpower and industrial might of the North, Lee's brilliance as a strategist gave the Confederacy many important military victories before his eventual defeat by General ULYSSES S. GRANT.

The son of a Revolutionary War hero—"Light Horse Harry"—Lee was born in Stratford, Virginia. In 1825, he entered West Point Academy, where he graduated second in his class. After graduation, he was commissioned as an engineer, and later served on the general staff during the Mexican War.

Lee had a successful career in the United States military and had even served, starting in 1852, as superintendent of West Point. When home, he led the life of a country gentleman on a plantation he had acquired through the family of his wife, Mary Anna Randolph Custis, the great-granddaughter of Martha Washington. Lee did not believe the South should secede, but he was loyal to his state of Virginia, and when that state seceded, he left what became the Union army to become an officer in the new Confederacy, where he eventually became general in chief of the Southern forces.

His forces often outmanned and outgunned, Lee compensated with brilliant tactics and strategy. His skill as a general is credited with keeping the Union army at bay for several years until the aggressive strategies of General Grant finally wore down his forces. With the surrender of Lee's army in 1865, the Civil War had, for all intents and purposes, ended.

After the war, Lee urged reconciliation between the North and South. He served as president of Washington College at Lexington in Virginia (now Washington and Lee) until his death.

In *Song of Solomon* (1977), Macon I's cow on his farm, Lincoln's Heaven, is named General Lee.

BIBLIOGRAPHY

Eicher, David J. *Robert E. Lee: A Life Portrait.* Dallas, Tex.: Taylor Publishing Company, 1997.

Freeman, Douglas Southall. *Robert E. Lee: A Biography*. New York: Charles Scribner's Sons, 1934.

Horn, Stanley F., ed. *The Robert E. Lee Reader*. New York: Konecky and Konecky, 1993.

Nolan, Alan T. *Lee Considered: General Robert E. Lee and Civil War History*. Chapel Hill: University of North Carolina Press, 1991.

Thomas, Emory M. *Robert E. Lee: A Biography*. New York: W.W. Norton, 1995.

Lindbergh, Charles (1907–1974)   Charles Lindbergh was an American aviator who was the first to cross the Atlantic Ocean alone and nonstop. Though other aviators had crossed the Atlantic before him, Lindbergh's solo flight was considered a major accomplishment that made him an instant hero among the public in both the United States and Europe.

Lindbergh was born in Detroit but grew up on a farm in Little Falls, Minnesota. At 18, he entered the University of Wisconsin to study engineering but dropped out to become a barnstormer—a pilot who performed aerial stunts at state fairs. In 1924, Lindbergh trained as an Army Air Service Reserve pilot, graduating in 1925 as the best pilot in his class. He later flew the mail between St. Louis and Chicago.

In 1927, Lindbergh turned his attention to the Orteig Prize, first offered by hotel owner Raymond Orteig in 1919 to anyone who could fly nonstop between New York and Paris. Several pilots were killed or injured in their attempt to win the $25,000 prize. Lindbergh persuaded nine St. Louis businessmen to help finance the building of a new plane, which he christened "the Spirit of St. Louis." After a transcontinental test flight, Lindbergh took off from Roosevelt Field in New York and flew more than 3,600 miles to land, 33.5 hours later, in a field near Paris. He was greeted by thousands of cheering people.

Dubbed "Lucky Lindy" and the "Lone Eagle" by the press, Lindbergh became an instant celebrity around the world and was honored with celebrations and parades. President Coolidge gave Lindbergh the Congressional Medal of Honor and the Distinguished Flying Cross.

After his epic fight, Lindbergh spent much of his time crisscrossing the country to promote the still-fledgling field of commercial aviation. His life in later years was marked by tragedy and controversy. In 1932, the 20-month baby of the Lindberghs was kidnapped and was later found murdered.

In 1938, Lindbergh accepted a German medal of honor from Hermann Goering, head of Nazi Germany's Luftwaffe. This caused an outcry back in the States. He later campaigned against American involvement in World War II until Japan's attack on Pearl Harbor in 1941.

In later years, Lindbergh continued to promote commercial aviation in the jet age. He also became a high-profile environmentalist. In 1974, Lindbergh died in Hawaii of cancer. He is buried there.

At the beginning of *Song of Solomon* (1977), the narrator states that the community had been more interested in Lindbergh's flight than it was in Robert Smith's suicide.

BIBLIOGRAPHY

Berg, Scott. *Lindbergh*. New York: G.P. Putnam's Sons, 1998.

Milton, Joyce. *Loss of Eden: A Biography of Charles and Anne Morrow Lindbergh*. New York: HarperCollins, 1993.

Lorain, Ohio   Lorain, Ohio, is the birthplace of Toni Morrison. Founded in 1807 with the original name of Charleston, Lorain is located on LAKE ERIE, approximately 30 miles west of Cleveland, Ohio. In the years before the Civil War, Lorain was an important station in the UNDERGROUND RAILROAD for escaped southern slaves headed for Canada, though many chose to stay in Ohio. Oberlin College, located in Lorain County, was the first institution of higher learning in the United States to enroll African Americans, as well as the first to become coeducational.

The 20th century saw Lorain grow with the arrival of the car and steel industries. Today, large sections of the city are devoted to the mills of United States Steel and Republic Steel. As a result, Lorain, with a population of approximately 68,000, has a strong blue-collar tradition, and its ethnic population is quite diverse, with over 70

When asked what kind of commemoration she would prefer in her hometown of Lorain, Ohio, Toni Morrison requested that a reading room be dedicated in the Lorain Public Library, an institution she credits with having a profound impact on her early intellectual development. The Toni Morrison Reading Room was dedicated on January 22, 1995. *(Photograph by Carmen R. Gillespie)*

different nationalities. Racially, Lorain's population is approximately 75 percent white and 15 percent African American, along with smaller percentages of other races, such as Native American, Asian, and mixed. Latinos, who may be of either race, make up approximately 20 percent of Lorain's population. In recent years, due to the downturn in the car and steel industries, Lorain has experienced some population loss.

BIBLIOGRAPHY

Lorain, Ohio. City of Lorain Web site. Available online. http://www.cityoflorain.org/. Accessed on September 14, 2006.

M

Maginot Line, the The Maginot Line was a line of fortifications extending hundreds of miles and was intended to protect France from invasion from Germany. It was built after World War I, when the two opposing nations had suffered millions of casualties. Its creation was influenced by that war's trench warfare, which slowed and often stopped armies from attacking each other. France felt the Maginot Line would compensate for its smaller army in any future attack from Germany.

Built during the years 1930 to 1935, the Maginot Line consisted of concrete forts, bunkers, tunnels, machine-gun nests, and tank obstacles. It originally ran only along the French-German border. It was later extended along the French-Belgian border in case Germany came through Belgium. The line there was not as strong, but the French had assumed that the supposedly impenetrable Ardennes Forest, located along this stretch, would compensate and act as a natural barrier. During World War II, however, the Germans invaded France primarily by way of the Ardennes. Thus, most military historians consider the Maginot Line to have been a failure.

In *The Bluest Eye* (1970), there is a character, a prostitute named Miss Marie, who is called the Maginot Line.

Malcolm X (1925–1965) Malcolm X was a U.S. Black Muslim leader who, for most of his career, spoke for black pride and separation of the races. A year before his assassination, he made a pilgrimage to Mecca, which transformed his thinking to a belief that all races shared a common brotherhood.

Malcolm X was born Malcolm Little in Omaha, Nebraska, where his father was a Baptist minister who spoke out against racism and was an avid supporter of black nationalist leader MARCUS GARVEY. The family had to move several times to avoid threats from white racists. In Michigan, the family's house was burned down by the KU KLUX KLAN. Two years later, Malcolm X's father, Earl, was found dead on trolley tracks. The police ruled it an accident, but the family was certain that members of a racist organization had murdered him. Several years later, Malcolm's mother, Louise, suffered an emotional breakdown and was committed to a mental hospital. Her eight children were then separated and sent to various foster homes and orphanages.

As a young man, Malcolm X became involved with narcotics, prostitution, and gambling. In 1946, he was sent to prison for burglary. He used his time there to pursue his education and, at the behest of his brother, read up on the Nation of Islam, led by Elijah Muhammad, who taught that white society worked to keep African Americans from attaining political and economic success. According to the Nation of Islam, the solution was a separate state for blacks. By 1952, when he was paroled, Malcolm converted to the Black Muslim faith and changed his last name, Little, to X to reject his "slave name."

As a member of the Nation of Islam, Malcolm X proved himself to be a brilliant organizer and became that sect's major spokesman. His speeches drew a huge number of converts. In keeping with the teachings of Elijah Muhammad, Malcolm X spoke out against the white exploitation of blacks and against much of the CIVIL RIGHTS MOVEMENT, which emphasized integration. He called for black separatism and the use of violence for self-protection.

In 1964, however, Malcolm X left the Nation of Islam when he learned that Elijah Muhammad was having affairs with six women, some of whom had his children. Elijah Muhammad asked him to use his skills to help him cover up the potential scandal, but Malcolm X refused. That same year, he made a pilgrimage to Mecca, which led him to convert to orthodox Islam and to consider the possibility that the races could live together in peace. Rival Black Muslims threatened his life, and he was shot to death at a rally in HARLEM. Some scholars have speculated that the federal government was involved in Malcolm X's assassination.

Toni Morrison refers to Malcolm X in several of her novels, including *Song of Solomon* (1977), *Paradise* (1998), and *Love* (2003).

BIBLIOGRAPHY

Breitman, George, ed. *By Any Means Necessary: Speeches, Interviews, and a Letter by Malcolm X.* New York: Pathfinder Press, 1970.

———. ed. *Malcolm X Speaks.* New York: Pathfinder Press, 1965.

Clark, Steve, ed. *February 1965: The Final Speeches.* New York: Pathfinder Press, 1992.

Cone, John H. *Martin and Malcolm and America: A Dream or a Nightmare.* Maryknoll, N.Y.: Orbis Books, 1991.

DeCaro, Louis A., Jr. *Malcolm and the Cross: The Nation of Islam, Malcolm X, and Christianity.* New York: New York University Press, 1998.

———. *On the Side of My People: A Religious Life of Malcolm X.* New York: New York University Press, 1996.

Dyson, Michael Eric. *Making Malcolm: The Myth and Meaning of Malcolm X.* Oxford: Oxford University Press, 1995.

Epps, Archie, ed. *Malcolm X and the American Negro Revolution: The Speeches of Malcolm X.* London: Peter Owen, 1968.

Karim, Benjamin, ed. *The End of White World Supremacy: Four Speeches by Malcolm X.* New York: Little, Brown, 1971.

Lee, Martha F. *The Nation of Islam: An American Millenarian Movement.* Lewiston, N.Y.: Edwin Mellen, 1988.

Lincoln, C. Eric. *The Black Muslims in America,* 3rd ed. Grand Rapids, Mich.: William B. Eerdmans, 1994.

Perry, Bruce. *Malcolm: A Life of the Man Who Changed Black America.* Barrytown, N.Y.: Station Hill Press, 1990.

Wolfenstein, Eugene Victor. *The Victims of Democracy: Malcolm X and the Black Revolution.* New York: Guilford, 1993.

Wood, Joe, ed. *Malcolm X: In Our Own Image.* New York: Anchor Books, 1992.

X, Malcolm, and Alex Haley, ed. *The Autobiography of Malcolm X.* New York: Grove Press, 1965.

Mammy stereotype Even before her generally unwilling arrival upon American shores, the African woman was beset with negative and pernicious rhetoric regarding the nature of her character. African-American women have suffered from societal representations as alternately bestial, primitive, hypersexual, and emotional. This depiction continues into the 21st century and remains an element in many characterizations of African-American women in the media. Depictions of African-American women polarize around the issue of sexuality. The sexualized black woman generally appears in American films as victimized and powerless, an antecedent to the literary tragic MULATTO or as hypersexual and out of control, fulfilling the persistent image of the wild and unrestrained black woman.

Perhaps one of the most famous lines from the film *Gone With the Wind* (1939) is Mammy's reprimand of Scarlett O'Hara when Scarlett insists that she will go to Atlanta to meet Ashley, on furlough from the war, as he visits his wife Melanie. Mammy angrily tells Scarlett that she will "be sitting there jes lak a *spider.*" Despite Mammy's advice and to the horror of Atlanta's Confederate society, Scarlett journeys to Atlanta to be by Ashley's side. What this iconographic moment in film history reveals is a classic representation of the mammy stereotype. The scene from *Gone With the Wind* illustrates the role cinematic mammies often play as the moral guardians of their white female charges.

In many Hollywood films the mammy character frequently functions as a moral arbiter and barometer for the white woman protagonist. One of Mammy's most frequently repeated reprimands of Scarlett in *Gone With the Wind* is "'taint fittin'. It just ain't fittin.'" Throughout the film Mammy chastises Scarlett with this refrain when Scarlett's behavior transgresses the boundaries of Mammy's superior moral code. Hattie McDaniel's powerful performance in *Gone With the Wind* as Mammy helped to reinforce in public consciousness the mammy's primary characteristics.

Like the several cosmetic changes Proctor and Gamble has made in the appearance of its trademark pancake symbol of Aunt Jemima, the Mammy stereotype has undergone a similar and equally superficial evolution. By excavating the roots of the Mammy stereotype, the source of many contemporary depictions of African-American women becomes evident. African-American women writers like Toni Morrison counter the Mammy stereotype in their work by presenting African-American female characters that have dimension and complexity.

BIBLIOGRAPHY

Alexander, Elizabeth. *Black Interior: Essays.* Saint Paul, Minn.: Graywoif Press, 2004.

Brody, Jennifer DeVere. *Impossible Purities: Blackness, Femininity, and Victorian Culture.* Durham, N.C.: Duke University Press, 1998.

Campbell, Cathy. "A Battered Woman Rises: Aunt Jemima's Corporate Makeover," *The Village Voice* 7 (November 1989): 45–46.

Cleage, Pearl. "Hairpiece," *African American Review* 27 (1993): 37–41.

Collins, Patricia Hill. "Get Your Freak On: Sex, Babies, and Images of Black Femininity." In *Black Sexual Politics: African Americans, Gender and the New Racism.* New York: Routledge, 2004.

Craig, Maxine Leeds. *Ain't I a Beauty Queen?: Black Women, Beauty, and the Politics of Race.* New York: Oxford University Press, 2002.

Gilman, Sander. "Black Bodies, White Bodies: Toward an Iconography of Female Sexuality in Late Nineteenth-Century Art, Medicine, and Literature." In *Race, Writing, and Difference,* edited by Henry Louis Gates Jr. Chicago: University of Chicago Press, 1985.

Gone with the Wind. (1939). Warner Home Video, DVD/VHS, (2005).

Haug, Kate. "Myth and Matriarchy: An Analysis of the Mammy Stereotype." In *Dirt and Domesticity: Constructions of the Feminine.* New York: Whitney Museum of Art, 1992.

hooks bell. *Black Looks: Race and Representation.* Boston: South End Press, 1992.

———. *Yearning: Race, Gender, and Cultural Politics.* Boston: South End Press, 1990.

Jones, Lisa. *Bulletproof Diva: Tales of Race, Sex and Hair.* New York: Doubleday, 1994.

Rose, Tricia. "Black Texts/Black Contexts." In *Black Popular Culture: A Project by Michele Wallace,* edited by Gina Dent. Seattle: Bay Press, 1992.

marcelling iron   A marcelling iron is a heated curling iron used to create a hairstyle called a marcel, which is characterized by deep waves. A marcelling iron is one of Violet's primary tools as a hairdresser in *Jazz* (1992). The irons are also referenced in *Sula* (1973).

Márquez, Gabriel García (1928–   Gabriel García Márquez is a Nobel Prize–winning Colombian novelist and short-story writer. His best-known work is the novel *One Hundred Years of Solitude* (1967).

As a university student, García Márquez studied law and journalism. He began his career as a journalist and worked in different cities in Latin America and Europe. In 1955, he wrote a series of articles exposing what happened in a Colombian naval accident in which a sailor was swept off a Colombian destroyer into the Caribbean Sea. These articles won him fame, and in 1970 they were collected in the book *The Account of a Shipwrecked Person.*

Márquez's most acclaimed novel, *One Hundred Years of Solitude* (1970), is an intergenerational family saga set in the fictional town of Macondo.

The town is modeled after the small town where Márquez was born, Aracataca, located in a tropical region of Colombia between the mountains and the ocean. The novel is written in a style that is often called magical realism, which mixes the literary elements of fantasy and realism. Strange occurrences are depicted as commonplace.

Other works of Márquez include the novel *The Autumn of the Patriarch* (1975), three collections of short stories, the novel *In Evil Hour* (1968), the novella *Chronicle of a Death Foretold* (1981), and the novel *Love in the Time of Cholera* (1985). Márquez won the Nobel Prize in literature in 1982.

Toni Morrison counts Márquez as an influence and a friend.

BIBLIOGRAPHY

Bell-Villada, Gene H. *Gabriel García Márquez: The Man and His Works.* Chapel Hill: University of North Carolina Press, 1990.

Bloom, Harold. *Modern Critical Views: Gabriel García Márquez,* New York: Chelsea House 1989.

Gallagher, D. P. *Modern Latin American Literature.* New York: Oxford University Press, 1973.

Gullon, Ricardo. "Gabriel García Márquez and the Lost Art of Storytelling," *Diacritics* (1971): 27–32.

Foster, David William. *Handbook of Latin American Literature.* New York: Garland, 1987.

Janes, Regina. *One Hundred Years of Solitude: Modes of Reading.* Boston: Twayne Publishers, 1991.

Márquez, Gabriel García. *Chronicle of a Death Foretold.* New York: Vintage, 2003. [1982]

———. *The General in His Labyrinth,* translated by Edith Grossman. 1990. New York: Random House, 2004.

———. *Innocent Erendira: And Other Stories,* translated by Gregory Rabassa. 1978. Harpercollins, 2005.

———. *Love in the Time of Cholera.* 1989. New York: Random House, 2003.

———. *Memories of My Melancholy Whores,* translated by Edith Grossman. New York: Random House, 2005.

———. *News of a Kidnapping,* translated by Edith Grossman. New York: Random House, 1997.

———. *J. S. Bernstei No One Writes to the Colonel: And Other Stories.* 1979. New York: HarperCollins, 2005.

———. *One Hundred Years of Solitude,* translated by Gregory Rabassa. 1971. New York: HarperCollins, 1991.

———. *Strange Pilgrims: Twelve Stories,* translated by Edith Grossman. 1979. New York: Random House, 1993.

McMurray, George R. *Gabriel García Márquez.* New York: Frederick Ungar, 1983.

Marshall Plan The Marshall Plan was a United States–sponsored program to provide economic aid to Europe after the devastation of World War II. It was considered a great success in restoring the European countries to economic health.

After six years of war, Europe lay in ruins—its infrastructure devastated, its economies destroyed, its population often hungry, even starving. Outlined in 1947 by Secretary of State George C. Marshall at Harvard University, the Marshall Plan offered as much as $20 billion in relief, provided that the European nations got together to plan how they would use the money. In this way, they would have to act as a single economic unit.

By 1953, the plan was deemed a success. The United States had contributed $13 billion, and Europe was on its way to recovery. A strong feature of the plan was that it included West Germany, which brought that country back into the European community. This was a very different approach to the defeated German nation (the western half) than was the retribution demanded by the victorious allies after World War I. George Marshall offered similar aid to the Soviet Union and its eastern European allies, but Soviet leader Joseph Stalin was suspicious of American aid and refused to participate.

In addition to bringing the European economy above its prewar levels, the Marshall Plan was also a major factor in uniting European countries for their common good and so was a catalyst for modern Europe's attempts to form a single economic and political union.

In *Tar Baby* (1981), Valerian's friends and acquaintances have conversations about current issues and events such as the Marshall Plan. Margaret does not participate in these conversations because she is uninformed and, as a result, feels isolated and alone.

BIBLIOGRAPHY

Agnew, John J., and Nicolas Entriking. *The Marshall Plan Today: Model and Metaphor.* London: Routledge, 2004.

Bonds, John Bledsoe. *Bipartisan Strategy: Selling the Marshall Plan.* Westport, Conn.: Praeger, 2002.

Mary Janes   Mary Janes are a candy created by the Charles N. Miller Company in 1914. Mary Janes were made from molasses and peanut butter. The Miller family named the candy after a much-loved aunt. Mary Janes are produced today by the New England Confectionery Company. Mary Janes are the candy that Pecola in *The Bluest Eye* (1970) buys from Mr. Yacobowski and then eats with tremendous, almost sexual pleasure.

BIBLIOGRAPHY

Necco. "Mary Jane." New England Confectionery Company Web site. Available online. URL: http://www.necco.com/OurBrands/Default.asp?BrandID=1. Accessed on September 10, 2006.

Massachusetts 54th Regiment   During the height of the Civil War, it became apparent that the policies that prevented African Americans from serving as soldiers in the Union army were counterproductive to the goal of winning the war. As the tide of the war seemed to turn in the direction of the South, the North authorized the use of African-American troops as soldiers in 1863, shortly after the signing of the EMANCIPATION PROCLAMATION. Following authorization, of the use of African Americans as troops the 54th Massachusetts Regiment was formed and subsequently became the first all-African-American regiment in the Union army.

Although African-Americans were not allowed to serve or to advance as officers in the regiment, news of the opportunity attracted more than one thousand recruits in less than six months. There were so many volunteers that a second unit was formed, the 55th Massachusetts Regiment.

The 54th Massachusetts Regiment fought valiantly throughout the remainder of the war. The resilience and bravery of the men was particularly apparent during a bloody battle at Fort Wagner in South Carolina where the regiment lost but demonstrated its resolve and skill. During the battle, almost half of the regiment were killed or seriously wounded.

The 54th Massachusetts Regiment was the first of many African-American units established during the Civil War on the side of the Union. The pay inequity between black soldiers and white soldiers became a major issue, and as a result of the 54th's persistence, in 1864 Congress passed a resolution that equalized the pay of white and black soldiers. The participation of nearly 200,000 African-American soldiers during the war made a significant difference in Union troop strength and was, most likely, a deciding factor in the ultimate victory of the Union troops over the Confederacy.

Morrison references the 54th Massachusetts Regiment in *Beloved* (1987) during the time that Paul D is engaged with the conflicts of the Civil War.

BIBLIOGRAPHY

Duncan, Russell, ed. *Blue-Eyed Child of Fortune: The Civil War Letters of Colonel Robert Gould Shaw.* Athens: University of Georgia Press, 1992.

Emilio, Luis F. *A Brave Black Regiment: History of the Fifty-Fourth Regiment of Massachusetts Volunteer Infantry 1863–1865,* 3rd ed. Salem, N.H.: Ayer Company Publishers, 1990.

Glathaar, Joseph T. *Forged in Battle: The Civil War Alliance of Black Soldiers and White Officers.* New York: Free Press, 1990.

O'Connor, Thomas. *Civil War Boston: Homefront and Battlefield.* Boston: Northeastern University Press, 1997.

Quarles, Benjamin. *The Negro in the Civil War.* New York: Da Capo Press, 1953.

Mau Mau   The Mau Mau was a guerrilla organization in Kenya fighting against British colonial rule in an uprising that lasted from 1952 to 1960. The uprising did not succeed militarily, but it did create momentum toward Kenyan independence in 1963.

The name Mau Mau is of uncertain origin. Sometimes referred to as the Mau Mau Rebellion, or the Mau Mau Revolt, the uprising was led by members of the Kikuyu tribe and was the result of unfair economic practices that cheated the Kikuyu of the prosperity enjoyed by the British white settlers.

In 1952, the Mau Mau began attacking Europeans, especially in the highlands claimed by the Kikuyu. The settlers retaliated. Jomo Kenyatta and other nationalist leaders were imprisoned. By 1956, British troops captured or executed most of the Mau Mau leadership. Later, the entire Kikuyu tribe was resettled within a guarded area.

Though the Mau Mau lost on the battlefield, their insurrection showed the British that ruling Kenya would be costly. In 1960, the state of emergency ended, and Kenyatta was released. In 1963, he became prime minister upon independence, and in 1964, president when the country became a republic.

In *Tar Baby* (1981), Son's locks before he shaves his head are described as Mau Mau.

BIBLIOGRAPHY

Askwith, Tom. *From Mau Mau to Harambee.* Cambridge: Cambridge University Press, 1995.

McNair, Carol Denise (1951–1963)   See COLLINS, ADDIE MAE

McPherson, James Alan (1943–)   James Alan McPherson is a short-story writer, essayist, and critic. In 1978, he became the first African American to receive the Pulitzer Prize in fiction for his 1977 story collection, *Elbow Room.*

Born in Savannah, Georgia, McPherson's early life was spent in the segregated world of the JIM CROW South. In 1962, he worked as a dining-car waiter on the railroad, but he went on to receive his B.A. degree from Morris Brown College in Atlanta, a law degree from Harvard University, and an M.F.A. in creative writing from the University of Iowa.

McPherson's central literary interest is the short story. He does not consider himself a black writer but a writer who happens to be black. In his view, his writing is culturally connected to the world of white culture, if from a black writer's perspective. His fiction explores racial tensions, but his characters also grapple with the common human concerns of love and isolation.

BIBLIOGRAPHY

Beavers, Herman. *Wrestling Angels into Song: The Fictions of Ernest J. Gaines and James Alan McPherson.*

Philadelphia: University of Pennsylvania Press, 1995.

McQueen, Thelma "Butterfly" (1911–1995)   Butterfly McQueen was an actress best known for her portrayal of Prissy, Scarlett O'Hara's maid in *Gone with the Wind* (1939).

Born Thelma McQueen to a dockworker and domestic worker in Tampa, Florida, McQueen took her nickname, Butterfly, from her appearance in the butterfly ballet in the HARLEM Theater Group's production of *Midsummer Night's Dream.*

Throughout her career, McQueen suffered many of the indignities of other African-American actors. She could not attend the premiere of *Gone with the Wind* because it was held in a whites-only theater, and she found it difficult to get work as an actress except in the role of maid. By 1947, tired of her limited roles, she quit her film career.

She turned to television, but she initially had no better luck. For two years, she played another stereotypical role on the series *Beulah* (1950–53). The program reunited her with another African-American actress whose roles were likewise limited, Hattie McDaniel, who had also played a maid in *Gone with the Wind.*

For the next several years, McQueen often worked at odd jobs, including waitress, receptionist, and dance instructor between acting jobs in small parts on Broadway. In 1975, at age 64, McQueen earned a bachelor's degree in political science from New York's City College. In 1980, she won an Emmy for her performance in a children's production, *The Seven Wishes of a Rich Kid.* In 1986, she was back in film with a role in *The Mosquito Coast.* McQueen had a radio show in Augusta, Georgia, when she died of burns from a fire at her home.

When Pilate comes to rescue Milkman and Guitar at the police station after they steal the green bag from her house in *Song of Solomon* (1977), Milkman thinks that she acts like Butterfly McQueen and LOUISE BEAVERS, another African-American actress whose career was limited by racism.

Mildred Pierce (1945)   *Mildred Pierce* was a 1945 movie thriller starring Joan Crawford. The movie is about a driven woman who must deal with not only her poor choice in men but also an angry, ungrateful daughter. Part soap opera, part mystery, it is narrated by the character of Mildred Pierce as she reveals in flashback the secrets of a murder.

Directed by Michael Curtiz, *Mildred Pierce* is shot in the style of film noir, which was a popular genre for directors in the 1940s. Its black-and-white images emphasize shadows, quirky camera angles, mystery, and dark secrets. Film noir is often used to present detective stories, murder mysteries, and psychological thrillers.

Adapted from the 1941 novel of the same name by James M. Cain, *Mildred Pierce* was a box-office hit and critical success. It remains a cult favorite.

Morrison refers to the film *Mildred Pierce* several times in her novels, including in L's monologue at the beginning of *Love* (2003).

BIBLIOGRAPHY

Cain, James. *Mildred Pierce*. 1941. New York: Vintage, 1989.

Mildred Pierce (1945). MGM/UA Home Entertainment, DVD/VHS, 1999.

mulatto Mulatto is a racial term of Spanish or Portuguese origin that originally referred to a person who had one African parent and one European parent. As used in the United States, mulatto became a term that described a biracial person, usually light-skinned, who was the offspring of one black parent and one white parent. It is considered by many people today to be a dated and objectionable term.

In American literary and film tradition, the mulatto was often portrayed as a tragic figure, both black and white, yet being neither and having no clear sense of identity. The mulatto also became the symbol of the supposedly forbidden but extremely common sexual contact between blacks and whites. In the days of slavery in the United States, the existence of the mulatto was often cited as proof that the white masters often used black female slaves as concubines.

The irony of any use of the mulatto designation in the United States today is that most African Americans have some European ancestry, due to often involuntary sexual unions throughout the centuries, whether it was between white masters and black slaves in the early years or the freer mixing and intermarriage today.

Also, with contemporary scientists saying that race has little biological validity, the term mulatto becomes a poor descriptor of a person except among those people who insist on using an outmoded racial categorization.

Toni Morrison references and rewrites the figure of the tragic mulatto in several of her novels, including *The Bluest Eye* (1970) and *Paradise* (1973).

BIBLIOGRAPHY

Basinger, Jeanine. *A Woman's View: How Hollywood Spoke to Women, 1930–1960*. New York: Knopf, 1993.

Bogle, Donald. *Toms, Coons, Mulattoes, Mammies and Bucks: An Interpretive History of Blacks in American Films*. New York: Continuum, 1997.

Byars, Jackie. *All That Hollywood Allows: Re-reading Gender in 1950s Melodrama*. Chapel Hill: University of North Carolina Press, 1991.

Dyer, Richard. *White*. New York: Routledge, 1997.

Funderburg, Lisa. *Black, White, Other: Biracial Americans Talk about Race and Identity*. New York: William Morrow, 1994.

Gates, Henry Louis. *Colored People*. New York: Knopf, 1994.

Gubar, Susan. *Racechanges: White Skin, Black Face in American Culture*. New York: Oxford, 1997.

Hall, Ronald, and Kathy Russell and Midge Wilson. *The Color Complex: The Politics of Skin Color among African Americans*. New York: Harcourt Brace Jovanovich, 1992.

N

NAACP (National Association for the Advancement of Colored People) The NAACP (National Association for the Advancement of Colored People) is the oldest and largest civil rights organization in the United States.

The NAACP was founded in 1909 by a large group of activists, including W. E. B. DuBois, Ida Wells-Barnett, Henry Moskowitz, Mary White Ovington, and William English Walling. The organization was—and is—dedicated to securing political, educational, social, and economic parity for African Americans. Its list of accomplishments throughout the decades is long and is only touched upon here.

Much of the motivation for starting the organization came from the Jim Crow laws of the South, which legalized racial discrimination. In its first years, these were the laws that the NAACP tackled, bringing suits in court to overturn laws that codified racial segregation.

The NAACP also organized opposition to President Wilson's introduction of racial segregation in federal policy, and it helped win the right of African Americans to serve as officers in World War I. As a result, hundreds of African Americans were commissioned as officers and 700,000 African Americans registered for the draft. Shortly after, the NAACP organized a nationwide protest against D. W. Griffith's *Birth of a Nation* (1915), a film that justified the presence of the Ku Klux Klan.

After World War I, the NAACP targeted the lynching of African Americans and in 1919 the organization also investigated the Elaine Race Riot in which more than 200 black tenant farmers were killed by white vigilantes and federal troops. The killings had been in response to the death of a white man who was killed in a sheriff's attack on a sharecroppers' union meeting.

After World War II, the NAACP continued in its efforts against segregation. In the late 1940s, the NAACP pressed for desegregation of the armed forces, which it accomplished by 1948, and in 1954 it sued for school desegregation in Brown v. the Board of Education. One of the NAACP's general counsels in the 1950s and 1960s was Thurgood Marshall, who went on to become, in 1967, the U.S. Supreme Court's first African-American justice.

Morrison references the NAACP in several of her novels, including *Paradise* (1998) and *Love* (2003).

BIBLIOGRAPHY

Finch, Minnie. *The NAACP: Its Fight for Justice.* Lanham, Md.: Scarecrow Press, 1981.

Harris, Jacqueline L. *History and Achievements of the NAACP (The African American Experience).* New York: F. Watts, 1992.

NAACP Legal Defense and Educational Fund. *It's Not the Distance, "It's the Niggers."* New York: NAACP Legal Defense and Educational Fund, Division of Legal Information and Community Service, 1972.

Zangrando, Robert L. *The NAACP Crusade against Lynching, 1909–1950.* Philadelphia: Temple University Press, 1980.

Nag Hammadi   The Nag Hammadi Library is a collection of 13 sacred texts discovered in 1945 in the village of Nag Hammadi in Upper Egypt on the Nile River. According to legend, Mohammed Ali, a resident of the village, discovered the texts in an old clay jar. Not understanding the significance of his discovery, Ali destroyed several of the documents. More than 1,000 years old, the 13 remaining texts contained 52 previously unknown chapters from the Egyptian branch of the early Christian Church. Documents from this early period in the development of Christianity, which were excluded from the Bible, are sometimes called the GNOSTIC GOSPELS. The word "gnostic" comes from the Greek word "gnosis," which means knowledge.

The recovered texts, found by Ali in 1945, are known as the Nag Hammadi Library and contain books not found in the contemporary Christian Bible. Experts believe that these chapters were excluded from the Bible because their messages often conflicted with the Bible's contents. These controversial passages include references to gods and goddesses, such as the Nag Hammadi verse Morrison uses as the epigraph in *Jazz* (1992). The texts of the Nag Hammadi Library emphasize self-discovery, self-guidance, and individual divinity. The relationship between the believer and Christ is a more personal, less hierarchical one, where Christ functions as a reflection of the divine in the individual. The epigraphs of *Jazz* (1992) and *Paradise* (1998) come from the Gnostic poem, *Thunder Perfect Mind*.

BIBLIOGRAPHY

Filoramo, Giovanni. A *History of Gnosticism*, translated by A. Alcock. Oxford: Blackwell, 1990.

Foerster, Werner. *Gnosis*, Vol. 1, *Patristic Evidence*. Oxford: Clarendon, 1972.

Hedrick, Charles W., and Robert Hodgson Jr., eds. *Nag Hammadi, Gnosticism and Early Christianity*. Peabody, Mass.: Hendrickson, 1986.

Layton, Bentley. *Gnostic Scriptures*. Garden City, N.Y.: Doubleday, 1987.

———, ed. *The Rediscovery of Gnosticism*, Vol. 2, *Sethian Gnosticism*. Leiden: Brill, 1981.

Logan, A. H. B., and A. J. M. Wedderburn, eds. *The New Testament and Gnosis: Essays in Honour of Robert McL. Wilson*. Edinburgh: T. and T. Clark, 1983.

Longenecker, Richard N., and Merrill C. Tenney, eds. *New Dimensions in New Testament Study*. Grand Rapids, Mich.: Zondervan, 1974.

Pagels, Elaine. *The Gnostic Gospels*. New York: Random House, 1978.

Pearson, Birger. *Gnosticism, Judaism, and Egyptian Christianity*. Minneapolis, Minn.: Fortress, 1990.

Perkins, Pheme. "Apocalypse of Adam: Genre and Function of a Gnostic Apocalypse," *CBQ* 39 (1977): 382–395.

———. "Gnostic Christologies and the New Testament," *CBQ* 43 (1981): 590–606.

———. *The Gnostic Dialogue*. New York: Paulist, 1980.

———. *Gnosticism and the New Testament*. Minneapolis, Minn.: Fortress, 1993.

Robinson, James M., ed. *The Nag Hammadi Library in English*. San Francisco: Harper and Row, 1988.

Rudolf, Kurt. *Gnosis*, translated by P. W. Coxon and K. H. Kuhn, edited by R. McL. Wilson. San Francisco: Harper and Row, 1983.

Scholer, D. M. "Bibliographia Gnostica: Supplementum XXII," [*Novum Testamentum*] 36, no. 1 (1994): 58–96.

New Negro   In Morrison's *Jazz* (1992), Joe Trace refers to himself as a New Negro, as re-created seven times. The origins of the idea of the New Negro are the subject of scholarly debate. In the early decades of the 20th century, African-American leaders expressed the desire to form an intellectual, artistic, and spiritual collective inhabited by fellow African Americans who would embrace a new definition of blackness, one based on a reformation of negative constructions of black identity. The New Negro was one who would be self-defined and who would excel in artistic and intellectual accomplishments in a space he or she could claim as home, namely Harlem, New York.

Philosopher Alain Locke wrote about the New Negro in a classic essay of the same name. The essay became an ideological manifesto for many of the artists of the Harlem Renaissance. The New

Negro movement also has complex intersections with American modernism.

BIBLIOGRAPHY

Berg, Allison. "The New 'New Negro': Recasting the Harlem Renaissance," *College Literature* 25, no. 3 (Fall 1998): 172–180.

Harris, Leonard. *The Philosophy of Alain Locke: Harlem Renaissance and Beyond.* Philadelphia: Temple University Press, 1989.

Holmes, Eugene C. "Alain Locke and the New Negro Movement," *Negro American Literature Forum* 2 (Fall 1968): 60–68.

Locke, Alain, ed. *The New Negro: An Interpretation.* 1925. New York: Arno, 1968.

Maxwell, William J. *New Negro, Old Left: African-American Writing and Communism between the Wars.* New York: Columbia University Press, 1999.

Nommo The Nommos are African ancestral spirits worshipped by the Dogon people of Mali, Sudan, and Burkina Faso. They are usually described as part-fish, part-person, similar to a mermaid or merman, or as part-snake.

There are variations in the stories surrounding the Nommos. In one story, the Nommos are part of the Dogon creation myth. They were the first life created by the sky god Amma. At first only one being, Nommo, multiplied into four pairs of twins. One of the twins—a TRICKSTER named Yurugu—rebelled against Amma. To battle the resulting chaos, Amma sacrificed another Nommo twin, whose dismembered body parts were scattered around the world.

Another myth surrounding the Nommo has some remarkable similarities to the story of Jesus. In the story, the Nommo descended from the sky and created a reservoir of water to live in. Also seen as a single figure, Nommo then divided his body to feed it to people. This sacrificial act is often referred to as having drunk of his body. He taught people about life and wisdom and was subsequently crucified on a tree. He was resurrected and returned to his home around the star Sirius. According to the legend, he will return to Earth in human form.

There is a character in TAR BABY (1981) named Nommo that Son befriends. He says that she reminds him of his sister Francine who is in a mental institution.

BIBLIOGRAPHY

Calame-Griaule, Genevieve. *Words and the Dogon World.* Philadelphia: Ishi, 1965.

Griaule, Marcell. *Conversations with Ogotemmeli—An Introduction to Dogon Religious Ideas.* London: Oxford University Press, 1965.

Temple, Robert K. G. *The Sirius Mystery.* New York: St. Martin's Press, 1976.

Norman, Jessye (1945–) An African-American soprano, Jessye Norman is regarded internationally as among the most celebrated of operatic artists. She is noted for her commanding stage presence, emotional performances, and a wide vocal range, which includes soprano, mezzo-soprano, and contralto. Among her roles, Norman has become particularly identified with her leads in *Aida, Les Troyens,* and *Fidelio.*

Born in Augusta, Georgia, Norman was introduced to music an early age by her mother, who played piano, and her father, who sang in a church choir. Norman studied music formally at Howard University, where she graduated in 1967 with a B.A. in music, and from the University of Michigan, where she received her master's degree in 1968. Much of her early singing career was spent in Germany. In 1969, she won the ARD International Music Competition in Munich and made her operatic debut that same year in Wagner's *Tannhauser* at the Berlin State Opera. She toured Germany for several years and, in 1972—a year that also saw her performing for the first time in Milan and London—Norman made her U.S. debut at the Hollywood Bowl as Aida. In 1983, during the New York Metropolitan Opera's 100th anniversary season, Norman made her debut with that company in the roles of Cassandra and Dido in Berlioz's *Les Troyens.*

Among Norman's nonoperatic performances are stage recitals that include arias, song cycles, French chansons, German *Lieder,* American spirituals, and jazz. Often collaborating with other artists, Norman premiered the song cycle *woman.life.song* in 2000 at Carnegie Hall, with music composed by Judith Weir and texts written by Maya Angelou, Clarissa Estes, and Toni Morrison. Previously she had worked with Morrison and RICHARD DANIELPOUR on the song cycle *Sweet Talk: Four Songs on Text*, which premiered in Carnegie Hall in 1997, featuring Norman singing.

OKeh Records The name of the record company, OKeh Records, came from the initials of its founder, Otto K. E. Heinemann. In 1918, Heinemann began the record company with a commitment to recording diverse artists. One of its first artists was the famous blues singer BESSIE SMITH, whose recording of "Crazy Blues" gave the company its first popular hit.

Eventually, the company was acquired by Columbia Records, but it maintained its commitment to African-American JAZZ and BLUES artists. It continued as a successful label until the 1960s when its succession of hits began to falter. The label is remembered for its support and promotion of blues, jazz, and soul songs and artists. OKeh was one of several recording labels that were said to produce race records.

In *Jazz* (1992), when Felice comes to visit Violet and Joe in search of the ring her mother gave her, she is carrying an OKeh record.

BIBLIOGRAPHY

Laird, Ross, and Brian Rust. *Discography of OKeh Records, 1918–1934.* Westport, Conn.: Praeger, 2004.

Oklahoma Territory The land known as the Oklahoma Territory was part of the land acquired by the U.S. government in the Louisiana Purchase of 1803. In 1819, the federal government made the land that is now Oklahoma a part of the Arkansas Territory.

In the southeastern United States, the U.S. government decided to take highly desirable lands from the Native American tribes known to the government as the Five Civilized Tribes and forced members of the Cherokee, Choctaw, Creek, Chickasaw, and Seminole to abandon their lands and their homes and move west into present-day Oklahoma. The government promised a new home to the Native Americans. This area, 31,000 square miles located west of the Mississippi River, was called Indian Territory and was so designated by an act of Congress in 1834.

The forced removal of Native Americans from the southeast to Indian Territory, known as the Trail of Tears, was responsible for the deaths of more than 4,000 Native Americans from exposure, starvation, and illness. The Trail of Tears occurred between 1838 and 1839. Beginning in 1866, the government began taking away the land it had promised to the Native Americans.

Because of the westward expansion that followed the Civil War, the land given to the Five Civilized Tribes became highly desirable, and the government began systematically to take the land back and give it to white settlers and ranchers. Congress created the Oklahoma Territory in 1890 out of lands formerly belonging to Indian Territory. Leaders of the Indian Territory tried to maintain their lands and attempted to become a state in 1905. That effort was undermined and the Oklahoma Territory and the Indian Territory were combined to create the state of Oklahoma in 1907. With the creation of the state of Oklahoma, Native Americans lost sovereignty over what remained of their land.

When they travel west in search of a home, the group in *Paradise* (1998) that founds Haven finds the land in the Oklahoma Territory.

BIBLIOGRAPHY

Foreman, Grant. *Indians and Pioneers: The Story of the American Southwest before 1830*. Norman: University of Oklahoma Press, 1936.

————. *Indian Removal: The Emigration of the Five Civilized Tribes of Indians*. Norman: University of Oklahoma Press, 1972.

McLoughlin, William G. *After the Trail of Tears: The Cherokees' Struggle for Sovereignty 1839–1880*. Chapel Hill: University of North Carolina Press, 1993.

Schultz, George A. *An Indian Canaan: Isaac McCoy and the Vision of an Indian State*. Norman: University of Oklahoma Press, 1972.

P

Philadelphia Negro, The (1899) *The Philadelphia Negro* is a sociological work by W. E. B. DuBois, exploring the lives of the African-American community in Philadelphia on the eve of the 20th century. In 1897, DuBois had been given a fellowship at the University of Pennsylvania as assistant professor in sociology in order to conduct his research, which was to be the first major empirical study of African Americans in U.S. society.

Convinced that bigotry in America was due to ignorance, DuBois focused his study on the slums of Philadelphia's seventh ward, hoping to uncover information that would help lead to greater understanding between the races. He points to the severe disadvantages that black Americans faced in finding jobs, suitable housing, and a competitive education in a society that was not far removed from the days of southern slavery, which continued to hurt the opportunities of blacks even in northern cities. DuBois insists that helping the Negro would also help American society as a whole: "There is no doubt that in Philadelphia the centre and kernel of the Negro problem so far as the white people are concerned is the narrow opportunities afforded Negroes for earning a decent living. Such discrimination is morally wrong, politically dangerous, industrially wasteful, and socially silly. It is the duty of the whites to stop it, and to do so primarily for their own sakes."

Published in 1899, *The Philadelphia Negro* incorporates historical, statistical, and ethnographical investigations, which made the work not only critical in understanding African Americans in a late 19th-century urban setting, but also made DuBois one of the founders in the field of sociology.

In *Jazz* (1992), Sydney Childs refers to and thinks of himself as a Philadelphia Negro.

BIBLIOGRAPHY

DuBois, W. E. B. *The Philadelphia Negro: A Social Study.* 1899. New York: Schocken Books, 1969.

Katz, Michael B., and Thomas J. Sugrue. *W.E.B. DuBois, Race, and the City: The Philadelphia Negro and Its Legacy.* Philadelphia: University of Pennsylvania Press, 1998.

Picasso, Pablo (1881–1973) Pablo Picasso is one of the best-known and highly regarded artists of the 20th century. Picasso was born into a middle-class family in Spain. Picasso's father was an art teacher and nurtured son's early interest in art. Picasso attended the Barcelona Academy of Art where he thrived and grew into a more mature artist.

Picasso's work is often thought of in phases that reflect the artist's development. Picasso's Blue Period was characterized by realistic works of subjects that were often the victims of class oppression. During this time his works had a predominantly blue tone both literally and figuratively.

Picasso's next phase was his Rose Period in which his palette consisted mostly of roses and pinks. He also painted a number of portraits during this time. Picasso is known as one of the innovators of visual modernism, and his Rose Period evolved into his experiments and developments in cubism.

Throughout the remainder of his life, Picasso continued to grow and change and was perpetually attracted to new forms of expression. Picasso was also moved to use his painting as a form of political commentary. His most well-known political painting is *Guernica* (1937). The painting protested German actions in the town of Guernica during the Spanish Civil War.

Picasso was widely respected and enjoyed international renown during his life. He died in 1973. Regard for Picasso's talents has only increased in the years following his death.

In *Tar Baby* (1981), Jadine values the art of Western culture, Picasso, over indigenous African art as represented by the Itumba mask.

BIBLIOGRAPHY

Boone, Daniele. *Picasso.* London: Studio Editions, 1993.
Hilton, Timothy. *Picasso.* London: Thames and Hudson, 1975.
Schiff, Gert, ed. *Picasso in Perspective.* Englewood Cliffs, N.J.: Prentice Hall, 1976.
Stein, Gertrude. *Picasso.* New York: Dover, 1984.

pickaninny In American literature, films, and television, stereotypes of African Americans abound. African-American men, women, and children are frequently portrayed in demeaning and dehumanizing caricatures that allow the consumer of the image to more readily accept justifications for slavery, segregation, and inequality. Some common stereotypes are MAMMY, Aunt Jemima, black buck, Uncle Tom, and the pickaninny.

The pickaninny stereotype caricatures African-American children. The common depictions of pickaninnies portray these children as incompetent, physically repulsive, and comical. Frequently, these children are victims of violence, particularly of wild animals who are about to kill these little ones in gruesome fashion.

The pickaninny emerges in early American fiction. One of the most famous examples is in Harriet Beecher Stowe's *Uncle Tom's Cabin* (1852) with the author's creation of the pickaninny character, Topsy. Another example exists in the 1939 film *Gone with the Wind* and the character Prissy, played by the actress BUTTERFLY MCQUEEN. Although Prissy is older than most pickaninnys, she exhibits all of the characteristics of the stereotype with her ineptitude, laziness, and histrionics.

Morrison may be trying to rewrite the pickaninny stereotype with several of her characters, including Pecola in *The Bluest Eye* (1970), the Deweys in *Sula* (1973), and Honor in *Jazz* (1992).

BIBLIOGRAPHY

Bogel, Donald. *Toms, Coons, Mulattoes, Mammies and Bucks: An Interpretive History of Blacks in American Films.* New York: Continuum, 2001.
Gone with the Wind. (1939). Warner Home Video. DVD, 2001.
Riggs, Marlon. *Ethnic Notions.* California News Reel. VHS, 1986.
Stowe, Harriet Beecher. *Uncle Tom's Cabin.* 1852. New York: Bantam Classics, 1983.

playing the dozens In African-American vernacular, playing the dozens refers to the bantering between two individuals in which insults are exchanged in accelerating intensity. Often the insults are personal, about an individual's features or body size, or they may be insults about an individual's family, quite frequently about a person's mother. Literary critic Henry Louis Gates has written extensively on this subject and connects playing the dozens with the literary critical conception of signifying where language is used by the disempowered to reclaim authority and to alleviate, if not eliminate, the impacts of inequality. Instances of playing the dozens, such as the scenes in *Song of Solomon* (1977) in Tommy's barbershop, occur in all of Morrison's novels.

BIBLIOGRAPHY

Gates, Henry Louis. *The Signifying Monkey.* New York: Oxford University Press, 1989.
Jones, Rhett. "Place, Politics and the Performing Arts in the African Diaspora," *Western Journal of Black Studies* 24 (2000): 71–85.

Plessy v. Ferguson   Although African Americans were emancipated by the end of the Civil War, their rights as citizens were far from secure. During the Reconstruction era, there were several measures passed by Radical Republicans in Congress designed to assure African-American men full citizenship. These measures included the Thirteenth (1865), Fourteenth (1868), and Fifteenth (1870) Amendments to the Constitution, a Civil Rights Bill (1875), as well as various Reconstruction Acts. While these measures were essential to the eventual acquisition of citizenship, they were all undermined by legal and illegal measures implemented in the southern United States and known as JIM CROW laws and the Black Codes. These measures were designed to ensure that African Americans could not exercise their right to vote, to use public facilities, or to move about freely, among other limitations.

The *Plessy v. Ferguson* decision occurred in this climate of retrenchment and backlash. The litigant in the case was Homer Plessy. Plessy was accused by officials of the East Louisiana Railroad of violating a Louisiana law that mandated that railroads provide separate accommodations on all of the passenger trains that traveled though the state. The law, passed in Louisiana in 1890, mandated that passengers who were found sitting in the "wrong" compartment would be fined $25 or could spend 20 days in jail.

Homer Plessy sat in the white section of the railroad car and was jailed as a result. Plessy's case was complicated by the fact that he was mixed-race. Racial law in the United States, however, has traditionally followed the one-drop rule, meaning that any percentage of black blood makes an individual African American. Plessy was found to be black and, therefore, in violation of the law.

Unwilling to accept this injustice, and the fundamental violation of the Thirteenth and Fourteenth Amendments that the Louisiana law represented, Plessy attempted to assert his rights in court. The initial court decision found Plessy guilty of violating the Louisiana law; he then decided to appeal the case to the Louisiana Supreme Court. When the Louisiana Supreme Court upheld the decision of the lower court, Plessy then decided to appeal his case to the U.S. Supreme Court.

In 1896, the Supreme Court heard the case, *Plessy v. Ferguson,* and concurred with the findings of the previous hearings. The Court made its decision with an eight to one ruling that asserted that there was a difference between the equality guaranteed by the Thirteenth Amendment and Fourteenth Amendments and the separation or distinction between the races mandated by the Louisiana law. In other words, the Court asserted that social and political equality could be considered as separate conditions. With this ruling, the Court established the legality and constitutionality of separate but equal.

The one dissenting justice was John Harlan who argued in his dissent that constitutional rights could not, if genuinely applied, be predicated on color. As Justice Harlan predicted, *Plessy v. Ferguson* would be the legal foundation for racial segregation in the United States until the issue was revisited by the Supreme Court in the BROWN V. BOARD OF EDUCATION OF TOPEKA, KANSAS decision in 1954.

BIBLIOGRAPHY

Brook, Thomas, ed. *Plessy v. Ferguson: A Brief History with Documents.* Boston: Bedford Books, 1997.

Lofgren, Charles A. *The "Plessy" Case: A Legal-Historical Interpretation.* New York: Oxford University Press, 1987.

Nelson, William E. *The Fourteenth Amendment.* Cambridge, Mass.: Harvard University Press, 1988.

Painter, Nell Irvin. *Standing at Armageddon.* New York: W. W. Norton, 1987.

Przybyszewski, Linda. *The Republic According to John Marshal Harlan.* Chapel Hill: University of North Carolina Press, 1999.

Olsen, Otto H., ed. *The Thin Disguise: "Plessy v. Ferguson."* New York: Humanities Press, 1967.

Rosen, Paul L. *The Supreme Court and Social Science.* Urbana: University of Illinois Press, 1972.

Thomas, Brook, ed. *Plessy v. Ferguson.* Boston: Bedford Books, 1997.

Trachtenberg, Alan. "The Machine as Deity and Demon." In *Major Problems in the Gilded Age and the Progressive Era,* edited by Leon Fink, 27–34. Boston: Houghton Mifflin, 2001.

Popeye Popeye is an iconographic American cartoon character who was first drawn in 1929 by cartoonist Elzie Segar. Segar wrote a comic narrative called *Thimble Theater* (1919) for the Hearst newspapers. Popeye was not originally a central character in the story but quickly became a favorite. Popeye was a gruff but big-hearted sailor who evolved into a likeable, if untraditional, hero. One of the interesting aspects of the Popeye character was his near-superhuman strength, which derived from his consumption of spinach. As Segar developed the strip, other notable characters began to recur, including Olive Oyl, Wimpy, and Popeye's arch-enemy, Bluto. The character found an even wider audience in television, and in 1980 the tale of the feisty sailor was made into a live-action film.

Popeye is referenced in Toni Morrison's *The Bluest Eye* (1970).

BIBLIOGRAPHY

Anobile, Richard. *Popeye: The Movie Novel*. New York: Avon, 1980.
Marschall, Richard. *America's Great Comic-Strip Artists*. New York: Abbeville Press, 1989.
Sagendorf, Bud. *Popeye: The First Fifty Years*. New York: Workman Publishing, 1979.

Postum Postum is a dehydrated powder that, when reconstituted, becomes a coffee substitute. Postum was invented by cereal manufacturer Charles William Post. Originally touted as a health coffee substitute, Postum became a popular drink with Americans through the late 19th and early 20th centuries. Postum is caffeine free. Postum, which is a combination of wheat, molasses, and barley, is still manufactured and sold today.

In *Tar Baby* Valerian Street does not like Postum, and his manservant, Sydney Childs, tries to substitute Postum for coffee because he thinks it is better for Street.

pot liquor Pot liquor or pot likker is the watery remains of cooking. When vegetables, such as greens, are cooked the water that is left over in the pot is called pot liquor. This liquid was highly prized in traditional African-American cooking as a base for other dishes or simply as a substance to be consumed for its healthful properties. As it turns out, the pot liquor often contains most of the nutrient value of the food.

In *The Bluest Eye* (1970), the community contributes various items, including HOG JOWLS, to make pot liquor when Aunt Jimmy is ill.

Previn, Andre (1929–) Grammy Award–winning Andre Previn is a celebrity composer and musical performer whose career has demonstrated his ability to excel in many mediums, including opera, JAZZ, and popular and classical music. Born in Germany, Previn came of age in Paris before his family moved to California.

Previn demonstrated his musical abilities at an early age and recorded his first album when he was only 16 years old. He went on to work as a composer for the giant movie studio, Metro-Goldwyn-Mayer. Previn excelled as a pianist and conductor and has been an innovator and become an expert in each field he has explored. Previn also gained a measure of fame because of his associations with, and marriages to, Hollywood starlets such as Mia Farrow. Some of Previn's most notable works include his 1998 opera, *A Streetcar Named Desire*, and his 1992 song-cycle collaboration with Toni Morrison, *Honey and Rue*, recorded by KATHLEEN BATTLE in 1995.

BIBLIOGRAPHY

Previn, Andre. *No Minor Chords — My Early Days in Hollywood*. New York: Doubleday, 1991.
———. *Honey and Rue*. (1992). Deutsche Grammophon (USA), 1995.

Prince Charming Prince Charming is a standard character in many fairy tales. Traditionally, he represents an ideal of masculine perfection. Prince Charming often is the catalyst for the rescue or salvation of the female protagonist from the evil villain who seeks, in some way, to harm her. The name Prince Charming became popular and widely used in American vernacular after the release of the 1950 Disney film, *Cinderella*.

Morrison critiques the myth of Prince Charming in each of her novels.

Princeton Atelier   In 1994, Toni Morrison began an arts program at Princeton University called the Princeton Atelier. The program was designed to support and nurture interdisciplinary collaborations between artists and students from different disciplines. The program attracts artists who are considered to be among the best in their fields because the artists are intrigued by the possibilities inherent in such fertile collaborations.

Historically the program has offered four course sections with different artists and themes in the spring semester. Each section of the Atelier enrolls 10 students and the size of the class allows for close and intimate interactions between faculty, artists, and students. The guest artists live in residency on the Princeton campus and therefore are more available for engaged participation. Morrison has said that she was inspired to begin the program because of the richness of her own interdisciplinary collaborations.

BIBLIOGRAPHY

Deborah A. Kaple. "Toni Morrison's Atelier: Students and Professors Join Together to Create Art from the Heart." September 10, 1997. Available online. URL: http://www.princeton.edu/~paw/archive_old/PAW97–98/01-0910/0910feat. html. Accessed on September 20, 2006.

Pullman porters   The Pullman porters were the men who worked as railroad porters for the Pullman train company. African-American men began working for the Pullman Company before the Civil War. These men worked as porters, waiters, chefs, and attendants. During the early 20th century, the Pullman Company employed more African Americans than most other companies in the nation. Many African Americans found economic mobility and gained middle-class status by working for the railroad. The porters were often among the most respected and admired individuals in their communities.

In spite of the advantages of working as a porter for the Pullman Company, the work was often difficult and even demeaning. On the trains, the porters were subjected to the racial climate of the time, which put them on the front line of racial conflict. No matter their individual names, the porters were often referred to by white passengers as George, which was the name of the Pullman Company founder. They were subjected to unfair, often dangerous working conditions, and had to indulge constant assaults on their personhood.

These difficulties and oppressive conditions led to the organization of the first black union, the Brotherhood of Sleeping Car Porters, under the leadership of activist A. Phillip Randolph. In 1937, the union entered into its first collective bargaining agreement. As a result of the union and its efforts, its African-American members were able to enter into an improved relationship with the company. The Pullman Company went out of business in 1969, but African-American employment in the company contributed substantially to the growth of the African-American middle classes.

In *Jazz* (1992), Felice's father works as a Pullman porter.

BIBLIOGRAPHY

Brazeal, Brailsford Reese. *The Brotherhood of Sleeping Car Porters, Its Origin and Development.* New York and London: Harper, 1946.

Briggs, Martha T., and Cynthia H. Peters. *Guide to the Pullman Company Archives.* Chicago: Newberry Library, 1995.

Harris, William Hamilton. *Keeping the Faith: A. Philip Randolph, Milton P. Webster, and the Brotherhood of Sleeping Car Porters, 1925–37.* Urbana: University of Illinois Press, 1977.

Perata, David D. *Those Pullman Blues: An Oral History of the African American Railroad Attendant.* New York: Twayne Publishers, 1996.

Santino, Jack. *Miles of Smiles, Years of Struggle: Stories of Black Pullman Porters.* Urbana: University of Illinois Press, 1989.

Wilson, Joseph F., ed. *Tearing Down the Color Bar: A Documentary History and Analysis of the Brotherhood of Sleeping Car Porters.* New York: Columbia University Press, 1989.

Q, R

Quakers See Society of Friends

Quilts, Quilting See African-American Quilting

Rastus Rastus was a fictional figure, a trademark forever associated in the minds of American consumers with the marketing and packaging of the grain breakfast cereal, Cream of Wheat. The trademark emerged as a symbol associated with Cream of Wheat in the late 19th century. The original product was called Middlin and was produced by the Diamond Milling Company, located in North Dakota. One of the owners of the company, Emery Mapes, renamed the product Cream of Wheat and developed an image of Rastus.

The image changed from the original in the 1920s when the face of Rastus was replaced by a drawing of the face of a man from Chicago who was employed as a waiter. Although the company has no record of this man's identity, a man named Jim White from Leslie, Michigan, claimed to have been the model for Rastus. In this new incarnation, Rastus appears to be an exceptionally happy and accommodating cook. He wears a white chef's hat and coat and holds a steaming bowl of Cream of Wheat in his right hand level with his broad grin. The product, Cream of Wheat, still bears this logo.

In *Tar Baby* (1981), Jadine playfully and scornfully asks Son if his real name is Rastus.

BIBLIOGRAPHY

Kern-Foxworth, Marilyn. *Aunt Jemima, Uncle Ben, and Rastus*. Westport, Conn.: Greenwood Press, 1994.

razor strop A razor strop (strap) is a soft leather strip or band used to sharpen an old-fashioned straight razor blade. The strop was also used by some as an implement for spanking children. In *The Bluest Eye* (1970), Aunt Jimmy beats Cholly's mother with a razor strap after the girl tries to abandon her infant son. Shortly thereafter, the girl runs away.

Robertson, Carole (1949–1963) See Collins, Addie Mae

Robinson, Bill "Bojangles" (1878–1949) Robinson was an innovative African-American tap dancer. His on-stage image was often that of a dapper gentleman, appearing in tails with top hat and cane. Considered one of the great dancers of all time, he also broke racial barriers when he started to perform for white audiences.

Born in Richmond, Virginia, Robinson was raised by his grandmother after the death of his parents when he was a baby. A precocious child, Robinson began dancing for a living at the age of six. He started to tour a couple of years later and never stopped. For most of his career, he stayed on the black theater circuit, becoming a great success as a musical comedy performer in nightclubs. He did not perform for white audiences until he was 50, when a white producer gave him a role in *Blackbirds of 1928*, an all-black musical revue intended for white audiences. His fame soared.

At a time when the entertainment world was racially segregated, Robinson often acted as an ambassador for African Americans to the white world. To that end, his public persona was that of a well-dressed, gracious man. As his career progressed, he lost more contact with the black circuit and concentrated on performing for the higher paying white audiences. His fame grew still further when he appeared in several movies, his most famous being his appearances in several movies with SHIRLEY TEMPLE in the 1930s.

When Robinson died of heart failure in New York City, schools in black neighborhoods were closed, thousands of people lined the streets to see his coffin, and he was eulogized by both black and white politicians. In *The Bluest Eye* (1970), Claudia bemoans the fact that in the movies Robinson dances with white Shirley Temple and not her.

BIBLIOGRAPHY

Haskins, James, and N. R. Mitgang. *Mr. Bojangles. The Biography of Bill Robinson.* New York: Welcome Rain Publisher, 1999.

Rogers, Ginger (1911–1995) Ginger Rogers was an American dancer, actor, and singer on both stage and in film, and she is best remembered as the romantic lead and dancing partner in a series of movies starring Fred Astaire. Born in Independence, Missouri, Rogers acquired her interest in the theater from her mother, who was a theater critic. As a teenager, Rogers performed in vaudeville, and in 1929 she made her film debut in several early talkies. She appeared in the Gershwin stage musical, *Girl Crazy* (1930), for which Astaire had been hired to assist in the choreography. In 1933, Rogers gained greater success in *42nd Street* and other films that followed, but she achieved her greatest fame and artistic success in the films she was to make with Astaire, the first of which was *Flying Down to Rio* (1933), in which the two were teamed up in nonstarring roles. Throughout the remainder of the 1930s, Rogers costarred with Astaire in several more musicals—including the *The Gay Divorcee* (1934), *Top Hat* (1935), *Follow the Fleet* (1936), and *Shall We Dance* (1937)—films in which Astaire had greater artistic control and which are respected by movie critics as great achievements in film musicals. Fans and film critics alike credit the success

of the partnership partly to Rogers's talent as an actress and dancer; Astaire acknowledged that she also contributed to the choreography. Throughout the 1940s, Rogers had continued success without Astaire, but they were reunited one last time in 1949 for the film *The Barkleys of Broadway.*

In *The Bluest Eye* (1970), Mr. Henry calls Frieda and Claudia by the names of movie stars such as Ginger Rogers.

BIBLIOGRAPHY

Faris, Jocelyn. *Ginger Rogers: A Bio-Bibliography.* Westport, Conn.: Greenwood Press, 1994.

Morley, Sheridan. *Shall We Dance: The Life of Ginger Rogers.* New York: St. Martin's Press, 1995.

Rogers, Ginger. *Ginger Rogers: My Story.* New York: HarperCollins, 1991.

Roots In 1974, Alex Haley published the first version of his classic American saga, *Roots. Roots,* the story of Haley's family from enslavement to the contemporary age, won a Pulitzer Prize and became a record-breaking best-seller and a miniseries with one of the largest television audiences ever. Many Americans are familiar with the story of Alex Haley's family as narrated in the novel *Roots* and as dramatized in the *Roots* television miniseries.

Particularly well-known is the tale of Haley's African ancestor, Kunta Kinte. After his kidnap from the African village of Juffure and his survival of the Middle Passage, in 1768 Kunta Kinte was sold to the Waller family in Spotsylvania County, Virginia. Kinte was the progenitor for the family that, eventually, produced Alex Haley. *Roots* traces the story of Kinte's descendants from Kunta Kinte to Haley.

Some have compared Morrison's *Song of Solomon* (1977) to Haley's *Roots.*

BIBLIOGRAPHY

August, Melissa. "Roots Mania: Spurred by New Resources on the Internet, the Ranks of Amateur Genealogists are Growing, and Millions of Family Trees Are Flourishing." *Time,* April 19, 1999, 54–64.

Eliot, Jeffrey. "The Roots of Alex Haley's Writing Career," *Writer's Digest* (August 1980): 20–26.

Haley, Alex. *Alex Haley's Queen.* New York: Morrow/ Avon, 1993.

———. "A Turtle Atop a Fence Post." *U.S. News and World Report,* February 24, 1992, 20–22.

———. *Different Kind of Christmas.* New York: Random House Value Publishing, 1988.

———. "How *Roots* Grew," *Writer's Digest* (August 1980): 23–25.

———. *Mama Flora's Family.* New York: Dell Publishing, 1999.

———. *Muhammad Ali.* New York: Little, Brown, 1999.

———. *The Autobiography of Malcolm X.* New York: Ballantine Publishing Group, 1968.

———. *Roots.* New York: Bantam Doubleday Dell, 1976.

———. "We Must Honor Our Ancestors." *Ebony,* August 1993, 16–19.

Royce, Josiah (1855–1916) Josiah Royce, born into a rural and laboring family in Grass Valley, California, was an American philosopher whose beliefs derived from the philosophical school of thought called absolute idealism. Absolute idealism can be summarized as a belief that individual experience and consciousness is, in actuality, a manifestation of a unified whole. Royce's views changed over time and he finally came to a belief that replaced the unified whole with the concept that reality exists as a complex community formed by the exchange of signs between individuals in a community in the form of language and ideas.

Josiah Royce is credited with developing the influential idea of the BELOVED COMMUNITY. According to Royce, the Beloved Community derives from the collectivity of individuals who have organized their lives by adhering and acting in service to a central purpose. The challenge for the individual is to coordinate desires into a harmonious entity. This coordination creates a self. Each self constitutes a miniature Absolute. The Beloved Community can emerge when the micro-Absolutes coalesce and work together. Royce believed that the emergence of the Beloved Community would bring about stability and peace among humanity. Royce's idea of the Beloved Community was expanded upon and popularized by MARTIN LUTHER KING JR. Morrison may employ aspects of the Beloved Community

in her novels, especially *Beloved* (1987), *Paradise* (1998), and *Love* (2003).

BIBLIOGRAPHY

Clendenning, J., ed. *The Letters of Josiah Royce.* Chicago: University of Chicago Press, 1970.

Hocking, W. E., R. Hocking, and F. Oppenheim, eds. *Metaphysics / Josiah Royce: His Philosophy 9 Course of 1915–1916.* Albany: State University of New York Press, 1998.

McDermott, J., ed. *The Basic Writings of Josiah Royce.* 1969. New York: Fordham University Press, 2005.

Robinson, D. S., ed. *Royce's Logical Essays: Collected Logical Essays of Josiah Royce.* Dubuque, Iowa: W. C. Brown, 1959.

Royce, J. *Primer of Logical Analysis for the Use of Composition Students.* San Francisco: A. L. Bancroft and Co., 1881.

———. *The Religious Aspect of Philosophy.* Boston: Houghton Mifflin, 1885.

———. *The Spirit of Modern Philosophy: An Essay in the Form of Lectures.* Boston: Houghton Mifflin, 1892.

———. *The Conception of God.* New York: Macmillan, 1897.

———. *Studies of Good and Evil.* New York: D. Appleton, 1898.

———. *The Problem of Christianity.* 1913. Washington, D.C.: Catholic University of America Press, 2001.

Rumpelstiltskin Rumpelstiltskin is the name of a character in a popular fairy tale collected by the Brothers Grimm in the 19th century. In the story, a maiden must spin straw into gold for a king or else face death. She is unable to accomplish the task, but Rumpelstiltskin, a gnome, volunteers to perform the task for her, provided she gives him her first-born child. She agrees. The maiden later marries the king, and when the gnome comes to collect the child, she begs him to let her keep it. Rumpelstiltskin says he will let her keep her child provided she can guess his name. After many false guesses, the maiden learns from a messenger what his name is. She tells the gnome, and he is so furious he tears himself in two.

Morrison alludes to *Rumpelstiltskin* in *Song of Solomon* (1977) when Ruth Dead is breastfeeding Milkman.

S

Sanchez, Sonia (1934–) Sanchez's earliest work as well as her most recent works are true to the essence of the BLACK AESTHETIC. Each of her texts expresses the subjective voices of the African-American community, utilizes formal strategies in order to privilege orality and performance as primary modes of conveyance, and affirms the cultural repository that is African-American vernacular. Sanchez's articulation of these fundamental precepts of the BLACK AESTHETIC are filtered through her positionality as a conscious black woman writer/activist.

Despite her seemingly uncompromising rhetorical stance on the feminist movement, careful analysis of Sanchez's poetry reveals a powerful commitment to the principles of gender equality and a recognition of the particular oppression experienced by black women. In her first four volumes of poetry, Sanchez's narrative voices reveal the tension experienced in the negotiations between her simultaneous identities as woman, black woman, and black person. The titles of Sanchez's early texts encode her expansion of Black Aesthetic rhetoric to include the specific concerns of black women.

The first volume, *Homecoming* (1969), marks her post-collegiate return to the black activist/intellectual community and her renewed commitment to the Black Aesthetic. The second volume, *We a BaddDDD People* (1970), celebrates that community while acknowledging its complexity. The third volume, *Love Poems* (1973), examines and demythologizes relationships between black men and women, and *A Blues Book for Blue Black Magical Women* (1973) particularizes Sanchez's narrator's role as a woman within the black community. Throughout these works, Sanchez retains her allegiance to the foundational precepts of the Black Aesthetic while giving voice to the gender-specific oppressions of black women.

Both Morrison and Sanchez are African-American women writers who came of age at roughly the same time. The women respect and count each other as influences and friends.

BIBLIOGRAPHY

Neal, Larry. "The Black Arts Movement," *Drama Review* 12 (Summer 1968): 29–39.

Sanchez, Sonia. *A Blues Book for Magical Blue Black Women*. Detroit: Broadside, 1974.

———. *Home Coming*. Detroit: Broadside, 1969.

———. *Love Poems*. Detroit: Broadside, 1973.

———. *We a BaddDDD People*. Detroit: Broadside, 1974.

Secessionists The Secessionists were those people in the American South during the first half of the 19th century who felt that the only solution to the political conflict between the North and the South was for the southern states to break away from the United States and form their own union—the Confederate States of America. The eventual secession of 11 southern states led to the Civil War.

The central disagreement between the North and South revolved around the question of slavery, which continued as an institution in southern states after it had been outlawed in the North. The North, led by ABOLITIONists, considered slavery to be immoral and tried to extend the ban on slavery to the South. The South, however, considered any attempt by the federal government to end slavery to be an infringement of their states' rights and a threat to their economic system. In 1861, South Carolina, Virginia, North Carolina, Georgia, Florida, Alabama, Mississippi, Texas, Arkansas, Tennessee, and Louisiana seceded from the United States, precipitating the Civil War.

The Seccesionists are referenced in Toni Morrison's novel *Beloved* (1987).

BIBLIOGRAPHY

Gallagher, Gary W. *The Confederate War.* Boston: Harvard University Press, 1997.

Paquette, Robert Louis, and Louis A. Ferleger, eds. *Slavery, Secession, and Southern History.* Charlottesville: University of Virginia Press, 2000.

Rable, George C. *The Confederate Republic: A Revolution against Politics.* Chapel Hill: University of North Carolina Press, 1994.

Stampp, Kenneth M. *And the War Came. The North and the Secession Crisis, 1860–1861.* Baton Rouge: Louisiana State University Press, 1970.

Wright, William C. *The Secession Movement in the Middle Atlantic States.* Cranbury, N.J.: Associated University Presses, 1973.

Seneca (American Indian Nation)   The Seneca—or Seneca Nation of Indians—is the largest of the six tribes of the Iroquois Confederacy, which includes the Oneida, Mohawk, Onondaga, Cayuga, and Tuscarora (the last of the tribes to join the confederacy). The Seneca's aboriginal lands include much of what is today upper New York State.

Before the Europeans arrived in North America, the Seneca economy depended on the cultivation of crops—corn, beans, and squash—and on hunting and fishing. Known as the People of the Long House, they lived in villages often surrounded by palisades as protection against other tribes. With the arrival of the Europeans, their economy expanded to include fur trapping.

During the American Revolution, the Seneca Nation underwent some division and weakening as many members sided with the British and raided the settlements of the American colonies while others sided with the colonists. Perhaps the biggest influence of the Seneca—and of all the Iroquois Confederacy—on the future American union was in their own democratic political system, including a constitution, which is considered to be an important model for America's founding fathers.

After the eventual independence and formation of the United States, much of the Seneca aboriginal lands in northern New York State were set aside as a reservation by the Treaty of Canandaigua in 1794. With a current population of over 7,200 enrolled members, the Seneca Nation holds title to three New York territories, including the city of Salamanca. The Seneca economy today is tied mostly to their reservation's casino and hotel industry.

In *Paradise* (1998), one of the central characters is named Seneca.

BIBLIOGRAPHY

Hass, Marilyn L. *The Seneca and the Tuscarora Indians.* Lanham, Md.: Scarecrow, 1994.

Seneca (Roman dramatist and statesman, Seneca, Lucius Annaeus)   (c. 3 B.C.–65 A.D.)   Lucius Annaeus Seneca, also known as Seneca the Younger, was a Roman philosopher and dramatist. His most influential works were his nine tragedies, though they were probably written for recitation and not for stage performance. Based on Greek models, the plays were not—and are not—often performed as theater, but they had a strong influence on Renaissance tragedies, especially in their use of dark moods, rhetoric, and stoicism. The nine plays attributed to Seneca include *Hercules Furens, Medea, Troades, Phaedra, Agamemnon, Oedipus, Hercules Oetaeus, Phoenissae,* and *Thyestes.*

Philosophically, Seneca was a Stoic. His essays known as the *Dialogi* include reflections on anger, on divine providence, emotional peace, and Stoic acceptance. His *De elementia* is an essay that calls on rulers to be merciful. The noble nature of his writings did not, however, necessarily reflect the life that he led, which was often dictated by political expediency. Born in Cordoba, Spain, Seneca went to Rome in his childhood, where he studied rhetoric and philosophy. Emperor Claudius exiled him in A.D. 41 because of his affair with the emperor's niece. He was recalled to Rome in 49 to tutor the young Nero, whom Seneca was to influence—for the better—when his student himself became emperor. In 62, he retired from the court, at the bidding of Nero's wife, but conspiracy accusations followed him into his retirement, and he was forced to commit suicide.

In *Paradise* (1998), one of the central characters is named Seneca.

BIBLIOGRAPHY

Cooper, John M., and J. F. Procopé. *Seneca: Moral and Political Essays.* Cambridge: Cambridge University Press, 1995.

Motto, Anna Lydia. *Seneca Sourcebook: Guide to the Thought of Lucius Annaeus Seneca.* Amsterdam: Hakkert, 1970.

Seneca Falls Seneca Falls is a small town in upstate New York. It was made famous by a women's suffrage convention that was held there in July of 1848. This meeting is often cited as the beginning of the suffrage movement in the United States. Seneca Falls was the home of one of the conference organizers and a key leader in the struggle for women's rights in the United States, Elizabeth Cady Stanton.

In *Paradise* (1998), one of the central characters is named Seneca.

BIBLIOGRAPHY

Banner, Lois. *Elizabeth Cady Stanton: A Radical for Women's Rights.* Boston: Little, Brown, 1980.

Gurko, Miriam. *The Ladies of Seneca Falls: The Birth of the Woman's Rights Movement.* New York: Schocken Books, 1976.

Melder, Keith. *Beginnings of Sisterhood: The American Woman's Rights Movement, 1800–1850.* New York: Schocken Press, 1977.

Seneca Village Seneca Village was founded in current-day Manhattan in 1820. On this site, which is now a part of Central Park, a group of African Americans held property and built a small,

stable community until 1857 when the community was disrupted by development.

In *Paradise* (1998), one of the central characters is named Seneca.

Shadrack Shadrack is a character from the Old Testament. Along with Meshack and Abednego, Shadrack is one of three Hebrew young men who refuse to bow down to a golden statue of Nebuchadnezzar, king of Babylon.

King Nebuchadnezzar sends for all the officials of his provinces to assemble to dedicate and bow to the statue. With everyone assembled before it, Nebuchadnezzar commands them all to fall down and worship his golden image. Everyone does so except for the three Hebrews. He threatens to have them thrown into a furnace, saying, "What god will be able to rescue you from my hand?" (Daniel 3:15). They still refuse. They are then thrown into the furnace, but they do not burn or even get singed. A fourth figure appears in the flames with them, a being with the image of God. Nebuchadnezzar is amazed, and he has the three Hebrews removed from the flames. They are unharmed. In awe of what he had witnessed, Nebuchadnezzar then decrees that no one shall blaspheme against the God of the Hebrews.

One of the central characters in *Sula* (1973) is named Shadrack.

sharecropping Sharecropping was a system of farming where the sharecropper lived on and worked land owned by someone else. The sharecropper contributed his labor, and the owner, or landlord, provided the animals, equipment, seed, tools, and living quarters.

The institution arose in the United States at the end of the Civil War. It grew out of the plantation system, whereby the newly freed slaves became sharecroppers on plantations because they had few other options. The ex-slave owners, and other planters, had land but little money for wages. In this way, the white landowners were able to keep ex-slaves in a subordinate position, and the cultivation of cotton continued. The system eventually included poor white farmers.

The system was generally abusive. The landlord kept the accounts and marketed the crops, and often he cheated the sharecropper out of his rightful share, which was generally half the profits. The landowner also gave the sharecropper advanced credit to meet living expenses, but the interest rates were typically so high that the sharecropper's portion of the profits went directly toward reducing his debt to the landlord. In this way, the sharecropper was tied to both the land and the landlord. The system can still be found in various parts of the world, and includes other cash crops besides cotton, but in the United States sharecropping faded for the most part when farm mechanization took over much of the manual work on farms, and fewer acres were devoted to cotton.

In *Jazz* (1992), Violet and Joe work for a time as sharecroppers before they relocate to HARLEM.

BIBLIOGRAPHY

Anderson, Eric, and Alfred A. Moss Jr., eds. *The Facts of Reconstruction: Essays in Honor of John Hope Franklin.* Baton Rouge: Louisiana State University Press, 1991.

Byres, T. J., ed. *Sharecropping and Sharecroppers.* Totowa, N.J.: Biblio Distribution Center, 1983.

Carter, Dan T. *When the War Was Over: The Failure of Self-Reconstruction in the South, 1865–1867.* Baton Rouge: Louisiana State University Press, 1985.

Cohen, William. *At Freedom's Edge: Black Mobility and the Southern White Quest for Racial Control, 1861–1915.* Baton Rouge: Louisiana State University Press, 1991.

Daniel, Pete. *Breaking the Land: The Transformation of Cotton, Tobacco, and Rice Cultures since 1880.* Urbana: University of Illinois Press, 1985.

Davis, Ronald L. F. *Good and Faithful Labor: From Slavery to Sharecropping in the Natchez District, 1860–1890.* Westport, Conn.: Greenwood Press, 1982.

Foner, Eric. *Reconstruction: America's Unfinished Revolution, 1863–1877.* New York: Harper and Row, 1988.

Harris, William H. *The Harder We Run: Black Workers since the Civil War.* New York: Oxford University Press, 1982.

Higgs, Robert. *Competition and Coercion: Blacks in the American Economy, 1865–1914.* Cambridge: Cambridge University Press, 1977.

Jaynes, Gerald D. *Branches without Roots: Genesis of the Black Working Class in the American South, 1862–1882.* New York: Oxford University Press, 1986.

Jones, Jacqueline. *Labor of Love, Labor of Sorrow: Black Women, Work, and the Family from Slavery to the Present.* New York: Basic Books, 1985.

Kousser, J. Morgan, and James M. McPherson, eds. *Region, Race, and Reconstruction: Essays in Honor of C. Vann Woodward.* New York: Oxford University Press, 1982.

Litwack, Leon F. *Been in the Storm So Long: The Aftermath of Slavery.* New York: Knopf, 1979.

Mandle, Jay R. *The Roots of Black Poverty: The Southern Plantation Economy after the Civil War.* Durham, N.C.: Duke University Press, 1978.

———. *Not Slave, Not Free: The African American Economic Experience since the Civil War.* Durham, N.C.: Duke University Press, 1992.

McGlynn, Frank, and Seymour Drescher. *The Meaning of Freedom: Economics, Politics, and Culture after Slavery.* Pittsburgh, Pa.: University of Pittsburgh Press, 1992.

McPherson, James M. *Ordeal by Fire: The Civil War and Reconstruction.* New York: Alfred A. Knopf, 1982.

Nieman, Donald G., ed. *From Slavery to Sharecropping: White Land and Black Labor in the Rural South, 1865–1900.* New York: Garland, 1994.

Orser, Charles E., Jr. *The Material Basis of the Postbellum Tenant Plantation: Historical Archaeology in the South Carolina Piedmont.* Athens: University of Georgia Press, 1988.

Otto, John S. *Southern Agriculture during the Civil War Era, 1860–1880.* Westport, Conn.: Greenwood Press, 1994.

Roark, James L. *Masters without Slaves: Southern Planters in the Civil War and Reconstruction.* New York: W. W. Norton, 1977.

Royce, Edward C. *The Origins of Southern Sharecropping.* Philadelphia: Temple University Press, 1993.

Stokes, Melvyn, and Rick Halpern, eds. *Race and Class in the American South since 1890.* Oxford: Berg Publishing, 1994.

Woodman, Harold D. *New South? New Law: The Legal Foundations of Credit and Labor Relations in the Postbellum Agricultural South.* Baton Rouge: Louisiana State University Press, 1995.

Wright, Gavin. *Old South, New South: Revolutions in the Southern Economy since the Civil War.* New York: Basic Books, 1986.

shotgun house   The shotgun house is a rectangular one-story dwelling where each room follows the one in front of it in single file. It has no hallways. The name comes from the idea that if a person fired a shotgun through the front door, the shot would pass through the doors of each room and exit the back door. In reality, the inside doors of shotgun houses do not always line up perfectly. The house is usually no more than 12 feet wide and three to five rooms deep. The style became particularly popular in the South from the late 19th century until the early 20th, spreading also into the North.

Shotgun houses appear in Morrison's novel *Sula* (1973).

Simone, Nina Eunice Kathleen Waymon   (1933?–2003)   Nina Simone was an American singer who gained initial success as a JAZZ singer but turned to songs of political and social import during the 1960s CIVIL RIGHTS MOVEMENT. She had a large following of fans who appreciated her rich, husky voice, her skill at the piano, and the messages of her songs, which particularly addressed racism and women's issues.

Born as Eunice Kathleen Waymon in Tryon, North Carolina, Simone showed great musical talent at the piano at the age of four. Through the years her family, which was poor, had to find various ways of supporting her musical lessons in classical piano. In her last year of high school, she studied piano at the Juilliard School of Music in New York City to prepare for an audition for the Curtis School of Music. She did not pass the Curtis audition. Simone believed it was due to racism.

To support her family, Simone worked as an accompanist for a music teacher and as a pianist in clubs. When she added singing to her playing, her new career began. She then started to use the stage name of Nina Simone. Over the years, Simone not only sang but also arranged and composed songs. Several of these became standards. Her version of "I Loves You, Porgy," from Gershwin's *Porgy and Bess* (1935), made her a star, and she soon performed at such venues as Carnegie Hall and the Newport Jazz Festival. Music fans were drawn not only to her unique voice but also to her improvising at the piano, which often combined jazz and classical influences.

It was the bombing of a church in Birmingham in 1963, in which four black children were killed, that compelled Simone to add songs of social commentary and protest to her repertory. Her song "Mississippi Goddam" was an angry denunciation of the racism that caused the deaths of those children.

Simone kept up an active schedule all her life, winning many honors along the way, until she became ill in 2003 and passed away in Carry-le-Rouet, France, where she had a villa.

In the novel *Love* (2003) the romance and perseverance represented in Simone's voice temporarily preserves the failing relationship of Christine Cosey and her boyfriend, Fruit.

BIBLIOGRAPHY

Kelly, Lisa Simone. *Nina Simone: Break Down and Let It All Out.* London: Sanctuary Publishing, 2004.

Simone, Nina. *I Put a Spell on You: The Autobiography of Nina Simone.* Cambridge, Mass.: Da Capo Press, 2003.

Simpson, O. J. (Orenthal James)   (1947–   )   Orenthal James Simpson was a major football star of the 1970s who developed a successful career as a film actor and company spokesman until he was charged with the murder of his wife, Nicole Simpson Brown, and her friend, Ron Goldman. The trial ended in acquittal in 1995, but Simpson was unable to resume his career.

During his football career, Simpson was a star player at the University of Southern California and won the Heisman Trophy in 1968. Nicknamed "The Juice," Simpson became a star running back for the Buffalo Bills and then the San Francisco 49ers. He retired from professional football in 1979 for a career as actor and spokesman.

In 1994, Simpson's ex-wife Nicole Brown Simpson was found murdered at her home along with her friend Ronald Goldman. Simpson was arrested a few days later after a car chase that was televised to a national audience. Simpson's eventual acquittal proved controversial, and support for or against it seemed to break along racial lines, with African Americans often supporting the trial's outcome, and whites often believing that he was guilty. In 1997, Simpson was held liable in a civil trial for the deaths of his wife and her friend.

The murder trial of O. J. Simpson was an unprecedented media spectacle. One explanation for the disproportionate interest in this trial lies in its resonance with American narratives surrounding issues of race and interracial relationships. Irrespective of O. J. Simpson's actual innocence or guilt, the murder of Nicole Simpson validated American mythologies regarding the dangerous consequences of interracial sexuality for white women and simultaneously portraits of the black male as a sexual predator.

The fascination with the purportedly threatening aspects of African-American sexuality is at the heart of America's love affair with the Simpson narratives. Characterizations of African-American men as sexual predators have roots in the genesis of the American experiment and the justification of slavery. Popular narratives abound that connect O. J. Simpson and Nicole Brown Simpson with these images. The pervasive presence of the Simpson trials in the media and interest in and knowledge of the case confirm America's ongoing obsession with the particulars of race. Toni Morrison reflects on these obsessions in her edited collection *Birth of a Nation'hood: Gaze, Script and Spectacle in the O. J. Simpson Trial* (1997).

BIBLIOGRAPHY

Barbieri, Paula. *The Other Woman: My Years with O. J. Simpson.* New York: Warner Books, 1997.

Bosco, Joseph. *A Problem of Evidence: How the Prosecution Freed O. J. Simpson.* New York: William Morrow, 1996.

Bugliosi, Vincent T. *Outrage: The Five Reasons Why O. J. Simpson Got Away with Murder.* New York: Dell Publishing Company, 1997.

Clark, Marsha. *Without a Doubt.* New York: Penguin USA, 1998.

Cochran, Jhonnie L. *Journey to Justice.* New York: Ballantine Books, 1996.

Dunne, Dominick. *Another City, Not My Own: A Novel in the Form of a Memoir.* New York: Random House, 1998.

Geis, Gilbert. *Crimes of the Century: From Leopold and Loeb to O. J. Simpson.* Boston: Northeastern University Press, 1998.

Gibbs, Jewelle Taylor. *Race and Justice: Rodney King and O. J. Simpson in a House Divided.* New York: Jossey-Bass, 1996.

Hoffer, William. *His Name Is Ron: Our Search for Justice.* New York: Avon, 1997.

Hutchinson, Earl Ofrai. *Beyond O. J.: Race, Sex, and Class Lessons for America.* Montreal: Black Rose Books, 1997.

Morrison, Toni. *Birth of a Nation'hood: Gaze, Script and Spectacle in the O. J. Simpson Trial.* New York: Pantheon Books, 1997.

Shapiro, Robert L. *Search for Justice: A Defense Attorney's Brief on the O. J. Simpson Case.* New York: Warner Books, 1996.

Weston, Crystal H. "Orenthal James Simpson and Gender, Class, and Race: In That Order." In *Critical Race Feminism: A Reader,* edited by Adrien Katherine Wing. New York: New York University Press, 1997.

slave narratives The slave narratives were first-person accounts by American slaves of their experiences as slaves. These were written both during and after emancipation. The narratives have become critical historical documents about life in the American South—and, to some degree, in the North—as well as philosophical treatises about freedom and the nature of the United States.

The American slave narratives may be dated back to Briton Hammon, who wrote *A Narrative of the Uncommon Sufferings and Surprising Deliverance of Briton Hammon, a Negro Man* (1760). There is some debate over whether he was an indentured servant or a slave, but his writing is considered the first African-American prose in North America.

Another slave narrative from the 18th century was *An Interesting Narrative of the Life of Olaudah Equiano* (1787). Equiano became one of the most widely read authors of African descent in the English-speaking world, and he is often credited with being among the most influential creators of the slave narrative.

The most famous of the slave narratives were written by such 19th-century writers as Nat Turner,

Frederick Douglass, William Wells Brown, and Harriet Jacobs. Their writings not only describe their personal experiences trying to survive and attempts at freedom, but also comment on the hypocrisy of a nation that allowed slavery and yet insisted, as Thomas Jefferson wrote, that "all men are created equal." Jefferson himself owned slaves. These first-person accounts of the cruelty and humiliation of slavery helped strengthen the ABOLITIONist cause.

At the turn of the 20th century, the most widely read slave narrative was *Up from Slavery* (1901), by BOOKER T. WASHINGTON. It described the rise of Washington from slavery to a position of leadership in the African-American community but also outlined his vision of how black Americans could eventually become fully accepted citizens of the United States through their labor.

An important source of slave narratives in the 20th century occurred between 1936 and 1938, during the Great DEPRESSION, when the Works Progress Administration financed writers to interview over 2,300 former slaves. Mostly born toward the end of slavery, these men and women described their experiences on plantations and in the cities. In these remarkable interviews, the former slaves discussed the lives they led, the nature of slavery, the relationships between masters and slaves, the role of religion in their lives and the slavery system, and their struggles for freedom.

Beloved (1987) is considered to be a fictional neo-slave narrative.

BIBLIOGRAPHY

Andrews, William L., and Henry Louis Gates Jr., eds. *Six Women's Slave Narratives.* New York: Oxford University Press, 1988.

———, eds. *Slave Narratives.* New York: Library of America, 2000.

Berlin, Ira, Marc Favreau, and Steven F. Miller, eds. *Remembering Slavery: African Americans Talk about Their Personal Experiences of Slavery and Emancipation.* New York: New Press, 1998.

Blassingame, John W., ed. *Slave Testimony: Two Centuries of Letters, Speeches, Interviews, and Autobiographies.* Baton Rouge: Louisiana State University Press, 1977.

Botkin, B. A., ed. *Lay My Burden Down: A Folk History of Slavery.* New York: Delta, 1994.

Curtin, Philip D., ed. *Africa Remembered: Narratives by West Africans from the Era of the Slave Trade.* Madison: University of Wisconsin Press, 1967.

Douglass, Frederick. *Autobiographies: Narrative of the Life; My Bondage and My Freedom; Life and Times.* New York: Library of America, 1994.

Ferguson, Moira, ed. *The History of Mary Prince: A West Indian Slave—Related by Herself.* Ann Arbor: University of Michigan Press, 1997.

Gates, Henry Louis, Jr., and Charles T. Davis, eds. *The Slave's Narrative.* New York: Oxford University Press, 1985.

Jacobs, Harriet. *Incidents in the Life of a Slave Girl, Written by Herself.* Cambridge, Mass.: Harvard University Press, 1987.

Mellon, James, ed. *Bullwhip Days: The Slaves Remember.* New York: Weidenfeld and Nicolson, 1988.

Meltzer, Milton. *The Black Americans: A History in Their Own Words, 1619–1983.* New York: Harper and Row, 1984.

Osofsky, Gilbert, ed. *Puttin' On Ole Massa. The Slave Narratives of Henry Bibb, William Wells Brown and Solomon Northup.* New York: Harper and Row, 1969.

Perdue, Charles L., Jr., Thomas E. Barden, and Robert K. Phillips, eds. *Weevils in the Wheat: Interviews with Virginia Ex-Slaves.* Charlottesville: University of Virginia Press, 1992.

Porter, Dorothy, ed. *Early Negro Writing 1760–1837.* Baltimore: Black Classic Press, 1994.

Taylor, Yuval, ed. *I Was Born a Slave: An Anthology of Classic Slave Narratives.* Chicago: Lawrence Hill Books, 1999.

Washington, Booker T. *Up from Slavery.* 1901. New York: Penguin, 1986.

Yetman, Norman R., ed. *Voices from Slavery: 100 Authentic Slave Narratives.* Mineola, N.Y.: Dover Publications, 2000.

Smith, Bessie (1895?–1937) Smith was one of the great BLUES singers of the 1920s and early 1930s. During her career, she became the most prominent black performer in the country as well as a great influence on both singers and instrumentalists in both the blues and JAZZ.

Born in Chattanooga, Tennessee, Smith began as a street musician. She later went on the road with Ma Rainey's traveling show, the Rabbit Foot Minstrels. Smith eventually ended up in the vaudeville circuit, where she became one of the most in-demand blues singers. Her first recording, *Down Hearted Blues,* released in 1923, was a hit, selling over two million copies in its first year. From then on, she continued to make recordings and tour the country, becoming the highest-paid black entertainer at the time.

Smith recorded with many of the jazz greats of her day, including Louis Armstrong, Fletcher Henderson, Charlie Green, and James P. Johnson. Her voice was rough and earthy, able to convey a great range of emotion, but it was also strong and clear, often soaring. Smith's career faltered somewhat in the 1930s. In 1937, she got into a car accident and was driven to a hospital for African Americans. Her arm was amputated, but she never regained consciousness.

Bessie Smith is referenced in Morrison's novel *Sula* (1973).

BIBLIOGRAPHY

Bessie Smith Songbook. Frank Music Corp., 1994.

Davis, Angela Yvonne. *Blues Legacies and Black Feminism: Gertrude 'Ma' Rainey, Bessie Smith, and Billie Holiday.* New York: Pantheon, 1998.

Feinstein, Elaine. *Bessie Smith: Empress of the Blues.* New York: Macmillan, 1975.

Fraher, James. *The Blues Is a Feeling: Voices and Visions of African-American Blues Musicians.* Mount Horeb, Wis.: Midwest Traditions, 1998.

Welding, Pete. *Bluesland: Portraits of Twelve Major American Blues Masters.* New York: E. P. Dutton, 1992.

Society of Friends (Quakers)   Known also as the Quakers, the Society of Friends is a Protestant denomination whose central tenet is that no official priest or rite is needed to establish communion between the soul and God and that all divine truth can be received by a person's inner light supplied by the Holy Spirit.

In their services—often called unprogrammed meetings—the Society's worship is often without a set form or leaders. Any member can follow his or her impulse of the moment and speak spontaneously in prayer or exhortation. It is possible that a meeting may be spent entirely in silent reflection. The Society's ministers are not generally required to have special training. Any sincere member who experiences the call may serve as minister.

Founded by George Fox in the 17th century, the Society of Friends was considered separatist in that it regarded the sacraments of the church as nonessential to Christian life. They refused to attend worship in the established church or pay tithes. They also refused to take oaths or fight in any war.

Another central tenet is their belief in the equality of all men and women. Quakers do not see religious or political superiors as above the common person. For this belief, they were persecuted until the passage of the Toleration Act of 1689. Because of their belief in the equality of all people, the Society of Friends provided some of the first and most vocal opponents of slavery in the United States. Slave traders could not join the Society. By 1775, the Society founded the first American antislavery group. The Society inspired other ABOLITIONists, and by the 1830s antislavery had become a major political issue in the United States.

In *Beloved* (1987) the Bodwins are Quakers and their intervention assists in Sethe's release from jail.

BIBLIOGRAPHY

Fletcher, J., and C. Mabee. *A Quaker Speaks from the Black Experience: The Life and Selected Writings of Barrington Dunbar.* New York: New York Yearly Meeting, 1979.

Harrison, E. C. *For Emancipation and Education: Some Black and Quaker Efforts 1680–1900.* Philadelphia: Awbury Arboretum Association, 1997.

Ives, K., ed. *Black Quakers: Brief Biographies.* Chicago: Progressive Publishers, 1991.

Soderlund, J. R. *Quakers and Slavery: A Divided Spirit.* Princeton, N.J.: Princeton University Press, 1985.

The Song of Solomon   The Song of Solomon—also called the Song of Songs—is a book from the

Hebrew Bible, or Old Testament. It is part of the Hebrew Bible called the Megillot, or Five Scrolls. The other books are Ruth, Lamentations, Ecclesiastes, and Esther. These books are often read as part of various Jewish festivals.

The Song of Solomon is a collection of poems about erotic love between a bride and bridegroom. It takes the form of a dialogue as the two take turns expressing their love and passion for one another. "Let him kiss me with the kisses of his mouth," says the bride in chapter one, "for thy love is better than wine." Says the groom in chapter seven: "Thy navel is like a round goblet, which wanteth not liquor: thy belly is like an heap of wheat set about with lilies."

The text implies that the bride is of more humble background than the groom, who might be Solomon himself. Her darker skin is a marker that indicates a life worked outdoors. "I am black, but comely," she says in chapter 1. She later implores: "Look not upon me, because I am black, because the sun hath looked upon me: my mother's children were angry with me; they made me the keeper of the vineyards . . ."

According to tradition, King Solomon is credited with having authored the book, along with two others in the Old Testament, Proverbs and Ecclesiastes. Song of Solomon is thought to have been written when he was a young man, and passionate love was uppermost on his mind. Proverbs is thought to have been written when he was middle-aged and gaining the wisdom of the passing years. Finally, Ecclesiastes is thought to have been written when he was old and wondering about the meaning of life as he faced his own mortality. Some theologians believe, however, that Song of Solomon was not written by Solomon, but might have simply been dedicated to him. The date of its writing is sometimes put after Solomon lived and as late as the third century B.C., several centuries after Solomon ruled Israel.

Though it is included in the both the Jewish and Christian Bibles, The Song of Solomon does not mention God. Its inclusion in the religious canon has been read and justified as an allegory of the love between God and Israel, with God being the groom, or, in the Christian tradition, between Jesus and his church, with Jesus being the groom.

The title of Morrison's *Song of Solomon* (1977) is an allusion to the biblical text.

BIBLIOGRAPHY

Dillow, Joseph C. *Solomon on Sex*. Nashville, Tenn.: Thomas Nelson, 1977.

Falk, Marcia. *Love Lyrics from the Bible: A Translation and Literary Study of the Song of Songs*. Sheffield: Almond Press, 1982.

Fuerst, W. J. *The Song of Songs*. Cambridge: Cambridge University Press, 1975.

Landry, Francis. *Paradoxes of Paradise: Identity and Differences in the Song of Songs*. Sheffield: Almond Press, 1983.

Olhsen, W. *Perspectives on Old Testament Literature*. New York: Harcourt, Brace, 1978.

Seerveld, Calvin. *The Greatest Song*. Amsterdam: Trinity Pennyasheet Press, 1967.

spirituals   In the United States, spirituals are songs, or hymns, that are sung in church. Though their expression has varied from one culture or region to another, the term "spiritual" is most often associated with the traditions of African-American services originating in southern congregations.

Early in U.S. history, the African-American spirituals were adapted from hymns sung in white churches. The lyrics were usually related to biblical passages. Of particular interest to black congregations were texts taken from the Old Testament that spoke of the Israelite struggles for freedom. In this way, American slaves were able to express their own yearnings to be free.

Black congregations added African musical forms to the spiritual. As sung in black churches, the spiritual became an outwardly emotional, often melancholic song characterized by syncopation and polyrhythms. Another African influence is the call-and-response and the freer improvisations during the singing. The more joyous spirituals have been an influence on gospel music.

There are spirituals and references to spirituals throughout Morrison's canon.

BIBLIOGRAPHY

Epstien, Dena J. *Sinful Tunes and Spirituals: Black Folk Music to the Civil War*. Urbana: University of Illinois Press, 1977.

Jones, Art. *Wade in the Water: The Wisdom of the Spirituals*. Maryknoll, N.Y.: Orbis Books, 1993.

Katz, Bernard, ed. *The Social Implications of Early Negro Music in the United States.* New York: Arno Press and the New York Times, 1969.

Levine, Lawrence. *Black Culture and Black Consciousness: Afro-American Folk Thought from Slavery to Freedom.* New York: Oxford University Press, 1977.

Reagon, Bernice Johnson. *If You Don't Go, Don't Hinder Me: The African American Sacred Song Tradition.* Lincoln: University of Nebraska Press, 2001.

Stagger Lee In African-American legend, Stagger Lee was a cold-blooded murderer and symbol of the bad man stereotype. His crime and character became the popular subject of various blues songs, folksongs, and tales.

The character is apparently based on a man named Lee Sheldon, whose crime took place in 1895 in St. Louis, Missouri. In that crime, Sheldon shot a man during an argument, and, while the man lay wounded, begging for his life, Sheldon apparently left him to die. The man's actual name and the events vary according to the historian and singer. Some historians actually place the source of the name Stagger Lee to events before 1895. Variations of the name of this figure are Stagolee, Stack O'Lee, and Stack-a-Lee.

Sung in African-American communities along the lower Mississippi River during the 1910s, the song was first recorded by folklorist John Lomax in 1919. There have since been hundreds of versions of the song, recorded by such artists as DUKE ELLINGTON, Woody Guthrie, the Isley Brothers, the Grateful Dead, and Lloyd Price. Mississippi John Hurt recorded what some music historians consider to be the definitive version of the song because its story has elements from all the other versions.

In African-American communities, Stagger Lee's badness became an archetype for a certain kind of black male character. In some versions of the song, he is so bad that the police are too frightened of him to arrest him. In other versions, the judge is too frightened to send him to prison because he is afraid Stagger Lee will somehow get back at him. In yet other versions, Stagger Lee is executed, but he is so bad that he takes over hell. Stagger Lee is an important figure in African-American culture as he represents defiance and resistance to institutionalized oppression.

In *TAR BABY* (1981), the narrator compares Son and other wandering men with Stagger Lee.

BIBLIOGRAPHY

Brown, Cecil. "The Real Stagger Lee," *Mojo* 126 (January 1996): 77–78.

Levine, Lawrence W. *Black Culture and Black Consciousness.* New York: Oxford University Press, 1977.

Lomax, John, and Alan Lomax. *American Ballads and Folk Songs.* New York: Macmillan, 1934.

Stepin Fetchit (Lincoln Perry) (1902–1985) Stepin Fetchit was the stage name of Lincoln Perry, an actor whose roles were limited to the African-American stereotype of the day as slow-witted, slow-moving simpleton. Though the role is still considered controversial, Perry's reputation has been somewhat rehabilitated in recognition of his great talent as a physical comedian.

Born Lincoln Theodore Monroe Andrew Perry in Key West, Florida, to West Indian immigrant parents, he became a comic performer as a teenager, eventually creating the character of "the laziest man in the world." Perry achieved tremendous success in film during the 1930s, becoming the first African-American actor to become a millionaire, and some film historians consider his fame as trailblazing for African Americans trying to enter the American film industry.

Perry's Stepin Fetchit can be traced to the coon figure stereotype, a caricature who was supposed to have undermined his white slave-owners by pretending to be lazy and stupid. Thus, the character has an element of the TRICKSTER in it, though it is primarily criticized for promoting a black stereotype. Perry's best roles were with Will Rogers, including *Steamboat Round the Bend*, directed by John Ford. By the 1940s, Perry no longer appeared in films meant for white audiences, instead acting in films meant for black audiences, where he continued to play the same role.

By the 1940s, his career suffered because his character was considered an insult to African-American audiences. Without his signature role, he could find no acting work. Due to mismanagement of his money, Perry was bankrupt by 1947. His reputation was rehabilitated late in life. In 1976, the NAACP gave Perry a Special Image Award for helping to open doors for blacks in the movie industry. In 1978, he was inducted into the Black Filmmakers Hall of Fame.

Stepin Fetchit is referenced in Morrison's *Sula* (1973).

BIBLIOGRAPHY

Bogle, Donald. *Toms, Coons, Mulattoes, Mammies, and Bucks: An Interpretive History of Blacks in American Films.* New York: Continuum, 2001.

Watkins, Mel. *Stepin Fetchit: The Life and Times of Lincoln Perry.* New York: Pantheon, 2005.

T

Tar Baby JOEL CHANDLER HARRIS is credited with publishing the classic American version of the tar baby tale, a story in his collection of Uncle Remus tales. The Uncle Remus tales came out of Chandler's experiences as an adolescent working for Joseph Addison Turner, the owner of Turnwold Plantation. While working for Turner, Chandler had the opportunity to interact with and to listen to the stories of Turner's slaves, particularly of those he knew as Uncle George Terrell, Old Harbert, and Aunt Crissy. Chandler also read collections of African-American folklore.

Chandler's "Wonderful Tar Baby Story" (1881) is the blueprint for the many versions of the story published subsequently, including the well-known Disney animated version incorporated into the live-action movie *Song of the South* (1946). The basic tar baby story is as follows: In an effort to catch and eat B'rer Rabbit, B'rer Fox creates a figure out of tar and turpentine, places a hat on top of the heap, and sets it by the side of the road. B'rer Fox hides and waits for B'rer Rabbit to pass by. When B'rer Rabbit discovers the tar baby, he attempts to speak to it and gets angry when the tar baby does not respond. B'rer Rabbit's anger grows until he hits the figure and becomes stuck in the tar. B'rer Fox emerges and mocks B'rer Rabbit's situation. B'rer Rabbit convinces B'rer Fox to throw him into the brier patch, claiming that the brier patch represents a worse fate than becoming B'rer Fox's dinner. Once in the briar patch, his home, B'rer Rabbit is able to free himself from the tar and B'rer Fox. B'rer Rabbit is a TRICKSTER figure who outsmarts his more powerful adversary. Morrison refers to the tar baby story with her novel of the same name.

In American history, the term tar baby has also had other meanings. The name has been used as a negative slang for an African-American person, particularly for African-American children. The words also have a history of use as a description of a difficult or sticky situation for which a solution or escape is hard to find.

BIBLIOGRAPHY

Bickley, R. Bruce. *Joel Chandler Harris.* Boston: Twayne, 1978.

Birnbaum, Mihele, "Dark Dialects: Scientific and Literary Realism in Joel Chandler Harris's, Uncle Remus Series," *New Orleans Review* 18 (Spring 1991): 36–45.

Harris, Joel Chandler. *Uncle Remus.* New York: D. Appleton and Company, 1895.

Keenan, Hugh. "Twisted Tales: Propaganda in the Tar-Baby Stories," *Southern Quarterly* 22 (Winter 1984): 54–69.

Montenyohl, Eric L. "The Origins of Uncle Remus," *Folklore Forum* 18, no. 2 (Spring 1986): 136–167.

Temple, Shirley (1928–   ) In contrast to the realities of the Great DEPRESSION, the Hollywood films of the 1930s were often produced with the deliberate intention of providing audiences with an escape by creating stories that portrayed a world of happy idealism. With her 56 blond ringlets, her bright blue eyes, her endearing lisp, and her song and dance routines, Shirley Temple was the star of the era and the symbol of an imaginary, trouble-free innocence. The fantastic world inhabited by Temple differs markedly from the one Morrison creates for her characters Claudia and Pecola in *The Bluest Eye* (1970).

Born on April 23, 1928, in California, Shirley Jane Temple was the youngest of three children. Her mother, Gertrude Temple, was the force behind her daughter's success. At the age of four, Temple was cast in a series of one-reel films entitled *Baby Burlesks* (1932). As Temple began to take bit roles in feature films, she was eventually cast in the movie, *Stand Up and Cheer* (1934). Her song and dance performances won her the attention of Hollywood's biggest producers. Within months of her performance, Temple began to receive contracts for lead roles.

In 1934, Temple received a special Academy Award in recognition of her contribution to American life in the midst of the Depression. Between 1934 and 1940, Temple appeared in 24 motion pictures. Among her most popular films were *Little Miss Marker* (1934), *The Littlest Rebel* (1935), *Poor Little Rich Girl* (1936), *Captain January* (1936), *Heidi* (1937), and *Rebecca of Sunnybrook Farm* (1938). Temple became especially well-known for her tap dance routines with African-American performer BILL "BOJANGLES" ROBINSON.

By 1938, Temple was a huge box office success and had become a national icon. Americans purchased representations of her likeness on books, buttons, paper dolls, cups, bowls, coloring books, ribbons, and soapboxes. Morrison uses such a bowl to demonstrate Pecola's obsession with Temple and blue eyes in *The Bluest Eye* (1970).

Contests were held across America featuring girls who looked, dressed, and performed like Temple. Eventually, the popularity Temple achieved deteriorated as she began to outgrow her baby-faced appeal. As an adult, Temple, known as Shirley Temple Black after her marriage to Charles Black, abandoned her film work for a career in politics and international diplomacy, but her indelible imprint on the popular culture of the United States and on the definition of ideal girlhood remains relatively undisturbed.

BIBLIOGRAPHY

Hammontree, Patsy G. *Shirley Temple Black: A Bio-Bibliography.* Westport, Conn.: Greenwood Press, 1998.

Thomas, Clarence (1948–)   Clarence Thomas is a Supreme Court associate justice and the second African American to hold that position in the Court's history, having replaced Thurgood Marshall, the first African American to serve on the high court. Unlike Marshall, however, Thomas is considered to be a political conservative.

His appointment to the Court by President George H. W. Bush in 1991 was particularly controversial. Though he replaced the only other African American to sit on the bench, Thomas's legal thought was far to the right of Marshall's. Organizations like the NAACP and the Urban League opposed Thomas because of his criticism of affirmative action. The National Organization for Woman (NOW) opposed his nomination because it felt he did not support the Supreme Court decision *Roe v. Wade* that legalized abortion. The American Bar Association was lukewarm about his nomination, rating him using their ranking system from qualified to unqualified.

In addition, a former colleague of Thomas's, Anita Hill, a University of Oklahoma law school professor, accused him of sexually harassing her when the two had worked together at the Equal Employment Opportunity Commission (EEOC). In a widely televised hearing, the Senate Judiciary Committee did not find Hill's position to be strong enough to deny Thomas a seat on the Court.

Since he has been on the bench, Thomas has fulfilled the expectations—of both critics and supporters—that his judicial philosophy is on the far right, voting consistently with fellow conservatives Antonin Scalia and, until his passing, Chief Justice William Rehnquist. In 1992, Morrison published her edited collection, *Race-Ing Justice, En-Gendering Power: Essays on Anita Hill, Clarence Thomas, and the Construction of Social Reality*, a book of essays on the Clarence Thomas hearings.

BIBLIOGRAPHY

Chrisman, Robert, and Robert L. Allen, ed. *Court of Appeal: The Black Community Speaks Out on the Racial and Sexual Politics of Clarence Thomas vs. Anita Hill.* New York: Ballantine Books, 1992.

Danforth, John C. *Resurrection: The Confirmation of Clarence Thomas.* New York: Viking, 1994.

Flax, Jane. *The American Dream in Black and White: The Clarence Thomas Hearings.* Ithaca, N.Y.: Cornell University Press, 1998.

Gerber, Scott Douglass. *First Principles: The Jurisprudence of Clarence Thomas.* New York: New York University Press, 1999.

Jordan, Emma C. *Race, Gender, and Power in America: The Legacy of the Hill-Thomas Hearings.* New York: Oxford University Press, 1995.

Mayer, Jane, and Jill Abramson. *Strange Justice: The Selling of Clarence Thomas.* Boston: Houghton Mifflin, 1994.

Morrison, Toni, ed. *Race-ing Justice, En-gendering Power: Essays on Anita Hill, Clarence Thomas, and the Construction of Social Reality.* New York: Pantheon Books, 1992.

Phelps, Timothy M. *Capitol Games: Clarence Thomas, Anita Hill, and the Story of a Supreme Court Nomination.* New York: Hyperion, 1992.

Roberts, Ronald Suresh. *Clarence Thomas and the Tough Love Crowd: Counterfeit Heroes and Unhappy Truths.* New York: New York University Press, 1995.

Simon, Paul. *Advice and Consent: Clarence Thomas, Robert Bork, and the Intriguing History of the Supreme Court's Nomination Battles.* Washington, D.C.: National Press Books, 1992.

Smith, Christopher E. *Critical Judicial Nominations and Political Change: The Impact of Clarence Thomas.* Westport, Conn.: Praeger, 1993.

Smith, Christopher E., and Joyce A. Baugh. *The Real Clarence Thomas: Confirmation Veracity Meets Performance Reality.* New York: Peter Lang, 2000.

Smitherman, Geneva. *African American Women Speak out on Anita Hill–Clarence Thomas.* Detroit: Wayne State University Press, 1995.

Thomas, Clarence. *Clarence Thomas—Confronting the Future: Selections from the Senate Confirmation Hearings and Prior Speeches.* Washington, D.C.: Regnery Gateway, 1992.

Till, Emmett (1941–1955) Born on July 25, 1941, Emmett Louis Till became a central symbol of the extreme barbarism of southern racism in the segregationist South. Born to Louis and Mamie Bradley Till outside of Chicago, Illinois, by all accounts Till was a bright and precocious young man. During the summer of his 14th year, Mamie Till, in the process of recovering from her second divorce, sent her son south to visit with her family in Tallahatchie County, Mississippi. Till stayed at the home of his great uncle, Moses Wright.

On August 24, 1955, a week after his arrival in Mississippi, Till and several other young boys traveled to the nearby town of Money, in Leflore County. While in Money, Till and his companions visited Bryant's Grocery and Meat Market, a small establishment owned by Roy Bryant that primarily served the black community in Money.

According to the boys accompanying Till, the young man, while standing outside of the store, took a picture of a white woman out of his wallet and boasted that the photo was of his girlfriend back in Chicago. Subsequently, some of the boys dared Till to go into the store and flirt with Mrs. Bryant. Till went into the store while his friends watched from outside through a window.

What transpired in the store is a matter of some controversy. By some accounts, Till is said to have grabbed Mrs. Bryant's hand while paying for candy and asked her on a date. Others present reported that Till paid for the candy, whistled, and said, "Bye, baby," to Caroline Bryant. In any case, Till's cousins, knowing that Till's actions were dangerous in the segregated South, hurried him away from the store.

Two days later, Roy Bryant returned from a trip to Texas. Learning of Emmett Till's interactions with his wife, Bryant, along with his half-brother J. W. "Big" Milam, went in search of young Till. Arriving at Moses Wright's house in the early hours of the morning, Bryant and Milam kidnapped Till and carried him in the back of their pickup truck to Milam's house. According to the men's later paid confession in *Look* magazine, they drove Till to Milam's house and pistol-whipped the boy in a tool house in the backyard. The men then drove Till to the Progressive Ginning Company near the town of Boyle, where they found a large, discarded gin mill fan. They made Till carry the fan down to the Tallahatchie River and undress. Bryant and Milam then shot Till near his ear, wrapped barbed wire around his neck and attached the wire to the fan. Thus weighed down, Milam and Bryant threw Till's body into the Tallahatchie River.

Three days later, the mutilated and decomposed body of Emmett Till was discovered and removed from the river. At the time of his murder, Till wore a ring, the one piece of evidence that allowed his mother to identify her son when his body was returned to Chicago. Heroically, Mamie Till demanded that her son have an open casket funeral so that "the world can see what they did to my boy." The shocking photographs of Emmett Till's corpse were published in newspapers and magazines throughout the United States and the world. Exposure of the brutality of Till's murder helped to generate support for the elimination of racial violence and segregation and motivated the continuing efforts of those who were fighting for African-American civil rights.

In spite of her courage, Mamie Till did not experience justice in the American legal system. On September 23, 1955, the all-white jury took less than 70 minutes to find Bryant and Milam innocent. Later the men told the story of their torture and murder of Emmett Till to *Look* magazine. The interview was published as an article entitled, "The Shocking Story of Approved Killing in Mississippi." In the article, Milam claimed that the brothers had only wanted to frighten Till in order to get him to admit that he had done something wrong. According to Milam, Till would not acknowledge blame and so the men killed him.

The Till story not only inspired civil rights activists, the crime also moved artists to memorialize the murdered boy. There have been poems, songs, and ballads written about Till by various artists, including Bob Dylan, GWENDOLYN BROOKS, and JAMES BALDWIN. Toni Morrison references the killing in *Song of Solomon* (1977) and *Love* (2003), and Till's story is the subject of her only play, *Dreaming Emmett* (1986).

BIBLIOGRAPHY

Colin, Mattie Smith. "Till's Mom, Digs Both Disappointed." *Chicago Defender*, October 1, 1955.

Colin, Mattie Smith, and Elliott Colin. "Mother Waits in Vain For Her 'Bo.'" *Chicago Defender*, August 28, 1955.

Dray, Phillip. *At the Hands of Persons Unknown.* New York: Random House, 2002.

Eisenhower, Dwight D. *Waging Peace.* Garden City, N.Y.: Doubleday, 1965.

Elliot, Robert. "Thousands at Rites for Till." *Chicago Defender*, September 3, 1955.

Ginzburg, Ralph. *100 Years of Lynching.* Baltimore, Md.: Black Classic Press, 1962.

Hampton, Henry, and Steve Fayer, with Sarah Flynn. *Voices of Freedom: An Oral History of the Civil Rights Movement from the 1950s through the 1980s.* New York: Bantam, 1991.

Huie, William Bradford. "The Shocking Story of Approved Killing in Mississippi." *Look*, January 15, 1956.

Kilgallen, James L. "Mose Wright Fingers Milam and Bryant." *Chicago Defender*, September 17, 1955.

Metress, Christopher. *The Lynching of Emmett Till.* Charlottesville: University of Virginia Press, 2002.

Newson, Moses. "Emmett's Kin Hang on to Harvest Crop." *Chicago Defender*, September 17, 1955.

Tolnay, Stewart E., and E. M. Beck. *A Festival of Violence.* Chicago: University of Illinois Press, 1995.

Vollers, Maryanne. *Ghosts of Mississippi.* Boston: Little, Brown, 1995.

Tillie the Toiler *Tillie the Toiler* was a newspaper comic strip that first appeared in 1921. Distributed by King Features Syndicate and created by Russell Channing Westover, *Tillie the Toiler* was about a working girl, Tillie Jones, who worked for a women's fashion wear company.

During World War II, Tillie aided the war effort and joined the U.S. Army, but she eventually returned to her fashion company, where she worked mostly in an office but also sometimes modeled. Always stylishly dressed, the story line often had her pursuing charming and wealthy men, who changed frequently. Clarence "Mac" MacDougall, a short, big-nosed co-worker, loved her but she never reciprocated.

Tillie the Toiler was one of several female characters in the comics that showed women working outside the home. She reflected the slowly changing attitudes of America toward women, which sometimes allowed for an independent "career girl." The strip ended in 1959. Films entitled *Tillie the Toiler,* based on the strip, were made in 1929 and in 1941.

Tillie the Toiler is referenced in Morrison's novel *Sula* (1973).

BIBLIOGRAPHY

Tillie the Toiler (1927). Metro-Goldwyn-Mayers, Film, 1927.

Tillie the Toiler (1941). Metro-Goldwyn-Mayers, Film, 1941.

Westover, Russ. *Tillie the Toiler.* New York: Cupples and Leon Company, 1927.

Toni Morrison Society   In 1993, Professor Carolyn Denard, then of Georgia State University, initiated the birth of the Toni Morrison Society at the annual convention of the American Literature Association, an organization that fosters the growth and development of societies devoted to the study and promotion of the works of individual American authors. The American Literature Association supports the Coalition of American Author Societies, and the Toni Morrison Society is one of the members of the coalition. The official founding date of the Toni Morrison Society is May 28, 1993, in Baltimore, Maryland.

According to its literature, the purpose of the society is "to initiate, sponsor, and encourage critical dialogue, scholarly publications, conferences and projects devoted to the study of the life and works of Toni Morrison." The Toni Morrison Society has more than 200 members worldwide. The Toni Morrison Society convenes at biennial meetings devoted to analysis and exploration of the works of Toni Morrison. Conferences have been held since 1998 in the cities of Atlanta, Georgia; LORAIN, OHIO; Washington, D.C.; and CINCINNATI, OHIO, each of which has a special relevance to Toni Morrison and her work. The Toni Morrison Society sponsors a book prize for the best work on Toni Morrison's writing in a given year.

BIBLIOGRAPHY

The Toni Morrison Society. Available online. URL: http://www.tonimorrisonsociety.org/. Accessed on September 22, 2006.

Toomer, Jean (1894–1967)   Jean Toomer's maternal grandfather was P. B. S. Pinchback, the first African American elected as lieutenant governor and then to serve as acting governor of the state of Louisiana. Pinchback was born free. His daughter, Nina Pinchback, was Jean Toomer's mother. Toomer was born December 26, 1894. Toomer's father abandoned the family, and Jean Toomer and his mother lived with P. B. S. Pinchback, who had relocated to Washington, D.C. As a boy, Toomer was frequently ill, a circumstance that seems to have colored his experience and perceptions of the world. When Toomer's mother died in 1909, he remained with his grandparents for the remainder of his childhood. Following his graduation from Dunbar High School in Washington, D.C., Jean Toomer attended many institutions of higher education, but he never graduated from any of them.

Jean Toomer published CANE in 1923 to strong reviews. Many literary critics note the publication of *Cane* as the beginning of what is known as the HARLEM RENAISSANCE, the literary time period, roughly between World War I and World War II, when African-American literary artists such as Claude McKay, Zora Neale Hurston, Langston Hughes, and many others produced a number of significant American literary works. The Harlem Renaissance was a period in which African-American artists in other genres, such as art, music, and theater, also produced a great number of significant works.

Cane is an elliptical work, meaning that its primary textual energy moves in circular patterns. The entire text creates a type of thematic circle that takes the reader through the experience of migration. During the time Toomer wrote *Cane,* many African Americans were in the process of migrating from the South to the North in record numbers. The causes of that movement, known as the GREAT MIGRATION, were complicated and various. Generally, African Americans left the South in search of economic opportunities, in an attempt to flee random and systematic racial violence, and in an effort to live in a place where segregation did not entirely control the ability to vote, to own land and property, and to attend schools.

Jean Toomer captured the violent, wistful, transient, poignant currents of this time period in African-American history with *Cane*. The novel moves from the South to the North and returns to end in the South again. With that movement, Toomer captures the feeling of the transition from rural south to city and back again. The city in which Toomer locates the urban section of his narrative is Washington, D.C., the city he was from, but also, and perhaps more importantly, the figurative and ideological center of the country. The movement to D.C. represents the hopefulness of the individuals relocating in the very site where they had, less than a century before, been granted citizenship and the rights therein with the ratification of the Thirteenth, Fourteenth, and Fifteenth Amendments to the Constitution. The return south in the final section of the novel is a wistful reminder that such a return is neither literally or figuratively possible. *Cane* represents the inauguration of the contemporary period of African-American literature. It shares many of the characteristics of the texts that are considered works of American modernism, such as ambiguity, fragmentation, experimentation with form, alienation, and, to some extent, hopelessness. *Cane* functions as a multi-genre text in that it is at once poetry, drama, and fiction.

Although Toomer has an extensive canon of other works, his literary reputation remains primarily linked to *Cane*. Contemporarily, Toomer is considered one of the most important American writers of the early 20th century. Morrison counts Toomer as an important influence on her work.

BIBLIOGRAPHY

Benson, Brian J., and Mabel M. Dillard. *Jean Toomer*. Boston: Twayne Press, 1980.

Byrd, Rudolph P. *Jean Toomer's Years with Gurdjieff: Portrait of an Artist, 1923–1936*. Athens: University of Georgia Press, 1990.

Jones, Robert B. *Jean Toomer and the Prison-House of Thought: A Phenomenology of the Spirit*. Amherst: University of Massachusetts Press, 1993.

Kerman, Cynthia E., and Richard Eldridge. *The Lives of Jean Toomer: A Hunger for Wholeness*. Baton Rouge: Louisiana State University Press, 1987.

Larson, Charles R. *Invisible Darkness: Jean Toomer and Nella Larsen*. Iowa City: University of Iowa Press, 1993.

McKay, Nellie Y. *Jean Toomer, Artist: A Study of His Literary Life and Work, 1894–1936*. Chapel Hill: University of North Carolina Press, 1984.

O'Daniel, Therman B., ed. *Jean Toomer: A Critical Evaluation*. Washington, D.C.: Howard University Press, 1988.

Scruggs, Charles W. *Jean Toomer and the Terrors of American History*. Philadelphia: University of Pennsylvania Press, 1998.

Toomer, Jean. *Cane*. New York: Liveright Publishing, 1997.

———. *Jean Toomer: Selected Essays and Literary Criticism*, edited by Robert B. Jones. Knoxville: University of Tennessee Press, 1997.

———. *The Collected Poems of Jean Toomer*, edited by Robert B. Jones and Margery Toomer Latimer. Chapel Hill: University of North Carolina Press, 1988.

Turner, Darwin T., ed. *The Wayward and the Seeking: A Collection of Writings by JT*. Washington, D.C.: Howard University Press, 1980.

———. *In a Minor Chord: Three Afro-American Writers and Their Search for Identity: Toomer, Cullen, Hurston*. Carbondale: Southern Illinois University Press, 1971.

Tower of Babel, the   The narrative of the Tower of Babel can be found in the Bible, specifically in the Old Testament book of Genesis. The narrative in Genesis 11:1–9 tells of the original inhabitants of the Earth, the descendants of Adam and Eve, who have a common language and identity. Fearing that they will disperse and be separated, they propose to build a tower to heaven so that they can establish a clear and unified identity.

God observes this endeavor and says that if this group is successful in what they are attempting to do, they will be limited only by their imaginations. In order to stop this from happening, God does not destroy the building, rather he causes the people to speak in other languages so that they cannot understand each other and thus are unable to complete building the tower. God then scatters the people to the far corners of the Earth. This story is an explanatory narrative that provides an answer for why there are different languages, cultures, and, perhaps, races.

The English word "babble" has its roots in this story. Toni Morrison refers to the Tower of Babel in her Nobel Prize acceptance speech. She challenges the idea that one language is superior to many different tongues and asks if the task of the people, rather than constructing a symbol of unification, should have been to learn to understand each other and to attempt to communicate.

BIBLIOGRAPHY

Gelb, I. J. "The Name of Babylon," *Journal of the Institute of Asian Studies* 1 (1955): 25–28.

Kramer, S. N. "The 'Babel of Tongues': A Sumerian Version," *Journal of the American Oriental Society* 88 (1968): 108–111.

Saggs, H. W. F. "Babylon." In *Archaeology and Old Testament Study,* edited by D. W. Thomas. Oxford: Clarendon, 1967.

trickster African-American trickster tales are a part of a larger tradition in folklore that is cross-cultural. Trickster characters appear in every type of story, and they are a part of both oral and written tales. African-American trickster tales began as a survival mechanism for slaves and borrow from African, European, and Native American storytelling traditions. African-American tricksters, like their African predecessors, often change shape from animal to human and sometimes appear as gods. The trickster in these tales reverses the roles of the powerful and the powerless by using wit. Always vulnerable to danger, the trickster outthinks and, inevitably, overcomes the adversary.

Although the trickster is a figure who just barely balances on the edges of danger and uncertainty, he or she also functions as a community role model by demonstrating subversive ways to survive. Most often the trickster manages to disrupt and triumph over the existing social order by bending and breaking its rules. The trickster is normally motivated by an overwhelming need to deceive and to consume food and/or common resources for selfish reasons, but often, inadvertently, brings prosperity, or at least the resolution of a problem, to his community. Possible Morrison trickster figures include Freddie from *Song of Solomon* (1977) and Son from *Tar Baby* (1981).

BIBLIOGRAPHY

Babcock-Abrahams, Barbara. "'A Tolerated Margin of Mess': The Trickster and His Tales Reconsidered," *Journal of the Folklore Institute* (November 1975): 147–186.

Biebuyck, Daniel, and Kahombo Mateene. *The Mwindo Epic: From the Banyanga.* Berkeley: University of California Press, 1971.

Bleek, Wilhelm. *Reynard the Fox in South Africa, or Hottentot Fables and Tales Chiefly Translated from Original Manuscripts in the Library of His Excellency Sir George Gray, K.C.B.* London: Trübner, 1864.

Doueihi, Ann. "Trickster: On Inhabiting the Space between Discourse and Story," *Soundings: An Interdisciplinary Journal* 67 (1984): 283–311.

Edwards, Viv, and Thomas J. Sienkewicz. *Oral Culture Past and Present: Rappin' and Homer.* Oxford: Blackwell, 1990.

Fine, Elizabeth C. *The Folklore Text: From Performance to Print.* Bloomington: Indiana University Press, 1994.

Goody, Jack, and Jan Watt. "The Consequences of Literacy." In *Literacy in Traditional Societies,* edited by Jack Goody. Cambridge: Cambridge University Press, 1968.

Truth, Sojourner (1797–1883) Sojourner Truth was an American evangelist and social reformer. As a self-taught speaker, she provided a compelling voice for the cause of ABOLITION directly from someone who had been a slave to white audiences. She also spoke out for the rights of women.

Born Isabella Baumfree to slave parents in a Dutch settlement in Ulster County, New York, Sojourner Truth spoke only Dutch until the age of 11, when she was sold from her family to an

English-speaking slaveholder. She was sold several times and experienced several cruel slave masters until 1827, when New York outlawed slavery. She initially made her living as a domestic servant.

She began preaching on street corners, adopting the name Sojourner Truth. She left New York for the Midwest to preach not only religion but also in behalf of abolition and women's rights. Using scripture to make her points, Sojourner Truth drew large crowds, which were moved by her oratory. She spoke firsthand of the cruelties of slavery.

When the American Civil War began, she helped gather supplies for African-American volunteers for the Northern army. In 1864, she helped integrate streetcars in Washington, D.C., where she also met with President Abraham Lincoln. After the war ended, she worked in the National Freedman's Relief Association, an organization dedicated to better conditions for the newly freed slaves.

Active into old age despite increasing medical problems, she died in a sanitarium in Battle Creek, Michigan.

Sojourner Truth is referenced in Morrison's novel *Beloved* (1987).

BIBLIOGRAPHY

Bernard, Jacqueline. *Journey toward Freedom; the Story of Sojourner Truth.* New York: Norton, 1967.

Fitch, Suzanne P., and Roseann M. Mandziuk. *Sojourner Truth as Orator: Wit, Story, and Song.* Westport, Conn.: Greenwood Press, 1997.

Mabee, Carleton, and Susan M. Newhouse. *Sojourner Truth—Slave, Prophet, Legend.* New York: New York University Press, 1993.

Painter, Nell I. *Sojourner Truth: A Life, a Symbol.* New York: W. W. Norton, 1996.

Stetson, Erlene, and Linda David. *Glorying in Tribulation: The Lifework of Sojourner Truth.* East Lansing: Michigan State University Press, 1994.

Truth, Sojourner. *Narrative of Sojourner Truth.* 1850. Salem, N.H.: Ayer Co., 1988.

Tulsa, Oklahoma, Riot   During the period following the end of the Civil War and until the years after World War I, African Americans were subjected to a backlash of racially based violence that was in part the catalyst for the GREAT MIGRATION of African Americans out of the Deep South states. Some of those individuals migrated to the western United States and settled in various locations, including the states of Kansas, Nebraska, and Oklahoma.

In the wake of World War I and with the return of African-American soldiers from Europe, riots broke out in various locations throughout the United States. One of the most ferocious and deadly occurred in 1921 in Tulsa, Oklahoma. The rioting in Tulsa began on the evening of May 31 and lasted for nearly 24 hours. The riot began after a false report in the *Tulsa Tribune* newspaper that a white woman had been assaulted in an elevator by a black man. Editorials in the newspaper called for vigilante violence. Although the official account of the events that occurred subsequently differs from the testimony of eyewitnesses, most historians believe that the riot included air bombings of the African-American community of Greenwood as well as widespread violence, looting, and burning perpetrated by white mobs that converged on the area.

According to most contemporary estimates, more than 300 African Americans were killed during the riots and approximately 36 blocks of residential and business property were destroyed. Following the riots, there are reports that African-American men were held for at least two months in internment camps. As a result of the violence, many African Americans fled the city permanently. The Greenwood section of Tulsa was rebuilt eventually, but it never regained the economic prosperity and social vibrancy it possessed before the riot.

In 1997, the Oklahoma legislature established the 1921 Tulsa Race Riot Commission. The commission determined that the surviving victims of the riot were entitled to compensation for the psychological, social, and economic trauma they experienced.

Morrison references the Tulsa Riots in her 1998 novel *Paradise*.

BIBLIOGRAPHY

Debo, Angie. *Tulsa: From Creek Town to Oil Capitol.* Norman: University of Oklahoma Press, 1943.

Ellsworth, Scott. *Death in a Promised Land*. Baton Rouge: Louisiana State University Press, 1982.

Halliburton, R. *The Tulsa Race War of 1921*. San Francisco: R and E Research Associates, 1975.

Haynes, Robert V. *A Night of Violence*. Baton Rouge: University of Louisiana Press, 1976.

Hower, Robert N. *1921 Race Riot and the American Red Cross: Angels of Mercy*. Tulsa, Okla.: Homestead Press, 1993.

Johnson, Hannibal. *Black Wall Street: From Riot to Renaissance in Tulsa's Historic Greenwood District*. Austin, Tex.: Eakin Press, 1998.

Parrish, Mary E. Jones. *Race Riot 1921: Events of the Tulsa Disaster*. Tulsa, Okla.: Out on a Limb Publishing, 1998.

Teall, Kaye M. *Black History in Oklahoma, A Resource Book*, Oklahoma City: Oklahoma City Public Schools, 1971.

U

Underground Railroad The Underground Railroad was a network of people, fund-raising, and safehouses that helped fugitive slaves in the American South escape to freedom in the northern states and Canada. No one person oversaw the railroad. It was instead a collection of local efforts.

The Underground Railroad began in the late 18th century and continued until 1862. The term "railroad" was inspired by the fledgling steam railroads, and the network even used railroad terms: safe-houses were stations run by stationmasters. The conductors moved passengers from one station to the next.

The conductors were sometimes whites or Native Americans, but usually they were free, or freed, blacks who snuck onto plantations and helped guide slaves north. Typically, the fugitive slaves—who traveled either singly or in small groups—covered 10 to 20 miles between stations, where they hid in barns or other out-of-sight structures. There they would rest and eat while the next stationmaster would be alerted to expect the fugitives. If the fugitives were lucky, and if there was money to pay for it, they sometimes traveled by boat, ship, wagon, or even an actual train, but usually their trek northward was on foot and at night in the backwoods.

Perhaps the most famous of the conductors was Harriet Tubman. An escaped slave herself, she made 19 trips to the South and helped conduct a total of about 300 slaves to freedom. She became known as the Moses of her people. In 1850, the compromise on the FUGITIVE SLAVE LAW gave slave owners the right to organize a posse anywhere in the country—north or south—to recapture their runaway slaves. Courts, police, and even private citizens were obligated to assist them. People who were caught helping slaves served jail time and were required to pay restitution to the slave owner. This law made it more dangerous for fugitives to stay in the North, so more and more of them continued on to Canada or to the Caribbean.

It is estimated that approximately 100,000 fugitive slaves escaped to freedom via the Underground Railroad between the late 18th century and the Civil War.

The network of individuals who assist Sethe and Denver's crossing of the Ohio River and secure passage to 124 Bluestone Road in *Beloved* (1987) can be understood as a representation of escape via the Underground Railroad.

BIBLIOGRAPHY

Blockson, Charles. *The Underground Railroad.* New York: Prentice Hall, 1987.

Brown, William Wells. *Narrative of William Wells Brown, A Fugitive.* New York: Markus Weiner Publishing, 1848.

Cockrum, William Monroe. *History of the Underground Railroad as It Was Conducted by the Anti-Slavery League.* Oakland City, Ind.: Press of the J. W. Cockrum Printing Co., 1915.

Coffin, Levi. *Reminiscences of Levi Coffin, the Reported President of the Underground Railroad: Being a Brief*

History of the Labors of a Lifetime in Behalf of the Slave with Stories of Numerous Fugitives, Who Gained Their Freedom through His Instrumentality, and Many Other Incidents. Cincinnati: Western Tract Society, 1876.

Douglass, Frederick. *Life and Times of Frederick Douglass.* New York: Gramercy Books, 1993.

Gara, Larry. *The Liberty Line: The Legend of the Underground Railroad.* Lexington: University of Kentucky Press, 1996.

Quarles, Benjamin. *Black Abolitionists.* New York: Oxford University Press, 1969.

Siebert, Wilbur. *The Underground Railroad from Slavery to Freedom.* New York: Macmillan, 1898.

Sprague, Stuart Seely. *His Promised Land: The Autobiography of John P. Parker, Former Slave and Conductor of the Underground Railroad.* New York: W. W. Norton, 1996.

Still, William. *The Underground Railroad: A Record of Facts, Authentic Narratives, Letters, etc.* Philadelphia: Porter and Coates, 1872.

UNIA (Universal Negro Improvement Association) The Universal Negro Improvement Association (UNIA) was founded by MARCUS GARVEY in 1914 in Jamaica to promote racial pride for people of the African Diaspora, their economic self-sufficiency, and the formation of an independent black nation in Africa. Garvey did not believe that blacks and whites would ever be able to live together. Though he campaigned against JIM CROW laws and lynching, he in fact believed the ultimate solution was separation of the races: ". . . Europe for the Europeans . . . Asia for the Asiatics . . . Africa for the Africans . . ."

In 1917, Garvey opened the first branch of UNIA and began to publish *The Negro World*, a journal that promoted African nationalism. By 1919, UNIA had become extremely popular, with 30 branches and over two million members. Garvey's fraud conviction in 1923 weakened the UNIA, but the association inspired other black nationalist movements.

Marcus Garvey's Universal Negro Improvement Association (UNIA) is referenced in Morrison's novel *Jazz* (1992).

BIBLIOGRAPHY

Cronon, E. *Black Moses: The Story of Marcus Garvey and the Universal Negro Improvement Association.* Madison: University of Wisconsin Press, 1969.

Vincent, Theodore G. *Black Power and the Garvey Movement.* Berkeley, Calif.: Ramparts Press, 1990.

V

Van Der Zee, James (1886–1983) James Van Der Zee was a prominent HARLEM photographer during the years commonly referred to as the HARLEM RENAISSANCE. Van Der Zee reached the height of his fame as a photographer during the 1940s when he was extremely well-known as a photographer of the dead, an art that reached its peak during these years. The practice involved photographing the dead as they lay in repose. The photographs were revered by family members and frequently displayed in prominent locations in African-American homes.

James Van Der Zee was born on June 29, 1886, in Lenox, Massachusetts. Van Der Zee began his life as a photographer when he was a young boy. Van Der Zee's parents had worked as maid and butler for Civil War general and U.S. president ULYSSES S. GRANT. Following the death of his mother, Van Der Zee, his brother, and his father relocated to Harlem in New York City. The family moved to the city in 1906 and, although they were not coming from the South, became a part of the mass relocation of African Americans to the city in the early years of the 20th century. This relocation was known as the GREAT MIGRATION.

Like many young African-American boys and men of the time, Van Der Zee held a number of service jobs, including employment as an elevator operator and as a waiter. In spite of these necessary detours to support himself and to assist his family, Van Der Zee maintained his interest in photography and eventually found work as a darkroom assis-

tant in a portrait studio in Newark, New Jersey. As a result of his talent and hard work, eventually he became a portrait artist and in 1915 returned to Harlem to open his own studio.

Van Der Zee's second studio was called Guarantee Photo Studio and it was there that he created what is now considered to be his most important work. Van Der Zee's photographs created a visual record of the Harlem Renaissance and captured the images of both the era's luminaries as well as its lesser-known constituents. Van Der Zee photographed black Americans as they inhabited urban life and appropriated its affectations.

Although James Van Der Zee was well-known by the residents of Harlem, he was not recognized for the artistry and historical significance of his photography until 1967. In that year, an official from the Metropolitan Museum of Art discovered that Van Der Zee had a collection of more than 40,000 prints and negatives that were the primary documentation of an era of American history. After the boom years between the turn of the century and the 1940s, Harlem fell into a time of economic and social decline. As a photographer, Van Der Zee found it increasingly difficult to find customers and to support himself and his family. When his collection was finally appreciated, the Van Der Zee family was in economically dire straits and welcomed both the financial compensation and the critical acclaim Van Der Zee's photographs finally acquired.

Van Der Zee's photographs were a significant feature of the Metropolitan Museum of Art's 1969 exhibition entitled *Harlem on My Mind*. This show brought attention to Van Der Zee and his work and renewed his career. Van Der Zee became an in-demand artist during the 1970s and found work displaying his older photographs, as well as creating new work with a body of more contemporary photographs. In 1978, James Van Der Zee's photographs of deceased African Americans were collected in a text entitled *The Harlem Book of the Dead*. Toni Morrison wrote the foreword to that collection while she was an editor at Random House.

James Van Der Zee enjoyed prominence and success in the later years of his life and continued to work up until his death on May 15, 1983. Van Der Zee still enjoys a reputation as a preeminent visual artist of the Harlem Renaissance. His work is frequently exhibited and there are many books that both collect and analyze his work. The National Portrait Gallery mounted an important retrospective of his work in 1993.

The idea for Morrison's novel *Jazz* (1992) originated with a James Van Der Zee photograph of a dead teenaged woman who, knowing she was dying, told her friends that she would tell them on the next day the name of the man who had shot her with a silenced gun at a rent party. The woman was dead the next day and so did not betray her lover, the man who had murdered her.

BIBLIOGRAPHY

Anderson, Jervis. *This Was Harlem 1900–1950*. New York: Farrar, Straus, and Giroux, 1982.

De Cook, Liliane, and Reginald McGhee. *James Van Der Zee*. New York: Morgan and Morgan, 1973.

Dodson, Owen, and Camille Billops. *The Harlem Book of the Dead: James Van Der Zee*. Dobbs Ferry, N.Y.: Morgan and Morgan, 1978.

Haskins, Jim. *James Van Der Zee: The Picture Takin' Man*. New York: Dodd, Mead, 1979.

Higgins, Chester Jr., and Orde Coombs. *Some Time Ago: A Historical Portrait of Black Americans, 1850–1950*. New York: Anchor Press, 1980.

Hughes, Langston. *A Pictorial History of the Negro in America*. New York: Crown, 1968.

McGhee, Reginald. *The World of James Van Der Zee: A Visual Record of Black Americans*. New York: Grave Press, 1969.

Willis-Thomas, Deborah. *Black Photographers, 1840–1940: An Illustrated Bio-Bibliography*. New York: Garland, 1985.

Wintz, Cary D. *Black Culture and the Harlem Renaissance*. Houston, Tex.: Rice University Press, 1988.

Washington, Booker T.

Washington, Booker T. (1856–1915) Washington was an American educator and reformer. Perhaps the most prominent African-American leader of his time, he believed that African Americans could best gain equality in the United States by first improving their economic situation through education rather than by demanding equal rights. Washington was born to an unknown white man and a slave on a tobacco farm in Virginia. After the Civil War, his family moved to West Virginia, where Washington started working at nine years old as a salt packer. A year later, he worked as a miner. He eventually became a houseboy for the mine's owner, whose wife encouraged Washington to study. In 1872, Washington attended Hampton Normal and Agricultural Institute, where he eventually joined the staff. In 1881, he helped start the new Tuskegee Normal and Industrial Institute, which emphasized a practical education for African Americans, in areas such as farming, carpentry, brick making, shoemaking, and printing. Under his guidance, Tuskegee became a successful institution. It later became Tuskegee University.

Washington's ideas about how African Americans could gain equality with whites were controversial. He did not believe that blacks should campaign for the vote but that they needed to first prove their loyalty to the United States through manual labor. He had many critics in the black community, the most prominent being W. E. B. DuBois. He had many supporters among white leaders who saw Washington's views as a way to keep blacks in an inferior position. Washington believed the surest way to equality for African Americans at that time was to earn a living and become property owners. In 1901, he published his autobiography, *Up from Slavery,* in which he not only presented his life but also defended his views. He died in Tuskegee, where thousands of people attended his funeral.

There are several references to Booker T. Washington in Morrison's canon, including a mention in *Jazz* (1992) of his meal at the White House.

BIBLIOGRAPHY

Harlan, Louis R. *Booker T. Washington; The Making of a Black Leader, 1856–1901.* New York: Oxford University Press, 1972.

———. *Booker T. Washington: The Wizard of Tuskegee, 1901–1915.* New York: Oxford University Press, 1983.

———. *The Booker T. Washington Papers:* Volumes 1–14. Urbana: University of Illinois Press, 1972.

Hawkins, Hugh. *Booker T. Washington and His Critics; The Problem of Negro Leadership.* Boston: Heath, 1962.

Thornbrough, Emma L. *Booker T. Washington.* Englewood Cliffs, N.J.: Prentice Hall, 1969.

Washington, Booker T. *The Future of the American Negro.* 1899. New York: Haskell House, 1968.

———. *Up from Slavery, An Autobiography.* 1901. Garden City, N.Y.: Doubleday, 1951.

———. *Working with the Hands.* 1904. New York: Arno Press, 1969.

Watts riots The Watts riots occurred in south Los Angeles in 1965 when a routine traffic stop provided the spark in a community already frustrated by racial injustices. The riots lasted for six days and left 34 people dead, over a thousand more injured, and hundreds of buildings destroyed. Nearly 4,000 people were arrested.

The cause of the riots can be traced to California's Proposition 14, which strove to block the fair housing section of the 1964 Civil Rights Act. In the summer of 1965, with anger and frustration in the south-central neighborhood already high, a Los Angeles police officer stopped a motorist for suspicion of driving while intoxicated. As officers questioned the driver and his passenger—the driver's brother—a crowd began to form. When the driver's mother showed, the police officers ended up struggling with the family. More officers arrived and began striking family members with their batons. After the police arrested the family and left the scene, the angry crowd began to riot. A commission ordered by California governor Pat Brown concluded that the riots were the result of stubborn racial disparities, in which people in the inner city suffered from a high jobless rate, poor housing, a drug epidemic, and bad schools. No attempt was made, however, to correct these injustices or to rebuild the blocks destroyed by the riots.

There are references to Watts in Morrison's novels *Paradise* (1998) and in *Love* (2003).

BIBLIOGRAPHY

Bullock, Paul. *Watts: The Aftermath; An Inside View of the Ghetto.* New York: Grove, 1969.

Conot, Robert. *Rivers of Blood, Years of Darkness: The Unforgettable Classic Account of the Watts Riot.* New York: Morrow, 1968.

Crump, Spencer. *Black Riot in Los Angeles: The Story of the Watts Tragedy.* Los Angeles: Trans-Anglo, 1966.

Fogelson, Robert. *The Los Angeles Riots.* New York: Arno, 1969.

Governor's Commission on the Los Angeles Riots. *Violence in the City—An End or a Beginning?* Los Angeles: The Commission, 1965.

Sears, David. *The Politics of Violence: The New Urban Blacks and the Watts Riot.* Boston: Houghton Mifflin, 1973.

Wesley, Cynthia (1949–1963) See COLLINS, ADDIE MAE

Wheatley, Phillis (1753–1785) In 1773, Phillis Wheatley became the first African American to publish poetry. Before she was allowed to submit her volume, she had to undergo a trial to prove her competence, to demonstrate that she was capable of writing her own poetry.

The act of public testimony has always been a precarious, high-stakes endeavor for black women, but black women have refused to accept silence as an option. Phillis Wheatley was the first African American—and the first slave—in the United States to publish a book of poetry.

Born in Gambia, West Africa, Wheatley was kidnapped at the age of eight and brought to Boston, where she was bought by John Wheatley. Her first name came from the slave ship, the *Phillis*. It was in the Wheatley home that she learned to speak and write English. Her great intelligence was obvious to the Wheatleys, and they encouraged her to study theology and the classics.

As a young teenager, Wheatley published her first poem, *On Messrs. Hussey and Coffin* (1767). Several years later, she published a poetry collection, *Poems on Various Subjects* (1773). She was freed that same year.

Her poetry was recognized widely, and Wheatley traveled to London to speak and promote her book. Political figures of the day, such as George Washington and Voltaire, sought to speak with her. The influences on her poetry were diverse, and included both the oral traditions of the African-American slaves as well as her knowledge of classic Latin. Her life, however, ended in poverty. A second volume of her poetry did not find a publisher, and the manuscript was lost.

In *Love* (2005), when Christine is nearly destitute, she is turned away from the Young Women's Christian Association (YWCA) and takes shelter in a Phillis Wheatley house.

BIBLIOGRAPHY

Flanzbaum, Hilene. "Unprecedented Liberties: Re-reading Phillis Wheatley," *Melus* 18, no. 3 (Fall 1993): 71.

Kendrick, Robert. "Re-membering America: Phillis Wheatley's Intertextual Epic," *African American Review* 30, no. 1 (Spring 1996): 71–89.

Levernier, James A. "Phillis Wheatley and the New England Clergy," *Early American Literature* 26, no. 1 (1991): 21–38.

Mason, Julian. *Poems of Phillis Wheatley.* Chapel Hill: University of North Carolina Press, 1966.

Nott, Walt. "From 'Uncultivated Barbarian' to 'Poetical Genius': The Public Presence of Phillis Wheatley," *Melus* 18, no. 3 (Fall 1993): 21.

Ogude, S. E. "Slavery and the African Imagination: A Critical Perspective," *World Literature Today: A Literary Quarterly of the University of Oklahoma,* 55, no. 1 (1981): 21–25.

O'Neale, Sondra. "A Slave's Subtle War: Phillis Wheatley's Use of Biblical Myth and Symbol," *Early American Literature* 21, no. 2 (1986): 144–165.

Richards, Phillip M. "Phillis Wheatley and Literary Americanization," *American Quarterly* 44, no. 2 (1992): 163–191.

Robinson, William H. *Phillis Wheatley: A Bio-Bibliography.* Boston: Hall, 1981.

Scruggs, Charles. "Phillis Wheatley and the Poetical Legacy of Eighteenth-Century England," *Studies in Eighteenth-Century Culture* 10 (1981): 279–295.

Shields, John C. "Phillis Wheatley's Use of Classicism," *American Literature* 52 (1980): 97–111.

Sistrunk, Albertha. "The Influence of Alexander Pope on the Writing Style of Phillis Wheatley." In *Critical Essays on Phillis Wheatley,* edited by William H. Robinson, 175–188. Critical Essays on American Literature. Boston: Hall, 1982.

Steele, Thomas J. S. J. "The Figure of Columbia: Phillis Wheatley Plus George Washington," *New England Quarterly* 54, no. 2 (1981): 264–266.

Watson, Marsha. "A Classic Case: Phillis Wheatley and Her Poetry," *Early American Literature* 31, no. 2 (1996): 103–132.

Wheatley, Phillis. *An Elegiac Poem, on the Death of that Celebrated Divine, and Eminent Servant of Jesus Christ, the Late Reverend, and Pious George Whitefield, Chaplain to the Right Honourable the Countess of Huntingdon.* Boston: Russel and Boyles, 1770.

———. *Poems on Various Subjects, Religious and Moral.* London: Printed for A. Bell, Bookseller, Algate; and sold by Messrs. Cox and Bery, 1773.

whites only   See COLORED ONLY

Williams, Bert (1874–1922)   Williams was a vaudeville performer at the end of the 19th century. Though he was an African American, he appeared in blackface. Before Jack Johnson's championship boxing matches, Williams was the most famous African American in the country.

Born in the West Indies, Williams and his family immigrated to California in 1888. With partner George Walker, Williams made his career in the vaudeville circuit at a time when black Americans had few roles open to them. One of the first African Americans to don blackface, Williams portrayed the clown stereotype of African Americans common at the time, acting as a dull-witted character with a shuffling gait.

Williams became, in the early 20th century, one of the highest-paid performers in the country. He had talents in many fields; in addition to being a comedian, he was a singer, recording artist, early film maker, dancer—he was a master of the cakewalk—and composer. His song "Nobody" was recorded years later by Perry Como, Johnny Cash, and NINA SIMONE.

Williams starred on Broadway at a time when African Americans could sit only in the balcony. In 1903, he starred in *In Dahomey,* the first all-African-American Broadway musical. He played a royal command performance in London. He was the first black performer to star in the Ziegfeld Follies. He also performed with Eddie Cantor, one of vaudeville's most popular performers, at a time when black and white performers rarely appeared on stage together. W. C. Fields, another famous vaudeville performer and film star, called Williams "the funniest man I ever saw—and the saddest man I ever knew."

Williams's personal life was marked by an impoverished youth, racism, and often heavy drinking. He collapsed during one of his performances and died a week later in the hospital.

Bert Williams is mentioned in Morrison's novel *Sula* (1973).

BIBLIOGRAPHY

Cockrell, Dale, and Don B. Wilmeth. *Demons of Disorder: Early Blackface Minstrels and Their World.* Cambridge: University of Cambridge Press, 1997.

Lhamon, W. T., Jr. *Raising Cain: Blackface Performance from Jim Crow to Hip Hop.* Cambridge, Mass.: Harvard University Press, 1998.

Lott, Eric. *Love and Theft: Blackface Minstrelsy and the American Working Class.* Oxford: Oxford University Press, 1993.

Rogin, Michael. *Blackface, White Noise: Jewish Immigrants in the Hollywood Meltingpot.* Berkeley: University of California Press, 1998.

Winfrey, Oprah (1954–) Oprah Winfrey is a talk show host, magazine publisher, film producer, and actress. The popularity of her television show and other business enterprises have made Winfrey one of the first African-American women to become a billionaire.

Born in Kosciusko, Mississippi, to poor, unmarried teenage parents, Winfrey was raised first by her grandmother on a farm. At six, Winfrey moved to Milwaukee to live with her mother. At 13, after suffering molestation, she ran away but eventually ended up living with her father in Nashville, Tennessee.

Winfrey got into journalism early. At 17, she started in Nashville radio, then moved on to other jobs in television as a reporter and news anchor. She earned her undergraduate degree in speech communications and performing arts at Tennessee State University. In 1984, Winfrey moved to Chicago, where she helped raise the ratings of a local TV talk show that was later renamed *The Oprah Winfrey Show.* It was first broadcast nationally in 1986.

The format of Winfrey's hour-long program entails Winfrey interviewing people from all walks of life, housewives, doctors, writers, and so forth, with an emphasis on celebrities. The subject matter is usually taken from the headlines or a celebrity cross-country tour. Winfrey is considered to be among the most influential celebrities of all time. In the late 1990s, her program unveiled a new segment, "Oprah's Book Club." Each month, Winfrey chose a book—a novel, history, work of philosophy—and interviewed the writer. Whether the book was by a famous or obscure writer, the book became an instant best-seller. Winfrey has featured several of Morrison's novels on her Book Club list.

Through her production company, Harpo, Winfrey produced several television movies, including *Tuesdays With Morrie* (1999), based on the best-selling book by Mitch Albom, *David and Lisa,* a remake of a 1962 film, and *Their Eyes Were Watching God* (2005), based on the Zora Neale Hurston novel of the same name. In 1998, Winfrey produced and starred in the film version of Toni Morrison's Pulitzer Prize–winning novel, *Beloved* (1987).

BIBLIOGRAPHY

Beloved (1998). Buena Vista Pictures, DVD/VHS, 1998.

David and Lisa (1998). American Broadcast Company, Movie, 1998.

Oprah.com. Available online. URL: http://www2.oprah.com/index.jhtml. Accessed on September 22, 2006.

Their Eyes Were Watching God (2005). Buena Vista Home Video, DVD/VHS, 2005.

Tuesdays With Morrie (1999). Walt Disney Video, DVD/VHS, 2003.

wintergreen Wintergreen is a lunar herb, meaning that its growth, development, and life span are influenced by the cycles of the moon. Wintergreen is purported to be a curative for both internal and external wounds and is described as having a creeping root that proliferates in forested areas such as the mountains and valleys of Virginia's Blue Ridge.

The word wintergreen appears only a few times in all of Morrison's novels, but the references to the herb seem connected with moments in her novels where she is examining the dangerous spaces women occupy and the often urgent need for repair of the bodies and spirits of her characters. She references wintergreen in her novels *The Bluest Eye* (1970) and *Paradise* (1998) as a trace, a nearly imperceptible, yet essential element in a healing ritual.

womanism Alice Walker, the architect of the concept of womanism, states in a September 1989 issue of *Essence* magazine the distinguishing characteristics of a feminist and a womanist posture. According to Walker's definition of womanism, feminism becomes a term that is inappropriately pale for African-American women. Walker emphasizes this distinction more completely when she states in the fourth part of her definition of the term "Womanism is to feminism as purple is to lavender." Primarily, what this statement implies is that the relationship between the terms womanist and feminist is analogous to that between the words flower and rose: A rose is a flower, but there are many different components of the word flower, only one of which is a rose. Likewise, feminism is a part of womanism, but it is less than the whole.

Walker's analogy also sparks comparisons between the regal and spiritual associations of purple and the pale and "lady-like" connotations of the color lavender. Although womanism shares commonalities with feminism, it represents an expansion beyond the traditional feminist critical agenda. The definitional introduction of the term womanism into the field of African-American women's writing in Alice Walker's 1983 collection of essays *In Search of Our Mother's Gardens* spawned a debate over its implications. Individual interdisciplinary critics who have embraced womanism as a foundational philosophy for their work include African-American women historians and theologians such as Darlene Clark Hine, Elsa Barkely Brown, and Katie Cannon. Attempting to establish or to confirm womanism as a literary critical movement, however, is a much more complex task. Although critics of African-American women's literature such as Barbara Christian, Marjorie Pryse, Hazel Carby, Valerie Smith, and others analyze literature in womanist terms (i.e., by relying on analyses of self-affirmation, tradition, matrilineal inheritance), they, for the most part, continue to label themselves black feminist or instead choose not to identify their critical allegiance at all.

Some academic critics interpret Morrison's fiction as having womanist characteristics.

BIBLIOGRAPHY

Baca Zinn, Maxine, and Bonnie Thornton Dill, eds. *Women of Color in U.S. Society.* Philadelphia: Temple University Press, 1994.

Beal, Frances M. "Slave of a Slave No More: Black Women in Struggle," *Black Scholar* 6, no. 6 (1975): 2–10.

Bell, Roseann P., Bettye J. Parker, and Beverly Guy-Sheftall, eds. *Sturdy Black Bridges: Visions of Black Women in Literature.* Garden City, N.Y.: Anchor Press, 1979.

Bell-Scott, Patricia, ed. *Life Notes: Personal Writings by Contemporary Black Women.* New York: Norton, 1994.

Brown, Elsa Barkley. "Womanist Consciousness: Maggie Lena Walker and the Independent Order of Saint Luke," *Signs* 14 (1989): 610–633.

Cade, Toni. *The Black Woman: An Anthology.* New York: Signet, 1970.

Cannon, Katie G. *Black Womanist Ethics.* Atlanta, Ga.: Scholars Press, 1988.

———. *Katie's Canon: Womanism and the Soul of the Black Community.* New York: Continuum, 1995.

Christian, Barbara. *Black Women Novelists: The Development of a Tradition, 1892–1976.* Westport, Conn.: Greenwood, 1980.

———. *Black Feminist Criticism: Perspectives on Black Women Writers.* New York: Pergamon Press, 1985.

———. "But Who Do You Really Belong to—Black Studies or Women's Studies?" *Women's Studies* 17 (1989): 17–23.

Combahee River Collective. "The Combahee River Collective Statement." In *Home Girls, A Black Feminist Anthology,* edited by Barbara Smith. New York: Kitchen Table Women of Color Press, 1983.

Dill, Bonnie Thornton. "The Dialectics of Black Womanhood," *Signs* 4 (1979): 543–555.

hooks, bell. *Ain't I a Woman?: Black Women and Feminism.* Boston: South End Press, 1981.

———. *Talking Back, Thinking Feminist, Thinking Black.* Boston: South End Press, 1989.

Hull, Gloria, Patricia Bell Scott, and Barbara Smith, eds. *All the Women Are White, All the Blacks Are Men, But Some of Us Are Brave.* Old Westbury, N.Y.: Feminist Press, 1982.

King, Deborah. "Multiple Jeopardy, Multiple Consciousness: The Context of Black Feminist Ideology," *Signs* 14 (1988): 42–72.

Lorde, Audre. *Sister Outsider: Essays and Speeches.* Trumansburg, N.Y.: The Crossing Press, 1984.

Smith, Barbara. *Toward a Black Feminist Criticism.* Trumansburg, N.Y.: The Crossing Press, 1977.

Walker, Alice. *In Search of Our Mother's Gardens: Womanist Prose.* San Diego, Calif.: Harcourt Brace Jovanovich, 1983.

Woolf, Virginia Stephen (1882–1941) Virginia
Woolf is one of the most well-known and revered
writers of the last century. Woolf created texts that
were experimental in form and explored familiar
subjects in unexpected and unique ways. In addition to her work as a fiction writer, Woolf also
wrote prolifically in the genres of nonfiction and
literary criticism.

Virginia Woolf was the child of Leslie and Julia
Jackson Duckworth Stephen. Woolf's abilities were
nurtured in her home where reading and intellectual pursuits were encouraged by her father and
mother's circle of literary friends. Both of Woolf's
parents died while she was relatively young, and
Woolf took up residence with her sister. As Woolf
matured, her family's group of friend and associates
became known as the Bloomsbury Group. The man
she ultimately married, Leonard Woolf, was one of
the Bloomsbury Group as well.

After three years of marriage, Woolf published
her first novel, *The Voyage Out*, in 1915. This publication was commercially and critically successful and was the beginning of an acclaimed writing
career. Other writing landmarks in Woolf's career
include *Jacob's Room*, published in 1922, *Mrs. Dalloway*, published in 1925, *To the Lighthouse*, published in 1927, *Orlando*, published in 1928, *A Room
of One's Own*, published in 1929, and *The Waves*,
published in 1931.

Throughout her life, Virginia Woolf suffered
from bouts of debilitating depression. Eventually,
the emotional toll of her mental illness cost her her
life when she committed suicide by drowning herself in 1941. Woolf's literary reputation continues
to flourish. Toni Morrison wrote her master's thesis
on the theme of suicide in the works of William
Faulkner and Virginia Woolf.

BIBLIOGRAPHY

Glenny, Allie. *Ravenous Identity: Eating and Eating Distress in the Life and Work of Virginia Woolf.* New
York: St. Martin's Press, 1999.

Gualtieri, Elena. *Virginia Woolf's Essays: Sketching the
Past.* New York: Palgrave, 2000.

Peach, Linden. *Virginia Woolf (Critical Issues)*. New
York: Palgrave, 2000.

Woolf, Virginia. "A Room of One's Own." London:
Hogarth Press, 1929.

———. *Jacob's Room.* London: Hogarth Press, 1922.

———. *Mrs. Dalloway.* London: Hogarth Press,
1925.

———. *Night and Day* (Collected Works of Virginia
Woolf). New York: Classic Books, 2000.

———. *Orlando: A Biography.* London: Hogarth
Press, 1928.

———. *To the Lighthouse.* London: Hogarth Press,
1927.

———. *The Waves.* London: Hogarth Press, 1931.

PART IV

Appendices

CHRONOLOGY OF TONI MORRISON'S LIFE

1906

Ella Ramah Willis, Toni Morrison's mother, is born in Greenville, Alabama.

1908

George Wofford, Toni Morrison's father, is born in Cartersville, Georgia.

1910 (approx.)

Solomon Willis and his wife, Ardelia Willis, leave their home in Greenville, Alabama. The farm, built on land given to John Solomon Willis by his Native American grandmother, was lost due to the theft of the land by unscrupulous and racist whites. The Willis family moves from Alabama to Kentucky.

1912 (approx.)

After finding Kentucky disappointing racially and economically, the Willis family relocates to LORAIN, OHIO, on the shores of Lake Erie.

1916 (approx.)

The Wofford family leaves Cartersville, Georgia, in the wake of several lynchings in the town and the unfair loss by Morrison's grandfather of his position as a railroad engineer to a white man. They relocate to Lorain, Ohio.

1929

Chloe Wofford's only sister, Lois, the oldest child of George and Ramah Wofford, is born.

1931

Chloe Wofford (Toni Morrison) is born on February 18. According to her birth certificate, Morrison is given the name Chloe Ardelia Wofford. As was the custom at the time, Morrison was born at home. At the time, the Wofford family lived

at 2245 Elyria Avenue. Morrison was the second child and second girl in the Wofford family.

1935

Toni Morrison's brother, George Carl Wofford, is born.

1937

Chloe Wofford begins her formal education at Hawthorne Elementary. She is the only African-American child in her class and also is the only child in the class who arrives already knowing how to read.

1943

According to some accounts, Chloe Wofford adopts as a middle name the name of her paternal grandmother Anthony, when she is baptized.

Toni Morrison's brother, Raymond Allen Wofford, is born.

1947–49 (approx.)

Chloe Wofford works as a library helper at the Lorain Public Library.

1949

Chloe Wofford's older sister, Lois, marries Wayne Albert Brooks.

Graduating with honors from Lorain High School, Chloe Wofford, with her parent's approval and support, decides to attend Howard University.

1953

After a successful experience at Howard University, Chloe Wofford graduates with a bachelor of arts degree. While at Howard, she majors in English, minors in Classics, and pursues her interest in theater. Amiri Baraka (LeRoi Jones) is one of her classmates. She also adopts the name Toni while at Howard and may have changed her middle name from Ardelia to Anthony.

Following her graduation from Howard, Wofford decides to pursue graduate studies in literature. She moves and begins studying for her master's degree at Cornell University in Ithaca, New York.

1955

Wofford graduates from Cornell University with a master's degree in English literature.

Wofford begins her career as a professor when she takes a position as an instructor at Texas Southern University. Later, she credits the experience with expanding and enhancing her understanding of black life in America.

1957–65

Wofford returns to Howard University as an instructor. While at Howard, she counts as her students Claude Brown, Stokely Carmichael, and Andrew Young.

1958

While at Howard, Chloe Wofford meets and marries Harold Morrison. Morrison is from Jamaica and is an architect. Chloe Wofford takes her husband's last name.

1961

The Morrisons welcome their first child, son Harold Ford Morrison.

1964

Morrison, pregnant with her second child, travels to Europe and lives there a brief while. She returns to the United States, divorces Harold Morrison, and relocates for a short time to her parent's home in Lorain, Ohio.

Morrison's second son, Kevin Slade Morrison, is born while the family is in Lorain, Ohio.

1965

Although Morrison's mother expresses concern about her daughter's move to a place where

she has no family, Morrison accepts a job as a textbook editor at Random House in Syracuse, New York, with hopes that, in time, she will be promoted and transferred to the main office of Random House in New York City.

1967

Morrison is promoted to senior editor and relocates to Random House's main office in New York City.

1970

Morrison achieves critical acclaim, but not commercial success, with the publication of her first novel, *The Bluest Eye*. *The Bluest Eye* is a coming-of-age story that tells of the plight of the protagonist, Pecola Breedlove. The young girl has no support for her maturation. Her family, her peers, and her community all denigrate her and destroy her self-esteem. Pecola's low self-regard and the violence she experiences at the hands of those who are supposed to protect her fractures her psychological well-being. Pecola's downfall is witnessed and mourned by the novel's narrator, Claudia MacTeer.

1971–72

While still an editor, Morrison resumes her teaching career when she takes a position at the State University of New York at Purchase. Morrison is appointed as an associate professor at the university.

1973

Morrison continues her success as an author when she publishes her second novel, *Sula*. *Sula* is the story of a girlhood friendship between the novel's two protagonists, Nel Wright and Sula Peace. The two girls come from homes that are nearly opposite in character. Those differences draw the girls to each other and make their friendship the most determinative factor in their lives. The friendship is neglected and, eventually, abandoned in the wake of the pressure to conform to traditional roles and the societal hierarchy that places relationships between men and women above other types of bonds.

1974

Morrison edits and publishes *The Black Book*. *The Black Book* is a landmark collection documenting the African-American experience.

1975

Toni Morrison's father, George Wofford, dies on September 9.

Morrison's second novel, *Sula*, is nominated for a National Book Award and receives an Ohioana Award.

1976

Toni Morrison serves as a faculty member at the Bread Loaf Writer's Conference in Vermont.

1976–77

Toni Morrison accepts a visiting lectureship at Yale University in New Haven, Connecticut.

1977

Song of Solomon is the third of Morrison's published novels, and it brings her the commercial success that her first two novels did not experience. The novel is the story of the Dead family, a family displaced from its roots by ignorance of their history. The central figure in the novel, Milkman Dead, is the benefactor of the upward mobility of his family. Ironically, it is that economic security that fosters Milkman's self-centeredness and myopia. Through the assistance of his aunt, Pilate Dead, Milkman begins to move toward a more compassionate and empathetic understanding of the world. He also discovers the lost family history and gains the abilities possessed by his ancestors. With *Song of Solomon*, Morrison also interrogates the question of the role of retributive violence in the struggle for justice and equality.

Toni Morrison wins the National Book Critics' Circle Award for *Song of Solomon*. *Song of Solomon* receives the American Academy and Institute of Arts and Letters Award. The novel is also selected as a Book of the Month Club choice.

1978

In the wake of the commercial success of *Song of Solomon*, Morrison purchases a house in the Hudson River valley, near Nyack, New York.

1980

President Jimmy Carter appoints Toni Morrison as a member of the National Council on the Arts.

1981

Morrison's fourth novel, TAR BABY, is published. The novel is a riff on the traditional love story. The characters in the novel represent the extremes that confront modern blacks—the struggle between colonial and postcolonial subjectivity, assimilation and nationalism, folk and high culture. The novel, unlike Morrison's others, takes place outside the United States. Set on a fictional island in the Caribbean, it centers on the intersections and conflicts of the two central characters, Jadine Childs and Son (William Green). The novel uses the folk image of the tar baby as its central metaphor.

In recognition of the quality of her work, Morrison receives the honor of election to the American Academy and Institute of Arts and Letters. Toni Morrison is also the first African-American woman to appear on the cover of a major national news magazine when she appears on the March 30, 1981, cover of *Newsweek* magazine.

Toni Morrison writes the story and lyrics for the musical *New Orleans: The Storyville Musical*, with Donald McKayle and Dorothea Freitag.

1983

After a successful tenure of nearly 20 years as an editor, Morrison decides to pursue teaching and writing full-time.

Toni Morrison publishes her only short story, "Recitatif."

1984

Morrison accepts an endowed chair at the State University of New York at Albany. Morrison becomes the Albert Schweitzer Professor of the Humanities, a position she holds for two years.

New Orleans: The Storyville Musical is workshopped at the Public Theater in New York.

1986

Following up on her childhood interests in theater and her horror at the murder of EMMETT TILL,

Morrison writes and assists in mounting a production of her play, *Dreaming Emmett*, in Albany, New York.

Morrison accepts a position as a visiting lecturer at Bard College in Annandale-on-Hudson, New York.

1987

Morrison publishes her fifth novel, *Beloved*. During this incredibly productive time in her life, Morrison turns again to history as a source when she chooses the story of MARGARET GARNER as a springboard for *Beloved*. Margaret Garner was a slave in Kentucky in 1851 when she and her husband decided to try to escape with their children to the other side of the Ohio River and freedom. The story of Margaret Garner was an inspiration for Morrison, but the novel that she wrote, *Beloved,* is more than a replication of the Margaret Garner story. *Beloved* is the story of Sethe Garner and Paul D Garner, two former slaves whose traumatic experiences as slaves on a Kentucky farm called Sweet Home cause them to share memories and bind them together even after they are no longer enslaved. Paul D's traumas emerge from the emasculation of slavery. He is uncertain about what it means to be a man since the autonomy and strength traditionally attributed to that label have been denied to him most of his life. Sethe tries to live in the wake of her decision to kill her children rather than have them returned to slavery after her successful escape with them is undone. Sethe struggles with the consequences of her decision and finds herself isolated and living half a life.

At the novel's beginning, Paul D arrives at 124 Bluestone Road, the home Sethe claims as a free woman. *Beloved* is the story of the two and of their attempt to find true freedom by achieving a kind of equilibrium between the memory of the horrors of the past, the demands of the present, and the fear of the uncertainty of the future. Morrison's artful handling of the difficult issues *Beloved* raises solidifies her reputation as a figure of major significance in the pantheon of American letters.

With the publication of *Beloved*, Morrison catapulted to literary superstardom by achieving the literary triple crown of an almost unconditionally positive critical reception, commercial success, and literary awards.

Like *Song of Solomon*, *Beloved* is selected as a Book-of-the-Month Club choice. The novel also receives nominations for, but does not win, the National Book Award.

Morrison is appointed as a lecturer at Bowdoin College and at the University of California, Berkeley.

1988

Almost 50 prominent African-American writers sign an open letter to the *New York Times Book Review* protesting the fact that Morrison has not yet won any major literary awards for *Beloved*.

As her one-year appointment at Bard College ends, Toni Morrison wins the Pulitzer Prize for fiction.

Morrison accepts a position as a Tanner Lecturer at the University of Michigan.

1989

Toni Morrison acts once again as a path-breaker when she becomes the first African-American woman to hold an endowed chair at an Ivy League university, becoming the Robert E. Goheen Professor in the Council of Humanities at Princeton University in Princeton, New Jersey.

1992

Toni Morrison publishes her sixth novel, *Jazz*. The novel becomes a *New York Times* best-seller. *Jazz* is the second of a trilogy of Morrison's novels reflecting on love and its manifestations. The idea for the novel originated with a JAMES VAN DER ZEE photograph of a dead teenaged woman who, knowing she was dying, told her friends that she would tell them on the next day the name of the man who had shot her with a silenced gun at a rent party. The woman was dead the next day and so did not betray her lover, the man who had murdered her.

The novel tells the story of the New York neighborhood HARLEM from the perspective of its ordinary inhabitants, namely Joe and Violet

Trace. The couple is at the center of the novel's investigation of the complexities faced by those million African Americans who moved from the rural South to the North during the GREAT MIGRATION in search of jobs and a better life in the cities.

Joe and Violet have to negotiate the stories from their pasts that continue to haunt and to define who they are even as they begin, or try to begin, new lives in the city. The skills, knowledge, and information that they acquire as they mature in the southern countryside both equip and disable them for their lives as urban residents. The novel bridges the post–Civil War era and the post–World War I generation in its portrait of the HARLEM RENAISSANCE and the NEW NEGRO from the inside out.

Morrison's literary critical text, *Playing in the Dark: Whiteness and the Literary Imagination,* is published and becomes a classic work of American literary criticism.

Morrison publishes *Race-Ing Justice, En-Gendering Power: Essays on Anita Hill, Clarence Thomas, and the Construction of Social Reality,* a book of essays on the CLARENCE THOMAS hearings.

Toni Morrison becomes a founding member of Elie Wiesel's Académie Universelle des Cultures.

1993

Toni Morrison's brother, Raymond Wofford, dies of colon cancer.

Toni Morrison joins American Nobel Prize in literature laureates Sinclair Lewis, Eugene O'Neill, Pearl S. Buck, WILLIAM FAULKNER, Ernest Hemingway, John Steinbeck, Saul Bellow, Isaac Bashevis Singer, Czeslaw Milosz, and Joseph Brodsky when she wins the award in 1993. She is the first black woman to win the prize.

Toni Morrison establishes the ATELIER program at Princeton University. Morrison begins the program as an interdisciplinary arts program that brings artists from various disciplines together to work closely with students to produce a work of art or a production. Atelier artists have included Richard Danielpour, GABRIEL GARCÍA MÁRQUEZ, Yo Yo Ma, Maria Tucci, Peter Sellars, Lars Jann, and Roger Babb.

Literary critic and professor Carolyn Denard initiates the birth of the TONI MORRISON SOCIETY at the annual convention of the American Literature Association. The official founding date of the Toni Morrison Society is May 28, 1993, in Baltimore, Maryland.

According to its literature, the purpose of the society is "to initiate, sponsor, and encourage critical dialogue, scholarly publications, conferences and projects devoted to the study of the life and works of Toni Morrison." The Toni Morrison Society has more than 200 members worldwide.

The Toni Morrison Society convenes at biennial meetings devoted to analysis and exploration of the works of Toni Morrison. Conferences have been held since 1998 in the cities of Atlanta, Georgia; Lorain, Ohio; Washington, D.C.; and CINCINNATI, OHIO, EACH OF WHICH HAS A SPECIAL RELEVANCE TO TONI MORRISON AND/OR HER WORK.

Toni Morrison's much-loved house on the Hudson River is damaged as a result of a Christmas Day fire. The author loses some original manuscripts and irreplaceable family heirlooms and mementos.

1994

Toni Morrison's mother, Ella Ramah Wofford, dies on February 17, the day before Morrison's birthday.

1995

Continuing to develop her interests in theater, dance, and music, Morrison creates the interdisciplinary work entitled *Degga* with composer Max Roach and dancer/choreographer BILL T. JONES.

When Toni Morrison's hometown of Lorain decides to honor her, Morrison suggests that they create a reading room in her name in the Lorain Public Library. The room is dedicated in 1995 in Lorain and Morrison returns for the ceremony.

Toni Morrison edits and publishes the writings of Huey P. Newton in a volume entitled *To Die for the People: The Writings of Huey P. Newton.*

Honey and Rue is recorded for distribution.

1996

When Toni Morrison is awarded the National Book Foundation Medal for Distinguished Contribution to American Letters she gives one of her most important and well-known speeches, *The Dancing Mind: Speech upon Acceptance of the National Book Foundation Medal for Distinguished Contribution to American Letters on the Sixth of November, Nineteen Hundred and Ninety-Six*. The speech is published in 1996 as a book.

Toni Morrison's fame and popularity, as well as sales of all of her novels, increase when *Song of Solomon* is chosen by talk show personality OPRAH WINFREY for her show's book club.

Toni Morrison edits and publishes the multi-genre collection of Toni Cade Bambara's writings, *Deep Sightings and Rescue Missions: Fiction, Essays and Conversations*.

In response to the national conversation about the racial issues raised by the O. J. SIMPSON murder trial, Morrison edits and publishes *Birth of a Nation'hood: Gaze, Script, and Spectacle in the O. J. Simpson Case*. She co-edits the text with Claudia Brodsky Lacour, a comparative literature professor at Princeton.

Toni Morrison writes the libretto for *Sweet Talk: Four Songs on Text*, with composer Richard Danielpour.

Toni Morrison is selected by *Time* magazine as one of America's 25 most influential people.

1997

Toni Morrison publishes her seventh novel, *Paradise*. *Paradise* is the final installment of Morrison's trilogy on the question of love in its myriad forms. In the novel, Morrison examines the ways in which love is abused and/or fulfilled. The novel demonstrates the way in which manifestations of love determine not only the course of individual and familial interactions, but also can affect the character, direction, and health of whole communities.

Specifically, *Paradise* tells the story of lost women who find themselves at the edge of an all-black town called Ruby. The members of the town,

as descendants of historical outcasts, might find common connections with the women living in the Convent just beyond Ruby's limits. Instead, the town leaders, enmeshed in fear of change and of the world outside of Ruby, see the women as threatening. They are so shaken by the women's presence and potential influence that they attempt to kill them rather than grapple with the realities of inevitable change.

1998

Oprah Winfrey produces and stars in the cinematic version of *Beloved*. The movie, directed by Jonathan Demme and also starring Danny Glover, is a critical and commercial failure.

Toni Morrison edits and publishes the collected works of James Baldwin under the title *James Baldwin: Collected Essays: Notes of a Native Son / Nobody Knows My Name / The Fire Next Time / No Name in the Street / The Devil Finds Work / Other Essays*.

Morrison, along with Stephen Holmes, Paul Berman, and Sean Wilentz organize a writers' and scholars' protest against the impeachment of Bill Clinton.

1999

Toni Morrison and her youngest son, Slade, begin a literary collaboration with their joint authoring and publication of *The Big Box*, the first in a series of children's books the mother and son produce. The book is illustrated by Giselle Potter.

2000

Toni Morrison is nominated for and receives the National Humanities Medal.

Toni Morrison publishes the poems "I Am Not Seaworthy," "The Lacemaker," "The Perfect Ease of Grain," and "The Town Is Lit" in the literary magazine *Ploughshares*.

2001

Toni Morrison publishes *The Book of Mean People* with her son, Slade Morrison.

Toni Morrison celebrates her 70th birthday a day early on February 17 at a gala bash sponsored by the Toni Morrison Society and held at the New York Public Library.

2002

Toni Morrison publishes the poem "black crazies" in *Ms. Magazine*.

2003

Toni Morrison publishes her eighth novel, *Love*. *Love* has received mixed reviews and, to date, does not enjoy the same reputation as some of Morrison's earlier novels. *Love* is another chronicle in Morrison's continuing exploration of the lives, communities, and histories of African Americans.

The story specifically questions the meanings of love for the post–CIVIL RIGHTS MOVEMENT African-American community. The novel has as its center the pre-integration gathering site of Cosey's Hotel and Resort, a beach escape for middle-class African Americans. This site becomes the locale for both the very particular conflict between the novel's main characters, Heed and Christine Cosey, as well as a stage for the exploration of the larger issues of assimilationism vs. nationalism, class conflicts, and sexism as they affect African-American communities.

Toni Morrison publishes the children's book, *The Lion or the Mouse? (Who's Got Game?)*, with her son, Slade Morrison.

2004

Toni Morrison publishes the children's book, *The Poppy or the Snake? (Who's Got Game?)*, with her son, Slade Morrison.

As commemoration of the 50th anniversary of the BROWN V. BOARD OF EDUCATION OF TOPEKA, KANSAS Supreme Court decision, which declared unconstitutional the legal practice of separate but equal, established in the 1896 PLESSY V. FERGUSON Supreme Court decision, Toni Morrison

publishes the book *Remember: The Journey to School Integration* for young readers.

2005

Toni Morrison serves as a Feature Films Jury Member of the Festival de Cannes.

Toni Morrison writes the libretto for the opera *Margaret Garner* with composer Richard Danielpour. The opera premieres in Detroit, Philadelphia, and Cincinnati.

Toni Morrison receives an honorary doctor of letters degree from the University of Oxford.

2006

Toni Morrison retires from Princeton University after 17 years of teaching at the institution.

The *New York Times Book Review* names *Beloved* as the best work of American fiction of the past 25 years.

In November, Morrison reads from her forthcoming novel, *Mercy* (2007), and serves as a guest curator at the Louvre in Paris at an event entitled "The Foreigner's Home Exhibit," co-sponsored by the Toni Morrison Society.

2007

November 14, 2007

Austrian Book Week Festival includes the distribution of 100,000 free copies of the German version of *The Bluest Eye*.

March 2007

Morrison collaborates with William Forsythe and other artists in her *Art is Otherwise* festival at the Baryshnikov Arts Center in New York.

September 11, 2007

The New York City Opera's 2007–08 season opens with the New York premier of Richard Danielpour and Toni Morrison's opera *Margaret Garner*.

CHRONOLOGIES OF INDIVIDUAL NOVELS

Beloved Chronology

1794

Baby Suggs is born in Carolina.

1803

Ohio becomes a state in the United States of America.

1829

Halle Suggs is born a slave to Baby Suggs. He is the only one of her children Baby is able to see become an adult.

1836

Sethe Garner born to Ma'am, an African woman who chooses to keep her daughter because she is conceived with a man that Ma'am loves. Sethe's mother killed the rest of her children because they were the product of rape.

1840

Mr. Garner purchases Baby Suggs and Halle and brings the two to work at Sweet Home.

1849

Garner purchases Sethe and brings the woman to work at Sweet Home. Garner tells Sethe that she can choose one of the Sweet Home men as her husband. Eventually, she chooses Halle.

Halle earns the money Garner deems Baby Suggs is worth and purchases his mother's freedom. Garner drives Baby Suggs to CINCINNATI and places her in the hands of his ABOLITION friends, the Bodwins.

1850

Sethe makes a "bedding" dress. Lillian Garner, seeing Sethe's efforts to be a bride, gives her earrings to wear when she marries Halle. Halle and Sethe consummate their relationship in the corn field at Sweet Home while the other Sweet Home men watch the corn stalks waving above the couple. Sethe is 14 years old when they get married.

1851

Sethe and Halle's first son, Howard, is born.

1852

Sethe and Halle's second son, Buglar, is born.

1853 (approx.)

The "crawling-already? baby" (Beloved) is born.

1855

The escape from Sweet Home fails almost completely. Sixo, Paul A, and Paul F are killed immediately. Halle seems to lose his mind after seeing Sethe violated by the nephews and schoolteacher. Sethe does get her children safely to the meeting place in the corn, and the other runaways take them to Baby Suggs in Cincinnati. Sethe, with the help of Amy Denver, gets to the Ohio River, gives birth to her daughter, Denver, and makes it to her children and to Baby Suggs in Cincinnati. Paul D is sold to Brandywine. He tries to kill the slave-trader and is sold to a CHAIN GANG and winds up in Alfred, Georgia.

Twenty-eight days after Sethe's escape, schoolteacher arrives at 124 Bluestone Road. Sethe, in an attempt to save them from slavery, kills Beloved and injures both Howard and Buglar.

1856

After finding himself on a chain gang in Alfred, Georgia, Paul D's hands tremble for 83 days in a row.

1862

Denver attends school with Lady Jane for a short time until another student teases her about Sethe's murder of her sister. As a result, Denver loses her hearing and stops speaking for a time.

1862

Saywer plants roses up and down the lumberyard fence.

1865

Baby Suggs dies before the end of the Civil War.

1873

The present tense of the novel occurs in 1873. Both Paul D and Beloved arrive at 124 Bluestone Road in 1873. When Paul D arrives, he has not seen Sethe in 18 years. He has never seen Denver, with whom Sethe was pregnant when she escaped from Sweet Home.

1874

Concerned about the deteriorating situation between Beloved and Sethe, Denver steps out the door of 124 Bluestone Road to get help for the family from the community. She eventually finds work with the Bodwins, the abolitionist brother and sister who own 124 Bluestone Road and who assisted Baby Suggs when Garner first brought her to Cincinnati.

Thirty women of the community come to 124 Bluestone Road to save Sethe from Beloved with song.

Paul D returns to 124 Bluestone Road.

Beloved disappears from 124 Bluestone Road forever.

Bluest Eye Chronology

Early 1800s

An ancestor of Soaphead Church, Sir Whitcomb, immigrates to Jamaica and produces a mixed-raced son who marries a woman of similar heritage.

1902 (approx.)

Soaphead Church (Elihue Micah Whitcomb) is born in Jamaica.

1904 (approx.)

Pauline Williams is born the ninth of 11 children to Ada and Fowler Williams.

In Georgia, Cholly Breedlove is born to a mother who is possibly mentally impaired. His mother abandons him on a railroad track where he is found and taken in by his Great Aunt Jimmy. Cholly is named after Aunt Jimmy's brother, Charles Breedlove. Cholly never knows either of his parents.

1906 (approx.)

Pauline experiences a permanent deformity when she steps on a nail.

1914 (approx.)

The Williams's, Pauline Williams's family of origin, move over the course of six months from Alabama to Kentucky. Pauline leaves school.

Cholly asks Aunt Jimmy who his father is and she tells him that she thinks that his name is Samson Fuller.

1915 (approx.)

When his wife, Velma, leaves him after two months of marriage, Soaphead Church, at the urging of his father, travels from Jamaica to the United States to study psychiatry. He dabbles in this and in other fields, but never completes any field of study.

1916 (approx.)

Cholly quits school and takes his first job where he meets a man named Blue who befriends him and becomes a kind of surrogate father.

1918

Aunt Jimmy falls ill and dies, leaving Cholly alone.

During his first sexual experience, Cholly and Darlene, the girl he is having sex with, are violated by hunters who force them to copulate while they watch. This event catalyzes in Cholly a lifelong hatred of women. Cholly, fearing he has impregnated Darlene, runs off to Macon, Georgia, to find his father, Samson Fuller. Samson rejects Cholly, which disconnects Cholly permanently from any feeling of accountability or responsibility.

1919 (approx.)

Cholly Breedlove wanders into the Williams's yard and he and Pauline fall in love.

Pauline and Cholly marry and relocate to LORAIN, OHIO. Shortly thereafter, Pauline loses her front tooth. After several months, Pauline takes a job as a domestic.

1921

Soaphead Church's father cuts him off financially.

1926

Cholly and Pauline Breedlove become parents when their first child, Sammy, is born.

1929

Pecola Breedlove is born.

There is a tornado in Lorain that destroys half the town. Mrs. MacTeer tells Claudia about the storm. Claudia associates the storm with her mother's youth and strength.

1930

Frieda MacTeer is born.

1931

Claudia MacTeer is born.

After wandering aimlessly for several years, Soaphead Church arrives in Lorain, decides to settle there, and tells people that he is a minister.

1940

Autumn. Beginning of novel.

Mr. Henry Washington becomes a boarder at the MacTeers'.

Pecola Breedlove come to live temporarily at the MacTeers' after her father, Cholly Breedlove, is responsible for his family "being put outdoors."

While Pecola is staying at the MacTeers', she has her first menstrual period.

The Breedloves move into an abandoned storefront at the corner of Broadway and Thirty-fifth.

The prostitutes, China, Poland (also known as the MAGINOT LINE), and Miss Marie, who live above the Breedlove's storefront, befriend Pecola.

Winter. Light-skinned Maureen Peale arrives in Lorain from Toledo. The general glowing reaction of the town to the girl is confusing and unsettling to Claudia and Frieda.

Claudia and Frieda find Mr. Henry in their house with the prostitutes China and the MAGINOT LINE. The girls do not tell their parents about what they see.

Junior lures Pecola into his house and throws his mother's cat at her. When Geraldine, Junior's mother, returns, she blames Pecola for the incident and calls the little girl a "black bitch."

1941

Spring. Mr. Henry molests Frieda.

Mr. MacTeer throws Mr. Henry out of the house.

Frieda worries that she has been "ruined." Because of the prostitute Miss Marie's weight, Frieda and Claudia think that being ruined means being fat. Claudia and Frieda believe that drinking alcohol will keep Frieda thin, so the girls go to Pecola's house to see if she can help them get some alcohol.

When Claudia and Frieda arrive at Pecola's house, they find that she is not home. While they are at the Breedloves', the girls inadvertently insult Miss Marie and she responds by throwing a coke bottle at the girls.

Claudia and Frieda find Pecola at the house on the lake where her mother, Pauline Breedlove, works. After Claudia and Frieda arrive at the house where Pauline works, Pauline screams at Pecola when the girl accidentally spills a blueberry pie she has just made.

Cholly rapes Pecola at least twice and she becomes pregnant.

Pecola goes to Soaphead Church to ask for blue eyes.

While she is there, Soaphead gets her to poison his landlady's dog, Bob.

Soaphead writes a letter to God, asking that he grant Pecola her blue eyes.

Summer. Claudia and Frieda spend their time selling marigold seeds. As they do they are appalled at the lack of sympathy and compassion they hear from adults about Pecola's plight. The girls try to devise a way to help her themselves.

Pecola loses touch with reality and develops an alter ego. She believes that Soaphead Church has given her blue eyes, but is insecure with wondering whether her eyes are the bluest eyes.

1941

Autumn. End of the novel.

Claudia says that in the fall of 1941, there were no marigolds.

Claudia and her sister Frieda plant marigold seeds in a vain attempt to save the life of Pecola's unborn child.

Pecola's baby dies.

Postscript

Sammy leaves town.

Cholly dies in the workhouse.

Pecola ends up living with her mother and spending her days picking through the debris on the edge of town.

Jazz Chronology

1828

True Belle is born.

1855

Colonel Wordsworth Gray disowns his daughter, Vera Louise Gray, when he discovers that the girl has become pregnant with Henry LesTroy's child. LesTroy is a black man, making Vera Louise's pregnancy an incomprehensible reality in the antebellum South. After both of her parents scorn her and cast her out, appeasing their consciences with the gift of a large sum of money, the pregnant Vera Louise relocates from Vesper County, Virginia, to Baltimore, Maryland. In addition to money, her family gives Vera Louise the enslaved woman, True Belle, to travel with her as she goes to begin a new life. Vera Louise is completely unconcerned with the fact that True

Belle must abandon her own family to accompany her to Baltimore.

Golden Gray is born in Baltimore.

1868

Alice Manfred is born.

1870

Honor, the boy who helps Golden Gray and Wild in Henry LesTroy's absence, is born.

1870–90s

African Americans begin to migrate from the South to the North in search of respite from the violence and segregation in the years following the Civil War.

1873

Vera Louise tells Golden Gray that his father is black and tells the boy where Henry LesTroy lives. Golden Gray sets off on an ill-conceived mission to confront his father. During his journey to Vesper County, Golden Gray encounters Wild who is pregnant with Joe. When Wild runs into a tree and knocks herself unconscious, Golden Gray is forced to pick the naked woman up and take her with him as he travels to Henry LesTroy's house.

After Golden Gray arrives at his father's house, Wild gives birth to Joe Trace. When she refuses to feed him and then disappears, the infant boy is adopted by Rhoda and Frank Williams, who raise the boy as their own child along with their biological son, Victory, who is three months older than Joe.

1876

Rose Dear, True Belle's daughter, gives birth to Violet near Rome, Virginia.

1888

Men come to the house where Rose Dear lives with her children and repossess her belongings before they force the family out of their home. In the process of reclaiming these goods, they knock Rose Dear out of the chair in which she sits, an act that serves as a last psychological insult for Rose Dear.

After learning of her daughter and granddaughters' predicament, True Belle returns from Baltimore to Vesper County as a free woman. She brings with her the money Vera Louise pays her after the end of the Civil War and emancipation. She also carries with her the stories of the child she raised until his 18th year, Golden Gray. True Belle's return helps restore the family, but her stories of Golden Gray infuse Violet with a sense of inferiority that pervades her adult life. Violet is 12 years old when True Belle returns.

1892

After ensuring that her children are safe in the care of her mother, True Belle, Rose Dear commits suicide by drowning in the family well.

Violet's father, Rose Dear's husband, returns by chance two weeks after Rose Dear's funeral and learns of his wife's suicide with regret. He leaves again 21 days later.

1893

The black residents are forced to leave their homes in Vienna, Virginia. Whites burn the town in their wake. Joe and his brother-friend, Victory, drift from place to place trying to find work and roots. Joe says that this event changes him for the third time. The first change happened when he identified himself as Joe Trace, the trace his parents left behind. The second change occurred when Henry LesTroy took him on as a hunting apprentice.

Using his skills as a master hunter, which he acquired from Henry LesTroy, Hunter's Hunter, Joe goes on three separate quests to find his mother, Wild.

True Belle sends Violet and two of her sisters to make money picking a bumper cotton crop in Palestine, Virginia.

Eventually, after much wandering, Victory and Joe find work picking cotton in Palestine and that is where Joe meets Violet when he falls out of a tree in which he has fallen asleep.

Shortly thereafter, the couple marries. They work for two years clearing crops for a man named Harlon Ricks.

1895

Harlon Ricks sells the farm where Violet and Joe Trace are share-cropping to Clayton Bede. The couple work for Bede, who exploits them terribly for the next five years.

1896

Alice Manfred's husband, Louis, leaves her for an affair with another woman.

For seven months after her husband's departure, Alice dreams of murdering his mistress.

After living with his mistress for seven months, Louis Manfred dies.

1899

After an illness of 11 years, True Belle dies.

1900

Joe gets a job with the railroad, Southern Sky.

1901

President Theodore Roosevelt invites BOOKER T. WASHINGTON to dine at the White House for an evening meal. The invitation is thought by some to be a sign of racial progress and interpreted by others as a symbol of the danger of Washington's philosophies.

After working at laying rails for the Southern Sky Railroad, Joe decides to purchase some land and to try to make a living as an independent farmer.

1906

Whites cheat Joe and Violet out of their land and the couple decide to head north to New York. Joe and Violet leave Tyrell in Vesper County, Virginia, and ride on the train called the Southern Sky from Rome, Virginia, to HARLEM. During the train ride through the South, they have to change trains several times due to JIM CROW laws, but when they arrive in the city, the movement of the train feels more like dancing. Joe says that this move is the fourth change in his identity.

1907

Dorcas is born in East St. Louis.

1916

At age 40, Violet begins to regret her decision not to have children.

1917

During the year 1917, race riots break out in many urban locations in the United States including East St. Louis where, on July 1, hundreds of African Americans are killed.

In East St. Louis, Dorcas's father is murdered by a gang when he is pulled off a streetcar and stomped to death; her mother dies in a fire instigated by the same riot.

During the summer, Joe is beaten up during a riot in New York City. He is nearly killed when a man hits him on the head with a steel pipe. This trauma brings about Joe's fifth transformation.

On July 28, black Americans respond to the national violence against African Americans by holding the Silent Protest Parade down Fifth Avenue in New York City. Estimates of the number of march participants range from between 10,000 to 15,000 people. The organizers of the march include intellectuals, artists, and political activists such as W. E. B. DuBois and James Weldon Johnson.

Alice Manfred witnesses and disapproves of a silent protest march held to bring attention to the violence of the riots and the American inequalities and racism they reflect.

1919

On Armistice Day, James Reese Europe and the Harlem Hellfighters Band, also known as the 369th Infantry Regiment, U.S. Army, hold a victory parade up Fifth Avenue and then to Harlem upon their return from fighting in France.

Joe walks with the parade and dances in the street with pride at the public display of personhood he feels the soldiers represent.

With the help of his friend, Gistan, Joe gets a job at a hotel that pays well in tips and Joe feels successful.

1920

According to Malvonne, Violet's behavior begins to become peculiar.

1925

Violet's unresolved issues come to the surface and she begins sleeping with dolls.

Joe meets Dorcas at her aunt's house, 237 Clifton Place, a fact that Alice Manfred later bemoans.

Joe and Dorcas begin their affair in October. Dorcas is 18 years old. Joe becomes new for the final time.

1926

Joe stalks and shoots Dorcas while she is at a rent party with her new boyfriend, Acton, on New Year's Day.

Dorcas's funeral is held on January 3. During the funeral, Violet tries to stab the dead girl in her coffin.

In March, Violet, obsessed with Dorcas and jealous of Joe's love of the girl, begins to visit Alice Manfred in order to discover what Joe found so appealing.

Violet returns Dorcas's photograph to Alice Manfred.

Felice comes to visit Dorcas to ask Joe if he knows what happened to the ring she loaned to Dorcas.

Felice's presence and her explanations of Dorcas help Joe and Violet to heal and the couple embark on a new, more quiet and content phase of their lives together.

The narrator reveals that she is the book itself.

Love Chronology

1890

William Cosey is born. His father is Daniel Robert Cosey.

1909

L is born in the middle of a thunderstorm.

1912

The jute mill closes in what will become Junior's hometown community. The lack of employment creates a permanent underclass of people who eventually come to be called rurals. The impoverished, dysfunctional community they form comes to be called the Settlement.

1913

Billy Boy Cosey is born to Julia and Bill Cosey.

1914

L is five and Bill Cosey is 24 when she sees him holding his wife, Julia, in the sea.

1923

L begins to work for Bill Cosey at Cosey's Hotel and Resort.

1925

Julia Cosey dies. Her son, Billy Boy, is 12 years old.

1929

May and Billy Boy Cosey marry.

1930 (approx.)

Bill Cosey purchases the hotel from a white man who has lost his fortune.

1930

Christine, Bill Cosey's granddaughter, born to May and Billy Boy Cosey.

Heed-the-Night Johnson born to Surrey and Wilbur Johnson.

1935

Billy Boy Cosey, Bill Cosey's son and only child, dies of walking pneumonia. Billy Boy's death leaves Bill Cosey disconsolate.

1940

Bill Cosey molests Heed and decides to marry the girl.

1942–1950

L reports that during these years the Policeheads lurk around the resort and are particularly dangerous around the time of the setting sun.

1942

Bill Cosey buys the silverware with the engraved letters CC on the stems. No one is ever absolutely certain what the letters signify.

Welcome Morning and Joy Johnson, Heed's brothers, drown when the boys are swimming in front of Cosey's Hotel and Resort. Bill Cosey pays for the boys' funeral. L accuses the boys of having hard heads and of refusing to pay attention to the safety ropes that were there to warn them of the dangers of the sea.

Bill Cosey marries Heed-the-Night Johnson in 1942. Heed is 11 years old. Bill Cosey is 52.

Sandler Gibbons is born.

1943

Bill Cosey, with May's permission, sends Christine away to Maple Valley School. Christine feels exiled.

1945

Bill Cosey builds the house at One Monarch Street and moves his family to Silk.

There is a celebration from May to August 14 at Cosey's Hotel and Resort to mark the building, relocation, and acceptance of the Coseys' house at One Monarch Street in Silk.

1947

In June, when Christine returns from Maple Valley School, Heed and Christine have not seen each other in four years.

Bill Cosey spanks his wife, Heed, in front of her sworn enemies, Christine and May, during dinner before Christine's sweet-sixteen party.

Bill Cosey has Christine's graduation and 16th birthday party at the Cosey Resort and Hotel. Heed ruins the evening for Christine by dancing with another man at the party and by setting Christine's bed on fire.

When Bill Cosey suggests that Christine, rather than Heed, leave, Christine abandons Silk and does not see her grandfather, Bill Cosey, alive again. She is sixteen years old.

After 1947, Bill Cosey never tells Heed that he loves her.

Christine marries Ernie Holder and moves to Germany with him to live, for a short while, on a military base. When Christine discovers Ernie cheating with another woman sometime later, she leaves him immediately and returns to the States.

1955

Emmett Till's lynching in Mississippi seems to destabilize May.

1958

The Policeheads appear at Cosey's Resort and Hotel.

Heed has an affair with a man, Knox Sinclair, who comes to the hotel to claim the remains of his brother who has drowned while staying at Cosey's. Heed believes that the relationship will last and makes plans with the man to run away and begin a life together. After the man returns to his home in Indiana, he never contacts Heed again and does not answer her calls.

Heed discovers that she is pregnant with Knox Sinclair's baby. Heed loses the baby and goes into denial about her miscarriage.

1960s

In the 1960s, the fish smell becomes a problem for the Up Beach community.

1961

Sandler and Vida Gibbons are married.

1962

Vida Gibbons gives birth to her daughter and only child, Dolly. Dolly's father and Vida's husband is Sandler Gibbons.

1963

Christine begins a relationship with Fruit that lasts for nine years.

1964

Sandler Gibbons is 22 old when he and then 74-year-old Bill Cosey first go fishing.

1964

Heed's hands are burned by fat from a meal L is cooking.

May takes the box with Rinso on it and the menus in it to the attic for safekeeping.

The sheriff, Boss Silk, threatens to close Cosey's Hotel and Resort.

A group of young people come out to the hotel to confront Bill Cosey and demand land from the man. They pour animal excrement on Cosey. He responds by diffusing their anger with cordiality.

May is 61 years old.

1971

Bill Cosey dies when he is poisoned by L after she discovers that he leaves no provision in his will for May, Heed, or Christine and that he leaves everything, except his fishing boat, to his mistress, Celestial.

L writes the false wills on the menus dated 1958 and 1959. The menu wills are vague and leave the Cosey fortune to "my sweet Cosey child."

Christine returns to Silk for her grandfather, Bill Cosey's, funeral.

Christine and Heed get into a fight at Bill Cosey's funeral. L breaks up the fight with her words, "I'll tell," which stops both women's efforts to hurt the other.

Christine leaves Silk again after Bill Cosey's funeral.

The relationship between Christine and Fruit ends. Christine begins a destructive relationship with a physician, Kenny Rio, who is married and ultimately sees her as expendable. Dr. Rio is 60 years old when the relationship begins.

Heed finds the 1958 menu will leaving everything to the "Sweet Cosey child."

1973 (approx.)

Cosey's Resort and Hotel closes.

1975

Junior Viviane is born. Her mother is Vivian and her father is probably Ethan Payne, Jr.

In 1975, there are about 50 Settlement dogs.

Christine returns to Silk with no suitcase and lays claim to the house at One Monarch.

1976

May dies at dawn with a smile on her face.

1993

Present tense of the novel.

Both Heed and Christine are in their sixties, approximately 63.

Junior Viviane arrives in Silk, gets a job working for Heed and begins her affair with Romen.

Heed goes out to the hotel with Junior to find menus upon which to get Junior to forge a will. Christine follows them out to the abandoned resort. Heed falls when Christine arrives. Junior leaves the women there alone, although Heed is mortally wounded, and returns to the Cosey house.

When Romen learns that the women are at the hotel alone, he drives out to the beach to get them. It is almost morning when he arrives. Heed is dead, but the women have spent the night reflecting upon their lives and determining that the problem was created and nurtured by Bill Cosey and May. They remember, restore, and express their love for each other before Heed dies.

Romen returns with the women, one dead and one alive, to the Cosey house. Junior is there and, although Heed is dead, Heed and Christine converse about what is to be done with Junior. They decide to treat her with more compassion than they were shown by the adults in their lives.

Paradise Chronology

1770s
Ancestors of the founding fathers of Ruby arrive in the United States.

1812
Louisiana becomes a state.

1875
Fairy DuPres is born.

1890
The 8-rock families migrate to Oklahoma from Louisiana and Mississippi.
Lone DuPres born and orphaned. She is rescued by Fairy DuPres during the journey to Haven.
The Disallowing occurs in Fairly, Oklahoma.
Walking man appears to Big Papa and leads the group to the land that will become Haven.

1891
Founding of Haven, Oklahoma.
The founders of Haven construct the Oven.

1900
One thousand residents live in Haven.

1910
There are two churches in Haven.
Big Daddy, Pryor, and Elder Morgan go on the First Grand Tour through Oklahoma, visiting other all-black towns.

1913
Mary Magna assigned to serve in Brazil.

1915
Consolata Sosa born in Brazil.

1918–19
Returning from World War I, Elder Morgan fights a white man in New York City after he sees the man attacking an African-American woman Elder believes is a prostitute. The event impacts Elder's perception of the world for the rest of his life.

1919
Worldwide influenza epidemic impacts residents of Haven.

1920
Big Daddy (Rector) Morgan takes a 65-mile journey from Haven for supplies for the residents of the sick and destitute town. He travels to a town called Pura Sangre. He is warned by strangers not to enter the town as they have posted a "No Niggers" sign.

1921
Tulsa, Oklahoma, riot and bombing.

1922
Convent built as embezzler's palace.

1924
Deacon and Steward Morgan born to Big Daddy (Rector) and Beck Morgan.

1924
Consolata kidnapped by Mary Magna in Brazil at age nine.

1926
Mary Magna and the other sisters, along with Consolata, occupy the embezzler's mansion and

attempt to convert it into a convent and school. The women attempt unsuccessfully to strip the mansion of its profanity.

1932

During the Second Grand Tour, Rector, Pryor, and Elder Morgan go on a journey to inspect other all-black towns. During the tour, young Deacon and Steward see the 19 black ladies.

1934

Haven falls on hard times.

1940s

Pecans first planted at the Convent by the nuns.

1941

Mavis Goodroe Albright born.

1942

Deacon and Steward Morgan enlist in the army for World War II.

1947

Deacon and Soane Blackhorse Morgan marry.

1948

Steward Morgan disapproves of Thurgood Marshall and NAACP desegregation efforts in Norman, Oklahoma.

1949

Led by the New Fathers, Haven residents move farther west to found a new settlement (Ruby).
Steward Morgan marries Dovey Blackhorse.
Billie Delia Cato is born to Billy and Patricia Best Cato.

1950

The town of Ruby is founded.
Anna Flood born to Ace Flood.
Grace (Gigi) Manley born.
Just as Connie approaches menopause, Lone DuPres teaches her how to use her powers to bring people back to life.

1952

Ruby Morgan Smith falls ill and dies. Eventually, the new town is named after the woman. The residents celebrate the naming of the town.

1953

SENECA born to Jean. Seneca believes that Jean is her sister.

1954

Consolata first sees Deacon at a horse race and has an affair with him that summer and fall.
A pregnant Soane Morgan visits the Convent in November, then has a miscarriage.

1958

Jean abandons five-year-old SENECA.
Steward sells his cattle at top dollar, but then loses a statewide election for church secretary.
There is a big blizzard in Ruby.

1959

Pallas Truelove is born to Divine (Dee Dee) and Milton Truelove.

1961

Manley Gibson (Gigi's father) is put on death row when Gigi is 11.

1962

Natural gas is discovered on Steward's ranch, but the subsequent development diminishes the beauty of the ranch.

1964

Dovey and Steward learn that they cannot have children.

1965

Consolata brings Scout Morgan back from the dead ("steps in" or "sees in") after his car accident.

1967

Sweetie Fleetwood begins six years of confinement in her house caring for her sick children.

1968

April 4, MARTIN LUTHER KING JR. assassinated in Memphis, Tennessee.

Frank and Mavis Albright's twins suffocate in the back seat of Frank's 1965 Cadillac.

After running away from her abusive husband Frank, Mavis arrives accidentally at the Convent after running out of gas.

June 5, Robert Kennedy is assassinated in Los Angeles, California.

Scout and Easter come home on furlough from service in Vietnam at Thanksgiving.

Scout and Easter die within two weeks of each other while serving in the Vietnam War.

1969

Scout and Easter's bodies are sent home from Vietnam.

1970

Richard Misner is called to Mount Calvary Church in Ruby.

Mavis Albright returns to Maryland to try to see her children.

After Connie's numerous resurrections of her over the course of 17 days, Mary Magna (Mother Superior) dies.

Grace (Gigi) Manley arrives in Ruby at the advice of Dice, the man on the bus.

Arnette Fleetwood and K. D. Smith's first baby dies at the Convent.

1971

Divine (Dee Dee) Truelove divorces Milton Truelove and relocates to Mehita, New Mexico, leaving her children, Pallas and Jerome, with Milton. Pallas does not see her mother again until after Pallas runs away from home with Carlos.

1973

Billie Delia fights with her mother and, after spending a short time at the Convent, leaves Ruby in October.

The town meeting about the Oven takes place at Mount Calvary Church.

Sweetie walks out to the Convent. It is her first time out of her house since 1967. Seneca helps her and ends up joining the women at the Convent.

A sudden blizzard buries a station wagon, killing the white family within, because they do not

heed the advice of the several residents of Ruby who warn them about the approaching storm.

Gigi Manley ends her four-year affair with K. D. Smith.

1974

Buzzards appear during the spring thaw.

Arnette Fleetwood and K. D. Smith marry in April. The evening of the wedding Arnette walks out to the Convent and accuses the women there of stealing or killing her baby.

After all of her work trying to reconstruct the histories of the families of Haven and Ruby, Patricia Best Cato burns the genealogies.

In September, Pallas Truelove meets Carlos at her high school and the two begin an affair.

In December, Carlos and Pallas Truelove run away to Pallas's mother Divine's (Dee Dee) home in Mehita, New Mexico.

The annual Ruby Christmas pageant occurs. It is, in part, a reenactment of the Disallowing.

1975

After Pallas discovers that her mother and Carlos are having an affair, the girl runs away and has a violent encounter with a group of boys.

At the advice of Billie Delia, Pallas is given refuge at the Convent.

K. D. and Arnette Fleetwood Smith's baby is born in March.

Pallas returns to her father's home in August, then comes back to the Convent after Christmas. She is pregnant.

Consolata has a visitation from the man in the cowboy hat who looks like her and she has a revelation. From then on, Connie takes charge of the redemption of herself and of the women who live at the Convent.

1976

In July, the men arrange and carry out their attack on the Convent. Lone DuPres overhears their plans and tries to intervene but arrives too late.

Roger Best goes out to the Convent to retrieve the women's bodies and finds no sign of them.

Richard Misner and Anna Flood go out to the Convent to see for themselves if they can figure out what happened. Anna retrieves five eggs from the hen house, then the two have a vision. In the field one sees a closed door, while the other sees an open window.

In September, Deacon Morgan takes a barefoot walk through town and goes to Richard Misner's house for consolation and counsel.

In November, Jeff and Sweetie Fleetwood's sick daughter, Save-Marie, dies. Her death marks the first death that has occurred in Ruby since the death of Ruby Morgan Smith.

Gigi (Grace) appears to her incarcerated father. She has shaved her head and wears army gear.

Pallas appears to her mother twice. Once Divine sees Pallas while she is painting. Later Pallas seems to be looking in the guest room for shoes that she left there. During both encounters, Divine is unable to speak to her daughter. Both times Pallas is carrying an infant.

Sally Albright meets with her mother Mavis in a diner. Mavis promises to meet with Sally's brothers as well. Mavis has also cut off her hair. Mavis tells her daughter that her side hurts.

Jean encounters Seneca in a parking lot. She thinks she is mistaken about her daughter's identity until she is back in her car with her husband and it is too late.

In *Paradise*'s final scene, Consolata and Piedade sit on a littered beach waiting for an incoming ship.

Song of Solomon Chronology

1869

Macon Dead I receives his name when a drunken Yankee soldier enters his birth location, Macon, Georgia, as his name.

Macon and Sing meet on a wagon headed north.

1891

Macon Dead born to Sing and Macon Dead.

1895

Pilate Dead born to Sing and Macon Dead.

Sing Dead dies giving birth to Pilate.

1896

Dr. Foster moves onto Mains Avenue into a big, dark house with 12 rooms. In honor of the only colored doctor's residence on the street, the African-American community begins to call the avenue, Doctor Street. Later, in ironic compliance with town officials, they call the street Not Doctor Street.

1901

Ruth Foster is born to Dr. and Mrs. Foster. Ruth bears a striking resemblance to her mother.

1907

Macon Dead I is shot by greedy whites while defending his farm in Montour County. Pilate says that her father was killed the year that they shot the Irish down in the street. She probably refers to the Orange Riot in New York, where Irish were killed due to anti-Irish sentiment in New York.

Six days after their father is shot, Macon and Pilate run to CIRCE, the community midwife, for shelter and advice. Circe takes them in and hides them in the Butler mansion, where she works.

With Circe's help, Pilate puts the scrap of Bible paper from which her father derived her name in a box and creates with the contraption an earring in her ear. Reverend Cooper's father, the blacksmith, creates the earring for Pilate. Macon is 16. Pilate is 12.

After two weeks, Pilate and Macon leave Circe and the Butlers. Several days later, out of fear, Macon kills an old white man in a cave. Macon and Pilate fight about whether to take the old man's gold. Macon leaves the cave. When he returns, the gold is gone. He believes Pilate has taken it.

After Macon and Pilate separate, Pilate is taken in by a preacher's family that makes her wear shoes and go to school. After a relatively short time, Pilate is forced to leave when the minister's wife catches the minister abusing Pilate.

After leaving the preacher's family, Pilate joins a group of migrant workers who pick beans in upstate New York. While she is with this group of people, she works with a root worker woman who shares with Pilate many of her secrets.

1908

Macon first has sex at 17.

1910

Pilate has a relationship with a male relative of the root worker. He discovers and shares with the group that Pilate has no navel. When the group learns of her difference, they send her away.

Pilate travels to Virginia and joins up with another group of migrant workers. After they discover her navellessness, they too abandon the child.

Pilate works briefly as a washer woman and then heads for West Virginia. Eventually, she finds her way to an island off the coast of Virginia.

1911

Pilate chooses a lover from among the islanders, making sure that he never sees her stomach completely and learns that she has no navel. When Pilate becomes pregnant, her fear that her lover will discover the secret of her stomach keeps her from marrying him and remaining on the island.

Reba is born on the island off the coast of Virginia to Pilate and her unnamed father.

Pilate's dead father, Macon I, visits her and she believes that he wants her to return to Pennsylvania to bury the man she believes she and Macon II killed. She returns to the cave in winter, with heavy snow covering the ground, and gathers the bones. From that point on, Pilate carries them with her wherever she goes.

1913

Pilate begins a wandering, nomadic life with her daughter Reba.

1917

Ruth and Macon get married.

1917

Magdalene, called Lena, is born to Ruth and Macon Dead.

1918

First CORINTHIANS is born to Ruth and Macon Dead.

During World War I, black soldiers begin to use Doctor Street as their official address. The town officials object to the renaming and the African-American community responds by calling the street, Not Doctor Street.

Soldiers return from World War I.

1921

Dr. Foster dies.

Macon discovers Ruth with her dead father. According to Macon, they both were naked and laying in the dead man's bed. According to Ruth, she had on a slip and was merely kissing her father's fingers.

Macon stops sleeping with Ruth.

Ruth begins to visit her father's grave, spending nights there periodically.

1923

The Deads take a family vacation to Honore Island.

1926

Hagar is born to Reba.

Guitar is born.

1927

CHARLES LINDBERGH's flight across the Atlantic Ocean.

1929

Pilate decides that Hagar needs more traditional and stable relationships and so Pilate tries to find Macon so that the families can live in the same community.

1930

Pilate arrives in the city in search of Macon.

Pilate helps Ruth to conceive Milkman.

1931

Guitar's father is killed in a saw mill accident. Then his mother abandons the family.

February 18, 1931

Robert Smith commits suicide by jumping off the roof of Mercy Hospital. (This date also happens to be Toni Morrison's birthday.)

February 19, 1931

Milkman is born to Ruth and Macon Dead and becomes the first African American born in Mercy Hospital.

1932

Winnie Ruth Judd, a criminally insane woman, is committed to a state asylum. The woman manages to escape two or three times each year. Unsolved crimes are often attributed to her.

1934 (approx.)

Macon Dead III gets his nickname of Milkman when Freddie discovers Ruth breastfeeding him.

1936

Macon refuses Mrs. Bains's request for leniency with her late rent money.

Porter screams and pees drunkenly out of the window.

Milkman pees on his sister, Magdalene, called Lena, while the Dead family takes one of its Sunday drives in the Packard.

1938

Michael-Mary Graham publishes her first volume of poetry, *Seasons of My Soul.*

1941

Michael-Mary Graham publishes her second volume of poetry, *Farther Shores.*

1942

Reba wins a diamond ring for being the 500,000th customer to walk into Sears.

1943

Milkman meets and is befriended by Guitar Bains.

Guitar takes Milkman to meet Pilate.

Milkman meets Hagar, and the two begin a relationship.

Milkman starts working with his father.

1945

Milkman develops a limp. He believes that one of his legs is shorter than the other.

1948

Milkman begins having sex with Hagar.

Pilate confronts the man who beats up Reba.

1953

Milkman confronts and threatens his father after his father hits his mother at the dinner table.

Macon tells Milkman his version of what happened between Ruth and her father.

EMMETT TILL is murdered at 14 in Money, Mississippi.

The Seven Days enact a revenge killing on a white boy in retribution for the killing of Emmett Till.

1955

The Seven Days enact a revenge killing on four white men in retribution for the killing of four black men.

1961

First Corinthians grows dissatisfied with the narrow confines of her life and decides to get a job. She finds employment as the maid of the former state poet laureate, Michael-Mary Graham.

1962

Milkman breaks off his relationship with Hagar by writing her a thoughtless, indifferent letter.

1962

Porter begins courting Corinthians.

1963

Hagar begins to try to murder Milkman each month to get revenge for his abandonment.

Milkman follows his mother one night and discovers that she, periodically, spends the night lying on her father's grave. By way of explanation, Ruth tells Milkman about his father Macon's attempt to kill him while she was pregnant.

Milkman confronts Hagar and her monthly attempts to kill him end. She turns her fury and pain inward and becomes self-destructive.

Guitar tells Milkman about the Seven Days.

Milkman mentions Pilate's mysterious green bag to his father, Macon. Macon believes that the bag contains the gold from the cave and sets up with Milkman and Guitar a plan to steal the bag from Pilate.

Four young black girls are killed by racists while in church in Birmingham, Alabama. Because of his involvement in the Seven Days, Guitar sets about to avenge their deaths.

On September 19 a strange, ginger odor fills the air the night that Milkman and Guitar steal Macon I's bones from Pilate's house believing that they have taken gold.

Corinthians and Porter have sex for the first time at Porter's apartment, 3 Fifteenth Street.

Pilate rescues Milkman and Guitar after they are arrested while carrying Macon I's bones.

Lena confronts Milkman about his selfishness and he decides to leave his father's house for the first time in his life.

Milkman travels to Danville, Pennsylvania, and to various places in Virginia in search of the gold he, his father, and Guitar believe Pilate took from the cave.

In Danville, Milkman experiences a new sense of community and learns more about his family history.

Circe tells Milkman about the cave. He visits it and does not find the gold. He journeys to Virginia based on the information Circe gave him.

In Shalimar, Virginia, Milkman learns more about himself and his family. He goes on a hunt during which Guitar tries to kill him. After the hunt, he loses his limp.

Milkman puts the pieces of his family narrative together after his second conversation with Susan Byrd.

Hagar dies of fever and heartbreak. Pilate saves her hair for Milkman's return.

Milkman returns from Shalimar and learns of Hagar's death. Pilate gives him the box of Hagar's hair and Milkman acknowledges his responsibility for her demise. He tells Pilate about what he has discovered about the family history.

Milkman and Pilate travel to Shalimar to bury Macon I's bones, the bones Pilate has been carrying with her without knowing it. After the burial, Guitar fatally shoots Pilate and attacks Milkman. Milkman surrenders to his fate and flies with the currents of his life and history.

Sula Chronology

Before 1803

According to legend, sometime before 1803, when Ohio became a state, and a free state, a white farmer promises land and freedom to his slave in exchange for the performance of some difficult tasks. The farmer has promised his slave land in the valley, but when it comes to making good on the deal, he gives the slave difficult land in the hills, and tells his slave that the land is the bottom of heaven. This story becomes the founding narrative of the Bottom, the central locale of the novel. The town that formed in the Bottom is called Medallion.

1872
Helene Sabat's mother, Rochelle Sabat, is born.

1885
Helene Sabat is born.

1890
Eva marries Boy Boy and the couple move from Eva's home in Virginia to Medallion.

Eva and Boy Boy's oldest child, Hannah, is born.

1892
Pearl is born to Eva and Boy Boy.

1895
Plum is born to Eva and Boy Boy.

Boy Boy abandons Eva and their three children.

December. After recognizing her desperation, Eva leaves her children with Mrs. Suggs for 18 months.

1897
SHADRACK is born.

Eva returns to Medallion. Upon her return, she has money and one leg.

She begins to build her house at Number Seven Carpenter's Road.

1898
Boy Boy returns to Medallion and pays a visit to Eva. She determines to spend the rest of her life hating him.

1901
Helene Sabat marries Wiley Wright and relocates from New Orleans to Medallion.

A. Jax is born.

1902
Construction is completed on Eva's house of many rooms.

1907

Pearl marries and moves to Flint, Michigan.
Jude Green, Nel's future husband, is born.

1910

Eva stops coming downstairs.
Nel is born the only child of Helene and Wiley Wright.
Sula is born to Rekus and Hannah.

1913

Rekus, Hannah's husband and Sula's father, dies. Hannah returns with her only child, Sula, to live with her mother, Eva.

1917

Shadrack is permanently traumatized by his experience in combat. He witnesses a fellow soldier having his face and head blown off by enemy fire. To Shadrack's horror, the headless soldier continues running for a short distance.
Plum goes to fight in World War I.

1919

Although still suffering from post-traumatic stress disorder and amnesia, Shadrack is released from the military hospital and wanders until he is arrested. After his arrest, Shadrack gains some psychological equilibrium, but not his memory. Shadrack then wanders into the Bottom.
Plum returns to the United States from his wartime service, but does not return to Medallion immediately.

1920

On January 3, Shadrack initiates the 1st National Suicide Day, frightening the inhabitants of the Bottom. National Suicide Day is Shadrack's attempt to control death and his fear of it.
Residents of the Bottom try to figure Shadrack out.
In November, Helene receives a letter from Mr. Henri Martin informing her about her grandmother Cecile Sabat's illness. She returns to New Orleans with Nel, but her grandmother dies before she and Nel arrive. Nel is 10 years old.
TAR BABY, an ambiguously raced, alcoholic man, takes up residence at Eva's house.
At the end of December, Plum returns from his travels to Eva's house. He is addicted to heroin.

1921

January 3. After spending the year making a home on the riverbank in the Bottom, in the shack where his grandfather lived many years before, Shadrack celebrates the second National Suicide Day. The residents of the Bottom are not as alarmed by his celebration since they have become familiar with his way of being. Shadrack gets money by selling fish to the residents and uses the money he earns to buy alcohol to drink. National Suicide Day becomes an organic part of life in the Bottom.
Eva sets her drug-addicted son Plum on fire, killing him. She sees it as a merciful act.
The Deweys arrive at Eva's and stay there.

1922

Sula cuts off the tip of her finger in an attempt to frighten off four white boys who threaten her and Nel.
Sula overhears her mother telling her friends, Patsy and Valentine, that she loves Sula, but does not like her.
Sula and Nel dig a hole together and place all the trash they can find in it.
Sula swings CHICKEN LITTLE in circles and accidentally throws the little boy into the river to his death. Shadrack witnesses the incident.

1923

Hannah asks her mother, Eva, if she ever loved her children. During the same conversation, she asks Eva why she killed Plum.
Hannah burns to death when her skirts catch on fire as she is doing laundry. Eva jumps from her bedroom window trying to save her daughter. Sula watches as her mother burns.

1927

Nel and Jude Greene get married in June.
Sula leaves Medallion for 10 years.
River Road is built, leading to the proposed tunnel under the river that would connect Medallion to the surrounding communities. No blacks are employed in the construction of the road.

1937

Medallion experiences a plague of robins.
Sula returns to Medallion.

In April, Sula has Eva committed to a nursing care facility out by Beechnut called Sunnydale.

The town starts to label Sula a pariah after Teapot falls on her stairs and Mr. Finley chokes on a chicken bone in her presence.

Sula has an affair with Nel's husband, Jude. Jude leaves Nel and, when Sula loses interest in him, moves to Detroit. Nel stops speaking to Sula.

Work begins on the long-promised, long-awaited river tunnel project. Hope runs high that blacks will be employed in the construction project.

1939

Ajax and Sula begin a relationship.

Tar Baby is beaten up by the police.

1940

After Ajax leaves her, Sula falls ill and Nel comes to visit her once.

Sula dies.

In October, Medallion experiences a sudden ice storm. The odd weather foreshadows a season of illness and misfortune in Medallion.

1941

The first three days of the year are unusually warm.

On January 3, Shadrack leads the last National Suicide Day. The warm weather draws more participants than usual. The group parades down to the river and begins to attack the long-promised river tunnel project that never materialized. Many die when the ground surrounding the site collapses.

Eva and Boy Boy's second child, Pearl, dies.

1965

Nel goes to visit Eva at Sunnydale and has an epiphany. Nel begins to see her own responsibility for the events and course of her life. She discovers that she has used Sula as a scapegoat rather than accepting that she is accountable for the events in her life and for her reactions to them. Most of all, she realizes that Sula was the most important person in her life and that she misses her terribly.

Tar Baby Chronology

Haitian laborers come to Isle des Chevaliers, an island near Dominique, and work to clear the land. The development causes a swamp to form on the island.

1906

Valerian Street is born. His family celebrates his birth with the introduction of a new candy called Valerians.

1907

Sydney is born in Baltimore.

1913

Valerian's father dies. The only person to acknowledge the boy's grief is a drunken washerwoman who provides an outlet for his grief by letting him wash clothes. The woman is fired as a result.

1924

Ondine is born.

1927

Therese is born.

(approx.) Sydney moves to Philadelphia from Baltimore.

1928

Margaret is born to Joseph and Lenora Lordi.

1929

Gideon born.

1934

Therese tastes apples for the first time.

1935

The Lordi family moves from a trailer to a house.

1937

Sydney begins working for the Streets.

1945

Valerian swears that he will retire at 65. He meets and marries Margaret, his second wife.

Sydney begins working for the Streets.

1947 (approx.)

The first house, L'Arbe de la Croix, is built on Isle des Chevaliers when Valerian purchases the island and commissions the house.

1948

March 10. Michael Street born to Margaret and Valerian Street.

1950

Valerian first discovers Michael hiding under the sink, singing a song.

(approx.) Son, the eldest son of William Green, is born in Eloe.

1951

Gideon immigrates to Canada.

1952

Jadine born in Baltimore, Maryland.

1953

Gideon moves to the United States.

1960

Michael goes to boarding school.

1962

Therese tastes apples for the second time in her life.

1965

Margaret begins to throw parties at L'Arbe de la Croix.

1966

Jadine's mother dies and she goes to live with Ondine and Sydney.

1968

Son serves in Vietnam and then is dishonorably discharged when he refuses to reenlist.

1969

Son accidentally kills his wife after finding her in bed with a teenager and then crashing his car into their house. He then leaves Eloe as a fugitive.

Jadine spends the summer in Orange County, California, with the Streets and Michael.

1971 (approx.)

Son leaves the United States and travels the world as a fugitive.

1973

As a result of Therese's deceptive, pleading letters stating her urgent need for assistance with tending their property, Gideon returns from the United States to Isle des Chevaliers. When he returns, he learns that he and Therese no longer own any property.

1975

Valerian finally retires from his family's candy business at age 68. Gideon begins working for the Streets at L'Arbe de la Croix.

1977

December. Son arrives at L'Arbe de la Croix after sneaking onto the boat that Margaret and Jadine take to town.

December 25. Ondine reveals Margaret's abuse of Michael during a verbal confrontation at Christmas dinner.

December 27. Son leaves Isle des Chevaliers and flies to New York using Gideon's passport and Jadine's money.

1978

Jadine follows Son to New York. They reside in the city in Dawn's apartment for four months.

March. Son and Jadine travel to Eloe. Jadine hates it and leaves after a couple of days. After promising to follow her the next day, Son remains in Eloe for more than a week and does not call Jadine to let her know what his plans are. This absence forever changes their relationship.

September 16. Son and Jadine have their final fight and Jadine leaves New York to return to Paris. She first stops at Isle des Chevaliers.

Son follows Jadine shortly after her departure. Therese says she will row him to Isle des Chevaliers, but instead takes him to the place where the One Hundred Horsemen are said to dwell.

SELECTED BIBLIOGRAPHY OF TONI MORRISON'S WORKS

Novels

Morrison, Toni. *Beloved.* New York: Knopf, 1987.

———. *The Bluest Eye.* New York: Holt, 1970.

———. *Jazz.* New York: Knopf, 1992.

———. *Love.* New York: Knopf, 2003.

———. *Paradise.* New York: Knopf, 1998.

———. *Song of Solomon.* New York: Knopf, 1977.

———. *Sula.* New York: Knopf, 1973.

———. *Tar Baby.* New York: Knopf, 1981.

Children's Books

Morrison, Toni. *Remember: The Journey to School Integration.* New York: Houghton Mifflin, 2004.

———. *Untitled Modern Aesop.* New York: Simon and Schuster Audio, 2006.

Morrison, Toni, and Slade Morrison. Illustrated by Giselle Potter. *The Big Box.* New York: Jump at the Sun, 1999.

Morrison, Toni, and Slade Morrison. Illustrated by Pascal Lemaitre. *The Book of Mean People.* New York: Hyperion, 2002.

———. *The Lion and the Mouse? (Who's Got Game?).* New York: Scribner, 2003.

———. *The Mirror or the Glass? (Who's Got Game?).* New York: Scribner, 2007.

———. *Who's Got Game: The Ant or the Grasshopper.* New York: Scribner, 2003.

———. *The Poppy or the Snake? (Who's Got Game?).* New York: Scribner, 2004.

Selected Essays and Interviews

Morrison, Toni. "A Conversation with Toni Morrison: 'The Language Must Not Sweat.'" By Thomas Le Clair. *New Republic,* March 21, 1981, 26–27.

———. "A Conversation: Gloria Naylor and Toni Morrison," *Southern Review* 21 (1985): 567–593.

———. "A Slow Walk of a Tree (as Grandmother Would Say), Hopeless (as Grandfather Would Say)." *New York Times Magazine,* July 4, 1976, 104.

———. "The Art of Fiction CXXXIV," *Paris Review* 128 (1993): 83–125.

———. "Behind the Making of *The Black Book,*" *Black World* (February 1974): 86–90.

———. "Clinton as the First Black President." *New Yorker,* October 1998.

———. "Home." In *The House That Race Built: Original Essays by Toni Morrison, Angela Y. Davis, Cornel West, and Others on Black Americans and Politics in America Today,* edited by Wahneema Lubiano. New York: Vintage, 1998.

———. "Memory, Creation, and Writing," *Thought* 59 (December 1984): 385–390.

———. "The Pain of Being Black." Interview with Bonnie Angelo. *Time,* May 22, 1989, 120–122.

———. "On the Backs of Blacks." *Time,* December 2, 1993, 57.

———. "Rootedness: The Ancestor as Foundation." In *Black Women Writers (1950–1980): A Critical Evaluation,* edited by Mari Evans, 339–345. Garden City, N.Y.: Anchor, 1984.

———. "Unspeakable Things Unspoken: The Afro-American Presence in American Literature," *Michigan Quarterly Review* 28, no. 1 (1989): 1–34.

———. "What the Black Woman Thinks about Women's Lib." *New York Times Magazine,* August 22, 1971, 14–15, 63–66.

Toni Morrison. "The Dead of September 11." *Vanity Fair*, November 2001, 48–49.

Nonfiction Books and Speeches

Baldwin, James, and Toni Morrison, ed. *James Baldwin: Collected Essays: Notes of a Native Son / Nobody Knows My Name / The Fire Next Time / No Name in the Street / The Devil Finds Work / Other Essays.* New York: Library of America, 1998.

Bambara, Toni Cade, and Toni Morrison, ed. *Deep Sightings and Rescue Missions: Fiction, Essays and Conversations.* New York: Pantheon, 1996.

———. *Those Bones Are Not My Child.* New York: Pantheon, 1999.

Bergman, Robert. *A Kind of Rapture.* New York: Pantheon, 1998.

Morrison, Toni. *The Dancing Mind: Speech upon Acceptance of the National Book Foundation Medal for Distinguished Contribution to American Letters.* New York: Knopf, 1996.

———. *Playing in the Dark: Whiteness and the Literary Imagination.* Cambridge, Mass.: Harvard University Press, 1992.

———. *Race-ing Justice, En-Gendering Power: Essays on Anita Hill, Clarence Thomas and the Construction of Social Reality.* New York: Pantheon Books 1992.

———. *Nobel Lecture in Literature.* New York: Knopf, 1993.

Morrison, Toni, and Boris I. Bittker. *Case for Black Reparations: The Groundbreaking First Book on Black Reparations Essential Reading for the Twenty-First Century.* Boston: Beacon Press, 2003.

Morrison, Toni, and Claudia Brodsky Lacour. *Birth of a Nation Hood: Gaze, Script and Spectacle in the O. J. Simpson Case.* New York: Knopf, 1997.

Newton, Huey P., and Toni Morrison, ed. *To Die for the People.* New York: Writers and Readers Publisher, 1995.

SELECTED BIBLIOGRAPHY
OF SECONDARY SOURCES

Abadi-Nagy, Zoltan. "Fabula and Culture: Case Study of Toni Morrison's *Jazz*," *European Journal of English Studies* 8, no. 1 (April 2004): 13–25.

Abel, Elizabeth. "Black Writing, White Reading: Race and the Politics of Feminist Interpretation," *Critical Inquiry* 19, no. 3 (Spring 1993): 470–498.

———. "(E)Merging Identities: The Dynamics of Female Friendship in Contemporary Fiction by Women," *Signs: Journal of Women in Culture and Society* 6, no. 3 (Spring 1981): 413–435.

Adams, Rachel. "The Black Look and 'the Spectacle of Whitefolks': Wildness in Toni Morrison's *Beloved*." In *Skin Deep, Spirit Strong: The Black Female Body*, edited by Kimberly Wallace Sanders, 153–181. Ann Arbor: University of Michigan Press, 2002.

Adrian, Stephanie McClure. "The Art Songs of Andre Previn with Lyrics by Toni Morrison: 'Honey and Rue' and *Four Songs for Soprano, Cello and Piano*, a Performance Perspective," *Dissertation Abstracts International, Section A: The Humanities and Social Sciences* 62, no. 11 (May 2002): 3613.

Agbajoh-Laoye, G. Oty. "Motherline, Intertext and Mothertext: African Diasporic Linkages in *Beloved* and The Joys of Motherhood," *Literary Griot: International Journal of Black Expressive Cultural Studies* 13, no. 1–2 (Spring-Fall 2001): 128–146.

Aguiar, Sarah Appleton. "'Everywhere and Nowhere': *Beloved*'s 'Wild' Legacy in Toni Morrison's *Jazz*," *Notes on Contemporary Literature* 25, no. 4 (September 1995): 11–12.

———. "Listening to the Mother's Voice in Toni Morrison's *Jazz*," *Journal of Contemporary Thought* 6 (1996): 51–65.

Aithal, S. Krishnamoorthy. "Getting Out of One's Skin and Being the Only Person Inside: Toni Morrison's *Tar Baby*," *Indian Journal of American Studies* 28, no. 1–2 (Winter-Summer 1998): 79–84.

Albrecht-Crane, Christa. "Becoming Minoritarian: Post-Identity in Toni Morrison's *Jazz*," *Journal of the Midwest Modern Language Association* 36, no. 1 (Spring 2003): 56–73.

Alexander, Harriet S. "Toni Morrison: An Annotated Bibliography of Critical Articles and Essays, 1975–1984," *College Language Association Journal* 33, no. 1 (September 1989): 81–93.

Als, Hilton. "Ghosts in the House: How Toni Morrison Fostered a Generation of Black Writers." *New Yorker*, October 27, 2003, 64–75.

Alwes, Karla. "'The Evil of Fulfillment': Women and Violence in *The Bluest Eye*." In *Women and Violence in Literature: An Essay Collection*, edited by Katherine Anne Ackley, 89–104. New York: Garland, 1990.

Andrews, Jennifer. "Reading Toni Morrison's *Jazz*: Rewriting the Tall Tale and Playing the Trickster in the White American and African American Humour Traditions," *Canadian Review of American Studies/Revue Canadienne d'Etudes Americaines* 29, no. 1 (1999): 87–107.

Angelo, Bonnie. "The Pain of Being Black: An Interview with Toni Morrison." In *Conversations with Toni Morrison*, edited by Danille Taylor-Guthrie, 255–261. Jackson: University Press of Mississippi, 1994.

Applegate, Nancy. "What's in a Name? Morrison's *Song of Solomon*," *Notes on Contemporary Literature* 27, no. 4 (September 1997): 2–3.

Ashley, Kathleen M. "Toni Morrison's Tricksters." In *Uneasy Alliance: Twentieth-Century American Literature, Culture and Biography,* edited by Hans Bak, 269–284. Amsterdam: Rodopi, 2004.

Atkinson, Yvonne. "Language That Bears Witness: The Black English Oral Tradition in the Works of Toni Morrison." In *The Aesthetics of Toni Morrison: Speaking the Unspeakable,* edited by Marc C. Conner, 12–30. Jackson: University Press of Mississippi, 2000.

Atlas, Marilyn Judith. "The Darker Side of Toni Morrison's *Song of Solomon,*" *Society for the Study of Midwestern Literature Newsletter* 10, no. 2 (1980): 1–13.

———. "The Issue of Literacy in America: Slave Narratives and Toni Morrison's *The Bluest Eye,*" *Midamerica: The Yearbook of the Society for the Study of Midwestern Literature* 27 (2000): 106–118.

———. "Toni Morrison's *Beloved* and the Reviewers," *Midwestern Miscellany* 18 (1990): 45–57.

———. "A Woman Both Shiny and Brown: Feminine Strength in Toni Morrison's *Song of Solomon,*" *Society for the Study of Midwestern Literature Newsletter* 9, no. 3 (1979): 8–12.

Awkward, Michael. *Inspiriting Influences: Tradition, Revision, and Afro-American Women's Novels.* New York: Columbia University Press, 1991.

———. "Roadblocks and Relatives: Critical Revision in Toni Morrison's *The Bluest Eye.*" In *Critical Essays on Toni Morrison,* edited by Nellie Y. McKay, 57–68. Boston: Hall, 1988.

Babbitt, Susan E. "Identity, Knowledge, and Toni Morrison's *Beloved*: Questions about Understanding Racism," *Hypatia: A Journal of Feminist Philosophy* 9, no. 3 (Summer 1994): 1–18.

Badode, R. M. "American Society as Reflected in Toni Morrison's *The Bluest Eye.*" In *Indian Views on American Literature,* edited by A. A. Mutalik-Desai, 84–94. New Delhi: Prestige, 1998.

Baillie, Justine. "Contesting Ideologies: Deconstructing Racism in African-American Fiction," *Women: A Cultural Review* 14, no. 1 (Spring 2003): 20–37.

Baker, Amy M. "On Toni Morrison: 1993 Nobel Prize-winner for Literature." In *Skoob Pacifica Anthology No. 2: The Pen Is Mightier Than the Sword,* edited by Y. C. Loh and I. K. Ong, 339–342. London: Skoob, 1994.

Bakerman, Jane. "The Seams Can't Show: An Interview with Toni Morrison." In *Conversations with Toni Morrison,* edited by Danille Taylor-Guthrie, 30–42. Jackson: University Press of Mississippi, 1994.

Banyiwa-Horne, Naana. "The Scary Face of the Self: An Analysis of the Character of Sula in Toni Morrison's *Sula.*" *SAGE: A Scholarly Journal on Black Women* 2, no. 1 (Spring 1985): 28–31.

Barksdale, Richard K. "Castration Symbolism in Recent Black American Fiction," *College Language Association Journal* 29, no. 4 (June 1986): 400–413.

Barthold, Bonnie J. *Black Time: Fiction of Africa, the Caribbean and the United States.* New Haven, Conn.: Yale University Press, 1981.

Basu, Biman. "The Black Voice and the Language of the Text: Toni Morrison's *Sula,*" *College Literature* 23, no. 3 (October 1996): 88–103.

Battles, Elizabeth H. "Slavery through the Eyes of a Mother: The Runaway Slave at Pilgrim's Point," *Studies in Browning and His Circle: A Journal of Criticism, History, and Bibliography* 19 (1991): 93–100.

Baum, Rosalie Murphy. "Alcoholism and Family Abuse in Maggie and *The Bluest Eye,*" *Mosaic: A Journal for the Interdisciplinary Study of Literature* 19, no. 3 (Summer 1986): 91–105.

Bawer, Bruce. "All That *Jazz,*" *The New Criterion* 10, no. 9 (May 1992): 10–17.

Beaulieu, Elizabeth Ann. "Gendering the Genderless: The Case of Toni Morrison's *Beloved.*" *Obsidian II: Black Literature in Review* 8, no. 1 (Spring-Summer 1993): 1–17.

———. *The Toni Morrison Encyclopedia.* Westport, Conn.: Greenwood Press, 2003.

Begley, Adam. "Toni Morrison's Public Persona," *Mirabella* 61 (June 1994): 50–54.

Bell, Pearl K. "Self-Seekers," *Commentary* 72, no. 2 (August 1981): 56–60.

Bender, Eileen T. "Repossessing Uncle Tom's Cabin: Toni Morrison's *Beloved.*" In *Cultural Power/Cultural Literacy,* edited by Bonnie Braendlin, 129–142. Tallahassee: Florida State University Press, 1991.

Benet-Goodman, Helen C. "*Sula* and the Destabilisations of Apocalypse," *Literature and Theology: An*

International Journal of Theory, Criticism and Culture 13, no. 1 (March 1999): 76–87.

Bennett, Juda. "Toni Morrison and the Burden of the Passing Narrative," *African American Review* 35, no. 2 (Summer 2001): 205–217.

Benston, Kimberly W. "Re-Weaving the 'Ulysses Scene': Enchantment, Post-Oedipal Identity, and the Buried Text of Blackness in Toni Morrison's *Song of Solomon*." In *Comparative American Identities: Race, Sex, and Nationality in the Modern Text*, edited by Hortense J. Spillers, 87–109. New York: Routledge, 1991.

Bent, Geoffrey. "Less Than Divine: Toni Morrison's *Paradise*," *Southern Review* 35, no. 1 (Winter 1999): 145–149.

Beppu, Keiko. "Toni Morrison." In *America Bungaku no Shintenkai: Dai 2-ji Sekaitaisen go no Shosetsu*, edited by Toshihiko Ogata, 203–224. Kyoto: Yamaguchi, 1983.

Berlant, Lauren. "Poor Eliza," *American Literature: A Journal of Literary History, Criticism, and Bibliography* 70, no. 3 (September 1998): 635–668.

Berret, Anthony J. "Toni Morrison's Literary *Jazz*," *College Language Association Journal* 32, no. 3 (March 1989): 267–283.

Berry, Wes. "Toni Morrison's Revisionary 'Nature Writing': *Song of Solomon* and the Blasted Pastoral." In *South to a New Place: Region, Literature, Culture*, edited by Suzanne W. Jones and Sharon Monteith, 148–164. Baton Rouge: Louisiana State University Press, 2002.

Beutel, Katherine Piller. "Gothic Repetitions: Toni Morrison's Changing Use of Echo," *West Virginia University Philological Papers* 42–43 (1997–98): 82–87.

Bhabha, Homi. "The World and the Home." In *Close Reading: The Reader*, edited by Frank Lentricchia and Andrew DuBois, 366–379. Durham, N.C.: Duke University Press, 2003.

Bidney, Martin. "Creating a Feminist-Communitarian Romanticism in *Beloved*: Toni Morrison's New Uses for Blake, Keats, and Wordsworth," *Papers on Language and Literature: A Journal for Scholars and Critics of Language and Literature* 36, no. 3 (Summer 2000): 271–301.

Bingham, Arthur. "A Linguistic Rationalization for the Universal Appeal of Toni Morrison's *Jazz*," *Language and Literature* 23 (1998): 1–12.

Bischoff, Joan. "The Novels of Toni Morrison: Studies in Thwarted Sensitivity," *Studies in Black Literature* 6, no. 3 (1975): 21–23.

Bishop, John. "Morrison's *The Bluest Eye*," *Explicator* 51, no. 4 (Summer 1993): 252–255.

Bisla, Sundeep. "Reading the Native Informant Reading: The Art of Passing on Empathy in *Beloved*." *Cultural Critique* 42 (Spring 1999): 104–136.

Bjork, Patrick Brice. *The Novels of Toni Morrison: The Search for Self and Place within the Community*. New York: Peter Lang, 1992.

Blanco, Angel Otero. "The African Past in America as a Bakhtinian and Levinasian Other. 'Rememory' as Solution in Toni Morrison's *Beloved*," *Miscelanea: A Journal of English and American Studies* 22 (2000): 141–158.

Bloom, Harold, ed. *Toni Morrison*. New York: Chelsea House, 1990.

Blyn, Robin. "Memory under Reconstruction: *Beloved* and the Fugitive Past," *Arizona Quarterly: A Journal of American Literature, Culture, and Theory* 54, no. 4 (Winter 1998): 111–140.

Boesenberg, Eva. *Gender-Voice-Vernacular: The Formation of Female Subjectivity in Zora Neale Hurston, Toni Morrison and Alice Walker*. Heidelberg, Germany: Carl Winter Universitätsverlag, 1999.

Bogus, S. Diane. "An Authorial Tie-Up: The Wedding of Symbol and Point of View in Toni Morrison's *Sula*," *College Language Association Journal* 33, no. 1 (September 1989): 73–80.

Booher, Mischelle. "'It's Not the House': *Beloved* as Gothic Novel," *Readerly/Writerly Texts: Essays on Literature, Literary/Textual Criticism, and Pedagogy* 9, no. 1–2 (Spring-Winter 2001): 117–131.

Boudreau, Kristin. "Pain and the Unmaking of Self in Toni Morrison's *Beloved*." In *Understanding Toni Morrison's Beloved and Sula: Selected Essays and Criticisms of the Works by the Nobel Prize-Winning Author*, edited by Solomon O. Iyasere and Marla W. Iyasere, 258–276. Troy, N.Y.: Whitston, 2000.

Bouson, J. Brooks. "'Quiet as It's Kept': Shame and Trauma in Toni Morrison's *The Bluest Eye*." In *Scenes of Shame: Psychoanalysis, Shame, and Writing*, edited by Joseph Adamson and Hillary Clark, 207–236. Albany: State University of New York Press, 1999.

Selected Bibliography of Secondary Sources   443

———. *Quiet as It's Kept: Shame, Trauma, and Race in the Novels of Toni Morrison.* Albany: State University of New York Press, 2000.

Boutry, Katherine. "Black and Blue: The Female Body of Blues Writing in Jean Toomer, Toni Morrison, and Gayl Jones." In *Black Orpheus: Music in African American Fiction from the Harlem Renaissance to Toni Morrison,* edited by Saadi A. Simawe, 91–118. New York: Garland, 2000.

Bowers, Susan. "*Beloved* and the New Apocalypse," *Journal of Ethnic Studies* 18, no. 1 (Spring 1990): 59–77.

Bowman, Diane Kim. "Flying High: The American Icarus in Morrison, Roth, and Updike," *PCL* 8 (1982): 10–17.

Bradfield, Scott. "Why I Hate Toni Morrison's *Beloved.*" *Denver Quarterly* 38, no. 4 (2004): 86–99.

Branch, Eleanor. "Through the Maze of the Oedipal: Milkman's Search for Self in *Song of Solomon,*" *Literature and Psychology* 41, no. 1–2 (1995): 52–84.

Bredella, Lothar. "Decolonizing the Mind: Toni Morrison's *The Bluest Eye* and *Tar Baby.*" In *Intercultural Encounters-Studies in English Literatures,* edited by Heinz Antor and Kevin L. Cope, 363–384. Heidelberg, Germany: Carl Winter Universitätsverlag, 1999.

Brenner, Gerry. "*Song of Solomon*: Morrison's Rejection of Rank's Monomyth and Feminism," *Studies in American Fiction* 15, no. 1 (Spring 1987): 13–24.

Broeck, Sabine. "Postmodern Mediations and *Beloved*'s Testimony: Memory Is Not Innocent," *Amerikastudien/American Studies* 43, no. 1 (1998): 33–49.

Brown, Caroline. "Golden Gray and the Talking Book: Identity as a Site of Artful Construction in Toni Morrison's *Jazz,*" *African American Review* 36, no. 4 (Winter 2002): 629–642.

Brown, Cecil. "Interview with Toni Morrison," *Massachusetts Review: A Quarterly of Literature, the Arts and Public Affairs* 36, no. 3 (Fall 1995): 455–473.

Bruck, Peter. "Returning to One's Roots: The Motif of Searching and Flying in Toni Morrison's *Song of Solomon* (1977)." In *The Afro-American Novel since 1960,* edited by Peter Bruck and Wolfgang Karrer, 289–305. Amsterdam: Gruner, 1982.

Buchanan, Jeffrey M. "'A Productive and Fructifying Pain': Storytelling as Teaching in *The Bluest Eye,*"

Reader: Essays in Reader-Oriented Theory, Criticism, and Pedagogy 50 (Spring 2004): 59–75.

Budick, Emily Miller. "Absence, Loss, and the Space of History in Toni Morrison's *Beloved,*" *Arizona Quarterly: A Journal of American Literature, Culture, and Theory* 48, no. 2 (Summer 1992): 117–138.

Buehrer, David. "American History X, Morrison's *Song of Solomon,* and the Psychological Intersections of Race, Class, and Place in Contemporary America," *Journal of Evolutionary Psychology* 25, no. 1–2 (March 2004): 18–23.

———. "Fragmentation and Beyond: Characterization in Toni Morrison's *Song of Solomon,*" *Journal of Evolutionary Psychology* 16, no. 1–2 (March 1995): 2–8.

Bulsterbaum, Allison A. "'Sugarman Gone Home': Folksong in Toni Morrison's *Song of Solomon,*" *Publications of the Arkansas Philological Association* 10, no. 1 (Spring 1984): 15–28.

Buma, Pascal P. "Black Female Bildungsromane: Complementary Selfhood in Toni Morrison's *Sula,*" *Literary Griot: International Journal of Black Expressive Cultural Studies* 11, no. 2 (Fall 1999): 70–96.

Burkhalter, Cindy. "Surrendering to the Air: Metaphors for Traditional African-American Wisdom in Toni Morrison's *Song of Solomon,*" *Journal of the American Studies Association of Texas (JASAT)* 26 (October 1995): 55–65.

Burton, Angela. "Signifyin(g) Abjection: Narrative Strategies in Toni Morrison's *Jazz.*" In *Toni Morrison,* edited by Linden Peach, 170–193. New York: St. Martin's Press, 1997.

Butler, Robert James. "Open Movement and Selfhood in Toni Morrison's *Song of Solomon,*" *The Centennial Review* 28–29, no. 4–1 (Fall-Winter 1984–85): 58–75.

Butler-Evans, Elliott. *Race, Gender, and Desire: Narrative Strategies in the Fiction of Toni Cade Bambara, Toni Morrison, and Alice Walker.* Philadelphia: Temple University Press, 1989.

Byerman, Keith E. "Intense Behaviors: The Use of the Grotesque in *The Bluest Eye* and *Eva's Man,*" *College Language Association Journal* 25, no. 4 (June 1982): 447–457.

Byrne, Dara. "'Yonder They Do Not Love Your Flesh': Community in Toni Morrison's *Beloved*: The Limitations of Citizenship and Property in the American Public Sphere," *Canadian Review of American*

Studies/Revue Canadienne d'Etudes Americaines 29, no. 2 (1999): 25–59.

Cadman, Deborah. "When the Back Door Is Closed and the Front Yard Is Dangerous: The Space of Girlhood in Toni Morrison's Fiction." In *The Girl: Construction of the Girl in Contemporary Fiction by Women*, edited by Ruth O. Saxton, 57–78. New York: St. Martin's Press, 1998.

Caldwell, Gail. "Author Toni Morrison Discusses Her Latest Novel *Beloved*." In *Conversations with Toni Morrison*, edited Danille Taylor-Guthrie, 239–245. Jackson: University Press of Mississippi, 1994.

Campbell, Jan. "Images of the Real: Reading History and Psychoanalysis in Toni Morrison's *Beloved*," *Women: A Cultural Review* 7, no. 2 (Autumn 1996): 136–149.

Campbell, Josie P. "To Sing the Song, To Tell the Tale: A Study of Toni Morrison and Simone Schwarz-Bart," *Comparative Literature Studies* 22, no. 3 (Fall 1985): 394–412.

Capuano, Peter J. "Singing beyond Frederick Douglass: Toni Morrison's Use of Song in *Beloved*," *MAWA Review* 16, no. 1–2 (June–December 2001): 60–66.

———. "Truth in Timbre: Morrison's Extension of Slave Narrative Song in *Beloved*," *African American Review* 37, no. 1 (Spring 2003): 95–103.

Carabi, Angels. "Interview: Toni Morrison on *Jazz*," *Belles Lettres* 10, no. 2 (Spring 1995): 40–43.

———. "Toni Morrison," *Belles Lettres* 9, no. 3 (May 1994): 38–39, 86–90.

Casler, Jeanine. "Monstrous Motherhood across Cultures: The Rejection of the Maternal," *JAISA: The Journal of the Association for the Interdisciplinary Study of the Arts* 5, no. 1 (Fall 1999): 43–54.

Chadwick-Joshua, Jocelyn. "Metonymy and Synecdoche: The Rhetoric of the City in Toni Morrison's *Jazz*." In *The City in African-American Literature*, edited by Yoshinobu Hakutani and Robert Butler, 168–180. Madison, N.J.: Fairleigh Dickinson University Press, 1995.

Christian, Barbara. "Beloved, She's Ours," *Narrative* 5, no. 1 (January 1997): 36–49.

———. "Community and Nature: The Novels of Toni Morrison," *Journal of Ethnic Studies* 7, no. 4 (Winter 1980): 65–78.

———. "Layered Rhythms: Virginia Woolf and Toni Morrison," *MFS: Modern Fiction Studies* 39, no. 3–4 (Fall-Winter 1993): 483–500.

Clark, Norris. "Flying Black: Toni Morrison's *The Bluest Eye, Sula,* and *Song of Solomon*," *MV* 4, no. 2 (Fall 1980): 51–63.

Clarke, Deborah L. "'What There Was before Language': Preliteracy in Toni Morrison's *Song of Solomon*." In *Anxious Power: Reading, Writing, and Ambivalence in Narrative by Women*, edited by Carol J. Singley and Elizabeth Susan Sweeney, 265–278. Albany: State University of New York Press, 1993.

Clasby, Nancy. "Sula the Trickster." *Tenfelde Lit: Literature Interpretation Theory* 6, no. 1–2 (April 1995): 21–34.

Clewell, Tammy. "From Destructure to Constructive Haunting in Toni Morrison's *Paradise*," *West Coast Line* 37, no. 36 (Spring 2002): 130–142.

Closser, Raleen. "Morrison's *Sula*." *Explicator* 63 (Winter 2005): 111.

Coleman, Alisha R. "One and One Make One: A Metacritical and Psychoanalytical Reading of Friendship in Toni Morrison's *Sula*," *College Language Association Journal* 37, no. 2 (December 1993): 145–155.

Coleman, James W. "Beyond the Reach of Love and Caring: Black Life in Toni Morrison's *Song of Solomon*," *Obsidian II: Black Literature in Review* 1, no. 3 (Winter 1986): 151–161.

Comfort, Susan. "Counter-Memory, Mourning and History in Toni Morrison's *Beloved*," *Lit: Literature Interpretation Theory* 6, no. 1–2 (April 1995): 121–132.

Conner, Marc C. "From the Sublime to the Beautiful: The Aesthetic Progression of Toni Morrison." In *The Aesthetics of Toni Morrison: Speaking the Unspeakable*, edited by Marc C. Conner, 49–76. Jackson: University Press of Mississippi, 2000.

Conner, Marc C., ed. *The Aesthetics of Toni Morrison: Speaking the Unspeakable*. Jackson: University Press of Mississippi, 2000.

"Conversation with Alice Childress and Toni Morrison." In *Conversations with Toni Morrison*, edited by Danille Taylor-Guthrie, 3–9. Jackson: University Press of Mississippi, 1994.

Cooper, Grace C. "Language in Morrison's Novels," *MAWA Review* 8, no. 1 (June 1993): 27–31.

Corey, Susan. "The Religious Dimensions of the Grotesque in Literature: Toni Morrison's *Beloved*." In *The Grotesque in Art and Literature: Theological Reflections,* edited by James Luther Adams and Wilson Yates, 227–242. Grand Rapids, Mich.: Eerdmans, 1997.

———. "Toward the Limits of Mystery: The Grotesque in Toni Morrison's *Beloved*." In *The Aesthetics of Toni Morrison: Speaking the Unspeakable,* edited by Marc C. Conner, 31–48. Jackson: University Press of Mississippi, 2000.

Corti, Lillian. "Medea and *Beloved*: Self-Definition and Abortive Nurturing in Literary Treatments of the Infanticidal Mother." In *Disorderly Eaters: Texts in Self Empowerment,* edited by Lilian R. Furst and Peter W. Graham, 61–77. University Park: Pennsylvania State University Press, 1992.

Croyden, Margaret. "Toni Morrison Tries Her Hand at Playwriting." In *Conversations with Toni Morrison,* edited by Danille Taylor Guthrie, 218–222. Jackson: University Press of Mississippi, 1994.

Cullinan, Colleen Carpenter. "A Maternal Discourse of Redemption: Speech and Suffering in Morrison's *Beloved*," *Religion and Literature* 34, no. 2 (Summer 2002): 77–104.

Cumings, Susan G. "'Outing' the Hidden Other: Stranger-Women in the Work of Toni Morrison." In *Dissent and Marginality: Essays on the Borders of Literature and Religion,* edited by Kiyoshi Tsuchiya, 45–57. Basingstoke, England: Macmillan, 1997.

Daily, Gary W. "Toni Morrison's *Beloved*: Rememory, History and the Fantastic." In *The Celebration of the Fantastic: Selected Papers from the Tenth Anniversary International Conference on the Fantastic in the Arts,* edited by Donald E. Morse, Marshall B. Tymn, and Csilla Bertha, 141–147. Westport, Conn.: Greenwood Press, 1992.

Dalsgard, Katrine. "The One All-Black Town Worth the Pain: (African) American Exceptionalism, Historical Narration, and the Critique of Nationhood in Toni Morrison's *Paradise*," *African American Review* 35, no. 2 (Summer 2001): 233–248.

Daniel, Janice Barnes. "Function or Frill: The Quilt as Storyteller in Toni Morrison's *Beloved*," *Midwest Quarterly: A Journal of Contemporary Thought* 41, no. 3 (Spring 2000): 321–329.

Daniels, Jean. "The Call of Baby Suggs in *Beloved*: Imagining Freedom in Resistance and Struggle," *Griot: Official Journal of the Southern Conference on Afro-American Studies* 21, no. 2 (Fall 2002): 1–7.

Daniels, Steven V. "Putting 'His Story Next to Hers': Choice, Agency, and the Structure of *Beloved*," *Texas Studies in Literature and Language* 44, no. 4 (Winter 2002): 349–367.

Darling, Marsha. "In the Realm of Responsibility: A Conversation with Toni Morrison." In *Conversations with Toni Morrison,* edited by Danille Taylor-Guthrie, 246–254. Jackson: University Press of Mississippi, 1994.

Dauterich, Edward. "Hybrid Expression: Orality and Literacy in *Jazz* and *Beloved*," *Midwest Quarterly: A Journal of Contemporary Thought* 47 (Autumn 2005): 26–39.

Davidson, Rob. "Racial Stock and 8-Rocks: Communal Historiography in Toni Morrison's *Paradise*." *Twentieth Century Literature: A Scholarly and Critical Journal* 47, no. 3 (Fall 2001): 355–373.

Davies, Jacqueline MacGregor. "More Than the Moral of the Story: Contributions to Narrative Ethics from Carol Gilligan, '*Beloved*' and Jephthah's Daughter," *Dissertation Abstracts International, Section A: The Humanities and Social Sciences* 58, no. 6 (December 1997): 2,240–2,241.

Davis, Christina. "An Interview with Toni Morrison." In *Conversations with Toni Morrison,* edited by Danille Taylor Guthrie, 223–233. Jackson: University Press of Mississippi, 1994.

Davis, Cynthia A. "Self, Society, and Myth in Toni Morrison's Fiction," *Contemporary Literature* 23, no. 3 (Summer 1982): 323–342.

———. "Self, Society and Myth in Toni Morrison's Fiction." In *Toni Morrison,* edited by Linden Peach, 27–42. New York: St. Martin's Press, 1997.

Davis, Kimberly Chabot. "'Postmodern Blackness': Toni Morrison's *Beloved* and the End of History." In *Productive Postmodernism: Consuming Histories and Cultural Studies,* edited by John N. Duvall, 75–92. Albany: State University of New York Press, 2002.

D'Cruz, Doreen. "The Liquid Alterity of the Maternal-Feminine in Toni Morrison's *Beloved*," *AUMLA: Journal of the Australasian Universities Language and Literature Association: A Journal of Literary Criticism and Linguistics* 92 (November 1999): 50–79.

De Angelis, Rose. "Morrison's *Sula*," *Explicator* 60, no. 3 (Spring 2002): 172–174.

———. "Rewriting the Black Matriarch: Eva in Toni Morrison's *Sula*," *MAWA Review* 16, no. 1–2 (June–December 2001): 52–59.

De Arman, Charles. "Milkman as the Archetypal Hero: 'Thursday's Child Has Far to Go,'". *Obsidian* 6, no. 3 (Winter 1980): 56–59.

DeLancey, Dayle B. "Motherlove Is a Killer: *Sula, Beloved*, and the Deadly Trinity of Motherlove," *SAGE: A Scholarly Journal on Black Women* 7, no. 2 (Fall 1990): 15–18.

———. "Sweetness, Madness, and Power: The Confection as Mental Contagion in Toni Morrison's *Tar Baby, Song of Solomon*, and *The Bluest Eye*." In *Process: A Journal of African American and African Diasporan Literature and Culture* 2 (Spring 2000): 25–47.

Delashmit, Margaret. "*The Bluest Eye*: An Indictment," *Griot: Official Journal of the Southern Conference on Afro-American Studies* 20, no. 1 (Spring 2001): 12–18.

Demetrakopoulos, Stephanie. "The Nursing Mother and Feminine Metaphysics: An Essay on Embodiment," *Soundings: An Interdisciplinary Journal* 65, no. 4 (Winter 1982): 430–443.

Denard, Carolyn. "The Convergence of Feminism and Ethnicity in the Fiction of Toni Morrison." In *Critical Essays on Toni Morrison*, edited by Nellie Y. McKay, 171–179. Boston: Hall, 1988.

De Vita, Alexis Brooks. "Not Passing On *Beloved*: The Sacrificial Child and the Circle of Redemption," *Griot: Official Journal of the Southern Conference on Afro-American Studies* 19, no. 1 (Spring 2000): 1–12.

DiBattista, Maria. "Contentions in the House of Chloe: Morrison's *Tar Baby*." In *The Aesthetics of Toni Morrison: Speaking the Unspeakable*, edited by Marc C. Conner, 92–112. Jackson: University Press of Mississippi, 2000.

Dickerson, Vanessa D. "The Naked Father in Toni Morrison's *The Bluest Eye*." In *Refiguring the Father: New Feminist Readings of Patriarchy*, edited by Patricia Yaeger and Beth Kowaleski Wallace, 108–127. Carbondale: Southern Illinois University Press, 1989.

———. "Summoning SomeBody: The Flesh Made Word in Toni Morrison's Fiction." In *Recovering the Black Female Body: Self-Representations by African American Women*, edited by Michael Bennett and Vanessa D. Dickerson, 195–216. New Brunswick, N.J.: Rutgers University Press, 2001.

Diedrich, Maria. "'Things Fall Apart?': The Black Critical Controversy over Toni Morrison's *Beloved*," *Amerikastudien/American Studies* 34, no. 2 (1989): 175–186.

Di Loreto, Sonia. "'Short and Flashy Results': *Beloved* and the Civil War." In *Red Badges of Courage: Wars and Conflicts in American Culture*, edited by Biancamarie Pisapia, Ugo Rubeo, and Anna Scacchi, 520–525. Rome: Bulzoni, 1998.

Dittmar, Linda. "'Will the Circle Be Unbroken?' The Politics of Form in *The Bluest Eye*," *Novel: A Forum on Fiction* 23, no. 2 (Winter 1990): 137–155.

Domini, John. "Toni Morrison's *Sula*: An Inverted Inferno," *High Plains Literary Review* 3, no. 1 (Spring 1988): 75–90.

Doughty, Peter. "A Fiction for the Tribe: Toni Morrison's *The Bluest Eye*." In *The New American Writing: Essays on American Literature Since 1970*, edited by Graham Clarke, 29–50. New York: St. Martin's Press, 1990.

Dowling, Colette. "The Song of Toni Morrison." In *Conversations with Toni Morrison*, edited by Danille Taylor Guthrie, 48–59. Jackson: University Press of Mississippi, 1994.

Dubey, Madhu. "'No Bottom and No Top': Oppositions in *Sula*." In *Toni Morrison*, edited by Linden Peach, 70–88. New York: St. Martin's, 1997.

Dudek, Debra. "The Magnificent Missing Leg: Masochistic Love in Toni Morrison's *Sula*," *Postscript: A Journal of Graduate School Criticism and Theory* 3, no. 2 (Spring 1996): 122–128.

Dudley, David. "Toni Morrison (1931–)." In *Gothic Writers: A Critical and Bibliographical Guide*, edited by Douglass H. Thomson, Jack G. Voller, and Frederick S. Frank, 295–302. Westport, Conn.: Greenwood, 2002.

Duvall, John N. *The Identifying Fictions of Toni Morrison: Modernist Authenticity and Postmodern Blackness*. New York: Palgrave, 2000.

———. "Parody or Pastiche? Kathy Acker, Toni Morrison, and the Critical Appropriation of Faulknerian Masculinity," *Faulkner Journal* 15, no. 1–2 (Fall-Spring 1999–2000): 169–184.

Dyer, Joyce. "Reading The Awakening with Toni Morrison," *Southern Literary Journal* 35, no. 1 (Fall 2002): 138–154.

Eckard, Paula Gallant. "The Interplay of Music, Language, and Narrative in Toni Morrison's *Jazz*," *College Language Association Journal* 28, no. 1 (September 1994): 11–19.

Elbert, Monika. "Maternal Dialogics in Toni Morrison's Fiction," *Lit: Literature Interpretation Theory* 6, no. 1–2 (April 1995): 73–88.

———. "Persephone's Return: Communing with the Spirit-Daughter in Morrison and Allende," *Journal of the Association for Research on Mothering* 4, no. 2 (Fall-Winter 2002): 158–170.

Elia, Nada. "'Kum Buba Yali Kum Buba Tambe, Ameen, Ameen, Ameen' Did Some Flying Africans Bow to Allah?" *Callaloo: A Journal of African-American and African Arts and Letters* 26, no. 1 (Winter 2003): 182–202.

Ellis, Kate. "Text and Undertext: Myth and Politics in Toni Morrison's *Song of Solomon*," *Lit: Literature Interpretation Theory* 6, no. 1–2 (April 1995): 35–45.

Emberley, Julia V. "A Historical Transposition: Toni Morrison's *Tar Baby* and Frantz Fanon's Post-Enlightenment Phantasms," *MFS: Modern Fiction Studies* 45, no. 2 (Summer 1999): 403–431.

Eppert, Claudia. "Histories Re-Imagined, Forgotten and Forgiven: Student Responses to Toni Morrison's *Beloved*," *Changing English: Studies in Reading and Culture* 10, no. 2 (October 2003): 185–194.

Epstein, Grace A. "Out of Blue Water: Dream Flight and Narrative Construction in the Novels of Toni Morrison." In *State of the Fantastic: Studies in the Theory and Practice of Fantastic Literature and Film*, edited by Nicholas Ruddick, 141–147. Westport, Conn.: Greenwood, 1992.

Erickson, Peter B. "Images of Nurturance in Toni Morrison's *Tar Baby*," *College Language Association Journal* 28, no. 1 (September 1984): 11–32.

Fabi, M. Giulia. "On Nobel Prizes and the 'Robinson Crusoe Syndrome': The Case of Toni Morrison," *Journal of Gender Studies* 2, no. 2 (November 1993): 253–258.

Fabre, Genevieve. "Genealogical Archaeology or the Quest for Legacy in Toni Morrison's *Song of Solo-*

mon." In *Critical Essays on Toni Morrison*, edited by Nellie Y. McKay, 105–114. Boston: Hall, 1988.

Falling-rain, Sunny. "A Literary Patchwork Crazy Quilt: Toni Morrison's *Beloved*," *Uncoverings: Research Papers of the American Quilt Study Group* 15 (1994): 111–140.

Farrell, Susan. "'Who'd He Leave Behind?': Gender and History in Toni Morrison's *Song of Solomon*," *Bucknell Review: A Scholarly Journal of Letters, Arts and Sciences* 39, no. 1 (1995): 131–150.

Feng, Pin-chia. "Memory and Identity: Engendering New Black Womanhood in *Sula*," *Studies in Language and Literature* 7 (August 1996): 89–111.

Ferguson, Rebecca. "History, Memory and Language in Toni Morrison's *Beloved*." In *Contemporary American Women Writers: Gender, Class, Ethnicity*, edited by Lois Parkinson Zamora, 154–174. London: Longman, 1998.

Fick, Thomas H. "Toni Morrison's 'Allegory of the Cave': Movies, Consumption, and Platonic Realism in *The Bluest Eye*," *Journal of the Midwest Modern Language Association* 22, no. 1 (Spring 1989): 10–22.

Fields, Karen E. "To Embrace Dead Strangers: Toni Morrison's *Beloved*." In *Mother Puzzles: Daughters and Mothers in Contemporary American Literature*, edited by Mickey Pearlman, 159–169. Westport, Conn.: Greenwood Press, 1989.

Fikes, Robert, Jr. "Echoes from Small Town Ohio: A Toni Morrison Bibliography," *Obsidian: Black Literature in Review* 5, no. 1–2 (1979): 142–148.

Fils-Aime, Holly. "The Living Dead Learn to Fly: Themes of Spiritual Death, Initiation and Empowerment in A Praisesong for the Widow and *Song of Solomon*," *MAWA Review* 10, no. 1 (June 1995): 3–12.

Finney, Brian. "Temporal Defamiliarization in Toni Morrison's *Beloved*," *Obsidian II: Black Literature in Review* 5, no. 1 (Spring 1990): 20–36.

Fishman, Charles. "Naming Names: Three Recent Novels by Women Writers," *Names: A Journal of Onomastics* 32, no. 1 (March 1984): 33–44.

FitzGerald, Jennifer. "Selfhood and Community: Psychoanalysis and Discourse in *Beloved*," *MFS: Modern Fiction Studies* 39, no. 3–4 (Fall-Winter 1993): 669–687.

———. "Signifyin(g) on Determinism: Commodity, Romance and Bricolage in Toni Morrison's

Jazz," *Lit: Literature Interpretation Theory* 12, no. 4 (December 2001): 381–409.

Flanagan, Joseph. "The Seduction of History: Trauma, Re-Memory, and the Ethics of the Real," *CLIO: A Journal of Literature, History, and the Philosophy of History* 31, no. 4 (Summer 2002): 387–402.

Folks, Jeffrey J. "Language and Cultural Authority in Toni Morrison's *Jazz,*" *Journal of Literary Studies/ Tydskrif vir Literatuurwetenskap* 15, no. 1–2 (June 1999): 146–159.

Foor, Sheila M. "Toni Morrison's Rhetoric of Assemblage: The Jigsaws of *Beloved,*" *Pennsylvania English* 19, no. 1 (Fall-Winter 1994): 37–52.

Fraile-Marcos, Ana Maria. "Hybridizing the 'City upon a Hill' in Toni Morrison's *Paradise,*" *MELUS: The Journal of the Society for the Study of the Multi-Ethnic Literature of the United States* 28, no. 4 (Winter 2003): 3–33.

———. "The Religious Overtones of Ethnic Identity-Building in Toni Morrison's *Paradise,*" *Atlantis: Revista de la Asociacion Espanola de Estudios Anglo Norteamericanos* 24, no. 2 (December 2002): 95–116.

Fritz, Angela DiPace. "Toni Morrison's *Beloved*: 'Unspeakable Things Unspoken' Spoken," *Sacred Heart University Review* 14, no. 1–2 (Fall 1993–Spring 1994): 40–52.

Fryar, Lillie B. "The Aesthetics of Language: Harper, Hurston and Morrison," *Dissertation Abstracts International* 47, no. 2 (August 1986): 529A.

Fultz, Lucille P. "Images of Motherhood in Toni Morrison's *Beloved.*" In *Double Stitch: Black Women Write about Mothers and Daughters,* edited by Patricia Bell-Scott et al., 32–41. New York: HarperCollins/ Beacon, 1993.

———. "Southern Ethos/Black Ethics in Toni Morrison's Fiction," *Studies in the Literary Imagination* 31, no. 2 (Fall 1998): 79–95.

———. *Toni Morrison: Playing with Difference.* Urbana: University of Illinois Press, 2003.

Fulweiler, Howard W. "Belonging and Freedom in Morrison's *Beloved*: Slavery, Sentimentality, and the Evolution of Consciousness," *Centennial Review* 40, no. 2 (Spring 1996): 331–358.

Furman, Jan. *Toni Morrison's Fiction.* Columbia: University of South Carolina Press, 1996.

Fussell, Betty. "All That *Jazz.*" In *Conversations with Toni Morrison,* edited by Danille Taylor Guthrie, 280–287. Jackson: University Press of Mississippi, 1994.

Fuston-White, Jeanna. "'From the Seen to the Told': The Construction of Subjectivity in Toni Morrison's *Beloved,*" *African American Review* 36, no. 3 (Fall 2002): 461–473.

Galehouse, Maggie. "'New World Woman': Toni Morrison's *Sula,*" *Papers on Language and Literature: A Journal for Scholars and Critics of Language and Literature* 35, no. 4 (Fall 1999): 339–362.

Garabedian, Deanna M. "Toni Morrison and the Language of Music," *CLA Journal* 41, no. 3 (March 1998): 303–318.

Garbus, Lisa. "The Unspeakable Stories of Shoah and *Beloved,*" *College Literature* 26, no. 1 (Winter 1999): 52–68.

Gauthier, Marni. "The Other Side of *Paradise*: Toni Morrison's (Un)Making of Mythic History," *African American Review* 39 (Fall 2005): 395–414.

Gerster, Carole J. "From Film Margin to Novel Center: Toni Morrison's *The Bluest Eye,*" *West Virginia University Philological Papers* 38 (1992): 191–200.

Gilbert, Katherine. "'The Best Hiding Place': Internalization and Coping Mechanisms in Toni Morrison's *The Bluest Eye,*" *MAWA Review* 8, no. 2 (December 1993): 48–52.

Gillan, Jennifer. "Focusing on the Wrong Front: Historical Displacement, the Maginot Line, and *The Bluest Eye,*" *African American Review* 36, no. 2 (Summer 2002): 283–298.

Gillespie, Diane, and Missy Dehn. "Who Cares? Women-Centered Psychology in *Sula.*" In *Understanding Toni Morrison's Beloved and Sula: Selected Essays and Criticisms of the Works by the Nobel Prize-Winning Author,* edited by Solomon O. Iyasere and Marla W. Iyasere, 19–48. Troy, N.Y.: Whitston, 2000.

Goldstein-Shirley, David. "Race/[Gender]: Toni Morrison's 'Recitatif'," *Journal of the Short Story in English* 27 (Autumn 1996): 83–95.

Gourdine, Angeletta K. M. "Hearing, Reading and Being Read by *Beloved,*" *NWSA Journal* 10, no. 2 (Summer 1998): 13–31.

Grant, Robert. "Absence into Presence: The Thematics of Memory and 'Missing' Subjects in Toni

Morrison's *Sula*." In *Critical Essays on Toni Morrison*, edited by Nellie Y. McKay, 90–103. Boston: Hall, 1988.

Greenbaum, Vicky. "Teaching *Beloved*: Images of Transcendence," *English Journal* 91, no. 6 (July 2002): 83–87.

Grewal, Gurleen. *Circles of Sorrow, Lines of Struggle: The Novels of Toni Morrison*. Baton Rouge: Louisiana State University Press, 1998.

Griesinger, Emily. "Why Baby Suggs, Holy, Quit Preaching the Word: Redemption and Holiness in Toni Morrison's *Beloved*," *Christianity and Literature* 50, no. 4 (Summer 2001): 689–702.

Groover, Kristina K. "The Wilderness Within: Home as Sacred Space in American Women's Writing—Jewett's *The Country of the Pointed Firs*, Morrison's *The Bluest Eye* and Gibbons' *Ellen Foster*," *MAWA Review* 12, no. 1 (June 1997): 13–29.

Guth, Deborah. "A Blessing and a Burden: The Relation to the Past in *Sula, Song of Solomon* and *Beloved*," *MFS: Modern Fiction Studies* 39, no. 3–4 (Fall-Winter 1993): 575–596.

———. "A Blessing and a Burden: The Relation to the Past in *Sula, Song of Solomon* and *Beloved*." In *Understanding Toni Morrison's Beloved and Sula: Selected Essays and Criticisms of the Works by the Nobel Prize–Winning Author*, edited by Solomon O. Iyasere and Marla W. Iyasere, 315–337. Troy, N.Y.: Whitston, 2000.

———. "'Wonder What God Had in Mind': *Beloved*'s Dialogue with Christianity," *Journal of Narrative Technique* 24, no. 2 (Spring 1994): 83–97.

Gutmann, Katharina. *Celebrating the Senses: An Analysis of the Sensual in Toni Morrison's Fiction*. Tübingen, Germany: Francke, 2000.

Gwin, Minrose C. "'Hereisthehouse': Cultural Spaces of Incest in *The Bluest Eye*." In *Incest and the Literary Imagination*, edited by Elizabeth Barnes, 316–328. Gainesville: University Press of Florida, 2002.

Haley, Shelley Pbb. "Self-Definition, Community, and Resistance: Euripides' 'Medea' and Toni Morrison's 'Beloved'," *Thamyris: Mythmaking from Past to Present* 2, no. 2 (Autumn 1995): 177–206.

Hardack, Richard. "'A Music Seeking Its Words': Double-Timing and Double Consciousness in Toni Morrison's *Jazz*," *Black Warrior Review* 19, no. 2 (Spring-Summer 1993): 151–171.

Harding, Wendy, and Jacky Martin. *A World of Difference: An Inter-Cultural Study of Toni Morrison's Novels*. Westport, Conn.: Greenwood, 1994.

Harris, Norman. "The Black Universe in Contemporary Afro-American Fiction," *College Language Association Journal* 30, no. 1 (September 1986): 1–13.

Harris, Trudier. *Fiction and Folklore: The Novels of Toni Morrison*. Knoxville: University of Tennessee Press, 1991.

———. "Reconnecting Fragments: Afro-American Folk Tradition in *The Bluest Eye*." In *Critical Essays on Toni Morrison*, edited by Nellie Y. McKay, 68–76. Boston: Hall, 1988.

———. "Toni Morrison: Solo Flight through Literature into History." *World Literature Today: A Literary Quarterly of the University of Oklahoma* 68, no. 1 (Winter 1994): 9–14.

———. "The Worlds That Toni Morrison Made," *The Georgia Review* 49, no. 1 (Spring 1995): 314–330.

Harting, Heike. "'Chokecherry Tree(s)': Operative Modes of Metaphor in Toni Morrison's '*Beloved*'," *ARIEL: A Review of International English Literature* 29, no. 4 (October 1998): 23–51.

Hebert, Kimberly G. "Acting the Nigger: Topsy, Shirley Temple, and Toni Morrison's Pecola." In *Approaches to Teaching Stowe's Uncle Tom's Cabin*, edited by Elizabeth Ammons and Susan Belasco, 184–198. New York: Modern Language Association of America, 2000.

Heffernan, Teresa. "*Beloved* and the Problem of Mourning," *Studies in the Novel* 30, no. 4 (Winter 1998): 558–573.

Heinze, Denise. *The Dilemma of 'Double Consciousness': Toni Morrison's Novels*. Athens: University of Georgia Press, 1993.

Heller, Dana. "Reconstructing Kin: Family, History, and Narrative in Toni Morrison's *Beloved*," *College Literature* 21, no. 2 (June 1994): 105–117.

Henderson, Mae G. "Toni Morrison's *Beloved*: Re-Membering the Body as Historical Text." In *Comparative American Identities: Race, Sex, and Nationality in the Modern Text*, edited by Hortense J. Spillers, 62–86. New York: Routledge, 1991.

Hendrick, Veronica Catherine. "Transgression and Reprisal in Toni Morrison's Fiction: Breaking the Codes of Race and Gender as a Way to Autonomy," *Dissertation Abstracts International, Section A:*

The Humanities and Social Sciences 59, no. 4 (October 1998): 1,165.

Hewlett, Peter. "Messianic Time in Toni Morrison's *Beloved.*" *Agora: An Online Graduate Journal* 1, no. 1 (Fall 2001). Available online. URL: http://www.humanities.ualberta.ca/agora/Articles.cfm?ArticleNo=121. Accessed on September 21, 2006.

Hilfer, Anthony C. "Critical Indeterminacies in Toni Morrison's Fiction: An Introduction," *Texas Studies in Literature and Language* 33, no. 1 (Spring 1991): 91–95.

Hindman, Jane E. "'A Little Space, a Little Time, Some Way to Hold Off Eventfulness': African American Quiltmaking as Metaphor in Toni Morrison's *Beloved,*" *Lit: Literature Interpretation Theory* 6, no. 1–2 (April 1995): 101–120.

Hirsch, Marianne. "Maternity and Rememory: Toni Morrison's *Beloved.*" In *Representations of Motherhood,* edited by Donna Bassin, Margaret Honey, and Meryle Mahrer Kaplan, 92–110. New Haven, Conn.: Yale University Press, 1994.

Hoem, Sheri I. "Disabling Postmodernism: Wideman, Morrison and Prosthetic Critique." *Novel: A Forum on Fiction* 35, no. 2–3 (Spring-Summer 2002): 193–210.

Hogle, Jerrold E. "Teaching the African American Gothic: From Its Multiple Sources to Linden Hills and *Beloved.*" In *Approaches to Teaching Gothic Fiction: The British and American Traditions,* edited by Diane Long Hoeveler and Tamar Heller, 215–222. New York: Modern Language Association of America, 2003.

Hogue, W. Lawrence. "Postmodernism, Traditional Cultural Forms, and the African American Narrative: Major's *Reflex,* Morrison's *Jazz,* and Reed's *Mumbo Jumbo,*" *Novel: A Forum on Fiction* 35, no. 2–3 (Spring-Summer 2002): 169–192.

Holland, Sharon P. "Bakulu Discourse: The Language of the Margin in Toni Morrison's *Beloved,*" *Lit: Literature Interpretation Theory* 6, no. 1–2 (April 1995): 89–100.

Holloway, Karla F. C., and Stephanie A. Demetrakopoulos. *New Dimensions of Spirituality: A Biracial and Bicultural Reading of the Novels of Toni Morrison.* New York: Greenwood, 1987.

———. "Remembering Our Foremothers: Older Black Women, Politics of Age, Politics of Sur- vival as Embodied in the Novels of Toni Morrison," *Women and Politics* 6, no. 2 (Summer 1986): 13–34.

Holton, Robert. "Bearing Witness: Toni Morrison's *Song of Solomon* and *Beloved,*" *English Studies in Canada* 20, no. 1 (March 1994): 79–90.

Homans, Margaret. "'Her Very Own Howl': The Ambiguities of Representation in Recent Women's Fiction," *Signs: Journal of Women in Culture and Society* 9, no. 2 (Winter 1983): 186–205.

Horvitz, Deborah. "Nameless Ghosts: Possession and Dispossession in *Beloved,*" *Studies in American Fiction* 17, no. 2 (Autumn 1989): 157–167.

Hostettler, Maya. "Telling the Past—Doing the Truth: Toni Morrison's *Beloved,*" *Women's History Review* 5, no. 3 (1996): 401–416.

House, Elizabeth B. "Artists and the Art of Living: Order and Disorder in Toni Morrison's Fiction," *MFS: Modern Fiction Studies* 34, no. 1 (Spring 1988): 27–44.

———. "Toni Morrison's Ghost: The *Beloved* Who Is Not *Beloved,*" *Studies in American Fiction* 18, no. 1 (Spring 1990): 17–26.

Hove, Thomas B. "Toni Morrison." In *Postmodernism: The Key Figures,* edited by Hans Bertens and Joseph Natoli, 254–260. Malden, Mass.: Blackwell, 2002.

Hovet, Grace Ann, and Barbara Lounsberry. "Flying as Symbol and Legend in Toni Morrison's *The Bluest Eye, Sula,* and *Song of Solomon,*" *College Language Association Journal* 27, no. 2 (December 1983): 119–140.

Huang, Hsin-ya. "Three Women's Texts and the Healing Power of the Other Woman," *Concentric: Literary and Cultural Studies* 28, no. 1 (January 2003): 153–180.

Hubbard, Dolan. "In Quest of Authority: Toni Morrison's *Song of Solomon* and the Rhetoric of the Black Preacher," *College Language Association Journal* 35, no. 3 (March 1992): 288–302.

Humphrey, Catherine Carr. "Toni Morrison's Sermon: A Gospel of Love and Imagination," *Dissertation Abstracts International* 56, no. 3 (September 1995): 931A.

Hunt, Kristin. "*Paradise* Lost: The Destructive Forces of Double Consciousness and Boundaries in Toni Morrison's *Paradise.*" In *Reading under the Sign of Nature: New Essays in Ecocriticism,* edited by John

Tallmadge and Henry Harrington, 117–127. Salt Lake City: University of Utah Press, 2000.

Hsu, Lina. "Aesthetic Experience of the Novel: The Narrative of Toni Morrison's *Sula*," *Studies in Language and Literature* 9 (June 2000): 289–329.

Iannone, Carol. "Toni Morrison's Career," *Commentary* 84, no. 6 (December 1987): 59–63.

Ibrahim, Huma. "Speaking in Tongues: The Living Past," *Thamyris: Mythmaking from Past to Present* 6, no. 2 (Autumn 1999): 195–214.

Inoue, Kazuko. "'I Got a Tree on My Back': A Study on Toni Morrison's Latest Novel, *Beloved*," *Language and Culture* 15 (1988): 69–82.

———. "A Study on Toni Morrison: The Quest for a Real Woman," *Language and Culture* 10 (1986): 133–144.

Insko, Jeffrey. "Literary Popularity: *Beloved* and Pop Culture," *Lit: Literature Interpretation Theory* 12, no. 4 (December 2001): 427–447.

Iyasere, Solomon O., and Marla W. Iyasere, eds. *Understanding Toni Morrison's Beloved and Sula: Selected Essays and Criticisms of the Works by the Nobel Prize–Winning Author.* Troy, N.Y.: Whitston, 2000.

Jablon, Madelyn. "The Art of Influence in Toni Morrison's *Tar Baby*," *MAWA Review* 10, no. 1 (June 1995): 33–38.

Jackson, Tommie L. "The Polyphonic Texture of the Trope 'Junkheaped' in Toni Morrison's *Beloved*," *Griot: Official Journal of the Southern Conference on Afro-American Studies* 18, no. 2 (Fall 1999): 19–33.

Jessee, Sharon. "Git Way Inside Us, Keep Us Strong': Toni Morrison and the Art of Critical Production," *MFS: Modern Fiction Studies* 52 (Spring 2006): 179–186.

———. "'Tell Me Your Earrings': Time and the Marvelous in Toni Morrison's *Beloved*." In *Memory, Narrative, and Identity: New Essays in Ethnic American Literatures*, edited by Amritjit Singh, Joseph T. Skerrett Jr., and Robert E. Hogan, 198–211. Boston: Northeastern University Press, 1994.

Johnson, Barbara. "'Aesthetic' and 'Rapport' in Toni Morrison's *Sula*." In *The Aesthetics of Toni Morrison: Speaking the Unspeakable*, edited by Marc C. Conner, 3–11. Jackson: University Press of Mississippi, 2000.

———. "'Aesthetic' and 'Rapport' in Toni Morrison's *Sula*," *Textual Practice* 7, no. 2 (Summer 1993): 165–172.

Jones, Bessie W., and Audrey Vinson. "An Interview with Toni Morrison." In *Conversations with Toni Morrison*, edited by Danille Taylor-Guthrie, 171–187. Jackson: University Press of Mississippi, 1994.

———. *The World of Toni Morrison: Explorations in Literary Criticism*. Dubuque, Iowa: Kendall/Hunt, 1985.

Jones, Jacqueline M. "When Theory and Practice Crumble: Toni Morrison and White Resistance," *College English* 68 (September 2005): 57–71.

Jordan, Elaine. "'Not My People': Toni Morrison and Identity." In *Black Women's Writing*, edited by Gina Wisker, 111–126. New York: St. Martin's Press, 1993.

Joyce, Joyce Ann. "Structural and Thematic Unity in Toni Morrison's *Song of Solomon*," *CEA Critic: An Official Journal of the College English Association* 49, no. 2–4 (Winter-Summer 1986–87): 185–198.

Kang, Ja Mo. "Toni Morrison's *Song of Solomon*: Milkman's Limited Moral Development," *Journal of English Language and Literature* 41, no. 1 (1995): 125–147.

Kang, Nancy. "To Love and Be Loved: Considering Black Masculinity and the Misandric Impulse in Toni Morrison's *Beloved*," *Callaloo: A Journal of African-American and African Arts and Letters* 26, no. 3 (Summer 2003): 836–854.

Kannammal, S. "Man-Woman Dichotomy Untenable: A Post-Structuralist Reading of Toni Morrison's Novels," *Indian Journal of American Studies* 23, no. 2 (Summer 1993): 99–104.

Kearly, Peter R. "Toni Morrison's *Paradise* and the Politics of Community," *Journal of American and Comparative Cultures* 23, no. 2 (Summer 2000): 9–16.

Kearney, Virginia Heumann. "Morrison's *Beloved*," *Explicator* 54, no. 1 (Fall 1995): 46–49.

Keenan, Sally. "'Four Hundred Years of Silence': Myth, History, and Motherhood in Toni Morrison's *Beloved*." In *Recasting the World: Writing after Colonialism*, edited by Jonathan White, 45–81. Baltimore: Johns Hopkins University Press, 1993.

Keller, James R. "Sethe and Lady Macbeth: Toni Morrison's Appropriation of Shakespeare in *Beloved*," *MAWA Review* 12, no. 1 (June 1997): 44–48.

Kellman, Sophia N. "To Be or Not to Be(loved)," *Black Issues in Higher Education* 18, no. 7 (May 24, 2001): 29–31.

Kelly, Robert W. "Toni Morrison's *Beloved*: Destructive Past Becoming Instructive Memory," *MAWA Review* 10, no. 1 (June 1995): 28–32.

Khushu-Lahiri, Rajyashree. "Matrilineage, Migrancy and Morrison's *The Bluest Eye*." In *New Waves in American Literature*, edited by A. A. Mutalik-Desai, et al., 17–22. New Delhi: Creative, 1999.

Kim, Ae-ju. "The Psychological Effects of Migration and Narrative Strategies in *The Bluest Eye, Song of Solomon,* and *Jazz*," *Journal of English Language and Literature/Yongo Yongmunhak* 45, no. 4 (Winter 1999): 1,021–1,032.

Kim, Min-Jung. "Expanding the Parameters of Literary Studies: Toni Morrison's *Paradise*," *Journal of English Language and Literature/Yongo Yongmunhak* 47, no. 4 (Winter 2001): 1,017–1,040.

Kim, Yeonman. "Involuntary Vulnerability and the Felix Culpa in Toni Morrison's *Jazz*," *SLH* 33, no. 2 (Spring 2001): 124–133.

King, Nicole. "'You Think Like You White': Questioning Race and Racial Community through the Lens of Middle-Class Desire(s)," *Novel: A Forum on Fiction* 35, no. 2–3 (Spring-Summer 2002): 211–230.

Klooss, Wolfgang. "Difference and Dignity: Problems of (Inter-)Cultural Understanding in British and North American Literature." In *New Worlds: Discovering and Constructing the Unknown in Anglophone Literature*, edited by Martin Kuester, Gabriele Christ, and Rudolf Beck, 239–259. Munich: Voegel, 2000.

Knadler, Stephen. "Domestic Violence in the Harlem Renaissance: Remaking the Record from Nella Larsen's Passing to Toni Morrison's *Jazz*," *African American Review* 38, no. 1 (Spring 2004): 99–118.

Knauer, Krzysztof. "Playing in the Wild: Toni Morrison's Play on Wild Guesses, Their Authors and the Wildness of Being in Her Novel *Jazz*, and Its Analogies in Non-Fictional Real." In *The Wild and the Tame: Essays in Cultural Practice*, edited by Wojciech Kalaga and Tadeusz Rachwal, 91–100. Katowice, Poland: Uniwersytet Slaski, 1997.

Koenen, Anne. "The (Black) Lady Vanishes: Postfeminism, Poststructuralism, and Theorizing in Narratives by Black Women." In *Explorations on*

Post-Theory: Towards a Third Space, edited by Fernando de Toro, 131–143. Frankfurt: Iberoamericana, 1999.

———. "The One Out of Sequence." In *Conversations with Toni Morrison*, edited by Danille Taylor Guthrie, 67–83. Jackson: University Press of Mississippi, 1994.

Krumholz, Linda. "Dead Teachers: Rituals of Manhood and Rituals of Reading in *Song of Solomon*," *MFS: Modern Fiction Studies* 39, no. 3–4 (Fall-Winter 1993): 551–574.

———. "Reading and Insight in Toni Morrison's *Paradise*," *African American Review* 36, no. 1 (Spring 2002): 21–34.

Kulkarni, Harihar. "Mirrors, Reflections, and Images: Malady of Generational Relationship and Girlhood in Toni Morrison's *The Bluest Eye*," *Indian Journal of American Studies* 23, no. 2 (Summer 1993): 1–6.

Kwon, Teckyoung. "Toni Morrison's *Sula*: 'We Was Girls Together,'" *Studies in Modern Fiction* 9, no. 1 (Summer 2002): 5–28.

Lakshminarasaiah, G. "The Wounded Black Psyche under White Duress in Toni Morrison's Novels," *Indian Journal of American Studies* 23, no. 2 (Summer 1993): 7–15.

Lange, Bonnie Shipman. "Toni Morrison's Rainbow Code," *Critique: Studies in Contemporary Fiction* 24, no. 3 (Spring 1983): 173–181.

Lawrence, David. "Fleshly Ghosts and Ghostly Flesh: The Word and the Body in *Beloved*," *Studies in American Fiction* 19, no. 2 (Autumn 1991): 189–201.

Leake, Katherine. "Morrison's *Beloved*," *Explicator* 53, no. 2 (Winter 1995): 120–123.

LeClair, Thomas. "The Language Must Not Sweat: A Conversation with Toni Morrison." In *Conversations with Toni Morrison*, edited by Danille Taylor-Guthrie, 119–128. Jackson: University Press of Mississippi, 1994.

LeClair, Thomas, and Larry McCaffery. *Anything Can Happen: Interviews with Contemporary American Novelists*. Urbana: University of Illinois Press, 1983.

Ledbetter, Mark. "An Apocalypse of Race and Gender: Body Violence and Forming Identity in Toni Morrison's *Beloved*." In *Picturing Cultural Values in Postmodern America*, edited by William G. Doty,

158–172. Tuscaloosa: University of Alabama Press, 1995.

———. "Through the Eyes of a Child: Looking for Victims in Toni Morrison's *The Bluest Eye*." In *Literature and Theology at Century's End,* edited by Gregory Salyer and Robert Detweiler, 177–188. Atlanta: Scholars, 1995.

Lee, Dorothy H. "The Quest for Self: Triumph and Failure in the Works of Toni Morrison." In *Black Women Writers (1950–1980): A Critical Evaluation,* edited by Mari Evans, 346–360. Garden City, N.Y.: Anchor-Doubleday, 1984.

Lee, Gui-woo. "The Ghosts of the Past and the Present: Toni Morrison's *Beloved," Journal of English Language and Literature/Yongo Yongmunhak* 43, no. 2 (1997): 365–380.

Lee, Kyung Soon. "Black Feminism: *Sula* and Meridian," *Journal of English Language and Literature* 38, no. 3 (Fall 1992): 585–599.

Lee, Rachel C. "Missing Peace in Toni Morrison's *Sula* and *Beloved*." In *Understanding Toni Morrison's* Beloved *and* Sula: *Selected Essays and Criticisms of the Works by the Nobel Prize–Winning Author,* edited by Solomon O. Iyasere and Marla W. Iyasere, 277–296. Troy, N.Y.: Whitston, 2000.

Lee, Soo-Hyun. "*The Bluest Eye*: Tragic Aspects of Black Consciousness of the Self," *Studies in Modern Fiction* 9, no. 1 (Summer 2002): 195–217.

Lee, Suk-Hee. "The Internalization of Colonial Discourse in *The Bluest Eye," Journal of English Language and Literature/Yongo Yongmunhak* 45, no. 3 (1999): 629–645.

Lee, Valerie Gray. "The Use of Folktalk in Novels by Black Women Writers," *College Language Association Journal* 23 (1980): 266–272.

Leonard, John. "Travels with Toni," *Nation* 17 (January 1994): 59–62.

Leontis, Artemis. "'What Will I Have to Remember?': Helen Papanikolas's Art of Telling," *Journal of the Hellenic Diaspora* 29, no. 2 (2003): 15–26.

LeSeur, Geta. "The Allegorical Nature of Toni Morrison's *Song of Solomon," MAWA Review* 6, no. 1 (June 1991): 11–15.

———. "Moving beyond the Boundaries of Self, Community, and the Other in Toni Morrison's *Sula* and *Paradise," CLA Journal* 46, no. 1 (September 2002): 1–20.

Lester, Cheryl. "Meditations on a Bird in the Hand: Ethics and Aesthetics in a Parable by Toni Morrison." In *The Aesthetics of Toni Morrison: Speaking the Unspeakable,* edited by Marc C. Conner, 125–138. Jackson: University Press of Mississippi, 2000.

Lester, Rosemarie K. "An Interview with Toni Morrison, Hessian Radio Network, Frankfurt, West Germany." In *Critical Essays on Toni Morrison,* edited by Nellie Y. McKay, 47–54. Boston: Hall, 1988.

Leusmann, Harald. "'Come and Do Wrong': Musical Memory in Toni Morrison's *Jazz," Notes on Contemporary Literature* 29, no. 1 (January 1999): 8–10.

Levy, Andrew. "Telling *Beloved," Texas Studies in Literature and Language* 33, no. 1 (Spring 1991): 114–123.

Lewis, Vashti Crutcher. "African Tradition in Toni Morrison's *Sula," Phylon: A Review of Race and Culture* 48, no. 1 (March 1987): 91–97.

Lindroth, James R. "Archetypes of Love, Hate, and Rebirth in Toni Morrison's *Jazz," JAISA: The Journal of the Association for the Interdisciplinary Study of the Arts* 1, no. 1 (Fall 1995): 113–119.

Lock, Helen. "'Building Up from Fragments': The Oral Memory Process in Some Recent African-American Written Narratives," *College Literature* 22, no. 3 (October 1995): 109–120.

Loris, Michelle C. "Self and Mutuality: Romantic Love, Desire, Race, and Gender in Toni Morrison's *Jazz," Sacred Heart University Review* 14, no. 1–2 (Fall 1993–Spring 1994): 53–62.

Ludwig, Sami. "Grotesque Landscapes: African American Fiction, Voodoo Animism, and Cognitive Models." In *Mapping African America: History, Narrative Formation, and the Production of Knowledge,* edited by Maria Diedrich, Carl Pedersen, and Justine Tally, 189–202. Hamburg, Germany: LIT, 1999.

Luebke, Steven R. "The Portrayal of Sexuality in Toni Morrison's *The Bluest Eye*." In *Censored Books, II: Critical Viewpoints, 1985–2000,* edited by Nicholas J. Karolides and Nat Hentoff, 87–94. Lanham, Md.: Scarecrow, 2002.

MacKethan, Lucinda H. "Names to Bear Witness: The Theme and Tradition of Naming in Toni Morrison's *Song of Solomon," CEA Critic: An Official Journal of the College English Association* 49, no. 2–4 (Winter-Summer 1986–87): 199–207.

Magness, Patricia. "The Knight and the Princess: The Structure of Courtly Love in Toni Morrison's *Tar Baby*," *South Atlantic Review* 54, no. 4 (November 1989): 85–99.

Malcolm, Cheryl Alexander. "Family Values? Father/Daughter Seduction in Toni Morrison's *The Bluest Eye* and Milcha Sanchez-Scott's Roosters." In *Reflections on Ethical Values in Post(?) Modern American Literature,* edited by Teresa Pyzik and Pawel Jedrzejko, 115–124. Katowice, Poland: Wydawnictwo Uniwersytetu Slaskiego, 2000.

Malmgren, Carl D. "Mixed Genres and the Logic of Slavery in Toni Morrison's *Beloved*," *Critique: Studies in Contemporary Fiction* 36, no. 2 (Winter 1995): 96–106.

———. "Texts, Primers, and Voices in Toni Morrison's *The Bluest Eye*," *Critique: Studies in Contemporary Fiction* 41, no. 3 (Spring 2000): 251–262.

Mandel, Naomi. "'I Made the Ink': Identity, Complicity, 60 Million, and More," *MFS: Modern Fiction Studies* 48, no. 3 (Fall 2002): 581–613.

Marks, Kathleen. *Toni Morrison's Beloved and the Apotropaic Imagination.* Columbia: University of Missouri Press, 2002.

Martin, Curtis. "A Bibliography of Writings by Toni Morrison." In *Contemporary American Women Writers: Narrative Strategies,* edited by Catherine Rainwater and William J. Scheick, 205–207. Lexington: University Press of Kentucky, 1985.

Martin, Jacky. "From Division to Sacrificial Reconciliation in Toni Morrison's Novels," *Obsidian II: Black Literature in Review* 5, no. 2 (Summer 1990): 80–99.

Martin, William. "Linear and Non-Linear Concepts of Time in Toni Morrison's *Song of Solomon*," *Notes on Contemporary Literature* 26, no. 3 (May 1996): 9–11.

Mason, Theodore O., Jr. "The Novelist as Conservator: Stories and Comprehension in Toni Morrison's *Song of Solomon*," *Contemporary Literature* 29, no. 4 (Winter 1988): 564–581.

Masters, Joshua J. "Milkman's Quest for Authenticity: Transgression and Transcendence in Toni Morrison's *Song of Solomon*," *MAWA Review* 10, no. 1 (June 1995): 13–18.

Mathieson, Barbara Offutt. "Memory and Mother Love in Morrison's *Beloved*," *American Imago: Studies in Psychoanalysis and Culture* 47, no. 1 (Spring 1990): 1–21.

Matus, Jill. *Toni Morrison.* Manchester, England: Manchester University Press, 1998.

Mayberry, Susan Neal. "Something Other Than a Family Quarrel: The Beautiful Boys in Morrison's *Sula*," *African American Review* 37, no. 4 (Winter 2003): 517–533.

Mayer, Elsie F. "Morrison's *Beloved*," *Explicator* 51, no. 3 (Spring 1993): 192–194.

Mayer, Sylvia. "'You Like Huckleberries?' Toni Morrison's *Beloved* and Mark Twain's *Adventures of Huckleberry Finn*." In *The Black Columbiad: Defining Moments in African American Literature and Culture,* edited by Werner Sollors and Maria Diedrich, 337–346. Cambridge, Mass.: Harvard University Press, 1994.

Mayo, James. "Morrison's *The Bluest Eye*," *Explicator* 60, no. 4 (Summer 2002): 231–234.

Mbalia, Doreatha Drummond. "*Tar Baby*: A Reflection of Morrison's Developed Class Consciousness." In *Toni Morrison,* edited by Linden Peach, 89–102. New York: St. Martin's Press, 1997.

———. *Toni Morrison's Developing Class Consciousness.* Selinsgrove, Pa.: Susquehanna University Press, 2004.

———. "Women Who Run with Wild: The Need for Sisterhoods in *Jazz*," *MFS: Modern Fiction Studies* 39, no. 3–4 (Fall-Winter 1993): 623–646.

McBride, Dwight. "Speaking the Unspeakable: On Toni Morrison, African American Intellectuals and the Uses of Essentialist Rhetoric," *MFS: Modern Fiction Studies* 39, no. 3–4 (Fall-Winter 1993): 755–776.

McCoy, Beth A. "Between Spaces: Meditations on Toni Morrison and Whiteness in the Classroom," *College English* 68 (September 2005): 42–71.

———. "Trying Toni Morrison Again," *College English* 68 (September 2005): 43–57.

McDermott, Ryan P. "Silence, Visuality, and the Staying Image: The 'Unspeakable Scene' of Toni Morrison's *Beloved*," *Angelaki* 8, no. 1 (April 2003): 75–89.

McDowell, Deborah E. "'The Self and the Other': Reading Toni Morrison's *Sula* and the Black Female Text." In *Critical Essays on Toni Morrison,* edited by Nellie Y. McKay, 77–90. Boston: Hall, 1988.

McKay, Nellie. *Critical Essays on Toni Morrison.* Boston: Hall, 1988.

———. "An Interview with Toni Morrison," *Contemporary Literature* 24, no. 4 (Winter 1983): 413–429.

McKee, Patricia. "Geographies of *Paradise*," *CR: The New Centennial Review* 3, no. 1 (Spring 2003): 197–223.

———. "Spacing and Placing Experience in Toni Morrison's *Sula.*" In *Toni Morrison: Critical and Theoretical Approaches,* edited by Nancy J. Peterson, 37–62. Baltimore: Johns Hopkins University Press, 1997.

McKenzie, Marilyn Mobley. "Spaces for Readers: The Novels of Toni Morrison." In *The Cambridge Companion to the African American Novel,* edited by Maryemma Graham, 221–232. Cambridge, England: Cambridge University Press, 2004.

McKinstry, Susan Jaret. "A Ghost of An/Other Chance: The Spinster-Mother in Toni Morrison's *Beloved.*" In *Old Maids to Radical Spinsters: Unmarried Women in the Twentieth Century Novel,* edited by Laura L. Doan, 259–274. Urbana: University of Illinois Press, 1991.

McWilliams, Mark B. "The Human Face of the Age: The Physical Cruelty of Slavery and the Modern American Novel," *Mississippi Quarterly: The Journal of Southern Cultures* 56, no. 3 (Summer 2003): 353–371.

Mendelsohn, Jane. "Harlem on Her Mind: Toni Morrison's Language of Love," *Village Voice Literary Supplement* 105 (May 1992): 25–26.

Menke, Pamela Glenn. "'Hard Glass Mirrors' and Soul Memory: Vision Imagery and Gender in Ellison, Baldwin, Morrison, and Walker," *West Virginia University Philological Papers* 38 (1992): 163–170.

Mermann-Jozwiak, Elisabeth "Re-Membering the Body: Body Politics in Toni Morrison's *The Bluest Eye,*" *Lit: Literature Interpretation Theory* 12, no. 2 (June 2001): 189–203.

Mezru, Rose Ure. "Sembene and Morrison: The Moral Quandary in Neo-Slave Narratives," *MAWA Review* 14, no. 2 (December 1999): 57–64.

Michael, Magali Cornier. "Re-Imagining Agency: Toni Morrison's *Paradise,*" *African American Review* 36, no. 4 (Winter 2002): 643–661.

Micucci, Dana. "An Inspired Life: Toni Morrison Writes and a Generation Listens." In *Conversations with Toni Morrison,* edited by Danille Taylor-Guthrie, 275–279. Jackson: University Press of Mississippi, 1994.

Middleton, Joyce Irene. "'Both Print and Oral' and 'Talking about Race': Transforming Toni Morrison's Language Issues into Teaching Issues." In *African American Rhetoric(s): Interdisciplinary Perspectives,* edited by Elaine B. Richardson and Ronald L. Jackson II, 242–258. Carbondale: Southern Illinois University Press, 2004.

———. "Toni Morrison and 'Race Matters' Rhetoric: Reading Race and Whiteness in Visual Culture." In *Calling Cards: Theory and Practice in the Study of Race, Gender, and Culture,* edited by Jacqueline Jones Royster. Albany: State University of New York Press, 2005.

Middleton, Victoria. "*Sula*: An Experimental Life," *College Language Association Journal* 28, no. 4 (June 1985): 367–381.

Miller, D. Quentin. "'Making a Place for Fear': Toni Morrison's First Redefinition of Dante's Hell in *Sula,*" *English Language Notes* 37, no. 3 (March 2000): 68–75.

Minakawa, Harue Kyushu. "The Motif of Sweetness in Toni Morrison's *Song of Solomon,*" *American Literature* 26 (October 1985): 47–56.

Miner, Madonne M. "Lady No Longer Sings the Blues: Rape, Madness, and Silence in *The Bluest Eye.*" In *Conjuring: Black Women, Fiction, and Literary Tradition,* edited by Marjorie Pryse and Hortense J. Spillers, 176–191. Bloomington: Indiana University Press, 1985.

Mitchell, Angelyn. "'Sth, I Know That Woman': History, Gender, and the South in Toni Morrison's *Jazz,*" *Studies in the Literary Imagination* 31, no. 2 (Fall 1998): 49–60.

Mitchell, Carolyn A. "'I Love to Tell the Story': Biblical Revisions in *Beloved,*" *Religion and Literature* 23, no. 3 (Autumn 1991): 27–42.

Mitchell, Leatha Simmons. "Toni Morrison, My Mother, and Me." In *In the Memory and Spirit of Frances, Zora, and Lorraine: Essays and Interviews on Black Women and Writing,* edited by Juliette Bowles, 58–60. Washington, D.C.: Institute for the Arts and the Humanities, Howard University, 1979.

Mix, Debbie. "Toni Morrison: A Selected Bibliography," *MFS: Modern Fiction Studies* 39, no. 3–4 (Fall-Winter 1993): 795–817.

Mobley, Marilyn Sanders. "A Different Remembering: Memory, History and Meaning in Toni Morrison's *Beloved*," In *Toni Morrison*, edited by Harold Bloom, 189–199. New York: Chelsea House, 1990.

———. "The Mellow Moods and Difficult Truths of Toni Morrison," *The Southern Review* 29, no. 3 (Summer 1993): 614–628.

———. "Narrative Dilemma: Jadine as Cultural Orphan in Toni Morrison's *Tar Baby*," *The Southern Review* 23, no. 4 (Autumn 1987): 761–770.

Mock, Michele. "Spitting Out the Seed: Ownership of Mother, Child, Breasts, Milk, and Voice in Toni Morrison's *Beloved*," *College Literature* 23, no. 3 (October 1996): 117–126.

Moffitt, Letitia. "Finding the Door: Vision/Revision and Stereotype in Toni Morrison's *Tar Baby*," *Critique: Studies in Contemporary Fiction* 46, no. 1 (Fall 2004): 12–26.

Moraru, Christian. "Reading the Onomastic Text: 'The Politics of the Proper Name' in Toni Morrison's *Song of Solomon*," *Names: A Journal of Onomastics* 44, no. 3 (September 1996): 189–204.

Moreland, Richard C. "'He Wants to Put His Story Next to Hers': Putting Twain's Story Next to Hers in Morrison's *Beloved*," *MFS: Modern Fiction Studies* 39, no. 3–4 (Fall-Winter 1993): 501–525.

Morey, Ann-Janine. "Toni Morrison and the Color of Life," *Christian Century* 105, no. 34 (November 1988): 1,039–1,042.

Morgan, Kathleen. "The Homeric Cyclops Episode and 'Otherness' in Toni Morrison's *Jazz*," *Classical and Modern Literature: A Quarterly* 18, no. 3 (Spring 1998): 219–229.

Morgenstern, Naomi. "Literature Reads Theory: Remarks on Teaching with Toni Morrison," *University of Toronto Quarterly: A Canadian Journal of the Humanities* 74 (Summer 2005): 816–828.

Mori, Aoi. "Embracing Jazz: Healing of Armed Women and Motherless Children in Toni Morrison's *Jazz*," *CLA Journal* 42, no. 3 (March 1999): 320–330.

———. *Toni Morrison and the Womanist Discourse*. New York: Peter Lang, 1999.

Morrison, Toni. "Black Matter(s)." In *Falling into Theory: Conflicting Views on Reading Literature*, edited by David H. Richter, 255–268. Boston: Bedford, 1994.

———. "Black Matter(s)," *Grand Street* 10, no. 4 (40) (1991): 205–225.

———. "City Limits, Village Values: Concepts of the Neighborhood in Black Fiction." In *Literature and the Urban Experience: Essays on the City and Literature*, edited by Michael C. Jaye and Ann Chalmers Watts, 35–43. New Brunswick, N.J.: Rutgers University Press, 1981.

———. "A Conversation." In *Conversations with Gloria Naylor*, edited by Maxine Lavon Montgomery, 10–38. Jackson: University Press of Mississippi, 2004.

———. "Faulkner and Women." In *Faulkner and Women: Faulkner and Yoknapatawpha, 1985*, edited by Doreen Fowler and Ann J. Abadie, 295–302. Jackson: University Press of Mississippi, 1986.

———. "How Can Values Be Taught in the University?" *Michigan Quarterly Review* 40, no. 2 (Spring 2001): 273–278.

———. "Memory, Creation, and Writing," *Thought: A Review of Culture and Idea* 59, no. 235 (December 1984): 385–390.

———. "On 'The Radiance of the King'," *New York Review of Books* 48, no. 13 (August 9, 2001): 18–20.

———. "Person to Person," *Black Seeds* 1, no. 1 (1980): 28–29.

———. "Romancing the Shadow." In *The New Romanticism: A Collection of Critical Essays*, edited by Eberhard Alsen, 51–67. New York: Garland, 2000.

———. "Unspeakable Things Unspoken: The Afro-American Presence in American Literature," *Michigan Quarterly Review* 28, no. 1 (Winter 1989): 1–34.

Moyers, Bill. "A Conversation with Toni Morrison." In *Conversations with Toni Morrison*, edited by Danille Taylor Guthrie, 262–274. Jackson: University Press of Mississippi, 1994.

Munafo, Giavanna. "'No Sign of Life': Marble-Blue Eyes and Lakefront Houses in *The Bluest Eye*," *Lit: Literature Interpretation Theory* 6, no. 1–2 (April 1995): 1–19.

Murray, Rolland. "The Long Strut: *Song of Solomon* and the Emancipatory Limits of Black Patriarchy," *Callaloo: A Journal of African-American and African Arts and Letters* 22, no. 1 (Winter 1999): 121–133.

Mutalik-Desai, A. A. "Conflicting Claims in Toni Morrison's Novels: Realism vs. Fantasy, Aesthetic Verisimilitude vs. Captious Ethnic Pride." In *Indian Perspectives on the U.S.: Literature and Foreign Affairs*, edited by P. M. Kamath and A. A. Mutalik-Desai, 34–42. Bombay: Prestige, 1993.

Myers, Linda Buck. "Perception and Power through Naming: Characters in Search of a Self in the Fiction of Toni Morrison," *Explorations in Ethnic Studies: The Journal of the National Association for Ethnic Studies* 7, no. 1 (January 1984): 39–55.

Nakatani, Hitomi. *Toni Morrison: The Making of a Politicized Muse*. Okayama, Japan: Daigaku Kyoiku Shuppan, 1999.

Napieralski, Edmund A. "Morrison's *The Bluest Eye*," *Explicator* 53, no. 1 (Fall 1994): 59–62.

Naylor, Carolyn A. "Cross-Gender Significance of the Journey Motif in Selected Afro-American Fiction," *Colby Library Quarterly* 18, no. 1 (March 1982): 26–38.

Naylor, Gloria. "A Conversation: Gloria Naylor and Toni Morrison." In *Conversations with Toni Morrison*, edited by Danille Taylor Guthrie, 188–217. Jackson: University Press of Mississippi, 1994.

Naylor, Gloria, and Toni Morrison. "A Conversation," *The Southern Review* 21, no. 3 (Summer 1985): 567–593.

Neubauer, Paul. "The Demon of Loss and Longing: The Function of the Ghost in Toni Morrison's *Beloved*." In *Demons: Mediators between This World and the Other: Essays on Demonic Beings from the Middle Ages to the Present*, edited by Ruth Petzoldt and Paul Neubauer, 165–174. Frankfurt, Germany: Peter Lang, 1998.

Neustadt, Kathy. "The Visits of the Writers Toni Morrison and Eudora Welty." In *Conversations with Toni Morrison*, edited by Danille Taylor-Guthrie, 84–92. Jackson: University Press of Mississippi, 1994.

Nicol, Kathryn. "Visible Differences: Viewing Racial Identity in Toni Morrison's *Paradise* and 'Recitatif'." In *Literature and Racial Ambiguity*, edited by Teresa Hubel and Neil Brooks, 209–231. Amsterdam: Rodopi, 2002.

Nissen, Axel. "Form Matters: Toni Morrison's *Sula* and the Ethics of Narrative," *Contemporary Literature* 40, no. 2 (Summer 1999): 263–285.

Nodelman, Perry. "The Limits of Structures: A Shorter Version of a Comparison between Toni Morrison's *Song of Solomon* and Virginia Hamilton's *M. C. Higgins the Great*," *Children's Literature Association Quarterly* 7, no. 3 (Fall 1982): 45–48.

Nowlin, Michael. "Toni Morrison's *Jazz* and the Racial Dreams of the American Writer," *American Literature: A Journal of Literary History, Criticism, and Bibliography* 71, no. 1 (March 1999): 151–174.

Nutting, Elizabeth Lofgren. "Remembering the Disremembered: Toni Morrison as Benjamin's Storyteller," *Schuylkill: A Creative and Critical Review from Temple University* 1, no. 1 (Fall 1997): 29–39.

Nwankwo, Chimalum. "'I Is': Toni Morrison, the Past, and Africa." In *Of Dreams Deferred, Dead or Alive: African Perspectives on African-American Writers*, edited by Femi Ojo-Ade, 171–180. Westport, Conn.: Greenwood, 1996.

Ogunyemi, Chikwenye Okonjo. "An Abiku-Ogbanje Atlas: A Pre-Text for Rereading Soyinka's Ake and Morrison's *Beloved*," *African American Review* 36, no. 4 (Winter 2002): 663–678.

———. "Order and Disorder in Toni Morrison's *The Bluest Eye*," *Critique: Studies in Modern Fiction* 19, no. 1 (1977): 112–120.

———. "*Sula*: 'A Nigger Joke,'" *Black American Literature Forum* 13 (1979): 130–133.

O'Reilly, Andrea. "Maternal Conceptions in Toni Morrison's *The Bluest Eye* and *Tar Baby*: 'A Woman Has to Be a Daughter before She Can Be Any Kind of Woman.'" In *This Giving Birth: Pregnancy and Childbirth in American Women's Writing*, edited by Julie Tharp and Susan MacCallum-Whitcomb, 83–102. Bowling Green, Ohio: Popular, 2000.

———. *Toni Morrison and Motherhood: A Politics of the Heart*. Albany: State University of New York Press, 2004.

O'Shaughnessy, Kathleen. "'Life life life life': The Community as Chorus in *Song of Solomon*." In *Critical Essays on Toni Morrison*, edited by Nellie Y. McKay, 125–133. Boston: Hall, 1988.

Osundare, Niyi. "Toni Morrison in Madison," *African Literature Association Bulletin* 17, no. 1 (Winter 1991): 18–19.

Othow, Helen Chavis. "Comedy in Morrison's Terrestrial *Paradise*," *CLA Journal* 47, no. 3 (March 2004): 366–373.

Otten, Terry. *The Crime of Innocence in the Fiction of Toni Morrison.* Columbia: University of Missouri Press, 1989.

———. "The Crime of Innocence: *Tar Baby* and the Fall Myth." In *Toni Morrison,* edited by Linden Peach, 43–51. New York: St. Martin's Press, 1997.

———. "The Crime of Innocence in Toni Morrison's *Tar Baby,*" *Studies in American Fiction* 14, no. 2 (Autumn 1986): 153–164.

———. "Horrific Love in Toni Morrison's Fiction," *MFS: Modern Fiction Studies* 39, no. 3–4 (Fall-Winter 1993): 651–667.

———. "Transfiguring the Narrative: *Beloved*—From Melodrama to Tragedy." In *Critical Essays on Toni Morrison's Beloved,* edited by Barbara H. Solomon, 284–299. New York: G. K. Hall, 1998.

Owusu, Kofi. "Rethinking Canonicity: Toni Morrison and the (Non)Canonic 'Other.'" In *Rewriting the Dream: Reflections on the Changing American Literary Canon,* edited by W. M. Verhoeven, 60–74. Amsterdam: Rodopi, 1992.

Page, Philip. *Dangerous Freedom: Fusion and Fragmentation in Toni Morrison's Novels.* Jackson: University Press of Mississippi, 1995.

———. "Furrowing All the Brows: Interpretation and the Transcendent in Toni Morrison's *Paradise,*" *African American Review* 35, no. 4 (Winter 2001): 637–664.

Pankhurst, Anne. "Recontextualization of Metonymy in Narrative and the Case of Morrison's *Song of Solomon.*" In *Metonymy in Language and Thought,* edited by Klaus-Uwe Panther and Gunter Radden, 385–399. Amsterdam: Benjamins, 1999.

Paquet-Deyris, Anne-Marie. "Toni Morrison's *Jazz* and the City," *African American Review* 35, no. 2 (Summer 2001): 219–231.

Parikh, Bharati A. "Heroines of Toni Morrison and Anita Desai: A Cross-Cultural Perspective," *Indian Journal of American Studies* 23, no. 2 (Summer 1993): 17–25.

Park, Sue. "One Reader's Response to Toni Morrison's *Beloved,*" *Conference of College Teachers of English Studies* 56 (September 1991): 39–46.

Park, Yup. "Toni Morrison's Historical Consciousness," *Journal of English Language and Literature/ Yongo Yongmunhak* 43, no. 2 (1997): 343–363.

Parker, Betty Jean. "Complexity: Toni Morrison's Women." In *Conversations with Toni Morrison,* edited by Danille Taylor-Guthrie, 60–66. Jackson: University Press of Mississippi, 1994.

Parker, Emma. "A New Hysteria in Toni Morrison's *Beloved,*" *Twentieth Century Literature: A Scholarly and Critical Journal* 47, no. 1 (Spring 2001): 1–19.

Peach, Linden. *Toni Morrison.* New York: St. Martin's Press, 2000.

———. "Toni Morrison: *Beloved.*" In *Literature in Context,* edited by Rick Rylance and Judy Simons, 225–238. Basingstoke, England: Palgrave, 2001.

Peach, Linden, ed. *Toni Morrison.* New York: St. Martin's, 1997.

Pearce, Richard. "Toni Morrison's *Jazz:* Negotiations of the African American Beauty," *Culture Narrative* 6, no. 3 (October 1998): 307–324.

Perez-Torres, Rafael. "Knitting and Knotting the Narrative Thread—*Beloved* as Postmodern Novel," *MFS: Modern Fiction Studies* 39, no. 3–4 (Fall-Winter 1993): 689–707.

Perry, Carolyn, and Tonya Maddox. "Repetition and Revision in Toni Morrison's *Jazz,*" *Publications of the Missouri Philological Association* 21 (1996): 62–68.

Peterson, Nancy J. "'Say Make Me, Remake Me': Toni Morrison and the Reconstruction of African-American History." In *Toni Morrison: Critical and Theoretical Approaches,* edited by Nancy J. Peterson, 201–221. Baltimore: Johns Hopkins University Press, 1997.

Peterson, Nancy J., ed. *Toni Morrison: Critical and Theoretical Approaches.* Baltimore: Johns Hopkins University Press, 1997.

———. "Toni Morrison Double Issue," *MFS: Modern Fiction Studies* 39, no. 3–4 (Fall-Winter 1993): 461–833.

Petric, Jerneja. "Up and Down in the World of War and Peace: Toni Morrison's Use of Tropes in *Sula* and *Song of Solomon.*" In *Literature, Culture and Ethnicity: Studies on Medieval, Renaissance and Modern Literatures,* edited by Mirko Jurak, 141–147. Ljubljana, Slovenia: Author, 1992.

Pettis, Joyce. "Difficult Survival: Mothers and Daughters in *The Bluest Eye,*" *SAGE: A Scholarly Journal on Black Women* 4, no. 2 (Fall 1987): 26–29.

Phelan, James. "Sethe's Choice: *Beloved* and the Ethics of Reading." In *Mapping the Ethical Turn: A Reader in Ethics, Culture, and Literary Theory,* edited by Todd F. Davis and Kenneth Womack, 93–109. Charlottesville: University Press of Virginia, 2001.

———. "Toward a Rhetorical Reader-Response Criticism: The Difficult, The Stubborn, and the Ending of *Beloved*," *MFS: Modern Fiction Studies* 39, no. 3–4 (Fall-Winter 1993): 709–728.

———. "Trading Meanings: The Breath of Music in Toni Morrison's *Jazz*," *Connotations: A Journal for Critical Debate* 7, no. 3 (1997–98): 372–398.

Pinsker, Sanford. "Magic Realism, Historical Truth, and the Quest for a Liberating Identity: Reflections on Alex Haley's *Roots* and Toni Morrison's *Song of Solomon*." In *Studies in Black American Literature, Volume I: Black American Prose Theory*, edited by Joe Weixlmann and Chester J. Fontenot, 183–197. Greenwood, Fla.: Penkevill, 1984.

Pitavy, Francois. "From Middle Passage to Holocaust: The Black Body as a Site of Memory." In *Sites of Memory in American Literatures and Cultures*, edited by Udo J. Hebel, 51–63. Heidelberg, Germany: Carl Winter Universitätsverlag, 2003.

Plasa, Carl, ed. *Toni Morrison: Beloved*. New York: Columbia University Press, 1998.

Pond, Wayne. "An Interview with Toni Morrison, and a Commentary about Her Work," translated by Maria Frias, *Atlantis: Revista de la Asociacion Española de Estudios Anglo Norteamericanos* 16, no. 1–2 (May–November 1994): 273–283.

Portales, Marco. "Toni Morrison's *The Bluest Eye*: Shirley Temple and Cholly," *The Centennial Review* 30, no. 4 (Fall 1986): 496–506.

Powell, Betty Jane. "'Will the Parts Hold?': The Journey Toward a Coherent Self in *Beloved*," *Colby Quarterly* 31, no. 2 (June 1995): 105–113.

———. "'Will the Parts Hold?': The Journey toward a Coherent Self in *Beloved*." In *Understanding Toni Morrison's* Beloved *and* Sula: *Selected Essays and Criticisms of the Works by the Nobel Prize–Winning Author*, edited by Solomon O. Iyasere and Marla W. Iyasere, 143–154. Troy, N.Y.: Whitston, 2000.

Pullin, Faith. "Landscapes of Reality: The Fiction of Contemporary Afro-American Women." In *Black Fiction: New Studies in the Afro-American Novel since 1945*, edited by Robert A. Lee, 173–203. New York: Barnes and Noble, 1980.

Puri, Usha. "Toni Morrison: Redefining Feminine Space in *Beloved*," *Indian Journal of American Studies* 23, no. 2 (Summer 1993): 27–34.

Rabinowitz, Paula. "Naming, Magic, and Documentary: The Subversion of the Narrative in *Song of Solomon*, Ceremony, and China Men." In *Feminist Re-Visions: What Has Been and Might Be*, edited by Vivian Patraka and Louise A. Tilly, 26–42. Ann Arbor: Women's Studies Program, University of Michigan, 1983.

Rainwater, Catherine. "Worthy Messengers: Narrative Voices in Toni Morrison's Novels," *Texas Studies in Literature and Language* 33, no. 1 (Spring 1991): 96–113.

Ramey, Deanna. "A Comparison of the Triads of Women in Toni Morrison's *Sula* and *Song of Solomon*," *Mount Olive Review* 6 (Spring 1992): 104–109.

Rand, Lizabeth A. "Female Discourse in *The Bluest Eye*—The Quest for Voice and Vision," *MAWA Review* 12, no. 2 (December 1997): 69–79.

———. "'We All That's Left': Identity Formation and the Relationship between Eva and Sula Peace," *CLA Journal* 44, no. 3 (March 2001): 341–349.

Randle, Gloria T. "'Knowing When to Stop': Loving and Living Small in the Slave World of *Beloved*," *CLA Journal* 41, no. 3 (March 1998): 279–302.

Ranveer, Kashinath. "African-American Feminist Consciousness in the Novels of Toni Morrison," *Indian Journal of American Studies* 23, no. 2 (Summer 1993): 35–45.

Rao, E. Raja. "African-American Women Writers and the Aesthetics of Marginality with Special Reference to Toni Morrison," *Indian Journal of American Studies* 23, no. 2 (Summer 1993): 47–58.

Rao, R. M. V. Raghavendra. "In Search of an Authentic Voice: Toni Morrison's *Beloved*," *Indian Journal of American Studies* 23, no. 2 (Summer 1993): 91–93.

Raphael, Heike. "A Journey to Independence: Toni Morrison's *Beloved* and the Critical Utopia." In *Flip Sides: New Critical Essays in American Literature*, edited by Klaus H. Schmidt, 43–60. Frankfurt: Peter Lang, 1995.

Ray, Arunima. "The Quest for 'Home' and 'Wholeness' in *Sula* and Meridian: Afro-American Identity in Toni Morrison and Alice Walker," *Indian*

Journal of American Studies 23, no. 2 (Summer 1993): 59–65.

Raynaud, Claudine. "The Poetics of Abjection in *Beloved.*" In *Black Imagination and the Middle Passage,* edited by Maria Diedrich, Henry Louis Gates Jr., and Carl Pedersen, 70–85. Oxford: Oxford University Press, 1999.

Reckley, Ralph. "On Looking into Morrison's *Tar Baby.*" In *Amid Visions and Revisions: Poetry and Criticism on Literature and the Arts,* edited by Burney J. Hollis, 132–138. Baltimore: Morgan State University Press, 1985.

Reddy, Maureen T. "The Triple Plot and Center of *Sula.*" In *Understanding Toni Morrison's* Beloved *and* Sula: *Selected Essays and Criticisms of the Works by the Nobel Prize–Winning Author,* edited by Solomon O. Iyasere and Marla W. Iyasere, 1–18. Troy, N.Y.: Whitston, 2000.

Reed, Harry. "Toni Morrison, *Song of Solomon,* and Black Cultural Nationalism," *The Centennial Review* 32, no. 1 (Winter 1988): 50–64.

Reid, Suzanne Elizabeth. "Toni Morrison's *Song of Solomon:* An African American Epic." In *Censored Books, II: Critical Viewpoints, 1985–2000,* edited by Nicholas J. Karolides and Nat Hentoff, 387–394. Lanham, Md.: Scarecrow, 2002.

Reinikainen, Hanna. "Embodiment of Trauma: Corporeality in Toni Morrison's *Beloved.*" In *Close Encounters of an Other Kind: New Perspectives on Race, Ethnicity, and American Studies,* edited by Roy Goldblatt, 95–102. Joensuu, Finland: Faculty of Humanities, University of Joensuu, 2005.

Reyes, Angelita Dianne. "Ancient Properties in the New World: The Paradox of the 'Other' in Toni Morrison's *Tar Baby,*" *Black Scholar* 17, no. 2 (March–April 1986): 19–25.

Rhodes, Jewell Parker. "Toni Morrison's *Beloved:* Ironies of a 'Sweet Home' Utopia in a Dystopian Slave Society," *Utopian Studies* 1, no. 1 (1990): 77–92.

Rice, Alan. "Erupting Funk: The Political Style of Toni Morrison's *Tar Baby* and *The Bluest Eye,*" In *Postcolonial Literatures: Expanding the Canon,* edited by Deborah L. Madsen, 133–147. London: Pluto, 1999.

———. "'It Don't Mean a Thing If It Ain't Got That Swing': Jazz's Many Uses for Toni Morrison." In *Black Orpheus: Music in African American Fic-* *tion from the Harlem Renaissance to Toni Morrison,* edited by Saadi A. Simawe, 153–180. New York: Garland, 2000.

———. "Jazzing It Up a Storm: The Execution and Meaning of Toni Morrison's Jazzy Prose Style," *Journal of American Studies* 28, no. 3 (December 1994): 423–432.

Rice, Herbert William. *Toni Morrison and the American Tradition: A Rhetorical Reading.* New York: Peter Lang, 1996.

Rice, Marcelle Smith. "Blue Note: Postmortem Photography and the Genesis of *Jazz* for Toni Morrison," *West Virginia University Philological Papers* 41 (1995): 143–147.

Rigney, Barbara. "Hagar's Mirror: Self and Identity in Morrison's Fiction." In *Toni Morrison,* edited by Linden Peach, 52–69. New York: St. Martin's, 1997.

———. "'A Story to Pass On': Ghosts and the Significance of History in Toni Morrison's *Beloved,*" In *Haunting the House of Fiction: Feminist Perspectives on Ghost Stories by American Women,* edited by Lynette Carpenter and Wendy K. Lynette, 229–235. Knoxville: University of Tennessee Press, 1991.

Rimmon-Kenan, Shlomith. "Narration, Doubt, Retrieval: Toni Morrison's *Beloved,*" *Narrative* 4, no. 2 (May 1996): 109–123.

Rodrigues, Eusebio L. "Experiencing *Jazz,*" *MFS: Modern Fiction Studies* 39, no. 3–4 (Fall-Winter 1993): 733–754.

———. "The Telling of *Beloved,*" *Journal of Narrative Technique* 21, no. 2 (Spring 1991): 153–169.

Rodriguez, Denise. "'Where the Self That Had No Self Made Its Home': The Reinscription of Domestic Discourse in Toni Morrison's *Beloved,*" *Griot: Official Journal of the Southern Conference on Afro-American Studies* 20, no. 1 (Spring 2001): 40–51.

Rody, Caroline. "Toni Morrison's *Beloved:* History, 'Rememory,' and a 'Clamor for a Kiss.'" In *Understanding Toni Morrison's* Beloved *and* Sula: *Selected Essays and Criticisms of the Works by the Nobel Prize–Winning Author,* edited by Solomon O. Iyasere and Marla W. Iyasere, 83–112. Troy, N.Y.: Whitston, 2000.

Rolfe, Keith E. "'She Seemed Receptive but She Was Hardly Anxious': The Influence of Racism, Patriarchal Control, and Gender Roles in Toni Morrison's *Sula*," *MAWA Review* 13, no. 2 (December 1998): 88–95.

Romero, Channette. "Creating the Beloved Community: Religion, Race and Nation in Toni Morrison's *Paradise*," *African American Review* 39 (Fall 2005): 415–430.

Rosenberg, Ruth. "'And the Children May Know Their Names': Toni Morrison's *Song of Solomon*," *Literary Onomastics Studies* 8 (1981): 195–219.

Rothberg, Michael. "Dead Letter Office: Conspiracy, Trauma, and *Song of Solomon*'s Posthumous Communication," *African American Review* 37, no. 4 (Winter 2003): 501–516.

Royster, Philip M. "Milkman's Flying: The Scapegoat Transcended in Toni Morrison's *Song of Solomon*," *College Language Association Journal* 24, no. 4 (June 1981): 419–440.

———. "A Priest and a Witch against the Spiders and the Snakes: Scapegoating in Toni Morrison's *Sula*," *Umoja* 2 (1978): 149–168.

Ruas, Charles. "Toni Morrison." In *Conversations with Toni Morrison*, edited by Danille Taylor Guthrie, 93–118. Jackson: University Press of Mississippi, 1994.

Rubenstein, Roberta. "Singing the Blues/Reclaiming *Jazz*: Toni Morrison and Cultural Mourning," *Mosaic: A Journal for the Interdisciplinary Study of Literature* 31, no. 2 (June 1998): 147–163.

Rummell, Kathryn. "Toni Morrison's *Beloved*: Transforming the African Heroic Epic," *Griot: Official Journal of the Southern Conference on Afro-American Studies* 21, no. 1 (Spring 2002): 1–15.

Rushdy, Ashraf H. A. "Daughters Signifyin(g) History: The Example of Toni Morrison's *Beloved*." In *Toni Morrison*, edited by Linden Peach, 140–153. New York: St. Martin's Press, 1997.

Russell, Mariann. "Toni Morrison's *The Bluest Eye*," *Sacred Heart University Review* 14, no. 1–2 (Fall 1993–Spring 1994): 35–39.

Ryan, Judylyn S. "Contested Visions/Double-Vision in *Tar Baby*," *MFS: Modern Fiction Studies* 39, no. 3–4 (Fall-Winter 1993): 597–621.

———. "Morrison's *Jazz*: 'A Knowing So Deep.'" In *Approaches to Teaching the Novels of Toni Morrison*, edited by Nellie Y. McKay and Kathryn Earle, 154–160. New York: Modern Language Association of America, 1997.

Salvatore, Anne T. "Toni Morrison's New Bildungsromane: Paired Characters and Antithetical Form in *The Bluest Eye, Sula*, and *Beloved*," *Journal of Narrative Theory* 32, no. 2 (Summer 2002): 154–178.

Samuels, Wilfrid D. "Liminality and the Search for Self in Toni Morrison's *Song of Solomon*," *MV* 5, no. 1–2 (Spring-Fall 1981): 59–68.

Sargent, Robert. "A Way of Ordering Experience: A Study of Toni Morrison's *The Bluest Eye* and *Sula*," In *Faith of a (Woman) Writer*, edited by Alice Kessler-Harris and William McBrien, 229–236. Westport, Conn.: Greenwood, 1988.

Sathyaraj, V. "'Dragon Daddies and False-Hearted Men': Patriarchy in Toni Morrison's *Love*," *Notes on Contemporary Literature* 35 (November 2005): 2–4.

Schapiro, Barbara. "The Bonds of Love and the Boundaries of Self in Toni Morrison's *Beloved*," *Contemporary Literature* 32, no. 2 (Summer 1991): 194–210.

Schmudde, Carol E. "Knowing When to Stop: A Reading of Toni Morrison's *Beloved*," *College Language Association Journal* 37, no. 2 (December 1993): 121–135.

———. "Morrison's *Beloved*," *Explicator* 50, no. 3 (Spring 1992): 187–188.

Schomburg, Connie R. "To Survive Whole, To Save the Self: The Role of Sisterhood in the Novels of Toni Morrison." In *The Significance of Sibling Relationships in Literature*, edited by JoAnna Stephens Mink and Janet Doubler Ward, 149–157. Bowling Green, Ohio: Popular, 1992.

Schopp, Andrew. "Narrative Control and Subjectivity: Dismantling Safety in Toni Morrison's *Beloved*," *The Centennial Review* 39, no. 2 (Spring 1995): 355–379.

Schramm, Margaret. "The Quest for the Perfect Mother in Toni Morison's *Sula*." In *The Anna Book: Searching for Anna in Literary History*, edited by Mickey Pearlman, 167–176. Westport, Conn.: Greenwood, 1992.

Schueller, Malini Johar. "Articulations of African-Americanism in South Asian Postcolonial Theory: Globalism, Localism, and the Question of Race," *Cultural Critique* 55 (Fall 2003): 35–62.

———. "Locating *Paradise* in the Post–Civil Rights Era: Toni Morrison and Critical Race Theory,"

Contemporary Literature 45, no. 2 (Summer 2004) 276–299.

———. "The Subject of Law: Toni Morrison, Critical Race Theory and the Narration of Cultural Criticism," *49th Parallel: An Interdisciplinary Journal of North American Studies* 6 (Autumn 2000).

Scruggs, Charles. "The Invisible City in Toni Morrison's *Beloved*," *Arizona Quarterly: A Journal of American Literature, Culture, and Theory* 48, no. 3 (Autumn 1992): 95–132.

———. "The Nature of Desire in Toni Morrison's *Song of Solomon*," *Arizona Quarterly: A Journal of American Literature, Culture, and Theory* 38, no. 4 (Winter 1982): 311–335.

Segal, Carolyn Foster. "Morrison's *Beloved*," *Explicator* 51, no. 1 (Fall 1992): 59–61.

Seidel, Kathryn Lee. "The Lilith Figure in Toni Morrison's *Sula* and Alice Walker's The Color Purple," *Weber Studies: An Interdisciplinary Humanities Journal* 10, no. 2 (Spring-Summer 1993): 85–94.

Shannon, Anna. "'We Was Girls Together': A Study of Toni Morrison's *Sula*," *Midwestern Miscellany* 10 (1982): 9–22.

Sherard, Tracey. "Women's Classic Blues in Toni Morrison's *Jazz*: Cultural Artifact as Narrator," *Genders* 31 (2000): 40.

Sheriff, Karen M. "Metonymical Re-membering and Signifyin(g) in Toni Morrison's *Beloved*." In *Semiotics 1996*, edited by C. W. Spinks and John Deely, 290–300. New York: Peter Lang, 1996.

Shourie, Usha. "The Morrison Music: Narrative Style in *Jazz*," *Indian Journal of American Studies* 23, no. 2 (Summer 1993): 67–73.

Simpson, Angela C. "Morrison's *Beloved*," *Explicator* 56, no. 3 (Spring 1998): 154–156.

Smith, Barbara. "Toward a Black Feminist Criticism." In *Falling into Theory: Conflicting Views on Reading Literature*, edited by David H. Richter, 186–193. Boston: Bedford, 1994.

———. "Toward a Black Feminist Criticism." In *In the Memory and Spirit of Frances, Zora, and Lorraine: Essays and Interviews on Black Women and Writing*, edited by Juliette Bowles, 32–40. Washington, D.C.: Institute for the Arts and the Humanities, Howard University, 1979.

Smith, Cynthia J. "Intertextuality as Agent of Representation in Toni Morrison's *Tar Baby*," *Genre: Forms of Discourse and Culture* 27, no. 3 (Fall 1994): 165–181.

Smith, Valerie. "The Quest for and Discovery of Identity in Toni Morrison's *Song of Solomon*," *The Southern Review* 21, no. 3 (Summer 1985): 721–732.

Softing, Inger-Anne. "Carnival and Black American Music as Counterculture in Toni Morrison's *The Bluest Eye* and *Jazz*," *American Studies in Scandinavia* 27, no. 2 (1995): 81–102.

Somerville, Jane. "Idealized Beauty and the Denial of Love in Toni Morrison's *The Bluest Eye*," *Bulletin of the West Virginia Association of College English Teachers* 9, no. 1 (Spring 1986): 18–23.

Spargo, R. Clifton. "Trauma and the Specters of Enslavement in Morrison's *Beloved*," *Mosaic: A Journal for the Interdisciplinary Study of Literature* 35, no. 1 (March 2002): 113–131.

Spearey, Susan. "Substantiating Discourses of Emergence: Corporeality, Spectrality and Postmodern Historiography in Toni Morrison's *Beloved*." In *Body Matters: Feminism, Textuality, Corporeality*, edited by Avril Horner and Angela Keane, 170–182. Manchester, England: Manchester University Press, 2000.

Stave, Shirley A. "Toni Morrison's *Beloved* and the Vindication of Lilith," *South Atlantic Review* 58, no. 1 (January 1993): 49–66.

Stein, Karen. "'I Didn't Even Know His Name': Name and Naming in Toni Morrison's *Sula*," *Names: A Journal of Onomastics* 28, no. 3 (September 1980): 226–229.

———. "Toni Morrison's *Sula*: A Black Women's Epic." In *Understanding Toni Morrison's Beloved and Sula: Selected Essays and Criticisms of the Works by the Nobel Prize–Winning Author*, edited by Solomon O. Iyasere and Marla W. Iyasere, 49–60. Troy, N.Y.: Whitston, 2000.

Stepto, Robert B. "'Intimate Things in Place': A Conversation with Toni Morrison," *Massachusetts Review: A Quarterly of Literature, the Arts and Public Affairs* 18 (1977): 473–489.

Stern, Katherine. "Toni Morrison's Beauty Formula." In *The Aesthetics of Toni Morrison: Speaking the Unspeakable*, edited by Marc C. Conner, 77–91. Jackson: University Press of Mississippi, 2000.

Stewart, Jacqueline. "Negroes Laughing at Themselves? Black Spectatorship and the Performance of Urban Modernity," *Critical Inquiry* 29, no. 4 (Summer 2003): 650–677.

Stewart, Michelle Pagni. "Moynihan's 'Tangle of Pathology': Toni Morrison's Legacy of Motherhood." In *Family Matters in the British and American Novel*, edited by Andrea O'Reilly Herrera et al., 237–253. Madison: University of Wisconsin Press, 1997.

Stockton, Kathryn Bond. "Heaven's Bottom: Anal Economics and the Critical Debasement of Freud in Toni Morrison's *Sula*," *Cultural Critique* 24 (Spring 1993): 81–118.

Storhoff, Gary. "'Anaconda Love': Parental Enmeshment in Toni Morrison's *Song of Solomon*," *Style* 31, no. 2 (Summer 1997): 290–309.

Story, Ralph D. "Sacrifice and Surrender: Sethe in Toni Morrison's *Beloved*," *CLA Journal* 46, no. 1 (September 2002): 21–47.

Stout, Janis P. "Playing in the Mother Country: Cather, Morrison, and the Return to Virginia." In *Willa Cather's Southern Connections: New Essays on Cather and the South*, edited by Ann Romines, 189–195. Charlottesville: University Press of Virginia, 2000.

Stratton, Kathryn Alice Abels. "Woman as B: Woman as A," *Dissertation Abstracts International* 43, no. 2 (August 1982): 447A–448A.

Stryz, Jan. "Inscribing an Origin in *Song of Solomon*," *Studies in American Fiction* 19, no. 1 (Spring 1991): 31–40.

———. "The Other Ghost in *Beloved*: The Specter of *The Scarlet Letter*," *Genre: Forms of Discourse and Culture* 24, no. 4 (Winter 1991): 417–434.

Subryan, Carmen. "Circles: Mother and Daughter Relationships in Toni Morrison's *Song of Solomon*," *SAGE: A Scholarly Journal on Black Women* 5, no. 1 (Summer 1988): 34–36.

Sullivan-Haller, Mary. "Ethical Authority and Women Writers of Color." In *Women of Color: Defining the Issues, Hearing the Voices*, edited by Diane Long Hoeveler and Janet K. Boles, 83–107. Westport, Conn.: Greenwood, 2001.

Tae, Heasook. "The Body in Black Women's Literature: Their Eyes Were Watching God and *Sula*," *Journal of English Language and Literature/Yongo Yongmunhak* 46, no. 1 (2000): 243–263.

Tally, Justine. "The Nature of Erotica in Toni Morrison's *Paradise* and the Em-Body-ment of Feminist Thought." In *Essays on the Culture and Literature of Desire*, edited by Cheryl Alexander Malcolm, 60–74. Gdańsk, Poland: Wydawnictwo Uniwersytetu Gdanskiego, 2005.

———. "Reality and Discourse in Toni Morrison's Trilogy: Testing the Limits." In *Literature and Ethnicity in the Cultural Borderlands*, edited by Jesus Benito and Anna Maria Manzanas, 35–49. Amsterdam: Rodopi, 2002.

———. *Toni Morrison's (Hi)stories and Truths*. FORECAAST: Forum for European Contributions to African American Studies 3. Hamburg, Germany: Lit, 1999.

Tate, Claudia. "Toni Morrison." In *Black Women Writers at Work*, edited by Claudia Tate, 117–131. New York: Continuum, 1983.

———. "Toni Morrison." In *Conversations with Toni Morrison*, edited by Danille Taylor Guthrie, 156–170. Jackson: University Press of Mississippi, 1994.

Taylor-Guthrie, Danille. "Who Are the Beloved? Old and New Testaments, Old and New Communities of Faith," *Religion and Literature* 27, no. 1 (Spring 1995): 119–129.

Taylor-Guthrie, Danille, ed. *Conversations with Toni Morrison*. Jackson, Miss.: University Press of Mississippi, 1994.

Teague, Shell. "Relational Breakdowns: Exploring the Emotional Legacy of Slavery in Toni Morrison's *Beloved*," *MAWA Review* 10, no. 1 (June 1995): 19–27.

Thomas, Helen. "Toni Morrison: A Profile," *Wasafiri: Journal of Caribbean, African, Asian and Associated Literatures and Film* 20 (Autumn 1994): 56–58.

Thomas, H. Nigel. "Further Reflections on the Seven Days in Toni Morrison's *Song of Solomon*," *Literary Griot: International Journal of Black Expressive Cultural Studies* 13, no. 1–2 (Spring-Fall 2001): 147–159.

Thompson, Carlyle V. "'Circles and Circles of Sorrow': Decapitation in Toni Morrison's *Sula*," *CLA Journal* 47, no. 2 (December 2003): 137–174.

Tibbetts, John C. "Oprah's Belabored *Beloved*," *Literature/Film Quarterly* 27, no. 1 (1999): 74–76.

Tignor, Eleanor Q. "Toni Morrison's Pecola: A Portrait in Pathos," *MAWA Review* 1, no. 1 (Spring 1982): 24–27.

Tobin, Elizabeth. "Imagining the Mother's Text: Toni Morrison's *Beloved* and Contemporary Law." In *Beyond Portia: Women, Law, and Literature in the United States*, edited by Jacqueline St. Joan and Annette Bennington McElhiney, 140–174. Boston: Northeastern University Press, 1997.

Todd, Richard. "Toni Morrison and Canonicity: Acceptance or Appropriation?" In *Rewriting the Dream: Reflections on the Changing American Literary Canon*, edited by W. M. Verhoeven, 43–59. Amsterdam: Rodopi, 1992.

Toman, Marshall B. "Un-*Beloved?*" In *Censored Books, II: Critical Viewpoints, 1985–2000*, edited by Nicholas J. Karolides and Nat Hentoff, 58–69. Lanham, Md.: Scarecrow, 2002.

Tonegawa, Maki. "Toni Morrison's Exploration of the Relational Self in *Sula* and *Beloved*," *Studies in American Literature* 29 (1992): 91–106.

"Toni Morrison: A Special Section," *Callaloo: A Journal of African-American and African Arts and Letters* 13, no. 3 (Summer 1990): 471–525.

"Toni Morrison's Narrative Strategies," *Texas Studies in Literature and Language* 33, no. 1 (Spring 1991): 89–123.

Toutonghi, Pauls Harijs. "Toni Morrison's *Beloved*," In *American Writers Classics*, Vol. 1, edited by Jay Parini, 19–33. New York: Thomson Gale, 2003.

Trace, Jacqueline. "Dark Goddesses: Black Feminist Theology in Morrison's *Beloved*," *Obsidian II: Black Literature in Review* 6, no. 3 (Winter 1991): 14–30.

Traore, Ousseynou. "Creative African Memory: Some Oral Sources of Toni Morrison's *Song of Solomon*." In *Of Dreams Deferred, Dead or Alive: African Perspectives on African American Writers*, edited by Femi Ojo-Ade, 129–141. Westport, Conn.: Greenwood Press, 1996.

Traore, Ousseynou B., ed. "Where to Dry Ourselves: Essays Celebrating Achebe and Morrison at 70," Special Issue of *Literary Griot: International Journal of Black Expressive Cultural Studies* 13, no. 1–2 (Spring-Fall 2001): 1–160.

Travis, Molly Abel. "*Beloved* and Middle Passage: Race, Narrative, and the Critic's Essentialism," *Narrative* 2, no. 3 (October 1994): 179–200.

———. "Speaking from the Silence of the Slave Narrative: *Beloved* and African American Women's History," *The Texas Review* 13, no. 1–2 (Spring-Summer 1992): 69–81.

Treherne, Matthew. "Figuring In, Figuring Out: Narration and Negotiation in Toni Morrison's *Jazz*," *Narrative* 11, no. 2 (May 2003): 199–212.

Turner, Darwin T. "Theme, Characterization, and Style in the Works of Toni Morrison." In *Black Women Writers (1950–1980): A Critical Evaluation*, edited by Mari Evans, 361–369. Garden City, N.Y.: Anchor-Doubleday, 1984.

Uma, Alladi. "The Significance of Class in Multiple Oppression: A Study of Toni Morrison," *Indian Journal of American Studies* 23, no. 2 (Summer 1993): 95–98.

Uma, Alladi, Alphy J. Plakkoottam, and Joseph L. Plakkoottam, eds. "Toni Morrison," *Indian Journal of American Studies* 23, no. 2 (Summer 1993).

Upot, Sherine. "Cultural Politics in Toni Morrison's *Song of Solomon*," *Indian Journal of American Studies* 23, no. 2 (Summer 1993): 75–80.

Valkeakari, Tuire. "Beyond the Riverside: War in Toni Morrison's Fiction," *Atlantic Literary Review* 4, no. 1–2 (January–June 2003): 133–164.

———. "Toni Morrison Writes B(l)ack: *Beloved* and Slavery's Dehumanizing Discourse of Animality," *Atlantic Literary Review* 3, no. 2 (April–June 2002): 165–187.

Vega Gonzalez, Susana. "A Comparative Study of Danticat's *The Farming of Bones* and Morrison's *Beloved*," *Estudios Ingleses de la Universidad Complutense* 13 (2005): 139–153.

———. "From Emotional Orphanhood to Cultural Orphanhood: Spiritual Death and Re-Birth in Two Novels by Toni Morrison," *Revista Alicantina de Estudios Ingleses* 9 (November 1996): 143–151.

———. "Memory and the Quest for Family History in *One Hundred Years of Solitude* and *Song of Solomon*," *CLCWeb: Comparative Literature and Culture: A WWWeb Journal* 3: 1 (March 2001): 13 paragraphs. Available online. URL: http://clcwebjournal.lib.purdue.edu/clcweb01-1/vega-gonzalez01.html. Accessed on September 21, 2006.

———. "Remembering the Ancient Properties: Visions of Death and Re-Birth in *Sula* and *Tar Baby*." In *Proceedings of the 20th International AEDEAN Conference*, edited by P. Guardia and J. Stone, 613–617. Barcelona: Universitat de Barcelona, 1997.

Verrico, Rose May. "Women and the Problem of Bildung," *MAWA Review* 8, no. 1 (June 1993): 7–10.

Vickroy, Laurie. "The Force Outside/The Force Inside: Mother-Love and Regenerative Space in *Sula* and *Beloved*." In *Understanding Toni Morrison's* Beloved *and* Sula: *Selected Essays and Criticisms of the Works by the Nobel Prize–Winning Author,* edited by Solomon O. Iyasere and Marla W. Iyasere, 297–314. Troy, N.Y.: Whitston, 2000.

Wade-Gayles, Gloria. "The Truths of Our Mothers' Lives: Mother-Daughter Relationships in Black Women's Fiction," *SAGE: A Scholarly Journal on Black Women* 1, no. 2 (Fall 1984): 8–12.

Waegner, Cathy. "Toni Morrison and the 'Other'-Reader: Oprah Winfrey and Marcel Reich Ranicki as Mediators?" In *Holding Their Own: Perspectives on the Multi-Ethnic Literatures of the United States,* edited by Dorothea Fischer-Hornung and Heike Raphael-Hernandez, 169–179. Tübingen, Germany: Stauffenburg, 2000.

Wagner, Linda W. "Teaching *The Bluest Eye*," *ADE Bulletin* 83 (Spring 1986): 28–31.

———. "Toni Morrison: Mastery of Narrative." In *Contemporary American Women Writers: Narrative Strategies,* edited by Catherine Rainwater and William J. Scheick, 191–207. Lexington: University Press of Kentucky, 1985.

Wagner-Martin, Linda. "'Closer to the Edge': Toni Morrison's *Song of Solomon*," In *Teaching American Ethnic Literatures: Nineteen Essays,* edited by John R. Maitino and David R. Peck, 147–157. Albuquerque: University of New Mexico Press, 1996.

Walker, Margaret Urban. "Moral Repair and Its Limits." In *Mapping the Ethical Turn: A Reader in Ethics, Culture, and Literary Theory,* edited by Todd F. Davis and Kenneth Womack, 110–127. Charlottesville: University Press of Virginia, 2001.

Wall, Cheryl A. "Extending the Line: From *Sula* to *Mama Day*," *Callaloo: A Journal of African American and African Arts and Letters* 23, no. 4 (Fall 2000): 1,449–1,463.

Wallace, Kathleen R., and Karla Armbruster. "The Novels of Toni Morrison: 'Wild Wilderness Where There Was None.'" In *Beyond Nature Writings: Expanding the Boundaries of Ecocriticism,* edited by Karla Armbruster and Kathleen R. Wallace, 211–230. Charlottesville: University Press of Virginia, 2001.

Walther, Malin LaVon. "'And All of the Interests Are Vested': Canon Building in Recent Morrison Criticism," *MFS: Modern Fiction Studies* 39, no. 3–4 (Fall-Winter 1993): 781–794.

———. "Toni Morrison's *Tar Baby*: Re-Figuring the Colonizer's Aesthetics." In *Cross-Cultural Performances: Differences in Women's Re-Visions of Shakespeare,* edited by Marianne Novy and Peter Erickson, 137–149. Urbana: University of Illinois Press, 1993.

Wang, Chih-ming. "The X-Barred Subject: Afro-American Subjectivity in Toni Morrison's *Song of Solomon*," *Studies in Language and Literature* 9 (June 2000): 269–288.

Wardi, Anissa J. "A Laying on of Hands: Toni Morrison and the Materiality of Love," *MELUS: The Journal of the Society for the Study of the Multi-Ethnic Literature of the United States* 30 (Fall 2005): 201–218.

———. "Breaking the Back of Words: The Language of the Body in *Beloved*," *Griot: Official Journal of the Southern Conference on Afro-American Studies* 17, no. 1 (Spring 1998): 44–52.

———. "Inscriptions in the Dust: *A Gathering of Old Men* and *Beloved* as Ancestral Requiems," *African American Review* 36, no. 1 (Spring 2002): 35–53.

Warner, Anne. "New Myths and Ancient Properties: The Fiction of Toni Morrison." In *Twayne Companion to Contemporary Literature in English,* Vol. 2, *Macleod-Williams,* edited by R. H. W. Dillard and Amanda Cockrell, 87–98. New York: Twayne/Thomson Gale, 2002.

Warner, Anne Bradford. "New Myths and Ancient Properties: The Fiction of Toni Morrison," *The Hollins Critic* 25, no. 3 (June 1988): 1–11.

Washington, Elsie B. "Talk with Toni Morrison." In *Conversations with Toni Morrison,* edited by Danille Taylor Guthrie, 234–238. Jackson: University Press of Mississippi, 1994.

Washington, Teresa N. "Re-embodiment of Mother-Daughter Relationship in *Beloved*," *Literary Griot: International Journal of Black Expressive Cultural Studies* 13, no. 1–2 (Spring-Fall 2001): 100–119.

———. "The Mother-Daughter Àje Relationship in Toni Morrison's *Beloved*," *African American Review* 39 (Spring-Summer 2005): 171–188.

Watkins, Lorie. "Hiding Fire and Brimstone in Lacy Groves: The Twinned Trees of *Beloved*," *Afri-*

can *American Review* 39 (Spring-Summer 2005): 189–199.

Watkins, Mel. "Talk with Toni Morrison." In *Conversations with Toni Morrison,* edited by Danille Taylor Guthrie, 43–47. Jackson: University Press of Mississippi, 1994.

Weathers, Glenda B. "Biblical Trees, Biblical Deliverance: Literary Landscapes of Zora Hurston and Toni Morrison," *African American Review* 39 (Spring-Summer 2005): 201–212.

Webster, William S. "Toni Morrison's *Sula* as a Case of Delirium," *Tennessee Philological Bulletin: Proceedings of the Annual Meeting of the Tennessee Philological Association* 38 (2001): 49–58.

Weever, Jacqueline de. "The Inverted World of Toni Morrison's *The Bluest Eye* and *Sula*," *College Language Association Journal* 22 (1979): 402–414.

———. "Toni Morrison's Use of Fairy Tale, Folk Tale and Myth in The *Song of Solomon*," *Southern Folklore Quarterly* 44 (1980): 131–144.

Wegs, Joyce. "Toni Morrison's *Song of Solomon*: A Blues Song," *Essays in Literature* 9, no. 2 (Fall 1982): 211–223.

Weinstock, Jeffrey Andrew. "Ten Minutes for Seven Letters: Reading Beloved's Epitaph," *Arizona Quarterly: A Journal of American Literature, Culture, and Theory* 61 (Autumn 2005): 129–152.

Weixlmann, Joe. "Culture Clash, Survival, and Trans-Formation: A Study of Some Innovative Afro-American Novels of Detection," *Mississippi Quarterly: The Journal of Southern Culture* 38, no. 1 (Winter 1984–85): 21–32.

Wessling, Joseph H. "Narcissism in Toni Morrison's *Sula*," *College Language Association Journal* 31, no. 3 (March 1988): 281–298.

West, John T., III. "*Sula*: Existentialist Heroine," *Publications of the Mississippi Philological Association* (1998): 74–79.

White, Vernessa C. *Afro-American and East German Fiction*. New York: Lang, 1983.

Widdowson, Peter. "The American Dream Refashioned: History, Politics and Gender in Toni Morrison's *Paradise*," *Journal of American Studies* 35, no. 2 (August 2001): 313–335.

Wilkerson, Margaret B. "The Dramatic Voice in Toni Morrison's Novels." In *Critical Essays on Toni Morrison,* edited by Nellie Y. McKay, 179–190. Boston: Hall, 1988.

Willis, Susan. "Eruptions of Funk: Historicising Toni Morrison." In *Reading the Past: Literature and History,* edited by Tamsin Spargo, 44–55. Basingstoke, England: Palgrave, 2000.

Wilson, Jean. "Toni Morrison: Re-visionary Words with Power." In *Frye and the Word: Religious Contexts in the Writings of Northrop Frye,* edited by Jeffery Donaldson and Alan Mendelson, 235–250. Toronto: University of Toronto Press, 2003.

———. "Toni Morrison's *Beloved*: A Love Story." In *The Conscience of Humankind,* edited by Elrud Ibsch, Douwe Fokkema, and Joachim von der Thusen, 349–359. Amsterdam: Rodopi, 2000.

Wilson, Judith. "A Conversation with Toni Morrison." In *Conversations with Toni Morrison,* edited by Danille Taylor Guthrie, 129–137. Jackson: University Press of Mississippi, 1994.

Woidat, Caroline M. "Talking Back to Schoolteacher: Morrison's Confrontation with Hawthorne in *Beloved*," *MFS: Modern Fiction Studies* 39, no. 3–4 (Fall-Winter 1993): 527–546.

Wolfe, Joanna. "'Ten Minutes for Seven Letters': Song as Key to Narrative Revision in Toni Morrison's *Beloved*," *Narrative* 12, no. 3 (October 2004): 263–280.

Wolff, Cynthia Griffin. "'Margaret Garner': A Cincinnati Story." In *Discovering Difference: Contemporary Essays in American Culture,* edited by Christoph K. Lohmann, 105–122. Bloomington: Indiana University Press, 1993.

Wolff, Janice M. "Teaching in the Contact Zone: The Myth of Safe Houses." In *Professing in the Contact Zone: Bringing Theory and Practice Together,* edited by Janice M. Wolff, 240–256. Urbana: National Council of Teachers of English, 2002.

Wolter, Jurgen C. "'Let People Know Where Their Power Is': Deconstruction and Re-membering in Toni Morrison's *Beloved*," *Zeitschrift für Anglistik und Amerikanistik: A Quarterly of Language, Literature and Culture* 45, no. 3 (1997): 236–246.

Wood, Michael. "Sensations of Loss." In *The Aesthetics of Toni Morrison: Speaking the Unspeakable,* edited by Marc C. Conner, 113–124. Jackson: University Press of Mississippi, 2000.

Wren, James A. "Morrison's *The Bluest Eye*," *Explicator* 55, no. 3 (Spring 1997): 172–175.

Wu, Yung-Hsing. "Doing Things with Ethics: *Beloved, Sula,* and the Reading of Judgment," *MFS: Modern Fiction Studies* 49, no. 4 (Winter 2003): 780–805.

Wyatt, Jean. "Giving Body to the Word: The Maternal Symbolic in Toni Morrison's *Beloved.*" In *Understanding Toni Morrison's* Beloved *and* Sula: *Selected Essays and Criticisms of the Works by the Nobel Prize-Winning Author,* edited by Solomon O. Iyasere and Marla W. Iyasere, 231–257. Troy, N.Y.: Whitston, 2000.

Yancy, George. "The Black Self within a Semiotic Space of Whiteness: Reflections on the Racial Deformation of Pecola Breedlove in Toni Morrison's *The Bluest Eye*," *CLA Journal* 43, no. 3 (March 2000): 299–319.

Yates, Kimberley A. "Explosions of 'Maternal Instinct': Images of Motherhood in Selected Novels by Toni Morrison." In *Fissions and Fusions,* edited by Lesley Marx, Loes Nas, and Lara Dunwell, 21–32. Bellville, South Africa: University of the Western Cape, 1997.

Young, John. "Toni Morrison, Oprah Winfrey, and Postmodern Popular Audiences," *African American Review* 35, no. 2 (Summer 2001): 181–204.

Yoo, JaeEun. "'*Talking to You and Hearing to You Answer—That's the Kick*': History and Dialogue in *Toni Morrison's Jazz,*" *Exit 9: The Rutgers Journal of Comparative Literature* 7 (2005): 87–101.

Yu, Jeboon. "A Study on Aesthetics of Fantasy and Mimesis: Identity and Representation of Ethnic Literature in the U.S.A.," *Journal of English Language and Literature/Yongo Yongmunhak* 49, no. 3 (2003): 651–669.

INDEX